D1106137

FV.

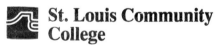

Dream Reader

SUNY Series in Dream Studies
Robert L. Van de Castle, Editor

Dream Reader

CONTEMPORARY APPROACHES TO THE
UNDERSTANDING OF DREAMS

Anthony Shafton

State University of New York Press

Published by
State University of New York Press, Albany

For information, address State University of New York Press,
State University Plaza, Albany, NY 12246

Printed in the United States of America

Production by Marilyn P. Semerad
Marketing by Terry Abad Swierzowski

Cover art: "Caribou Women," papercut by Mado Spiegler

Library of Congress Cataloging-in-Publication Data

Shafton, Anthony, 1937–
    Dream reader: contemporary approaches to the understanding of
dreams / Anthony Shafton.
        p.   cm. — (SUNY series in dream studies)
    Includes bibliographical references and indexes.
    ISBN 0-7914-2617-3 (alk. paper). — ISBN 0-7914-2618-1 (pbk. :
alk. paper)
    1. Dreams.   2. Dream interpretation.   I. Title.   II. Series.
BF1091.S54   1995
154.6'3— dc20   94-42405
                                                                    CIP

10 9 8 7 6 5 4 3 2 1

Also by Anthony Shafton

*Conditions of Awareness: Subjective Factors in the Social Adaptations
of Man and Other Primates*

Grateful acknowledgement is made for permission to reproduce excerpts from the following material.

From Alfred Adler, *What Life Should Mean to You*, New York: Capricorn, 1958. Copyright © 1931, 1958 by Raissa Adler, renewed 1959 by Kurt A. Adler. Reprinted by permission of the Estate of Alfred Adler.

From Merrill Aldighieri and Joe Tripician, producers and directors, *METAPHORIA* (an Emmy Award-winning TV program). Copyright © 1991 by Co-Directions, Inc.

From Judith S. Antrobus, John S. Antrobus & Charles Fisher, "Discrimination of dreaming and nondreaming sleep" *Archives of General Psychiatry* 12: 395-401, 1965. Copyright © 1965 by American Medical Association. Reprinted by permission.

From Arthur M. Arkin, John M. Hastey & Morton F. Reiser, "Post-hypnotically stimulated sleep-talking," *Journal of Nervous and Mental Disease* 142:293-309, 1966. Copyright © by Williams & Wilkins. Reprinted by permission.

From A. M. Arkin, M. F. Toth, J. Baker & J. M. Hastey, "The frequency of sleep talking in the laboratory among chronic sleep talkers and good dream recallers," *Journal of Nervous and Mental Disease* 151:369-74, 1970. Copyright © by Williams & Wilkins. Reprinted by permission.

From Martin Barad, Kenneth Z. Altshuler & Alvin I. Goldfarb, "A survey of dreams in aged persons," *Archives of General Psychiatry* 4:419-23, 1961. Copyright © 1961 by American Medical Association. Reprinted by permission.

From Deirdre Barrett, "The 'committee of sleep': a study of dream incubation for problem solving," *Dreaming* 3:115-22, 1993. Copyright © by Association for the Study of Dreams. Reprinted by permission of Plenum Publishing Corp. and Deirdre Barrett.

From Leo H. Bartemeier, "Illness following dreams," *International Journal of Psycho-Analysis* 31:8-11, 1950. Copyright © by Institute of Psycho-Analysis. Reprinted by permission.

From Basho, an untitled haiku, in *An Introduction to Haiku*, Harold G. Henderson, editor and translator, Garden City: Doubleday Anchor Books, 1958. Copyright © by Harold G. Henderson. Reprinted by permission of Doubleday, a division of Bantam Doubleday Dell Publishing Group, Inc.

From Aaron T. Beck & Clyde L. Ward, "Dreams of depressed patients," *Archives of General Psychiatry* 5:462-7, 1961. Copyright © 1961 by American Medical Association. Reprinted by permission.

From Henry W. Beck, "Dream analysis in family therapy," *Clinical Social Work Journal* 5:53-7, 1977. Copyright © by Human Sciences Publishing Corp. Reprinted by permission of Human Sciences Publishing Corp. and Henry W. Beck.

From Carlotte Beradt, *The Third Reich of Dreams*, Chicago: Quadrangle Books, 1968. Copyright © 1966 by Nymphenburger Verlagshandlung GmbH, Munich. Translation copyright © 1968 by Quadrangle Books, Inc. Copyright © by Robin Shohet. Reprinted by permission of Robin Shohet.

From Yoram Bilu, "The Other as a nightmare: the Israeli-Arab encounter as reflected in children's dreams in Israel and the West Bank," *Political Psychology* 10:365-89, 1989. Copyright © by Plenum Publishing Corp. Reprinted by permission of Plenum Publishing Corp. and Yoram Bilu.

From Susan Blackmore, "Dreaming, out-of-body experience, and reality: an interview with Susan Blackmore," interview by Tore Nielsen, *Association for the Study of Dreams Newsletter* 6(6):7-10, 1989. Copyright © by Association for the Study of Dreams. Reprinted by permission.

From Mark Blagrove, "A critical review of neural net theories of REM sleep," *Association for the Study of Dreams Newsletter* 7(1):1-2, 1990. Copyright © by Association for the Study of Dreams. Reprinted by permission.

From H. Robert Blank, "Dreams of the blind," *Psychoanalytic Quarterly* 27: 158-74, 1958. Copyright © by The Psychoanalytic Quarterly. Reprinted by permission.

From Fariba Bogzaran, "Expressive dream art," *Association for the Study of Dreams Newsletter* 7(2):8-9, 1990. Copyright © by Association for the Study of Dreams. Reprinted by permission.

From Walter Bonime, *The Clinical Use of Dreams*, approximately 1,500 words. Copyright © 1962 by Basic Books Publishing Company, Inc. Copyright renewed. Reprinted by permission of BasicBooks, a division of HarperCollins Publishers, Inc.

From Robert Bosnak, *A Little Course in Dreams*, Boston: Shambhala, 1988. Copyright © 1986 by Robert Bosnak. Translation © 1988 by Shambhala Publications, Inc. Reprinted by arrangement with Shambhala Publications, Inc., 300 Massachusetts Avenue, Boston, MA 02115.

From Robert Bosnak, *Dreaming with an Aids Patient*. Boston: Shambhala, 1989. Copyright © 1989 by Robert Bosnak. Reprinted by arrangement with Shambhala Publications, Inc., 300 Massachusetts Avenue, Boston, MA 02115.

From Medard Boss, *"I dreamt last night . . ."*, New York: Gardner Press, 1977. Copyright © by Gardner Press, Inc. Reprinted by permission.

From Jackson Browne, "Colors of the Sun" (a song). Copyright © 1970, 1974 by Atlantic Music Corp. and Open Window Music. Reprinted by permission of Criterion Music Corp.

From Jackson Browne, "For Everyman" (a song). Copyright © 1973 by Swallow Turn Music. All rights reserved. Reprinted by permission.

From Linda Anne Camino, *Ethnomedical Illnesses and Non-orthodox Healing Practices in a Black Neighborhood in the American South: How They Work and What They Mean*, unpublished Ph.D. dissertation, University of Virginia, 1986. Reprinted by permission of Linda Anne Camino.

From Patricia Carrington, "Dreams and schizophrenia," *Archives of General Psychiatry* 26:343-50, 1972. Copyright © 1972 by American Medical Association. Reprinted by permission.

From Rosalind D. Cartwright, *Night Life: Explorations in Dreaming*, Englewood Cliffs: Prentice-Hall, 1977. Copyright © 1977 by Prentice-Hall, Inc. Reprinted by permission of Prentice Hall/A Division of Simon & Schuster, Englewood Cliffs, N.J.

From Rosalind Cartwright, "Affect and dream work from an information processing point of view," *Journal of Mind and Behavior* 7:411-27, 1986. Copyright © by Institute of Mind and Behavior. Reprinted by permission of Institute of Mind and Behavior and Rosalind Cartwright.

From Rosalind D. Cartwright, "'Masochism' in dreaming and its relation to depression," *Dreaming* 2:79-84, 1992. Copyright © by Association for the Study of Dreams. Reprinted by permission of Plenum Publishing Corp. and Rosalind D. Cartwright.

From Rosalind Cartwright, Ph.D. & Lynne Lamberg, *Crisis Dreaming: Using Your Dreams to Solve Your Problems*, approximately 500 words, New York: HarperCollins, 1992. Copyright © 1992 by Rosalind Cartwright & Lynne Lamberg. Reprinted by permission of HarperCollins Publishers, Inc.

I'm not try'ng to tell you that I've seen the plan
Turn and walk away if you think I am—
But don't think too badly of one who's left holding sand
He's just another dreamer, dreaming 'bout Everyman

> — Jackson Browne, "For Everyman"

Wake to understand you are not dreaming
It is not seeming just to be this way

> — Jackson Browne, "Colors of the Sun"

Contents

□

Introduction

I have the poet Allen Ginsberg to thank for getting me interested in writing this book. Ten years ago in London, I attended a lecture/conversation he gave together with R. D. Laing. They soon got onto the subject of meditation, and spent most of a fascinating evening recounting their personal histories with it. In the end they both conceded, with very little explanation, that they no longer kept up a meditative practice. Nevertheless, Ginsberg's remarks and songs inspired me to take up a practice myself, something I had been meaning to do for a long time.

Almost as soon as I undertook meditation, my dream life began to flourish (not an unusual effect, I found out later). I had always recalled dreams pretty well and they had always pleased and mattered to me. But now a vertical channel seemed to clear itself. Stirred and intrigued, I started keeping a dream journal. I looked for workshops, joined a dream group, and began to read about dreams. One book led to the next, one thing led to another, and eventually I decided to research and write this book.

So in one sense, the 'reader' in the title *Dream Reader* is myself. This book is in large part a product of reading the literature about dreaming and dreamwork. The book comprises a review of that literature. Naturally I have my own views, and they will be apparent; but they do not, I feel confident, detract from the survey.

The book itself is a 'reader', in the sense that it contains a selection of excerpts from other writings. Perhaps a quarter of the text consists of passages from the literature. Virtually every excerpt includes a dream. Reports of over 500 dreams are quoted, in about 350 selections drawn from some 200 authors (see List of Dreams). Sources include popular as well as clinical and scholarly writings; for as Alan Moffitt, a researcher and past president of the Association for the Study of Dreams, has commented: "Dreams can be studied by anyone with equal legitimacy."[1]

Here will be found discussions of most aspects of dreams and dreaming, and within those discussions, a sampler, giving the flavor of many different schools and individual styles of thinking about and using dreams, from recent decades but also from earlier decades. In these respects, I believe, this book is unique in its coverage.

As to the dreams related here, I have made it a point to select short ones, or at least to avoid very long ones, for the most part. When I read a dream, I try to 'enter' it as I read, and to guess at possible meanings before the interpreter tells me her/his view. Then I do my best to keep the whole dream and my conjectures in mind while the interpreter speaks. This is hard to do with long, complicated dreams. Probably my preference is influenced by the fact that my own dreams tend to be short and episodic.

Besides relevance and length, another criterion for selection has been esthetic appeal—of dreams, in some cases, but more generally, of their treatments. Wilhelm Stekel, an early defector from Freud (in 1912), remarked: "There are some interpretations whose luminousness and intrinsic vigor instantly produces conviction of their truth."[2] But satisfying treatments do not necessarily sew the dream up, as Stekel implies. His own do—he was known for it in psychoanalytic circles.* But interpretations by people such as Patricia Garfield or Gayle Delaney can feel remarkably apt without seeming to foreclose other possibilities; and Robert Bosnak often lets his equally appealing interpretations trail off quite unresolved.

The first entry under 'reader' in the *Oxford English Dictionary* says: "An expounder, interpreter (of dreams, etc.)." Thus the title *Dream Reader* also conveys that this book is about the reading, the interpreting of dreams.

The expression 'dream interpretation' has to some extent been supplanted of late by 'dreamwork': 'work' encompasses both interpretive and non-interpretive approaches, whereas 'interpretation' suggests to some the discredited belief that we need clinicians to tell us what our dreams mean. But the older expression has an historical resonance predating by eras the clinical conception of dreamwork. So I will use it where appropriate, but with a meaning nearly as broad as that of the newer term. Still, interpretation in the strict sense is the chief focus, although other issues come in. These issues include not only non-interpretive approaches to dreamwork, but also the background issues of psychological function, social usage, physiology, and so on.

---

* Freud wrote to Jung before their own break in 1914: "Stekel's method of presentation will be hard to stomach in the long run, even though he is usually right." "[T]he pig finds truffles. . ." (W. McGuire 1974, pp. 257 and 404). And Jung to Freud: "He is a slovenly, uncritical fellow who undermines all discipline; I feel the same as you do about him. Unfortunately, he has the best nose of any of us for the secrets of the unconscious" (p. 259).

Briefly, the book has three parts. The first part consists of a single chapter centered on the basics of sleep laboratory research. Few nonspecialized books on dreams being published now bother with much if any introduction to dream psychobiology. This probably reflects the circumstance that the research has not proven to be as illuminating as it once promised to do. Consequently, the volume of research has ebbed since the 1970s, and it "now faces skepticism, disillusionment, and lack of funding."[3] That may be true. Nevertheless, the findings constitute a foundation and a filter for many other ways of thinking about dreams. Facts from the sleep lab do bear on all sorts of questions concerning dream meaning and function. Besides, the research is inherently interesting.

The next part consists of a group of chapters discussing the major Euro-American schools of dream interpretation as they developed this century. I should say a word about the Freud chapter. His psychology is another subject given little space recently, except within psychoanalysis proper. As a result, there are readers of the dream literature who have never encountered a Freudian interpretation, unless perhaps in caricature. Not only that, but it is astonishing how many mental health professionals have never read a page written by Freud himself.[4] Yet he established the ground for almost all other psychologies, and certainly for other dream theories. In a book such as this, he fully deserves at least a chapter.

The last and largest part, chapters 7–16, is organized by topics. The best way to get a quick idea of the scope of topics covered is to glance through the List of Dreams. Please note that many topics which are discussed do not have their own chapters. Thus the question of laboratory vs. home dreams comes up in the chapter on dream incubation (13), the social implications of dreamwork, in the chapter on culturalism (5), content analysis of dreams, in the chapter on Jung (3), Jung's method of active imagination, in the chapter on dream re-entry (15), and so on. In general, the style of this book is digressive. Digressive and eclectic. Readers seeking information on particular subjects are encouraged to make use of the indexes.

I will declare up front that if we were playing desert island dream book, I would certainly choose to bring something of Jung's as my one and only book on dreams. But the eclecticism of my point of view is conspicuous in the fact that the chapter on lucid dreaming (14) is as long as the chapter on Jung—the significance of which is that Jung refrained from the sort of control of dreams favored by many lucidity enthusiasts. Moreover, the authors whose names keep coming up in various chapters are not necessarily Jungians (for example, Rosalind Cartwright, David Foulkes, Emil Gutheil, Harry Hunt, Milton Kramer, and Montague Ullman).

In this time and place, it would be difficult (though not impossible*) to think seriously about the subject of dreams and *not* be eclectic. Even Freud, who persistently reiterated his theme that dreams fulfill wishes, recognized that dreaming may be "of as many different sorts as the process of waking thought."[5] And he informed us that each dream has a "navel, the spot where it reaches down into the unknown."[6] And Jung, whose appetite and tolerance for the unknowable were certainly greater than Freud's, said: "Dreams may give expression [besides to Freudian wishes] to ineluctable truths, to philosophical pronouncement, illusions, wild fantasies, memories, plans, anticipations, irrational experiences, even telepathic visions, and heaven knows what besides."[7] Thus both Freud and Jung left their inventories of dream types open-ended.

Euro-American culture lacks any generally accepted system or systems for classifying dreams such as many cultures have. In part this reflects the small value we have placed on dreams historically,[8] our schooled skepticism about dreams. But it also reflects our eclecticism.

Within the dream literature, diverse lists of dream types are encountered. Some of their authors aim to classify the distinct types of dreams; others, to identify possible levels of any given dream. Some intend to clarify only a specific aspect of dreaming;** others intend to be comprehensive, and do not mind mixing categories of form, function, and meaning.*** No two lists are quite the same, and none is really satisfying.

The best must be Harry Hunt's "diamond of dream types."[9] Hunt's "system is based on dimensions that vary continuously across all dream formation," and "all dimensions of dream formation may be more or less nascent in all dreams."[10] The moral is that we should take to heart Hunt's title, *The Multiplicity of Dreams*, and enjoy ourselves with the fact that dreams are in-

---

* Cognitive psychologist and dream researcher John Antrobus is "persuaded that the study of dreaming outside of the cognitive and neurosciences will retard our ability to understand this most fascinating state of consciousness" (1993, pp. 549–50). What keeps Antrobus fascinated is not the adaptive function of subjective dreaming, for he finds there to be none (p. 553).

** Loma Flowers (1988), for example, categorizes dreams according to the kinds of insight they yield ("emphasis," "reconceptualization," "confrontation," and "discovery"). Don Kuiken & Shelley Sikora (1993) discern three types of "impactful dreams" ("transcendent dreams" with "rapture and mythic capabilities"; "existential dreams" characterized by "agony and separation"; and "nightmares" involving "intense fear and harm avoidance").

*** Robin Shohet (1985, pp. 42–3), for example, lists: "nightmares, shadow dreams, recurring dreams, creative dreams, problem-solving dreams, precognitive dreams, warning dreams, lucid dreams, wish-fulfillment dreams, clearing dreams, 'big dreams', information dreams, communication dreams and social dreams." Other comprehensive lists are those of K. L. West (1977); M. Kelsey (1978); J. Campbell (1980); S. K. Williams (1980); H. A. Wilmer (1987); J. Windsor (1987); S. Cunningham (1992); R. Watts (1992a) and (1992b). (See also 'dream types' in the General Index.)

herently ambiguous and multi-layered.* Jeremy Taylor counsels that "The best dreamwork is carried out in this context of openness and an acceptance of irony, paradox, ambiguity, uncertainty, and multiple possibility."[11]

Hunt sums up the state of affairs in contemporary dream psychology by saying, "All this adds up to a postmodern 'self-deconstruction'. . . ."[12] Gordon Globus likewise invokes postmodern textual criticism in arguing that the various approaches to interpretation "are not mutually exclusive, but correlated. . . ."[13] Jungian Carl Meier also affirms that the schools all contribute "to the understanding of one or the other of the untold aspects of this inexhaustible phenomenon."[14] And Ullman, when introducing a set of interpretations of a single dream series by practitioners from different schools, finds himself "not in complete agreement with any one approach," but "enriched by the totality."[15]

Ullman elsewhere observes that, in a given therapeutic situation, only one interpretation may be "appropriate."[16] That could be debated, but very few maintain that "one and only one interpretation is correct."[17]

Even within any particular school, interpreters often disagree. Investigations show that when presented with a dream for 'blind analysis', Freudian psychoanalysts interpret it in very different ways—all propagated from the Freudian theory. Not only that, but when provided with more information about the dreamer, their interpretations diverge even further.[18] The existentialist Medard Boss, who discusses this circumstance, adds that the same holds true for Jungian psychologists. And in fact a Jungian, Patricia Berry,

---

* Hunt (p. 93ff.) offers "a three-dimensional diamond representing basic dream forms and their interrelations. . . ." • "The vertical dimension depicts vividness or intensification of the dreaming process." At the bottom, where memory processes predominate in dream formation, dreams are less vivid, less memorable, more mundane, more clouded. At the top come archetypal dreams, lucid dreams, and some nightmares. These types, which share a predominance of imaginative processes with psychedelic, sensory deprivation, and deep meditative experiences, are more vivid, more memorable, more bizarre—and less frequent. • The horizontal dimension depicts degrees of symbolic complexity, from less complex, more realistic dreams dominated by the single mode of "the deep structures of ordinary language" to more complex dreams integrating the former with "imagistic visual-kinesthetic intelligence." This "unfolding of multiple frames of mind" culminates in the unusual but normal dreams of "abstract self-reference": white light, mandala imagery, etc. • To the above is somewhat confusingly coordinated a "two-dimensional depth diagram" which factors in: complexity of story narrative (time); complexity of setting (space); and, especially, the degree of dream-ego participation in the narrative. This last specifies activity vs. receptivity, where receptivity is associated not with that passivity which ego-psychology rating systems devalue, but with the receptivity of meditative states.

Hunt proposes that all types of dreams, including telepathic, inventive, medical, archetypal, etc. can be located on this diamond. The major dream types are universal, he says, only the valuation placed on them in different cultures varies (p. 90).

has demonstrated as much by framing seven interpretations of a dream, all equally supportable, by seven hypothetical Jungians who approach the dream each with a different Jungian orientation.[19]

This calls to mind the well-known Talmudic story told by Rabbi Bana: "There were twenty-four interpreters of dreams in Jerusalem. Once I had a dream and went to everyone of them and what any one interpreted, none of the others interpreted in the same way, and yet all of them were fulfilled."[20]

I wondered if I could find twenty-four interpretations of a single dream motif by contemporary experts, and was not surprised when I found at least that many. The motif is flying.

1. Vestibular stimulation (e.g., from turning in bed).
2. Labyrinthitis and/or mid-brain disease.
3. Precoronary personality.
4. An ancestral vestige, of life in the sea or in the trees.
5. A memory trace of childhood games of movement (e.g., being tossed).
6. Infantile grandiosity.
7. A symbol of death (ghosts and angels fly).
8. Desire to escape, from anxiety, responsibility, parents, the limits of nature, etc.
9. A will to dominate others.
10. Dread of contamination by others.
11. High self-esteem or sense of personal power.
12. Optimism or stimulation for success.
13. Freedom.
14. Rising above difficulties.
15. Being ungrounded.
16. A warning of overstepping oneself in waking life.
17. Feeling good ('high').
18. *Not* feeling good.
19. Genital eroticism, romantic eroticism, and/or sexual liberation.
20. Kundalini power, often preceding out-of-body experience.
21. Really flying in an astral body.
22. A prelude to lucid dreaming.
23. Spirituality.
24. A sense of fun or playfulness.[21]

I do not mean to make psychologists "come off sounding stupid,"[22] which they might if only one of the twenty-four interpretations were 'right'. But the point of the Talmudic story is just that all twenty-four are right. So differences of opinion betoken not the stupidity of the interpreters but the complexity of their subject, which is nothing less than life. For the most part, the authors of these interpretations appreciate that flying (or any motif) has more than one cause or meaning at the same time, or at different times, in different dreamers, in different cultures. As Cartwright says: "The uses of dreaming may turn out to be as many and complicated as the uses of waking thought. . . ."[23]

In this spirit, Kelly Bulkley speaks of a "coat of many colors" approach to the study of dreams, a comprehensive approach which he contrasts to a "triumphant science" conception, overconfident of hard answers, but which he also contrasts to a "self-actualization" conception, overconfident of soft ones.[*]

Gutheil likens the aspects of dream meaning to "cross sections through a globe from many directions."[24]

Hunt takes it a step further: "Like the endless permeable consciousness of wakefulness, dreaming may have no set or fixed nature. Dreaming may simply have no essence."[25]

Dreams, says Werner Wolff, are "as complex as man is and thus admit a great variety of possible interpretations. . . ."[26]

And Eugene Gendlin gives the pragmatic assurance that "[a]lthough the experts differ, you can tap the dream with a question from one, then a question from another and another. With different dreams different questions lead to a breakthrough. . . ."[27]

This book is meant to expose readers to a large array of those questions.

---

[*] K. Bulkley (1990). Bulkley has recently restored his surname to its genealogically original form of 'Bulkeley'. I will use 'Bulkeley' only when referring to recent works published under that name. Bulkeley develops his own interdisciplinary approach in a book about "ways that dreams may have religious meaning in the modern context" (forthcoming in 1994, manuscript p. 43). Bulkeley's definition of "religious" is so broad as to include virtually anything and everything life-relevant. His net conclusion is that much of what people do with dreams *is* religious, in such a broad sense. He leans on several thinkers in religious studies, critical theory, and linguistics to critique and synthesize eight major contemporary dream theories in this light. Bulkeley demonstrates the virtue of eclecticism, even while he reiterates Hunt's warning against "'empty eclecticism' that admits everything and explains nothing" (ms. p. 129, quoting H. T. Hunt 1989, p. 92). "An empty eclecticism is the great danger all interdisciplinary studies face, for when we try to reconcile serious disputes we risk ignoring genuine differences; when we try to synthesize extremely different ideas we risk draining away their critical force" (ms. p. 315).

Part I

REM, ETC.

As a child I could never understand why grown-ups took dreaming so calmly when they could make such a fuss about any holiday. This still puzzles me. I am mystified by people who say they never dream and appear to have no interest in the subject. It is much more astonishing to me than if they said they never went out for a walk.

— J. B. Priestley, *Delight*

We think by feeling. What is there to know?
I hear my being dance from ear to ear.
I wake to sleep, and take my waking slow.

— Theodore Roethke, "The Waking"

□ 1 □

REM, etc.

Under this excited headline Harry Fiss, a laboratory dream researcher, several years ago re-evoked the news of the birth of his field.[1] In 1953, a University of Chicago graduate student Eugene Aserinsky and his professor Nathaniel Kleitman had published findings that a hitherto unremarked type of *rapid eye movement* occurs during sleep. Clusters of these *REMs* (a term coined by William Dement, another of Kleitman's students[2]) occur at intervals.[3] Furthermore, REMs are associated both with a pattern of electrical activity in the brain, and—here was the big news—with dreaming. So scientists had found a way, if not actually to eavesdrop on the dream itself, at least to measure the dream's physical correlates and, most importantly, to collect an all-but-living specimen in the dream laboratory by awakening the dreamer during REM to solicit a report.

Venerable misconceptions about dreaming promptly fell: that some people rarely or never dream; that dreams transpire instantaneously; and so forth. Other misconceptions introduced by the Freudian revolution in dream theory at the turn of the century, such as that dreaming is essentially "the guardian of sleep" (or "preserves sleep"), have proven tenacious[4] but have generally given way as well. Mistakes generated by the early laboratory studies themselves, such as that dreaming is confined to REM sleep, were gradually rectified. In the years since Aserinsky & Kleitman's discovery, a considerable amount of dependable information has been gathered about the physiology of sleeping and of dreaming, as well as about the psychological contours of dreaming.

This correction of old wrong ideas and development of good, 'hard' information has not, however, brought about a consensus concerning what if anything dreams mean or how if at all to interpret them. Indeed, the polarity of views in the nineteenth century, surveyed by Freud in *The Interpretation of Dreams*, can easily be matched by views prevailing now in various circles as we near the end of the twentieth.

Thus the nineteenth century medical concept of dreams as "*somatic* processes, which are in every case useless and in many cases positively pathological,"[5] has its equivalent in the current concept of dreams as "parasitic modes of [mental] activity," produced nightly as the memory-and-learning system evacuates itself of useless or mistaken memory traces.[6]

And at the positive end of the polarity, Freud sneered at "remarks by the young Fichte . . . and others, all of which represent dreams as an elevation of mental life to a higher level . . . ; today they are repeated only by mystics and pietists."[7] Well, as for pietists, we have many a Jungian pastor plausibly preaching dreamwork for personal growth;[8] and as for mystics, the passionate lucid dreamer Patricia Garfield, among others, beckons us toward "the glory, ah, the glory. . . ."[9]

Numerous evaluations of dreams and their relation to the rest of life will be sampled in the pages to follow. For background, we begin with a look at findings from the sleep labs. That discussion will lead into a brief presentation of information theories about dreaming.

Sleep Stage Basics

As a soon-to-be sleeper relaxes, cerebral cortex activity shows up on the electroencephalogram (EEG) as *alpha*, a pattern characteristic of waking repose. Next a person enters *sleep onset*, or *descending stage 1* sleep, when their eyes make slow, rolling, uncoordinated movements (SEMs). Then, in more or less short order, s/he passes through *stage 2* to *stage 3* to *stage 4*, normally reached within half an hour of sleep onset. Apart from some EEG 'spikes' and 'spindles' in stage 2 which linger into stage 3, this passage from 1 to 4 is marked by a slowing of cortical activity, with waves of greater voltage (amplitude) becoming more regular (synchronized) until in stage 4 the EEG tracing of delta waves "closely resembles that of coma."[10]

Eye movements are absent during stages 2 to 4, which collectively are termed *non-rapid eye movement sleep* (*NREM*, pronounced and sometimes spelled *non-REM*, *NONREM*), or *S-sleep* (for the synchronized brain wave pattern), or *quiet* sleep. During NREM, blood pressure lowers, and respiration and heart rates become slower and regular. Sleep is "deepest," at least in the sense that a sleeper is harder to awaken than from REM, under most conditions.[11]

Typically, after 30-40 minutes in stage 4, the sleeper returns to stage 1 sleep, now to have the first REM dream(s). REMs are bouts of readily visible, coordinated, up-down or sideways eye movements, "faster and sharper than [one] could execute while awake."[12] REM bouts are separated by up to several minutes. This phase of sleep goes by several names, among them *ascending* or *emergent stage 1* sleep. Though ascending stage 1 is designated by the same number as *descending* stage 1 of sleep onset, the electrical signatures of the two "are not really identical."[13] It is also called *D-sleep*, variously for *dreaming sleep* or *desynchronized sleep*, in reference to its pattern of cortical activation with features resembling full wakefulness. For this reason the terms *active* and *activated sleep* are also found. The term *REM sleep* is most current, though the functional connection between eye movements and dreaming is still by no means evident.*

One final term is *paradoxical sleep*, offered by the French physiologist Michel Jouvet[14] (who first identified the importance of the brain stem in regulating sleep[15]): the paradox is that REM sleep shows both light- and deep-seeming features. As for light-seeming features, in addition to REMs and to EEG activation level (which has been compared to that of "panic states"[16]): brain temperature and cortical blood flow increase; respiration rate, blood pressure, and heart rate increase and become irregular; middle ear muscles contract, as if in response to sounds; and the sleeper has vaginal swelling or penile erection. As for deep features: the body during REM sleep undergoes *atonia* (or *atony*), an almost complete immobilization by loss of muscle tone (excepting the eyes and respiratory system), accompanied by suppressed reflex responsiveness;[17] and there is some loss of body temperature regulating functions (shivering, sweating, etc.).[18] In sum, the sleeping body seems most asleep while the sleeping mind seems most 'awake'. Most dream researchers conclude that 'light' and 'deep' do not usefully describe REM sleep. Some think of it as a third state, or cluster of states, apart from waking and from NREM sleep.

A night of sleep follows a fairly predictable pattern, though with many variations such as brief awakenings or stages skipped. REM is reached after a first *NREM period* (*NREMP*) of 70–120 minutes or longer, but not much

---

* Researchers of the evolution of sleep and dreaming may avoid the term *REM sleep* because other parameters of ascending stage 1 occur without concurrent eye movements in some animal species (T. Allison & H. Van Twyver 1974 [1970], p. 344). In humans, however, the close connection of REMs to ascending stage 1 sleep is shown by the fact that even the congenitally blind have REMs at the expected times (J. Gross, J. Byrne & C. Fisher 1965). Theirs are especially jerky, smaller, occasionally unpaired, and often in one direction only. The dreams of the blind will be discussed in chapter 9.

shorter, except with certain disorders affecting sleep (narcolepsy, posttraumatic stress, depression, and some acute schizophrenia[19]). The first *REM period* (*REMP*) is typically the briefest of the night, lasting only up to 10 minutes. Most of the laboratory awakenings from REM which yield no dreams occur now.[20] The first REMP is faltering, writes Rosalind Cartwright, "as if the subject is 'trying' to get into REM but not quite making it."[21] Next the sleeper returns to stage 3 and perhaps briefly to stage 4 before ascending a second time to stage 1 and REM. Thereafter the sleeper may touch stage 3 again, but basically s/he alternates between stages 1 and 2, from either of which awakening occurs after four, five, or more REMPs.

We have more dreams than that per night, however, since some REMPs contain two or more distinct episodes. By one assessment, only 10% of lab awakenings yield "two or three apparently unrelated scenarios," but Dement judges we have 10-20 episodes per night.[22*]

The interval separating stage 1 sleep periods varies from one species to another according to body size. In mice the average interval is only 9 minutes, in monkeys and human children it is 50 minutes, and in human adults, 90 minutes.[23**] Perhaps the REM cycle is the expression during sleep of a "biologic rhythm" of rest and activity present during all twenty-four hours but obscured during wakefulness.[24] We seem to have "a tendency for a shift of attention to subjective stimuli every ninety minutes," whether asleep or awake.[25] But superimposed over this rhythm while we are awake is a world of stimulations. And superimposed over it while we sleep is a tendency for REMPs to come closer together through the night until by morning as little as twenty minutes may separate them.[26] In part this is because REMPs also tend to last longer as the night advances, finally up to 40 minutes or more.

---

* According to Cartwright (1977, p. 34), when we awaken spontaneously with dreams combining unrelated episodes, the earlier may have been registered in memory during a brief awakening such as often occurs during or at the end of a REMP, without our remembering the awakening as such in the morning. In that event, the two episodes would come from separate REMPs. This probably does not apply to the majority of multiple-episode dreams recalled.

Ideas about connections between episodes vary as do ideas about the general meaningfulness of dreams. On the negative side, Robert McCarley & J. Allan Hobson (1979, p. 118) see abrupt shifts as due not to symbolic or motivational processes, but to random physiological activations (see later this chapter). Walter Bonime (1982 [1962]) (see chapter 5), on the other hand, thinks temporally connected episodes reflect the same underlying issue and may show "a progression toward or retreat from a more realistic solution or perception" (p. 239), or may show, disjointedly, different aspects of the issue (p. 245).

** Slightly different results are reported by W. Moorcroft (1986, p. 11), citing R. L. Williams, I. Karacan & C. J. Hursch, *Electroencephalography (EEG) of Human Sleep: Clinical Applications*, New York: Wiley, 1974: newborns, 60 minutes; preschoolers, 90 minutes (girls less); grade schoolers, 111 minutes; young adults, 105 minutes; retirees, 100 minutes.

Thus most REM is concentrated in the final third of sleep—we dream more richly toward morning.

While some of us dream more than others,[27] a typical adult spends about 25% of each night in REM sleep. Newborns, however, spend 50% of their total sleep time in REM, and prematures[28] and infants *in utero*[29] even longer. REM sleep is thought to contribute to the maturation of the young nervous system. REM can be detected from the 26th–32nd week of gestation,[30] when it apparently occupies almost 24 hours a day.[31]*

Whether infants recognizably dream is another question. It was recently asserted in the introduction to an authoritative book that REM dreaming begins between 3 and 5 years, NREM dreaming not until after 5.[32] However, experimenters have elicited REM dream reports from children as young as 1½ and 2 years.[33]**

The adult level of REM as a percentage of total sleep time is pretty well reached by age 5. Thereafter, except for a peak during puberty, the level remains quite constant until it declines in old age to near 20%. The total of hours spent in NREM, on the other hand, remains unchanged from infancy through adulthood, until the decline of total sleep time in old age. By age

---

* After 5 months, the fetus frequently shows increased movement during the *mother's* REMPs (J. Tolaas 1986, pp. 363–4, citing N. B. Sterman, "Relationship of intrauterine fetal activity to maternal sleep stage," *Experimental Neurology*, Supplement 4, pp. 98–105, 1967). The channel through which the mother's state is communicated to the fetus is obscure. In Jon Tolaas's view, it may be psychic. There are also indications of postnatal synchrony between maternal and newborn sleep stages (Tolaas, p. 366, citing M. Bertini, D. Gambi & F. Gagliardi, "Polygraphic and behavioral observations of mother-infant sleep-patterns," paper presented to the 2nd International Congress of Sleep Research, Edinburgh, Scotland, 1975).

** David Foulkes, the leading researcher of dreaming development, holds that because dreaming is a constructive process of thought and imagination, bound up with language skills, it is beyond the capacity of children before 1½–3. But Harry Hunt (1989, p. 54) believes Foulkes's developmental timetable is distorted by the procedures of experimental collection and the inhibitions it imposes on young subjects. Hunt (p. 43) points to the anecdotal reports supplied by parents of very young children. He relates John Mack's account of "a thirteen-month-old boy's terrified sleep cries of *'boom! boom!'* after the child had so shouted in response to the vacuum cleaner on the preceding day" (p. 44, quoting Mack, "Nightmares, conflict, and ego development in childhood," *International Journal of Psychoanalysis* 46, pp. 403–28, 1965; see also S. L. Ablon & J. E. Mack 1980, pp. 181–2). Denyse Beaudet (1990, p. 130) relates that instance and two more, one of "a fourteen-month-old child who had awakened frightened saying that *a rabbit was about to bite her*" (citing S. Isaacs, *The Nursery Years*, New York: Vanguard, 1932), the other of "a fifteen-month-old boy who during his sleep yelled, *'Let me down, let me down.'* He had been tied to the examination table at the doctor's that day" (quoting S. H. Fraiberg, "Sleep disturbances of early childhood," *Psychoanalytic Study of the Child* 5, p. 286, 1950). Such examples can only be gathered from children with some language skills, but Fiss (1986, p. 178 and 1993, p. 403) conjectures that infants dream from birth, on the basis of those innate perceptual tendencies already functioning or about to function when they enter the world.

80, an average person sleeps only 6 hours per night and spends little or even no time in deep sleep.[34]*

There is some gender difference: adult women have slightly more deep and REM sleep than men, and do not lose as much REM time in old age.[35]

The amount of time we spend nightly in REM is marginally sensitive to a number of known influences, among them the *wish to dream*.[36] REM time goes up through the *menstrual cycle*, possibly due to hormonal changes, and secondarily, to premenstrual tension.[37] If our *psychological defenses become stressed*, we will reach REM more quickly and dream somewhat longer, as if needing to resolve our conflict by dreaming.[38] Engaging in *solitary activities* all day causes REMPs to last longer and increases total REM time by considerable amounts as compared to being socially busy.[39]

Substances which elevate REM time include LSD and natural hallucinogens in the peyote family, which Jeremy Taylor says increase "dream recall dramatically," even when taken in quantities too minute to alter waking consciousness.[40] It is found by some people that B vitamins with lecithin make dreaming more vivid. B_6 may increase recall, but it is toxic if misused, and should not, warns Gayle Delaney, be experimented with.[41] Taylor is not as concerned about it. He suggests that toxicity results only from "massive" intake.** Other elevators of REM include the antibiotics, said to "increase the length of the first two REM periods of the night";[42] tryptophane, an amino acid found in dairy products (if taken as a dietary supplement, tryptophane causes drowsiness which may persist the morning after[43]); and a low carbohydrate, high fat diet.[44] In addition, various aromatic 'dream pillows' have been recommended.***

As for *substances which suppress REM* sleep, alcohol certainly has that effect on normal drinkers,[45] though the situation is complicated for chronic

---

* Dream recall from REM awakenings also declines with advanced age, in one sample to about 55% (E. Kahn, C. Fisher & L. Lieberman 1969, p. 1123). Kahn et al. attribute this change to factors such as "anxiety, repression, and resistances . . . inhibiting dream memory" rather than to loss of dreaming per se during REM (p. 1124). P. R. Robbins (1988, p. 54) adds the factor of loss of short-term memory.

** Symptoms of B vitamin overdose include "increased urination," sometimes with "mild discomfort"; then "tingling" and "progressive loss of sensation in the fingers and toes" (J. Taylor 1992a, p. 86).

*** Henry Reed (1988 [1985], pp. 69-70) suggests a pillow filled with mugwort, a fragrant herb. And here is Katherine L. West's herbal "dream pillow" recipe (1977, p. 10): one part each of barberry root, lemon verbena, lemon grass, and mistletoe; two parts each of raw dandelion root and eucalyptus. The dreamer is advised to fill a 3" x 4" cotton pillow with the mix and to sleep with it "*directly* under the middle of the forehead" while lying on one's back. Enhanced dreams are anticipated after ten nights.

alcoholics. "In the chronic alcoholic [total] REM sleep is both fragmented and decreased, but with the cessation of drinking, REM time increases but fragmentation continues."[46] Marijuana and cocaine both decrease dream recall.[47] Withdrawal from heroine causes a rebound effect of increased REM time, suggesting a suppression of REM with use.[48] Tobacco withdrawal also elevates REM time.[49] But these withdrawal effects might simply be due to stress. Amphetamines and other stimulants generally reduce REM time. So do barbiturates, benzodiazepines, and most of the sedative-hypnotic sleeping pills, tranquilizers, muscle relaxants, etc.[50] Barbiturates cause "dreams to be more conceptual and thoughtlike. . . ."[51] Some mood stabilizing drugs, such as lithium, reduce REM sleep, as do the antidepressants with the exception of trimipramine.[52] Antipsychotic drugs have mixed effects on sleep.[53] Stelazine, Haldol, and Tegretol are said to reduce dream recall, but effects vary with dosage, and during drug withdrawal REM time decreases.[54]

Many supposedly "non-psychotropic" medications actually have effects of one sort or another on REM sleep.[55] And finally, caffeine has no effect on REM sleep.[56] Caffeine withdrawal, however, usually brings an increase of dreaming. That is the effect of withdrawal from any stimulant.[57]

Certain of the bodily changes that take place during ascending stage 1, when dreaming is most active, have been noted: genital arousal, loss of muscle tonus, and the rapid eye movements themselves. What if any connection do these have to the content of dreams they accompany?

Genital arousal. Penile erection in sleep was first reported by German scientists before the REM era. They noted the periodicity (85 minutes), but of course were in no position to make the correlation to dreaming.[58] Men—including psychologically impotent men[59]—have erections in 80–95% of their REMPs, between a half and a third of these full erections, the rest partial.[60] This largely accounts for the familiar experience of awakening with an erection. Penile tumescence (accompanied by nipple erection[61]) can begin a couple of minutes before or after REM begins. Tumescence typically becomes full about five minutes into a REMP, and is mostly maintained throughout it. Gradual detumescence starts half a minute after REM ceases.

It should be noted that men also have erections which are confined entirely to NREM. This leads some to consider whether the phenomenon may be related to physiological mechanisms other than REM sleep[62] (see below).

Garfield reviews literature confirming the more recent observation of a comparable cycle in women, with these differences: vaginal-clitoral changes mostly occur within the first half of the REMP, and last an average of about 8 minutes; they reach maximum levels less often than do erections in men; and women have more of these events during NREM than do men.[63]

Is genital arousal during REM connected with sexual drive or the sexual content of dreams? The greatest vaginal blood flow, the firmest erections, and sudden erections are said to be associated with sexual dreams.[64] So sexuality can obviously be a factor. Interestingly, in men "castration anxiety" (induced by having to view, before bedtime, a documentary film showing ritual genital mutilation) sometimes causes what amounts to REM-erection impotence.[65] Such anxieties, when they crop up during a dream, can trigger detumescence[66] (in general, anxiety inhibits erection, asleep just as awake[67]). These negative effects probably have as much to do with the psychophysiology of aggression as of sexuality.

Arguing against a *necessary* connection between genital arousal and sexuality is the fact that the occurrence of erection is not diminished by orgasm before sleep or even by a 'wet dream' in the REMP just preceding. Moreover newborns have frequent erections, and erections diminish and disappear only with very advanced age,[68] while younger adults obviously have many more REM erections than sexual dreams (much less sexy ones).[69]

Perhaps most interesting is that erections generally come at 90 minute intervals even in the absence of REM sleep, as when a REMP is spontaneously skipped or is eliminated by sleep lab procedures.[70] Thus erection appears to be linked with the 90 minute periodicity of the deep physiological arousal system underlying the sleep cycle. In this light we might ponder Garfield's thought, that the phenomenon exhibits our "Kundalini . . . serpent power" in readiness.[71]

Atonia and muscle movements. On top of the general inhibition of movement in sleep, the muscles becomes especially slack during REM.* The brain stem's REM-on system sends "go" signals to the motor centers of the brain, finds Allan Hobson, but effectively cancels them by simultaneously sending "no go" signals to the spinal cord.[72] REMPs are often framed by a shift of

---

* The combination of cortical activation plus motor arrest, together with a cluster of other physiological measures, leads Adrian Morrison to conclude that the REM state is "a specialized version of . . . the orientation response" (H. T. Hunt 1989, pp. 28, citing A. R. Morrison & P. B. Reiner, "A dissection of paradoxical sleep," in D. J. McGinty, R. Drucker-Colin, A. Morrison & P. L. Parmeggiani, editors, *Brain Mechanisms in Sleep*, New York: Raven, 1985; see also A. R. Morrison 1983). In waking, an orienting episode proceeds from an unconscious sensory awareness, to the orienting response (OR) itself, to a conscious perception, or image. In sleep, speculates Raymond Rainville (1988, pp. 20–1), the direction is reversed: from an unconscious image, to the OR, to a sensory experience of the image. Hunt (p. 30) considers the OR to be "a common organismic background for dreaming and altered states of consciousness" in general. He might have said, for consciousness overall, as E. N. Sokolov (1963) proposed (see A. Shafton 1976, pp. 29–37). Other treatments of dreaming in connection with the OR include M. Koukkou & D. Lehmann (1993) and D. Kuiken & S. Sikora (1993).

the whole body.[73] The REMP itself is conspicuously quiet, but when major movements do intrude they often mark a transition from one distinct dream episode to the next: either the first episode closes naturally, or else the body movement breaks in and a new episode starts up. Dreamers often remember only the last episode from such a REMP.[74]

While large movements are inhibited during REM sleep, very fine movements of limb muscles actually increase.[75] These small, twitchy actions seem roughly related to the concurrent dream scenario, both with respect to the part of the body moved (upper or lower), and with respect to intensity. Fine movements of both upper and lower body reflect a globally active dream.[76] Moreover, in lucid dreams (the dreamer knows s/he is dreaming: see chapter 14), body muscles make "shadow" movements which are electrically detectable, and which match intentional actions performed in the dreams.[77]

Relevant fine movements of the facial muscles which produce expressions also occur. Inge Strauch, a Swiss investigator, finds that the smiling muscles are active during dreams which contain positive emotions (and also during dreams of speaking), whereas brow-knitting muscles are active during negatively toned dreams (and also during dreamt social signals of attention and concentration).[78]

What of those coherent physical activities we associate with sleep, namely, talking and walking? As for talking, "episodes are distributed more or less randomly throughout the night."[79] Consequently, over 75% occur during NREM sleep.[80] Words spoken during REM quite often (80%) bear a relation to a simultaneous dream action, more often than those spoken during NREM; but this may only be because recall from NREM is not as good. As Arthur Arkin et al. remark:

> [T]he experimenter is prone to feel astonishment when a subject utters a dramatic, emotion-infused speech, and following immediate awakening fails to report content. . . .
> . . . [This speech is from stage 4 sleep, for example:] *No! No! No, wait Sam! Wait!! No Sam, Sam, no wait a minute no—no—no—no, no I, I, I was, I was awake a little—mm-hm* [pause] *mm.*[81]*

---

* Quotes containing dream reports have been edited with the following conventions throughout this book. Dreams themselves are italicized. When introduced into the main body of text, dreams are occasionally edited or paraphrased. But when quoted in insets—the large majority of cases—the dreams themselves are transcribed exactly and completely, as published (only in exceptional, clearly indicated instances have I edited very long dreams quoted in insets). Where added italics make quotation marks superfluous, they have been omitted. Original italics have been bolded where necessary to differentiate them from italics added by me. Obvious typos have been corrected. Occasionally, ellipses indicate transposition of text for the sake of clarity.

Awakened twenty seconds later, the man could remember no dream, neither images nor feelings.

As for sleepwalking, almost all of it takes place during NREM stages 3 and 4,[82] "usually about an hour after the start of sleep, before REM sleep begins."[83]

Failure of REM atonia received attention in the media not long ago: in *REM sleep behavior disorder* (*RBD* or *RSBD*), an untimely loss of motor inhibition usually accompanies "dreams that are excessively vivid, action-filled, and violent,"[84] leading to complex behaviors often resulting in injuries to self or others. Carlos Schenck, Mark Mahowald and their colleagues have written about such cases, some involving actions which would be held criminal were they performed awake:

> A REM sleep behavior disorder vignette involves a 67-year-old man who was awakened one night by his wife's yelling as he was choking her. He was dreaming of *breaking the neck of a deer he had just knocked down*. The patient had tied himself to his bed with a rope at night for 6 years as a protective measure, owing to repeated episodes of jumping from bed and colliding with furniture and walls.[85]

Other examples include jumping from windows, driving cars, and climbing ladders. Most sufferers of RBD are men. Its causes can be neurological. Advanced age is predisposing, because the physiological mechanism of atonia begins to fail. Causes can also be psychological. "[A]dverse life events resulting in adjustment disorders or posttraumatic stress disorder can herald the onset" of RBD.[86]

Note that similar violent or self-destructive behaviors can also take place during night terrors and sleepwalking, which are NREM phenomena. Cartwright points out that such ordinary "[s]leepwalkers are not acting out their dreams."[87]

Besides failing to function when it should, the mechanism of sleep atonia sometimes does function when it should not. This mechanism is implicated in the disorders of cataplexy ("motor paralysis occurs suddenly without loss of consciousness") and sleep paralysis ("motor paralysis . . . persists after consciousness has been recovered" upon awakening).[88]

Eye movements. In 1892, George T. Ladd, a philosopher, surmised that the direction of eye movements during sleep corresponds with the direction of the dreamer's gaze within the spatial dreamscape.[89] This became known as the 'scanning hypothesis' when early dream lab scientists made the same surmise about REMs. Examples such as these were offered:

> [Awakened after a bout of vertical eye movements, the dreamer reported] *watching a blimp that hovered above him. The occupants of the blimp began dropping*

leaflets and [the dreamer] recalled alternately looking up at the blimp and down at the dropping leaflets.[90]

Only one instance of pure horizontal movement was seen. . . . *[The dreamer] was watching two people throwing tomatoes at each other.*[91]

[We have the report of] a highly active dream from a subject who was showing long periods of REM quiescence. This was puzzling until the subject pointed out that in the dream *she saw all the action on a television screen.*[92]

In the last of the studies just quoted, judges were able to *predict* the direction of eye movements by first reading the dreams, with about 80% success.

Lately it has been put forward by Hobson, on the basis of his theory of dream generation (see below), that correlations could just as well result from matching dream imagery to preceding eye movement nerve impulses as from matching eye movements to preceding imagery. To this extent, the dream is "a response to eye movement commands in the visual motor system."[93]

Be that as it may, the case is that the early, convincing demonstrations have not been duplicated, giving rise to skepticism about the supposed connection. It has been noted that the early blind, who lack visual dreams (see chapter 9), do have REMs; and that no directional eye movements accompany dreams occurring in NREM.[94] Recently John Herman et al. did have statistical success predicting eye movements from REM dreams, but only in instances when dream narratives gave pronounced indications. Even then, no outstandingly obvious examples arose. Their work "raises the question of whether this association is partial and intermittent or, alternatively, ubiquitous but difficult to discern uniformly."[95]

One suggested possibility is that correspondences do occur, as above, but only occasionally, and usually after single REMs.[96] But there is no conspicuous correlation between dream actions and eye movements. In fact, the eye movement may even be opposite the one expected:

One subject, for example, stated that at the end of her dream *she was looking at vertical rows of buttons from a distance of about 2 feet.* When asked how she looked at them, she replied, *I was looking vertically,* but the EOG record was almost entirely horizontal before awakening. . . .[97]

The exception, as in many regards, is lucid dreaming. Stephen LaBerge and others have shown that there is "a very direct and reliable relationship between gaze shifts" voluntarily carried out in the dreams and observed eye movements.[98] In an experiment by Morton Schatzman et al., for example, the triangular eye movements of an experienced subject corresponded to *the triangles he had agreed to draw on a chalkboard* in his lucid dream. Other successes involved writing, tracking, and so forth.[99]

The nature of the link between REM and dreaming remains a puzzle. (1) REMs (along with atonia and respiratory changes) occur in the presumable absence of dreams. This happens with people, and cats, who have lost their cerebral cortex.[100] Moreover, (2) dreams occur in the demonstrable absence of REMs. This happens during stage 1 sleep, in between REM clusters.[101] And more importantly, it happens outside of REM sleep altogether.

REM and NREM

At first it seemed conveniently simple: during REM sleep we dream; during NREM we do not. Lab awakenings from REM have consistently yielded dream reports at a rate of 80 to 90–95%, when awakenings are timed to coincide with REM clusters.[102] A person awakened without a reportable dream often says s/he was dreaming but cannot recall the content (so-called 'white dreams'). Even that fraction of awakenings with no trace of a dream is assumed to represent failure of recall, not dreamless sleep.[103] Awakenings from NREM, on the other hand, initially produced as little as 0% recall of anything.[104] But evidence of mental activity during NREM sleep soon grew. By one recent theory of memory, we recall from NREM sleep awakenings less well only because our brain state then is less like waking than it is during REM.[105] Findings of mentation during NREM have varied widely over the years, but by one estimate based on many studies, only 50% of lab awakenings from NREM yield nothing at all, whereas 10% yield dreams, while a full 40% yield something more like ordinary thinking.[106]*

So in place of the absolute distinction between REM and NREM with respect to mere recall, a distinction was found in the qualities of the dreams gathered from each. According to this well-known contrast, REM dreams are more storylike, NREM dreams more thoughtlike. Cartwright provides a pair of generic examples:

---

* Hunt (1989, p. 52) proposes that some NREM thinking may result from psychological defense against the intrusiveness of the lab setting. In one procedure, "when experienced senior researchers well used to the laboratory environment used themselves as subjects, levels of NREM thinking fell from the 70% found by most studies to 20 percent" (citing A. Kales, F. Hoedemaker, A. Jacobson, J. Kales, M. Paulson & T. Wilson, "Mentation during sleep: REM and NREM recall reports," *Perceptual and Motor Skills* 24, pp. 556–60, 1967). Further, Hunt thinks it possible that *all* types of NREM reports may result from defense, "created by an artificial vigilance carried into normally restitutive sleep." Blank sleep, in this event, "may be the functional norm" for NREM (p. 53). Hobson (1988, p. 145) suspects that many stage 4 reports are actually not memories of foregoing dreams but sleep talking, caused by the attempt to process environmental inputs while still physiologically in deep sleep.

When awakened from REM sleep, the report might begin: *"Holy smokes! I was skiing down a mountain. Somehow I wasn't touching the ground at all, and I was dressed only in a pair of ladies pink panties. . . . "* If the awakening had been from a NREM sleep period, the report would be quite different in character: "I was thinking about skiing, wondering if I could learn to do it at all at my age without looking ridiculous."[107]

Though both REM and NREM dreams tend to become more "dreamlike" as the night progresses,[108] they are generally considered to preserve certain differences. As listed by Ann Faraday, "NREM dreams are . . . shorter, less vivid, less visual, less dramatic, less elaborated, less emotional, less active; more plausible, more concerned with current problems, more purely conversational, more thoughtlike."[109] Faraday also finds NREM dreams less likely to be composed of distinguishable episodes. Allan Rechtschaffen et al. mention among other traits that NREM dreams seem to the dreamer typically to be more pleasant. They give this example of the more thoughtlike variety of NREM dream:

> This time I recall no dreaming at all. 'Thought' I guess you would call it. These thoughts, there was no obvious correlation between them. They were just *various things that I would like to do*, going from *wanting a sailboat*, say, which is one of them, to *doing something with various interests, chemistry particularly, and metallurgy*, which I happen to be interested in. Then it would drift back to the *sailing*. Then I would think about *school—going back to school.*[110]

John Antrobus thinks the apparent REM/NREM difference might merely be an artifact of better recall from REM, due to higher cortical activation.[111] But Harry Hunt counters that when dream reports are controlled for length, NREM dreams are indeed less dreamlike, i.e., they have fewer characters, less definite settings, and less bizarreness.[112] David Foulkes also thinks the difference arises at the time of dream generation.[113]

Some people have more consistently thoughtlike NREM experiences than others. Apparently the deeper a sleeper you are (i.e., difficult to awaken), the more likely it is that your NREM mentation will be of the thoughtlike type.[114] On the other hand, a small number of people have frequent dreamlike NREM experiences. They are psychologically normal, says Cartwright, but she compares them to schizophrenics insofar as REM dreaming appears to spill over into another state[115] (schizophrenia is sometimes called a "waking dream"[116]) (see chapter 9).

A few individuals "report more thoughts than images even during REM sleep."[117] And with most of us, it is not that we never 'think' in REM sleep; on the contrary, REM thoughts can be elaborate and sometimes very cogent (if usually not). This is particularly the case with lucid dreams.[118] But unlike prototypical NREM thinking, thinking in REM is usually bound up with the dream's hallucinated imagery. Very striking are those instances where the thinking consists of the dreamer interpreting the dream in the act of dreaming it. This occurs in ordinary non-lucidity, but especially in semi-lucidity and full lucidity,[119] where the quality of self-interpretation may (but does not necessarily) surpass any available to unprompted waking consciousness on that day (see chapter 14). NREM thoughts, by distinction, often seem "nonprogressive,"[120] nebulous, drifting and unconstructive. Little if anything gets "thought *through*."[121] The thinking of a person awakened from NREM quite often appears congested. S/he may complain, "I can't think." This is something which does not normally happen after REM awakenings.[122]

There is one type of dream report which is fairly unique to NREM awakenings, namely, of isolated, static imagery, lacking characters and setting. Foulkes mentions these instances: "*[A] pen writing on a drum, shelves with jars of purple liquid on them,* and *a big piece of yellow cake with whipped cream and a cherry on top.*"[123]*

In sum, there are several varieties of reports more common from NREM than from REM awakenings: no recall of anything, mere thinking, and isolated imagery.

Then are we actually dealing with two distinct types of dreams, REM and NREM? Their standard differences were noted above. A really full-blown REM-style dream is "rare" in NREM.[124] Judges have proven almost 95% successful telling which is which.[125] And lucidity may be confined to REM sleep[126] (although the rare event of lucidity maintained throughout a night's sleep[127] might suggest otherwise; see ch. 14, pp. 476-8). Another finding: someone exposed to a subliminal stimulus configuration tends to incorporate its more dreamlike aspects into REM mentation, its more thoughtlike aspects into NREM mentation.[128] Then there is Fiss's intriguing experiment showing that paying close attention to one's REM dreams and their meanings "is significantly associated with increased self-awareness and decreased psychopathology," whereas attending to NREM dreams is not.** Moreover, there do

---

* These NREM reports resemble, besides hypnagogic images (see below), certain schizophrenic dreams (W. Dement 1955, p. 226) (see chapter 9). Intuitively, they might seem age-regressive in character, but in fact their type emerges relatively late in development, not until age 13–15, during which epoch they also occur in REM sleep. Because they appear earliest in highly analytic children, Foulkes believes they are connected with the development of conceptualizing abilities (1985, pp. 135–6).

** H. Fiss (1979), pp. 59–60, citing H. Fiss & J. Lichtman, "Dream enhancement: an experimental approach to the adaptive function of dreams," paper presented to the Association for the Psychophysiological Study of Sleep, Cincinnati, Ohio, 1976. Fiss cites this paper in another place (1993, p. 402), where he also summarizes, somewhat inaccurately, a related experiment by Cartwright (R.

appear to be functional differences between the sleep stages, relating to organic regeneration, learning, emotional coping, and such matters.

But all of these indicators of difference notwithstanding, it remains that *most* NREM reports are not *radically* different from most ordinary narrative dreams. One early study had found dreams in only 7% of NREM awakenings, because it held NREM reports to a rigorous criterion of being "dreamlike."[129] But this jumped to 54% when the criterion was relaxed to include "any occurrence with visual, auditory, or kinesthetic imagery [or] in which the subject either assumed another identity than his own or felt that he was thinking in a physical setting other than that in which he actually was."[130] A "content analysis" by Calvin Hall concluded that "many non-REM reports were indistinguishable from REM reports."[131] And in contrast to the estimate based on many studies, mentioned above (p. 22), another such estimate determined that as many reports from NREM are of "dreaming" as of "thinking."[132] Two examples of NREM reports, which were actually adduced by Faraday to illustrate the REM/NREM contrast, also show their likeness:

> [1] It was all very vague. *I was in a street with two shadowy figures, and we were talking about something. I think one of them was a woman, the other male, but I couldn't see their faces and have no idea who they were. I was saying, "Go here, go there" or something. I was telling them where to go. . . .*
>
> [2] *I was drinking a cup of milk in bed here. And I was talking to somebody but I don't know who it was.* That's all.[133]

These both convey the impression of simple, vague, but veritable dreams as we think of dreams.

With the intent of puncturing yet one more received lab finding, William Domhoff concludes that between REM and NREM dreams "the similarities far outweigh the differences. . . ."[134] And Foulkes proposes that there is only a single dream-making system, one usually operating at fullest pitch during REM sleep.[135] True, there is not a simple gradient of dream production efficiency from NREM stage 4 through 3 and 2 to REM stage 1, since dreams from NREM stages 4 and 2 cannot be told apart for their 'dreamlike' qualities.[136*] But NREM dreams as a whole may just be incompletely developed

---

Cartwright, L. Tipton & J. Wicklund 1980): "[P]atients trained in attending to their REM dreams remained longer in treatment and made better progress than patients trained in attending to their non-REM dreams." What Cartwright actually found was that of patients who are not "psychologically minded" and therefore at risk of dropping out of treatment, those who discuss "dream-like" experiences, whether obtained from REM or NREM awakenings, have better therapeutic outcomes than those who discuss undreamlike material from NREM awakenings.

* LaBerge (1985, p. 48) states, however, that particularly toward morning and for light sleepers, "lengthy and vivid dreams" may be reported from stage 2.

'REM dreams'; the more 'undreamlike' ones would, if that were so, reveal some of the unorganized components of potential 'dreams'. These Foulkes studies, like embryos, to discover the primitive features of the dream formation process which they reveal.

Hypnagogic Dreams, and Stages of Sleep Onset

Not yet mentioned is a further and rather special category of dreaming outside of REM sleep: so-called *hypnagogic* (leading-to-sleep) *dreams* or *images*, which occur during descending stage 1 sleep. These are the dreamlets many people have while falling off to sleep.

As mentioned, the EEG profile of descending stage 1 differs slightly from ascending,* presumably due to residual waking activation. In someone who falls asleep quickly, this stage may last only 30–60 seconds. Virtually 100% of lab awakenings then yield mental activity, very little of which resembles NREM 'thoughts'; but it is not fully like most REM dreams, either. Coherent narratives may develop if the stage lasts awhile, but they are usually less well elaborated than REM dreams, and seemingly accelerated sometimes— more like a sequence of still shots than a movie.** The 'self' or 'dream-ego' is much likelier to be missing from a hypnagogic dream than from any other, and they are typically emotionally flat, if often exceptionally vivid.

What makes hypnagogic dreams so engaging is this vividness, together with the often seemingly fractured, decoupled, or embryonic nature of the imagery. "There may be 'incomplete' images (such as *a number hanging in mid-air*) or 'superimposed' images (such as *a train station overlaying an image of strawberries*)."[137]

Such fragments may occur in isolation, or follow one another in bizarre sequence:

1) *Two dogs fighting over a piece of cloth.* 2) *Storming the barricades and trying to penetrate something.* 3) *The gait of a hemiplegic.* 4) *Trying to get a look inside a cube.*[138]

Sometimes, a hypnagogic image constitutes a symbolic transformation of the last pre-sleep thoughts:

---

* Unless otherwise indicated, information in this paragraph comes from D. Foulkes & G. Vogel (1965) and from D. Foulkes (1978) and (1985).

** One culture has been written about, the Yolmo of Nepal, where dreams are dreamt, recalled, selected for sharing, and/or styled for telling in the form of discrete images rather than narratives (R. R. Desjarlais 1991, p. 220).

Last remembered thought: I had been asked to get a certain job done that was not my responsibility. I, in turn, assigned it to a coworker, Bob. Much to my chagrin, he made a mess of it.

Hypnagogic image: *We were playing football. I tossed the ball to Bob, feeling certain that he would make a touchdown. Instead he fumbled the ball.*[139]

This insight about hypnagogic dreams is owed to Freud's contemporary Herbert Silberer, who published examples of what he termed the "auto-symbolic" process active at sleep onset:

> While lying in bed at night, I remember that I have to correct a passage in a paper I have written. While considering this fact I become drowsy, and the following hallucination occurs: *I am busy smooth-planing a piece of wood.*[140]

Silberer found auto-symbolic transformations of three types of material: (1) the content of thoughts (as above), (2) the thought process (including images of falling asleep itself), and (3) somatic sensations (see chapter 8). Here is an example of the symbolic rendering of a thought process:

> I am pondering a problem, and because of my drowsiness, detail escapes me. The image shows *me asking for information at an office. A sullen officer, who appears to have mislaid the file, refuses the information.* The interpretation is obvious.[141]

Silberer thought auto-symbolic phenomena worthy of attention because, he felt, they are "rudimentary dreams."[142] Images of the type he described resemble hypnotically induced dream images in being obviously significant, while "relatively poor in multiple meanings."[143] Waking associations to sleep onset dreams are more likely to reference specific real life episodes than are associations to REM dreams.[144]

Other hypnagogic events are less obviously if at all relevant in this relatively immediate way. While most seem less bizarre, more "lifelike" than REM dreams,[145] yet at the same time, "paranormal, apparitional, and out-of-body experiences occur most commonly at sleep onset."[146] "Hypnagogic effects can include the sense of uncanniness and unreality, bizarre visual, somatic, and auditory hallucinations, geometric patterns, synaesthesias, and brief 'cosmic' delusions that are also typical of psychedelic drugs."[147] The following such dream, of an "archetypal character and significance," will also serve to exemplify a well-developed hypnagogic 'dream'. LaBerge relates a subject's image:

> *I saw the huge torso of a man,* she reported, *rising out of the depths of a profoundly dark-blue sea. I knew, somehow, that he was a god. Between his shoulders, in place of a head, he had a large golden disc engraved with ancient designs. It reminded me of the high art of the Incas. He continued to rise out of the*

sea. The rays of light streaming out from behind him told me the sun was setting. People, clothed in dark garments, were diving into his face—the golden disc. I knew they were dead, and it seemed to me they were being "redeemed" by this action.[148]

Underlying this variety of sleep onset phenomena, Foulkes, Gerald Vogel and coworkers have discerned a pattern of steps 'downward' from a waking state into a sleeping state. Described in 1966 in terms of "ego functions,"[149] it amounts to a pattern of changes for breaking the grip of waking reality. One of the ego functions involved is *"maintaining contact with the external world,"* being aware of oneself in the actual environment; the other function is *"maintaining nonregressive content,"* where 'regressive' implies bizarre, incomplete, implausible, and so on.

There are three downward steps:

(1) In presleep alpha relaxation, both functions are fairly intact. Reality contact weakens, but though mental imagery increases it is usually not mistaken for the external world.

(2) In the hypnagogic period proper (just described above), usually during descending stage 1 sleep, *both* ego functions are lost. It is as though the mind needs to "destructuralize," to scramble itself in order to let go of the waking world and subside into sleep. The dream world is fully hallucinated and the dream content may be exceptionally "regressive." An emotional flatness in this period also facilitates the letting go.

(3) Usually reached with stage 2 sleep, this step is still marked by non-contact with the real environment, but also by a considerable return from regressive to nonregressive content—in short, to typical NREM 'thinking', the simpler, less lively NREM 'dreaming'.

Here is an engaging illustration of the three-stage downward progression:

[(1) "relatively intact ego"] *I was thinking of sending clippings to a Russian pianist and I saw an envelope with 15¢ postage.*

(The subject is a concert pianist. The content is not regressive. The subject had lost volitional control over content, was unaware of his surroundings, but knew that the image was in his mind and not in the external world.)

[(2) "destructuralized ego"] *I was observing the inside of a pleural cavity. There were small people in it, like in a room. The people were hairy, like monkeys. The walls of the pleural cavity are made of ice and slippery. In the midpart there is an ivory bench with people sitting on it. Some people are throwing balls of cheese against the inner side of the chest wall.*

(The report contains bizarre, implausibly-associated elements, distortions, etc. There was a complete loss of contact with external reality during the reported experience.)

[(3) "restructuralized ego"] *I was driving a car, telling other people you shouldn't go over a certain speed limit.*
(In this report it will be noted that the content is again plausible and realistic. There was a complete loss of contact with external reality during the reported experience.)[150]

So there are two ways of describing falling asleep: one, in terms of EEG sleep stages, and the other, in terms of a psychological progression. Foulkes gives more details of the psychological side than repeated here, in particular concerning the vicissitudes of our directive, reflective self. But for the present purpose the interesting thing is that these two dimensions, the physiological and the psychological, usually but not always parallel each other. The EEG sequence is relatively invariable; and the psychological sequence, although showing considerable deviation from one person to another,[151] is also quite invariable for each individual. But the two sequences are often enough and far enough out of sync with each other to suggest that changes in our dream state depend on a set of *psychological* conditions, ones subserved by but not wholly dependent upon physiological correlates.[152]*

---

[*] M. Bosinelli (1991) mentions additional correlates possibly explaining the characteristics of sleep onset mentation. Hunt (1989, p. 187) makes a suggestion involving brain hemispheric functions. When one passes from Foulkes's step (1) to step (2), overall brain activation lowers to the point where the usual, waking dominance of the left, verbal hemisphere is reduced, disinhibiting the right, imagistic hemisphere. Step (3) comes with still lower activation: the right hemisphere subsides and the left partially reasserts itself.

The association between dreaming and right hemisphere activation in people with the usual pattern of hemispheric dominance (R. E. Ornstein, *The Psychology of Consciousness*, San Francisco: Freeman, 1972, cited by J. Antrobus 1987, p. 359) has been said recently to be small or nonexistent (R. W. McCarley & J. A. Hobson 1979, p. 110). Moreover, "[w]hen found, activation of the right hemisphere prior to waking is associated with poorer rather than richer dream phenomenology" (A. Moffitt & R. Hoffmann 1986, p. 149). Hunt (1989, p. 169) cites the same article as saying that right hemisphere activation correlates to dream bizarreness, even though Moffitt & Hoffmann conclude that the association "seems to be incorrect rather than tenuous and indirect" (p. 149). Conceding that hemispheric dominance is highly variable among individuals, Hunt (p. 168) says that generally the same balance of right and left hemispheric functions obtains in dreaming as awake, but with somewhat more prominence of right functions, lending dreams their "intrinsically bizarre visual-spatial imageries, powerful affect, and kinesthetic self-awareness" (p. 170).

John Antrobus's (1987) "review finds no support for early proposals that the [right hemisphere] is the primary location for dream production" (p. 359). The right hemisphere may, Antrobus concedes, make some unique contribution to the visual content of dreams (p. 366). However, the left hemisphere "is capable of independently producing dreamlike mentation . . ." and most of the cortical structures implicated in dreaming are in the left not the right hemisphere.

LaBerge (S. LaBerge & H. Rheingold 1990, pp. 22–3) has determined, by having lucid dreamers signal at critical moments during preagreed dream events, that such events have physiological correlates which largely, though not completely, correspond to those of the same events in waking. Activities tested thus far include singing (right hemisphere) and counting (left hemisphere).

Less often discussed than dreams of sleep onset are dreams which occur sometimes while leaving sleep, called *hypnopompic dreams* or *images*. Like their counterparts from sleep onset, hypnopompic images may exhibit auto-symbolism, as Jean Piaget illustrates with one based on somatic sensations (Silberer's third category; see above, p. 27):

Half-wakened by cramp in a bent leg, the subject stretched it out, and just as he stood up *he saw a frog with its legs moving from a state of flexion to an upright position. He had the feeling that he was still dreaming, and was himself the frog.*[153]

Waking Dreams

It emerges from these discussions that dreaming is not only not necessarily tied to REM sleep, it is not tied to any physiological condition, at least by current knowledge. In fact, it is not even necessarily tied to sleep.[154] It was noticed by Foulkes that his sleep lab subjects would sometimes report small dreams if questioned while still awake but fully relaxed. These *waking dreams** are sometimes but not always quite realistic, and their hallucinatory nature may be ambiguous, coming as they do as transient snatches between spells of knowing where one really is. An example from Foulkes illustrates the more realistic type of waking dream:

One young woman believed, on successive signals that: *she had been back in her old home town, standing in front of the drug store; her boyfriend had been sitting in her dormitory room drinking beer, as she thought about how upset she was with him; she had been in her dormitory room again, this time smoking a cigarette; a man had been leaning out a window, taking pictures of the clouds (she had been concerned that he might be leaning out too far and might fall).*[155]

Frank Heynick (1986, p. 323), who has studied reports of speech in REM dreams, concludes that there is "little to suggest loosening of integration between the two hemispheres, since (. . . in contrast to many cases of sleeptalking [usually a NREM phenomenon; see above, p. 19]) dream dialogue, apparently generated by the left hemisphere, seems closely related to the visual scenario presumed to be generated by the right hemisphere."

R. T. Pivik (1991, pp. 222–3) lists studies affirming and disfirming a special role for the right hemisphere in dreaming.

* The term 'waking dream' is found used to refer to any number of ways in which waking mental activity shows resemblances to dreaming. For example, I am using it here to label the small intrusions of dreaming into relaxed wakefulness described by Foulkes. Taylor (1983) applies it, in a negative sense, to waking behavior unconsciously governed by unwholesome psychological patterns. Mary Watkins (1984 [1976]) applies it, in a positive sense, to conscious participation in altered states having psychological or spiritual value.

Another example shows how transient these images may be:

> One subject, for instance, gave a nonhallucinatory report, but stated that just the moment before, she had believed that *she was inside a refrigerator, staring down at a sandwich on a lower shelf.*[156]

And another, how bizarre:

> *I was picturing this thing, this animal kind of thing. . . . It was gray, grayish white in color; it was really scaly. I pictured it in midair; it wasn't moving or flying or anything. It had little bowed legs, and regular hands and feet and all, and a face—no, there wasn't a face, there was sort of a helmet, you know, going down over his head, and it had these huge wings that were spreading out, but it was like a statue falling from somewhere, but it was more lifelike than a statue.*[157]*

What accounts for such intrusions of dreaming into the waking state? One possibility is that we are always dreaming, that we live above an aquifer of dream activity which we become conscious of only when the ground conditions allow it to surface. Freud (see chapter 2) conceived of several currents of unconscious dream-related activity. One current is our proto-mental *infantile wishes* bound to biological drives; another, our *dream-thoughts*, a current of formally rational but unconscious musings and fantasies, related to our day lives but energized by the infantile wishes which they evoke; and then, the *dream-work*, by which the other activities are disguised and made acceptable to us in the form of the actual dreams we experience. The dream-work, if not a constant process, does at least begin during the waking day: the dream "is like a firecracker, which takes hours to prepare but goes off in a minute."[158] This is supported by experiments which detect unconscious transformations of subliminally perceived images, indicating that the 'dream-work' is already in play before sleep.[159]

Jung wrote, "It is on the whole probable that we continually dream, but that consciousness makes such a noise that we do not hear it."[160] L. J. West compares dreams to the stars, "there all the time" but invisible through daylight.[161] Donald Meltzer likens dreaming to digestion, an ongoing process, in this case of "unconscious fantasy."[162] E. Klinger "suggests that fantasy forms a baseline, or background activity, in the waking state and dreaming forms a baseline during sleep. He suggests that these conditions make up a

---

* P. Cicogna, C. Cavallero & M. Bosinelli (1991, p. 415) cite J. Antrobus, "Mental processes during sleep and waking," *Sleep Research* 12, pp. 25-7, 1983 and several other studies confirming Foulkes regarding the similarities of "mental productions in sleep and relaxed wakefulness in an understimulated environment. . . ."

single waking and sleeping stream of ideation whose properties are modulated by fluctuations in the states of arousal and whose flow is interrupted only by certain incompatible activities."[163] Jon Tolaas cites reports of a 70–120 minute periodicity of daydreaming and inclination to fantasy during the waking day, and himself conjectures about a similar rhythm of psi receptivity, based on one and the same "image tide."[164] Many others similarly hold the opinion that we either do, or are able to do, something dreamlike just about all of the time.

Foulkes, in reflecting on the waking dreams he found in the lab, wonders "how much of what we consider characteristic of dreaming is already anticipated by a stream of perceptual consciousness available to waking introspection?"[165] He is talking not so much about a background or underground of continuous dreaming, as about shifts of state in which front-and-center consciousness momentarily trips over into dream production. For Foulkes, the gist of the matter is that "the sleeping mind is not functionally distinct from the waking mind; hence dreaming does not depend on mental processes or systems that are in any way unique to sleep."[166]

Not to deny that most of our accessible dreaming is done asleep, or that most dreams we recall are in fact REM dreams. But, Foulkes points out, observations of waking hallucinatory experience have been registered repeatedly in the past, only to be ignored or forgotten.[167] Historically, the West has held to dichotomies of waking/sleeping, sane/insane, self/other, now/then, real/unreal—ethnocentric dichotomies (anthropologists and minority psychologists also tell us[168]), which make it awkward for us to acknowledge hallucinatory episodes as normal, or even to identify them. This assessment by Foulkes should be congenial to those who approve the shift of Euro-American attitudes away from rigid dualisms. Many people interest themselves in dreams nowadays, and take enrichment from the dream state. Quite a few have heard of Native American vision questing, of Senoi dream control, or of Tibetan dream yoga. Many of us have used hallucinogenic drugs or techniques which cultivate altered states: meditation, visualization, hypnosis, lucidity. Foulkes's levelling of waking and sleeping with respect to dreaming might appear to be up this street.

'Nothing-but' Theories of Dreaming

But in fact, Foulkes does not lead us in that direction. It has to be disappointing that this most prolific of dream experimenters and theorists should have so little to say in favor of the value of our dreams. Foulkes tells us that the conditions favorable for dream production consist basically of a turning of the mind inward and a slackening of the voluntary 'I'. At such times, our cognitive faculties may not be operating in full, but neither do they change their nature. What does change is the object our minds are brought to bear on: no longer the impinging sensory world. Now, we have to make sense and order of a jumbled array of "mnemonic elements,"[169] which is to say, everything mental happening in our heads, but without the sense and order which attunement to the outside world contributes. The mnemonic array is most chaotic during high cortical activation, and consequently stage 1 tends to produce dreams which are relatively flourishing and bizarre. But fundamentally the same thing is happening whenever conditions for dreaming are right, namely, that a cognitive system designed for making proper sense of the outer world sets to work making spurious sense of the random dischargings of our memory system. Dreaming comes off as an inferior product of cognition.

Foulkes does not particularly quarrel with Freudian theories of infantile sexuality and neurosis,[170] so much as he does with Freud's fundamental proposition about dreams, that they come into being like neurotic symptoms and therefore expose our unconscious to view in a particularly revealing way. But whereas many spurn the Freudian view as too restrictive with respect to the meanings and functions dreams may have, Foulkes finds it too comprehensive. He writes: "When laboratory experimenters say that adequately sampled REM dreams are relatively 'mundane,' 'dull,' or 'uninteresting,' they're suggesting that the run-of-the-mill dream is *not* highly self-revelatory."[171] And: "Since it seems that the activation of mnemonic elements during dreaming and their selection for dream processing *is* random and arbitrary, it's not likely that the *particular contents of our dreams*—in and of themselves—serve any adaptive function."[172] These views are diametrically different from those of interpreters who hold the belief that "nothing appears by chance in a dream . . . ," that "[n]o minor aspect of the dream is extraneous. . . ."[173] Foulkes considers it "quite likely that REM dreaming could be only the fortuitous by-product of the evolution of other systems that independently have significant adaptive value (e.g., REM sleep, representational intelligence), but whose convergence in REM dreaming typically conveys few if any additional adaptive advantages."[174]

Not to say dreams are entirely devoid of meaning. Although there is no framed message in a dream, nor any part of the mind coherently trying to have its say, nevertheless, a dream "can still be read for its *indications* of the mind of the person who dreamt it." However, the dream has no special claim in this respect, it only contains "the kind of information that inevitably is contained in any spontaneous and organized act of the human mind."[175]

So if we examine a dream series we may well pick up trends of personality, but not any more than "from systematic study (or even casual observation) in wakefulness."[176]

Dreams are very much worth study for what they can tell us about how minds in general work, says Foulkes, but only marginally so for understanding individual minds, which is the interest of dream interpreters.

Much the same position has been taken by John Antrobus, another cognitive psychologist[177] (they study reasoning, memory, imagination, and other dimensions of mental performance). But of contemporaries whose thrust is to diminish the dream as a vehicle of self-understanding, their views are less known popularly than the *activation-synthesis hypothesis* of psychiatrists Allan Hobson & Robert McCarley. Using Freudian orthodoxy as a foil (not to say straw man), Hobson means to establish that neither in its motivation nor its form is a dream a psychodynamically supercharged fantasy.

As to dream motivation, Hobson describes in detail the periodic spontaneous arousal of the brain stem during sleep. He elaborates what has been obvious since the first revelations of sleep lab monitoring, that the brain will go on spontaneously arousing itself to dream, apart from Freudian infantile wishes seeking expression or any other putative psychodynamic factors. The brain stem has, or is, a "dream-state generator." According to this hypothesis, there exist two competing populations of nerve cells in the brain stem, one of which turns REM on, but only when the other periodically reduces its instruction to keep REM turned off. The cycle which "reciprocal-interaction" of these cell populations produces is probably driven by the inhibitory "REM-off" cells.[178] Hobson has little to say about top-down, mind-to-body feedback from the dream experience to the brain stem arousal system[179] (see remarks on the orienting response above, p. 18n).

What he says about the forms dreams take evokes nineteenth century somatic explanations reviewed by Freud. He reduces typical dreams and prominent dream features to central nervous system causes. The large amount of motor activity in dreams (possibly overestimated by Hobson[180]) correlates with the regular activation of the motor system during sleep.[181] Bizarreness correlates with a "heightened degree of simultaneous activation of multiple sensory channels," and "[d]ifficulty fleeing," with conflicting activations and inhibitions.[182] "[S]uch features as scene shift, time compression, personal condensations, splitting, and [even] symbol formation" are nothing but the psychological aspects of unruly central nervous system stimulations.[183]

So much for the "activation" side. As for "synthesis," Hobson says, like Foulkes, that the sleeping mind does the same thing the waking mind does, it tries to make sense. Where for Foulkes, randomly activated memory is the raw material, for Hobson the raw materials are random sensory signals, muscle impulses, and emotional discharges, while the memory system is the synthesizer where current information is compared to stored information.[184]

Whether or not these are two ways of conceptualizing the same process, under both theories "the forebrain may be making the best of a bad job in producing even partially coherent dream imagery from . . . relatively noisy signals. . . ."[185] If the Freudian wish does not generate the dream, neither does the Freudian "dream-work" apparatus "disguise" to conceal any such latent wish. Noise prompts the composition of dreams.[186] Hunt characterizes Hobson's notion: "The cortex obliges with its tenuous and confused tales, mostly mundane and signifying nothing."[187]

Where, if anywhere, does life-relevant meaning come in? Again as for Foulkes, only in the dreamer's style of making sense out of the dream's raw makings. Hobson concedes that these constitute a sort of Rorschach field for the dreamer to project onto as the dream becomes organized.[188] The ad hoc order made of primary chaos "is a function of our own personal view of the world, our current preoccupations, our remote memories, our feelings, and our beliefs. That's all."[189] But at the same time, "[a]ny number of psychological functions can be superimposed upon the process—integrating daytime experiences with those memories already stored away, allowing the dreamer to deal with upsetting ideas and events, addressing one's unsolved problems, and coming up with tentative solutions." "As a result, dreams may be worthy of scrutiny when one reviews life strategies."[190] Hobson sincerely affirms the creative and problem-solving capacity* of the synthesized dream; he mentions positively the benefits of controlling dreams to provide favorable outcomes (see chapters 13–16); and he states that he consults his own dreams daily (though his published analyses of particular dreams tend to be superficial). In short, Hobson claims to "be able to avoid throwing out the psychodynamic baby with the psychoanalytic bathwater."[191] That sounds reasonable and promising.

Alan Moffitt et al. have criticized Hobson in terms which actually reiterate Hobson's own self-defense: "The usual understanding that dreaming is both meaningless and functionless because it is random, is incorrect. . . . Part of the popular confusion on this point derives from the failure to appreciate that the apparent randomness of dreaming at the physiological level is neutral with respect to the functional significance of dreaming at the psychological level."[192]

---

* For an excellent brief summary of famous anecdotal cases and experimental demonstrations of problem-solving in dreams, see D. Barrett (1993), pp. 115–7.

Moffitt could have emphasized more strongly Hobson's responsibility for the "confusion." In Hobson's view, observes Kelly Bulkley, the meanings of dreams must be "'transparent'" to be legitimate.[193] Further reaches of interpretation are "in the eye of the beholder—not in the dream itself."[194] In this regard Hobson professes to align himself with Jung,[195] which is accurate only in the negative sense that neither agrees with Freud's account of dream disguise (see chapters 2 and 3). But beyond that, his reading of dreams is not in the least Jungian. "Indeed," comments Bulkley, "Hobson ominously hints that looking beyond the transparent meaning and engaging in 'symbolic' interpretation may be 'unhealthy,' even 'dangerous'—although he never says exactly how."[196] He demands scientific proof of symbolic meaningfulness before he will recognize it.[197] In sum, Hobson thinks dreams are worth studying for what they can tell us about psychoneurology in general, but only marginally so for understanding individual minds.

Hobson's biological reductionism does not take account of an important element of evolutionary theory. Evolving biological systems incorporate and build upon preexistent systems. Human evolution may well have selected for adaptations of dreaming which incorporate the primitive bursts of brain stem activity studied by Hobson. That is, the dream-synthesizing mind-brain may exhibit systematic properties of meaning, beyond personal idiosyncracies of ad hoc remedies to chaos. The various types of dreaming—problem-solving, precognitive, archetypal, and such—may possess their own psychobiologies, superimposed on the "dream-state generator."*

On other grounds, Foulkes criticizes the fundamental project of explaining dreams by neurophysiology. "[I]t is functional/psychological research, and not neural modeling, that advances our understanding of complex mental phenomena."[198] As things stand in the pertinent disciplines, "[m]ental phenomena require mentalistic (non-reductionistic, functional) explanations." To Hobson's activation-synthesis hypothesis in particular, Foulkes raises these objections: that there has been no verification with "point-for-point, brain-event-to-mind-event correspondences" (a problem with any neurophysiological theory); that the mental role of the brain stem is poorly understood; and that the hypothesis is weakened by the fact that "dreaming can and does occur in other states."[199]** Hobson himself concedes that "[w]e have only frag-

* S. J. Ellman & L. N. Weinstein make a similar argument concerning Crick's reverse learning theory (see below).

** Cognitive psychologist Robert Haskell endorses Foulkes on the point that psychophysiology has gone as far as it can with dreams (1986a, p. 141)—but not that cognitive psychology is the sole legitimate successor discipline. Haskell rejoins: "What is there to say in the face of such disciplinary arrogance and ecumenical single mindedness, except to wonder how a mind like Foulkes's could be-

mentary details of how human physiology influences these mental process-es."[200] He allows that we do not even "really know the origin of the voltages that are measured" by EEG on the skin surface.[201]

But as we have seen, it is the *activation* side of the activation-synthesis hypothesis which Hobson renders in neurobiological terms; the *synthesis* of dreams he does describe largely, if not very appreciatively, in terms of func-tion. And to that extent, the theories of Hobson and Foulkes have much in common. They differ as to the precise source of random stimulation and the role of memory; but both account for dreaming as the mere attempt to make some sort of sense out of actual disorder.

In rejoining to Hobson, Cartwright speaks for many others: "When we study dreams of people in the sleep laboratory in the order in which they oc-cur, we find the images much more relevant to the dreamer's life than Hob-son and McCarley suggest."[202] (See also ch. 9, p. 318n.)

Hunt, whose "diamond of dream types" was mentioned (introduction, p. 4), takes exception to both theories, Hobson's and Foulkes's, with regard to randomness. Speaking of Hobson, Hunt simply questions the randomness of brain stem activity: "It may be, in fact, that the assertion of physiologi-cal 'randomness' is actually based more on a judgment about the experience of dreaming than on anything demonstrable within brain stem activation."[203] Speaking of Foulkes, Hunt does not accept that the dream is merely "syntax imposed on diffuse memory activation, but without any underlying intention-al semantics." Foulkes takes in only a part of what goes on in dreams, the part related to language, memory, and sequential, "representational" sym-bolic thought processes; the part Foulkes neglects is "presentational," imag-istic, and simultaneous more than sequential. Hunt's dream types result from a mix of these parts.*

To epitomize his differences with Foulkes, Hunt refers to the polarity in Western thought between rationalism (narrative-linguistic) and romanticism (imagistic-esthetic). Hunt comes down for romanticism. All the more inter-esting dream phenomena lean heavily on *meaningful* "imagery and metaphor

---

lieve this proposition" (p. 147). Haskell does not subscribe to Foulkes's idea of there being a single cognitive system for dreaming and waking (p. 145), and insists that dream meaning is a proper focus for research (p. 148).

* "It is difficult to imagine two researchers more disparate. . . ." "For Hunt," writes Haskell (1986b, p. 352), "symbolic consciousness is constituted by nonconscious 'meanings' that are repre-sented in symbolic consciousness; for Foulkes, symbolic consciousness is simply the ability to think about things that are not physically present." Haskell himself (p. 353) means to reach "beyond the historical dichotomies that have pervaded dream research," and, among other varied interests (see References), he undertakes what he hopes will become an adequate deciphering of the logic whereby meaning is expressed in dreams and other symbolic processes.

as an abstract cognitive ability in its own right." The dreaming mind spontaneously generates metaphors meaningful for the dreamer's life.[204] Dreams (as well as the imageries born of other altered states) are more, he argues, than mere "faces in clouds" into which we project significance upon awakening. Hunt attempts to give a foundation in cognitive psychology to Jung's convictions about "an abstract intuitive self-reference in the very fabric" of dream imagery.[205]

Hunt characterizes his cognitive approach as science with "heart," in distinction to Foulkes's "head" science. Foulkes depicts the mind as a computational device, which can theoretically be described by models of artificial intelligence. Hunt's model "emerges out of and rests on the senses—in sentience, not computation."[206]

Several other recent dream theories should be mentioned here, theories which like those just considered rest on some consolidation of REM findings with cognitive psychology, neurophysiology, and information theory.

Christopher Evans uses a computer analogy for the dreaming mind as a learning device. Evans envisions the raw stuff of dreams as derived more immediately from the life experience of the dreamer than does Foulkes or Hobson, but still dismisses the dream itself as just spurious mental byplay. During wakefulness, short-term memory keeps current inputs on hold; then during REM sleep, with sensory inputs reduced, information is processed for long-term memory, without the intercession of consciousness. A dream is nothing but "a momentary interception by the conscious mind of material being sorted, scanned, sifted, or whatever." Again as for Foulkes and for Hobson, confused consciousness seeks to "'interpret' it as a kind of pseudo-event and a dream is remembered."[207] But as Bert States insists when he endorses Evans's theory as a basis for his own speculations, "[d]reams are not intended for our conscious understanding. . . ." Dreams are "impersonal artifacts" with "no intrinsic meaning."[208]

A learning-and-memory theory of dreaming which is still more dispiriting for dream appreciators must be that of Francis Crick (of DNA fame) together with Graeme Mitchison,[209] according to whom the mind comes after itself like a night janitor to dispose of erroneous or superfluous learning accumulated during the day. We dream in order to unlearn, "in order to forget." This outlook was anticipated in the nineteenth century by Roberts (reviewed by Freud), who said that dreams are an "excretion" of "undigested thoughts" and "worthless impressions" of the day.[210] Where Evans has us eavesdropping on the nightly clean-up, Crick regards dreams as the very wastepaper itself, being tended to in the closed offices of the mind. Therefore we ought positively to avoid dream recall as "interfer[ing] with rational thought and memory"[211]—remembering a dream is like studying a rejected document on its way to the incinerator.*

Evans, in comparing dreaming to a computer clearing its memory before running a new program, had "likened dreams to the residue of a memory filter: disposable bits of irrelevant information."[212] Crick uses a neurological framework. To the activation-synthesis theory he adds the concept of "neural nets," a noncomputer model of brain circuitry. As I understand it, nets are also hard-wired (not a 'field'), but supposedly have operating principles which better correspond with human cognition. Reverse learning cleans up mistaken overlaps and connections in the neural net.[213]

Moffitt et al., while allowing that Crick's theory "has stimulated a great deal of rethinking of the functional significance of dreaming," reject it on these simple and cogent grounds: "Dreams and their waking interpretations can be correct rather than erroneous."[214]

In a related theory, J. Hopfield et al. say that when the neural memory network gets overloaded, memories begin to contaminate one another. REM sleep is a "random stimulation which preferentially evokes the mixed, or 'parasitic,' memory states. These are then unlearned. . . ." So paraphrases Mark Blagrove, who concludes regarding this and other unlearning theories, that they "rel[y] on an outmoded theory of memory as the collection and retrieval of independent items, rather than the view that the interactions and mixing of memories is an adaptive feature of both storage and retrieval."[215]

There exists here, with Foulkes, Hobson, Evans, Crick, and Hopfield, a family of theories which, with a little forcing, can all be fitted by a certain characterization. Employing the language of information processing or the computer metaphor, they describe the dream, at some stage of production, in terms of memory elements or learning processes. Furthermore, they are reductionistic toward the dream, and that, not only in the sense of stipulating the dream's supposed underlying causes (whether cognition awry, neural activations, or mnemonic housecleaning); but they are also reductive inasmuch as they devalue the dream (whether as a marginal source of information concerning the dreamer, as an accidental sideshow to another, more essential process, or as mental effluent or toxin). The net effect of these theories is the sort of scientific 'nothing but'-ism which demystifies to the point of depreciating the object of study.

---

* In response to criticism, Crick retreated slightly from the "slogan . . . we dream in order to forget." But he went on to make an equally contrary suggestion, that the seed of poetry and other products of the imagination is the residue of mistaken memory connections the dream clean-up process misses (F. Crick & G. Mitchison 1986, pp. 236–7).

Indications of Constructive Functions

It might well be that a portion of dreaming *is* system noise of some sort, while the rest of it serves the kinds of functions to be discussed throughout this book.[216] But even staying within the frame of memory, learning, information, computation, and/or network theory, it can be argued that dreaming is dynamically constructive rather than merely superfluous, mechanical, or janitorial.

Take Gordon Globus's application of network theory to dreaming. Raw activation is random, just as for Hobson, but the sequel to activation is not. "The networks are randomly activated, [then] certain intentional, instinctual, and affective tunings left salient at the end of the day become operative, and the networks begin to reorganize."[217] Self-reorganization is the main thing. "There is no program of serial rule-governed steps acting on input, as in a computer, but only a disturbed, fluidly reorganizing whole, constrained in its reorganizing movements by its connection weights."[218] Dreaming is "intrinsically problem-solving" insofar as it "harmonizes" conflicting networks. "[I]t may be that [when we dream] our knowledge even increases (that is, less probable solutions become available)."[219]

Less speculative is the laboratory finding with mammals and birds, that difficult learning tasks of all sorts are followed by augmented REM time.[220] Of course we cannot know for sure if other animals subjectively dream.* But

---

* V. S. Rotenberg (1993, p. 261) asserts that any adequate functional explanation of dreaming "should apply equally to humans and higher mammals." Jon Tolaas (1987, p. 144) believes that "basic drives like hunger, sex, and aggression [must] manifest themselves . . . in dream metaphors that truly depict [a mammal's] relatedness to its environment." Stanley Krippner (1993, p. 24) advances what he terms a "'survival hypothesis'. I think rapid eye movement sleep serves a survival function for mammals giving them an opportunity to rehearse and process strategies for survival during sleep in some sort of imagery form." Bulkeley (forthcoming), who proposes that we think of dreams in terms of "play" instead of "work" (as in 'dreamwork'), implies that since all mammals play, then all probably dream as well. LaBerge (1985, p. 192) assumes that if animals have REM, they dream. The same assumption is made by Hobson (1988) and by Taylor (1983, p. 6), a Unitarian Universalist minister and Jungian. Taylor goes so far as to suggest that because there are metabolic processes in animals and plants similar to REM in being cyclic, therefore *"all* living things may participate in the dream state." Elsewhere (1992a, p. 220) he endorses the animist-shamanic world view, that *"everything is alive"*—so perhaps he concludes that everything dreams. (Personally, I hold to a dual aspect theory, whereby what we call matter when regarding it from the outside is mind when regarded from inside. If one system, a human being, can have mentality, then perhaps every system (organic or inorganic) has mentality of a kind commensurate with its complexity. Dreaming would be found only in very complex, organic systems.)

Saying no, animals do not dream, is Foulkes (1985, p. 121), who argues that dreaming is not like just perceiving something, as animals obviously can, but rather is a constructive process of thought and imagination, beyond the capacity even of human children before age 1½–3, much less

whether they do or not, Darwinian considerations suggest an essential learning function for what goes on during sleep. Jouvet proposes that REM sleep serves the growth and conditioning of the nervous system.[221] Among mammals, fetal and neonatal REM sleep helps complete the innervation of innate action patterns—of feeding, homing, mating, etc. Early and late in life, it serves to integrate learned information with innate patterns, completing and updating them. Human REM sleep presumably does the same. The capacity for learning should be seen as an evolved dimension of any species' innate endowment.[222] As greatly as the learned component of human behavior may have expanded, and although it includes much of personality, it remains anchored to a bed of innate predispositions. REM sleep helps integrate inherited with acquired facets of behavior, subjective facets included.

Jouvet's approach allows us to see the human dream in an evolutionary context: dreaming is an evolved mechanism of the mammalian way of maturation. In the human case, this includes the development and maintenance of such psychological features as the self-concept,[223] the body-image,[224] and

---

animals. The spirit of this difference is plain enough: Foulkes does not believe that dreaming connects us to our deeper being, touching what we primitively share with fellow creatures. He does not indulge in the science fiction, in the best sense, of imagining the infrahuman homologues or analogues of human dreaming. These might not be tied to REM, if a species lacks it—note that the two species of dolphins tested have no REM (F. Crick & G. Mitchison 1986, citing L. M. Mukhametov, "Sleep in marine mammals," *Experimental Brain Research*, Supplement 8, pp. 227–38, 1984). Homologues and analogues might even not occur in sleep, if a species happens not to sleep (T. Allison & H. Van Twyver 1974 [1970]; T. Allison & D. V. Cicchetti 1976; J. A. Hobson 1989).

A reasoned response to Foulkes is offered by Hunt, who argues that because perception in lower species has the same constructive (not merely passive sensational) aspect as in humans, they too can dream (1986, p. 259). Hunt maintains that an animal's capacities for anticipation and recall seem to implicate some kind of "imagery," and that consequently "any creature with an activated cortex in sleep dreams—presumably of its species-specific 'life-world' as hitherto experienced in wakefulness" (1985, pp. 5–6). Hunt believes that Foulkes's data on child dreaming, and their implications for animals, relate only to the *recall* of dreams, the ability to detach the dream from its ground of experience (H. T. Hunt et al. 1982).

Hunt refers in this connection to the well-known experiment by M. Jouvet which provides presumptive evidence that animals do dream (M. Jouvet, "The function of dreaming: a neurobiologist's point of view," in M. Gazzinaga & C. Blakemore, editors, *Handbook of Psychobiology*, New York: Academic Press, 1975, cited by E. Rossi 1985, p. 205; see also A. R. Morrison 1983). Operating on cats, Jouvet disconnected that part of the brain which causes motor inhibition (atonia) during REM. This is how Truett Allison and Henry Van Twyver (1974 [1970], p. 355) describe what appears to be such a cat's acting out of a dream: "It will rise, walk about, attack invisible enemies, stalk an imaginary prey, or sit quietly and follow an unseen object with its eyes for periods of several minutes—all while deeply asleep!" Another piece of experimental evidence was earlier offered by Charles Vaughan (1964). He conditioned rhesus monkeys to press a bar when any visual stimulus appeared. Asleep, and temporarily blinded, the monkeys spontaneously pressed the bar during REM (how is not stated), suggesting that they were experiencing visual dream imagery.

a sense of the past and the continuity of life*—to mention just several functions linked by various theorists to dreaming. For Jungians, it entails actualization of the archetypes, conceived of as innate action potentials and inbuilt patterns of perception. The Jungian individuation process is, then, the genetically prescribed master plan of maturation, which gets implemented in part by dreaming (see chapter 3).

Studies generally support a connection between dreaming and learning in the case of humans as of animals.[225] It was first reported in 1914 by R. Heine that "recall of recently learned information was significantly better after a period of sleep than after an equal period of wakefulness."[226] A recent finding is that *students in an intensive foreign language course* whose REM time increases do better than students whose REM time does not.[227] This suggests that REM sleep assists the "integration of unfamiliar information. . . ."[228] Among *aphasics*, who have to relearn the use of their own language due to neurological problems, REM levels are higher in those recovering speech, lower in those not.[229] With *narcoleptics*, who often fall asleep directly into REM, Lawrence Scrima demonstrated that learning is better after a period of REM sleep alone than after a period of NREM sleep alone, and better in both cases than after an equivalent period of wakefulness. In Scrima's opinion, REM sleep assists learning actively, whereas NREM sleep assists it passively, merely by providing a period of time without interference from waking distractions.[230] Studies also show that *people subjected to stress* before sleep have increased REM activity,[231] and that dreams generated in stressful circumstances, e.g., before and after surgery, actually help the dreamer to cope.[232] This is certainly also a kind of information processing and learning, as is having to adapt to *wearing prismatic glasses* reversing the visual field, which also augments REM time.[233]

---

* Stanley Palombo (1978, p. 7) writes that Samuel Lowy (*Foundations of Dream Interpretation*, London: Keegan, Paul, Trench & Trubner, 1942) "sees the dream as a series of connections between past and present experience." Quoting Lowy (as quoted by Richard Jones, *The New Psychology of Dreaming*, New York: Viking, pp. 201–2, 1970): "By means of the dream-formation, details of the past are continually reintroduced into consciousness, [and] are thus prevented from sinking into such depths that they cannot be recovered." Moreover, through formation of symbols which represent "a whole period of the dreamer's life," dreams keep alive not only "single details" but also "whole 'conglomerations' of past experience. . . . [T]he constancy and continuity existing in the process of dreaming . . . greatly [contribute] to the preservation of the cohesion and unity of mental life as a whole." "Lowy believes that the dream is not primarily destined for conscious memory," writes Emil Gutheil (1967 [1951], p. 95), "'but for intrapsychic affect-energetic purposes.'" The very forgetting of dreams speaks, in his view, strongly against their function being that of guiding waking life (R. M. Jones 1979a, pp. 287–9). Rather, by dreaming the unconscious forms "antibodies," as it were, against psychic situations. Memory of the dream is secondary to this.

Dream deprivation. Another way to assess the relation between learning and dreaming is by so-called 'deprivation' experiments. In these experiments sleep is denied to the subject during a chosen sleep stage or stages, in order to see what effect this has. One very suggestive finding with animals is that whereas being reared in an enriched environment increases the brain weight of young rats, the effect is obviated when the animals are deprived of REM sleep.[234] In another suggestive experiment, young mice reared in social isolation, when kept awake following what would otherwise be socializing exposure to other mice, failed to develop normal social responses. Other mice kept awake for an equal amount of time, but *before* social exposure, did develop normal responses.[235*]

REM deprivation requires mention in this chapter anyway because of the widespread misconception associated with it. Dement's original study of it noted effects of "anxiety, irritability, and difficulty in concentrating," and one case of "serious anxiety and agitation" after five days. Dement floated the possibility "that if the dream suppression were carried on long enough, a serious disruption of the personality would result."[236] This compelling conjecture, perhaps confounded with findings concerning *sensory* deprivation and *total* sleep deprivation, gave rise to a popular belief that when deprived of dreams, we soon go crazy. Subsequent experiments, however, could only generate minor mood effects, even with longer-lasting REM deprivations.[237] "We have deprived human subjects of REM sleep for sixteen days," wrote Dement, "and cats for seventy consecutive days, without producing signs of serious psychological disruption."[238] (Quite possibly Dement's few first subjects were "unstable" to begin with.[239]) It continues with a life of its own, but the maddening effect of dream deprivation should have gone the way of other early misconceptions from sleep lab history, such as that we only have dreams during REM.

However, other less dramatic early REM deprivation findings have been confirmed in numerous studies over the years. A REM-deprived subject may appear "more animated and activated than usual," and show some memory deficit,[240] as well as increased appetite.[241] Most significantly, in sleep following deprivation there is a so-called *rebound* effect, an increase beyond the usual proportion of sleep given to REM, as if making up for the loss. The deprived person shows denser REMs and longer REMPs (if permitted them);

---

* Although it does not bear directly on learning, I have to mention here another, crueler sleep deprivation experiment with animals. Employing what can only be described as a torture apparatus, Allan Rechtschaffen established that *total* sleep deprivation causes rats to die in as few as 5 days (A. Rechtschaffen, M. A. Gilliland, B. M. Bergman & J. B. Winter 1983).

and the person returns to REM sleep sooner than usual and more often, even scores of times, as if in urgent need of it.* Cartwright nicely describes the battles between watchers and sleepers, whose "sleep records look as if they are trying more and more insistently to get into REM the longer researchers prevent it. Both sides wind up the night worn out from the effort and with a great respect for the possibility that there is a 'need to dream,' or at least a need for REM sleep."[242]

On the other hand, depriving subjects of stage 4 sleep rather than stage 1 has comparable effects: stage 4 urgency, rebound during subsequent sleep, and minor mood worsenings when awake (more depressed than anxious).[243] Moreover, if subjected to total sleep deprivation, stage 4 delta wave sleep is made up before lost REM sleep, the onset of which is delayed.[244]

Is it dreaming itself that we need, or some organic restorative processes accompanying and underlying dreaming? William Domhoff for one thinks that the need to dream per se cannot be extricated from the medley of deprivation study results.[245] But some observations do sustain the idea of a need to dream. One is that REM rebound can be reduced by interposing 'waking dream' activity between deprivation and subsequent sleep.** Another is the

---

* Some studies indicate that not deprivation of REM time per se, but rather of phasic events during REM (such as PGO spikes) is "the crucial variable in the occurrence of REM rebound. . ." (L. N. Weinstein, D. G. Schwartz & S. J. Ellman 1991, p. 378, citing several studies by W. C. Dement and colleagues). Such phasic events, when they occur outside of REM sleep, are also then associated with dreamlike mentation. On these grounds some researchers dispute that REM sleep, as defined by its "tonic" EEG characteristics, is a unitary 'third state' (R. T. Pivik 1991, p. 216).

** In evidence of this, Cartwright (R. Cartwright, L. Monroe & C. Palmer, "Individual differences in response to REM deprivation,"*Archives of General Psychiatry* 16, pp. 297–303, 1967, cited by H. Fiss 1979, pp. 51–2) has found that people with more native facility with waking fantasy show less REM rebound effect than those with less. Evidently they make up for the lost dream-time by functionally substituting waking fantasy. A related finding by Cartwright, with subjects not deprived of sleep, is "a dramatic reduction in the amount of time in REM sleep" on nights following hallucinatory fantasies induced by drugs. Cartwright concludes that waking dreamlike hallucinations in some measure satisfy a need to dream (P. A. Faber, G. S. Saayman & R. K. Papadopoulos 1983, p. 143, citing R. D. Cartwright, "Dream and drug induced fantasy behaviour," *Archives of General Psychiatry* 15, pp. 7–15, 1966 and other sources to the same effect). Other studies show that REM rebound following deprivation can be reduced by asking subjects to reflect on their own previous dreams or engage in visualizations before going back to sleep (D. Koulack 1991, pp. 156–7, citing R. D. Cartwright & L. J. Monroe, "Relation of dreaming and REM sleep: the effects of REM deprivation under two conditions," *Journal of Personality and Social Psychology* 10, pp. 69–74, 1968 and D. Koulack, "Effects of a hypnagogic type situation and a dull task on subsequent REM-rebound: a preliminary report," in M. H. Chase, W. C. Stern & P. L. Walter, editors, *Sleep Research 2*, Los Angeles: University of California, p. 167, 1973).

It has also been said that REM sleep "abruptly shortens in a state of high creative activity. . ." (V. S. Rotenberg 1993, p. 273, citing W. Mendelson, J. Gillin & R. Wyatt, *Human Sleep and Its Disorders*, New York: Plenum, 1977).

carry-over of dreamlike mentation into waking when a dream is interrupted, moreso than when dreaming is altogether prevented. To Fiss this indicates a need to complete one's dream independent of the need for REM per se.[246]

Another observation concerns the effect that REM deprivation has on the quality of the dreams gathered from REMPs following deprivation. Not only does dream imagery intensify,[247] but also the unfolding of the dream drama accelerates. Subjects consistently interrupted during REM learn to speed up their dreams in order to complete them before anticipated awakenings. Fiss reasons "that being prevented from completing a dream is far more disruptive than not being allowed to dream at all, and that therefore *the need to dream must be psychologically more important than sheer amount of dreaming*. . . . [This] suggests that dreams be regarded . . . as organized, meaningful, integrating, and synthesizing experiences."[248] Much the same point will be made in different ways throughout this book.

All the same, one is entitled to wonder just how essential the integrating and synthesizing role of dreams can be, if people deprived of REM by drugs for as much as six months show little if any adverse effect,[249] and if others (presumably suffering sleep disorders) do without REM for years "without showing any signs of mental breakdown."[250] All theories about the functions of sleep and dreaming, as Carl Sagan justly points out, should contend with the fact that not a few people get by on two hours of sleep or less habitually, without either physical or psychological deficit.[251] (But almost certainly no one never sleeps.[252])

Beyond questions of a 'need to dream' and global effects of deprivation, there is a literature examining the effects of deprivation on specific learning tasks set to animals and humans. With animals, the general finding is that a rat, for example, if set to learn a *difficult* task, will later remember what it has learned better if it experiences REM sleep in the meantime than if deprived of it. Performance on very *simple* learning tasks, on the other hand, is not similarly affected.* Comparable results with humans are very suggestive. For example, Isaac Lewin & Hanania Glaubman started their sleep lab subjects on two types of tasks to be performed the following morning. One task was simple rote learning ("serial memory of a list of 21 nonsense syllables"). The other, more difficult task required some "creativity" (the subject "lists as many uses as he can think of for a common brick, a wooden pencil,

---

* This literature is surveyed by M. J. McGrath & D. B. Cohen (1978). Doubts to the contrary are raised by H. Fiss (1979, p. 35). But alternative explanations for the learning deficit, such as hyperarousal caused by REM deprivation, or stress caused by the experimental procedure (M. Blagrove 1992), do not seem weighty enough to invalidate all such results.

etc.").[253] REM deprivation impaired performance on the creative task, but somehow actually enhanced simple serial memory.

Another line of inquiry examines the effect of REM deprivation, not on simple-rote vs. complex-creative, but on emotionally neutral vs. emotionally charged learning. One of many experiments by Ramon Greenberg and his colleagues indicates that "NREM sleep facilitates retention of non-emotional material, while REM sleep deals with material containing affective components."[254] Elsewhere, to examine emotional learning not in the sense of retaining something in memory but of coping emotionally with stress, Greenberg proceeded by showing his subjects a grisly autopsy film before sleep. Among subjects upset by the viewing, some were deprived of REM sleep before a second viewing, some not. Most of those allowed their REM sleep were less stressed at the second viewing than those deprived.[255]

Greenberg concludes that "REM sleep is involved in information processing in the service of emotional adaptation. . . . *[E]motionally* significant waking experiences touch on conflictual material from the past, arousing affects which require either defensive operations or an adaptive shift of response. Dreaming (REM sleep) provides an opportunity for integrating the recent experiences with the past, with a concomitant institution of characteristic defenses or a new resolution of the conflict."[256]

It is perhaps significant in connection with emotional learning that after REM deprivation, "low neurotics" rebound with more REM, shorter REM onset latency, and more intense dreams than do "high neurotics."[257]

Information Theories and Freud

Recognizable here, in new attire, is a Freudian principle of dream formation: waking events stir up unconscious impulses which then seek expression during sleep, when the repressive ego is in partial abeyance (see chapter 2). While distinctly *neo*-Freudian in its emphasis on ego defenses and conflict resolution, Greenberg's formulation aims at once at saving the Freudian theory from obsolescence, and the informational approach from inconsequence, by transposing the one into the frame of the other.

Cartwright largely endorses Greenberg, who in turn draws on a model of information processing developed by Louis Breger[258] as the basis of "a cognitive or information-processing interpretation of Freud's (1900) dream theory."[259] In Breger's model "there are two main information processing systems. The first is the rapid, action-oriented system primarily concerned with objective reality information . . . [while t]he second is a slower system which pertains more to subjective information geared to the development and maintenance of an organized pattern of personality traits known collectively as the self." The first system usually predominates in waking, whereas "[i]nformation relevant to the self . . . is for the most part carried over into the slower, off-line processing of sleep."[260]

Breger thinks that an informational approach actually does more justice to Freudian psychological observations than Freud's own "drive-discharge model," which lingers as "an anachronistic carry-over from nineteenth century science."[261] Certain important features of the Freudian theory, such as disguise, are rejected in favor of more neutral informational constructs. The central thesis about dream formation is that a day event, which constitutes new, affectively arousing information, activates a schema laid down in early life. In dreams, the current information is assimilated by the early solution, which is variously "defensive, magical, or realistic."[262] While the symbolic dream process is superficially "creative," Piaget's term "assimilation" (see ch. 7, p. 244) is borrowed to underscore the principle that the dream "plays no role in adaptation to the world. . . . Something must be done with dreams [awake] if they are to have an effect on a person's life."[263]*

Perhaps the most painstaking attempt to integrate Freud with information theory is that undertaken by Stanley Palombo. He compares sleep to down time on a large computer;** and he envisions a two-tiered dream process, the one a "computation" of information, the other a psychodynamic or "communication" process.[264] In the former, information gets moved from "temporary short-term memory . . . to permanent long-term storage." Extraneous bits of new information are eliminated, while pertinent bits are integrated.[265] In the psychodynamic process, which is superimposed over the computation, there operates "the conflict observed by Freud between the emergence of repressed childhood wishes and the countervailing action of the dream censor-

---

* A similar conclusion is reached by Swiss researchers Martha Koukkou & Dietrich Lehmann (1993), according to whose "state-shift hypothesis" the sleep stages entail "physiological regression to earlier stages of development" (p. 53). REM sleep is the most regressed stage (p. 95). The regression brings about comparison of recent memories with earlier experience as well as with innate information (p. 84), all of which is therapeutically useful though not inherently therapeutic (p. 93). Discussing this theory among other "Deficiency Views of Dreaming," Sheila Purcell et al. point out that "regression" derives from psychoanalytic reductionism (see chapter 2), and that "present data do not support the idea of all dreams as regressions to developmentally earlier levels of functioning. . ." (S. Purcell, A. Moffitt & R. Hoffmann 1993, p. 244).

** Palombo (1987a) argues that computers themselves—more precisely, large computer systems which require down time to process inputs from terminals—do in fact dream; not phenomenological dreaming, which is a "late refinement" in the evolution of REM sleep (p. 74), but dreaming in the sense that REM sleep is functionally the same kind of down time, for processing daytime inputs. Palombo asserts that study of such computer systems can enable a reconstruction of phylogenetic "precursor states" in premammalian animals (p. 61).

ship."[266] The two processes may complement one other, but often they work at cross-purposes, for the censor's agenda of disguising unacceptable wishes causes "mismatches" in the comparison of current and past information, and a mismatch causes anxiety. Palombo investigates the effect of mismatch on recall and subsequent dreaming.

Something which distinguishes Palombo's, as well as Breger's and Greenberg's informational models of dreaming from others we have looked at, is the aim of psychotherapeutic relevance. Palombo intends to help practitioners understand actual dreams of their clients. I wonder whether Palombo's somewhat ponderous formulations have actually had any appreciable influence on psychoanalytic practice—whether Freud and computation really mix in clinically fruitful ways. In Palombo's description of "mismatch" due to an incompatibility between psychodynamic and computative functions of the dreaming mind, I cannot help seeing a symbol—a waking dream symbol, as it were—of the conceptual mismatch of re-editing Freudian psychodynamics with a computational model, Palombo's project. But at least Palombo does not reduce dreams to cognitive trivia or computational dregs. Any psychodynamic theory of dreaming is virtually bound to assign it a constructive, recognizably life-pertinent role. Beside that of a Crick, Hobson, or Foulkes, a Freudian assessment of dream significance seems almost expansive.

Part II

SCHOOLS

"I've dreamt in my life dreams that have stayed with
me ever after, and changed my ideas; they've gone
through and through me, like wine through water, and
altered the colour of my mind."

— Emily Bronte, *Wuthering Heights*

Everywhere my dreams are bastardized.

— Lotus Lacey, *The Billboard Dolphin*

□ 2 □

Freud

In a letter to his confidant Wilhelm Fliess not long after the inconspicu-ous first publication of *The Interpretation of Dreams*, Sigmund Freud (1856–1939) indulged in the fantasy that someday a landmarks commission would install a plaque thus engraved to memorialize his insight and himself for a grateful world.[1] The revealed secret was that "*a dream is the fulfillment of a wish.*"

Wish-fulfillment as he conceived of it did not prove to be the most dura-ble element in the theory of dreams which Freud derived from it. Nonethe-less, Freud was not really so very grandiose about his pet idea's landmark status for the century's culture. True, the world is nowadays understandably less reverential toward the Freudian brainstorm than it once was. Still, those dreamworkers who make little of Freud might be faulted for disrespecting the basis for much of what they themselves think about dreams.

Freud's dream theory and neurosis theory developed together, and they parallel one another. He described the infant and small child as a creature striving for gratification of instinctive cravings which are organized around bodily functions and pleasure zones, and around basic but theretofore mis-perceived family relations. Its adult handlers tame the child by instilling fear and guilt over its wishes, which are consequently repressed from conscious-ness. These wishes enter the unconscious, where they persist in their origi-nal childish forms and, importantly, with their original energies. Though the socialized child's, then adult's, own psyche unwittingly collaborates in this repression, the dammed-up instinctive drives still seek release; and if for a variety of reasons the energy is not diverted into wholesome relationships

51

or constructive substitutes, it will force its way to light in the form of neurotic symptoms. As symptom, the original wish-energy gets discharged in a disguised form, admissible to consciousness.

It came to Freud that a comparable compromise between drive and censorship governs dream formation. Reinvigorating an idea as old as Plato,* Freud concluded that, during sleep, repression slackens and the old wishes surge up. Freud's is an "excretion theory"[2] (ch. 1, p. 38), whereby excess sexual or aggressive excitation from the unconscious gets excreted through dreaming.** The wishes must have release, but were they to find the surface in their own guise, they would shock the sleeper awake—not to speak of unsettling her/his self-image. Dreaming prevents that; it acts as a *guardian of sleep*. A *censor* kicks the wishes over to the *dream-work*, a set of functions which *disguise* the wishes, rendering them unrecognizable, while still allowing them to play out in dream hallucination so as to achieve a devious fulfillment.*** Disguise transforms wishes more or less identically in symptom formation and in dream formation.

This amounts to saying that in sleep we are all neurotic.

The Dream-work

In his detailed discussions of disguise mechanisms, Freud laid the foundation for all subsequent descriptions of dream form. This much has to be conceded, whether or not one thinks that dreams actually do disguise forbidden content. Without prejudging the question of disguise, we can enumerate the Freudian mechanisms, taking examples from Freudian as well as neo- and post-Freudian authors. The mechanisms Freud described are *representation, condensation, displacement, symbolization*, and *secondary revision*.

---

* Plato said in *The Republic* that when reason is suspended in sleep, lower impulses—desires and angers—reveal themselves in dreams. H. G. McCurdy (1946, p. 226) mistakenly claims that Freud failed to acknowledge his predecessor; M. H. Stein (1991, p. 199) cites Freud's references to Plato in the Standard Edition of *The Interpretation of Dreams* (pp. 67 and 620), and remarks that "he gave credit in spite of his reservations about philosophers. . . ."

** Freud first wrote of an aggressive drive which could motivate dreams in 1920 (1955 [1920]), and introduced the point in the 1925 edition of *The Interpretation of Dreams* (M. N. McLeod 1992, pp. 47–8). But actually, the first analyzed wish of the original edition—Freud's wish to pass blame for Irma's illness to Otto, in the dream of "Irma's injection"—is in fact aggressive, not sexual.

*** Freud's term for the resources of disguise is translated in the Standard Edition as 'dream-work', with a hyphen, and will be so spelled in this book, except where quoted from other sources in a variant spelling. In this book, as in current usage, 'dreamwork' without a hyphen signifies any work done with dreams.

Representation. Even apart from disguise, dreaming is predominantly a pictorial, sensorial mode of mentation. At the same time, explicit logical-linguistic operations ('but then', 'what if', 'even so', 'therefore', etc.) exist beneath a dream's surface in the *latent dream-thoughts* (see below). Dream-thoughts have to be represented as a sequence or juxtaposition of images. But images are not as explicit as language. Consequently, we easily miss the dream-thoughts underlying the picture story, which Freud called the *manifest dream.* A simple example from Erich Fromm:

> The dreamer may, for instance, dream of *a person standing up and raising his arm and then being transformed into a chicken.* In waking language the dream thought would be expressed as meaning, "He gives the appearance of being strong, BUT he is really weak and cowardly like a chicken."[3]

Condensation. No dream image, thought Freud, stands for one single underlying meaning only, there is no one-for-one symbolism—that would be too easy to solve, too undisguised. An image cannot enter the dream unless more meanings than one converge in and complexify it. Every image is thus 'over-determined'. Condensation is responsible for hybrid imagery. Partly a matter of "efficient representation,"[4] condensation—of which Freud stipulated several varieties—also serves to obfuscate. From Wilhelm Stekel:

> *I have gone swimming, and embrace a girl who wears two bathing suits, one of them a loose black one, and, underneath that, one which is light-green and fits tightly. I think: "She is wearing two because she has lost flesh lately, and the black one is now too large for her."*
>
> In this dream there is a condensation of two persons, . . . [the dreamer's] dead mother and Erna his betrothed. The black bathing suit symbolizes death; the light-green one, life. Past and future are conjoined in his mind (the water symbolizes his mind). . . .[5]

One obvious and often amusing form of condensation is the dream pun. A woman feeling guilty about her sexual misdemeanor dreams *she is being apprehended by undercover agents.*[6] A psychoanalyst tells a patient that his brief dream, "*I am going to Budapest,*" epitomizes to his behavior toward the analyst, "whom you pester with your hostility and envy while wearing a Buddha-like mask."[7] And Rosalind Cartwright gives this example, adduced primarily to illustrate another matter, the way in which sensations received during sleep can be incorporated into the dream story (see chapter 13):

> An infamous dream, from my own family history, was told by a cousin, an inveterate card player. The dream occurred on a winter night. Her back was to an open window and a cold wind was blowing. The blanket slipped down, and her nightie up. She dreamed that *she was playing cards. Someone looking over*

her shoulder at her hand questioned why she was not betting more on such a good hand. She replied that she couldn't because her "assets were frozen."[8]*

Described but unlabelled by Freud, there is another principle of dream formation which is essentially the opposite of condensation, whereby each component of meaning in the latent dream-thought goes along "associative paths"[9] to find representation in more than just one single dream image. The term 'over-determination' is used by some authors to signify this process of *splitting*, the opposite of the condensation to which Freud applied the term. Thus over-determination has come to mean both that multiple meanings converge in a single symbol and that "multiple symbols may repeat or reinforce a single meaning."[10] Between condensation and splitting, the dream imagery constitutes a puzzling display of masks and decoys.

Displacement. Purely for the sake of disguise, says Freud, the charge of meaning and energy gets transferred from where it really pertains to some relatively neutral other place where its nature will not be recognizable. By a covert condensation of meanings, something trivial gets endowed with vital interest, and contrariwise, something truly important gets treated flatly or never enters the dream imagery. From Leon Altman:

A woman troubled by intense competitiveness with her brother for their parents' love dreamed:
I was standing in a very definite place in a very definite house. It was the house we lived in when my brother was born. I stood in what had been my play area. I saw a ball lying in front of me and gave it a hard kick.
She had talked, the day before, to a man who resembled her brother, and had arrived home feeling unaccountably irritable. Without any provocation from her husband, she criticized him scathingly and then retired to bed, in tears. The husband at home and the ball in the dream suffered what was intended for her brother.[11]

An important subtype of Freudian displacement is *reversal*, whereby anything can be represented by its very opposite. Reversal, or interpretation by contraries or opposites, is a venerable principle found in indigenous cultures around the world. Reversal features in the oldest and most influential dream books of the ancient Occident, and it survives in contemporary U.S. popular

---

* Jack Maguire, a former editor of *Dream Network Bulletin*, speculates: "[I] wonder how many of our unusual dream images, especially punning images, date to our preliterate childhood, when we were confused about the meaning of words or expressions, or when we made no distinction among words with similar phonetic properties. At any rate, I have a category of dreams of this type that I call 'kiddie hangovers.' It includes a Christmastime dream that features *the mysterious appearance in Bethlehem of a fat man named 'Round John Vershun'* and a foggy dream where *I find myself in the 'mist' of my enemies*" (1989, p. 43).

dream culture.* In Freud's version, reversal may be simply wishful—"If only it had been the other way around!"[12]—but characteristically, it enters to confound understanding. Thus affection may really signify hostility; a crowd means something is secret; diving into water equals coming out of water, or birth—these examples from Freud.[13] Other examples: not touching refers to masturbation;[14] strangers are really relatives;[15] a rival's success conceals a wish for his failure.[16] Moreover, not only can anything be represented by its opposite, but sometime the reversal is accomplished "by some *other* piece of the dream content being turned into its opposite—as it were by an afterthought."[17]

Freudian reversal has often been considered to be a flawed principle of interpretation, because it seems to render all interpretation arbitrary and any interpretation feasible. But here is an example from Ella Sharpe where the actuality of a reversal seems to be confirmed by a second dream:

> [Sharpe's patient awakened suddenly.] *I was standing in a street looking up at a window which was open. A woman was standing there. I was only able to see the woman's head and shoulders and the upper part of her body which was fully clothed.* The patient, already acquainted with the [Freudian] theory of dreams, was interested in the sudden awakening and thought, "What can there be in a dream like this to make me wake?" She fell asleep and again woke suddenly. This time she had further dreamt that *she was inside the room where the woman was* whom she had seen in the previous dream at the windows from the street. *The dreamer, now a child, was on the floor, and she looked up and saw* not the woman's head and shoulders and face from the front, but *her back, and the body was naked*; a repressed memory of a bedroom scene in early childhood. . . .
>
> . . . [A]ll dreamers are not so obliging as to produce a second dream in which the truth is given, and one finds some types of reversal dreams difficult to elucidate.[18]

Notice the multiplicity of the reversal: front for back, clothed for naked, and adult for child. Sharpe also mentions reversals in the form of puns. She says

---

* A Northern Rhodesian (Zimbabwe) tribe believes that "[t]o dream that one is killed by a lion means great success in the chase" (F. H. Melland, *In Witchbound Africa*, London: Seeley Service, p. 247, 1923, quoted by W. Morgan 1932, p. 396). In many indigenous cultures, reversed or straight interpretations may be offered at different times, or by different interpreters (J. S. Lincoln 1970 [1935], p. 203; B. Tedlock 1981, pp. 313–4 citing her own work and several other sources). Likewise, the Chester Beatty papyrus from Egypt in 2000 B.C. also sometimes interpreted by contraries (e.g., a dream of death signifies long life) (M. Ullman & N. Zimmerman 1979, p. 34). The Greek Artemidorus (about 140 A.D.) also selectively employed the principle. His influential *Oneirocritica* is in the direct lineage of modern popular dream books and superstitions (A. Brelich 1966, p. 284), where, for example, a dream wedding means a death in the offing, a funeral foretells a marriage, or the birth of a son means a daughter should be expected.

she often finds herself referred to in patient dreams by a "flat" or a "block of flats."[19]

There is one variety of reversal which is much spoken of by dreamworkers without being identified as such: that where a disowned aspect of the self is projected onto a dream figure (see chapters 6 and 16). Thus Robin Shohet concludes that a woman's dream of *two youths driving dangerously at her in a car* means that "she fears her own destructiveness."[20]

Symbolization. Condensation and displacement generate the great majority of dream symbols, the ones which are idiosyncratic, deriving from the dreamer's personal history and associations. But there is another, universal set of symbols, the cliche 'Freudian' ones, deriving from humanity's collective experience. These symbolize such themes as birth and death, parents, siblings, body parts, and sex. Thus all pointed objects (pencil, pistol, etc.) stand for penis, all receptacles (vase, purse, etc.) for vagina. These are, a Jungian might say, a poor man's archetypal images.

Secondary revision (secondary elaboration). With their low opinions of it as a mental product, a David Foulkes or an Allan Hobson (ch. 1, p. 32ff.) would not dignify the dream by likening it to art. But the comparison, familiar to the Romantic tradition before Freud, has become commonplace since Freud and in spite of him. The thought is that a dream as dreamt and/or as remembered is a sort of para-art which arises from the same deep springs of creativity as art and which does for its creator/audience-of-one the good things art does. Beginning with Jung, and in numbers, virtually every twentieth century appreciator of dreaming as an alternative, co-equal, and/or in respects superior mental mode has been led to make the comparison: of the dream to poetry, drama, fiction, movie, painting.* Most popular for compar-

---

* Examples: • *Poetry:* E. F. Sharpe (1978 [1937]); E. S. Tauber & M. R. Green (1959); C. Downing (1977); M. Ullman (1987 [1978]); C. Rycroft (1981 [1979]); J. D. Clift & W. B. Clift (1984); L. Hudson (1985); R. M. Jones (1987); W. B. Webb (1992). • *Drama:* C. G. Jung [1945/-1948], CW 8; J. A. Hadfield (1954); C. S. Hall (1966a); H. C. Shands (1966); G. Delaney (1979); H. Reed (1988 [1985]); S. Resnik (1987); B. O. States (1988). • *Fiction:* L. Hudson (1985); H. Reed (1988 [1985]); R. Langs (1988); B. O. States (1988). • *Movie:* A. Faraday (1976 [1974]); G. Delaney (1979). • *Painting:* R. E. Fantz (1987 [1978]); H. T. Hunt (1989); J. Maguire (1989); K. A. Signell (1990).

Here is a typical appreciation, from Eva Renée Neu (1988, p. 12): "Dreams are everyone's art in that they express us metaphorically, and also in the very fact that they baffle the conscious mind. Like art, they do not seem to be purely functional means of informing, warning, and guiding us. They are playful and self-sufficient. They have style. Like art, they are compelling presences without seeming to care whether they communicate or not. Yet, like the art of any individual artist, they tend to repeat messages over and over, and in that way they try to tell us something."

Comparing dreams to the mystery genre, Robert Langs (1988, p. 4) says: "Paradoxically, although we are all superb mystery writers, none of us are very good detectives."

ison is poetry. Poetry criticism has even been adapted as a method of dream interpretation, for example, by Jean & Wallace Clift and by Liam Hudson,[21] and earlier by Sharpe.[22] For her, as for Erich Fromm[23] and for Edward Tauber & Maurice Green,[24] the esthetics of the dream gave a footing from which to revise the dominant Freudian paradigm.

One exception to this view was Alfred Adler's. He saw poetry in dreams, but thought admiration of it tempts us to indulge our maladjustments and diverts us from common sense[25] (see chapter 4).

As for Freud, he recognized the "poetic speech" of dream images,[26] but like Adler his commitment to straightforwardly communicated, consensual waking reality precluded complete appreciation of poetic means. But apart from that (and perhaps setting aside those styles which draw inspiration from the Freudian scheme itself, such as surrealism), a dream is unartlike in the Freudian scheme because art has form, has integrity, while dreams have not. Or more precisely, what form dreams have is an aspect of disguise, and is therefore antagonistic to communication or honest expression.

Freud strongly disparaged "'symbolic' dream-interpreting,"[27] by which the entire structure of the dream's surface—the *manifest dream*—is thought

---

Psychoanalytic discussions of music sometimes make the comparison to dreaming (references in S. Sand & R. Levin 1992), but with rare exceptions (that article and L. van den Daele 1992), psychoanalytic discussions of dreaming do not make the comparison to music, nor do other authors. (R. E. Fantz 1987 [1978] compares dreaming to choreography.) This is interesting in view of the fact that songs learned in dreams are a source of spiritual power in some indigenous cultures. In the case of the Northern Paiute (Numa), shamanic initiation dreams can be entirely auditory, including songs (W. Z. Park 1975 [1938], p. 115).

Important qualifications, some related to Freud's (see text), have been expressed about the comparison. M. Bartels states a reservation in relation to poetry, one which if accepted would apply to other arts as well: "As the dreamer's own 'product or statement,' the dream-text is unlike the poetic text, in that it is neither an independent nor isolated image, but rather becomes meaningful only when incorporated into the life-text of the dreamer" ("Ist der Traum eine Wunscherfüllung?" *Psyche* 33, pp. 97–131, 1979, quoted by R. Zwiebel 1985, pp. 87–8). Similarly, John Briggs (1988, pp. 111–2) points out that art (literature) "creates or evokes its own context" which is sufficient for its appreciation, whereas "the dreamer's life experience is . . . the actual context of the dream," involving "private significance" and "idiosyncratic connotations." This observation applies within a given culture, with its many spoken and unspoken common assumptions. Between cultures, it becomes apparent that art incorporates contextual cultural elements which may be opaque to an outsider, but no more so than the cultural elements incorporated in dreams (B. Tedlock 1992a [1987]).

A different reservation is voiced by Thomas Meyer (1971, p. 178). He compares three years of dream journal entries with poems written over the same period. Meyer finds that whereas the poems evolved in style as well as substance, the dream entries—whatever changes they may have undergone in substance—showed no stylistic evolution. And "it's apparent that whereas poetry's untranslatable, dream [like myth] *is* translatable; it can bear the passage from one language to another." One could argue with Meyer, both as to the absence of stylistic evolution in dreams and the full translatability of dream or myth.

to convey the dream's real meaning as an allegory or metaphor. To the contrary, each item of the manifest dream comes to birth out of its own psychic resources and each undergoes its own distortion by the censorship. Thus the manifest, the visible dream is "like a piece of breccia, composed of various fragments of rock held together by a binding medium, so that the designs that appear on it do not belong to the original rocks embedded in it."[28] The "binding medium" is the superficial form bestowed from the outset by the sheer fact of being a representation, and then, by secondary revision, a process rendering a sequence of discrete disguise-images into a text which is at least minimally intelligible to a waking ego.

Freud's notion of the breccia composing dreams has contemporary counterparts in Hobson's and Foulkes's ideas of random activations or memories cobbled together into dreams (ch. 1, p. 32ff.), and is opposed at the other extreme by Daniel Deslauriers's notion that dreams have governing "scripts" from the start, into which contextual "deviations" enter only as symbolic exploration of new psychological territory.[29]

Secondary revision has much in common with those processes by which we give coherence to waking experience which lacks it. In the case of the

---

Lawrence Kubie (1975 [1958]) and Fritz Perls (1969, p. 67) say dreams are art, but not good art. Wendy Doniger O'Flaherty (1984, p. 127) makes a similar evaluation, comparing dreams to myths. In dreams, "the thread of the plot is replaced by a pattern of images that suggest but never actually spell out the story." Harry Hunt (1991a), besides noticing that dreams differ from ordinary metaphors insofar as the reference of the metaphor is "deleted" in dreams, finds that some (but only some) dreams are on their "way *towards* the patterns and tropes of literature" (p. 241), but that they fall short as stories, according to P. Ricouer's (*Time and Narrative*, vols. 1 & 2, Chicago: University of Chicago, 1984-5) stipulations (Hunt, p. 239): (1) "successful resolution of the unexpected"; (2) "structured in terms of beginning middle and end"; (3) "expand and foreshorten temporal perspective in terms of plot requirements"; and (4) "reflect and potentially vary a distinct narrative voice or point of view." Hunt adds: "It is the way we handle dreams when we wake up that in a now quite interesting way may be taken as *finishing* the dream and finally meeting these criteria." (See also Hunt 1989, pp. 174-9.) Robert Bosnak (1988 [1986], p. 7) draws this contrast sharply: "A dream is not a story, not a movie or a text or a theatre play. . . . [W]e experience things we can talk about upon awakening as a dream story. But the dream story is not the dream itself. The dream itself is a texture woven of space and time inside which we find ourselves."

This survey has looked only at the literature on dreams. A different and larger whole field is the literature on literature, where a tradition exists of seeing art as dream (rather than dream as art). Kay Stockholder (1987) undertakes to bridge these fields by treating art (and specifically, the theater) as dream, not by the familiar approach of psychoanalyzing the author from his work, but rather by using methods of dream interpretation to get at the text itself. Her method involves treating a character—usually but not always the protagonist—as the dream-ego of a theatrical dream/work.

A majority of the writers interviewed by Naomi Epel (1993) about dreaming as it relates to their writing said in one way or another that the state in which they write is a sort of dream state. This is a variant of the theme that art is a dream; some, but many fewer, described their dreaming as a sort of writing.

dream, this finishing work is described by Freud in different places (1) as beginning in conjunction with other dream-work, (2) as occurring after the dream breccia consolidates, and (3) as continuing on into waking recall and narration.[30] Further, secondary revision has three functional aspects, according to a recent discussion by Martin Stein: "critic," "editor," and "plagiarist." The critic evaluates, usually in the service of defensive resistance ("It was only a dream," etc.). The editor renders the dream coherent, puts it into verbal form if it is told, repairs gaps due to forgetting, and arouses or misdirects interest in the listener. The plagiarist imposes the forms of previous conscious or unconscious fantasies, including cultural forms.[31]

Secondary revision artfully decoys attention toward the dream's spurious esthetic surface, which always lays at least minimal claim to stylistic cohesion; hence attention is drawn away from latent dream-thoughts coded in the images. The implication is "that we should disregard the apparent coherence between a dream's constituents as an unessential illusion, and that we should trace back the origin of each of its elements on its own account. A dream is a conglomerate which, for purposes of investigation, must be broken up once more into fragments."[32]

To "trace back" or decipher each separate dream element, Freud chiefly employed *free association*: starting from some element, the dreamer lets his imagination and his tongue flow uncensored farther and farther from the element. Psychological determinism is such that the dream-making process gets approximately unfolded in reverse by the chain of 'free' associations, to arrive near to the original, unconscious, latent content. In one of those unexpected exhibitions of obvious circularity which occasionally intrude into his usually persuasive argumentation, Freud asserted that a "far-fetched" associative chain could not arise "unless it had already been constructed by the dream-work."[33] By seeing where associations to the various dream elements lead, we are able to reconstruct the latent dream-thought, that real coherence underlying the "breccia" of components, which in turn underlies the sham coherence of the manifest dream. The main point upon which Freud insisted is that his upper level of coherence, the manifest dream, is a mere facade and not a direct analog for, not a helpful metaphor for his lower and more essential level of coherence, the latent dream-thought.

Dream-thought and Wish

So each dream has its latent dream-thoughts (or latent meanings, or latent contents), its authentic lower layer. And every dream is also the veiled expression of unconscious infantile wishes. Then are the latent dream-thoughts infantile wishes? In fact they are not, but this is a common confusion, one perpetuated by some popularizations of Freud's dream psychology. It is even shared by some Freudian analysts, on partial account, says Jacob Spanjaard, of Freud's own "imprecise formulations."[34]

This is how Freud describes the latent dream-thoughts: he says they "are dominated by the same material that has occupied us during the day and we only bother to dream of things which have given us cause for reflection in the daytime."[35] Therefore dreaming may be "of as many different sorts as the process of waking thought."[36] He would also, confusingly, speak of the dream-thoughts as "formed by a repressed wish,"[37] but more consistently as "not in themselves inadmissible to consciousness,"[38] as "characterized by all the signs of normal intellectual functioning,"[39] and as "immediately intelligible to us."[40]

He pointedly differentiates infantile wish from dream-thought: "If we disregard the unconscious contribution to the formation of the dream and limit the dream to its latent thoughts, it can represent anything with which waking life has been concerned—a reflection, a warning, an invention, a preparation for the immediate future, or, once again, the satisfaction of an unfulfilled [current, not infantile] wish."[41] Notice that this list could come from any one of a score of today's dreamworkers who, if asked, would contrast their own broad sense of dream relevance with Freud's narrow wish-fulfillment theory.

Within the manifest dream imagery, Freud could almost always discover material related, but indirectly, to one or more of these important day concerns—whether concerns consciously available to the dreamer, or "preconscious" ones retained below the surface. The concern itself, however, "is nevertheless withdrawn from consciousness till it emerges in distorted form in the [manifest] dream content."[42] But why should these "not inadmissible" concerns just not represent themselves wholly or intelligibly in the manifest dream? Why, instead, do they get deviously, cryptically represented there by relatively trivial, inessential day images, called *day residues*,* which the dream-work takes up for its manifest dream breccia? Not because dreaming is inherently trivial, as thought those of the nineteenth century against whom Freud defined *him*self, but rather for the sake of "dream-distortion" serving "censorship."[43]

But why should the "not inadmissible" dream-thoughts need censorship at all? Because before we actually dream them out, said Freud, they always become connected first with inadmissible unconscious infantile wishes.

---

* It is 'day's residues' in James Strachey's translation in the Standard Edition, but usually 'day residues'. Day residues are discussed in chapter 13, p. 394ff., in connection with dream incubation.

In Hermann Hesse's novel *Magister Ludi* there is an account of the writing of a poem. An inspired line of verse comes to the poet. From that start he then composes the rest of the poem, polishes it, and finds it satisfying, except for some one thing that bothers him. But he cannot say what—until he realizes that it is the inspired line itself which is out of keeping and needs to be changed. Freud's inspiration was the idea of the infantile wish as the "indispensable motive force"[44] of dreams, and he never really acknowledged a need to change it.

In seeking the cause of dreams, Freud operated from a view of psychophysiology which required there to be a first billiard ball, an energy source to initiate the causal sequence whose outcome is dreaming. Though upheld by some psychoanalytic diehards even in the face of dream lab findings,[45] "[s]uch a mechanistic energy model, . . ." Louis Breger et al. point out (ch. 1, p. 47), "is an anachronistic carry-over from nineteenth century science. It has long lived a life separate from Freud's clinical theory. . . ."[46] Freud found the energy source in the infantile wish-energy, which, since it cannot be admitted to consciousness, supposedly builds up pressure like water or steam. This excitation seeks conduits or valves through which to discharge. In the day, it uses neurotic and sublimated behavior. But at night, its expedient is to exploit the dream-thoughts: they are "drawn into the unconscious"[47] and there loaded with energy which empowers them to force their way back up into dream consciousness. But since the dream-thoughts have been made bearers of the infantile wish, they need now to be disguised by the dream-work before appearing in the manifest dream.

It seems that with his penchant for reductive analysis, Freud has provided us with not one but two authentic lower layers of dream meaning: the latent dream-thought related to present concerns, and the repressed infantile wish. There is always some kinship between these, since the infantile wish needs a hook in the dream-thought to attach by. But from the ego's point of view the kinship is often as remote as that, say, between a "reflection" or "invention" and a longing for mother.

So what is the task of Freudian dream interpretation? To discover the infantile wish or the dream-thought? In other words, to orient toward archaic infantile situations or present adult concerns?

Certainly both. But so often is Freud criticized nowadays for having focused only on infantile formations that it needs to be re-emphasized: Freud's actual interpretive practice had very much to do with the dreamer's present life.

In point of fact, *The Interpretation of Dreams* has been doubly criticized: for reducing everything to the infantile, and at the same time for failing actually to show the infantile genesis of particular dreams. It has been noticed that the infantile dimension is entirely absent from Freud's famous interpretation of his dream of "Irma's injection," the dream he offered as the key "specimen" of his argument.[48] In addition to that, he incorporates a manifest dream element, his reproach of Irma, into his interpretation.[49] The pattern is maintained throughout the book.

In 1911, in reply to Freud's invitation to suggest changes for a new edition, Jung brought up just this point.[50] Freud acknowledged in response that the book had the shortcoming of distorting interpretations by omitting the infantile, personally painful level, and he made a pledge—to be left unfulfilled—that the published version would be replaced by another which would make good this deficit.[51] His stated reason for his incomplete procedure had been the need to preserve an area of privacy, since most of the dreams discussed in the book are his own. But actually, he approached other people's dreams in much the same way.[52]* Richard Jones overstates the case when he claims that not a single dream in the book is traced to its repressed infantile wish.[53] But it certainly needs to be underscored just how much space Freud does devote to dream-thoughts, which, as he says, "can represent anything with which waking life has been concerned."[54]

During subsequent decades Freud occasionally attached riders to his original insight that infantile wish-energy is the sole fuel of dreaming. In 1920,[55] he remarked upon a type of dream which sometimes follows severe trauma. In these dreams, the traumatizing event re-presents itself night after night. He thought that, like certain neurotic repetitive patterns, such dreams "are attempts at mastering, under one's own control, events that one could not deal with originally."[56] Such an interpretation, which is in keeping with current thinking on nightmares in posttraumatic stress disorder (see ch. 9, p. 311), stipulates a dream function apart from drive discharge.

---

* Jung, who sometimes cleaned up interpretations of his own dreams (not always identified as such) for reasons of privacy and careerism (M. V. Adams 1990, p. 53), as well as did Freud, recognized Freud's right to privacy, and suggested that a *"ruthlessly* disclosed" patient's dream be substituted as the specimen dream (McGuire 1974, p. 392). Freud (p. 395) responded that he had omitted such a demonstration because material for it could only come from a neurotic, a patient, "and it was not possible to communicate their dreams, because I could not presuppose the secrets of neurosis, which were precisely what the interpretation of dreams was intended to disclose."

Meredith Sabini (1988, p. 389), a Jungian analyst, makes this interesting observation: "In the seven decades that psychiatric literature has been catalogued, there are only four papers in which the dreams of therapists are the explicit subject of study . . . ." (See her bibliography; actually, there are additional references to literature on this subject to be found in at least one of the articles listed there: M. H. Spero 1984.) This "dearth" surprises Sabini, considering that Freud inaugurated modern dream studies with his own dream about a patient of his own, Irma.

This drift came about with Freud's modification of his model of mind. The so-called *topological model* of *The Interpretation of Dreams* is named for its spatial projection of psychic stratigraphy: the conscious forms the surface, the unconscious is layered beneath. In the so-called *structural model*, psyche is instead imagined as a dynamic organization of autonomous formations—id, ego, super-ego.[57] Among his reasons for this modification were Freud's clinical observations of ego-related "complex mental activity in the unconscious," and of unwishlike anxiety and super-ego activity in dreams.[58] With this shift came an implicit suggestion that something other than the energy of the most primitive drives may be potent in the generation of dreams; and that the manifest dream deserved to be paid attention.

These threads were picked up by the 'ego psychologists' of the thirties, forties and beyond. They focused on adaptation to the outside world by ego functions which generate personality patterns, and especially patterns of defense (denial, projection, etc.), affecting dreaming as they affect other behavior. Ego functions operate independently from instinctive drives.

Further evolution of psychoanalytic theory followed with object relations theory, self psychology and other developments.*

---

* In ego psychology, "dreaming has become viewed more as an expression of conflicts between three psychic agencies, that is, between the sexual and aggressive wishes of the id, the prohibitions of the superego, and the management functions of the ego" (J. L. Fosshage 1987b, p. 25). "[C]onflicts are viewed as ubiquitously present in dreams, with little possible movement toward resolution (because conflict resolution is a higher-order ego function rarely operative in dreams . . .)" (J. L. Fosshage 1987a, p. 304). Object relations theory, associated especially with the English school of Fairbairn and Winnicott, stresses careful description of formative social dynamics over constructs of psychic structure (J. H. Padel 1987 [1978]). "Dreams [are] portrayals of attempts at finding solutions to these object-related conflicts" (P. H. Ornstein 1987, p. 89). Kohut's self psychology (ch. 10, p. 343 n.) added a focus on the status and repair of the self, rejecting Freud's reductionism and pessimism, considering the individual potentially "complete," "strong," and "unified" rather than inherently conflicted (A. M. Cooper 1983, pp. 9–10). Other recent psychoanalytic models are still engaged in "extricating" theory from Freud's biological energetics (J. L. Fosshage 1987a, p. 300). Of his "revised psychoanalytic perspective," James Fosshage (1983, p. 651) writes that it supplants Freud's "energy-based definitions" of the dream-work mechanisms (displacement, etc.), which accentuate disguise and defense, with a view of the dream-work mechanisms as "organizing principles" serving the "integration and organization of experiences and memories (which includes, but is not limited to a defensive function)."

All these elaborations of Freudian theory qualify the ubiquity of disguise and permit interpretation of the manifest dream. "In general, there appears to be a shift in emphasis from the wish-fulfillment-censorship model to one that focuses more on the integrating, organizing, problem-solving functions of dreams. . . . [T]he manifest content assumes greater importance as a metaphorical presentation of various intrapsychic issues . . . whether or not connected with earlier childhood experiences" (M. L. Glucksman 1987, p. 13). Silas Warner (1987, p. 102ff.) notes Erik Erikson's observation as early as 1954 (p. 17) that "unofficially" psychoanalysts make use of the manifest content in their dream analyses. In 1985, Warner tested this by surveying case reports in four current psy-

Freud himself, however, "never really updated" his drive-discharge theory of dream causation.[59] Much has been made of a distinction he drew in 1923 "between dreams from above and dreams *from below*. . . ."[60] Actually, his dream from below is substantially nothing but one instigated—as in *The Interpretation of Dreams*—by an unconscious wish which has latched onto day residues; while his new dream from above merely emphasizes the contribution of the dream-thoughts, i.e., "thoughts or intentions of the day before which have contrived during the night to obtain reinforcement from repressed material which is debarred from the ego." What Freud here adds to the distinction is that dream-thoughts are not necessarily present; and that when they are, they deserve special attention. "When this is so," i.e., when a dream from above is suspected, "analysis as a rule disregards [the] unconscious ally. . . ." He follows this up with the puzzling avowal that the "distinction calls for no modification of the theory of dreams"—puzzling, since according to the theory there must always be both components, the above (the dream-thought) and the below (the repressed wish), for a dream to occur. Then he must be fudging the theory a little when he now suggests that dreams from above occur only sometimes, and implies that the day residues of dreams from below do not necessarily pertain to dream-thoughts.

What he evidently means is that sometimes investigating links to a dreamer's present life through the dream is more productive than a search for infantile meaning. The bit of theoretical awkwardness stems from his stubborn adherence to the wish-fulfillment dogma.

In *The Interpretation of Dreams* itself there is a discernible lapse of empirical grounding when Freud insists that only an infantile wish can have the punch to initiate a dream, and that the dream-thought, even if it is an adult wish, cannot be "strong enough" to do so.[61] Oddly enough, all that really upholds this dogma is the sober assertion that after childhood "we are more and more inclined to renounce as unprofitable the formation or retention of such intense wishes as children know."

But while in theoretical passages he would not permit dream-thoughts to empower dreaming, in interpretive practice he not only often concentrated

---

choanalytic journals. "Out of 57 dreams the manifest content was used mainly for interpretations in 23 instances, and partly in 32. This means that in 55 out of 57 dreams there was from approximately 50 percent up to 100 percent use of the manifest dream. In only 2 dreams was the dream interpretation made mainly from the latent content, as Freud had suggested." It is no longer unofficial. An American Psychoanalytic Association panel report concludes that "on the basis of the panelists' presentations we must award the manifest dream, a favored, but not unique place in clinical work . . ." (S. Pulver & I. Renik, "The clinical use of the manifest dream," *Journal of the American Psychoanalytic Association* 32, p. 161, 1984, quoted by Warner 1987, p. 104).

on the dream-thoughts but could even discover the obligatory wish in adult as against infantile matters. For instance, Freud's analysis of a dream of his own, "Otto was looking ill,"[62] brought to light vengeful dream-thoughts of disparagement toward his friend and family doctor Otto, who had agreed to watch over Freud's children should he die. "But where was [the dream's] wish-fulfillment to be found?" In a different but equally adult and current issue: in Freud's ambition to be recognized by the academic establishment, which the dream vicariously accomplished. In the dream below, the dream-thought and the wish are not differentiated, and are both of the present:

"You're always saying to me," began a clever woman patient of mine, "that a dream is a fulfilled wish. Well, I'll tell you a dream whose subject was the exact opposite. . . . How do you fit that in with your theory? . . .

I wanted to give a supper-party, but I had nothing in the house but a little smoked salmon. I thought I would go out and buy something, but remembered then that it was Sunday afternoon and all the shops would be shut. Next I tried to ring up some caterers, but the telephone was out of order. So I had to abandon my wish to give a supper-party.

. . . My patient's husband, an honest and capable wholesale butcher, had remarked to her the day before that he was getting too stout and therefore intended to start on a course of weight-reduction. He proposed to rise early, do physical exercises, keep to a strict diet, and above all accept no more invitations to supper. . . . She was very much in love with her husband now and teased him a lot. . . .

. . . The associations which she had so far produced had not been sufficient to interpret the dream. I pressed her for some more. After a short pause, such as would correspond to the overcoming of a resistance, she went on to tell me that the day before she had visited a woman friend of whom she confessed she felt jealous because her (my patient's) husband was constantly singing her praises. Fortunately this friend of hers is very skinny and thin and her husband admires a plumper figure. I asked her what she had talked about to her thin friend. Naturally, she replied, of that lady's wish to grow a little stouter. Her friend had enquired, too: "When are you going to ask us to another meal? You always feed one so well."

The meaning of the dream was now clear, and I was able to say to my patient: "It is just as though when she made this suggestion you said to yourself: 'A likely thing! I'm to ask you to come and eat in my house so that you may get stout and attract my husband still more! I'd rather never give another supper-party.' What the dream was saying to you was that you were unable to give any supper-parties, and it was thus fulfilling your wish not to help your friend grow plumper. The fact that what people eat at parties makes them stout had been brought home to you by your husband's decision not to accept any more invitations to supper in the interests of his plan to reduce his weight." All that was now lacking was some coincidence to confirm the solution. The smoked salmon in the dream had not yet been accounted for. "How," I asked, "did you arrive at the salmon that came into your dream?" "Oh," she replied, "smoked salmon is my friend's favourite dish."[63]

It is easy to forget how much we owe to Freud for a style of dream interpretation which probably seems to most of us to be pretty straightforward, commonsensical, almost obvious in its approach. One important qualification needs to be made, however. Notice that when Freud paraphrases the dream-thought for his patient, he does not place its formation within the time frame of dreaming. Rather, he has it form during the daytime incident: "It is just as though when she made this suggestion you said to yourself. . . ." According to Freud, a dream-thought is not a follow-on or development of a line of thought, conscious or unconscious, initiated earlier in the day; rather, a dream-thought is a *repetition* of a day-thought. He held that the dreaming mind could not think anything original. The Freudian Robert Fliess put it plainly: "What appears as the dreamer's judgment is actually the individual's when he was still awake."[64] Freud was thus a forerunner of the low estimation of cognition in dreams on the part of Foulkes and others (chapter 1). Freud himself even came to the untenable position that whatever actual language appears in the dream must be lifted from day residues, since language production entails original thinking and cannot therefore be generated by the dream itself.

So it is only in a restricted sense that dreaming may be "of as many different sorts as the process of waking thought."[65] The dream is relevant to daily life, but never in its own right contributory. The contribution comes from waking interpretation. Nevertheless, even if Freud strictly adhered to this description, which is doubtful, dream treatments such as the above are a far cry from the unforgiving refrain of natal/anal/oral/genital which is the stereotyped version of Freudian dream analysis.

Freudian Reductionism

But there are of course good reasons for the latter view, and having now played devil's advocate for the overlooked Freud, it is time to look briefly at Freud the ogre of reductionism. To begin with, here is a presentation by Freud of a patient's dream. He offered it to illustrate points about symbolism and did not exactly specify the wish he thought it must embody, but the analysis well illustrates his orientation to psychosexual causations:

[The dreamer's] mother sent [the dreamer's] daughter away, so that she had to go by herself. Then she went in a train with her mother and saw her little one walk straight on to the rails so that she was bound to be run over. She heard the

*cracking of her bones. (This produced an uncomfortable feeling in her but no real
horror.) Then she looked round out of the window of the railway-carriage to see
whether the parts could not be seen from behind. Then she reproached her mother
for having made the little one go by herself.*

. . . In the first place, the patient declared that the train journey was to be
interpreted historically, as an allusion to a journey she had taken when she was
leaving a sanatorium for nervous diseases, with whose director, needless to say,
she had been in love. Her mother had fetched her away, and the doctor had appeared at the station and handed her a bouquet of flowers as a parting present.
It had been very awkward that her mother should have witnessed this tribute. At
this point, then, her mother figured as interfering with her attempts at a love
affair; and this had in fact been the part played by that severe lady during the
patient's girlhood.—Her next association related to the sentence: "she looked
round to see whether the parts could not be seen from behind." The facade of the
dream would of course lead one to think of the parts of her little daughter who
had been run over and mangled. But her association led in quite another direction. She recollected having once seen her father naked in the bathroom from behind; she went on to talk of the distinctions between the sexes, and laid stress on
the fact that a man's genitals can be seen even from behind but a woman's cannot. In this connection she herself interpreted "the little one" as meaning the genitals and "her little one"—she had a four-year-old daughter—as her own genitals.
She reproached her mother with having expected her to live as though she had
no genitals, and pointed out that the same reproach was expressed in the opening
sentence of the dream: "her mother sent her little one away, so that she had to
go by herself." In her imagination 'going by herself in the streets' meant not having a man, not having any sexual relations. . . . Her accounts all went to show
that when she was a girl she had in fact suffered from her mother's jealousy owing to a preference shown her by her father.

The deeper interpretation of this dream was shown by another dream of the
same night, in which the dreamer identified herself with her brother. She had
actually been a boyish girl, and had often been told that she should have been a
boy. This identification with her brother made it particularly clear that "the little
one" meant a genital organ. Her mother was threatening him (or her) with castration, which could only have been a punishment for playing with her penis; thus
the identification also proved that she herself had masturbated as a child—a memory which till then she had only had as applied to her brother. . . . Further, the
second dream alluded to the infantile sexual theory according to which girls are
boys who have been castrated. . . .

Thus the sending away of the little one (of the genital organ) in the first dream
was also related to the threat of castration. Her ultimate complaint against her
mother was for not having given birth to her as a boy.

The fact that "being run over" symbolizes sexual intercourse would not be
obvious from this dream, though it has been confirmed from many other
sources.[66]

We read here a sample of the Freudian psychosexual tool kit: erogenous zones, especially the genitals; sexual interpretations; sexual scenes of childhood; oedipal conflict; masturbation; and in this instance, a hapless dreamer who, like Woody Allen, suffered simultaneously from castration anxiety and penis envy. Despite the other, less celebrated side of Freud to which I have wanted to call attention, there is no doubt that his own karma, if you will— and also perhaps, as is often suggested, the repressive atmosphere of bourgeois Viennese society*—, compelled him always to come back to childhood sexuality. This is the side of Freud which gave its style to psychoanalysis. Objectors such as Jung, Adler, and Stekel were pretty much anathemized.** Not until after World War II would neo-Freudians such as Fromm and Erik Erikson begin substantially to break the commitment to psuchosexual reductionism within the Freudian camp itself. But during the decades of Freudian hegemony and even beyond, the reductive style was only too familiar among Freudian partisans.

That style has various aspects as it affects dream interpretation. As for the psychosexual aspect, even such an innovative and relatively independent Freudian dream expert as Sharpe in the 1930s would believe, for example, that music in dreams signifies sublimated oral desire,[67] or that "[t]he number five often ultimately refers to the five fingers and hence to infantile masturbation."[68] In the 1950s Geza Roheim, whom Freud encouraged to pursue an interest in psychoanalytic ethnography,[69] would still be oppressively insisting that "the central conflict in life is always oedipal."[70] We behold in Roheim's writing the kind of depersonalizing analysis by psychological determinism which, as Jung aptly put it, "is like losing one's way, where even what is right seems an alarming mistake";[71] and from which Erikson feelingly dissociated himself in the 1960s: "[W]e were dismayed when we saw our purpose

---

* Andrew Samuels (1992b, p. 137) remarks that Jungian "psychology has to free itself from similar cultural blunders rooted in [Jung's] Germanic ideas. . . ." Interestingly, the accusation made by European contemporaries of the first decade or so of psychoanalysis was, in Freud's words (1966a [1914], p. 39), that it "could only have originated in a town like Vienna—in an atmosphere of sensuality and immorality foreign to other cities. . . ." In ridiculing this perception (p. 40), Freud himself pointed out how much more plausible it would be to connect his sexual theories with an atmosphere of sexual inhibition, but he observed that Vienna was if anything a bit less prudish than some other capitals.

** Stekel (1943) broke with Freud in 1912. He believed the analyst should be able to draw important conclusions about the patient from the manifest dream, and should deliver these to the patient, thus short-cutting the treatment process. Free association, he thought, only encourages the patient's efforts to avoid the issue. His "active psychoanalysis" is the forerunner of all so-called brief psychotherapies. He himself treated over 10,000 patients (N. MacKenzie 1965, p. 197). Stekel also wrote a book about telepathic dreams (Der Telepatische Traum, Berlin: Johannes Baum, no date, cited by C. A. Cannegieter 1985, p. 42).

of enlightenment perverted into a widespread fatalism, according to which man is nothing but a multiplication of his parents' faults and an accumulation of his own earlier selves."[72] Roheim out-Heroded Herod by maintaining the theory that the basis of every dream is a symbolic return to the womb. He called this the "basic dream."

Roheim also serves as an example of that smug dismissiveness toward the Jungian point of view found until quite recently among Freudians, a stance which Freud himself legitimized by his conduct. The Naskapi Algonquins, Roheim wrote, believe that in dreams we communicate with our own soul, called the "Great Man." Their pictorial representation of the Great Man is a "typical *mandala*," or circular form. But, Roheim comments in a footnote, the mandala "does not mean what Jung thinks [i.e., precisely the soul, or self, or as it were the "Great Man"], but simply the uterus."[73]

Reading Roheim is like reading intemperate political ideology. It was a suffocating mentality. As with the "Little one run over" dream, the question is not so much whether the 'Freudian' level is there, but whether it is *all* that is there. Commenting respectfully on the role of Freud in his own spiritual development, Richard Grossinger remarks that "the problem of seeing a fish, for instance, as a penis is not the gaining of those fishy qualities of the penis (movement, origin), but the loss of those things which make a fish. . . ."[74] Grossinger contrasts this to the broader scope of Jungian symbolism: "Jung says that Freud has cheated us, and his message is received most heartily by dreamers who in their guts agree."[75]

Freud's penchant for reductionism, which permeates his entire enterprise, can be traced in part to the classical scientific tenet that you can best find out how reality works by taking it apart. This is reductionism in the strict and narrow sense. Likening Freud to Francis Crick (ch. 1, p. 38), Hudson notes Freud's faith that "the deficiencies of the psychoanalytic description of the mind 'would probably vanish if we were already in a position to replace the psychological terms by physiological or chemical ones.'"[76] He says "already," as if the day must come.* This is the vision which sees that the true meaning of the dream can only be found by its decomposition, if not to cellular or chemical, at least to hidden psychological constituents. Nothing is what it seems. The manifest dream is only a facade which, even when it appears meaningful, not to mention beautiful or moving, is really mean-

---

* Allan Hobson (1989, p. 146) remarks that "Freud's theory falls into the idealist camp because it ignores the physical condition of the brain completely." On the contrary, Freud had a *Project for a Scientific Psychology* (1966 [1895], Standard Edition, vol. 18, London: Hogarth), but could not complete it for lack of scientific means. Foulkes's criticism of Hobson's own approach is based on the fact that means are still lacking (ch. 1, p. 36).

ingless on its own terms. A Freudian of the 1970s informs us "that it is only in the manifest content that dreams are joyful or happy; there are only painful elements in the latent content. It is [my] belief that every dream is a potential nightmare,"[77] enjoyable only to masochists and self-deceivers.[78] This forbidding assessment merely carries to an absurd conclusion Freud's idea that dreams form like neurotic symptoms, an aspect of the theory often justly singled out for overemphasizing the negative aspects of dream activity. Charles Rycroft complains that "by categorizing dreams as 'abnormal psychic phenomena' [Freud] succeeded in explaining them to his satisfaction as analogous to neurotic symptoms, but at the cost of obliterating the distinction between health and illness."[79] The whole Freudian theory, says Erikson, "is heavily weighted in favor of insights which make dysfunction plausible. . . ."[80] Donald Meltzer puts it that Freud was prevented "from coming very close to the problem of mental *health* because his model of the mind could only clearly imagine mental *illness*."[81]

The "illness" was imagined to comprise the distorted expression of that instinctive energy which generates dreams, energy we repress asleep as well as awake. But it is not as if Freud championed the liberation of instinct. For all that his name has been correctly associated with sexual liberation in the century's cultural history, his own attitude toward the instincts was if anything censorious. Freud's human being is "ridden by primitive instincts."[82] As James Hillman nicely sketches, while Freud took from the Romantics the view that a dream is an intrapsychic event not meant for communication and mostly inscrutable to the dreamer's waking consciousness, he did not romanticize the dream but instead "took his stand with the dayworld view of sanity. . . ."[83] This "dayworld" is the consensual reality of Western science, the conceptualization of which, interestingly, has been traced precisely to the repudiation of dream experience by Heracleitos of Ephesos, around 500 B.C.: "The waking have one world in common, but the sleeping turn aside each into a world of his own." Heracleitos also said: "We must not act and speak like sleepers. . . ."[84] Freud wrote: "The ideal condition of things would of course be a community of men who had subordinated their instinctual life to the dictatorship of reason."[85]

But actually, the Freudian dayworld comes across as little more authentic than the manifest dream; it is also a facade in many respects. "Freud holds that the benevolent, loving, constructive impulses in man are not primary; he claims that they are a secondary production arising from the necessity to repress his originally evil strivings."[86] That is Fromm's description. Karen Horney's in the same mood: "Creativity and love (*eros*) were for him sublimated forms of libidinal drive." He could not allow "that inherent in man are evolutionary constructive forces, which urge him to realize his given potentialities."[87]*

Nowadays perhaps the most criticized aspect of Freudian psychology is this spiritual poverty, as regards both conscious and unconscious phenomena. Attitudes about psychology in general, and dreams in particular, have changed in recent decades—since Karl Stern could damn his contemporaries with this indictment: "Unfortunately, the reductive philosophy is the most widely acclaimed part of psychoanalytic thought. It harmonizes so excellently with a typical petit bourgeois mediocrity, which is associated with contempt for everything spiritual."[88]

Freud's personal lifelong conflict over his own spirituality has been fascinatingly explored by Werner Wolff, whose analysis of several of Freud's dreams is unfortunately too long to quote in full.[89] Wolff takes as his text the Latin epigraph which Freud gave to *The Interpretation of Dreams*, "If I cannot move heaven, I shall move hell." Being Jewish in an Austria where conventional avenues of advancement were blocked to Jews, and being son of a deprecating father, the ambitious Freud made a sort of implicit Faustian pact with the Devil which colored his whole life: he would find immortality by directing all his efforts downward in an "inquiry into the secrets of existence."[90] Wolff analyzes a key dream where Freud's associations led to an incident during which he had been prevented from entering a church. In the dream, *he turns aside into a beer cellar*. And in another dream, *Freud seeks safety by pretending to be blind*, that is, blind to life in its positive, spiritual aspects. Freud struggled with spiritual leanings, and sometimes "longed to be away from all this grubbing about in human dirt. . . ."[91] But his darker, down-looking, reductive complexion prevailed.

Wolff concludes his portrait by commenting on this anecdote: "'Freud, at one of the sessions of the Vienna Psychoanalytic Society, told the legend of the Devil as Churchbuilder. Freud compared himself with the hapless devil who having made an unfavorable pact with Saint Wolfgang had to labor hard and to keep on going down to the bowels of the earth (the unconscious) to haul heavy rocks—and still was unable to finish the church's edifice.' This is the anxiety of never finishing the church edifice of his soul, which never lets Freud and Faust rest."[92]

So there exists a pretty broad bill of indictments against Freudian psychology and dream interpretation. We should consider, however, how it is that this indubitable giant has come to serve as a straw man for any theorist to knock down by way of introducing his own contribution. Freud generated

---

* For a more generous interpretation of eros in Freud, see S. R. Palombo (1992).

a paradigm shift which is now so much a part of how we understand things that Freud's own shortcomings stand out against the background which he himself created.

If we become oppressed by the determinism of the Freudian psyche, we should remember that the sheer idea of the unconscious determination of behavior, with its vast explanatory power, is virtually Freud's discovery. If he insisted too much on the primacy of childhood formations throughout life, remember that he revolutionized our understanding of childhood and of how the personal past affects the personal present. And while we may not choose to look upon the unconscious as a sink of amoral infantile sexual fantasies, it was Freud who alerted us that erotic energy pervades life in unexpected ways—even if he himself held unnecessarily dark views about that energy.

Specifically on dreams, as outlandish as it must strike us to be told, for instance, that déjà vu in dreams always refers to mother's genitals,[93] *The Interpretation of Dreams* is still chock-full of good maneuvers for dream analysis. There is many a 'non-Freudian' dreamworker who knows that numbers in dreams may refer to important ages, perhaps without realizing that this dreamwork commonplace, as well as many others (such as that everything being oversized probably reflects a child's perspective and therefore an important memory), are Freud's.[94] And Freud devised free association, a method which stands in god-parental relationship to virtually every subsequent technique of verbal elicitation of a dream's meaning. Discussed earlier were Freud's enduring descriptions of dream formation, particularly condensation and displacement. Almost nobody still holds strictly to Freud's scheme of manifest dream disguising latent dream-thoughts and infantile wish, but it was the breakthrough idea of all modern dreamwork. Recall the self-gratulatory epitaph Freud coined for himself (". . . the Secret of Dreams was Revealed . . ."). I do not know if Hudson had this in mind when he observed that in the long run the fame of Freud's theory rests not on its accuracy in detail but on "its status as revelation."[95]

The dream can surely not be reduced to neurotic symptom. But if Freud's insight that dreams and symptoms have similar structures is even partially true, it is an astonishing one. We must thank Freud for relaxing the boundary between the normal and the abnormal. He firmly rooted dream psychology in general psychology, which is to say that he taught us to connect the reality of sleeping with that of waking in meaningful ways, and not only as regards unconscious infantile energies, but also as regards dream-thoughts spawned during the waking day. Moreover, although he saw life as a kind of disease process, he was also the first significant advocate of the modern idea of the patient curing her/himself, with therapist not as administrator of a treatment but rather as facilitator of the patient's own processes of recovery. The problem is that he gave us no clear vision of health, beyond the removal of symptoms.

That probably has to be the last word. When the average interested person speaks disparagingly nowadays of 'Freudian' dream interpretation, very often what s/he means is the mood "of hopelessness and doom,"[96] the sheer absence of positive expectations, of a growth dimension, of prospective ambitions for the dreamer's life, of spirituality in a broad or a narrow sense, rather than anything more technical or specific. "[Freud] suggests that the dream is a kind of mirage in our desert. The purpose of interpretation from that perspective is to challenge our illusions and eradicate them." So writes Eva Renée Neu. "[But] dreams talk to us about what we want and how we may get it, about the choices inherent in our lives. To seek to live without hope is to throw one's compass overboard. The best way to read one's compass is to listen to dreams respectfully."[97] And Grossinger, as quoted above (p. 69): "Jung says that Freud has cheated us, and his message is received most heartily by dreamers who in their guts agree."[98]

□ 3 □

Jung

Jung said, "I have no theory about dreams, I do not know how dreams arise. And I am not at all sure that my way of handling dreams deserves the name of a 'method'. I share all your prejudices against dream-interpretation as the quintessence of uncertainty and arbitrariness. On the other hand, I know that if we meditate on a dream sufficiently long and thoroughly, if we carry it around with us and turn it over and over, something almost always comes of it. . . . I may allow myself only one criterion for the result of my labors: does it work?"[1]*

Even allowing for disingenuousness, Jung's relatively modest self-assessment stands out against that of "Dr. Sigm. Freud" who—granted, in private —boasted ambitiously of fame in store for his dream theory and himself (ch. 2, p. 51). I have contrived this particular contrast of passages to highlight the fact that the two giants are sometimes posed against each other virtually as Manichean opposites. Bad Freud the egocentrist shows us the cup of life half empty. He is the reductionist, who sees dreaming as a disease process, and spirituality as denial. Good Jung teaches ego-transcendence. He shows us the cup of life half full, and filling. His impetus is always progressive, he lets the dream be healthy, and he cherishes the spirituality in normal human development.

Of course it is usually Jungians and the many influenced by Jung's 'analytical psychology' who offer such comparisons, where the high ground can

---

* T. A. Greene's (1979) chapter on Jung introduces him with this quotation, which I have borrowed for the same purpose. And here is a recent expression of humility resembling Jung's, from the prominent Jungian Robert Bosnak (1988 [1986], p. 89): "Generally I have no idea how to start on a dream. At such moments absolutely nothing comes to mind. Then a painful feeling of inferiority develops regarding the dream, and in this way my rational consciousness begins to sense its limits and my other faculties get their chance. Thus a wretched feeling at the beginning of work on a dream is completely normal."

so easily be taken. Thus I reveal my own partiality. But I agree with Montague Ullman, who said in a certain context that it is not necessary to swallow Jung whole in order to "resonate to whatever it is" his vision helps us see more clearly.[2]

The Freud-Jung comparison need not be completely lopsided. Ullman's is not, and I trust mine will not seem so. But where such comparisons *are* lopsided, there is a rough justice operating, getting back for the virtual conspiracy of silence during decades when the Freudian party treated Jung like a nonperson. Jungians Edward Whitmont & Sylvia Brinton Perera can still comment today about psychoanalysis: "Much of the new material 'rediscovers' Jung's basic ideas regarding the dream's function and some of his methodology of dream interpretation, without adequately, we feel, crediting that fact. It often seems as if Jung's seminal work has been generally defended against, first by denial of its existence or by derogation, then by claiming that it is obvious, or that it is a newly-made discovery of the psychoanalytic revisionists."[3]*

Mary Ann Mattoon asserts of Jung's dream "theory" (forget his claim not to have one) that it still remains less well-known than Freud's.[4] As reasons, she suggests that Jung's is inherently harder to understand; that Jung composed in a poetic style, difficult to access (but elsewhere, I add, in a style that is Germanically dense); and that he left no single comprehensive text on the subject, while Freud did. Mattoon's book and James Hall's,[5] as well as other primers, go a long way to make good for these deficits, if such they are. Also, some of Jung's primary texts concerning dreams have been edited into a single volume.[6] But in any event, I am not sure Mattoon is any longer right about whose theory is the better known. Probably in the less well educated public, it is true, a larger number may have a shadowy conception of Freudian wish-fulfillment than have even heard of Carl Jung. Also, members of the mental health bureaucracies still associate dream therapy with Freud's name—although their idea of *his* theory is often embarrassingly little more complete than the public's.[7] However, among those who actively pursue an interest in dreams, Jung has probably overtaken. I noticed in a prominent intellectual bookstore in London that Jung has three times the shelf space of Freud. Jung was Freud's Trotsky, but unlike Trotsky, Jung came back.

---

* Even Ullman, a revisionist psychoanalyst, who in 1979 (M. Ullman & N. Zimmerman 1979, p. 56) offered a balanced chart of the "Freudian View," "Jungian View," and "My View," had earlier (1982 [1962], pp. ix–x), before the ascendancy of Jung, written the following when introducing Walter Bonime's treatise: "Interestingly enough, there is much in Dr. Bonime's approach that is reminiscent of some of the early insights of Jung into the nature of the dream." Why "interestingly enough"? Why "reminiscent"? As though a direct influence could not come into it.

Wholeness and the Archetypes

If Freud's dream theory comes from his model of neurosis, then Jung's, it is fair to say, comes from his model of health. Jung's model is one of organismic balance, of wholeness. Of course Freud's model is also biologically based and prominently includes the notion of balance, or homeostasis: instinctive energies build up and need to find direct or devious release. This is a legitimate biological concept, but a narrow and rather mechanistic one. Its natural cousins are reflex and stimulus-response chains. Though the analogy of the thermostat comes to mind, Freud discerned the feedback process only in certain parts of the whole. He did offer what is called the "structural model" (super-ego, ego, id), but it is a structure which is not yet a system in the contemporary sense: he did not undertake to describe the dynamics of the whole in relation to the parts. One could apply Arthur Koestler's observation, that "feedback, without the concept of hierarchic order, is like the grin without the cat."[8]

Not to suggest that Jung was a cybernetician, but that his psychology was informed by a spirit akin to the holistic trend of systems thinking. Cousins to Jung's biological perspective are ethology, which shows how whole systems of goal-directed animal behavior are composed of smaller units, and embryology, which studies the purposive differentiation of organs toward the final pattern of the whole organism. Jung's inclination was to discern how the parts of the psyche operate if the natural target of their operations is the the whole's well-being—is its wholeness, in fact. Jung's 'compensatory function' of dreams and his 'individuation' are such operations (see below).

The governing whole in question is termed the *Self* (customarily capitalized by Jungians), which Whitmont characterizes as "an a priori wholeness potential or gestalt principle."[9] Jung says the concept of Self "expresses the unity of the personality as a whole," or "psychic totality," insofar as we can know it. "Self" is also an "archetypal idea," indeed, the archetype holding a "central position."[10] So before discussing the Self and the compensatory function of dreams further, something must be said about archetypes and the unconscious.

The Jungian unconscious broadly comprehends the entire "unknown in the inner world" from the point of view of ego consciousness.[11] It has two levels, the *personal* and the *collective*. The personal unconscious is roughly like the Freudian unconscious, with this noteworthy difference, that it contains not only what has been repressed because of being selfish, prohibited, and painful, but also, what is too good, too spiritual, or too beautiful for the ego identity presently to assimilate.

The collective unconscious—also called the *objective psyche* because it transcends personal, subjective experience—is comprised of *archetypes*. Like Platonic Ideas, from which they may be said ultimately to derive, archetypes can never be known directly; in themselves they are only formal potentials. We seem to know their actualizations in at least two interconnected ways: in the recurrent forms of human behavior (e.g., having or being a mother), and in *archetypal images*, symbolic imagery related to myth (e.g., the Great Mother, Astarte, Eve, etc.). Jolande Jacobi traces the development of Jung's thinking: "At first the notion of the archetype was applied by Jung primarily to psychic 'motifs' that could be expressed in images. But in time it was extended to . . . dynamic processes as well as static representations."[12] Treatments of archetypes in the Jungian literature tend to emphasize one aspect or the other, the biologic-behavioral or the mythic-imagic; and if the compatibility of the two aspects is less than perfect, that can be forgiven in view of the breadth of Jung's reach.

Approaching archetypes from the biologic side, Jung freely used a dominant biobehavioral concept of his time and place, 'instinct': he speaks of the "collective a priori beneath the personal psyche" as "forms of instinct, that is, archetypes."[13] And elsewhere, Jung writes: "Just as the migratory and nest-building instincts of birds were never learnt or acquired individually, man brings with him at birth the ground-plan of his nature. . . . These inherited situations correspond to the human situations which have existed since primeval times: youth and old age, birth and death, sons and daughters, fathers and mothers, mating, and so on. Only the individual consciousness experiences these things for the first time, but not the bodily system and the unconscious. . . . I have called this congenital and pre-existent instinctual model, or pattern of behaviour, the *archetype*."[14]

Jungians speak of the archetypal processes of the collective unconscious as being related "directly to the phylogenetic, instinctual bases of the human race."[15] Mattoon explains archetypes with the help of Konrad Lorenz's concept of innate behavior,[16] focusing on innate perceptual endowments (releasers) more than on the motor side of behavior (action potentials), as is understandable when someone is writing about how archetypes express themselves in dream imagery. Anthony Stevens, in his book titled *Archetypes*, gives a more balanced and biologically better informed treatment.[17] He quotes Jung saying that the archetype is not actually "an inherited idea, but rather an inherited mode of functioning, corresponding to the inborn way in which the chick emerges from the egg, the bird builds its nest, . . ." etc.[18] Complex behavior sequences of the sort involve innate patterns both of action and of perception, just as archetypes entail both life experiences and images.

So far, we find archetypes to be generally in the spirit of contemporary biology. While Jung's framing of the issue is somewhat inconsistent*—Jung was never inhibited by slavish self-consistency**—, there is no mistaking the biological direction of his thinking. It is when Jungians expound the more renowned mythic aspect that the biology gets murky.

James Hall quite correctly stipulates that in an evolutionary perspective, "for all practical purposes" archetypes "may be considered as fixed within historical time."[19] So what can Jung mean, that some archetypes are peculiar to "peoples or epochs"?[20] Wotan, he asserts, "is a fundamental attribute of the German psyche. . . ."[21] But Wotan cannot have become implanted in the "German psyche" in mere centuries by Darwinian mechanisms. Yet Jungians often explore the *unremembered* "tradition" and "belief" of a nation (June Singer), or the "collective history" of a "race" (Murray Stein), in search of the references of dream images.[22]

Of course archetypal *images* (actualizations of archetypes, as opposed to archetypes per se—a distinction which is easily muddied***) may be implanted by cultural influences during development, without awareness.[23] But once again, difficulties arise here because, if many Jungian interpretations are to be credited, very detailed information must be supposed to enter the psyche

---

* In another writing, Jung explicitly differentiates the archetypal bases of psyche from the "instinctual substrate," and "psychic processes" from "instincts" (*Aion* [1951], CW 9-II, excerpted in V. S. de Laszlo (1958), where the quoted phrases appear on p. 6). We can say that he is resorting here to a conventional distinction between higher and lower functions, psyche and instinct, to make his point in that context, that the higher is as lawful as the lower. But in yet another context we find archetypes, as "typical modes of apprehension," contrasted to instincts as "typical modes of action" ("Instinct and the unconscious" [1919], CW 8, para's 280 and 273, respectively). Here, in yet a different distinction, 'archetype' seems to designate the substrate of the perceptual side of behavior, 'instinct', the parallel substrate of the motoric side. The archetype "might suitably be described as *the instinct's perception of itself*, or as the self-portrait of the instinct. . ." (ibid., para. 277). But in no event did Jung regard archetypes as "totally transcendent entities" (C. E. Scott 1977b, p. 3), as metaphysical, unevolving absolutes (E. Lauter & C. S. Rupprecht 1985b, p. 13) in contrast to instincts, as some commentators perceive them to be. Or did he? "Empirically considered, however, the archetype did not ever come into existence as a phenomenon of organic life, but entered into the picture with life itself" ("A psychological approach to the dogma of the Trinity" ([1942/1948], CW 11, para. 222). "Whether . . . the archetypes . . . ever 'originated' at all is a metaphysical question and therefore unanswerable" ("Psychological aspects of the mother archetype" [1938/1954], CW 9-I, para. 187).

** Jean Piaget (1962 [1945]), p. 196), whose complexion was rather opposite Jung's, considered that Jung showed "a certain contempt for logic and rational activity, which he contracted through daily contact with mythological and symbolic thought. . . ."

*** Thus Jeremy Taylor (1992a, chapter 9) treats short-term cultural and even personal changes in consciousness as evolutionary changes at the archetypal level, without spelling out the biological implications.

by a sort of osmosis, and as a result of no plausible exposure. Consider this passage from *Psychology and Alchemy* (based on dreams of Nobel laureate Wolfgang Pauli), where Jung discusses what he takes to be a reenactment, in his patient's dream series, of certain historical expressions of archetypal motifs : "[C]onsciously the dreamer has no inkling of all this. But in his unconscious he is immersed in this sea of historical associations, so that he behaves in his dreams as if he were fully cognizant of these curious excursions into the history of the human mind. . . . Hence one could say—*cum grano salis*—that history could be constructed just as easily from one's own unconscious as from the actual texts."[24]

Thus it seems that two processes configure the contents of the collective unconscious: phylogenetic evolution creates the archetypes of the entire species, while some extragenetic process adds an historical gloss to the psyches of races and of nations. In the last analysis one can tolerate this imprecision with boundaries between biology and history for the sake of receiving Jung's wealth of insight, or not tolerate it. But in any event it is best to have it on the table. For myself, genetic transmission of psychic potentials which show up in dreams is not only a plausible idea but an inescapable one; while any sort of innate transmission on the time scale of history or even near prehistory is fanciful. Therefore I find archetypal analysis of dreams problematical, but only when neither a phylogenetic nor a developmental basis can be detected for the supposed presence of very detailed cultural-historical information in the psyche of the dreamer.*

---

* Andrew Samuels writes about this question in a pair of articles concerning Jung's regrettable association with National Socialism in the 1930s. "When we look a little more closely at Jung's not-absolutely-collective layer of the collective unconscious, we find that it is not 'race', not 'tribe', and not 'family' that engage Jung, but *nation*." And nationality comes less from race than from culture and—in a literal, causal sense—from "soil," from "earth." "'The mystery of the American earth','" for example, "was so powerful that, according to him . . . [t]he skull and pelvis measurements of second-generation Americans were becoming 'indianized'" as well as were their psyches (1992a, p. 20, quoting C. G. Jung, "The role of the unconscious" [1918], CW 10, para's 18–9). This supposed influence from the soil is more than ontogenetic: "national psychology" is for Jung "in some mysterious manner, an innate factor" (1992b, p. 128).

Jung cannot be exonerated from racial anti-semitism, however. For a while he "became a devotee of Wotan," and "became so excited by the potential of the Aryan consciousness that he developed a corresponding 'problem' about Jews" (1992a, p. 14). Since German Jews shared the soil with their Aryan countrymen and, to a very large degree, shared their culture, then the unique standing of Jews must have been a consequence of 'blood', as Hitler maintained.

Jung's racism toward blacks was altogether less subtle. "He said the black person has 'probably a whole historical layer *less* (of collective unconsciousness) than you. The different strata of mind correspond to the history of the races.' He continued to say that living with 'barbaric races' tends to exert a 'suggestive effect' on the 'tamed instinct of the white race and tends to pull it down'" (P. Young-Eisendrath 1987, p. 49, quoting C. G. Jung, "The Tavistock lectures. Lecture II," CW 18,

The use of cultural-historical parallels is termed *archetypal amplification*, and is to be applied by a qualified analyst—although in fact any interpreter can act as amateur historian-folklorist-ethnologist. Archetypal amplification is by no means applied to every dream. In a sense all experience and hence all dreaming has an archetypal basis, so "it is always possible to amplify any motif in the direction of its archetypal foundation." But "many archetypal elements are too trivial to attract attention."[25] Furthermore, the gist of most dreams pertains to the personal, not the collective unconscious. Jung held such dreams to be simply allegorical (i.e., not symbolic), insofar as a rational translation from dream story to meaning is possible in principle, without recourse to archetypal amplification.

Usually archetypal amplification is reserved for *archetypal* or *big dreams*, dreams more conspicuously involving deep springs of our nature, important events of the life cycle, and archetypal imagery.* Such dreams are emotionally charged, sometimes mystical. Motifs with mythic parallels predominate, although not necessarily in an obvious manner. "Usually they present themselves in some fragment or variation of their theme and/or in a contemporary frame of reference. Thus *a dreamer was warned by an electrician that he might be accidentally executed by a high tension wire if he did not stop fooling around.* This was his symbolic encounter with the transpersonal lord of the thunderbolt and ruler of the energies, Zeus."[26]

As with 'Freudian symbols', the dreamer may be at a loss for personal associations.** Amplification aims to hit upon "the collective associations that the human race as a whole has" to a given archetype.[27] Such big dreams are held to be symbolic rather than allegorical, in the sense that the ego cannot fully comprehend, and certainly never fully verbalize their meaning: dreams

---

para. 93). For further remarks by Jung about "primitives" and Africans, see (1984 [1938]).

* The term 'big dream' is found used with several different meanings. Sometimes it refers to archetypal dreams, especially to obvious and numinous ones; sometimes, to any dream of particular vividness or narrative coherence; sometimes, to a dream of notable significance for the dreamer; and sometimes, to dreams of significance for the dreamer's community, dreams dreamt for the benefit of the social collective, especially by prominent individuals and/or in heightened circumstances.

** Besides touching on archetypal notions with his universal so-called 'Freudian symbols', Freud suggests briefly that phylogeny may be recapitulated in the dream life, if we could only read it there (1953 [1900], p. 548). Speaking of "primal scene" fantasies of parental sexual intercourse, he says, "I believe that these primal fantasies, and no doubt a few others as well, are a phylogenetic endowment. In them the individual reaches beyond his own experience into primeval experience . . ." (*Introductory Lectures on Psycho-analysis*, 1916–7, Standard Edition, vol. 22, London: Hogarth, pp. 370–1, quoted by A. Samuels, 1985b, pp. 114–5).

Whitmont & Perera (1989, p. 38) mention other reasons besides archetypality that a dreamer may fail to find associations. The dreamer may simply be blocked, the material may be too threatening, "or there may be too little free imagination available for associating."

(and other symbolic events) resolve contradictions and thus surpass obstacles to wholeness.

Everyone has archetypal dreams. They tend to come most frequently at transitional epochs: early childhood, puberty, young adulthood, midlife, and approaching death. Illness, danger, and psychic impasse evoke them. But it is not clear whether the psychically well or unwell have more of them. Certainly they occur with psychosis (see the dream "Rotten tree of life," marking the onset of delusional schizophrenia, ch. 10, p. 340). The more ordered images of the Self archetype (e.g., the mandala) are said to crop up in the dreams of those whose "ego is confused and in disarray."[28] And archetypality is bound up with neurosis to the extent that the less conscious something is, the more likely that it will present itself in archetypal dream imagery.[29] Nevertheless, some research has found a "negative correlation between the proportion of recalled archetypal dreams and neuroticism and psychological distress,"[30] while high archetypality scores are associated with "psychological well-being."[31] Those who have done a good job of integrating their personal unconscious seem to enjoy archetype-rich dreaming. And some people (such as Jung) simply have a bent for archetypal dreaming.

As to the actual frequency of 'big' archetypal dreams, Jung's own assessment was that "the collective unconscious influences our dreams only occasionally."[32] If you have ever known a self-styled 'Jungian' enthusiast for amplification, you will understand the need to bear Jung's conservative estimate in mind. Peter O'Connor says that finding archetypal meanings everywhere "reflects an ego-inflation that one is so special that the only dreams occurring will be archetypal ones."[33] Hall warns that the result of "archetypal reductionism" is that "the dreamer's actual life issues are obscured in the exploration of mythic and other such motifs."[34] Kathrin Asper speaks about "a dangerous tendency to interpret dreams in a kind of vacuum. . . ."[35] Stephen Martin describes clients who undertake Jungian therapy hoping to repeat the experiences of Jung and other "big" dreamers and who consequently undervalue "small" dreams, those without obvious archetypal markers.* Whitmont adds that "symbol-hunting" can be abused by the therapist out of vanity or to avoid difficult issues in the therapeutic relationship.[36] Another Jungian, Roland Cahen, puts the matter more strongly: "This method of amplification must be handled with the utmost reserve and prudence. Otherwise it opens the door to all types of abuse and to the worst, most unspeakable kinds of proselytism."[37]

---

* S. A. Martin (1992), p. 41: "All dreams are big dreams, carriers of personal and archetypal meaning that can and must be assessed for the sake of individuation."

There is nothing unspeakable about the following interpretation, offered by Whitmont to exemplify amplification. (For another Jungian amplification, see "Extinct animals in a drained pond" in ch. 8, p. 267). Whitmont's amplification does, however, give an instance of the problematical procedure mentioned above, of analyzing dream images by resort to specific cultural parallels which, on the one hand, are unknown to the dreamer's ego, but the archetypal basis of which, on the other, cannot have entered the collective psyche by any plausible evolutionary process.

A middle-aged businessman in a state of depression dreamed:
I was in bed with a young girl and had just finished intercourse. Then I heard a voice saying in Hungarian—my mother tongue—that I did not deserve the 'fa' or 'fasz'. I was not sure which, perhaps both.

In Hungarian 'fa' means wood, 'fasz' means penis. Taken on the personal level, allegorically this dream might show the dreamer that he undervalues sexuality. . . . This level of interpretation should be checked out first in every case; often it will apply.

But in this instance it did not. There was no question of any repression of sexuality or masculine aggressiveness. . . . The dreamer was a self-confident and successful go-getter and felt himself quite deserving of his successes both in and out of bed. . . . Often the seemingly irrelevant or irrational details of a dream supply the most helpful pointers for its interpretation. In terms of associations, the wood motif drew a relative blank from the patient. He liked wood as a material and as a youth had tried his hand at wood carving.

Viewed symbolically, however, as a best possible representation of a transpersonal, essentially indefinable reality, the dream opens a new dimension of understanding. . . .

The phallus that is also wood is a widespread cult object. At the spring festival Indian men dance with wooden phalli. In ancient Egypt the wooden phallus represented the generative power of Osiris, restored to life by Isis from death and dismemberment; his natural phallus was lost and Isis substituted a wooden one by means of which he begot the child, Horus, on her. The wooden phallus, then, . . . signifies creativity that is not of the flesh, of natural being, but of the striving of the spirit, of immortality. An analogous image is found in the phallus carved upon antique grave monuments bearing the inscription 'Mortis et vitae locus' (the place of death and life). Purportedly this is a replica of the phallus which Dionysus, the god who dies and is reborn, erected before the portals of Hades.

. . . Amplification is essential for interpretation in such a case, but, equally important, it appeals to the dreamer's feeling imagination rather than simply to an intellectual understanding. The symbolic significance of the image cannot be grasped without such an involvement of feeling and intuition. It is to the mystery of spiritual renewal that the symbol of the wooden phallus points, and in respect to this, not to overt sexual prowess, the worthiness of the dreamer is questioned in the dream.

The validity of this assumption is borne out by the associations and descriptions of the young lady, the bed partner in the above example. She was an acquaintance whom he described as a grossly opportunistic go-getter, an unscrupulous success hunter whom in actual life he found quite repulsive.[38]

There are two issues: whether correspondences between dreams and culture items have a biological provenience, and whether, even if they do not, they help to understand dreams. In the example, one need not quarrel with Whitmont's characterization of his dreamer, in order to query the implication that wood and phallus are innately linked in the collective unconscious, not simply connected both in cultural history and in this dreamer's personal unconscious by their affinities (hardness, tubularity, growth, productivity, rhythm, ascent, etc.).

Jung's clinical evaluation of Freudian free association can be turned back on his own mythic amplification. One's complexes, said Jung, may be arrived at by free-associating to any arbitrary image.[39] Therefore a train of free associations leading away from a dream image will inevitably arrive at the dreamer's complexes, without necessarily showing which ones operated in the particular dream. Jung's corrective was to *circumambulate* the dream: an immediate 'free' association to an image, some directive probing, then a return to that image, another association, then the next image, a further association, more probing, etc.—suggesting a pattern like "daisy petals."[40]*

---

* The term 'complex', though sometimes used in Jungian writings to designate an aspect of neurosis (e.g., M. A. Mattoon 1984 [1978], pp. 4 and 10), as in everyday and Freudian usage, usually means rather the nexus of personal ideas, images and emotions—whether neurotic or healthy—which actualize an archetype. Each complex has its "archetypal core" (J. A. Hall 1983, p. 12). Complexes "constitute the structure of the unconscious part of the psyche and are its normal manifestations" (J. Jacobi 1959 [1957]), p. 20). Jung (*The Psychology of Dementia Praecox* [1907], CW 3, para. 137) said that the complexes "are like little secondary psyches having their affective roots in the body, by means of which they always keep awake." Though it would not be dreaming in the sleep-lab sense, it was the supposed perpetual activity of these component sub-psyches which caused Jung to say that we dream continuously (*Seminar on Children's Dreams, 1938-9*, unpublished, quoted by C. Rycroft, 1981, p. 32).

Hunt (H. T. Hunt, R. Ogilvie, K. Belicki, D. Belicki & E. Atalick 1982, p. 563) compares free association to reading Tarot cards or casting the *I Ching*, where "the pattern is *turned into* a symbol by the interpretive set of the subject—which may in turn, be influenced by the power and impact of the pattern. Done well there is no choice but to link the dream with the background of one's life. . . . Where else can it go?" (p. 564).

Werner Wolff (1972 [1952], pp. 189–90) devised an associational method of dreamwork which he probably derived from Jungian circumambulation, and which has since been recommended as one alternative by Patricia Garfield (1976 [1974], p. 185), Janice Baylis (1976, p. 40), Jill Morris (1987 [1985], pp. 89-95), Henry Reed (1991, pp. 24 and 74–82) and, in a computer program for dream-

Jung pursued both personal and archetypal associations in this fashion, minimizing *dis*sociation of dream and discussion by adhering to the dream itself. Archetypal amplifications do, however,—as the cautions of O'Connor, Hall, Whitmont, and Cahen suggest—, tend to exercise a fascination of their own. One or another can certainly be adduced for any dream image, without that in itself establishing that the dream was formed by an archetype they have in common, or even that the purported significance of the culture item has much to do with the dreamer's present state. As with free association, the success of the procedure probably depends more than anything else upon the acuity and intuition of the practitioner. Jung's own intuition was obviously prodigious.

Objections to archetypal interpretations are least likely to arise where amplification concerns plausible universals of the human condition, those with a plausible phylogenetic history. Some archetypes undoubtedly correspond to innate predispositions to occupy certain social roles which have antecedents reaching back at least to our troop-living primate past. The 'trickster', to speculate, might correspond to the peripheralized juvenile pioneer common in troop-living higher primate species. Other archetypes more obviously concern essential functions and transitions of the life cycle—birth, puberty, sexuality, death, and such. Additionally, and most importantly for practical Jungian dream interpretation, there are the archetypes governing the psyche itself: *persona*, *shadow*, the *animus/anima* pair, and the *Self*.

Short definitions of the Self were earlier quoted: "wholeness potential or gestalt principle," "psychic totality," the "central" archetype. Similar capsule definitions of the other three are easily extracted from the Jungian literature. Grasping them in depth and interrelation is another matter, partly for reasons of profundity and partly, again, for a certain imprecision. However, even if they sometimes weaken into cliches, they are extremely useful tools of dream interpretation.

Persona. 'Persona' is one of those concepts ('complex' is another) which has entered common usage without its users always knowing that it comes from Jung. Taken from the Greek word for 'mask', it refers to "the outer personality . . . the outer face . . . ,"[41] to "those aspects of the personality

---

work, by Sarah Lillie (personal communication, 1992). The method consists of first making an association to each element of the dream, and then assembling a new thought sequence out of the associations. The new sequence is parallel to the original dream and, hopefully, reveals its underlying meaning. Baylis calls this the "single association" method, Reed, interpretation by "key words." A wrinkle in Wolff's method not picked up by the others is to scramble the dream elements before associating to them, to prevent interference to the "freedom" of association, before reassembling the associations in correct order.

by which one adapts to the outer world. . . ."[42] Someone's persona is understood in terms of the specific social roles s/he adopts,, which have their own archetypal templates; but the persona proper is the very propensity to have a social role. A particular persona expresses "the ego's archetypal drive toward adaptation to external reality and collectivity."[43] For obvious reasons, the classic 'persona dream' involves clothing. A good example appears in Jean and Wallace Clift's excellent small book, a member of that minor genre of the 1970s and 1980s in which a Jungian approach to dream interpretation is combined with Christian perspectives. Incidentally, note that the interpretation is reached with personal but no mythic amplifications:

> The first year that we were studying Jung, an analyst from Zurich came to lecture at the Jung Center where we were studying. . . . [W]e invited him to our home for tea one afternoon. . . . [This] was pretty heady stuff for us at the time, when the whole field of study still seemed so esoteric to us. It was this event which inspired Jean finally to write down a dream one morning—the first time she had done so[—] . . . the morning our guest was coming to tea:
>
> *I was in a house. My mother was there. Some guests came and I was still in my pajamas, so I ran out and hid. I then went upstairs and went into a room to get something to put on.*
>
> *It was an extremely large room—huge—I couldn't see its sides and it was very, very still. There were some large plastic cases hanging on hangers. I knew that there were some dresses of mine stored there. In one plastic case where I looked there were a number of dresses of mine.*
>
> *One was a gold dress I had years ago, the one I had on when I was so embarrassed at that party. There were two which were my size, but they were exact replicas of dresses I made my daughters for their dolls last Christmas. I no longer remember the others.*
>
> . . . This dream suggests that Jean was at the time existing in a house with her mother—. . . "That's where she was coming from." . . .

The next event in the story presents another common persona motif: Jean was inappropriately dressed for what happened. Sometimes in dreams the dreamer is completely naked when everyone else is dressed. Such dreams suggest that the dreamer is not adequately protected from the world, that the necessary security of an appropriate persona is lacking. So this imagery suggests that in some current situation Jean was experiencing (or perhaps fearing?) that she did not have an appropriate way of being in relation to others.* Could the guests who came to her house be connected with the expected guest of the next day? It seems likely, and probably also the "guests" who were coming "into her house" were from the

---

* Another Jungian, Karen Signell (1990, p. 24), gives a different significance to nakedness: it "probably doesn't mean you're secretly exhibitionistic or seductive; rather it could mean that you're being open and vulnerable, being yourself without pretense, protection, or cultural accoutrements."

Jungian studies—those visitors of the ideas new to her—and were troubling her with insecure feelings. How could these new ideas be reconciled with her adaptive persona as a clergy wife and leader of prayer and study groups? Jean didn't really know; she was still dressed for sleeping, not for waking up to new possibilities.

The drama does not stop there, however. She runs "upstairs" (up to the mind to try to think of new reconciling persona adaptations?) to look for something else to put on. This presents another common persona motif: looking for the right clothes, looking for something else to put on. When such a motif appears in a dream, it can be instructive to examine carefully what the associations are with the offered choices. In many cases, as in this dream, they seem to review possibilities which have been used in the past. Sometimes, probably in the forgotten dresses of this dream, there are new, future possibilities portrayed.

The gold dress which appeared from Jean's past was associated in her memory with a particularly painful evening from her university days, an evening when her behavior made her feel exposed as foolish—a memory connected with a shadow aspect (the archetype to be discussed in the next chapter [here, the next section]. When she thought of the evening in relation to the persona, she realized that her behavior in the past arose out of her own sense of an inadequate persona —she didn't really know how to act—but instead of working with that problem sensibly, she had tried to cover up her insecurity with extraverted acting out and ended up feeling foolish. The appearance of this gold dress is a caution not to fall into the same error again. The other two dresses are replicas of doll dresses, which seem also to be a caution not to regress to a young, helpless, doll-like adaptation, but instead to move toward a genuine adult persona.[44]

Shadow. In acknowledging that the shadow is not a "clearly defined archetype," Stevens quotes Jung's frustrated response to a discussion aiming to make the term precise: "This is all nonsense! The shadow is simply the whole unconscious."[45] But in usual usage, including Jung's, the shadow refers to the unconscious in a certain aspect: the dark side of the personal unconscious, everything "repressed for the sake of the ego ideal."[46] Shadow formation is an "indispensable aspect of normal ego development."[47]

Habitually, we project our repressed shadow qualities onto 'the other': other individuals, other types, and dream elements other than the dream-ego. An example, from E. A. Bennet via Charles Rycroft, shows the dreamer's shadow impulses appearing in their most common personification, that of a shady, unpleasant character of the dreamer's own gender:

According to Jung, people who identify excessively with their persona are apt to have dreams in which a person conspicuously unlike their persona appears, this other 'opposite' person being the dreamer's 'shadow'. . . . [The dreamer was] a punctilious bank official who recurrently dreamt that *while looking up at night*

*he became aware of a figure trying to break into his house. This figure would
move from window to window, each of which he closed in the nick of time, but
eventually the intruder outstripped him, burst in through a door*—at which point
the dreamer woke with a start. The implication is that the intruder represented
all that the bank official had disowned of himself.[48]*

As already intimated when discussing the personal unconscious, not all
that the ego ignores, hides, or rejects is inherently dark or nasty. We also
repress strengths and virtues. In one place Jung says that positive qualities
are repressed in "rather rare cases,"[49] but elsewhere he speaks of those positive and "insufficiently developed functions and contents of the personal unconscious" as the norm.[50]

This so-called 'positive shadow' becomes manifest as the shadow typically does: repression turns it negative. This hypothetical example from Marie-
Louise von Franz, Jung's protege, shows a repressed positive impulse taking
the dream-form of beasts, a frequent shadow image:

> [A] man has a feeling impulse to say something positive to someone and he
> blocks it off through some inhibition. He might then dream that *he had driven
> over a child with his car*—he had had a spontaneous feeling impulse on the level
> of a child and his conscious purpose had smashed it. The human is still there, but
> as a hurt child. Should he do that habitually for five years, he would no longer
> dream of a child who had been hurt but of *a zoo full of raging wild animals in
> a cage*. An impulse which is driven back loads up with energy and becomes in-
> human.[51]

Naturally the negative shadow also intensifies when it has been repressed:
"If you see a herd of cattle or pigs and say they are non-existent, they are
immediately all over the place, the cows will eat up the rose garden and the
pigs will climb into your bed and sleep there!"[52]

Besides agressive or pathetic characters or animals, anything unpleasant,
monstrous, or destructive can represent the shadow in dreams. (For more
examples of shadow dreams, see especially chapter 16.)

Animus/Anima. The anima archetype constitutes an "imprint . . . of all
the ancestral experiences of the female. . . ."[53] It gives a man his images of
the other gender. As expressed in individuals, the 'anima complex' accrues

---

* On the question of shadow gender, Peter O'Connor (1986, pp. 142-3) suggests that in today's
climate, when animus issues may "have been awakened prematurely" before shadow issues have
been confronted, a woman's shadow may become "in some way involved with an animus image."
Signell (1990), a feminist Jungian, does not specifically address the issue of shadow gender, but
gives examples of male shadow figures in women's dreams without any implication of growth stages
being out of sequence.

peculiarities from family, cultural traditions and other exposures which help determine choice of partners and other relationships.

The anima is also seen to be the "unconscious, feminine side of a man's personality."[54] Freud also spoke of genetic bisexuality, but whereas he had in mind homosexual inclinations, Jung considered one's contrasexual aspect variously as a "personification" of one's unconscious or as the mediator or guide to it[55]—as entirely essential, therefore, to wholeness of the psyche. As we (men) mature, and particularly around midlife, we assimilate more and more of the anima into consciousness; if we do not, then our relationships are governed by projections (ch. 6, p. 221) and we fail to see ourselves and others as we really are.

Corresponding to a man's anima is a woman's animus. Jung described each with qualities opposite to those which he regarded as belonging natural-ly to the personality of each sex.[*] Thus "anima speaks of imagination, fan-tasy and play, while animus refers to focused consciousness, authority and respect for facts. Nowadays," continue Andrew Samuels et al., "it is widely regarded as fallacious to link such psychological traits to sex."[56] This reser-vation notwithstanding, something which a feminist must consider sexism is indelible in the animus/anima distinction, for good or ill. Notorious in this respect, for giving credence to objectionable stereotypes, is Jung's character-ization of women possessed by a negative animus as stubborn and argumen-tative, and of men possessed by a negative anima as petulant and tempera-mental.[**]

---

[*] Signell (1990, p. 200) argues that animus dynamics in women and anima dynamics in men are not strictly symmetrical, because men have a stronger "need to identify with consciousness, to be different from their mothers; . . . since a woman is freer to retain some identification with the moth-er and [thereby] the unconscious, her animus doesn't have to carry such a load, to represent all the unconscious."

[**] The archetypal *images* of a given culture reflect its "social structures, institutions, and roles" (D. S. Wehr 1985, p. 24). Jung, say feminists, treated culturally determined traits as if inbuilt, and in so doing reinforced the inequality of women by assigning thinking, which the culture values, to men (E. Lauter & C. S. Rupprecht 1985b, pp. 5-6). Riane Eisler (1990, p. xiii): "As Demaris Wehr writes in *Jung & Feminism: Liberating Archetypes* [Boston: Beacon, 1989], through archetypes that define their thinking side as masculine, women are left in 'a deficit position with regard to natural female authority, logic, and rationality'—they are effectively distanced from their thinking side, just as men are distanced from their more feeling and vulnerable side by personifying it as 'feminine.' And yet, unlike Freudian and other psychoanalytic approaches, Jung's work with archetypes and dreams did allow women and men to claim these qualities via their 'feminine' or 'masculine' side—an important first step toward a more integrated psyche for both sexes." All the same, Jung's high valuation of the feminine did not extend to "the actual experiences of women" or to "products of the female imagination" (E. Lauter & C. S. Rupprecht 1985b, p. 7 and 1985c, p. 224, respective-ly). His treatment of the animus is often "pejorative" (D. S. Wehr 1985, p. 34), and it is true that "[d]isparaging comments about women can be found throughout Jung's writings . . ." (p. 41), espe-

The example for this section is an animus dream, excerpted from a case study by Amy Allenby:

> My patient was a little over forty when she began analysis, and unmarried. An acute breakdown . . . had made her realize the need for reorientation. . . . [T]he first half of her life had been entirely governed by the consequences of the identification with her father, which dated from her early childhood. . . . The ensuing stresses and strains of life had led to a further weakening of the ego position until her ego was in danger of being completely overwhelmed by the unconscious. . . .
>
> During several years prior to her breakdown she had frightening dreams about her father, who turned into a negative figure, persecuting her and trying to destroy her. . . .
>
> As regards the father image, a threefold differentiation gradually took place into what I would call the image of the personal father, the positive animus, and the father archetype proper.
>
> The positive animus made his distinctive appearance in a dream in which he was introduced to the dreamer as *the landowner of a neighbouring estate, recently returned from abroad.* . . .
>
> One of the key dreams in which the collective nature of the animus came to dramatic expression occurred a few months later. . . .
>
> *I was in a large hall with about an equal number of Chinese people and English people. They were well mixed but one could feel how suspicious they were of each other, and the atmosphere was very tense. Suddenly a Chinaman flourished a knife, and I knew it would be a riot unless something was done. (The dreamer then suggests that a chosen member of each side should search the other party for weapons, and a number of them are found and taken away*

---

cially the earlier ones, which reveal the complacent sexism characteristic of the majority thinking of the era (M. V. Adams 1990, p. 55).

Robert Hopcke (1990, p. 122 passim) develops Jung's observation (1984 [1938], p. 489) that the anima may appear in the dreams of gay men as masculine rather than feminine. Hopcke argues that to identify the anima with a man's unconscious feminine is sexist, the result of patriarchal thinking, and that as the archetype of the "soul" the anima is without gender, before it is given a manifestation (p. 85 passim). Hopcke loses contact with the biological, the evolutionary origin of the archetypes when he says that "it makes no sense to confine an archetype's appearance to human categories of gender" (p. 127).

Hopcke's book is the most extended of the surprisingly small number of writings which approach the dreams of homosexuals in a 'politically correct' way, i.e., which do not treat homosexual preference as inherently pathological. Other such writings include Robert Bosnak's *Dreaming with an Aids Patient* (1989) and Gregory Bogart's article on sexual abuse and homophobia (1993), as well as passages in D. L. Hart (1977), P. R. Koch-Sheras, E. A. Hollier & B. Jones (1983, p. 169ff.), C. S. Rupprecht (1985, p. 214), S. Krippner & J. Dillard (1988, pp. 152–3), and K. A. Signell (1990, pp. 235–6 passim). Even, surprisingly, a book on contemporary dreamwork for couples by a San Francisco Bay Area author barely mentions homosexuals, and gives not a single example of dreams of a homosexual couple (P. Maybruck 1991, p. 60).

[Allenby's paraphrase]*). Every scrap of tension disappeared; I wanted every- one to express their happiness, and I started to dance. I became completely lost in what I was doing, and saw that everyone was watching me, enthralled. As I circled round I noticed a tall, stately, fine Chinese figure; he was obvi- ously the leader of all the Chinese people who were present. I held out my hand to him and he joined me. Together we circled round the room, and as we passed people we invited them to join us. Soon everyone was dancing and all were completely happy.*

After this the dream repeated itself with slight variations, the most noteworthy of which was that this time *the leader of the Chinese people revealed himself as the Chinese emperor, wearing a wonderful silver kimono which radiated a silver light, while from his forehead shone a brilliant light.* This time *the dance devel- oped into a kind of orgiastic Dionysian frenzy.*

. . . It should perhaps be noted that the dreamer herself still plays the role of the favored child. . . . But the important thing is that the dreamer here enters voluntarily and with abandon into an experience in which the memory image of the relation to her father in childhood is repeated on a collective, symbolic level. One is inclined to say that the incest motif, originally concealed in the rela- tionship with the actual father, is here transmuted into a ritual 'hieros gamos' [sacred marriage] with the animus in his positive aspect. In entering into the ritual, the dreamer takes an active role in reconciling the opposites which in the dream are represented by the Chinese and the English respectively—the masters of the inner life, and the masters of social adjustment and of disciplined activ- ity.[57]

The Self-system. Adding the ego, or I-centered consciousness, these—the persona, shadow, and animus/anima—are the proximate components of the whole which is the Jungian Self. They are usually mentioned in this order, one of increasing distance from the ego. The sequence has a dynamic sense as well, roughly indicating the sequence of key issues arising during matura- tion, which culminates in issues surrounding the Self itself.

As to how the components (not to mention their sub-components, other archetypes) interrelate to compose the whole, the literature contains no more than suggestions; and these do not combine to convey any very precise plan of the Self-system. Jung pairs the persona, as the face we turn toward the outer world, with the animus/anima, the face we turn inward to the uncon- scious,[58] our "skin of adaptation for" the unconscious world.[59] Hence Hall calls persona and animus/anima "relational structures," while shadow and ego are "identity structures."[60] The shadow is the shadow of the ego, but it is also in an obvious way, as our hidden aspect, the opposite of the persona, our presentational aspect. Meanwhile, both shadow and animus/anima per- sonify the unconscious. Jung also said that the ego is a "personification of the unconscious."[61] Make a diagram of this if you can.

Taking persona, shadow, and animus/anima conjointly with the ego, Hall classes them as "special structures of the personal parts of the psyche. . . ."[62] Whitmont emphasizes their collective aspect, in a passage which conveys the spirit if not the specifics of a view of the Self as a hierarchically arranged system: "The transpersonal psyche may be likened to an unconscious background personality or personalities" which "are as though related to an unconscious center which Jung called the Self and are what is depicted in the persona, shadow and animus-anima figures of the dream. The Self appears like an organizing totality. . . ."[63]

Of key importance is the systemic relation between Self and ego, a relation found characterized in several ways which are at least intuitively compatible. Firstly, the Self is the archetype of the ego. Just as for example the shadow archetype gives rise to an individual's 'shadow complex', so the Self gives rise to one's 'ego complex'. But at the same time, Self is an all-inclusive designation for the whole human being, as we would find one if we actually could perceive one, ego and all else, in organic unity. While the Self is "the subject of [the] total psyche, which also includes the unconscious,"[64] the ego, "a specialized outgrowth of the unconscious . . . ,"[65] is itself "never more and never less than consciousness. . . ."[66] The ego acts for the Self, but is not the center of the Self. In diagrams, the Self gets represented both as the center and as the circumference of a circle, while the ego is a much smaller circle acentrically located at or near an edge. The ego is "the center of the field of consciousness" but not the "center of the personality."[67] This eviction of the ego constitutes a "copernican revolution" for Western (if not for Oriental) psychology.[68]

Additionally, from the ego's point of view the Self, being comprehensive, gives rise to images of order and value, including the well-known 'mandala', the Buddhist meditation aid whose motifs of circularity and squareness universally (if not always consciously) symbolize the wholeness of the Self, as do, thought Jung, all variants of those motifs. Indeed, without prejudging the metaphysical question, Jung thought that the comprehensive Self archetype is the core of ideas of god. Thus the Self archetype is seen as directly actualizing itself variously as the ego, as the total personality, and as images of totality, including mandala and god. Other images of the Self include a king, a hero, a holy woman, a savior, an indigenous maiden, a cross, an infant or child, the number four, and a process such as a journey.[69]

Jung seems to have held a view not unlike Teilhard de Chardin's, that everything in nature evolves toward consciousness.[70] He probably thought that psychic existence of some kind is a general property of systems, for he saw archetypes as comparable to the structures of all living systems and even to inorganic structures.[71] But human consciousness is special, for a world without anyone saying 'This is the World' recedes to what Jung variously called "non-being," "nothingness," or "mere being."[72] The human Self, a highly developed system striving to maintain and enhance its wholeness, strives in so doing to manifest itself, to "experience itself as a whole,"[73] to become conscious; to become ego. Jung calls it man's "destiny . . . to create more and more consciousness."[74] However, the Self, like all in existence, remains forever founded in unconsciousness. The ego is Self's organ, the functional organ of consciousness, but it can never become the organism itself. That tension always holds. Though the ego is the indispensable "administrator of the personality,"[75] the Self in its comprehensiveness is ultimately inscrutable to the ego. It is at once inscrutably more primitive than ego and inscrutably wiser—"a superior, if archaic intelligence."[76] Our life plays out in the polarity of conscious and unconscious.*

Compensatory Dreaming

On the time scale of the lifespan, the dynamic between unconscious Self and conscious ego constitutes the process Jung called *individuation*, in which ego serves as "executant of the archetypal blueprint for the whole life-cycle which is systematically encoded within the Self"[77] (see below). On the scale of daily life, the Self-ego dynamic gives us *compensatory dreaming*. Wrote Jung: "The relation between the conscious and unconscious is compensatory. This is one of the best-proven rules of dream interpretation. When we set out to interpret a dream, it is always helpful to ask: What conscious attitude does it compensate?"[78] So as to frame this important contribution of Jung's, several pages will be taken to mention some alternative views of the relation between waking and dreaming.

Alternatives. Terms for the relation between waking and dreaming are diverse and do not have consistent acceptations. The relation is said to be

---

* Cf. also the section "Ego and Self" below. A special question is the relation between *dream-ego* and Self. Elie Humbert (1990, p. 115) says: "The dreamer who acts in the dream can then be three different realities: the ego-complex, the conscious personality dominated by this or that psychic content, the whole personality." Whitmont & Perera (1989, pp. 18–22) analyze the relation into several more possibilities. "Sometimes the dream-ego may represent *the dreamer's actual felt sense of identity* as observing witness or actor." Sometimes the dream-ego "*appears as the Guiding Self sees her or him.*" "At other times a dream may point up the Self's view of the dreamer's *identification (merger) with an ego-ideal or an inflated grandiosity.*" "At still other times the dream-ego appears to image *the Self.*" "At still other times the dream presents the dreamer with a diffusion or conflicting *fragments of identity* seemingly floating in some uncertain relationship to the dreamer. . . ."

one of 'correspondence', or of 'reciprocity', or to be 'parallel', 'congruent', 'complementary', 'discontinuous' (or 'continuous'), or 'compensatory'. In these pages, I will operate with the following minimal definitions: dreams are continuous insofar as they repeat waking issues and/or repeat the style of waking in some respect. If not continuous, then dreams are discontinuous or compensatory, that is, they do or provide something different from waking. Jungian compensatory dreaming is a special case.

A Freudian dream is discontinuous between waking and the latent wish, but continuous respecting day residues and dream-thoughts. Jung also found "a certain continuity"[79]—as indeed anyone must. This self-evident aspect of dreams has, since the late 1940s, been delved into in detail by Calvin Hall and others through *content analysis*, a method by which large numbers of dreams are statistically surveyed for their manifest features. This method can shed light on individual personalities,* but is chiefly used to typify classes of dreamers and to investigate dream universals.

In his earliest book (1953), Hall evenhandedly acknowledged the discontinuous side of dreaming, which "reveal[s] what we really think of ourselves when the mask of waking is removed."[80] He emphasized certain unexpected findings, such as that A-bombs did not enter the dreams of his students at the end of World War II, that "[b]usinesmen ordinarily do not dream about their business affairs," etc.[81] In later writings, the continuous side would impress Hall more. Now he said that "bankers dream of banking activities," etc.[82] He nodded to a compensatory function of dreaming[83] and allowed that "[d]reams often open our eyes to our true feelings, which we close our eyes to when awake,"[84] but he asserted the "continuity hypothesis" in these unmistakable terms: "We remain the same person, the same personality with the same characteristics, and the same basic beliefs and convictions whether awake or asleep."[85]

Following are some examples of continuities, drawn from content analyses as well as other types of sources. (All these examples, bear in mind, are statistical generalizations). Women dream more of babies than do men, and show relatively more verbal than physical aggression in their dreams compared to men[86] (ch. 9, p. 292ff.). Such gender features are probably quite universal,[87] whereas others depend more on one's culture: boys in the U.S. dream far more often of deadly weapons than do Asian Indian boys;[88] Mex-

---

* Hall demonstrated, for one intriguing example, that Freud's and Jung's dream styles each exhibited many gross features in common with what is known of their waking personalities—sociable Freud had more populous dreams than solitary Jung, and so on (C. S. Hall & B. Domhoff, "The dreams of Freud and Jung," *Psychology Today*, pp. 42–5, 64–5, June, 1968, cited by G. W. Domhoff 1985, pp. 108–10).

ican-American women with strong cultural roots dream more of death motifs than do Anglo women.[89]

Depressed patients often dream of reproach, rejection, and other depressive themes.[90] However, apparently they do so only when trying somehow to cope with their problems; when mired in chronic depression, patients typically have bland or even pleasant dreams (ch. 9, p. 322ff.).[91] This shows the complexity of the whole question. To the same effect, it is unclear how to reconcile findings, on one hand, that people more overt about sexuality also manifest somewhat more sex in dreams[92] (continuity), and, on the other, that people "with ongoing sexual gratification in their lives" have "less sexual symbolism in their dreams" than those without[93] (discontinuity).

Weighing for continuity is the fact that people generally reveal the same trends in dreams and in projective personality tests, such as the Rorschach and the Thematic Apperception Test.[94] Authoritarian personalities both think awake and dream "in terms of rigid dichotomies."[95] Those who play active roles in their dreams tend to do so awake.[96] Those who think of themselves as friendly are also friendly in dreams.[97] Paranoia "in therapy and in dreams tends to covary positively."[98] Also, one's daydream and night dream styles tend to show the same emotional tones.[99] What is more, as some neo-Freudians emphasize, one's characteristic waking ego defenses show up again in dreams, right along with emotionally charged issues of the day.*

Turning now to other frames of reference. In Vedantic and Buddhist traditions,[100] though waking and dreaming differ from the point of view of ordinary waking, from that of absolute reality or enlightened mind, which is what matters, they arise out of the very same illusory mental processes; and so dreaming is essentially continuous with waking. There is some parallel to this in the Western view that dreaming is just degraded cognition (chapter 1). Moreover, the Eastern perspective directly influences the 'dream movement'. In particular, lucid dreaming is thought to be wrapped up with parallel skepticisms, dreaming and awake, about naive reality (see chapter 14). Thus Linda ("Ravenwolf") Reneau's *Waking Dreamer's Manual* teaches that lucid dreaming is brought by "lucid living," and that when we live awake in "false clarity" we get only normal, unclear dreams.[101]

But if high civilization tends to see waking and dreaming as comparably illusory, indigenous peoples begin from the opposite assumption, that both

---

* For example, "Melvin's characteristic waking mode of coping with the stress of his impending operation was to seek nurturance and support from others. His dreams reflect this: 47% of the preoperative dreams involved him in a dependent position" (L. Breger, I. Hunter & R. W. Lane 1971, p. 139). See also: L. J. Saul (1940); E. Sheppard & L. J. Saul (1958); E. Sheppard (1963) and (1969); R. Greenberg & C. A. Pearlman (1975), p. 447.

are real. Anthropologist E. B. Tylor (*Primitive Culture*, 1871) planted the idea that "primitive thought" confuses waking and dreaming.[102] In fact, animist no less than Buddhist or scientist knows waking and dreaming to be different to common sense and rarely mistakes them.* Anthropologist Douglas Price-Williams remarks that for someone not to regard a talking deer differently from "a neighbor's cow or dog, would mean psychosis, and we may suppose that indigenous people have, on the whole, quite clear notions of madness."[103] L. Lévy-Bruhl (*Primitive Mentality*, 1922) corrected Tylor's misapprehension: primitives tell waking and dreaming apart, but in contrast to us find dreams more "'mystical'" and therefore more trustworthy than ordinary reality.[104] This is the compensatory aspect of the typical indigenous view: dreams partake of a sacred realm, a separate though equal or greater reality which complements waking.** Lévy-Bruhl was closer to the truth than Tylor, although he vastly oversimplified the variations on this theme as revealed by subsequent ethnography.

Still, what is likely to catch the eye of a literate Westerner about the indigenous view is the element of continuity. Thus a Cherokee snake-bitten in his dream was given treatment awake.[105] Adulterous in dream, an Ashanti was assessed the adultery fine.[106] A Macusi blamed his ill-health on being over-worked in dreams by his employer.[107] Also, dreams may presage happenings which must be enacted "lest some irremediable split occur in the tissue of events capable of causing the dreamer's death."[108] The Iroquois and Huron "believed that they would die if they did not execute their dreams. One of them tried to kill a Frenchman because he dreamed that this would cure him."[109] However, as Barbara Tedlock emphasizes, indigenous ideas about dreams and the waking state are not as simplistic as anecdotes such as these might lead us, with our own ethnocentric prejudices, to believe. Realities interpenetrate for preliterate peoples in quite subtle ways.***

---

* Tylor's characterization of "primitive" psychology betrays the prejudice of the imperial "ruling race" toward "lower races" (E. B. Tylor, quoted by G. O. Ferguson, Jr., *The Psychology of the Negro: An Experimental Study*, New York: The Science Press, p. 407, 1916, quoted by R. V. Guthrie 1976, pp. 34–5).

** "Crazy Horse dreamed and went into the world where there is nothing but the spirits of all things. That is the real world that is behind this one, and everything we see here is something like a shadow from that world" (J. G. Neihardt 1979 [1932], p. 85).

*** B. Tedlock (1992c [1987]). In the same volume, Gilbert Herdt (1992 [1987], p. 62) remarks from his field experience that in cultures where waking and dreaming have collateral realities, even members of the group may be unclear whether an incident being related is a dream or a day incident, unless the speaker clearly identifies the category, but the dreamer her/himself is not confused. William Merrill (1992 [1987], p. 200) describes one of numerous variants of indigenous views contained in this volume: "For the Ramámuri [of Northern Mexico], dreams are real events. On numer-

Turning in another direction, existential-phenomenological theorists such as Medard Boss (chapter 4), himself influenced by Asian philosophy,[110] try in their own fashion to reduce the anomalous distance separating dreaming and waking in Western culture.[111] The two states, in which "the same fundamental existential structures operate,"[112] are regarded as "modes of existing of an ever-integral and whole human being."[113] This is wholeness in a different sense from Jung's. Like waking perceptions, dream images are not symbols generated by an unconscious with its own, discontinuous agenda, they simply 'are'. In rejecting the concept of the unconscious, existentialists were anticipated by Alfred Adler, who likewise put all the stress on direct connections of dreams to life situations and waking ways of being.[114] "The dreamer carries into sleep the full range of thoughts and events that preoccupied him during the day. . . . [T]here is, therefore, continuity of thought and feeling from waking to sleeping."[115] Dreams mostly maintain one's waking "life style" by reiterating waking defensive strategies. In this respect Adler also anticipated neo-Freudian ego psychology, as well as such eclectics as Walter Bonime,[116] who like Adler sees "in dreams a symbolic extension of the problems and adaptive maneuvers of the waking state."[117] These and oth-

---

ous occasions, people would describe to me quite incredible personal experiences but fail to mention that the events had taken place in dreams until I asked. This does not mean that they do not distinguish between waking and dreaming lives but that they attribute comparable reality to both. The main difference . . . is that during dreaming people's souls operate independently of their bodies, while in waking life they act in conjunction with them." This is a commonly held view throughout the world. Merrill continues (p. 203): "In my experience, a Ramámuri man would not beat his wife for being unfaithful if the only evidence of her infidelity appeared in a dream. . . . [H]owever, he would be more attentive and cautious. . . . Their reticence to act upon dream experiences, despite considering them to be real, can be attributed in part to the fact that they distinguish between a person and his or her souls." Dream behavior of a soul "may reveal propensities that will find expression in waking life."

The first novel written in the Americas, which was published in London in 1769, contained this passage: "The Indians preserve the greater part of their old superstitions. I would underscore their faith in dreams, a lunacy of which they are unable to cure themselves in spite of repeated disappointments. . . . A savage was telling us a prophetic dream, which according to him announced the death of an English officer, and I was unable to contain a smile. 'You Europeans,' he said to me, 'are the least reasonable people in the world. You mock our faith in dreams, and nevertheless expect us to believe things a thousand times more incredible." This is my back-translation of Eduardo Galeano's (1990 [1984], pp. 45–6) Spanish translation of Frances Brooke, *The History of Emily Montague*, Toronto: McClelland & Stewart, 1961 [1769].

Jean Piaget (1962 [1945], cited by Carl O'Nell 1976, p. 15) observed three stages of development a child passes through to achieve what most of us regard as the correct idea about the reality status of dreams. (1) The young dreamer believes the dream "both originates and occurs outside himself." (2) Next, s/he believes it originates in her/his own head but takes place outside. (3) "Finally, the child comes to realize that his dreams both originate and occur totally within himself." Later observers have added refinements to this progression, but what is most interesting is that stage

er authors differ, however, as to the extent dreaming also finds novel solutions to waking problems.

Coming now to compensatory views. Dreams are compensatory insofar as they do or provide anything different from what the waking state is doing or providing. Dreams are compensatory in the Jungian sense, if they bring up material from the unconscious to equilibrate the Self-ego system and advance its development. There are certainly compensatory aspects of dreaming which may or may not fit Jung's idea, but do not require it.

Any of the various ways dreams tend to adjust imbalances from the day can be called compensatory. This is so of dream house-cleaning a la Crick (ch. 1, p. 38), who nevertheless views day and night activities as fundamentally continuous. It is so insofar as dreams re-engage day concerns to relieve conflict and lower stress. And it is so of drive states which carry over from day to night. Thus Freud called it "compensatory" when a dream fulfilled a child's frustrated day wish: the dream-thought was continuous, the drive release compensatory.[118] Experimentally, people kept in social isolation for the day dream more social dreams that night.[119] A waking overindulgence, by the same token, may be followed by dream abstinence:

> [O]ne subject, after pedaling a stationary bicycle for six hours, dreamt that *he was lying in a hammock on a tropical isle while a gentle breeze turned the pages of a book he was reading.*[120]

Similarly, those alcoholics who act out when drunk have dreams containing decreased sexual and aggressive content, whereas alcoholics inhibited by intoxication have dreams with increased sex and aggression.[121] And males, it has been reasoned, may have more violent dreams than women to relieve a naturally greater aggressive drive with insufficient opportunities for daytime release.[122] It is noteworthy that delinquent boys have less aggression in their

---

3 appears to be attained by children living in cultures where adults hold a more 'primitive' view. O'Nell (p. 16) cites work done by Lawrence Kohlberg ("Cognitive states and pre-school education," *Human Development* 9, pp. 5–17, 1966) with the Atayal, a Formosan people whose adults believe dreams may be encounters with supernatural beings. By age 11–12, Atayal children have attained Piaget's stage 3. "At that time, pressures for them to accommodate to the native belief system caused them to regress to a concept they held at an earlier age. . . ." Richard A. Shweder & Robert A. LeVine find the same trend among the Hausa of Niger: "Adult theory tells them that their 10-year-old understanding of dreams (which of course is *our* adult understanding of dreams) was inadequate—that dreams are a type of 'vision' giving access to an external, objective numinous realm of the soul and its wanderings" ("Dream concepts of Hausa children: a critique of the 'doctrine of invariant sequence'," *Ethos* 3, pp. 209–30, 1975, quoted by Wendy Doniger O'Flaherty 1984, p. 58). O'Flaherty suggests that the same so-called 'regression' occurs in India. M. C. Jędrej (1992, p. 111) finds the same pattern in the Ingessana of Sudan, and suspects it is general among traditional cultures.

dreams than non-delinquents;[123] and that dream aggression may actually diminish during periods of community violence.[124]

Such findings are, however, open to different interpretations. If, for example, the dreams of women are more sexual during just that phase of menstruation when they feel subjectively least sexy, as Ethel Swanson & David Foulkes observe, it is probably not because their drive is lower then, but because they repress it while awake. One could take this as compensation: the frustrated drive gets released, and repressed awareness finds an outlet. Swanson & Foulkes, however, prefers to emphasize the aspect of continuity here, between "waking drive strength" and "dream expression."[125] One can look at it in either way, but it seems to me that the more conspicuous the element of repression is in the dreaming process, the more compelling the notion of compensation becomes. Consider this dream, from Emil Gutheil's book:

> *I was intimate with Mrs. W. We were lying on a bed on top of my wife. My wife was covered with a black cloth and did not seem to object to our doings.* The "black cloth" symbolizes death. The dream contains a death wish against the dreamer's wife.[126]

The tired bicyclist with his "Hammock on a tropical isle" dream probably fancied a good rest while still awake, but this husband might well not have acknowledged to himself his conjugal morbidity or even his appetite for a Mrs. W.—the unconscious expresses itself in a compensatory dream. The case with Freud's repressed infantile wishes is even plainer. During dreams, the theory says, something profoundly alien to the ego achieves disguised expression.

Another compensatory aspect of dreaming is raised by Mattoon, a Jungian. It is that dreaming, which arises largely from the non-dominant (usually) right hemisphere of the brain, compensates for the predominance of the left hemisphere during waking.[127] The same point can be made without Jungian entailments, and has been by Rosalind Cartwright. She observes that a person whose waking life gives adequate play to right-hemispheric activities may have dreams which are "short, direct, and easy to understand," whereas someone whose day-life is ruled by left-hemispheric activity may dream "in complicated symbolic images" which enrich her/his waking life.[128]

Essentially the same point can also be made without neuroanatomical entailments, and perhaps should be so made, in view of doubts about the connection between dreaming and hemispheric specialization (ch. 1, p. 29n). Thus Liam Hudson simply recognizes in dreaming a salutary "destabilizing influence on habits of mind and patterns of thought. . . ."[129] Hudson transmits evidence showing that heavily rational people, although they may not recall their dreams well, on average enter REM sooner into sleep. This suggests that they require a supplement of irrationality.[130] (Counter-evidence, as so often, comes from Foulkes, who reports that the more bizarre one's waking mental style, the more bizarre one's dreams. The observation holds for both REM and NREM dreams.[131])

Cartwright maintains that within any given series of dreams, some may be compensatory ("complementary"), and some continuous. Predominance of one or the other mode depends "on the dreamer's prevailing psychological balance." For example, someone frustrated during the day may compensate in dreams, whereas "persons with well-balanced waking functioning" may have dreams "more continuous with daytime experiences."[132]

Jungian compensation. What sets Jung's compensatory dreaming apart is that all dream compensations, great and small, show the Self's "wholeness potential" at work in a "self-healing balancing process."[133]* Through its native imagery, the unconscious lifts just those matters, often quite alien to the ego, which will keep the Self-system in regulation by correcting a disequilibrium in consciousness. "For dreams are always about a particular problem of the individual about which he has a wrong conscious judgement. . . . *Dreams are the natural reaction of the self-regulating psychic system.* This formulation is the nearest I can get to a theory about the structure and function of dreams."[134] "Although the effect of any one dream may not be dramatic, the cumulative effect of compensatory dreaming is 'a new level of consciousness'. . . ."[135] But "particularly when the conscious attitude tends too exclusively in a direction that would threaten the vital needs of the individual . . . ," then "[v]ivid dreams with a strongly contrasting but purposive content will appear as an expression of the self-regulation of the psyche . . . , just as the body reacts purposively to injuries or infection."[136]

To begin with an obvious example of dream compensation, from Hall:

> Images of alcohol and drug abuse appear in dreams particularly when there is some waking problem with them. . . . [I]t is sometimes possible to see the unconscious ready for a change in the addiction pattern—suggesting, supporting or even pushing one—before any steps are taken by the waking ego. . . .

---

* A position with similarities to Jung's and probably influenced by Jung's, but without acknowledgement, was put forward by Karen Horney (1970 [1950]). When a person is in denial or unaware of some trend, then dreaming is compensatory; when s/he is arriving at consciousness of the trend, dreaming is continuous; and in practical fact, dreaming proceeds in a shifting balance between these poles, depending how close the match between the dreamer's "actual self" and potential or "real self." Information brought by dreams moves one toward self-realization, though the information may consist simply of hidden aspects of one's neurotic attitudes. Thus, for example, a person with an inflated self-image may be confronted with self-loathing in a dream, or a self-effacing person with vindictiveness.

An impressive example is the case of a man in his mid-thirties whose heavy use of marijuana had dulled his judgment and damaged his marriage. Soon after he entered analysis he had a series of dreams in which *crowds held up large signs and even billboards, proclaiming: DON'T SMOKE DOPE.*[137]*

Compensations range all the way from incidental corrections of attitude to momentous adjustments such as reconciling the ego to death. An example of the former is this often-quoted dream which Jung had, before speaking next day with a client about the fact that her treatment had stalled:

> *I was walking down a highway through a valley in late-afternoon sunlight. To my right was a steep hill. At its top stood a castle, and on the highest tower there was a woman sitting on a kind of balustrade. In order to see her properly, I had to bend my neck far back.* I awoke with a crick in the back of my neck. Even in the dream *I recognized the woman as my patient.*

The interpretation was immediately apparent to me. If in the dream I had looked up at the patient in this fashion, in reality I had probably been looking down on her. Dreams are, after all, compensations for the conscious attitude. I told her of the dream and my interpretation. This produced an immediate change in the situation, and the treatment once more began to move forward.[138]

---

* One of the pioneers of REM research, William Dement (1974 [1972], p. 102), quit smoking after a dream of *"an ominous shadow in my chest X-ray,"* then a physical exam confirming *"widespread metastases,"* and *"the incredible anguish of knowing my life was soon to end. . . ."* Dement cites his dream as an illustration of "problem-solving," not compensation. Patricia Garfield (1991, pp. 89-90) gives two more examples of warning dreams about smoking involving chest X-rays which appall and alarm the dreamer; and Jeremy Taylor (1991, pp. 11-2; 1992a, pp. 202-3) describes a lucid dream of a noxious *"Puff the Magic Dragon"* with the same stiffening effect.

Recovering smokers and drinkers are commonly beset by dreams of relapse and despair which resonate unmistakably as warnings. Novelist Robert Stone (N. Epel 1993, p. 261) speaks for smokers: "The one I used to get all the time was: *I find myself smoking, which horrifies me because I've wasted all that time and suffering quitting and I'm smoking again. . . .* I wake up with great relief to find that I'm not really smoking again." Norman Denzin (1988, pp. 136-7) relays this dream told at an Alcoholics Anonymous meeting: "This happened last year around Christmas time. I dreamed *I was drinking gin in front of the fireplace. Everybody had gone to bed. I was burning papers in the fire and suddenly the mantle caught on fire and the kids' stuffed animals started burning. I threw my drink on the fire* and woke up in a cold sweat. Actually this was pretty realistic because one Christmas I did start a fire that burned the mantle." A member with 15 years of sobriety commented about his own drinking dreams (pp. 137-8): "They remind me of how bad it was. . . . If I have to drink in my dreams in order to stay sober when I'm awake that's okay." I still occasionally have the smoker's version of this dream myself, after thirteen years not smoking, and so has virtually every other recovering smoker I have asked about it. (But also, I have heard wish-fulfilling variants of the pattern: *Oh my God, I'm smoking (drinking) again, and I don't know how it happened! But I didn't intend it, and there's nothing I can do to change it, so I'll smoke (drink) and just enjoy it.*)

Compensatory guidance dreams are not confined to substance abuse, of course. Karen Signell (1990, p. 282) tells of "a middle-aged divorced woman [who] had decided to get involved . . . with a man very similar to her ex-husband, with whom she had a destructive relationship. At this crucial

It is apparent from this example that by "conscious attitude," Jung meant an attitude of the waking mind, but not necessarily an attitude of which one is fully aware—it was only from his dream that Jung learned that he had been "looking down" on his patient.

Alan Siegel, an eclectic psychologist who leans strongly toward compensatory interpretations, tells this dream which has an opposite configuration from Jung's dream. It was dreamt by a man about his wife, and involves a more momentous change of attitude:

> I am encouraging Bev to climb up on a stand that is something like a pedestal for a statue. She doesn't really want to but she complies. I keep asking her to raise her arm higher, like the Statue of Liberty raising her torch. Suddenly she begins to teeter and fall off. I am terrified that she might get hurt or killed, but I'm paralyzed and can't do anything to stop her from falling.

As Adam related his dream to an old friend, he realized that he had put Bev on a pedestal. He had idealized her so much that he had been blinded to who she really was. Yes, she was creative, assertive, and successful, but she had been giving him a clear message for over a year: her career was more important than having a family or deepening their marriage. To his dismay, his idol had fallen.[139]

Only slightly less obvious is the compensation in the next dream, reported by Randa Diamond in an article about dreamwork with rape victims:

> [A]fter the rape, when affect seemed dulled, several of these women had vivid dreams in which the presence of blood had a significant and jolting effect. . . .
>
> The following is Nancy's dream, two weeks after she had been raped: "I was in the hospital, in an alternative birth center. There was a baby born. The father had a big erection and was rubbing the baby with his penis. There was blood all over." I commented on how hurt and helpless she must be feeling inside. Nancy was startled; until then she had shown herself to be calm, composed, and affectless. The image of the infant bleeding was an accurate compensatory reflection of her internal reality. The dream provided a vehicle through which to begin to talk about the rape experience and its associated affect which until then had been unavailable to the waking ego. After it, Nancy was able to admit, "I feel chopped up inside, all bloody, torn, as if someone had taken a knife and cut me up and torn me apart."[140]

---

turning point, she had a dream of *her analyst suddenly appearing before her with arms raised in a strong gesture, saying, 'No. Absolutely No.'"* Joel Covitz (1990, p. 122) tells of another woman "who seemed never to be sufficiently satisfied with a man to tie the knot, [who] dreamed that *Cary Grant called her up for a date. She said, 'Cary, I'm sorry, but no.' A voice was then heard proclaiming: 'Mary, if not him, who?'* This challenge from her unconscious humorously brought home the message that she needed to reexamine her standards for matrimonial eligibility."

The person who dreamt the next dream also readily made out its compensatory message. This dream comes from an article about dreams of surgical sex change candidates, by Vamik Volkan & Tajammul Bhatti:

> [A man conscious of feeling no ambivalence about a pending sex change operation dreamt that] *he saw the death of a brother, and this saddened and depressed him.* Since in actual fact he had no brother, he could easily make an association of the 'brother' with the penis he wanted to lose.[141]

Compensations are not usually as conspicuous as in the examples adduced thus far. Jung indeed cautions against simplistic application of the principle. A pessimist, he says, might have bright dreams correcting his conscious attitude, or he might have bleak dreams outdoing the conscious attitude to call attention to it.[142]

Since by the same token an optimist could likewise have bright or bleak dreams, it seems to follow that Jung's principle of compensation has in common with Freud's principle of reversal—which gets dismissed sometimes for the very reason—that it can be used arbitrarily to support any interpretation. Obviously what is required is to pay careful attention to the context of the dream, the dreamer's actual situation, as Jung illustrated with this example, another dream having to do with esteem. I have abridged the text quite a lot. A young man dreams:

> *My father is driving away from the house in his new car. He drives very clumsily, and I get very annoyed over his apparent stupidity. He goes this way and that, forwards and backwards, and manoeuvres the car into a dangerous position. Finally he runs into a wall and damages the car badly. I shout at him in a perfect fury that he ought to behave himself. My father only laughs, and then I see that he is dead drunk.* This dream has no foundation in fact. . . . [The father never acts that way, nor does the son.] His relation to his father is positive. He admires him for being an unusually successful man. . . . [But] the dream presents a most unfavourable picture of the father. What, then, should we take its meaning to be for the son? Is his relation to his father good only on the surface . . . ? If so, . . . we should have to tell the young man: "That is your real relation to your father." But . . . I could find nothing neurotically ambivalent in the son's real relation to his father. . . .
> But, if his relation to his father is in fact good, why must the dream manufacture such an improbable story in order to discredit the father? . . . If we regard this as a compensation, we are forced to the conclusion that his relation to his father is not only good, but actually too good. . . . His particular danger is that he cannot see his own reality on account of his father; therefore the unconscious resorts to a kind of artificial blasphemy so as to lower the father and elevate the son. . . . [I]t forces the son to contrast himself with his father, which is the only way he could become conscious of himself.

. . . [T]his interpretation was only possible when the whole conscious phenomenology of the father-son relationship had been carefully studied. Without a
knowledge of the conscious situation the real meaning of the dream would have
remained in doubt.[143]

Here is an example from Sonja Marjasch which shows mythic amplification used to arrive at a compensatory interpretation of a dream which, like
the foregoing one, moves the dreamer's ego toward "a closer adaptation to
the individuation process":[144]

A man in his early thirties was in conflict whether to pursue his personal inclinations, especially his interest in psychology, or to accept a breadwinning job.
He dreamed:

*There is a thunderstorm in the air. I am in a lonely place in the mountains. At
my feet a calm lake is inviting me to bathe. But the water is too cold and too
pure. On the water I see the reflection of my dark figure surrounded by a glim-
mering flickering aura. I should like to remain here in this quiet of nature. But
the family-chorus calls: "Come back, we need you!" And with heavy heart I decide to cross the mountain, following one of the dangerous passways that leads
through the dark, gloomy woods and past craggy rocks.*

The dream tended to overcome the conscious ambivalence whether at the
moment the outer or the inner world should be given preference. It revealed that
the dreamer's psychological studies could end in a fatal kind of self-fascination
and stressed his obligation toward his family. The moment had come for the patient to give his full attention to exterior tasks and the dream encouraged him that
this was possible, although it meant a sacrifice for him and he started his journey
with a heavy heart. Soon afterward the analysis came to an end and the patient
got a job that allowed him to support his family and to a certain extent also corresponded to his interests.

In the dream the mountain lake invited the dreamer to take a bath yet he
refrained from it because the water was too cool and too pure. He remained on
shore staring into the water and becoming fascinated with his own image. It was
dark yet had an aura, a dream image that could mean he was inclined to see himself in too dark or too bright a light: he was wavering between self-dejection and
self-idealization. The main point of this part of the dream was the purely reflective relation to the unconscious. How dangerous this could become was seen
clearer when this dream fragment was enlarged [amplified].

The dreamer had written down his dream and spontaneously used the word
"family-chorus". . . . With the chorus we enter the world of the antique stage
and the world of symbols. . . . [Marjasch tells the Greek myth of Narcissus, who
died of fascination with his own image reflected in the water.]

. . . Dreams of this kind are like plays acted on a double stage: In the foreground we see the dreamer contemplating his own image in the water, called
back by the family-chorus, voicing the will of destiny. At the back of the stage

we see Narcissus bending over his own reflection in the spring and the nymph Echo vainly appealing to him. The dream portrays the conflict between self-love and love for others. It is in these terms that it expresses the dreamer's dilemma whether to pursue his studies or take a job. The dream shows the general human aspect of the problem and, using the myth of Narcissus, it tells the dreamer that he is making a choice toward life or death and, more than that, weighs the scale in favor of choosing the hazardous path forward into life.[145]

In these dreams exemplifying compensation, the aspect of continuity is nevertheless very conspicuous insofar as the dreams re-present the life situation in dramatic-symbolic form. Jung's customary question for every dream, "What conscious attitude does it compensate?" is by no means incompatible with most findings of continuity. Many authors in the academic mainstream seem to miss this point, and in putting forward an inadequate conception of compensation maintain, as does David Koulack, that compensation is sufficiently disproven if it can be shown that "incorporation of presleep events into dreams takes place. . . ."[146] The fact that, for example, adolescent boys dream of acquiring male roles,[147] or that the failing aged dream of "loss of resources,"[148] argues for gross continuity, but does not speak to the possibility of compensations in finer dream dynamics. Their particular dreams may well be promoting compensations within a dream environment with general features of continuity.

Are all dreams compensatory? Jung said so,[149] but in the same book he added that if the conscious attitude is well-balanced, a dream will reinforce it.[150] He "spoke of *parallel* dreams, 'dreams whose meaning coincides with or supports the conscious attitude.'"[151] Strephon Kaplan Williams and others call these "confirming" dreams.[152] Jung indicated that confirming dreams are "comparatively rare."[153]

He did allow that dreams may fulfill unrelated functions. Dreams born from trauma deplete the fixating event of its power through realistic repetition.[154] Telepathy and prophesy are other non-compensatory functions. None of these functions precludes compensation within the same dream.[155]

Bordering on the prophetic is a further dream function listed by Mattoon as non-compensatory, the "prospective function."[156] When a mere rebalancing will not suffice, then a dream may offer a new direction for consciousness to take, an admonition/premonition of radical change. Such dreams are said to be "more or less unrelated to the conscious position" and to "anticipate . . . future conscious achievements. . . ."[157]

But in effect, prospective dreaming is a sort of heavy-duty compensation. So it is that Hall uses the term 'prospective' to refer to the general purposiveness or finality of dreams, that forward-turning which is the essence of the compensatory function.[158] It is often stressed that compensations need to be actualized in the future. Thus Marion Woodman: "[T]he last image [of a dream] usually shows where the energy wants to go to correct the psychic imbalance. . . ."[159] For Eugene Gendlin, every dream points to a "growth-direction."[160] For Robert Johnson, an interpretation is incomplete unless it answers the question, "What are you going to *do* about your dream?"[161] Thus though Jung did differentiate "anticipation in the unconscious of future conscious achievements"[162] (prospective function) from rebalancing in the present (compensation), the distinction is not sharp.

Not all compensatory dreams successfully perform their function. Some authors create the impression that the psyche is always "exactly" self-regulating,[163] but Jung himself cautioned that the process is fallible. Sometimes consciousness is radically unprepared to take on board what the unconscious brings up: "no matter how good, useful, and wonderful the new thing may be, it might have a bad effect if it hits upon an immature condition."[164] In the case of badly disturbed dreamers, compensation itself can precipitate a breakdown, or even suicide.[165] As Cahen writes, "When things have gone awry seriously enough, it can be that an attempt at compensation may be just as off-balance and off-balancing as the initial factor for which balance is being sought."[166] This should be no more surprising than that the somatic system sometimes reacts catastrophically to injury or pathogens. The imperfect organism can do the wrong thing, even as it mobilizes to preserve and enhance itself. John Sanford transmits the unpleasant story of such an outcome:

> [A] Jungian analyst [Anneliese Aumüller] . . . found herself caught in Berlin during World War II. She reports the case of a Nazi fighter pilot, a man 22 years of age, who . . . had developed hysterical color blindness; although there was nothing organically wrong with him, he could no longer distinguish colors, and consequently was unable to fly. . . . "Analysis was rough going at first. The patient was cooperative but entirely uncomprehending. His philosophy of life had no room for dynamics hidden behind simple facts. Everything that was useful to Germany, Hitler and the victory, was good; everything else was bad. It was as simple as that—black and white."
>
> . . . He had a brother and a sister in his family. His brother he adored; he was a member of the SS and an ideal Nazi. His sister he hated, for she had joined the underground resistance and, in his eyes, was a despised traitor.
>
> Eventually the young pilot had dreams. He found them puzzling and disturbing, for in his dreams everything seemed to be reversed from the way it should have been. He dreamt, for instance, of *his beloved brother: "He was wearing his SS uniform,"* he related, *"but everything was the wrong way. The uniform was white instead of black, and his face was entirely black. It was just the opposite*

of life." Then he dreamt . . . [that] *his sister was dressed in black prison garb, but her face was shining white.* The young pilot commented, "I could have understood if the face had been black for that would have shown her guilt." . . .

Some time after these dreams he was with his adored brother, who was then stationed at a concentration camp. The brother had drunk too much and in his drunkenness talked about what was going on at the concentration camp. That night the young man dreamt, *"A long column of concentration camp inmates with radiant white faces marched past Hitler. Hitler's face was black and he raised his hand, the color of which was the deep red color of blood."* . . . His confidence in his beliefs was finally shaken under the impact of the dreams, and an individual desire to know for himself was beginning to work. . . .

Not long [after a visit to the camp,] . . . another note came from the young pilot. It said simply, "I believed too long that black was white. Now the many colors of the world won't help me any more." The analyst never saw him again. He had committed suicide.[167]

Since, in the Jungian view, it is a "conscious attitude" being compensated by a dream, there is usually a tendency for us consciously to reject or misconstrue exactly what the dream has to offer. It is "the dreamer's fallacy" to trust one's own conscious position.[168] Marjasch's narcissist dreamer of "The family-chorus calls 'Come back!'" might well have said, 'There, you see? Heeding the family-chorus will bring me nothing but gloom. What I need is more courage to bathe in the cold waters of spirituality!' As Bosnak explains: "One of the tasks in working with dreams is to trip up our daytime consciousness again and again in order to unhinge our fixed positions. It is an unpleasant kind of work that often feels like torture to our habitual consciousness."[169] Not only do we draw back from specific insights with which compensatory dreams challenge us, but in a more general way, we fear "the revelation of unchanging depths;"[170] our egos resist loss of control to "the automatisms of the unconscious psyche."[171]

For these reasons, Jungians (like Freudians) have historically discouraged working on one's dreams alone. But Jungians of the self-help decades have joined the trend and suggested guidelines for self-interpretation, including measures for combatting "the dreamer's fallacy." For example, Johnson offers several tips: "Choose an interpretation that shows you something you didn't know." "Avoid the interpretation that inflates your ego or is self-congratulatory." "Avoid interpretations that shift responsibility away from yourself."[172]

The most complete anti-fallacy advice for those who interpret their own dreams is offered by Gendlin, another eclectic Jungian (and phenomenologist[173]). Gendlin devised a helpful method of which he calls *bias control.* He has us challenge ourselves: have we forced an interpretation on the dream story, ignoring what the story itself says? Or made the dream "take one side of a known conflict?"[174] Much simplified, Gendlin's basic maneuver has us turn our spontaneous interpretation on its head. Where we find ourselves in agreement with the dream, we should—just within the context of the interpretive activity—playfully take on and exaggerate the opposite attitude or attribute. If, for example, a dream brings something frightening, as when the "Intruder bursts in" through the banker's door, it should in some manner be welcomed by us during our dreamwork[175] (see chapter 16).

Intention vs. purpose. Inspiring Gendlin's instructions is Jung's concept of dreaming as a compensatory self-regulation of the Self-system. Gendlin's version says that the "dream is exactly what 'the other side' sent last night—how can it be anything but positive if I interact with it and allow myself to become more whole?"[176] Formulations such as this of Gendlin's—"what 'the other side' sent"—evoke ideas of a presiding dream-maker, of a "shadow intelligence," in Gordon Globus's skeptical phrase, who looks out at the ego, or in on it, and who deliberately sends it edifying communications.[177]* Certain statements of Jung's own possess this coloration: he says that "dreams fetch up the essential points, bit by bit and with the nicest choice,"[178] and that "conscious observation pays the unconscious a tribute that more or less guarantees its cooperation."[179] Such diction has permitted some followers as it were to anthropomorphize the compensatory process. At least they do not always make it clear that the Jungian Self does not literally experience what we would recognize as intentions toward us, when they talk about dreams as being "messages" (Ann Mankowitz),[180] or as providing a "highly refined [channel] of communication . . . so that the unconscious and conscious levels may speak to one another and work together" (Johnson).[181]

But Jung's own language concerning intentions of the unconscious was strictly metaphorical. Whitmont gets it right when, after saying that dreams "attempt to convey" something to the ego, he stipulates that "[a] dream may be read *as if* [stress added] saying 'Self addressing ego: . . .'."[182] Only "as if." And lest we believe that the Self's selections of imagery must be intentional, just because so apt, Cahen would have the unconscious operate "with a sleepwalker's self-assurance."[183] Cahen offers this unequivocal quote from Jung on the question of dream intentionality: "The dream reflects a certain functioning which is . . . devoid of any appearance of intentionality, similar,

---

* The problematical nature of such a socialized unconscious leads Globus (1987, p. 151) to this variant view: "[D]uring waking there is intense attachment to one way of Being, so that the alternatives are not available. The dream does not compensate for waking excess but expresses a more balanced presentation of all of our possible ways of Being."

in this, to all natural phenomena."[184] In the same vein, von Franz, speaking of the "diffuse intuitive knowledge" exhibited in dreams, stresses "the impersonal aspect of this 'knowledge' that, without intention, simply reflects our being."[185]

But though lacking *intention*, "the unconscious mind is capable at times of assuming an intelligence and purposiveness which are superior to actual conscious insight."[186] The *purpose* is "the self-regulation of the psyche."[187]

Such a distinction, between subjective intentionality and objective purposiveness, is one which is familiar in animal psychology. First with stimulus-response constructs, but better with the feedback constructs of information theory, it became feasible to model the evident goal-directedness of animal behavior without making 'unscientific' assumptions about an animal's subjective experiences. In a curious way, we are in the same position vis-a-vis Jung's objective psyche as we are vis-a-vis the subhuman psyche: in a manner of speaking, we (our egos) can never quite know it from inside. So it is helpful that the planned behavior of organisms can be analyzed, without it being required to say what an organism 'intended' to do. It is another question, whether strict observance of objectivity about animal minds is always good science.[188] And of course by no one's reckoning are we obliged completely to renounce mentalistic constructs when it comes to Jung's objective psyche. That would be awkward, not to say absurd. Jung himself speaks of a "sense of purpose."[189] But in fact, Jung's account of the compensatory behavior of the Self has precisely this in common with theories of the "objective purposiveness"[190] of animal behavior, that it discerns purposes without intentions. The immediate purpose, the sub-goal of the dreaming Self-system, is the compensation of some particular imbalance in the conscious attitude. The grand goal or purpose—and here is where both Jung and general systems theory seem to touch on vitalism—is the Self-system's maintenance and enhancement of itself, as systems by their nature 'try' to do.

The purposive, holistic trend is so pronounced in Jung, and so opposite to Freud's causal-reductive standpoint, that it is hard to imagine Freud ever wanting Jung for his scientific heir. In this as in other regards, the theories of the two men appear to mirror profoundly different intellects and personalities. Freud had great gifts of hindsight. He could sometimes reconstruct childhood events on the scantiest evidence. Jung, by contrast, had the gift of foresight. He sometimes prognosticated illness from dreams, or showed outright prescience.

Compare these anecdotes. First one about Freud. A woman named M. Choisy wrote about a dream she told him in an early session of her analysis. After hearing just several associations, "'Freud pondered for a few minutes over my dream, then muttered without warning: "Such and such an event happened in your family when you were still in the cradle." " "[191] The woman rejected what she took to be irresponsible guesswork on Freud's part, and angrily quit treatment. She returned to her home in Paris and told the story to her aunt, only to discover that Freud's conjecture was correct. This caliber of clinical intuition can only have predisposed Freud to the retrospective standpoint of causality, when it came to theory. Now contrast this extraordinary but not untypical story told by Jung:

> It concerns a colleague of mine, a man somewhat older than myself, whom I used to see from time to time and who always teased me about my dream-interpretations. Well, I met him one day in the street and he called out to me, "How are things going? Still interpreting dreams? By the way, I've had another idiotic dream. Does that mean something too?" This is what he had dreamed: *I am climbing a high mountain, over steep snow-covered slopes. I climb higher and higher, and it is marvelous weather. The higher I climb the better I feel. I think, 'If only I could go on climbing like this forever!' When I reach the summit my happiness and elation are so great that I feel I could mount right up into space. And I discover that I can actually do so: I mount upward on empty air, and awake in sheer ecstasy.*
>
> After some discussion, I said, "My dear fellow, I know you can't give up mountaineering, but let me implore you not to go alone from now on. When you go, take two guides, and promise on your word of honour to follow them absolutely." "Incorrigible!" he replied, laughing, and waved good-bye. I never saw him again. Two months later the first blow fell. When out alone, he was buried by an avalanche, but was dug out in the nick of time by a military patrol that happened to be passing. Three months afterwards the end came. He went on a climb with a younger friend, but without guides. A guide standing below saw him literally step out into the air while descending a rock face. He fell on the head of his friend, who was waiting lower down, and both were dashed to pieces far below. That was *ecstasis* with a vengeance![192]*

---

* Jung wrote about this incident in at least three other places, in one of which the man tells Jung "very emphatically that he would never give up his mountain climbing because he had to go to the mountains in order to get away from the city and his family. . . . Jung wrote[:] 'It occurred to me that his uncanny passion for the mountains must be an avenue of escape from an existence that had become intolerable to him. . . . I told him quite frankly what I thought, namely that he was seeking his death in the mountains, and that with such an attitude he stood a remarkably good chance of finding it'" (J. Covitz 1990, p. 108, quoting C. G. Jung, "Child development and education" [1928], CW 17, para's 117–22; see also "The transcendent function" [1957], CW 8, para. 164 and "Symbols and the interpretation of dreams" [1961], CW 18, para. 471). Covitz relates the story in a chapter entitled "The Art of Positive Dream Interpretation." He speculates that "Jung's forecast may have functioned as a negative suggestion that reinforced the man's self-destructive tendency" (p. 109). Speaking of another case in which Jung forewarned someone of dire consequences, Salomon Resnik

Whatever Jung's natural penchant for the forward-looking "standpoint of finality,"[193] he did of course well understand that psychological events have a causal as well as a purposeful dimension. "[A] well-trained analyst in the Jungian tradition gives careful attention to a full anamnesis of the patient's life and seeks to relate present neurotic symptoms and behavior to early development."[194] Jung, however, "relativized reductive analysis." It should be used for treating involvements of the personal unconscious, but without losing sight of "what the life process is moving *toward*."[195]

Concerning dreams, in a significant passage he credits Freud for teaching us reductive psychodynamics, then rather deftly confines their relevance to a "reductive function of the unconscious which raises infantile-sexual issues of the past [in dreams], much as the prospective function reveals prospects for the future."[196] Both functions serve compensatory purposes. The reductive function, for example, besides filling in missing information, may generate a dream which punctures an over-inflated ego,[197] or which connects the dreamer to her/his "natural and childlike side."[198] Thus not only do not all dreams have reductive content, but even those which do do not come about as Freud said they do. We get to glimpse oedipal strivings, etc. through the dream's purposive good offices, and not in spite of a dream censor. And this is the gist of the matter. Jung in a sense compensated for Freud on our behalf by rejecting disguise, and with it, the essentials of dream causation as conceived by Freud.

Dream imagery: disguise vs. honesty. The spontaneity of dreaming is the very basis of the compensatory function. For Jung, the unconscious is natural, just as, say, a beehive is natural, while consciousness is unnatural in the sense that architecture is. Of Freudian disguise, of dream as "facade," Jung wrote, "I kn[o]w no reasons for the assumption that the tricks of consciousness can be extended to the natural processes of the unconscious."[199]

"Jung insisted that 'a dream is quite capable . . . of naming the most painful and disagreeable things without the least regard for the feelings of the dreamer'."[200] If that is true, why do dreams not assault us more often with unvarnished disclosures? There are several reasons. First, with his characteristic absence of dogmatism Jung conceded, according to Mattoon, that repression does in fact produce some dream distortions.[201] A dream figure's true identity might be changed to distance painful emotions,[202] or some content tidied up for "moral" reasons.[203] But this is not the ubiquitous principle of dream composition Freud proposed, only incidental.

(1987, pp. 64–5) similarly accuses Jung of making unscientific mystical predictions which lead the person toward catastrophe by the force of his own, Jung's, counter-transference.

Second, not everything to emerge in dreams is despicable, and quite often the reverse. This theme of Jung's, that positive compensations bring out the good, true, and beautiful, imbues much of contemporary dreamwork. It was earlier taken up by Stekel, Wolff, Fromm[204] and others, not always with due acknowledgement of Jung, but always against the foil of Freud, whose cynicism is epitomized in this dreadful aphorism of his: "Dreams . . . reveal us as ethical and moral imbeciles."[205]

A third and crucial reason why dreams do not hit us more bluntly with plain facts is that the dreaming mind naturally composes in a symbolic style, which does not require censorship to account for it. Freud said that a dream censor takes originally verbal, easy to understand dream-thoughts and converts them into an imagery calculated to obfuscate them. Jung said that "as a plant grows or an animal seeks food,"[206] so dreaming spontaneously composes imagery which, like a parable, "does not conceal but it teaches."[207] A dream is not a "facade" but a "text,"[208] or a "little hidden door."[209]

There is a sizeable school of thought, influenced by Freud, which for diverse reasons has found the bizarreness of dream imagery, its distance from waking thinking and perception, to be associated with anxiety, repression, maladjustment, ego deficit, or psychosis.[210] But some findings have the opposite import. Scott Moss did not detect increases of "semantic distance"[211] between dream symbols and their references with elevations of anxiety. Noting also that one's dream vocabulary tends to remain stable regardless of familiarity with its meanings, Moss concluded—for reasons unrelated to Jung's —that dreams are naturally figurative whether disguising or not. Louis Breger et al. observed from dreams of surgical patients that symbolic transformation does not so much disguise a source of anxiety as render it into a form in which—again, for reasons unrelated to Jung's—the psyche can work with it constructively.[212] Thus, with regard to bizarreness, Moss and Breger belong by implication in that other diverse school which includes and sustains Jung. It connects dream bizarreness with coping, creativity, freedom, healing, growth, natural symbolic/metaphoric functions,[213] and/or the "superior, if archaic intelligence" of the unconscious.[214]

It is reasonable to suppose, and many do, that dream imagery has both 'Freudian' and 'Jungian' characteristics.[215] But insofar as dream imagery is honest, constructive, and (if difficult) direct in its meaning, it belies Freud's characterization of the dream surface as an incoherent "breccia" fit only to be decomposed for free association. Instead, it more resembles art, to be approached with appreciation (ch. 2, p. 56). Jung's own favorite art in this respect was classical drama, perhaps for its connections with myth and legend. Dreams have dramatic structure because both dreams and theater are rooted, thought Jung, in the same psychological structures, structures by means of which we grasp "the human drama."[216] Hence a fully realized dream generally follows a timeline containing the same elements as a classical drama: (1) exposition (or situation), (2) complication (or plot, or development), (3) crisis (or peripeteia), and (4) catastrophe (or lysis).

Whitmont & Perera distinguish between lysis, the satisfactory outcome of the crisis, and catastrophe, an unsatisfactory outcome. "The lysis shows the possible way out; the catastrophe may attempt to shake up the dreamer's consciousness by an urgent warning or (less frequently) acquaint him or her with an unalterable situation."[217] Whitmont & Perera employ dramatic structure as a tool in the following interpretation:

[A]n early analytic dream of . . . [a] woman who was very obsessive and self-controlled portrayed her in a dangerous position.
"I am lying in a stream that ran through my house, floating like Ophelia [from Shakespeare's *Hamlet*]."
She said that the dream experience felt good, like a relief, unlike her conscious sense of miserable rejection and "driven craziness and need for control." The dream compensates her conscious position, but also shows danger to the dream-ego.
. . . It reveals the fact that the naturally compensatory factor against her obsessive control tendencies is of a potentially harmful nature: it goes too far.
. . . [It] shows a dangerous situation . . . of being prone to a suicidal floating and giving up and feeling "good" about it. . . . [T]he impasse is in the exposition, not where the resolution ought to be; it does not at present lead to a potentially catastrophic deadlock, but is a situational picture that, showing neither crisis nor lysis, leaves open which way response and development might go.[218]

This interpretation notwithstanding, I am not sure the model of classical drama actually has much practical use for dreamwork. I have read an amount of Jungian literature and have seldom run across a dream interpreted by it, except those sampled to expound the model itself. That Jung chose to make the comparison does, however, testify to his respect for the manifest dream surface, in contrast with Freud's disrespect.*

---

* For interpretations employing the model of classical drama, see C. A. Meier (1990 [1972]), pp. 88 and 124ff.
The Jungian Patricia Berry wrote an influential paper (1974) which expressed reservations about making narrative the dream's "primary category," as do Jung's model of classical drama and many other approaches (including Freud's), which, she feels, do not sufficiently honor the dream on its own imagistic terms. Narrative entails coherence: "But I am beginning to question our idea of coherence. Is it truly the dream that is coherent or does our verbal approach to it make it so? . . . Images do not require words to disclose their inherent sense . . ." (p. 68). "An image is simultaneous. No part precedes or causes another part, although all parts are involved with each other. . . . We might

Harry Hunt conjectures that the two men's dream styles predisposed them to their differing evaluations of the manifest dream.[219] "Freud's dreams are unusually clouded and confused," and they show "a lack of narrative coherence," while "Jung's dreams are more overtly bizarre, with a numinous 'archetypal' quality" and "an unusual clarity." Correspondingly, for Freud the dream's manifest surface is ambiguous and heterogeneous, while the latent dream-thoughts, once discerned, turn out to be simple and in an important sense trivial; whereas for Jung, the manifest dream has the integrity of any effective symbol, while its references are ambiguous—that is, in the sense of being rich and complex. For Freud, the dream is a conglomeration pasted together at various levels of defense, quasi-symptomatic, with no inherent worthiness; for Jung, dreaming is a primary mode of experiencing, and the dream is a product of the psyche's gift for imaging, story-telling, myth-making. Freud said that we have to outwit dream symbolism in order to benefit from it; Jung that said symbolism (in the everyday sense, including allegory) is the natural medium in which the psyche regulates itself in dreams by compensation, so we ought to honor the dream and to heed it.*

Ego and Self

Not to say that the waking ego should be, in Jung's opinion, mere audience to the symbolic play of the great unconscious. The ego has a nature to be honored as well. Thus we come back to this central question of Jung's psychology: What is the relation of the ego to the Self of which the ego is a part? Here the question takes the form, What is the job the conscious ego needs to do to support the purposive compensatory function of dreams?

First of all, if dreams are not remembered, do they nevertheless compensate consciousness? "Even civilized man can occasionally observe," wrote Jung, "that a dream which he cannot remember can slightly alter his mood for better or worse. Dreams can be 'understood' to a certain extent in a sub-

---

imagine the dream as a series of superpositions . . . inseparable in time. . . . It does not matter which phase comes 'first' because there can be no priority in an image—all is given at once" (p. 63). To get in touch with the non-temporal aspect of dreams, Eva Renée Neu (1988, p. 31) suggests that it sometimes serves to tell a dream backwards.

    * Elsewhere (1992, pp. 28–30) Hunt portrays Freud and Jung as arch representatives, and advocates, of two necessary and "complementary ways of being in the world": Freud was keyed to "the dynamics of social relationships" (especially oedipal triads), to "doing/relating," while Jung was keyed to "more solitary 'individuation,'" to "being." Hunt (p. 32) illuminates (but overstates for symmetry's sake) Jung's avoidance of the 'Freudian' level of his own dreams: "his approach to his own dreams is as one sided as . . . Freud's corresponding transpersonal blindspot."

liminal way, and that is mostly how they work."[220] Cartwright represents it as Jung's thinking, that "automatic compensation"[221] is sufficient for healthy people, and that only neurotics need, as it were, to compensate their maladjusted compensation by paying conscious attention. That should be of some reassurance to non-recallers. Jung felt, however, that civilization renders us all effectively unhealthy, because it "drown[s] the quiet voice of nature" and "back[s] up all the aberrations of the conscious mind." Compensation works reliably by itself only in what he supposed were the "ideal conditions" of a certain primitive life. A price the civilized pay for the bulking up of our egos is the need to give "deliberate attention" to the unconscious for compensation to succeed.[222]

What if we remember a dream without understanding it?—the situation of most of us with most of our remembered dreams. Jung's simplest and forgiving answer is that we are influenced by many things of which we have no conscious understanding.[223] Whether understood or not, the dream image makes a vital connection to the dreamer by "the bridge of emotion,"[224] and that in itself is therapeutic.[225] Such is the meaning of Signell's title, *Wisdom of the Heart*.[226] Of important archetypal dreams, Jung believed that "[e]ven if the dream is not understood, it enriches the individual's experience; Jung described such dreams as 'stand[ing] out for years like spiritual beacons.'"[227]

But Jung also expressed himself strongly on the other side of the issue: "A dream that is not understood remains a mere occurrence; understood, it becomes a living experience."[228] And this: "The most beautiful and impressive dreams often have no lasting or transformative effect on the dreamer. He may be impressed by them, but he does not necessarily see any problem in them. The event then naturally remains 'outside', like a ritual action performed by others."[229]

The resolution of these views, and Jung's basic position, is expressed in a favorite alchemical saying of his: "What nature leaves imperfect is perfected by the art."[230] To the question, "Can you dream and derive the benefit of consciousness without understanding the dream?" Jung answered: "To a certain extent. It is the tidal wave that lifts you up, but you are in danger of being swept back down again with it. If you can cling to a rock and stay up, all right."[231] As the Clifts express it, "transformation thus involves both *experiencing* the emotion carried by the image and *understanding* the symbolic significance of the image. The understanding contains the meaning of the image, and the emotion contains the energy to bring about the needed change of transformation."[232]

How are we to understand the symbolism of dream imagery? We are to circumambulate the entire dream and to amplify it, as prompted by each detail of imagery, in two directions: mythic amplifications, which find resemblances between mankind's collective imagery and our own products of the collective unconscious; and personal amplifications, which show linkages to our personal unconscious and waking life—past, future, and especially present. But bear in mind that not just collective imagery but also personal life has an archetypal basis. Myths and other cultural forms universalize the aspects of life which our actual lives manifest in the particular. Dreams, having attributes of both the collective and the personal, help us consciously to place our particular experience in the context of universals, and that way lies wholeness and health.

What we are not to do, is to abdicate waking ego functions in favor of symbolic indications from dreams. Against this abuse of his teachings, Jung warns his readers not "to suppose that the dream is a kind of psychopomp which, because of its superior knowledge, infallibly guides life in the right direction."[233] "Experience has shown me that a slight knowledge of dream psychology is apt to lead to an overrating of the unconscious which impairs the power of conscious decision. The unconscious functions satisfactorily, only when the conscious mind fulfills its tasks to the very limit."[234] "[T]he ego," writes Hall, "must always take a stance toward the contents of the objective psyche . . . not simply evoke them, like the sorcerer's apprentice." "It is absolutely necessary for the waking-ego to know its own position in order for dreams to have a clear compensatory role."[235] And Jung: "Then dreams may perhaps add what is still lacking or lend a helping hand when our best efforts have failed."[236]

One sort of "overrating of the unconscious," already commented upon, is intemperate amplification with cultural parallels to the dream, or "archetypal reductionism."[237] This may take the form of over-intellectualization, but is more pernicious as a passive, anti-rational indulgence of symbolic resonances, where any and every echo of a myth or fairy tale is welcomed not only as self-validating but as self-explanatory. This leads not toward individuation but away from it.[238]

We are to show respect for the territories of both the conscious and the unconscious, and for the boundaries between them. Not only does each have its functions, but each can be abused by the other, to the detriment of the whole. On one hand, the unconscious can be vulnerable to conscious prying. John Grant has commented on this viewpoint of Jung's:

> In 1915 Jung wrote in a letter to the Swiss psychotherapist Hans Schmid (1881–1932) of a dream in which *he had been digging a hole in his garden. From the hole gushed forth water from a spring, and so the dreaming Jung had to dig another hole down which he could channel the water back into the ground.*

His interpretation of this dream is expressed with his usual charming opacity, but as far as I can understand he relates it to the role of the analytical psychologist: while it is important that he 'cracks' a particular symbol of the individual's unconscious to find the 'seed' within, he must remember that the symbol is there to **protect** the seed, and that this protection should not be removed. The dream, then—which took place some years before the letter and before Jung's break with Freud—signified his latent dissatisfaction with psychoanalysis, which he felt left the individual's 'seeds' exposed and vulnerable.[239]

Jung must have felt very protective toward his own "seeds." His very first remembered dream, from age 3–4, was of *an underground chamber containing a monumental phallus.*[240] This remarkable dream, which Jung says preoccupied him throughout his entire life, he did not relate to anyone—not his readers, not Freud, not his wife—until he was 65 years old![241]*

Jung expressed himself, on the other hand, more often and more forcefully about the vulnerability of the ego to the power of the unconscious. His respect for its destructive potential stands in contrast to the sanguine encouragements of popular Jungianism. Usually, it is true, the ego defends itself, by denial or other mechanisms, from material beyond its capacity to assimilate. For that reason, retrieving many extra dreams by sleep lab awakenings does not swamp the dreamer's ego (nor does it significantly accelerate therapy[242]). But there are times, Jung gravely warned, when premature disclosure of unconscious contents can be overwhelming: "I never force the issue if a patient is unwilling to go the way that has been revealed to him and take the consequences. . . . Resistances—especially when they are stubborn—merit attention, for they are often warnings which must not be overlooked. The cure may be a poison that not everyone can take, or an operation which, when it is contraindicated, can prove fatal."[243]

Inflation. A common maladaptive reaction of the ego to overwhelming unconscious contents is to identify with them: the ego becomes *inflated*, or even *possessed.* Yet Signell insists that "some inflation is necessary at times

---

* Many (but not all) cultures consider it imprudent to share good dreams, lest their effect be lost (while bad dreams are best shared for that very reason), e.g., Ojibwa (A. I. Hallowell 1975 [1960], p. 172); Kagwahiv (W. Kracke 1992 [1987], p. 33); Zuni (B. Tedlock 1992d [1987], p. 116); Judaism (J. Covitz 1990). In his old age, The Sioux Black Elk (J. G. Neihardt 1979 [1932], pp. 205–6; see below, ch. 5, p. 176) poignantly expressed the same attitude with respect to his transforming vision: "To use the power of the bison, I had to perform that part of my vision for the people to see. . . . I carried the pipe to Fox Belly, a wise and good old medicine man, and asked him to help me do this duty. He was glad to help me, but first I had to tell him how it was in that part of my vision. I did not tell him all my vision, only that part. I had never told anyone all of it, and even until now nobody ever heard it all. . . . It has made me very sad to do this at last . . . for I know I have given away my power when I have given away my vision, and maybe I cannot live very long now."

to sweep you into a new vision of your potential. . . . Inflation becomes a problem, and even a danger, only when it persists. . . ."[244] But even if the short-term effect of inflation may be euphoria, soon the ego loses its standpoint and individuality.

Dreams, in extreme cases, can contribute to the onset of a psychosis or neurosis, if the dreamer becomes inflated with their archetypal contents.[245]

Apparently as a result of painful experience, Jung seems ever to be warning about the hazards of inflation. In his autobiography, for example, when describing a psychological close call he had with a powerful and dangerous figure which arose from his unconscious, he warns: "Thus the insinuations of the anima, the mouthpiece of the unconscious, can utterly destroy a man. In the final analysis the decisive factor is always consciousness, which can understand the manifestations of the unconscious and take up a position toward them."[246]

Inflation, however, comes in two varieties: (1) that just mentioned, where the ego loses itself to the unconscious, and (2) the opposite, where the unconscious loses itself to the ego. Jung viewed this second inflation, which divorces us from vital contact with the collective unconscious, as the endemic tendency of our materialistic, I-centered civilization. It was his life's work to reproportion our egos and to repotentiate the collective unconscious in a constructive way. He undertook this project in psychological, spiritual, and even in moral terms. As to dreams, with the first type of inflation, with ego-loss, "reality ha[s] to be protected against an archaic, 'eternal', and 'ubiquitous' dream state; [but with] the second, room must be made for the dream at the expense of the world of consciousness."[247]

James Hillman's *The Dream and the Underworld* is an extreme development, verging on caricature, of Jung's project against inflation of the second type. Hillman tells us to regard dreaming, not as the compensation of "dayworld" ego consciousness, but as "initiation" of the ego into the personality in its irrational, mythic, or "underworld" aspect,[248] which seems to be Hillman's variant of Jung's Self. The function of initiation is not that of bringing contents up to the ego, but rather of bringing the ego down—in fact, to use his verb, of 'voiding' the ego.

But in the upshot, Hillman's project is really not unlike Jung's: exposure to the dream underworld on its own terms is to provide something missing from the dayworld which is crucial for our culture at large as well as for individuals.[249] This is compensation in all but name. Dreamwork is to lead us, through immersion in archetypal material from the "underworld," back to waking consciousness, now enhanced.[250] It is just that Hillman expresses his beliefs in a paradoxical, one-sided style which virtually invites an abdication of ego functions and an inflation of the first type (for those whose egos are perhaps not as powerful as Hillman's*).

The transcendent function and individuation. Be that as it may, the two inflations represent extremes of tendencies we all have, to give either (1) too much weight to the unconscious and its symbols, or (2) too little. Balance is of course recommended. For most of us, obtaining it entails concessions respecting the realistic boundaries of ego consciousness and its resources. We must learn, thought Jung, that the Self is fundamentally inscrutable and needs to be experienced via symbols; that the depths of the shadow remain forever darkly impermissible for any acceptable form of conscious assimilation; and so forth. In cardinal areas of psychic structure such as these, but equally, at the level of week-in, week-out compensatory dreaming, we profit from accepting that the psyche is busy with conflicting configurations whose meanings and energies can only be reconciled in the formation of irreducible symbols. The capacity of the psyche spontaneously to produce such symbols Jung termed its *transcendent function*, signifying by the expression not metaphysical transcendence, but the emergence of figurative resolutions which transcend the power of conscious thinking to achieve. Bosnak instructs: "[I]f you process the opposites long enough without taking sides with one or the other, an *identity of opposites* can develop, as the alchemists would say."[251]

We have noted Jung's admonition, that "[t]he unconscious functions satisfactorily only when the conscious mind fulfills its tasks to the very limit."[252] The tasks of the conscious mind may well include interpretation of dreams, with amplifications, sometimes with reductive analysis as well. Nevertheless, a transforming symbolic event is not likely to take place except as an aftermath of interpretation, and without the immediate impetus of analysis. Hall says that "[c]onscious attention may, for the more profound changes entailing reconciliations of opposites and therefore the transcendent function, be able to do no more than cultivate a helpful environment for the change to proceed in its own way—for ego consciousness cannot perform these reconciliations."[253] Here is an example, from Max Zeller, of a dreamer who paid his dues of conscious attention, to be rewarded by his transcendent function:

> The psyche does its transforming work in its own way.
>
> I saw this with a man who was in a deep, deep depression. He didn't know how he could shake the negative attitude toward life that had swallowed him. He was absolutely hopeless, and it went on and on. One day he came in, and he was totally changed. I mean, so changed that I asked, "WHAT has happened?" He sat down and said, "Listen to this dream.

---

* Cp. Richard Jones's (e.g., 1987) advocacy of immersion in the "non-I" through dreams.

"I hear birds singing. There are several different songs. I think of the wonderful range and variety in them. I am learning to differentiate between them and to identify them. One, a very simple little song, comes from a very large force from below, a much bigger source than any bird or animal.

"I see many ceramic roof tiles. They are stacked in rows. On top of them are several ceramic, tick-like objects which together form the feet of a bird. They are an art form from an early civilization, probably from the far east.

"I am in a rather small space with several other men. Upon entering, I nod a greeting to one man whom I recognize. It seems to be a conveyance that I enter, and we are all going off to work. It is dawn, and as the light grows I hear a voice narrating an epic poem to the sun, as a symbol of divine power. It begins, 'Comes now the creative spirit . . . ,' and goes on to tell of the sun's relation to mankind. It is a force that does not intervene directly in man's affairs, but is an inspiration and an example. I have heard it before, perhaps at some lecture, perhaps Yeats, perhaps it was a vision.

"The conveyance stops and the men prepare to leave. I awake. It has been rather crowded in the small space. Dawn is just breaking."

He was very, very moved. He had tears in his eyes and he said, "Now I am out of this narrow space!" After this dream he has a completely different attitude to everything that happened. It was the breaking of the new day, the new dawn. He could now be related to the Self, and the birds announced it.

The tick-like forms are of interest because the tick is an insect that waits as long as sixteen years until a furred animal passes under the branch; and then it drops down. It depends on the outer to touch it but it has an inner mechanism that tells it when it is time. It was that way with this man. The moment came, and everything changed. His work with the unconscious led to and prepared him for this irrational and totally unexpected moment of transformation.

In his next dream:

He gets into his car in order to drive off, we don't know where, and there stands his mother. She comes to the window of the car and hands him a compass as a farewell present.

This man had a very difficult mother problem. Apparently she had had the compass until now. Now she gives it to him, the means of finding his way. Until this moment the unconscious has kept his orientation from him. . . . He has won the treasure from the depths of his depression, and from now on he will go his own route.[254]

Consciousness may not micromanage a transformation such as this, but consciousness indispensably participates in it. It is, in fact, an absurdity, a denial of the human condition, to imagine psychic life progressing without the conscious component. Jung describes our life as a continual adjustment between conscious ego and unconscious Self. Dreams and other compensatory mechanisms help this happen daily, while the unfolding pattern of such adjustments is what Jung called the *individuation process*: "This process is, in effect, the realization of the whole man. . . . [S]ince everything strives for wholeness, the inevitable one-sidedness of our conscious life is continually being corrected and compensated by the universal human being in us, whose goal is the ultimate integration of conscious and unconscious, or better, the assimilation of the ego to a wider personality."[255] Individuation is what our life is. Conscious/unconscious is not merely a frame or context in which individuation takes place: their integration, the one with the other, is itself the transformation, the meta-transformation accomplished by the transcendent function. Thus conscious experience of a symbolic nature is the very stuff of human life.

We need to bear in mind that just as the compensatory process is fallible in its daily operations, so individuation, the grand compensation, does not always complete itself. Thus Meredith Sabini & Valerie Maffly describe the dreams of a man with terminal cancer, a man who had not paid his dues of conscious attention: "David's dreams poured out at a very rapid rate; that indicates that the individuation process would not be realisable. . . . [N]o one could integrate material brought up at this rate."[256] (For more regarding this dreamer, see ch. 8, p. 288.)

Stevens was earlier quoted concerning individuation, that the ego acts as the "executant of the archetypal blueprint for the whole life-cycle which is systematically encoded in the Self."[257] Individuation is not random. Compensations assume recognizable patterns, and they tend to summate in a coherent direction. One of Jung's stipulations of our blueprint is the stewardship of consciousness. Another is the division, which he so helpfully describes, between the first half of life, when the ego establishes itself by differentiation—I am this, I am that—, and the second half, reversing this trend. The second half of life is given to individuation in the strict sense, to "the assimilation of the ego to a wider personality." "Only when ego-consciousness is well-established can a true dialogue and relationship develop between it and the unconscious. Otherwise the ego simply falls into the clutches of the unconscious powers."[258]*

Our optional sub-plans within this scheme show up in the great archetypal motifs of myths, fairy tales, art and dreams. What is important to emphasize here is that Jungians consider themselves devoted to the same revelation, but

---

* Whitmont & Perera (1989, p. 186n7) indicate that whereas the term 'individuation' used to be applied only to this so-called second half of life, it is now applied to the entire life-cycle with respect to the process whereby the blueprint of wholeness realizes itself. This change obscures the very real transition most people experience at midlife. On the other hand, the change makes sense, in view of the fact that until extremely recently in evolutionary time, the average life expectancy of women was about 25 years, of men, 40.

in a contemporary guise, as that embodied in the very mythologies and other sources they explore. "Mythology is the psychology of antiquity," declares Hillman. "Psychology is the mythology of modernity."[259] Dreams share this ground. They give a sort of orientation, by prompting a prepared consciousness in the right direction according to the archetypal plan.

So the symbolic imagination is not just a mode of knowing in a diffuse sense, rather it is our direct access to the body of knowledge contained in the patterns of the objective psyche. This is what sharply separates Jung's perspective from the perspectives of most others who have celebrated symbolic awareness.

From our perspective, less 'advanced' societies may well seem better off than us in relation to that knowledge. Their myths provide them with a received, socially reinforced, and locally adaptive symbolic version of the archetypal scheme. Familiar mythic motifs often color their dreams, and not only "official"[260] or "culture pattern"[261] dreams which occur around rites of passage, but ordinary dreams also. In Ullman's view, we are more ignorant than they insofar as we lack a collective framework of myth and ritual which can enter our dream life from our day life, to link the two adaptively. And by the same tokens, we lack sanctioned means of sharing dreams, and thus are all the more deprived of the benefit inherent in the collective dimension of dreaming[262] (ch. 5, p. 172ff.). Ullman has in mind the social collective, not Jung's collective unconscious, but from a Jungian point of view it comes to much the same thing.

Writing on a related theme, the cultural historian Mircea Eliade has said that dreams are less satisfactory than myths for bridging between universals and our personal lives. Just as for Lawrence Kubie dreams are art, but bad art (ch. 2, p. 56n), for Eliade they are bad myth, or bad religion. Dreaming of a tree may restore psychic balance, but that is not the same as "awakening the whole consciousness . . . and 'opening' it to the universal" imports of renewal, immortality, ultimate reality and so on which the mythic symbol of a tree conveys.[263] But our luck is, we do not have myths—not, at least, an intact mythology. Things change too much and too fast.* We do have our dreams, however, and also the same archetypes in our genome as any noble savage, and a transcendent function to generate reconciling symbols (such as trees). Our own symbolism works, when we bring to it just that component of experience which Eliade faults dreams for not having: full consciousness. It works for us when "the conscious mind fulfills its tasks to the very

---

* David Feinstein & Stanley Krippner (1988, p. 22) speak of "the disorienting grip of a world in mythic turmoil." The remedy they promote is for each of us to develop a *Personal Mythology*.

limit."[264] We may have no received mythology to nourish our dreams and guide our interpretations, but with heightened individuality and less uncritical projection of the unconscious, we can draw on world mythologies to elucidate our own spontaneous symbolism, with the guidance of a conceptual psychology. As the world stands, this more advanced path to individuation is not going to solve the problems of alienated masses as tribal culture could solve the problem of alienation for hundreds or thousands. But Jungians, at least, have Jung's psychology, elitist though it necessarily be.

Jung as Myth

The "image of wholeness"[265] imparted by Jung's biological psychology provides us with an equivalent of, a successor to, those images of wholeness from man's cultural history which Jung's psychology studies. He gives us a conscious context, suitable to our time and place, in which to receive our own symbolic experience and complete our individuation. He is himself a symbol-maker at the collective level, therefore. In one sense, the symbol he created is the whole conceptual mandala of his psychology, with the world's symbolisms adorning it. Though his medium is expository prose, the effect of exposure to it is ultimately irrational, intuitive. In another sense, the mind of Jung seeking its own individuation is the symbol. If psychology is the religion of modern man, then Jung himself has to be a central symbol of that religion. And while to dream may not, as Eliade says, be adequate religious experience in itself, dream plus dreamwork is an important element of the spiritual practice Jung exemplifies. This is not, I think, to inflate Jung, but simply to recognize how these things work.

If religion is what helps us experience connectedness between our own particular existences and the universal, then there is no doubt of Jung's calling. "The feeling for the infinite," he writes in his autobiography, "can be attained only if we are bounded to the utmost. . . . Only consciousness of our narrow confinement in the Self forms the link to the limitlessness of the unconscious. In such awareness we experience ourselves concurrently as limited and eternal, as both the one and the other. In knowing ourselves to be unique in our personal combination—that is, ultimately limited—we possess also the capacity for becoming conscious of the infinite. But only then!"[266] And reciprocally, "the more one faces the unconscious and makes a synthesis between its contents and what is in the conscious mind, the more one derives a sense of one's unique individuality."[267]

This all-important tension between the particular and the universal is what is captured by the term 'individuation', with its paradoxical implication that one becomes not less but more individual even as the ego undergoes "assimilation . . . to a wider personality." The dynamic principle of individuation is the transcendent function, the making and using of symbols through which the ego relates to what it otherwise cannot. Symbols link conscious with unconscious, ego with collective, particular with universal. If we live symbol poor, then to be aware of being a speck of life going through the same motions as billions more is depersonalizing. Symbolically enriched, to be a particular instance of something universal is validating, stimulating, liberating. "It seems as if it were only through an experience of symbolic reality that man, vainly seeking his own 'existence' and making a philosophy of it, can find his way back to the world in which he is no longer a stranger."[268]

As Jung's farthest goal of individuation, perhaps to be attained in later life, we are to withdraw all our projections and come to perceive existence with "objective cognition,"[269] an emotionally detached condition yet not an emotionally untoned condition—Jung calls it "cosmogonic 'love'."[270] Jung's psychology of the Self-ego system and its progress toward individuation has aspirations beyond those normally associated with Western psychology. It is not misleading to speak of Jung as a spiritual teacher, nor of individuation as his 'path'.*

Jung's Spirituality

Since I have characterized Jung as a spiritual teacher, I need to acknowledge that in drafting this presentation I have expurgated his spiritual beliefs to an extent, omitting what I personally found most problematical in them. My reservations concern what might be called the spirit world.

If I have been able to organize a summary of Jung's thinking with such matters edited out, and if other summarizers have, that is because Jung him-

---

* Although individuation is everyone's innate potential, not everyone fulfills it: "I doubt my ability to give a proper account of the change that comes over the subject under the influence of the individuation process; it is a relatively rare occurrence which is experienced only by those who have gone through the wearisome but, if the unconscious is to be integrated, indispensable business of coming to terms with the unconscious components of the personality" (C. G. Jung, *Spirit and Nature*, Eranos Yearbook 1, p. 433, 1946, quoted by J. A. Sanford 1977, p. 117; also in "On the nature of the psyche," CW 8, para. 430).

All the same, "Jung considered death to represent a purposeful objective of the individuation process, a specific and archetypally determined 'goal and fulfillment'. . . . [T]he unity of the personality is attained at death" (M. Welman & P. A. Faber 1992, pp. 64 and 77, quoting C. G. Jung, "The soul and death" [1934], CW 8, para. 797, where the phrase is: "a goal and a fulfilment"). Von Franz (1986 [1984], p. xiii) says that individuation, "if not consciously experienced before death, may be 'telescoped' by the pressure of impending death." (See also A. Mindell 1989, p. 11.)

self enabled us to do so. He was a scientist in a scientific time, but a thinker whose ideas already placed him at the fringe. It was important to persuade. Accordingly, he not only made a point of showing deference to scientific assumptions and conventions (even his use of the "medical" concept 'instinct' has been attributed, if mistakenly, to the same motive[271]), he also censored himself to a degree. Letters and personal communications were less masked by a scientific persona, of course, as were his later writings. But over his career he remained wary.

In 1961 he commented upon this wariness, in a letter responding to Bill Wilson's expression of gratitude for the indirect role Jung had played many years earlier in the founding of Alcoholics Anonymous. Jung's influence had come by means of the clinical advice he had given to Rowland H., whose friend Ebby T. in turn influenced A.A. co-founder Wilson. Jung's advice had been that his American visitor's only hope of a reprieve from drinking was "a genuine conversion."[272] Jung wrote to Wilson that in his exchange with Rowland H. there had a dimension of which the latter was not aware. "The reason that I could not tell him everything was that those days I had to be exceedingly careful of what I said. I found out that I was misunderstood in every possible way. . . But what I really thought . . . [was that his] craving for alcohol was the equivalent on a low level of the spiritual thirst of our being for wholeness, expressed in medieval language: the union with God. How could one formulate such an insight in a language that is not misunderstood in our days? . . . I am strongly convinced that the evil principle prevailing in this world leads the unrecognized spiritual need into perdition, if it is not counteracted either by a real religious insight or by the protective wall of human community. An ordinary man, not protected by an action from above and isolated in society, cannot resist the power of evil, which is called very aptly the Devil. But . . . such words arouse so many mistakes that one can only keep aloof from them as much as possible. These are the reasons why I could not give a full and sufficient explanation to Rowland H., but am risking it with you. . . ."[273]

Notice the switch from past tense (in "those days") to present ("in our days . . . such words arouse so many mistakes"). Jung was still wary. One can sense his hunger to speak forthrightly to a kindred mind, but how far did he really go "risking it" here? He wrote that "Union with God" is equivalent to "wholeness." This equation, not quite anchored at either end, recalls Jung's observation that the Self is the archetype from which we derive our ideas of god, a formulation which leaves fully open, if it does not positively invite, a scientifically presentable interpretation without metaphysical entailments, namely, that our ideas about god amount to projections of the

Self. One can accept the gambit and still remain free to call an inexplicable ultimate reality 'God' if one chooses, while foreclosing ultimacy to anything remotely like a bearded man.*

This 'as if' diction is familiar and congenial. To draw a comparison, Buddhism teaches that while there is an ultimate reality, our specific ideas and perceptions of everything, including Buddha himself, are projections of our own minds. A deity upon whom a Buddhist may meditate, say a Tara, is to be understood as the projection of an aspect of the meditator's mind, much as, for example, Demeter or dream figures like Demeter are projections of the Jungian anima. The Buddhist visualizes deities even while seeking the enlightened realization that all forms, even forms of divinity, are empty, just as Jung cherished his symbols even while aiming to the withdrawal of projections.

But it seems to me that one moves into an altogether different register, when accepting as literal that the ultimate intrudes into our finite experience in a supernatural fashion. There are, for example, profound understandings of reincarnation which do not involve such literal beliefs as that the soul of a dying lama or rimpoche passes into the body of his successor, who then becomes identified when, as a child of three or so, he can recognize the old lama's belongings as 'his own,' or recite from memory sacred texts he has never heard.[274] I choose this example deliberately, because there is a strong presumption that Jung thought himself to be in some literal sense a reincarnation of Goethe, who may have been the biological father of Jung's grandfather.[275] Saying things like this (i.e., about reincarnation) is where risking it really comes in. Bill Wilson, as it happens, would have been a receptive listener. Also a spiritual teacher, Wilson likewise speculated at the esoteric fringe, and likewise guarded the fact for the sake of preserving credibility.

What follows is a sampling of risky esoterica from Jung, in connection with dreams. The items are plausible and implausible to differing degrees, as the reader will judge for her/himself.

---

* James Gollnick writes: "Jung's own position on the meaning of God and the spiritual world changed radically over his long career. James Heisig traces three distinct stages in the development of Jung's position. In the first stage (c. 1900–1921), Jung tended to reduce religious experience to the projection of emotional states. . . . The second stage . . . (c. 1921–1945) reflects his theory of the archetypes. Here religious experiences are viewed as projections from the deep layers of the psyche. . . . In this case he considers religious experience as the result of transpersonal dynamics . . . yet he does not relate the religious experience to an external and transcendent reality. The third stage . . . (c. 1945–1961) is not so clearly reductionistic as the first two stages. In this period there is evidence that Jung suspended judgment on the relationship of archetypal patterns of imagination to the spiritual entities they may symbolize" (1987, pp. 111–2, citing J. W. Heisig, *Imago Dei: Jung's Psychology of Religion*, Lewisburg, Pennsylvania: Bucknell University, pp. 31–43, 1979).

I mentioned Jung's gifts of foresight, as predisposing him to give his psychology a prospective orientation. His gifts included psi. The first example is of precognition. It can be explained as ordinary speculation, since it concerns a yet to be realized future. But what matters is that Jung appeared to reckon it as precognitive. It is worth quoting in any event, as evidence of Jung's religious visioning of his work. Again from Zeller:

When I was in Zurich in 1949, the first time after the war, I was terribly occupied with the question, "What am I doing as an analyst?" With the overwhelming problems in the world, to see twenty or twenty-five patients, that's nothing. What are we doing, all of us?

I stayed in Zurich about three months and saw Jung quite [often]. . . .

. . . [The last time, Zeller told Jung a dream:]

A temple of vast dimensions was in the process of being built. As far as I could see—ahead, behind, right and left—there were incredible numbers of people building on gigantic pillars. I, too, was building on a pillar. The whole building process was in its very first beginnings, but the foundation was already there, the rest of the building was starting to go up, and I and many others were working on it.

Jung said, "Ja, you know, that is the temple we all build on. We don't know the people because, believe me, they build in India and China and Russia and all over the world. That is the new religion. You know how long it will take until it is built?"

I said, "How should I know? Do you know?" He said, "I know." I asked how long it will take. He said, "About six hundred years."

"Where do you know this from?" I asked. He said, "From dreams. From other people's dreams and from my own. This new religion will come together as far as we can see."

And then I could say goodbye. There was the answer to my question what we, as analysts, are doing.[276]

The next item is more straightforward. It is a case of apparent clairvoyance, as related in Jung's autobiography:

I dreamed that *my wife's bed was in a deep pit with stone walls. It was a grave, and somehow had a suggestion of classical antiquity about it. Then I heard a deep sigh, as if someone were giving up the ghost. A figure that resembled my wife sat up in the pit and floated upward. It wore a white gown into which curious black symbols were woven.* I awoke, roused my wife, and checked the time. It was three o'clock in the morning. The dream was so curious that I thought at once that it might signify a death. At seven o'clock came the news that a cousin of my wife had died at three o'clock in the morning.[277]

In a letter to a man who had dreamt of meeting a dead brother's ghost, Jung spoke of "the continual presence of the dead and their influence on our dream life" in "genuine experience[s] which cannot be 'psychologized.'"[278] In the autobiography, Jung relates such a dream, one which recurred with elaborations during the course of one night:

"This is really strange," I thought. I was certain that the footsteps, the laughter and talk, had been real. But apparently I had only been dreaming. I returned to bed and mulled over the way we can deceive ourselves after all, and what might have been the cause of such a strange dream. In the midst of this, I fell asleep again—and at once the same dream began: *Once more I heard footsteps, talk, laughter, music. At the same time I had a visual image of several hundred dark-clad figures, possibly peasant boys in their Sunday clothes, who had come down from the mountains and were pouring in around the Tower* [Jung's residence], *on both sides, with a great deal of loud tramping, laughing, singing, and playing of accordions. Irritably, I thought, "This is really the limit! I thought it was a dream and now it turns out to be reality!"* At this point, I woke up. . . . Then I thought: "Why, this is simply a case of haunting!" . . .

. . . [It may have been a compensatory dream, but] it is also possible that I had been so sensitized by the solitude that I was able to perceive the procession of "departed folk" who passed by. . . .

It would seem most likely to have been a synchronistic phenomenon. Such phenomena demonstrate that premonitions or visions very often have some correspondence in external reality. There actually existed, as I discovered, a real parallel to my experience. In the Middle Ages just such gatherings of young men took place. . . .[279]*

Further along in the letter in which Jung spoke of "genuine experience[s] which cannot be 'psychologized,'" Jung characterized possession in a very different way from his own psychologized version, where it referred to an ego overwhelmed by contents from the unconscious. In the letter, he said: "There are experiences which show that the dead entangle themselves, so to speak, in the physiology (sympathetic nervous system) of the living. This would probably result in possession."[280]

Jung evidently lived in confidence of going to the other side after death. He accepted as genuine the near-death experiences he underwent in a critical illness: "It was not the product of imagination. The visions and experiences

---

* Synchronicity: "The synchronistic principle asserts a meaningful relationship with no possible causal connection between a subjective experience within the human psyche and an objective event which occurs at the same time but at a distant place in the outer world of reality" (H. A. Wilmer 1987, p. 169).

Belief in an afterlife, the reality of spirits of the dead, and even of communication with them is, to my skeptical mind, surprisingly common in the dream literature. For example, G. Delaney (1979, pp. 153–4); E. B. Taub-Bynum (1984, pp. 3–4 and 16); J. Windsor (1987, p. 180); A. Mindell (1990, pp. 15 and 33).

were utterly real. . . ."[281] In her book *On Dreams and Death*, Jung's spiritual heir von Franz says in effect that near-death dreams provide the ultimate compensation: "All of the dreams of people who are facing death indicate that the unconscious, that is, our instinct world, prepares consciousness not for a definite end but for a profound transformation and for a kind of continuation of the life process which, however, is unimaginable to everyday consciousness."[282] Jung had written to von Franz that the psyche exists both in and out of space-time. "Yes, we ourselves may simultaneously exist in both worlds, and occasionally we do have intimations of a two-fold existence." And: "We may therefore expect postmortal phenomena to occur which must be regarded as authentic."[283]

The reader will have opinions about these things. For skeptics, the point I wish to emphasize is that the conception of reality implied by survival after death, or even by phenomena on a nearer reach such as clairvoyance, was kept successfully segregated by Jung from his main psychology, a psychology which is spiritual but in a different sense.

Interestingly, Jung's last known dream, supposedly dreamt very near to death, is typically 'Jungian' and spiritual in that other sense. Miguel Serrano heard it from Jung's caretaker Ruth Bailey:

> *He saw a huge round block of stone sitting on a high plateau and at the foot of the stone was engraved these words: "And this shall be a sign onto you of Wholeness and Oneness."*[284]

□ 4 □

Existentialism

Adler broke with Freud in 1911, Jung did in 1914. Comparing defectors in the latter year, Freud dubbed Adler as "indubitably the more important"[1] (either from wishful thinking, or a conscious motive to diminish the worse betrayer). But when, in the late 1970s, James Fosshage & Clemens Loew edited a valuable book in which partisans of six different dream approaches took turns with the same dream series,[2] no Adlerian was included. Nor is one missed by many readers, presumably. In her book about Jungian dream interpretation, Mary Ann Mattoon epitomizes the consensus about Adler's dream theory: "Alfred Adler was, with Freud and Jung, one of the original 'big three' of psychoanalysis, but his contribution to dream theory was minor."[3] So far has his star fallen that none of the six practitioners in Fosshage & Loew mentioned his name once.

And yet, Adler's thoughts foreshadowed, and in respects influenced, fully three of their six approaches: the existential-phenomenological, whose best-known proponent is Medard Boss; the culturalist, represented in the book by Walter Bonime; and the Gestalt, developed by Fritz and Laura Perls. All of these have their greater or lesser debts, as did Adler himself, of course, to Freud, and also to Jung. But with Adler, they all share at least one outstanding feature in disagreement with the dominant schools. The common denominator of Adler with the existential, culturalist, and Gestalt approaches concerns the unconscious. They reject its existence or minimize its role. In this important regard, they stand in contrast to Freud and Jung, however differing the conceptions of the unconscious which these two held. And just as Freud's reductive approach and Jung's prospective one comprise a thesis/-antithesis which answers a need, so there is something necessary about the opposition of the Freud-Jung thesis of the unconscious to the antithesis first constellated by Adler.

Rejection of an autonomous unconscious carries with it this idea, that the important thing about dreams is their continuity with (not compensation of) waking. In the case of Adler, this implication took the form of his pivotal view about dreams, that they reinforce the dreamer's waking *life style*. Another emphasis of Adler's, one shared to differing extents with these others, was the bearing of societal factors. Not only do these influences shape a person, but beyond that, good health depends on developing, in Adler's phrase, strong *social interests*. Together, these features constitute an orientation to the dreamer's here-and-now reality which, though certainly not absent from Freud's and Jung's approaches, does not carry the same burden for them. Adler and the others mentioned are chief proponents among dream theorists of what can be called the existential pole of psychology; Freud and Jung occupy the oposite pole, of depth psychology.

If the influences of Boss, Bonime, and Perls are better appreciated now than the influence of Adler himself, their original contributions must certainly be one reason; but in addition to that, they probably made the points they share with Adler better and more fully than Adler did himself. Adlerians say that he was a gifted teacher but not much of a writer. Like Jung—who, however, wrote prodigious amounts—, he composed no single unifying book on the subject of dreams. In fact dreams do not figure nearly as largely in his *individual psychology* as in those of the other 'big three'. Adlerian psychology has made something of a comeback in recent years, but without much focus on dream interpretation,* or much notice in that field. His influence and precedence there deserve recognition, however.

The present chapter first surveys Adler's psychology with respect to the themes of waking-dreaming continuity and minimization of the unconscious in dream formation. It proceeds to discuss the existential-phenomenological dream approach, the approach which most emphatically propounds this configuration of ideas.

Chapter 5 takes up Adler's concept of social interest, and introduces the culturalists and others whose philosophies of dreamwork follow broadly in the same tradition.

Chapter 6 will then discuss the Gestalt approach—the one among those mentioned which is least conspicuously indebted to Adler.

---

* A search of the Adlerian journal *Individual Psychology* during a recent ten year stretch discovers only four articles with titles concerning dreams. One discusses what kinds of cultures nurture "creative dream work" (L. K. Ackerknecht 1985). The remaining three articles, totalling thirteen pages, present conflicting findings on a possible correlation between birth order and the incidence of nightmares (T. L. Brink & F. Matlock 1982; S. J. H. McCann & L. L. Stewin 1987; S. J. H. McCann, L. L. Stewin & R. H. Short 1990).

Adler

A *life style* is a person's adaptation to experience under Adler's "supreme law," which governs dreaming as well as waking: "the ego's sense of worth shall not be allowed to be diminished."[4] We are always striving for *superiority*, by which Adler meant not authority so much as competence and self-acceptance, not blunt power so much as freedom of action and expression. And we are more or less afflicted by contrary feelings of *inferiority*. Jung gave us the complex, Freud the oedipus complex, and Adler the inferiority complex, which he defined as follows: "The inferiority complex appears before a problem for which an individual is not properly adapted or equipped, and expresses his conviction that he is unable to solve it."[5] Though the term sounds dated now, it points to the same phenomena as 'low self-esteem' or 'shame', that is, "awareness of ourselves as fundamentally deficient in some vital way as human beings."[6]

Needless to say, we do not always acknowledge such feelings to others honestly, or even to ourselves. Instead, we develop strategies which provide us with compromised or specious superiority. Our battery of strategies and goals constitutes our life style. The farther our style deviates from reality, the more neurotic we are. A neurosis is a maladaptive strategy for turning feelings of inferiority into feelings of superiority or self-worth. But we are all more or less involved in these maneuvers, which in effect restrict rather than expand our "field of action."[7]*

Striving for superiority is a lifelong attempt to compensate for the experience of being a child in an adult world. Adler believed that our life styles usually get established by age four or five. He illustrated young life styles with this "anecdote of three children who were taken to the zoo for the first time. As they stood before the lion's cage, one of them shrank behind his mother's skirts and said, 'I want to go home.' The second child stood where he was, very pale and trembling, and said, 'I'm not a bit frightened.' The third glared at the lion fiercely and asked his mother, 'Shall I spit at it?' All three children really felt inferior, but each expressed his feelings in his own way, consonant with his life style."[8]

When commencing therapy, Adlerians solicit the client's earliest five or ten memories. From them—whether they happen to be historically accurate or not—can be obtained a quick read of the adult life style. This exercise is

---

* Harold Mosak (1989, pp. 69–71) comments that Adler's concept of psychological ill-health as distorted superiority has had an acknowledged influence on many neo-Freudians, notably Karen Horney. She elaborated on "the need for glory" and "perfection" as traits of neurosis, while faulting Adler for "staying too much on the surface of the problems involved" (1970 [1950], p. 372).

well worth trying out for oneself: the set of early recollections turns out to be much like an episodic allegorical dream of one's life.

Dreams are the night expression of the same underlying strategies of the life style, brought to bear on our current life situation. "The dream must be a product of the style of life, and it must help to build up and enforce the style of life."[9] As a prototypical example, the Adlerian Leo Gold offers the dream of a man whose style of life Gold calls that of a "getter":

Since the odds are that his approach to life is based on being deprived or never having enough, his expectation is that others should be constantly available to supply his needs. His goals are always geared to acquisition, and in the dream life this is a consistent pattern. He dreams as follows:

I was in a great hall standing to one side. I was feeling alone and very hungry. At first others did not realize who I was and passed me by. Then an older man came by and recognized me and took me to a large well-lit chamber. People surrounded me and placed a beautiful robe on my shoulders. I was led to a banquet table and all kinds of food were brought to me. The older man kept urging things on me. He said, "Here you can take anything you want." I felt a great sense of contentment.

The dream lends itself to quick interpretation. It states simply that the dreamer feels uncertain, a little frightened and empty. When others pay attention to him and give him many things, he feels better. When the dreamer can easily get what he wants and others bend to his service, he feels great. When he is told he can have what he wants, he feels more secure. . . . What is of interest in the dream is the passivity of the dreamer. He does not initiate but rather expects others to take the initiative in supplying his needs. . . .

. . . From this it is possible to create a hypothesis about how he relates to others and the kinds of difficulties he can get into as he stresses his need to get in his social milieu.[10]

Gold's interpretation makes no room for Freudian wish fulfillment (paternal permission to indulge), much less for a Jungian guide showing the ego the way to the bounty of the Self. Instead, the interpretation says, in effect, "Look. Here is how this person is." The governing assumption is that the dreamer must be resorting to the same maneuvers in the dream as he would do awake to overcome feelings of inferiority and to generate feelings of adequacy. This approach no doubt has something in common with neo-Freudian ego psychology—a life style is like a profile of ego defenses. Adler, however, focused even more exclusively on ego concerns than did the ego psychologists, by deemphasizing instinctual drives and by "reject[ing] the notion of an unconscious."[11] Without it, "such [ego defense] mechanisms as repression and sublimation" lose their meaning;[12] while dreams cannot be regarded as the "eruption of an unconscious mode of thought."[13]

Gold nevertheless speaks of an entry to "inner ideation" provided by the dream.[14] So it is not that no mental processes are hidden from view, but that there is no special mental place or entity with special properties which can be called *the* unconscious, and which is responsible for dreams. No different part of the mind—no infantile or collective unconscious—presides over the night. "In the Freudian view," explained Adler, "'[c]onscious' and 'unconscious' are placed in contradiction to each other, and the dream is given its own special laws contradictory to the laws of everyday thinking. . . . Any theory which treats sleep and waking, dream thoughts and day thoughts, as contradictions is bound to be unscientific."[15]

This is as strong a phrasing of the continuity hypothesis as one could ask for. Of course it overlooks Freud's technical characterization of the dream-thoughts, which he also found to be continuous with day thoughts, indeed virtually to be replicas of them (ch. 2, p. 60ff.). But Adler here meant by "dream thoughts" the whole dreaming process. He was contrasting his own ideas to Freud's repressed infantile unconscious and the dream-work devices which supposedly disguise its nightly upsurges. Similarly, though like Jung Adler viewed the dream as a whole metaphor and not as a Freudian "breccia" of symbolic fragments, he did not entertain Jung's idea of a compensatory unconscious (in Adlerian terminology, 'compensation' refers to maneuvers, awake or dreaming, to cope with feelings of inferiority). Instead, it is precisely the "continuity of thought and feeling from waking to sleeping" which dreams capture and convey.[16]

There is likewise continuity which proceeds from sleeping to waking, and herein lies the function of dreaming, according to Adler. The task of dreams is "to meet the difficulties with which we are confronted and to provide a solution."[17] Dreams process our problem situations, and then prime us, *emotionally*, to meet them in the coming day. Emotions generally are regarded by Adler as catalysts to action (or to inaction), along lines determined by the personality, or life style. If someone is feeling fearful, for example, Adler wants to know what life style goal the fear is serving. He wants to know, in other words, what the implicit fantasy is about the consequence of having the fear. In many cases, this means to determine the "basic mistake" under which the person is operating.[18]* The same questions need to be posed about fear in a dream as about a waking fear. A dream prepares us to meet an anticipated problem situation by arousing and leaving behind emotions which

---

* Mosak (1989, p. 87) categorizes basic mistakes as follows: "overgeneralizations"; "false or impossible goals of 'security'"; "misperceptions of life and life's demands"; "minimization or denial of one's worth"; and "faulty values."

will stimulate action (or inaction) congenial to the life style in that situation. And this is the essential function of dreams.[19]*

Unfortunately, the solutions generated by dreams follow the routines of our preestablished life styles, and if anything exaggerate their deficiencies. Adler actually had very little positive to say about dreams. Comparing them with waking by the criteria of waking, as he does, they are bound to come off second best. Although there is "no break with reality" when we dream, a "greater distance from reality . . . prevails," because "in dreaming more relations with reality are excluded."[20] Not needing to communicate with real others, we are not so bound by consensual reality, nor are our responses so constrained by convention. In consequence, dreams lose track of the objective features of our problem situations and they magnify our feelings. This accounts for exaggeration in dreams as well as for their narrowness.[21] Adler, like Freud but for different reasons, observed a parallel between dreams and neurosis: "[E]very neurotic restricts his field of action, his contacts with the whole situation."[22] Thus for Adler as for Freud, and in contrast to Jung, the dream is not constructive or healing in itself, but only becomes so when interpreted with a therapeutic eye. Solutions which dreams develop are merely subjectively gratifying ones, harmonious with the style of life. Dreams are "not more intelligent and prophetic than everyday thinking, but more con-

---

* Contemporary researchers continue to consider the role dreams may have in the regulation of emotion. Milton Kramer (1990, 1991a and 1991b) has studied the relation between bedtime and morning mood, finding "enormous variability" in that relation (1990). However, there is a general tendency for whatever feeling is present at night to be less intense after waking. This pattern is most pronounced for "unhappy" feelings. And whereas feeling fresh and thinking clearly in the morning depend on getting NREM sleep, a "decrease in unhappiness from night to morning" depends on having dreams which function as an "'emotional thermostat'" (1991a, p. 279; cf. R. D. Cartwright, *A Primer on Sleep and Dreaming*, Reading, Pennsylvania: Addison-Wesley, 1978, cited by W. Moorcroft 1986, p. 26). Like Adler, Kramer thinks that mood is regulated by some sort of problem resolution accomplished by dreaming, without waking processing or even dream recall. Kramer gives new life to Freud's old principle, that the function of dreaming is to act as a guardian of sleep, to prevent awakening: "[D]uring REM sleep there is a surge of emotion. We speculate that a function of dreaming is to contain or attempt to contain this surge" (1993, p. 145). The more successful the dream, the less the dream enters awareness (p. 148).

According to Mortimer Ostow (1992), people with affective disorders—"whether excessive excursions on the upside or downside, or excessive volatility" (p. 9)—have dreams presenting polar tendencies: not, as so commonly in dreams, poles of a conflict, but poles of the affect itself. When fully expressed in the manifest dream, the polarity takes the form of sequential tendencies: "a primary tendency corresponding to the prevailing waking aspect, a secondary correction, and a defeat of the correction by reassertion of the primary tendency. Only when the patient is about to recover from his illness or to switch from one mood to the opposite, is the final defeat absent" (p. 12). Ostow proposes that this exaggerated pattern provides "a window onto spontaneous attempts to regulate affect" (p. 11).

fused and confusing."[23] Their problem-solving is inferior to that of ordinary common sense, and beyond that, "[d]reaming is the adversary of common sense." Common sense was Adler's golden rule. "In dreams we are fooling ourselves. Every dream is an auto-intoxication, a self-hypnosis."[24]

This is not Freudian disguise Adler is talking about—the scrambling of threatening unconscious contents by special dream-work mechanisms. Rather it is ordinary self-deception, of the sort people employ awake as well as in dreams to protect themselves from reality. In dreams, the self-deception is even more conspicuous. And since the natural function of dreams is to rouse feelings which will prompt waking actions compatible with our self-deceptions, dreams do not require us to be aware of them to do their job, indeed they actually work better if we forget them; that is, if they stay out of the view of common sense. The operative feelings carry into the day as well or better, when the dream they come from is not recalled. "If dreams were understood, they would lose their purpose."[25]

As an illustration of how feelings roused by dreamt self-deceptions lead to waking actions, Adler scrutinizes an experience of his own. I include his interpretation here, partly for the surprising conclusion to which it leads:

> During the war I was the head of a hospital for neurotic soldiers. When I saw soldiers who were not prepared for war, I tried to relieve them as much as I could by giving them easier tasks. . . . One day a soldier came to me who was one of the best built and strongest men I have ever seen. He was very depressed and as I examined him I wondered what could be done with him. I should have liked, of course, to send home every soldier who came to me; but all my recommendations had to pass before a superior officer and my benevolence had to be kept within bounds. It was not easy to decide in this soldier's case; but when the time came I said, "You are neurotic, but you are very strong and healthy. I will give you easier work to do so that you need not go to the front."
>
> The soldier looked pitiable and answered, "I am a poor student and I have to support my old father and mother by giving lessons. If I cannot give lessons they will starve. They will both die if I can't help them." I thought that I should have to find him still easier service—send him back home to work in an office; but I was afraid that if this was my recommendation my superior officer would get angry and send him to the front. In the end I decided to do the utmost I honestly could. I would certify him as fit for service on guard. When I went home at night and slept I had a terrible dream. I dreamed that *I was a murderer and was running round in dark, narrow streets trying to think whom I had murdered. I could not remember who, but I felt, "Because I have committed murder I am done for. My life is over. Everything is finished." And so,* in the dream, *I stood still and sweated.*
>
> My first thought when I awoke was, "Whom have I murdered?" Then it occurred to me, "If I don't give this young soldier service in an office, perhaps he

will be sent to the front and killed. Then I should be the murderer." You see how I stirred up feelings to deceive me. I had not been a murderer; but if this disaster really occurred, I should still not be guilty. But my style of life would not permit me to run the risk. I am a doctor; I am to save life, not to endanger it. I thought again that if I gave him an easier job my superior would send him to the front and the position would be no better. It occurred to me that if I wanted to help him the only thing to do was to follow the rules of common sense and not bother about my own style of life. I, therefore, certified him as fit for service on guard. Later events confirmed the fact that it is always better to follow common sense. My superior read my recommendation and struck it out. . . . [He] wrote, "Six months' office service." It turned out that this officer had been bribed to let the soldier off easily. The youth had never given a lesson in his life and nothing he said had been true. . . . Since that day I have thought it better to give up dreaming.[26]

Adler's decision to "give up dreaming" can only strike us as an historical oddity in view of current knowledge. I cite it not to hold him to account for what he cannot have known, but to give the measure of his low estimation of dreaming. Adler claimed actually to have "stopped dreaming because he became so well able to interpret his dreams that they could not perform their function any longer,"[27] that is, they could no longer deceive him. Bernard Shulman, who reports this claim, tries to rescue it by implying that Adler only meant he stopped troubling to remember his dreams. But a number of Adler's own comments demonstrate that he meant it literally that he stopped dreaming. Thus: "We shall probably find that people who do not like to be deluded by their feelings, who prefer to proceed in a scientific way, do not dream often or do not dream at all."[28] Dreaming is "in itself a sign that the dreamer feels inadequate to solve the problems by common sense alone."[29] "The more the individual goal agrees with reality, the less a person dreams. Very courageous people dream rarely, for they deal adequately with [problems] in the daytime."[30] In other words, healthy people do not have healthy dreams, they stop dreaming.

It should be mentioned in fairness to Adler that some traditional Eastern belief systems also recognize dreamless sleep and regard it as a worthwhile accomplishment (ch. 14, p. 475ff.). There, however, the dreamless state is held to be the reward of spiritual discipline, and the sleeper in this state is supposed to become positively aware of ultimate reality—whereas Adler's standard of reality is the everyday, and his dreamlessness is merely a sound night's sleep, albeit earned by courage and a no-nonsense "scientific" outlook. This is simply a pre-REM misconception. It sounds very much as if Adler adapted his theory to accommodate the fact that at some point he personally stopped remembering his dreams.

Contemporary Adlerians. Adlerians today obviously take REM, etc. into account. Additionally, they qualify Adler's conclusion that dreaming is antithetical to a good psychological orientation. They uphold, however, Adler's fundamental view of dream function, by which dreaming prompts the dreamer to action after waking, and is thus future-oriented and purposive. This is, of course, different from Jung's view of dream purposiveness, by which a dynamic unconscious compensates the waking mind for the sake of psychic wholeness. Adler's purposiveness, while also professedly holistic, is in continuity with conscious life. The goals toward which dream-roused feelings tend are the same goals as those of our waking tendencies. In dreams, we rehearse scenarios, much as, awake, we anticipate and imagine before we act; only in dreams, we do so with less correction from reality. For Adler himself, the dream-rehearsed solutions are substantially unrealistic and dishonest, even if by chance they lead to helpful outcomes.[31] For later Adlerians, by contrast, dreams can develop helpful solutions which are more than merely subjectively gratifying and compatible with the life style. Dreams can upgrade the life style.

Thus Gold comments favorably on the poetic "private language of symbol and metaphor" in dreams, "which allows a much richer range of facts, information, ideas, fantasies, feelings, emotions, excitement, and passivity to interplay" than in waking. This "broader fictional world," Gold concludes, "becomes extremely important, since by going beyond the framework of common sense, the dreamer is . . . able to create new perspectives on seemingly unsolvable situations in waking life."[32] In conceding dreams this constructive role of invention and rehearsal, Gold permits them a certain compensation to waking life. His outlook also unseats Adler's "common sense" from its rather inflated position. In the same spirit, Shulman allows that reason itself can be abused for self-deception, while on the other hand dreaming is "a legitimate way of experiencing life."[33] And since dreams can have a constructive bearing on waking life, their meanings can become intelligible to us without that necessarily vitiating their purpose.[34]

Whether any given dream contributes life-effective promptings depends upon many conditions, and is by no means assured. Still, this is a long way from Adler's severe observation, that "a metaphorical conception of one's situation is a way of escape from it."[35]

Here from a contemporary Adlerian, Shulman, is an episode which shows a dream creating a feeling which prompts the dreamer toward a constructive correction of his life style:

> The following example was given me by Rudolf Dreikurs: A patient reported a dream in which *he was in jail*. He did not recall other dream elements. He did

not understand the dream and could not offer associations except to say that he would not like being in jail. Dreikurs asked him if he had done something wrong or illegal or if he contemplated or had contemplated the same. The patient then confessed that he had compiled a fraudulent income tax return, but the next morning had thought better of it and redid the return to remove the fraudulent features and then posted the honest return with his check. He had made this decision the morning after the dream. However, he did not see the connection between the dream and his subsequent behavior until Dreikurs pointed it out to him.

The dream created a mood through a metaphor. It was the complete equivalent of a conscious decision to redo the tax return, but, couched as a metaphor, was much more evocative of emotions than would be rational thinking which tends toward objectivity and dispassion.[36]

To summarize, Adlerians have dispensed with Adler's more unfavorable ideas about dreams—that they are less frequent in healthy people, are always inferior to common sense, are always self-deceptive, and serve their natural function best when forgotten—while adhering to essential features of Adler's approach. Thus, dreams are future-oriented, purposive. Their function is to arouse and leave behind feelings, which will prompt the awakened dreamer toward a course of behavior in her/his real-world current life situation. The very same coping mechanisms against inferiority operate in dreaming and waking. Though we are unaware of much in our minds, our blind spots are intrinsically the same awake and asleep. There is really no such 'thing' as *the* unconscious which determines dreams. Dreams are continuous with, not alien and/or compensatory to, the interests of the ego.

Existential Dream Psychology: Boss and Others

Over fifty years ago, a biographer wrote of Adler that he was "the first founder of an existence psychology."[37] Of course Nietzsche and other existential philosophers had concerned themselves with psychological matters. Adler, however,—while not labelling himself 'existential' any more than had Nietzsche—was first within the discipline called 'psychology' to take a generally existential approach.

Of later existential psychologists, Boss is the best known for focusing on dreams. The balance of this chapter looks at his approach, bringing in other existential writers as appropriate in drawing comparisons with the Adlerian configuration of ideas about dreams just presented.

In an account he gives of Boss, Heinz Lehmann explains that existential psychology applies the phenomenological method associated with the philosopher Husserl. This coupling obtains to the point where some speak of the 'existential-phenomenological' approach (but the coupling is not obligatory, as witness Adler himself). Husserl's method entails "a radical return to the phenomena as they present themselves. This is achieved by eliminating—or, as Husserl calls it, 'bracketing out'—all preconceived notions, attitudes and theories."[38] Bracketing out, says Erik Craig, requires us to "suspend belief" about what we suppose something is, to "bracket out what doesn't show in the thing itself."[39] Although the language which results at time sounds off-puttingly stilted, the purpose is simplification.

Boss begins his last book about existential dreamwork with this string of attractive quotations. The first is from Wittgenstein: "I am reminded of the wonderful saying that 'Every thing is what it is, not something else.'" Next Goethe: "Do not look for anything *behind* phenomena; they themselves are the lesson!" And Husserl: "Return to the things themselves!"[40]

Existentialists ask us to accept the dream with sophisticated naivete. The fact is that, while we dream, the dream-world is almost always taken to be real. There is no definitive distinction between waking and dreaming experiences, just in terms of the sense of "being there," of "being-in-the-world"—or in the terminology of Heidegger, which Boss adopted, of "Da Sein."[41] "If there is a single feature that distinguishes this existential approach to dreams from others, it is this very notion that the dream is real, so real in fact, that it might well be considered a bona fide autobiographical episode. . . ."[42]

A dream is not something we "have" or "make," rather it is a "mode of human existence."[43] Once we bracket out our waking predisposition to say the dream is merely this or really that, then, whatever other differences we may detect between the two states, dreaming appears to be "as autonomous a way of existing as is the waking life,"[44] and, by this reckoning, "equal in importance to waking reality,"[45] which deserves "no special priorities."[46]

"Had these events all occurred in his waking life we would readily agree that [a certain dreamer] led an exceptionally rich existence. And yet should we consider him any less rich simply because these events occurred while he was asleep and dreaming?" asks Craig.[47]

But if dreaming is an autonomous mode of existence, equal in importance to waking, it may appear puzzling that in practice Boss and other existential interpreters seem actually to give nearly complete preeminence to waking.

On the one hand, Boss will state that "[w]aking and dreaming . . . [are] but two different modes of carrying to fulfillment the one and same [*sic*] historical human existence. . . ."[48] Craig concurs that an existentialist "believes in the unity and indivisibility of human existence."[49] Moreover, we are to "shine these two lights of dreaming and waking on our single human existence. It is this *combined luminosity* of dreaming and waking that is so effective. . . ."[50] But on the other hand, "[m]an, as mere dreamer, cannot have a continuous development of his life. There is no dream history running parallel to his waking life history"[51] (Boss). So dreams are "autobiographical" only in this sense of being embedded in a waking history.* There can be no mistaking which mode of 'being-in-the-world' has priority in practice. After all, dreams change only as the "life historical problems they contain are . . . experienced as such in the dreamer's waking life, there to be faced. . . ."[52] It is apparent that actual dream interpretation always gravitates toward the waking condition.

Lehmann, for example, who speaks radically of there being "no special priorities" between the dreaming and waking states, nevertheless concludes his first exemplary interpretation by saying that the subject's dream "is simply a way of expressing his narrow-minded, waking life existence."[53] This is typical. The thrust, the entire thrust of existential interpretation is to bring the dream "into relationship with the dreamer's waking life,"[54] on the expectation of a continuity of meaning between the one and the other.

There is not, however, an appeal to common sense reality in the manner of Adler; although a "waking life is . . . presupposed in all dream interpretation, . . . dreams themselves force all future investigations to pay heed to the structure of waking life, instead of taking it for granted"[55] (Boss). Just such a critical application of dream studies to the study of waking mind is David Foulkes's project,[56] as it is of some others who share Boss's phenomenological approach, but for whom applied dream interpretation is an interest secondary to investigation of mentality per se.

Thus Harry Hunt, who aims to "'bracket' standard views . . . that there is an inherent and necessary difference between dreaming and waking,"[57] ascertains that, apart from some "relative," quantitative differences, the possibilities for the two conditions are, in fact, identical. These possibilities go from normative "'everyday reality'" through the various "'altered states,'" all of which have waking and dreaming manifestations.[58] Gordon Globus, in reference to Allan Rechtschaffen's often-cited essay on the "single-minded-

---

* This same point has been made for centuries by philosophers, to establish a criterion for determining we are not dreaming when awake. Norman Malcolm calls this "the coherence principle" and quotes its originator Descartes: "[O]ur memory can never connect our dreams one with the other, or with the whole course of our lives, as it unites events which happen to us while we are awake" (1967 [1959], p. 105, quoting R. Descartes, The Philosophical Works of Descartes, Cambridge, pp. 198–9, 1934). Malcolm himself refutes the coherence principle with the same irksomely complacent reasoning as he employs throughout his book: "The objection that should occur to anyone is that it is possible a person should dream that the right connections hold, dream that he connects his present perceptions with 'the whole course of his life'."

ness" of dreams,[59] argues: that all differences are of degree; that the main difference is the accessibility of 'self-reflection' awake ("I am awake"); and that the causation of the differences of degree comes down to the scarcity of sensory inputs during dreaming.[60] The sensory contribution notwithstanding, both conditions of mentation are equally self-creative, or "formative." Neither ever forms from a mere shuffling of inputs and/or memories.[61] So reality, in both cases, is substantially a product of the mind. Departing from strict phenomenology, Globus leads us toward radical solipsism and the essentially Eastern position on waking-dreaming continuity, that the two states are equally and comparably illusory.[62]

This turns out to be a sort of opposite to Boss's philosophical position, whereby we 'make' neither world, and whereby both are equally real (not unreal) as phenomena. However, the contrast is more apparent than actual; at least, the underlying sense of waking-dreaming continuity in terms of reality status is much the same. Boss was, in fact, deeply influenced by Indian philosophy, where he found confirmation of the co-equal status of waking and dreaming worlds.[63] But as he relates in *A Psychiatrist Discovers India*, his chief guru advised him not to use his Indian experience in psychotherapy in the West.[64]

Boss is foremost a clinician and dream interpreter. Here, his obligation is to find continuity of meaning between the dream and the dreamer's experience. Again, the thrust of existential interpretation is to bring the dream "into relationship with the dreamer's waking life." Thus in the last analysis, Boss gives the whole matter the Western slant: waking reality gets the last word.

Then to reverse the original problem: if waking has this pragmatic pre-eminence, why insist on the autonomy of dreaming? For one thing, to do so is a feature of clinical tactics, as will be seen in an example to follow. But also, it is vis-a-vis any supposed *un*conscious that existentialists unequivocally maintain the autonomy of dreaming. As with Adler, the unconscious is held not to exist. Also as with Adler, mental happenings are acknowledged to occur hidden from conscious view, "and there is not the slightest objection to apply the *adjective* 'unconscious' to all that escapes us"—so concedes a phenomenological psychiatrist, continuing: "There . . . is nothing however that would lead us to assume 'an' unconscious (substantive), which would be supposed to exist as a second reality. . . ."[65]

So existentialists maintain the autonomy of dreaming against the anti-phenomenological assumption made by most other psychologies, that "[d]reams originate in an estranged unconscious mind."[66] "They s[ee] in dreams the expression of something else, something merely assumed to exist beyond the phenomena, some mental construct."[67] Freud's construct of an unconscious involves disguise in the production of dreams, Jung's construct, compensation. Naturally, rejection of the unconscious entails rejection of disguise and compensation, and, with them, the interpretive tools of free association and amplification.[68] "The phenomenological attitude requires a radical commitment to conscious experience and therefore to the consciously remembered manifest dream."[69]

As for disguise, Boss objects that, since the self is unitary, it cannot, logically, deceive itself; so that Freud's unconscious dream censor amounts to a personality within a personality.[70] Mention was made in chapter 3 (p. 108) of Globus's parallel objection to Jungian compensation, that it seems to require a "shadow intelligence." The rejoinder, here as there, is that mental systems can behave purposively by virtue of their components, without our needing to attribute personal intentions to the part or even the whole.

The more fundamental existential objection to disguise is that it makes no sense, if dreaming "is a fully experienced way of living. . . ."[71] Disguise is not the reason we have difficulty understanding our dreams. Commenting on the fact that frequently even obvious and nonthreatening interpretations do not occur to the dreamer her/himself, Hunt suggests that "Freud's strict insistence on the universality of disguise may come ultimately from the inherent limitations of any self-analysis."[72] Moreover, Boss insists that opacity of meaning also complicates waking, and is not so much a matter of disguise as "of that prehuman, in fact, preontological concealment from which every human existence must wrest a region of illumination of the world."[73] This perspective, which raises to the cosmic Adler's idea that dreaming involves ordinary self-deception, no doubt contains a lot of truth, even if it does not answer all questions.

As for compensation, Boss contents himself—after a full critique of Freud —with a dismissive remark: "There are no traces of Jungian 'compensation' for waking consciousness."[74] But consider a hypothetical case discussed by existentialist Werner Mendel: "[I]f the dreaming existence creates a dream in which it is overwhelmed by the consequences of expressing an assertive attitude, such a patient is certainly not ready to express his assertiveness in the real world."[75] Other possibilities are readily imaginable, both compensatory and not; but existentialists are constrained by their working assumption of continuity between waking and dreaming ways of being-in-the-world to expect a mirroring which precludes compensation.

This conjunction of ideas—to emphasize the existential authenticity and the autonomy of dreaming, while yoking its meaning to waking; and to deny that the unconscious is its source—results in a sort of hesitance about dream imagery which recalls Adler's antipathy to the metaphor. Mere "images" are tainted by unreality,[76] in contrast to the dream when regarded as an authentic world. Importantly, symbolism is thought imposed by the waking mind, and not to be inherent in the dream. Boss illustrates with a patient's dream:

> "My dream last night began with *me in my mother's house. I saw my pet turtle, Jacob. Some force started to tear the turtle apart, pulling the top shell away from the bottom one. It was torture for me to watch, so I screamed and said to my mother: 'There is only one way to free the animal from its pain, by killing it.'"* . . .
>
> . . . [T]he therapist must strictly guard against the self-contradictory contention that, in the dreaming state, the turtle's armor "really" was the dreamer's own existential barriers, or that the tearing apart of the turtle "symbolized" the analytic exposure of the patient's waking life.[77]

It would appear to be Boss's existentialism which accounts for this prohibitive attitude, rather than the phenomenological method, for both Hunt and Globus more than allow, they celebrate dream symbolism. Hunt, while discarding the unconscious like Boss, and likewise placing dream imagery on the same phenomenological continuum as waking, nonetheless lets some dream imagery be symbolic (depending on dream type). Hunt points out that waking consciousness functions symbolically as well.[78] Globus also endorses dream symbolism, and even embraces the Jungian unconscious as a source of archetypal formats (if not of purposeful compensations).[79] Both praise the symbolic creativity of dream imagery.

But Boss himself, in fact, allows dreams to convey meaning, in ways not materially different from other interpreters. Returning to the turtle dream, we find that therapy leads to these questions:

> "Isn't it striking that the only animal that gained admittance into your dream world was one with a shell of armor?" . . .
>
> "Are you, waking, now perhaps more aware than you were in your dreaming that the meaningfulness of being torn apart has something to do with your own existence and not only with a turtle in your external environment?"[80]

These questions, although framed in a characteristically contrived existential diction to avoid the implication of symbolism, seem nonetheless to be about the symbolic meaning of the turtle image. But Boss refuses to see symbolism, and he finesses the difficulty by maintaining that dreams are *analogous* rather than symbolic.[81] Here is another example:

> [This] dreamer *saw himself standing on a rubbish heap near his church. The rubbish came from the ongoing total renovation and expansion of the church.* . . .
> [T]he previous day, the subject had realized the large extent to which the reli-

gious commands imposed on him . . . had given way during the maturing process of analysis to a far freer, and more loving, relationship to the divine. While awake, then, he could recognize the crumbling of a narrow "intellectual" relationship to God, and its replacement by a novel relationship of freedom, whereas his dreaming perception responded only to . . . the material, sensory presences of the church and rubbish heap. The alteration of his "intellectual" relationship toward God, so clear to him during his preceding waking state, was totally inaccessible to his dreaming perception.[82]

Pinning everything on the viewpoint of the dream-ego, Boss will not see here an imagery, an apt symbolic way of perceiving, one solidifying or refining the previous day's consciousness. He sees instead a beclouded parallel world—an autonomous world, yet one analogous to waking by reason of the dreamer being the same sort of person in both states, and so finding himself in comparable situations. As with the turtle dream, what results is a specialized, not to say a contrived procedure, one requiring prohibitions which will diminish its appeal to the average dreamer, inhibiting as it is to spontaneous interpretive inclinations. This predicament leads Craig to make an accommodation: a dream image is not a symbol when generated, but to say, "That is symbolic of . . ." is a practical way of speaking, when trying to grasp how the dream is analogous to waking life.[83]

If Boss appears to labor to make distinctions without a difference, it is not just to maintain a philosophical position. It is also a therapeutic choice, one claimed justified by its effects. In this excerpt, Boss is shown speaking at more length about the virtue of his therapeutic style of address:

[A] thirty-year-old woman with two children, who began Daseinsanalytic treatment because of frigidity [had this dream].

I dreamed I was supposed to decline a Latin noun, one of the ones whose masculine ending disguises its feminine gender. I was supposed to decline it with an adjective, so that the feminine endings of the adjective would betray the true gender of the noun, despite its masculine forms. But I had a hard time performing this task; in fact, I never managed to finish it. Even while I was dreaming, I wasn't sure which word was involved. . . .

Here the therapist t[ook] an initial step by just repeating the substance of her dream to the reawakened dreamer. . . .

In order to allow the patient to gain an insight into her present overall condition on the basis of her dreaming behavior, it was imperative not to distort her dreaming Being-in-the-world with symbolic interpretations. . . . Both [dreamer and therapist] would then overlook the extent to which the dreamer failed to perceive that it was she herself who was hiding her femininity behind a masculine appearance . . . known to her only through an alien component of a "dead" language: a Latin noun whose presence was incontrovertible but whose meaning was left vague. Consequently, she was not yet able to grasp, either waking or dreaming, that she needed to change, to "decline," her own masculine demeanor, so that her femininity could begin to shine through. . . .

Whenever a therapist uses symbolic interpretations . . . , he fails to see and to evaluate correctly how far the patient still is from becoming aware of that existential trait of his own existence whose significance corresponds with the meaningfulness of a dreamed object or a dreamed fellow human being. . . .

. . . [But] an analyst who is existentially free to recognize what significances pervade a thing . . . [will] not seize on events from outside the dreaming itself, pointing to these as indicators of the dreaming's "actual," "unconscious," or "symbolic" content. . . . [T]here is something worse than the theoretical inadequacy . . . : namely, disruption of therapy. To consider what great harm may result from this, we have only to consider the extent to which our subject is cut off, while dreaming, from any essential insight into her existential state, and how she can respond only to peripheral commands having to do with grammar beyond her ken. . . . If the woman has been fortunate enough to avoid an "education" in psychology, the symbolic content which the analyst suggests for the Latin word will simply go in one ear and out the other. If the therapist pushes his interpretations, she may find it at best "very interesting." This will make her begin to think about it. Yet it is this very "intellectualization" which prevents her from actually experiencing feelingly important insights into the foundations of her being. . . .

In sum, then, only the following inquiries and suggestions have enough scientific and therapeutic value to be addressed to the reawakened dreamer:

a. "As a person who doesn't know what to live for in your waking life, might not the appearance of a task in your dreaming state signify a first step toward a freer, more meaningful existence? In the world of your dreaming, that task even consisted in a most precise claim on you, i.e., in declining a Latin noun that looks masculine, but is really feminine, as the adjective accompanying it shows.". . .

b. . . . "On the other hand, does it not strike you as strange that in your dreaming you are given a task so separate from yourself, involving only a word from a dead foreign language, and that the task entails highly abstract, intellectual labor, namely, a grammatical declension?"

Once the patient became aware of her dreaming distance from the Latin word, she spontaneously remembered dozens of things, dating as far back as early childhood, toward which her behavior had been similarly distant. It was not long before she began to see the reasons behind her behavior: her parents had encouraged her to maintain an unnatural distance from things so many times that it had become second nature to her.

If, by contrast, the therapist begins searching for early childhood memories before the patient has had a chance to grow fully aware of the behavioral modes that govern her present waking and dreaming existence, the therapy is liable to wind up a Sisyphean labor. . . This insight into the historicity of [neurotic impairment] . . . is itself highly liberating. . . .

Now the time had come when the Daseins-analyst had to repeat and to complete his therapeutic interventions . . . :

"All that happened in your dreaming state has nothing at all to do with your own existence. During the whole time of your dreaming state you were only able to hear of a task referring to a Latin word. But now that you are awake could you not already be more clear sighted than you were while dreaming? Could it not be that now you are able at least to have a presentiment of quite a different task which is awaiting you . . . but one having nevertheless the same essential content of meaningfulness? Could there be a task, for instance, faintly appealing to you and demanding of you as a waking person to bring to light the femininity not only of an external distant Latin word, but the feminine character traits of your own existence? . . . Your dreamt task was of unknown origin, but can you not feel that this task of your waking clearly originates from the essential claim of your own existence, i.e., its demand to carry out all the relational possibilities of which your existence is made up?"

c. At last the therapist may add the encouragement:

"Do you not think yourself that this task will be one which you shall be able to accomplish, in sharp contradiction to the purely intellectual task of your dreaming state, where you finally failed in spite of all your efforts?"[84]*

This dreamer, Boss tells us, is typically "cut off, while dreaming, from any essential insight into her existential state. . . ." But he also considers her dream to be "a first step toward a freer, more meaningful existence." Boss's regard for the dream contains this ambivalence, that while the dream state is fundamentally inferior to waking, it also constitutes a space for discovery or rehearsal of new ways of being-in-the-world—"though he does not even try to explain how this might be possible," a commentator notes.[85]

As for the inferiority of dreams, Boss makes an assessment not unlike the one by Adler, who judged dreams by the standards of the waking state, and found dreams wanting. Dreaming, thinks Boss, is inferior to waking by degrees: while dreaming, we have less insight into the complex meanings of things and are more restricted to mere perceptions; we are less self-reflective, less able to make choices.[86] It adds up to the opinion that waking is the freer state—and freedom is the existentialist's condition for right living. To live right is to take full responsibility for one's being.

---

* Eugene Gendlin (1977) argues that "Boss interprets dreams with phenomenological concepts, but . . . imposes his scheme of ideas and also his personal values onto a dream with as little justification as is done in the method of interpretation he attacks" (p. 57). "Only the general concepts are phenomenological; the interpretations are seemingly quite arbitrary" (p. 64). This comment is a platform for Gendlin's own program for purging the arbitrariness from phenomenological interpretation, a program which led to "focusing" and to verification of interpretation by a "felt shift" in the dreamer (1986).

Rollo May, one of the first to bring existential therapy to the U.S. from Europe, asserts (with Irvin Yalom) that "the human being is responsible for and the author of his or her own world, own life design, own choices and actions. The human being, as Sartre puts it, is 'condemned to freedom.'"[87] A person "will be victimized by circumstances and other people until he or she is able to realize, 'I am the one living, experiencing. I choose my own being.'"[88]

Existential therapy sets itself the task of nurturing free choice. Dream interpretation helps by turning the dream's less free condition to advantage. In both states, says Boss, the "same fundamental existential structures" operate.[89] But the very limitations of the dreaming condition make those structures stand out with highlighted objectivity, when viewed from the vantage of waking.[90] The interpreter looks at dreams, then, for configurations of inhibited freedom: closure, defense, barrier, repulsion.

Note the similarities to Adler's thinking. For Adler, the dream is an inferior product of one's prevailing "life style," and exploitable on that basis. The goal of therapy is to liberate one's "field of action" (being-in-the-world) from neurotic constraints. Adler deemphasizes unconscious causation in favor of conscious responsibility: Adlerians "try to impress the patient with their [sic] power of self-determination."[91] Realization of a sound life style was his equivalent of existential self-actualization.

A notable area of difference between Boss and Adler concerns emotions. Boss has nothing comparable to Adler's idea that the sole function of dreams is to stimulate feelings which prime actions upon awakening. All the same, dream feelings do tell us about the dreamer's *potential* for waking action. Feelings influence actions comparably in the dream world and in the "analogous" world of waking. So looking at the dream, we first ask what actually fills the dream reality and to what is it closed, what is missing; and second, what is the feeling, "particularly the mood that predicates [the dreamer's] way of behaving."[92] These together yield the full phenomenology of the person's dreaming existence, from which to extrapolate an interpretation which bears on waking.*

---

* The interpreting process itself should involve feelings. On the one hand, Boss's is a so-called 'enlightenment therapy', and he tips his hat to Freud for realizing that "self-enlightenment is equivalent to healing" (M. Boss 1977, p. 55). This must not, on the other hand, take the form of intellectualized interpretation. The dreamer "must be made to reexperience [the dream] and reintuit it" (p. 142). Boss is not advocating an immersion in symbolic resonances, of course, nor even 'redreaming' as a sufficient self-healing process. The dreamer needs a certain detachment, a certain conceptual readiness, in order to feel out analogous constellations in her/his waking existence. But as he says discussing the dream "She declines a Latin noun," "'intellectualization'" is inimical to "actually ex-

One emotion considered pivotal by many existentialists is anxiety. They contend that other approaches regard anxiety merely as a symptom, to be removed. Anxiety can be that, agrees May,[93] when it is "neurotic anxiety," i.e., "not appropriate," "destructive," and/or "repressed." But there is also "normal anxiety," which arises inevitably from the very "'givens' of existence." Hence its importance. By Yalom's reckoning, these givens include death, isolation, and meaninglessness—and the freedom with which we confront these.[94] In contrast to the neurotic sort, normal anxiety is appropriate; it does not in itself reflect unfreedom. It can become a stimulus of "awareness and vitality;" it can be used "creatively."[95] May & Yalom contrast two cases of "the empty-nest syndrome" by way of illustrating wrong and right ways to manage existential anxiety:

A 46-year-old mother accompanied the youngest of her four children to the airport, from where he departed for college. She had spent the last 26 years rearing her children and longing for this day. . . . Finally she was free.

Yet as she said good-bye she unexpectedly began sobbing loudly, and on the way home from the airport a deep shudder passed through her body. "It is only natural," she thought. It was only the sadness of saying good-bye to someone she loved very much. But it was much more than that, and the shudder soon turned into raw anxiety. The therapist whom she consulted identified it as a common problem: the empty-nest syndrome. . . . For years she had based her self-esteem on her performance as a mother and suddenly she found no way to validate herself. . . . Gradually, with the help of Valium, supportive psychotherapy, an assertiveness training group, several adult education courses, a lover or two, and a part-time volunteer job, the shudder shrunk to a tremble and then vanished. She returned to her premorbid level of comfort and adaptation.

This patient happened to be part of a psychotherapy research project and there were outcome measures of her psychotherapy. Her treatment results could be described as excellent on each of the measures used—symptom checklists, target problem evaluation, self-esteem. . . . Yet, despite this, it is entirely possible to consider this case as one of missed therapeutic opportunities.

Consider another patient in almost precisely the same life situation. . . . [T]he therapist, who was existentially oriented, attempted to nurse the shudder rather than to anesthetize it. This patient experienced what Kierkegaard called "creative anxiety." The therapist and the patient allowed the anxiety to lead them into important areas for investigation. True, this patient suffered from the empty-nest syndrome; she had problems of self-esteem; she loved her child but also envied him for the chances in life she had never had; and, of course, she felt guilty because of these "ignoble" sentiments.

periencing feelingly important insights into the foundations of [one's] being" (p. 61).

The therapist did not simply allow her to find ways to help her fill her time but plunged into an exploration of the meaning of the fear of the empty nest. She had always desired freedom but now seemed terrified of it. Why?

A dream illuminated the meaning of the shudder. The dream consisted simply of *herself holding in her hand a 35-mm photographic slide of her son juggling and tumbling. The slide was peculiar, however, in that it showed movement; she saw her son in a multitude of positions all at the same time.* In the analysis of the dream her associations revolved around the theme of time. The slide captured and framed time and movement. It kept everything alive but made everything stand still. It froze life. "Time moves on," she said, "and there's no way I can stop it. I didn't want John to grow up. . . . [T]ime moves on for John and it moves on for me as well."

This dream brought her own finiteness into clear focus and, rather than rush to fill time with various distractions, she learned to appreciate time in richer ways than previously. She moved into the realm that Heidegger described as authentic being: she wondered not so much at the way things are but that they are. Although one could argue that therapy helped the second patient more than the first it would not be possible to demonstrate this conclusion on any standard outcome measures. In fact, the second patient probably continued to experience more anxiety than the first did; but anxiety is a part of existence and no individual who continues to grow and create will ever be free of it.[96]

By a compensatory theory of dreaming, this dream of frozen time might be presenting a symbolic insight, as if saying, "Consciousness, here is how you distort life." But for an existentialist, this woman's dream world simply labors under constraints matching those of her waking world, and all of the insight belongs to a subsequent waking state. This is in keeping with Boss's view of the inferiority of insight while dreaming.

I remarked earlier that Boss's regard for dreams contains an ambivalence: while dreams are qualitatively inferior to waking experience, they constitute at the same time a space for existential discovery and rehearsal. If the two worlds are autonomous and contain comparable existential structures, it follows that both should avail for constructive change. Existentialists stress that all existence is oriented more to the future than to the past, and they direct their interventions "toward the future's becoming the present" through the "emergent evolution" of the personality.[97] Dreams partake of that emergent evolution. Adler, by contrast—despite his generally prospective orientation, and despite his finding the whole function of dreams to be future-oriented—, only allows dreams to reinforce the waking life style. Later Adlerians, as we saw, moderate that view. They perceive that dreams contribute helpful solutions. Their position very much resembles that of Boss (and of many other contemporary dreamworkers): "It is most common that certain patterns of human behavior address themselves to people for the first time in their lives in dreaming states. . . ."[98]

It should be noted that Boss is not talking about insight per se within the constitution of the dream; insight he still reserves for waking. He is talking rather about experimentation in living, and usually tentative at that. It might become manifest as the action of a dream stranger, as some feature of the dream scene, or as an experience not yet understood or fully owned by the dream-ego.

The final example of existential dreamwork will be an extended excerpt from Craig, who focuses on this aspect of discovery and rehearsal in dreams more than Boss himself does. Craig indicates that the possibilities revealed in dreams include ones we already recognize, ones we recognize but ignore, and ones we have yet to recognize.[99] He calls dreaming an "existential open house." However, although "[w]e don't keep as tight a guest list dreaming as waking," still, "the guests come from the neighborhood." The object of dreamwork is to enhance the guest list. In the example, therapist and client work with three dreams, one of which evidently shows the dreamer beset by the same constraints as his waking "being-in-the-world"; another, a recurrent dream, shows a thwarted impetus toward change; while the third is said to contain an actual discovery of new experience:

Bob, as I shall call him, was a thirtyish business school graduate student whose initial phase of therapy had focused primarily on his sense of powerlessness, entrapment and shame in his emotionally enmeshed Italian family of origin. For as long as he could remember he had been ambivalently scorned as the "golden boy" and "the black sheep" of the family and he felt hopelessly entwined in this double bind. . . . One day, in his sixth month of therapy, Bob recalled that the previous night he had dreamt of *being at a family gathering where he was being alternately ignored and harassed by siblings and relatives. Throughout his dream, he felt diminished, hurt, helpless, and ashamed.* . . . [Now Bob] was reminded of another dream, a recurring nightmare which he had had for many years . . . of *falling out of a castle tower.* . . .

. . . [I]t typically opened with *his observing a castle from some nearby woods. He* usually *saw a figure, whom he knew to be himself, standing in the window of a turret.* Typically, *he then found himself tumbling out of the window and plunging toward a moat below. At this point, however, Bob was never a distant observer, but suddenly "in" his own body as he plummeted, terrified, toward the water's surface.* He always woke up before landing in the moat, feeling anxious and then relieved.

When Bob's therapist asked him to describe the castle, Bob said it was a great stone structure with high, thick walls around it. Bob was puzzled, however, that . . . he kept "wanting to say it [was] like a prison or a dungeon." . . . Regardless, he imagined it to be a "self-sufficient world" with "lots of feasts and celebrations" and that the family that lived there must have been "powerful," aristocratic, and "aloof," "isolated from the people who lived around them." Bob added that he had no idea how he had ended up in the tower since he was "just there" from the very beginning of his dream. He imagined that he might have been "trying to get away" from the others or that he had been "sent there as a punishment" for something. Bob assumed that, prior to his fall, he had been leaning out of the window, perhaps "to see the countryside or the moat down below," when he had "leaned too far" and "lost his balance." As Bob continued to describe the life-world of his dream he became increasingly animated and articulate. Aspects of his dreaming which had lain unacknowledged in the horizons of this recurrent experience became increasingly visible.

. . . The therapist offered no symbolic interpretations but simply underscored a few of the details of Bob's recall of his dream as such. He . . . then added that he thought it especially interesting that Bob had consistently experienced himself **as himself** only after he had left the confines of this situation, that is, fallen out of his tower. Finally he said he was impressed by Bob's courage, over the years, in being repeatedly open to getting out of these castle-prison walls in spite of the fact that this could only appear as a frightening, catastrophic event. He then paused and inquired, incidentally, if it had ever occurred to Bob that he might actually enjoy his splash in the moat and that he might go for a swim or for a walk in the nearby fields and woods? Although Bob was initially astonished with this last question, as he left the session he was sporting a subtle, slightly mischievous grin.

It is important to notice that neither Bob nor his therapist discussed any of the details of his original "shameful dream" about being alternately ignored and harassed by his family of origin. However, in his next session the following week, Bob reported another dream, this one involving one of his sisters who had been prominent in that previous undiscussed dream. . . . *[H]is sister was crudely speaking about his wife. When his sister continued, Bob suddenly (and uncharacteristically) interrupted her and told her that if that was the way she was going to talk about his wife, she would have to leave his home. He then showed her out immediately!* Bob said he was surprised, when he woke up and remembered the dream, that he had had such a distinct sense of pleasure and relief. He was amazed that he hadn't felt the "least regret!" Bob then added that he believed that the process of reliving his recurrent nightmare the previous day had somehow enabled this new dream. . . . "Somehow just . . . looking all around at the moat and the fields and the castle, just really looking at all this opened something up in me." . . .

In reflecting on this modest vignette, we see that . . . repeatedly, over the years, Bob had found the courage, while dreaming, to leave his ambiguous sequestered heights in th[e] family domain. But the possibility of this event seemed so catastrophic that he could entertain the happening only as unintended and as something he must arrest by waking up before its final, fateful conclusion. So over and over, while dreaming throughout the years he had boldly relived the reality of his terror at becoming himself.

By reconsidering this recurrent nightmare, acknowledging the reality of the dream as such, Bob actually began to feel immediately, in his own viscera, a concrete sense of liberation. This was then followed by the imminent actualization of new possibilities for being-in-the-world. Specifically, in dreaming that very night, Bob achieved what he had never achieved, asleep or awake; for in telling his sister to leave his home, he initiated his own possibilities for autonomous, adult intention, thought and action in relation to his family. . . . Though the months ahead held recurrences of Bob's difficulties in relation to his family, the palpable reality of this latest dream offered him, at last, **a concrete experience of autonomy** with which to compare his all too familiar experiences of flustered confusion. It is important to remember that Bob's experience was no mere symbolic achievement, but rather a tangible actualization while dreaming of hitherto disenfranchised human possibilities.

Here we see how in dreaming we may be open to possibilities which we still dare not acknowledge while fully awake. . . . We might say that dreaming provides us with a sanctuary in which we may take up our own future, entertaining as real and immediate that which is imminent in our development as individuals.[100]

I have characterized Adler's psychology as existential, and in the course of this chapter have pointed out the broadly Adlerian features in Boss and other existential-phenomenological dream theorists. There are also notable differences: in the phenomenological method; in the idea of an autonomous dream world; in different regards for common-sense reality; and in the treatment of feelings. But quite an array of features joins Adler and later existentialists, and sets their approach apart from the depth psychology of Freud and Jung, to which the existential approach forms, as I began by saying, a worthwhile antithesis.

Those common features include the following. Neither accepts that there is such a place or thing as 'the' unconscious. The dream and waking worlds are thought continuous (cp. Freud's dream-thoughts). But judged by waking standards, the dream is held to be generally inferior. On somewhat different bases, both show disregard for the dream as metaphor or symbol. Dreams are believed obscured by ordinary self-deception, not disguise. Emphasis is placed on freedom of self-determination. Both are strongly future-oriented (cp. Jung's purposiveness). And neo-Adlerians, perhaps influenced by existentialism, look for creative experimentation in dreams.

The strength of the existential approach is that it keeps dreamers grounded in their actual experience, in immediacy. Dreamers are to see themselves (and therapists are to see them) "as they really are"[101] in the dream world, and hence the waking one. Insofar as patterns of behavior (life styles) are continuous across the two worlds, the existential attitude facilitates discernment of those patterns.

By treating the dream as a display of the life possibilities we *can* experience, we become positioned to realize those possibilities we *cannot*. This is especially helpful if one follows one's dreams over time, noting the sorts of possibilities which never enter in, or rarely, or only in distanced or distorted ways. Moreover, clearsightedness about such actualities is encouraged by setting aside constructs of the unconscious, which can distract us from seeing how things really are—and also distract us from a sense of responsibility for how things are, and how we can change them. Boss maintains that Jungian amplification "often enough seduces the patient to take refuge, from the personal and concrete, in something distant and alien,"[102] and he says much the same about Freudian focus on causality stemming from the past and the unconscious.

However, the strength of the approach is also its weakness, for in denying the unconscious and narrowing the field of vision to waking-dreaming continuities, it risks sacrificing the wealth of insights which depth psychology draws from its various approximations of unconscious structures, which we may plausibly believe to have some reality of their own.

May & Yalom concede as much, when they profess that the existential contribution "is not a specific technical approach,"[103] but instead involves "the *presuppositions underlying therapy of any kind*."[104] The "'I-Am' experience" they aim to arouse "is not in itself a solution to an individual's problems. It is, rather, the *precondition* for the solution."[105] And Lehmann says: "The existential understanding of the meaning of a dream, of course, does not explain the *causes* for an individual's own world design; nor does it provide material that might be helpful in changing this design. All it can do is demonstrate the nature of the design to the dreamer and to the therapist."[106] Lehmann agrees with Ludwig Binswanger, a pioneer of European existential psychotherapy, who, in trying to achieve a synthesis with psychoanalysis, allowed that existentialism by itself is "clinically almost impotent."[107]* Student psychotherapists may consequently obtain their training "at any number of schools of therapy," say May & Yalom, and remold what they learn there "in existential form."[108]

---

* Binswanger was first a pupil of Jung's, who introduced him to Freud in 1907 (W. McGuire 1974, p. 24). Freud cordially rejected Binswanger's endeavor to apply phenomenology in psychiatry (C. Downing 1977, pp. 86-7), while "Jung was directly acquainted with Boss's own adaptation of Heidegger, and seems even less sympathetic to it than Freud had been to Binswanger's" (p. 87).

Perhaps, but this is somewhat disingenuous about the fundamental contradiction between existential and depth psychology views of the unconscious. Actually, May & Yalom—unlike Adler, Boss, and others cited—do not deny the unconscious. *Man's Unconscious Language* is the subtitle of May's chief contribution to the dream literature, in fact. There he attempts to conform existentialism to psychoanalysis.[109] At the same time, he withholds from the unconscious its classic role as "a reservoir of tendencies, desires and drives from which the motivation of behavior arises."[110] This qualification pretty much voids the concept and levels May's position to the existential norm, whereby the crucial notions of freedom and responsibility are premised on the belief that unconscious structures do not constrain the ego in its choices. Such a belief is bound to conflict with insights from depth psychology. The existential dictum 'I choose my own being' certainly invites Jungian observations of ego inflation and Freudian observations of denial.

Inherent in the existential approach there is a related difficulty: radical adherence to the continuity hypothesis as conceived existentially, with its incordiality to imagery as such and to the capacities of symbolism, means that dream bizarreness can find no positive basis as a feature standing in contrast to waking experience. There results a tendency to equate healthy dreaming exclusively with dreaming which reproduces healthy waking behavior.

This tendency is carried to extremes in the Boss-influenced "functional analysis" (also called "feeling therapy") of Richard Corriere, Werner Karle, and their associates, who say that healthy dreams are "not bizarre."[111] They believe that dreams are feelings trying to express themselves realistically.[112] A symbol, they insist, is an inadequately expressed feeling.[113] Their therapy aims for "transformative" shifts from symbolic, i.e., confused dreaming[114] toward its supposedly natural condition,[115] which is "distortion-free"[116] and realistic ("bodily sensations and nonsymbolic images"[117]). By their lights, a good dream is one which is, in Hunt's paraphrase, "true to the deliberate activity, forcefulness, and extraversion that they value in everyday waking life. So much for the diversity of living," chides Hunt, "let alone in dreaming."[118]*

---

* This anti-symbolic posture of Corriere, Karle et al. is only slightly ameliorated by the interesting few pages these authors devote to the marginal values of symbolism (R. Corriere, W. Karle, L. Woldenberg & J. Hart, 1980, p. 75ff.; W. Karle, R. Corriere, J. Hart & L. Woldenberg, 1980, pp. 23–4). Hunt himself does not draw the implication of his remarks about these authors for Boss's existentialism, and treats Boss kindly. These authors do, however, largely endorse Boss's dream theories, just not his clinical methods (ibid., p. 26). Looking at "*the way the dreamer is functioning in the dream* . . . frees us from the need to figure out what the symbols mean" (R. Corriere, W. Karle, L. Woldenberg & J. Hart, 1980, p. 12).

In the case of Boss, the obligation he places himself under to maneuver around a supposedly nonexistent symbolism produces an artificiality of language which would make me, for one, impatient if I were his client. Some other existentialists read less doctrinaire. Take Craig's treatment of the three dreams including "He falls from a turret toward a moat" several pages back. On the one hand, Craig describes as "no mere symbolic achievement" the dreamer's personality development within his dream world. But on the other hand, Craig states that "Bob had found courage, while dreaming, to leave his ambiguous sequestered heights in the family domain." This is nothing if not symbolic interpretation. No need to count May's hybrid neo-psychoanalytic position, receptive to the art, wisdom, and healing potential of dream symbols, in his chapter "Dreams and Symbols."[119] And as pointed out, some of Boss's interpretations are also symbolic in all but name.

If the approach can be hedged in this way, and also hedged by acknowledging the need for supplementation by other psychologies (May & Yalom), then perhaps the best way to regard existentialism is as a dialectical position not requiring to be sustained singlemindedly. In that role, the existential approach makes its claim for inclusion in an eclectic dreamwork toolkit. For some people, and for everyone sometimes, an existential orientation to reality and to dreamwork is unquestionably beneficial. The insistence on seeing things as they are and the lesson of freedom are good antidotes to fatalism, inertia, or doctrinaire excess. One need not agree to discard the fundamental assumptions of Jung and Freud in order to find in existentialism a helpful foil to Jungian fancy or Freudian reduction.

It has been the aim of the originators of existential psychotherapy that "it would influence therapy of all schools."[120] So recall May & Yalom in 1989, confident that this has in fact transpired.

This chapter has juxtaposed Adler with later existential dream psychologies, particularly that of Boss. Without reiterating the points of comparison (many of which will be touched upon again in the next chapter, which follows Adler's influence in another direction), I think it will be seen that the Adlerian heritage has been carried into the present by means of existentialism and the influence of existentialism on other approaches.

□ 5 □

Culturalism

Together with existentialism and Gestalt, culturalism is one of the three schools of dreamwork mentioned in chapter 4 as following lines originally drawn by Adler. In the collaborative volume of Fosshage & Loew, which I cited there to exemplify the absence of acknowledgement given Adler's influence, culturalism is represented by Walter Bonime. His approach will be discussed now to illustrate the fundamentals of culturalism and its points of congruence with Adler. This will be followed by a survey of contemporaries who emphasize social and societal aspects of dreamwork, with particular attention to Montague Ullman.

Walter Bonime

As its title suggests, Bonime's *The Clinical Use of Dreams* (1962) is in large part a handbook for practitioners. It does not mention Adler. Ullman's foreword, however,—which Bonime elsewhere commends to readers as "a clear, extensive statement of the 'culturalist' orientation"[1]—, leaves no doubt as to Adler's place in the trend of psychoanalysis labelled culturalist. The major representatives of culturalism, by Ullman's reckoning (modestly excluding himself), include Horney, Kelman, Robbins, Fromm, Sullivan, and Bonime. Ullman states that "[i]t was Adler who took the first steps in creating a social base for psychoanalytic theory."[2] And a contemporary Adlerian can say of Bonime's book that he "could find nothing with which an Adlerian could disagree."[3]

As do Adler and the existentialists, Bonime defines himself in contrast to Freud by deemphasizing instinct: "[M]an's personality is not basically determined by the presence, nature, and vicissitudes of sexuality or any other instinct. . . ."[4] But whereas for existentialists the focal contrast to instinct is freedom, Bonime and other culturalists focus on social influences and learning. Bonime regards "personality as a product of culture. . . ."[5] The relation between culture and dream life is the aspect of culturalism of chief interest here, and to which we will turn after first noting some general features of Bonime's dream psychology.

A conspicuous common feature of Bonime, Adler, and the existentialists is minimization of the unconscious, and with it, the concept of instinct. Like Boss, Bonime makes "no employment of a construct of an 'unconscious'." And in contrast to Freud and Jung, Bonime is together with Adler and Boss when he sees "a continuum between sleeping and waking consciousness, and between awareness and unawareness."[6] Bonime concentrates on the dreamer's present; effort is devoted to "uncovering the referents of the dream to the characterological and social realities of the patient's life."[7] This orientation corresponds to Adler's notion of 'life style' and to the identification of coping devices operating in both states.

As for Adler and Boss, dreaming engages no special disguise process, but instead operates along the ordinary spectrum from honesty and awareness to self-deception and ignorance. But whereas Adler thought self-deception more pervasive in dreams, Bonime seems to find it moreso awake, when a person is generally in some denial. "It is the awake patient who disguises his own feelings and thoughts . . . in order to maintain his self-image. . . ."[8] This sounds like "repression," a concept Bonime professes to discard, along with instincts and the unconscious.[9] But this repression does not drive a beclouding Freudian 'dream-work'. Here Bonime's sense of dreams approaches Jung's. The dream's figurative language is not disguise, as difficult as it often is to understand. Dreams reveal, they do not conceal.

There is even an implicit recognition of compensation at work, much as there is in the neo-Adlerian interpretation of the tax cheat's dream "He was in jail" (ch. 4, p. 139), where a truer feeling is raised by the dream to compensate a misguided conscious intention. Adlerians talk about constructive rehearsal and invention of new perspectives in dreams. Bonime speaks even more strongly of dreams as being capable of "leaping forward into symbolic insight."[10] But this is a compensatory function which is ego-based and fortuitous, without the dynamics of a Jungian Self-system. So when Bonime calls dreams "probably the most authentic presentation of the personality," he is saying "authentic" not as centered or enlightened, but only as unvarnished, showing fears, needs, hopes, and coping mechanisms. Dreams exhibit to the awake dreamer "accurate information about his own attitudes,"[11] if s/he is ready to appreciate it.

Feelings. If Bonime is known for anything, it is for an insistent emphasis on feelings as the keystone of dream interpretation. "The clinical usefulness of dreams is, in fact, directly proportional to the attention paid to feelings in dreams."[12] This may or may not show the influence of Adler, whose dream theory turns on the schema *dream → feeling → behavior*. Bonime does not employ that formula, but it is interesting, in view of their other congruences, to note this common emphasis.

Of the four elements, actions, characters, settings, and feelings, feelings are the best "indicators of the total personality."[13] For awake behavior also, feelings give the best clue to its essential drift. Unless psychological work keeps feelings in focus, the other elements of both waking and dreamt situations often "remain hopelessly tangled in self-deception and confusion."[14] One reason Bonime gives feelings such importance is that they are irreducibly authentic; they constitute "an immediate, undeniable datum."[15] Just as waking emotions are, in a sense, true even when, for reasons of denial or ignorance, "the attendant meaning is not clearly conceptualized,"[16] so feelings dreamt are "always an authentic response to something in the patient's life."[17] As such, they offer a secure bridge between the waking and dreamt configurations of the dreamer's existence.

Freud also advised that "the interpretation of a dream might well begin with its affect, for it is likely to be 'real,' even if, in the dream, it most often is attached to an 'unreal'" manifest image.[18] One writer states the principle as absolute: "The affect accompanying the dream is always appropriate to the latent content."[19] Freud and most Freudians, however, believe that the feelings are only partially immune to disguise and that they may well turn up reversed, distorted, or omitted.[20]*

A Jungian, Mary Ann Mattoon, recommends a certain suspicion of dream feelings, for a different reason: not because disguise can make them unauthentic, but because they may belong to the ego, and so represent resistance to the compensatory unconscious. Thus we may devalue something positive or value something negative because "woven into the dream is an evaluative response that is characteristic of the dreamer in waking life. He or she is happy, sad, repelled, or attracted by the dream experiences as would be the

---

* The following interpretation of the dream of an 8-year-old girl by Robert Gillman (1987, p. 30) ostensibly illustrates reversal of a feeling: " '*I went to see the Mona Lisa but the museum had tables we were eating at. I looked up and saw the Mona Lisa was missing from its frame. It had torn cut edges. I was the first to see and told the guard and the next day told my class in school and felt proud I was the first to know.*' . . . She was stuck with the analyst while her sister, toward whom she was intensely jealous, was out having a fine time eating with her mother. And she had been stuck on a museum trip with her mother while her sister had enjoyed an outing with her father. Her pride in the dream represented the opposite, the disappointment and humiliation over being cut out of the fun."

case if they actually happened." Dreamt feelings found to be of this sort are best "ignored, on the ground that they are accretions from consciousness."[21]*

Both the Freudian and Jungian reservations about the reliability of dream feelings arise from constructs of the unconscious. To Bonime, who does not hold with disguise and who thinks that the ego, not an unconscious Self, is the center of reference, no reason presents itself to question the authenticity or bearing of dream feelings.

That dream feelings are always authentic does not mean to Bonime that they are necessarily obvious to us. Our culture, in Bonime's view, typically breeds denial of feelings.[22] Along that line, a survey by Robert McCarley & J. Allan Hobson finds explicit mention of emotions in a mere one-eighth of lab-collected dreams.[23] Such a result must surely be due to obtuseness, or lack of fluency, about one's own emotions.** The profit from developing discriminating attention to emotions, which many of us do lack, is well expressed by Ernest Rossi:

> With some sensitivity the typical dream report can be enriched by an awareness of the multiplicity of feelings behind even simple behaviors in the dream. *The irate husband walks out on his wife and children* in a dream. But as he now looks

---

* Dreams which compensate by exaggeration can also present feelings which are not directly true to the compensatory purpose of the dream. Recall the dream "He mounts upward on empty air" (ch. 3, p. 110). Joel Covitz (1990, pp. 110-1) describes a comparable dream in which euphoria is interpreted as a warning to the dreamer. Another positively toned dream which compensates by exaggeration of a feeling is discussed by Max Zeller (1990 [1975], pp. 23-6).

** Another study, by Frederick Snyder, similarly found that emotion appears in less than 35% of dream reports, and that when present it is often "vague in quality" ("The phenomenology of REM dreaming," in H. Madow & L. H. Snow, editors, *The Psychodynamic Implications of Physiological Studies on Dreams*, Springfield, Illinois: Charles C. Thomas, 1970, cited by T. A. Nielsen, D. Deslauriers & G. W. Baylor 1991, p. 287). But studies such as that by Nielsen et al., more sensitively designed to elicit reports of emotions, show that emotion is present in virtually every dream, and that usually there is a sequence or complex of emotions. Ariane Loepfe (1989, p. 5) finds that only about 10% of countable perceptual events in dreams are emotional (the rest are sensory and cognitive in roughly equal proportions), but that over 90% of dreams are governed by a global emotion, apart from other transitory emotions. Rosalind Cartwright observes that "[f]eelings serve as the thread that links one dream image to the next and all the dreams of a night to one another" (R. Cartwright & L. Lamberg 1992, p. 59).

Bert O. States (1988, p. 47) makes a point about dream images and feelings made previously by Coleridge and reiterated by Jorge Luis Borges: "Coleridge wrote that in waking, images inspire feeling, while in sleep feelings inspire images. . . . If a tiger should come into this room, we would feel fear; if we feel fear asleep, we engender a tiger" (J. L. Borges 1976, p. 8). This formula contains much truth, but it oversimplifies a process in which image and affect can have a feedback or feedforward influence on one another. Borges continues: "I have said a tiger, but since the fear precedes the apparition improvised to understand it, we can project the horror onto any figure, which in waking is not necessarily horrifying."

into his dream feelings more deeply he also senses the genuine sorrow he felt for them, the bluff quality of his anger and the inner fear he also experienced on leaving.[24]

Some of us, on the other hand, are less receptive to our feelings awake than in our dreams, and Bonime uses dreamt feelings, with their authentic references in the dreamer's waking life, to draw the dreamer toward waking self-awareness.* In an article about the dreams of nonpsychotic depressives, for example, Bonime shows how, by focusing on dream affects, one gets to the "living emotion underlying much of [the] depressive practice."[25]

A last point from Bonime on feelings: another reason we may not notice them in dreams is that they can represent themselves in two ways, experientially and symbolically. "Experiential" fear, for example, is felt as fear, but "symbolized" fear may not be attended by that emotion:

> In one dream, for example, *feces on the leg, after* what would ordinarily be considered *a harrowing experience*, betrayed associatively that a patient had really been "scared shitless," although she reported having experienced *no feeling. . . .*
> . . . [A man] who looked for sexual solace with other women when he was angry at his wife, symbolized **anger** in a dream in which *a small valve for letting off steam, like that on top of a boiler, was situated on the end of his erect penis.*
> . . . Another woman patient depicted depression in her dream by *heavy leaden feet. . . .*
> . . . In each of these examples, the specific affect was not felt during the dream, but its presence was symbolized.[26]

Sometimes the complexity of feelings, which can include feelings about having other feelings, comes to light by seeing how experiential and symbolized feelings interplay:

> Symbolized feeling was exemplified in the dream of the engineer whose **anger** was represented by *a cap popping off the top of an otherwise carefully regulated machine. . . .*
> . . . *[H]e experienced annoyance* as an affect during the dream. The popping cap was a symbolized feeling, anger (blowing his top, flipping his lid). The annoyance (occurring as experiential feeling) was his response to his own failure to achieve perfect control.[27]

What follows is a fuller sample of Bonime's style of work with dreams. Bonime finds that the manifestly sexual imagery of this dream expresses a fundamentally nonsexual issue. Here where an Oedipal interpretation offers

---

* Writing 30 years later, Cartwright likewise teaches that dreams help us get in touch with our waking feelings (R. Cartwright & L. Lamberg 1992, pp. 108–10).

itself, he pointedly foregoes examination of Freudian psychosexual motivations from a supposed unconscious. He views sexuality as "neither prior nor governing, but interrelated with all other aspects of the personality as this evolves out of interpersonal experience."[28] While concerned with antecedent experience, the interpretation shows the dream moving toward resolution of a current situation. Notice the attention given feelings:

This was reported by a thirty-year-old bachelor, experiencing, as he approached marriage, a mixture of anxiety and depression. . . . He had been raised as an only child by a superficial, falsely gracious, middle-class mother who considered most people beneath her family in quality. Both parents had hovered over the patient throughout his childhood. . . . [E]ven after he had become a successfully developing ophthalmologist, she would still call him on snowy mornings to advise his wearing galoshes. After he was already comfortably self-supporting, it had once been a momentous and anxiety-ridden step, as he took leave of his parents at the end of a routine visit, for him finally to use his own money for the subway.

By the time of the dream reported below, he had made much progress in becoming independent of his parents, had concluded several relatively long-term affairs with women, was well-established professionally, and was on the verge of marriage to a sound and affectionate woman. The occasional dutiful visits to his parents were, as in the past, unrewarding.

After visiting them one sunday afternoon when his fiancee was out of town, he had the dream: *"Three people were sleeping, wearing three condoms. They were all in one very big bed. They were supposed to be using condoms for some active sexual activity, not necessarily with a prostitute, but certainly someone with whom there was no attachment. Instead they each had a nocturnal emission with the condoms on, and the thought crossed my mind in the dream that it would be messy and wet and a waste of the condom. The three condoms cost forty-five cents.*

"It was weird. *I had a feeling that the three people were vaguely me, my* **father,** *and my* **mother,** *and that my mother had given out the condoms,* but her having a condom doesn't seem right—a female doesn't need a condom."

His first association was, "Yesterday afternoon I went with my parents to a neighborhood movie. I got up and bought chocolate bonbons for the three of us. They cost forty-five cents. In one scene of the movie a girl who reminded me of my girl said something about the difference between genuineness and superficial trappings." Then he went on to discuss a relationship with a woman in which he had sought to avoid superficiality and to have a meaningful contact. I asked him what his **feeling** was in the dream and he answered, **"Death warmed over. . . ."**

When I asked what he thought was the meaning of the dream, he replied slowly, "I don't know—something about sterileness, our family's sterileness—I'm included." He was silent for a few moments and then added, "I think it's a concern about my ability to bear fruit in a relationship."

"So you really see yourself with the same kind of sterility as your mother and father?"

"Yes," he said, "I've had no relationships that have really born fruit. What was the forty-five cents for condoms? Oh, that was the forty-five cents I paid for the bonbons. That was the extent of my participation with my parents."

Again I carried his thought along, saying, "That's as much as you have to offer them, or they you? The relationship among you is about as fruitful as the three of you lying there having wet dreams into condoms."

His thoughts shifted to his future wife. "I suppose I'm concerned about not having much to offer the girl I'm marrying."

Often he spoke with contempt of his mother's emotional stinginess and falseness, of the inhospitable atmosphere in his home as he grew up, of the lack of family friends, of the lack of affection between his parents, and of his mother's having "worn the pants." He had often spoken of his mother's quick smile but complete lack of warmth. The patient in his own life had, in spite of many contacts, experienced little intimacy or friendship. . . .

. . . I said, "You felt in the dream that your mother had given out the condoms. At the movies it was actually you who had given out the bonbons. It's as though you feel that what you have to offer is the same as what your mother offers, that you are like your mother. That is the sterility in your relationships with your parents and others. What could be emptier, more sterile, than a wet dream into a condom?"

He concluded the hour with the remark, "But I've been feeling warm toward my girl. It goes in cycles."

My own final comment was to the effect that he did feel his greatest warmth toward the woman he was going to marry—that the problem of the dream was not his warmth, which he did show at times, but his concern about the lack of it . . . , the sense that his engagement in human relationships was like "death warmed over."

. . . A few weeks later . . . he added, "I remember going to that movie—the three of us sitting there. There was no intercourse—the only intercourse was my getting them the bonbons. The movie was the ejaculation—a pleasant sensation, no more. My mother being masculine that way and distributing the condoms— she's been the initiator of that kind of sterile activity." It was this kind of sterile human intercourse that became illuminated by the dream as an important aspect of the patient's feeling and behavior. . . .

Naturally the presence in the dream of the adult patient in bed with both of his parents in a sexual context, and at a time in his life when he is disturbed by the prospect of marriage, offers rich speculative possibilities for Oedipal interpretation. Such an interpretation would, however, be arbitrary. It would be the application of a construct from outside of the patient's biography, and would result merely in substituting one set of symbols for another. There was a real and immediate problem to tackle—the problem of his unwillingness to fructify a relationship, to give himself to the enhancement of another.[29]

Social Dimensions of Culturalism

We see that Bonime frames his assessment of the immature ophthalmologist's well-being in terms of interpersonal capacity. In deflecting the oedipal interpretation, he guides attention away from the unconscious to the ongoing social dynamics of the family. This brings us to the interpersonal and societal dimensions of culturalism, and, briefly, their foreshadowings in Adler.

Adler. Adler had pioneered in founding family therapy clinics. He emphasized the influence of family configuration on the formation of life style, exploring among other topics the effects of birth order on personality. Both Adler's and Bonime's are interpersonal psychologies. Moreover, both factor in larger societal influences. Adler celebrated "the feeling of being socially embedded, the willingness to contribute to the communal life for the common weal," a quality he called *social interest.*[30] One Adlerian rates social interest as Adler's fundamental biological concept, comparable to Freud's instincts and Jung's archetypes.[31] Social interest should set the tone for all relations, from marriage and friendship to work and other connections with society at large. Its opposite, self-centeredness, is the signature of mental ill health. "All failures—neurotics, psychotics, criminals, drunkards, problem children, suicides, perverts and prostitutes—are failures because they are lacking in fellow-feeling and social interest."[32] They "concern themselves with their own superiority, protecting themselves from threats to their sense of personal worth." But, adds Harold Mosak, "[i]f we regard ourselves as fellow human beings with fellow feeling, we are socially contributive people interested in the common welfare and, by Adler's pragmatic definition of *normality*, mentally healthy."[33]

Reconsider, from this point of view, the Adlerian dream interpretations quoted in chapter 4:

The "getter" in the dream "'Take anything you want'" (p. 134) is deemed unhealthy for his self-centered expectations of his social milieu.

Adler's dilemma as military doctor is resolved by recourse to objective, common-sense standards of social equity ("He was a murderer," p. 137).

The tax cheat's stroke of conscience returns him to the civic straight and narrow ("He was in jail," p. 139). All these dream readings concentrate on social relations of the ego to other persons and one's society, rather than on issues of the instincts or of the inner psyche.

His conventional tone notwithstanding, Adler's 'normality' was not that uncritical adjustment to social norms, that conformity, which Erich Fromm was to accuse psychiatry in the 1950s of instilling.[34] If no radical, he was a "social reformer" who spoke on crime, education, war, mass psychology, nationalism, etc.[35] He drew connections between the conditions of industrial society and neurosis, explaining that a healthy individual rejects "the faulty values that culture projects."[36]

Walter Bonime. There is likewise a social critique implicit in Bonime's book from 1962. His diagnosis, which sounds a little dated now, identifies two mutually reinforcing social attitudes which our culture inculcates, namely "cynicism" and "competitiveness." Cynicism he calls disbelief in genuine affection and friendliness. "It denies the possibility of a primary concern for another's welfare." Cynicism develops out of family life where affection "is subtly combined with exploitative and manipulative practices." The parents "exploit the children for the fulfillment of their own 'needs,' under the guise and with the self-delusion that this is love." This false element is an effect of "the pervasively manipulative, competitive" values of our culture, which drives the parents to be successful—among other ways, as parents.[37] Bonime depicts the ophthalmologist in these terms: "[W]hile depriving him of adult respect, his parents were introducing him around as 'my son, the doctor.' The man was able to 'see through' everyone," and this crippled his capacity for intimate ties.[38] In another context Bonime describes how parental competitiveness reappears in the developing cynic. "Vying with others to fend off their influence becomes itself an important basis of his sense of effective functioning." He nurtures a sense of "personal power" by imitating the manipulations used on him. He becomes adept at detecting, masking, and simulating feelings.[39]

Transposed into Adlerian terminology, Bonime identified our culture's dominant *life style*, by which we strive for false *superiority*. And the young ophthalmologist's cynicism and competitiveness, his unpreparedness "to give himself to the enhancement of another," is his lack of *social interest*.

Erich Fromm. In his still widely read book on dreams from 1951, *The Forgotten Language*, Fromm's description of the unconscious approximates the Adlerian-existential axis of continuity: "[C]onscious and unconscious are only different states of mind referring to different states of existence." The unconscious is simply mentation during sleep inactivity. This unconscious "is neither Jung's mythical realm . . . nor Freud's seat of irrational libidinal forces."[40] Nevertheless, elsewhere Fromm avows the Freudian unconscious as "a truly irrational force."[41] While rejecting, as did Jung, the prepotency of Freudian instincts—sex, aggression, hunger—, he retains Freud's notion of what an instinct is. Thus he passes over the possibility that man's more specifically human needs, which Fromm registers among the crucial "conditions of his existence,"[42]—relatedness, transcendence, rootedness—, may also possess an instinctual core. Moreover, Fromm's dream theory, while it emphasizes the constructive trend in night mentation, also incorporates the fundamentals of Freudian disguise. But where Fromm definitely parts from Freud is in regard to societal influences on the individual.

There is a certain parallel between Freud's dream theory and his view of society. Just as dreaming involves a quasisymptomatic repression of primitive energies, so culture comprises a collective defense mechanism against those energies. If we had any choice, it could only be between instinctive bestiality, without culture, and repression and sublimation with it. The latter condition prevails, and renders individual neuroses inevitable. This is truly a dark assessment of society, but not one which suggested to Freud a basis for differential criticism of specific societies. A point which Bonime made about Freud is by now commonplace, that he was blind to the idiosyncracies of his own Viennese middle-class culture, whose patriarchal repressiveness bred the sexual neuroses which Freud observed as universal sexuality, not Viennese patriarchy[43] (ch. 2, p. 68). Fromm contributed to this reevaluation of Freud by reinterpreting the Oedipus myth in terms of "interpersonal relationships" and "attitudes to authority" instead of infantile sexuality.[44]

The culturalist social critique begins from the beliefs that man is not inescapably maladjusted by virtue of his biological endowment; that culture can be adaptive; and, therefore, that specific cultures can be criticized for being maladaptive.[45] This line is not prominent, unfortunately, in *The Forgotten Language*. There, Fromm merely tips his hand by saying that societies become distorted by the struggle for limited means of production, which has an impact on the minds of both oppressors and oppressed; and he comments that our society being what it is, our spontaneous values during sleep are often better than our waking values.[46] But in *The Sane Society*, Fromm makes a full "critical evaluation of the effect of contemporary Western culture . . . [on] mental health and sanity."[47]

Fromm develops the thesis that sick societies create "socially patterned defects," superimposed over personal neuroses, or "individual defects."[48] His diagnosis of our sickness draws heavily on an updated Marxist analysis of class and alienation of labor, to which is added a liberal's emphasis on the value of the individual, together with an account of existential alienation under conditions of mass culture, engulfing owner and worker alike. Fromm criticizes Marx, Soviet communism (as was) and British socialism (also as was) for their narrow preoccupation with the economic and political structure of society, thereby losing track of the humane aspirations of socialism. His own socialist solution he terms "humanistic communitarian socialism,"[49] with goals owing more, Fromm says, to the idealism of early socialists such as Owens and Proudhon than to Marx.

Montague Ullman. If, regrettably, *The Sane Society* has nothing to say about the social dimension of dream life, the omission has in part been made good by Ullman. Ullman calls himself a "neoculturalist."[50] He has not articulated a full socialist agenda—the climate has discouraged that in a number of ways—, but in showing how dreamwork and social consciousness bear on one another, he acknowledges the influence of Fromm's social analysis.[51]* With it, he combines Adler's penchant for community outreach. Ullman is the major promoter (in the best sense) of self-help dream groups.

Besides its social emphasis, Ullman's dream approach has other culturalist features with Adlerian resonances: Ullman emphasizes the feeling aspect of dreams, their purposiveness and future orientation, and their continuity with waking. And he generally demotes the unconscious.

Ullman, like Bonime, particularly focuses on feelings for dream interpretation. "Asleep and dreaming, we move into the feeling dimension of our existence."[52] His group dreamwork method suggests that after a member has related a dream, and has satisfied requests for simple clarifications, then the dreamer should become the listener while the others make "the dream their own."[53] This they do first by verbalizing the feelings they empathetically experienced while hearing the dream.** The purpose is to remind the dreamer

---

* It gives an interesting historical perspective, to recall that in the very shadow of Joe McCarthy a prominent U.S. intellectual such as Fromm would still publish a widely circulated book of expressly socialist ideas. As a young man, Ullman himself did publish an article "under a pseudonym during the McCarthy era" (personal communication, 1993) revealing the influence of Marxism on his culturalism. "L. S. Williamson" (1955) asserted that while everyone distorts reality out of psychological "expediency," all things being equal, a worker is better integrated than a capitalist, because the capitalist has to rationalize his complicity in unjust class relationships (pp. 26–7). But neurosis and psychosis can result on both sides from "exploitative activity," so that one aspect of psychotherapy is political education (p. 28). Reality shapes dreams, so political realities must be understood to understand dreams (pp. 28–9). Dreams in turn expose political realities. Socioeconomic as well as personal "contradictions" are "deepened and brought closer to full awareness" by dreaming (pp. 29–30). More recently, Jeremy Taylor (1992a, pp. 23 and 27) has expressed similar thoughts, but couched in the more diffuse radicalism of the 1990s. Dreaming is "inherently 'radical' because it gets to the truth." Dreams "regularly offer specific creative inspiration for our collective struggles. . ." (p. 118). With his habitual bent for overstatement, Taylor calls "paying attention to our dreams . . . the single best and most reliable way" of priming the mind for "collective liberation and self-determination" (p. 114).

** Briefly, the group members continue to make "the dream their own" by reflecting on the metaphors in the dream. At this and only at this stage of the process, "the game," members are free to range as far afield as they care to, e.g., introducing theoretical constructs from Freud, Jung or whatever. They may relate the dream feelings and meanings to their own actual lives, or they may fish for meaning in what they know of the dreamer's life, as long as they pretend they are speaking of themselves, saying, "In my dream," or "If it were my dream and I had a mother who," etc. At this stage, the convention of calling the dream one's own is strictly observed. This keeps everyone alive to the fact that everything being said is no more than projection. (I notice that Jeremy Taylor 1992a,

of the subtleties of her/his own dreamt feelings. This awareness is critical for interpretation, because feelings "register the state of our relations with others. It is this aspect of our lives that dreams monitor most sensitively."[54] Feelings also link the present and past: "Residual emotional loose ends from the day before seem to pry open vulnerable areas. These in turn link up with historically antecedent but related experiences."[55] The sleeper's orientation, however, "is not primarily to his own past, but to the kind of immediate future situation to which he may awaken."[56]* Dreaming provides "a steering mechanism that orients us to the future."[57]

With the caveat that "dream life does seem to have a reality of its own," and that "its relationship to what we call 'waking reality' remains to be defined,"[58] Ullman's practical position is that, as an operation for addressing pending problems, dreaming is continuous with waking, but with a certain division of labor: the dream is better at epitomizing the problem, waking, at reaching solutions.

Ullman finds that dreams tend to have a three-act dramatic structure. The first two acts present the problem and give it a life-historical context. They do so, he believes (with Bonime), without disguise in the Freudian sense.

---

p. 106, claims "the 'if it were my dream' form" as a development of his own.) The dreamer listens to these contributions without responding until they are completed. At that point, the dream is firmly returned to the dreamer for the remainder of the process. Now without being interrupted, the dreamer responds to member projections, introduces associations, and speculates about the dream's meaning. When finished, a dialogue begins. The dreamer is first prompted for thoughts just before sleep, and for events from the dream day and the recent past which may connect with the dream. Next, the members "play back" the dream by reading sections of it and asking for further associations (members had copied the dream verbatim at first telling). Anyone can jump in with suggestive questions, as long as they are not leading, that is, are confined to the dream itself and what the dreamer has already owned to. The same restrictions apply when the members now "orchestrate" their final thoughts about the dream. Finally, the dreamer offers concluding thoughts. The only remaining step is for the dreamer to share any further insights at the beginning of the next session.

Ann Shuttleworth-Jordan & Graham Saayman (1989) conducted an experiment which they interpret to show that the 'if it were my dream' step tends either to cause (1) distancing, if the comments do not touch upon the dreamer's issues, or (2) anxiety and defensiveness due to premature intrusion, if they do. Ullman in a personal communication to the authors responded that such effects occur, if at all, only as a new group familiarizes itself with the process and each other (p. 519).

* This statement bears a relation to Snyder's "sentinel hypothesis" of dreaming, according to which a function of REM sleep is to prime an animal to awaken to external, predatory dangers in an alert condition (F. Snyder, "Toward an evolutionary theory of dreaming," *American Journal of Psychiatry* 123, pp. 121–42, 1966, cited by J. Tolaas & M. Ullman 1979, p. 192). A similar suggestion was earlier made by W. H. R. Rivers (1923, pp. 182–5), with respect to dreaming (but of course not REM). According to a related set of hypotheses, REM sleep is a "general arousal mechanism" which maintains the "tonus" of the cerebral cortex to prevent severe disorganization and thus to allow an adaptive level of interest and a capacity to act in the outside world once awakened (H. S. Ephron & P. Carrington 1966; H. P. Roffwarg, J. Muzio & W. C. Dement, "The

"When I talk about honesty [in dreams], I'm not saying we are angels without defenses, I'm just saying that our dishonesty is honestly portrayed; it's confronting us, that's all."[59] The unconscious is "unknown but not unknowable,"[60] and "[t]he dream is a kind of emotional range finder that locates our deeply felt and true position. . . ."[61]

Now comes the third act, which "is devoted to an effort at resolution."[62] Here I find a certain ambivalence in Ullman's evaluation of dreams. On the positive side, he writes that "[t]ransformation and change and, with them, the element of novelty, are just as much features of dream consciousness as they are of waking consciousness."[63] Sometimes "some internal rearrangement occurs that exposes new sources of genuine strength, creativity, and mastery."[64] Just as Bonime sees "leaping forward into symbolic insight" in dreams,[65] Ullman discerns a "surging, forward-looking, exploring, chance-taking operation. . . ."[66] Further, dreams connect us with "our uncorrupted core of being. . . ."[67]

But there is also a negative side to Ullman's evaluation of dreams, perhaps unexpectedly so from one whose theory of dream function turns on its future-orientation, and who is a convinced explorer of dream telepathy.[68] On the negative side, Ullman more or less follows Adler and the ego psychologists in asserting that dream solutions are confined to "the range and extent of [the dreamer's] existing characterological strengths and weaknesses."[69] Our dreams "come somewhere out of our life history and they are limited by that life history." Their helpfulness is circumscribed by the past, "they cannot promise solutions to life situations where no solution yet exists."[70] Solutions "have to be found in further experience in the waking state."[71]

I am not certain these two sides can be logically reconciled, though they seem to balance out to a moderate position. Dreams reflect "the balance be-

---

ontogenetic development of the human sleep dream cycle," *Science* 152, pp. 604–18, 1966, cited by I. Lewin & J. L. Singer 1991, p. 399; S. J. Ellman & L. N. Weinstein 1991, p. 472).

Ullman formulated his "vigilance" hypothesis in a talk given in 1953, a decade before Snyder's sentinel hypothesis and without knowledge of the sleep monitoring undertaken in the same year (M. Ullman, personal communication, 1993). "With the evolution of human society, the nature of the vigilance mechanism connected with dreaming was transformed from one involving physical danger to one involving psychological danger" and "relatedness to society" (M. Ullman 1986b, pp. 375 and 380). Social vigilance superseded 'sentinel' vigilance, after vigilance for the *awake* human had become substantially concerned with the social milieu (M. Ullman 1969b, p. 699). Dreaming provides further processing of social information absorbed during the day. Now the function of dream-caused awakening per se—no longer that of readiness to react to predatory danger—is two-fold: to facilitate dream recall and confrontation with the truthful information in the dream (L. S. Williamson 1955, pp. 39–40; M. Ullman 1962, pp. 24–5), or to terminate the dream to avoid an overload of painful affects (M. Ullman 1962, pp. 22–3; 1986b, p. 380).

tween the defensive and growth-potential aspects of the personality involv-ed."[72] Resolutions can be achieved by "denial, evasion, and self-deception"[73] and/or by "creative utilization of positive resources and growth potential."[74] While dreams are virtually always creative in the weak sense of generating meaningful metaphors, dreams are only occasionally creative in the strong sense of generating feasible solutions to the problems metaphorically repre-sented.

But what tilts the balance in favor of creative problem-solving, and what distinguishes Ullman's description of the dream's natural creativity, is that he treats not only the dream and its recall, but also dream appreciation and even dream sharing, as natural phases of the dreaming process.

The dream may not spontaneously heal, but "the remembered dream is an invitation to an emotionally healing experience."[75] The dreamer obtains new insights by contemplating the dream; and even insights others help her/-him to obtain—or those which the dream helps *them* to obtain—belong to the natural dream in this expanded sense. "Dreams are a most private, intimate and personal experience, but paradoxically, they can be fully realized only through a social process."[76*]

Culture is integral to man's biological adaptation.[77] Like other biological aspects of our nature, dreaming gets adapted with more or less success into specific culture arrangements, and that process of adaptation itself needs to be viewed as natural, if highly variable. One sign of a maladaptive society is that dream life gets divorced from social life. In this line of thinking, Ull-man cites and follows French dream sociologist Roger Bastide, who in 1966 framed a stern indictment of recent Western civilization for lacking customs and institutions which integrate social life and the psyche, particularly social life and dreaming. Bastide says that in traditional cultures, "the door is al-ways open between the two halves of man's life."[78] With Bastide, Ullman (as mentioned in chapter 3, p. 122) complains that the door has become ob-structed for us, in both directions:

(1) We lack sanctioned means of making our dreams social, of sharing them meaningfully.

---

* In a thought-provoking challenge to the problem-solving paradigm of dream function, Mark Blagrove (1992) argues that dreams do excellently at focusing in on genuine problems and translating them into metaphor, but generally produce solutions either already known to the waking dreamer or inapplicable to the actual problem. Dreams are "meaningful but functionless" (p. 213). Appro-priate solutions, if any, come from contemplation of the dream in the waking state. This case needs to be made as a counterbalance to idealizations of dream problem-solving, but its force is largely mooted when waking/dreaming boundary restrictions are relaxed so that waking consciousness is regarded as part of the natural dream process, as by Ullman.

(2) We lack a recognized body of myth and ritual which can pass from social experience into the dream, to socialize our night life.*

Dreaming as a Social Process

Indigenous and traditional societies: examples. Undoubtedly the most widely known example of traditional dream sharing is that attributed to the *Senoi*, first by Herbert Noone in the early 1930s, and later by Kilton Stewart.[79] Stewart described Malayan villages made idyllic by dream sharing every morning, first in the extended family, then in councils. Stewart's ideas were introduced to California at the Esalen Institute in the 1960s, by Charles Tart, the investigator of states of consciousness. Patricia Garfield, Strephon Williams,[80] and others then popularized the Senoi, though more from interest in their reported techniques of dream control than in sharing per se.

Stewart's account of the Senoi has since been seriously questioned, if not conclusively debunked.[81] But he was on an important track, for sanctioned forms of dream sharing are extremely common (though not universal**). Barbara Tedlock describes the semi-Christianized *Quiché Mayas* in Guatemala, where 10,000 out of 45,000 individuals are initiated "daykeepers" or dream interpreters; children are encouraged to remember their dreams and to share them each morning.[82] The *Huichol* Indians of Mexico with whom Brant Secunda lived gather by families and tell their dreams to "Grandfather fire" in the morning—and thereby presumably tell them to other family members as well.[83] Mubuy Mpier finds dream sharing every morning by the *Yansi* of Zaire.[84] Lydia Degarrod describes the *Mapuche* Indians of Chile, who share dreams and interpret them daily within the family, especially when a dream is bad or the dreamer sick. (Only very difficult or dangerous dreams merit consultation with a shaman.)[85]

Other instances are reported in Tedlock's *Dreaming: Anthropological and Psychological Perspectives*, a book devoted to reforming the once-prevalent application of content analysis to dreams in anthropology. That approach, which treated dreams as "quantifiable objects for testing cross-cultural hypo-

---

* Harry Hunt (1993, p. 8) remarks that just those dream types which in traditional societies most "pull people together"—archetypal and lucid dreams—sometimes lead dreamers among us into self-indulgent narcissism, because we have "lost the cultural context" for dreaming.

** Thus the Berti of North Africa "are not encouraged to dream and to remember their dreams," "have no sought or induced 'culture-pattern' dreams," have no dream "specialists," "only rarely tell others in the morning what they dreamt about or discuss their dreams with others," and reported to the ethnographer only "brief, concrete and realistic" dreams—in which, all the same, they did find signs to interpret by a simple code (L. Holy 1992, pp. 86–8).

theses,"[86] "is based on the assumption that there are neutral 'dream reports' out there, and that these reports are not only collectible in large numbers but are somehow free from the effects of cultural categorization, interpretation, and intercultural interaction. Our field experience led us to question all of these assumptions."[87]

If dream reports are collected outside culturally 'natural' contexts, says Tedlock, critical dimensions of meaning are never glimpsed. Anthropologists "began to focus their attention on studying dream interpretation systems as complex communicative processes. . . ."[88] Today anthropologists and ethnologists "are relying more on participant observation, in which they interact within natural communicative contexts of dream sharing, representation, and interpretation."[89]

"[T]o understand the culture and experience of dreams," writes Gilbert Herdt, "we need to know not just what people dream about, but how and what parts of their dreams they share," what interpretive codes they employ, and even "the modes of discourse through which dreams are interpreted and why."[90] The factors influencing how and when dreams are shared—factors which color the sampling an ethnographer can record—include: "Life-style stages" (proprieties of dream sharing by different age and/or ritual groups); "modes of discourse" ("public, secret, and private"); and "social status factors" (e.g., in a Melanesian society, men, who have higher status than do women, are entitled to share more dreams).[91]*

In the same vein, and two decades after Bastide (p. 172), J. P. Kiernan states the requirements of a sociology of dreams in these terms: "[T]he sociological emphasis . . . demands that as much attention be directed to the act of recounting as to the content of the narration. . . . The second methodological requirement is to connect narration to social action, social relations and social organization, and to demonstrate the tactical use of dreams in social encounters."[92]

Mary-Therese Dombeck is one of very few to study "social functions of dream telling" in a Euro-American society from such a viewpoint. Her book is about dream sharing in the context of Eastern U.S. community health centers. She draws a discouraging picture of the incidence of dream sharing, the importance afforded it, and the competence shown in its use.[93]

---

* To illustrate further: Among the Temne of West Africa, with whom "dreaming is not held to be a universal phenomenon," a diviner may actually tell a person s/he has had a certain dream s/he is—naturally—unaware of having dreamt (R. Shaw, pp. 42 and 47). M. C. Jędrej (1992, p. 112) considers that the Ingessana of Sudan draw a line between classes of dreamers which we draw between reality and imagination: only certain diviners are accorded the right to dream certain dreams of spiritual import.

Much of dream sharing in other societies is based on the conviction that dreams have a social as well as a personal bearing. For us, a dream is significant only for its dreamer. But most peoples also recognize *big dreams* (ch. 3, p. 81), big in the sense of significant for the community as well. The Roman Augustus "had a law enacted which required the citizens of certain provinces to publish in the marketplace any dream they might have concerning the state."[94] Recall Pharaoh's dreams interpreted by Joseph in the Old Testament. Dreams punctuate the mission of Mohammed,[95] and feature in the myths arising with the spread of Islam.* Examples can be multiplied. Of historical interest for U.S. Americans is the vision of the Nevadan Northern Paiute (Numa) visionary Wovoka, giving rise to the 1890 *Ghost Dance* religion which spread especially to the northern plains. "The North American Indian Ghost Dance, a kind of Messianic cult showing traces of Christian influence," describes Jackson Steward Lincoln, "arose at the end of the last century from the spontaneous vision of its founder or 'prophet.' The vision is similar in form to the usual Indian dream of the next world but definitely shows its Christian influence. . . ."[96] Here is one account:

Wovoka's father, Numa Taibo (White-Indian), a doctor and a vision seeker among his people, followed Wodziwob, who had originated the 1870 Ghost Dance on the Walker River Reservation. Both his father's influence and . . . Bible readings probably inspired Wovoka's beliefs and prompted him to become a vision-seeker.

Wovoka received special power and wisdom from Numanah [the father of all the Numa]; he told James Mooney that he had been taken up to the other world and given his powers:

He saw God and all the people who had died long ago engaged in their old time sports and occupations, all happy and forever young. It was a pleasant land and full of game. After showing him all, God told him he must go back and tell his people that they must be good, and love one another, have no quarreling, and live in peace with the whites; that they must work and not lie or steal; that they must put away all the old practices that savored of war; that if they faithfully obeyed his instructions, they would at last be reunited with their friends in this other world where there would be no more death or sickness or old age. He was then given the dance which he was commanded to bring back to his people. By performing the dance at intervals, for five successive days each time, they would secure this happiness to themselves and hasten the event. Finally, God gave him control over the elements so that he could make it rain, snow, or be dry at will, and appointed him to be his deputy and to take charge of the affairs in the West. . . .[97]

---

* Black Africa: H. J. Fisher (1979). Indonesia: R. Jones (1979).

Wovoka's history is an example of the "upsurge of religious dreaming" found to occur when traditional cultures come into sudden contact with the West. "What often results is the development of new symbols, myths, rituals, and movements that help people respond" to cultural disruption, write Wendy Doniger & Kelly Bulkley.[98] Vittorio Lanternari has described various other movements around the world whose founders blended Christian and traditional elements under conditions of culture contact. Dreams and visions have been instrumental in the origin and conduct of new messianic religious movements with the aim of political liberation in Africa, North and South America, the Caribbean, Melanesia, Polynesia, Indonesia, and South Asia, from the eighteenth century up to the present.[99]*

As Lanternari recounts, there had been numerous forerunner sects to the Ghost Dance, rejuvenating indigenous beliefs and teaching salvation for the tribes and a return of the dead. These sects included more than one known as "the Dreamers" on account of their trance visions.[100]

The Peyote cult also arose from a vision. It spread rapidly as the Ghost Dance was disappearing and largely took its place. The Peyote cult visionary was known as John Wilson (by coincidence, Wovoka was known to whites as *Jack* Wilson). He experienced his first peyote vision in 1890, at a Ghost Dance called by Sitting Bull. The peyote cult also merged indigenous and Christian religious features in an end-of-the-world redemptive vision. "[B]ut whereas the Ghost Dance promised the restoration of the past, Peyotism announced a new dispensation and a renewal of Indian culture" under conditions of forced acculturation.[101]

Another renowned Native American vision with social significance is the lengthy vision of the nine-year-old Ogalala Sioux *Black Elk*. As mentioned (ch. 3, p. 117n), by Sioux belief, to share a vision completely is to vitiate its power. Black Elk only related the total vision as an old man who tragically felt that he had already lost most of the power once given to him. On the other hand, such a vision was held to be useless, or even damaging to its visionary, unless and until shared with the community through ritual enactment. On different occasions during his young adulthood, he enlisted the cooperation of various shamans to direct the communal pageantry enacting one and another portion of the vision.

Black Elk believed that the vision had been bestowed on him so that he might keep "the nation's hoop" intact, that is, preserve the Sioux from the disasters overtaking them. Eventually, Black Elk with other Sioux became

---

* In (1975), Lanternari describes new, not necessarily political movements of "Africanized Christianity" among the Nzema of Ghana and "in a poor Negro neighborhood in Kingston, Jamaica."

caught up in Wovoka's Ghost Dance religion, but not in its original, pacifist form. In the northern plains, it developed into a cult of holy war, featuring ghost shirts supposed to grant invulnerability to bullets.* Black Elk himself, who as a boy had taken part in Custer's defeat at Little Big Horn, witnessed as an adult the massacre of the Sioux at Wounded Knee.

Robert Dentan remarks that "[p]rophetic dreams or visions trigger many, if not most, anti-colonial popular movements"—adding, "often with tragic consequences."[102] Black Elk ended his narrative: "And I, to whom so great a vision was given in my youth,—you see me now a pitiful old man who has done nothing, for the nation's hoop is broken and scattered. There is no center any longer, and the sacred tree is dead."[103]

Most socially significant dreams are not 'big' in the sense of influencing communal decisions and political destiny; rather, their social function is to integrate the individual into the community. Rites of passage often involve *culture pattern dreams* (see also ch. 13, p. 402), usually though not always deliberately sought, into which enter culturally determined imageries with understood meanings. Mircea Eliade relates a Siberian shaman's harrowing and beautiful dream which contains features, some or all of which must be present for a shaman's initiation to proceed (there are similarities to Wovoka's and Black Elk's visions): "*Dismemberment of the body, followed by the renewal of the internal organs and viscera; ascent to the sky and dialogue with the gods and spirits; descent to the Lowerworld and conversations with spirits and the souls of dead shamans; various revelations, both religious and shamanic (secrets of the profession).*"[104]**

Tedlock is one of various scholars who lately have taken exception to the distinction between culture pattern dreams and individual dreams,[105] Tedlock on the grounds that the distinction does not "correspond with the classificatory schemes" of the cultures themselves.[106] But surely that is true of many anthropologists' categories. Moreover, in the same volume one anthropologist writes about Kagwahiv "dreams which incorporate myths wholesale,"[107]

---

* Immunity to the white man's bullets by use of a fetish or rite was a recurrent theme of North American shamanism, and has also been reported in messianic liberation movements in South America, Africa, and Polynesia (V. Lanternari 1963 [1960]).

** The motif of dismemberment and reassembly shows up in various times and places. In the Roman period, the "oneiromancer" Aelius Aristedes "speaks, like the shamans, of the dismembering and reassembling of the body at the moment of dream ecstacy" (S. Resnik 1987, p. 23, citing Elemire Zolla, "Conoscensa religiosa," *Le Nuova Italia* 1, p. 54, 1976). Rossi (1985, p. 125ff.) tells a dream on the same pattern, dreamt by a patient at the culmination of therapy. Rossi does not say whether or not she was acquainted with the ethnographic material. Some schizophrenics dream a similar dream, except that whereas the shaman undergoes reassembly during the experience, the schizophrenic does not (H. T. Hunt 1989, p. 137; cf. J. Halifax 1982) (see ch. 9, p. 333).

and another, about Kalapolo dreamers who "receive metaphorically encoded visions of themselves" from their culture;[108] while a third, William Merrill, makes explicit reference to the concept of culture pattern dreams:

[T]he Rarámuri [of Mexico] say that God bestows these [curing] abilities upon people, usually males but sometimes females, in a specific type of dream, what Lincoln (1935) might have called a 'culture pattern dream.' In this dream, *God offers the individual three (or four if the dreamer is female) light-colored pieces of paper. If one takes the paper, then God provides the knowledge to cure and will assist in future curing endeavors.* Sometimes *the devil stands beside God* in such dreams, *holding three (or four) dark-colored papers. The person can then choose to become a doctor, a sorcerer, or both, or neither, according to whether he or she accepts a set of papers and the color of the papers selected.* The role of doctor is the only position in the society that requires legitimization through a dream.[109]

Jackson Steward Lincoln's classic about culture pattern dreaming "represents the first intensive use of psychoanalytic theory to analyze cultures, as well as the first and most extensive anthropological comparative research on dreams and dream telling."[110] Here is an excerpt concerning the *dream quest* of a ten-year-old Menomini boy seeking his spirit helper:

There were about seven of us fasting at the same time. All day we would play together, watching each other lest anyone eat during the day. We were to keep this up for ten days. . . .

After a while, they built me a little wigwam. It was standing on four poles and about three to four feet from the ground. This was my sleeping-place. My little wigwam was built quite a distance from the house, under an oak tree. . . .

The first morning my grandmother told me not to accept the first one that came, for there are many spirits who will try to deceive you, and if one accepts their blessings he will be surely led on to destruction.

The first four nights I slept very soundly and did not dream of anything. On the fifth night, however, I dreamt that *a large bird came to me. It was very beautiful and promised me many things. However, I made up my mind not to accept the gift of the first one who appeared. So I refused, and when it disappeared from view, I saw that it was only a chickadee.*

The next morning, when my grandmother came to visit me, . . . [s]he assured me that the chickadee had deceived many people who had been led to accept this offering.

Then a few nights passed and I did not dream of anything. On the eighth night, *another big bird appeared to me and I determined to accept its gift, for I was tired of waiting and of being confined to my little fasting-wigwam.* In my dream of this bird, *he took me far to the north where everything was covered with ice. There I saw many of the same kinds of birds. Some were very old. They of-*

fered me long life and immunity from disease. It was quite a different blessing from that which the chickadee had offered, so I accepted. Then the bird who had come after me, brought me to my fasting-wigwam again. When he left me, he told me to watch him before he was out of sight. I did so and I saw that he was a white loon.

In the morning when my grandmother came to me, I told her of my experience with the white loons and she was very happy about it, for the white loons are supposed to bless very few people. Since then, I have been called White Loon.[111]*

Such a dream is sought and then shared in a communal framework. Into its content go the dreamer's cultural exposure and education; out of it come the dreamer's spiritual, maturational, and perhaps occupational status in the community. This dream is also 'big', in the sense that most things in indigenous societies have a communal aspect. Henry Reed writes about the Native American dream quest: "Having been blessed by the dream, the young adult also would incur the responsibility of applying the gifts in a prescribed manner for the benefit of the community, often on penalty of contracting an untreatable disease."[112] Ritual songs and dances (such as those of Wovoka and Black Elk) often have their origins in dreams.

Bastide and Ullman say we pay a price of anxiety and worse for lacking the equivalents of this and other traditional dream functions in our culture.

But what equivalents can exist in contemporary societies? Ullman laments that we have relegated the dream to the therapist's office.[113] As recently as 1965, Norman MacKenzie warned in his widely circulated book *Dreams and Dreaming* that "the unskilled use of dreams outside the therapeutic situation is invariably misleading and may actually be harmful."[114] Remembering in fairness that in his time Freud restored at least some legitimacy to the dream by bringing it to a therapeutic setting from cultural limbo, what fuller sanction can dreams find nowadays, what social legitimacy?

Contemporary Societies: Examples. Big Dreams. First I will mention several dreams, each of which had an historical impact. The first was related to the Iranian parliament in May of 1951 by Mohammed Mossadegh, after the success of the democratic, anti-imperialist movement to nationalize oil which Mossadegh headed, and before his assassination by the C.I.A. The Argentinean author Jorge Luis Borges published this account:

In the summer of 1950 preceding the vote for the nationalization of oil, my doctor prescribed prolonged rest for me. A month later, while I was sleeping *I*

---

* For adults as well as children, I recommend Victor Barnouw's novel *Dream of the Blue Heron* (1975 [1966]), which tells the story of the dream quest of a Chippewa boy.

saw in my dream a radiant person, who said to me: "This is no time for rest; arise and go break the chains of the people of Iran." I responded to the call, and in spite of my extreme fatigue I resumed my work on the oil commission. When the commission accepted the principle of nationalization two months later, I had to acknowledge that the person of my dream had inspired me well.[115]

Dreams have an acknowledged relevance and a communal import in traditional Islam quite foreign to Euro-American culture.[116] G. E. von Grunebaum relates another historical vignette from the same land and some fifty years earlier:

> As recently as 1902, when the request for a loan from Russia was uppermost in his mind, did Muzaffar ad-Din, Shah of Persia from 1896 to 1906, ask a leading divine to interpret a dream in which he himself had appeared to the ruler. The theologian explained: "Whereas *Your Majesty saw me in the primitive Moslem garb throw a sack at your feet whence flowed gold and silver*, this means that my ancestor the Prophet bids you to make no fresh loans from unbelievers, but to trust for the restoration of your finances to your subjects and fellow servants of the faith." There was some disagreement at the time whether the dream had been invented by the Shah to test the feelings of the clergy.[117]

In the run-up to the Gulf War, Saddam publicized a dream—authentic or invented—as an instrument of policy. Journalist Thomas J. Friedman in the *New York Times*:

> Last week a Kuwaiti newspaper now publishing in Saudi Arabia reported that President Saddam Hussein of Iraq had dreamed that *the Prophet Mohammed appeared before him and said that Iraq's missiles "were pointed in the wrong direction."* Middle East experts were quoted as saying that this dream indicated that the Iraqi leader could be preparing for a withdrawal from Kuwait. But the White House spokesman, Marlin Fitzwater, asked for his reaction, responded: "No comment on dreams. I have enough problem dealing with reality." . . .
>
> "The reason we got the initial reaction we did from the Saudis was because they were scared to death," said one Administration Arabist. "But I fear that we may be moving out of that phase. Saddam let it be known that he had a dream, and we joke about it. But it sounds very different to Arab ears. He is speaking Arabic again and that worries me."[118]*

The dark side of Islamic dream culture was demonstrated a few years ago more forcibly than Salman Rushdie intended, with the Iranian reaction to the offending passages of *Satanic Verses*. It also features in the history of noto-

---

* Saddam must be aware that there exists a "widely known and frequently cited tradition to the effect that the Devil cannot masquerade as the Prophet. If the Prophet himself appears in a dream, that dream must be true" (H. J. Fisher 1979, p. 220).

rious Ugandan dictator Idi Amin, a Muslim. This is a contemporaneous account by Africanist John Mbiti:

[A]fter he came to power in a military coup d'état in January 1971, Amin let it be known that long before that he had had a dream in which *it was 'revealed' to him that one day he would become the ruler of Uganda*: his dream had now been fulfilled. He said also that *he was shown* in the same dream *the date and circumstances of his death*: but this he has not disclosed to the public. He says, however, that he fears nobody except God. . . .
. . . Early in August 1972 . . . Amin . . . announced that he had a dream in which *God directed him to expel the Asians from the country*. . . . In obedience to this dream, . . . within a short period of three months, he managed to expel an estimated 35,000 Asians of British, Indian, Pakistani and other citizenships.[119]

Another example of a big dream of a political personality is that of Cory Aquino, transmitted by Karen Signell from *Newsweek*:

When the Filipino people began to turn against Ferdinand Marcos, she was asked to accept the nomination for the presidency. While she was trying to reach a decision, she had a recurrent dream that *she was going to church and seeing a casket that she expected to contain Ninoy's (her assassinated husband's) body. But the coffin was empty: Ninoy, she felt, had been reborn in her.*[120]

Jeremy Taylor relates how Mohandas Gandhi, following many frustrating failures to put across his message of non-violence in the face of riots against renewed British colonial tyrannies, was motivated to instigate a successful general strike centered on religion by the following dream: "*[T]he Congress Party organizers should call upon the leaders of the many diverse and warring religious groups in India—Hindu and Moslem, Parsi and Jain, Buddhist and Sikh—to abandon their respective traditional calendars for public ritual gathering and practice their respective festivals of prayer and public procession at the same time.*"[121]

Another, less portentous big dream concerns the feminist movement here in the U.S. It was dreamt by the poet Adrienne Rich. Phyllis Koch-Sheras et al. include it in their dream book for women:

I dreamed *I was asked to read my poetry at a mass women's meeting, but when I began to read, what came out were the lyrics of a blues song.* I share this dream with you because it seemed to me to say something about the problems and the future of the woman writer, and probably of women in general. The awakening of consciousness is not like the crossing of a frontier—one step and you're in another country. Much of women's poetry has been of the nature of a blues song: a cry of pain, of victimization . . . charged with anger. I think we need to go through the anger, and we will betray our own reality if we try . . . for an objectivity, a detachment.[122]

Tima Priess of Alaska recounts a dream of *animals in spilled oil* following the Prince William Sound disaster. "I felt as though I was asked to do something with the dream other than to just integrate it on a personal level." That day, she wrote a poem inspired by the dream and the events. "I put the poem and the dream on a flyer and distributed it all over the country. In response, I received letters, dreams, and visions from people touched by the oil spill. . . ."[123]

Sam Sapiel, a Penobscot Indian, became an antinuclear activist in New England after dreaming of *deciding to lead his people to their sacred mountains when he saw them, from afar, at war and in disarray on their reservation.* "'There was a big explosion . . . [with] a lot of things going into the sky like fireflies, shooting around. The whole country's on fire.'"[124]

Marion Stamps is a community activist at Chicago's Cabrini Green housing project. I first heard about her in a National Public Radio news feature concerning the gang truce there which followed the shooting death of a boy, Dantrell Davis, in October of 1992. NPR asked Stamps about an open letter she had earlier written to her community which eventually contributed to the truce after the shooting. She mentioned that she had been moved to write the letter by a dream. As I learned when I interviewed her in February of 1993, the dream concerned *a four-day feast*, and it prompted her to convene a sort of festival for the gangs and civilians of Cabrini Green. An adequate account of this dream and its relation to events would be too long to include here, but is appearing elsewhere.[125]

A significant early phenomenon in the dream movement (see below) was a journal called *Gates—A Sausolito Waterfront Community Dream Journal*, which appeared in 1977. *Gates* published dreams and artwork from dreams, produced by artists and others in its community. It made 'big dreaming' an axis of organization for a community's resistance to commercial developers. Its example spawned a number of imitators.[126]

In 1988, Charles Upton attempted to establish a *dream bridge* between the Soviet Union and U.S. by having people in both lands incubate dreams (see chapter 13) about new ways of achieving peace.[127] (The rest is history.)

More dreams of ordinary, private dreamers which have social and political involvements will be discussed in several contexts below.

The dream movement. This development represents a spontaneous restitution of cultural sanctioning of interest in dreams. Deborah Jay Hillman, an anthropologist, dates the dream movement (or *dreamwork movement*) to the early 1970s.[128] Jack Maguire, in an excellent chapter about the history of the movement, typifies it as a "hybrid product of the self-help, alternative health therapy, consciousness-raising, and human potential movements of the

1960s and 1970s. . . ."[129] The term, says Hillman, entered "popular usage" about 1982–1983.[130]

Building on Freud, Jung, Fromm, Perls and others, and on the interest generated by REM science, the movement's first notable was Ann Faraday with her books *Dream Power* and *The Dream Game*.[131] She was followed by Patricia Garfield and Gayle Delaney.[132] They and other dreamworkers have become minor celebrities. Some demonstrate their talents and discuss their books on talk shows. All sorts of workshops and short courses on dreams can be found now, particularly on the coasts. Delaney is "required reading at Stanford School of Business."[133] Popular magazines carry articles, and a few specialized journals are devoted to dreams.*

General features of the movement are deprofessionalization and "an emphasis on the value of dream sharing and on the creative and practical uses of dreams."[134] Other frequent interests include spirituality in both religious and nonreligious senses, psychic events, and lucidity, not to exclude healing as in conventional therapy. All of this signifies a renascence of cultural legitimacy for dreams.

Perhaps the most significant development of these years is the emergence of dream sharing groups. There are groups led for a charge by professionals, both clinicians and self-styled 'dreamworkers', in offices, special dream centers, and various public venues. There are free groups led by lay leaders. And there are peerled and leaderless groups, mostly meeting in participants' homes. Some of these are loosely tied together and nurtured by grassroots community dreamwork networks.**

---

* *Association for the Study of Dreams Newsletter* as well as *Dreaming*, an interdisciplinary scholarly journal, come with membership in the ASD, PO Box 1600, Vienna, VA 22183. *Dreaming* may be subscribed to separately at Subscription Department, Human Sciences Press, Inc., 233 Spring St., New York, NY 10013. The best and oldest nonscholarly periodical is *Dream Network Journal* (formerly *Dream Network Bulletin*), PO Box 1026, Moab, UT 84532. *The Montreal Centre for the Study of Dreams Bulletin*, 4482 de Bullion, Montreal, Canada, H2W 2G1 is a smaller, semi-scholarly, bilingual periodical. *Lucidity Letter*, 43 Midland Avenue, Berwyn, PA 19312 is a scholarly journal concerned with lucid dreaming and related phenomena. More for lucid dreamers than for scholars, but with summaries of research, is *NightLight*, the newsletter which comes with membership in the Lucidity Institute, Box 2364, Stanford, CA 94309. For East Coast dream sharers, there is the six-page *Dream Switchboard*, Dreamsharing Grassroots Network, PO Box 8032, Hicksville, NY 11801.

** A few reservations about dream groups and/or sharing. Delaney (1990c, p. 13) thinks groups are not necessarily advisable for dreamwork beginners, "[b]ecause groups often attract leaders who like a lot of control, and need disciples. . . . And groups can be very hurtful to individuals—I don't think damaging in the long run . . . [b]ut groups can hurt your feelings a lot, because people usually . . . have no idea how tender people are about telling their dreams." For beginners, Delaney recommends reading books instead (p. 24). Robert Langs (1988, pp. 101–3), reflecting on dream sharing in general, thinks we merely embroil one another in our unconscious compulsions. Dream sharing

There are also groups which meet for specialized purposes. These include "Dreams & Nightmares Anonymous," a twelve-step program operating as of this writing in New York City. Another type of group devotes itself to so-called "cross-dreaming"[135] or "shared dreaming," which "involves "two or more dreamers apparently meeting in the same dream space and experiencing similar events." Linda Magallón & Barbara Shor make this claim: "This state of awareness can be used to create a forum in which a group of any size can hold conferences, create new projects and ideas, resolve conflicts, enhance cooperative efforts, and tap into the kind of information that appears to be available only in dreams shared with others."[136]

Ullman groups and other groups. A great many groups are patterned or influenced by the guidelines developed by Ullman. These groups may have trained facilitators, whose role is to be an authority about the process, but not about the meaning of the dream. Leadership can rotate when more than one member knows the process.[137] Besides in homes, Ullman envisions his groups functioning in churches, classrooms, hospitals, training centers, halfway houses, prisons, senior facilities, etc. A book he co-edited contains articles on groups of mothers, artists, parishioners, and even of psychoanalytic trainees.[138] Other venues reported include a managerial training program in India,[139] a research institute, a Catholic nunnery, and a kibbutz.[140]*

The following example of work in an Ullman group does not fully illustrate the guidelines, which were outlined above (pp. 169–70). Work with a dream by the guidelines easily lasts an hour and a half. This digested report does give a good sense of a typical Ullman group interaction. I particularly selected it, because the dreams concern the dreamer's relation to the dream group and to groups in general, a culturalist theme:

> At the second meeting Dotty (a widow with grown children and a highly responsible job with the Federal Government) recounted an experience of that week.
> . . .
> "Nan [Zimmerman, Ullman's collaborator] said I must dream a short dream. No way, I thought. All my dreams are long and complicated. I went to bed and my dream was this:

---

works, he believes, only in societies where there is less developed individuality, where sharing reinforces communal integrity. Jung of course did not comment on dream movement sharing groups, but he "had everything possible of a disdainful nature to say . . . against therapeutic work in groups. . . ." H. Barz (1990, p. 172) says that Jung's attitude, which continues to exert an influence among Jungians, is "rooted in the 'group psychology' of the turn of the century. . . ."

* C. H. Reid (1983, p. 88) mentions groups, not specifically run by Ullman's guidelines, of cancer patients and of psychologists. R. Parker (1988) discusses sharing in Protestant fellowships. J. Taylor (1992a, p. 100ff.) relates his experience of dreamwork in a group of political activists.

"*'I am alone.'*
. . . I went back to sleep and dreamed again:
"*'I am alone.'*
"I woke up and thought, 'Aha! I've dreamed two short dreams.' I didn't give them any consideration, just wrote them down. Then I had a third dream:
  "*I was introducing my group to someone else. I cut two round circles of white paper as representing them. They were like small, luncheon-size place mats.*
  "*There were two square napkins. I started to trim them round, then realized they were O.K. as they were.*
"I dreamed three short dreams!"

The group agreed there was obvious loneliness, and beyond that the desire for acceptance and belonging. Dotty cared very much that she produce a dream which fit the necessary criteria for the group's attention. . . .

Lenore asked if circles had a universal meaning. In response Dotty told us what she had been reading before going to sleep:

"I had been studying John Sanford's book **God's Forgotten Language**. . . . Sanford said that persons developing both inwardly and outwardly will have balance. In circles all points are equidistant from the center. Squares have four sides of equal length.

"When I think of small circles I think of a small group of people. White means pure and clean . . . whiter than snow . . . forgiveness. These are the only thoughts that seem to go with the dream at all. But I never came up with anything that hangs right."

Ben suggested that Dotty was trying to fit something (the squares) into a small group and it wasn't working. What did the squares represent? After a good deal of speculation about this Dotty shared some additional day residue.

"The night before the dreams I was with my church group and was in a devastating discussion of our life together. I felt that most of us didn't feel any 'real' sharing had taken place. Recently I've been much alone, far removed from family and without closeness anywhere."

Dotty traveled farther than any other member to attend our sessions, driving some forty-five minutes alone. We knew that the dream group was an important experience for her. And we knew that her church group also gave her a vital sense of belonging. She was concerned over her place in both groups. She needed a place. This connected with her image in the dream, place mat. We also noticed the importance of the number two: two circles; two squares; saying two times, "I am alone."

The two short dreams create the setting for evaluating her relationship to the two groups to which she belongs. She felt herself alone and lonely. She made a point of saying this twice, once for each group. After affirming that she was a part of two groups (the white circles) she asked what her place was in the groups (circular place mats) and saw herself as a square napkin. This was not enough to certify her belonging. Her sharp edges didn't fit into the circles. The temptation was to force herself to look exactly like her conception of the group image.

Then she realized that was not necessary. By combining both square and circle she made a new setting, a new place; a setting for eating, where needs may be satisfied, and quite often with pleasure.[141]

Robin Shohet has written a valuable book entitled *Dream Sharing*.[142] He talks about groups, some led, some self-help, in British hospitals, day centers, classrooms, and training programs, and with white adults tending black children, with other young children, and with disadvantaged teenage girls. The latter two of these endeavors were reported in the journal *Self and Society*, edited by Shohet.[143] His professional specialty is facilitating "temporary dreaming communities" at conferences, religious retreats, and the like. His work is guided and also limited by the nature of the larger gatherings within which his dream groups meet. He uses an eclectic mix of dreamwork techniques, plus some group work techniques not specific to dreaming.

Shohet's book also has a chapter on starting up a self-help dream group which can serve as a supplement or alternative to Ullman. Other such guidelines will be found in Delaney's and Taylor's popular books,* and in other sources.**

Group therapy. Ullman's and these other types of dream groups should not be considered means of clinical therapy, but of personal growth. They are meant to help the dreamer be "in a better position to work on his problems himself."[144] Among other differences between therapy and growth, or "experiential" groups, Ullman mentions these:

The unequal relationship between therapist and client should not exist between group facilitator and other members.

At an experiential dream group meeting, "the dream is the only item on the agenda. . . ."[145]

In therapy, vulnerabilities and defenses may be intentionally irritated. In dream groups, the object is to lower defenses by cultivating an atmosphere of safety.***

---

* G. Delaney (1979), pp. 192–203 and (1991), pp. 400–9. J. Taylor (1983), pp. 76–99, and especially (1992a), which offers advanced advice for group facilitators as well as basic information for beginners.

** E. R. Neu (1988) adds practical advice to Ullman's and Shohet's guidelines. J. Friedman (1981) writes about Bossian groups. D. Whitmore (1981) writes about groups using a psychosynthetic approach. See also: P. R. Koch-Sheras, E. A. Hollier & B. Jones (1983), p. 77ff.; J. Morris (1987 [1985]), p. 57ff.; R. Bosnak (1988 [1986]), pp. 27–36 passim; J. Maguire (1989), pp. 213–9; D. McLeester (1991); R. Cartwright & L. Lamberg (1992), pp. 261–6; N. Wessling (1993); articles in H. R. Ossana (1993).

*** Eva Renée Neu, who wrote a small book for self-help dream groups (1988), wisely cautions that while such groups always implicitly involve a therapeutic intention in a broad sense (p. 14), they often lack the basis of skepticism, natural to therapy, for tempering "the myth of change" (p. 97).

All the same, I would have to say on the basis of experience in growth dream groups that the boundary between the two types is not precise. Much depends on the aptitudes, training, purposes, and mental health of the participants. Moreover, the pattern for Ullman groups and for most other dream groups was undoubtedly derived from group therapy, which underwent an explosion of interest in the 1950s along with small group psychology in general. It is noteworthy that the article to which surveys of dreamwork in psychoanalytic therapy groups[146] give priority, written by Eva Klein-Lipshutz in 1953, foreshadowed Ullman's 'if it were my dream' technique by having each member free associate "as if it were his own dream."[147]

Klein-Lipshutz and many others give their primary attention to how the group's interactions induce dreams which reveal the individual dreamer. In essence, prior group sessions become the semi-controlled 'day residue' for subsequent dreams.[148] This sentence from analysts Thomas French & Erika Fromm has been quoted as stating the rationale of such work: "Almost all the problems that our patients bring us have arisen out of difficulties or failures in their attempts to find satisfying ways of fitting into some group."[149] The therapy group becomes the transference object, or projection screen, for these internalized conflicts, which are stimulated to express themselves in dreams.[150]

Group dreams. But besides "how group process influences the individual," a second but complementary interest has been explored in studies of therapy groups, and later of other groups where dreams are shared, namely, "how dreams may reflect group process."[151] Certain dreams are thought to give "an unconscious reflection of occurrences in the group,"[152] to concern "the preconscious or implicit communication in the group,"[153] or to reveal group structure and dynamics[154] or group "fantasies" and "mythology."[155] Often termed 'group dreams', such dreams are in effect the 'big dreams' of the small and temporary culture of the sharing group, as Jung observed,[156] and their interpretation within the context of the group will reflect the conventions of that culture.* The group may appear realistically in the dream, or metaphorically, as in the following example, published by a psychoanalytically oriented therapist, David Zimmermann:

By this she means the penchant for seeing all psychic events as always trending to the good. The group can detrimentally reinforce what psychoanalysts have called 'flight into health,' or improvement founded on denial (p. 98).

    * It should be borne in mind that dreams brought to individual therapy often concern that relationship. In that circumstance as well as in groups, the dream may be dreamt as a form of communication, to be shared. Communication is achieved both by the content of the dream and the manner of sharing it—with trust, suspicion, etc. (R. Shohet 1985, p. 121).

The unconscious meaning of th[is] dream provides a picture or cross-section of the latent current conflict of the whole group. . . .

. . . A group member reported:

I dreamed about an octopus which, with its innumerable tentacles, was fighting with a man. It was a horrible fight, and I was anxious as if it were fighting with me. Suddenly, I noticed that the octopus had a giant-sized mouth with teeth and a pair of green eyes. I was awakened by my husband, who had been roused by my agitation. I was full of anguish.

The first association, the green eyes which resembled the lenses of my glasses, compared the octopus to the therapist. The innumerable tentacles of the animal seemed to the group to indicate the innumerable possibilities of the therapist in his interpretative activity in the group. But then the complaints and questions which followed and the attempts to involve the therapist with rationalizations concerning their symptoms indicated that the octopus and his tentacles represented the patients trying to subdue, immobilize, swallow, and annihilate the therapist. In fact, the two interpretations complemented each other. The octopus shows the therapist as, on the one hand, a domineering and voracious mother, and, on the other, it represents each of the patients (the tentacles) forming a whole with their central object. . . .

. . . The situation expressed in the dream exists not only in the dreamer but in the whole group. The dreamer is an interpreter of the group because, as [s]he demonstrates, [s]he is able to catch and express the latent aggressive impulses of them all. On the other hand, it may be equally valid to say that the dreamer's expressive capacity has been stimulated by h[er] companions whose unconscious attitudes [s]he sensed.[157]

Family therapy and dream sharing. A specialized kind of group therapy, where dream sharing can be encouraged to continue beyond the sessions, is family, marital and couple therapy.[158] Therapist Patricia Maybruck discusses how couples can learn to share their dreams without professional guidance, and she gives guidelines. She describes the manner in which Ullman's procedures can be adapted for couples working on their own, and for groups of larger size, working on male-female issues.[159] Garfield, Delaney and others recommend dream sharing between couples and with children.[160]

Dream sharing commune. A unique instance, combining therapeutic and nontherapeutic models, is the collective created by Richard Corriere, Werner Karle, Lee Woldenberg & Joseph Hart. Their "functional" or "feeling therapy" was touched upon skeptically (ch. 4, p. 156). They propose that a personal "breakout" by means of "transformative dreaming" is actualized only by the full sharing of feelings brought into waking from the dream.[161] The essential thing about traditional dream sharing cultures, they say, is not their dances, dream songs, trances, and such, but their custom of "making the private public."[162] Moreover, "[l]ong-term transformations in dreams for individuals cannot be achieved or sustained without the support of the community. Individual therapy sessions and workshops are inadequate to bring about the major transformations which are possible."[163] Accordingly, they organized a therapeutic urban dream sharing community, where most members lived in adjacent homes in a communal arrangement. This was an all day, everyday approach to life-as-therapy which is obviously impracticable for widespread adoption, whatever else we may think of it. I believe that the commune no longer exists.

Education. Dreamwork has been introduced into secondary education,[164] and, by Richard Jones, into college education. He designed a course where dreamwork and creative writing are combined to teach each other.[165] Dreams have also been used by other dreamworkers, including Maguire,[166] in their teaching of poetry writing. This is not surprising, considering that literature is the one area of Euro-American culture where dreams possessed any real legitimacy through the nineteenth century prior to Freud.

There is a growing number of courses on dreamwork and dream theory being offered in universities, community colleges, Ys, alternative learning centers, dream centers, etc. The Association for the Study of Dreams has an active education committee, chaired as of this writing by Kelly Bulkeley.

Borrowings from Native Americans and other cultures. A notable strand of the dream movement is dreamwork which borrows its methods, symbols, and sanction from other traditions. Especially, interest in Native American spirituality has manifested itself in the dream movement with professional dreamworkers who borrow Native American beliefs and practices, in that way compensating the paucity of immigrant dream traditions.

Alexa Singer invokes the Sun Dance and the medicine wheel, as well as Quetzalcoatl.

Robert Krajenke writes about "The Mt. Rushmore Full Moon Medicine Wheel Dream Quest" (see below).

Alan Siegel leads a "Dream Quest wilderness backpacking workshop" at a place "considered to be a sacred site to the Ohlone Indians."

Fred Swinney took the name Graywolf and incorporates shamanic vision questing in his psychology practice.

The "Temagami Vision Quest" is staffed by Jungians in Ojibway land in Ontario.

Jack Zimmerman conducts "dream sharing in council," a method which borrows from Quaker philosophy and ancient Greek practices as well as Native American formats.

Elizabeth Cogburn employs the talking staff, aromatic smoke, and drumming at a retreat house in Hopi New Mexico.[167]

I will summarize the borrowing by Henry Reed, whom Maguire (perhaps debatably) calls "[b]y common agreement, the father of the modern dream-work movement. . . ."[168]

Inspired by Native American dream questing, and by the incubation of curative dreams in the temples of Asclepius in the ancient Greek world (ch. 13, p. 405ff.), Reed has devised a contemporary equivalent.[169] It is a four-step process. (1) The "incubant" must get an "invitational dream," showing readiness to work on a given problem with Reed. (2) As "preparation," the incubant meditates on her/his purpose. Importantly, s/he selects "personal symbols of a sacred place [equivalent to the temple] and a revered benefactor [equivalent to Asclepius]" to employ during the incubation. Also left to one's own choice are details of a symbolic purification undergone 24 hours in advance. (3) For the "incubation," s/he spends 4 to 6 hours in a "dream tent," with Reed as guide. Their discussions of the invitational dream and the issues wanting healing entail conventional psychotherapeutics as well as role-playing, of the dream elements, the benefactor, and the sacred place. Next, the incubant is coaxed asleep with suggestion, imagery, and music. (4) After awakening, the incubated dream is similarly discussed. Finally, the incubant writes a "testimony" regarding the entire experience. Here is an abbreviated example:

> [O]ne young boy (14 years), concerned with his involvement with psychedelic drugs, brought to the incubation ceremony *an epic seafaring dream portraying the plight of some pitifully adrift, waterlogged creatures who longed desperately for dry land.* The young incubant empathized with these creatures, and recognized in their desire for dry land his own longing for a surefooted alternative to his psychedelic voyages. Yet he resented the pressures of socialization he encountered in the "straight" environment of home and school. His incubated dream gave him the needed experience of navigating satisfactorily on dry land: *He was walking down a hot, dry road in the middle of a forest, the dust choking him, when he came to a dead end. He climbed up a tree to survey the surrounding forest, and spotted an axe a short distance away. He climbed down, picked up the axe, and began making his own trail through the forest. In contrast to the dry, dusty road, the path he cut for himself was cool and refreshing.* Encouraged by this image of blazing his own trail, when he returned to school he successfully initiated his own study projects. His use of drugs declined significantly, and his subsequent dreams provided him with additional images. . . .[170]

With Robert Van de Castle (who happens also to have been a star of Ullman's telepathy experiments,[171] as well as Calvin Hall's collaborator in content analysis research,[172] and a prominent researcher in his own right), Reed adapted his incubation methods to groups.[173] Inspiration for this work came from the psychic Edgar Cayce,[174] and from the Sun Dance. The Sun Dance is a Native American communal ritual, originating in the northern plains but later (and presently) widely disseminated, in which some participants experience visions.[175] Reed's and Van de Castle's "helpers" tap their "telepathic healing ability" by incubating dreams for the benefit, usually, of two members, who keep the nature of their problems or needs secret until after the dream night. The morning-after discussion draws on general psychological insights to explore possible problem-to-dream correspondences.

From 1977 (the year of *Gates*) to 1979, Reed and Van de Castle published six issues of the *Sundance Community Dream Journal*, attempting to utilize their small group incubation methods within a larger system. "A community can prepare itself to have a dream that will move the community as a whole closer to its ideals."[176] "People pool their dreams to obtain guidance to a common problem."[177] It was a Sun-Dance-by-mail experiment. Through dreams and discussions, contributors explored Sun Dance equivalents arising in their own images. These prominently included a world tree with a dance around it, the central ritual of the Sun Dance. In effect, contributors were dream helpers to the world. Hearkening to Native American reverence for nature and the belief, common to many indigenous cultures, that their rituals sustain the order of nature, Reed and Van de Castle sought the well-being of the planet in the spirit of the "New Age."[178]

Reed, it should be recognized, was careful to keep a toe on the ground. After citing a dream of his which intimated to him the possibility of evolution toward "supra-individual consciousness," he ended the article initiating the *Journal* with this caution against inflation:

> Be that as it may, community consciousness is no substitute for self-knowledge. The mystery of the community dance can only be revealed when each individual is attuned to his or her personal source of identity. If the forces of unification aren't properly balanced by the forces of individuation, we might simply storm together to make a mob. One of my dreams expressed the problem more constructively:
>
> *We are getting ready to go to the dream dance. Some of us have our dream shields, others of us don't. Since the dance can't start until all the dancers have made their shields, the shielded dancers are cheering on the others.*
>
> The meaning is clear. Each of us who wishes to play the dream game will have to learn for himself the personal meaning of his dream symbols. But we can certainly help one another learn. . . .[179]

That Reed conceived of real-world ambitions for collective, 'big' dreamwork, at least in principle, is demonstrated by the following quote from him. With it, Krajenke introduced an article about his own "Full Moon Dream

Community" and its journal *Awakening Arts*, modelled after Reed and Van de Castle's experiment, and borrowing the imagery and philosophy of the medicine wheel. Reed wrote: "There may be political ramifications to the process of a group of people focusing their dreams on a central topic. We know the unconscious shapes society. If we can become aware of this process, we can nurture it and foster its growth into some visible and practical consequences."[180] The consequence sought by Krajenke's group was a healing of the spirit of the U.S.*

Recall now Ullman's (and Bastide's) concern about our shallow and fragmented dream culture. The foregoing survey indicates that we have made a certain progress in learning to respect the dream and to sanction its sharing. What continues to be more problematical is the second aspect of Ullman's analysis: we lack a recognized body of myth and ritual to pass from social experience into the dream. Reed means his Sun Dance to "help give birth to a contemporary mythology"[181] and presumably other borrowers have similar intentions. These are times of cultural dissemination and invention, and it remains to be seen how changeable—some would say redeemable—we are. But for the time being, it can be said without implying criticism of Reed or others that such borrowings are peripheral, perhaps even in most of the lives actually exposed to them, not to speak of other dream-conscious people, still more the culture-at-large.

Another question which needs to be raised is, how do Native Americans feel about having their spiritual traditions borrowed? This question has been ignored in the writings of the borrowers of dream traditions.

No doubt many Native Americans are glad for the respect belatedly paid their heritage. Some promote the borrowing, from sincere belief in the saving power of Indian spirituality. But there are others who object strongly, out of reverence for their own traditions, combined with acute political consciousness.

"According to Matthew King, an elder spiritual leader among the Oglala Lakota, 'Each part of our religion has its power and its purpose. Each people has their own ways. You cannot mix these ways together, because each people's ways are balanced. Destroying balance is a disrespect and very dan-

---

* This is reminiscent of Charles Upton's (1988a and 1988b) dream bridge to the U.S.S.R. Contrast Delaney's (1990c, p. 27) no-nonsense remarks about dreamwork as a vehicle of social change on a national and international scale: "Dreams will not get us there on time; it's going to take much too long. Unless dreamworkers get really smart and go for people in power, and people in power are very afraid to tell their dreams. . . . I try, through individual contacts, to deal with people in power, but it's very hard; they're very inflated. So, I'd love to say: 'This is going to save the world', but I don't think we can wait for dreams to do it."

gerous. That's why it's forbidden.'"[182] Russell Means of the American Indian Movement voices the position radically: "As to white people who think . . . they have some fundamental 'right' to desecrate our spiritual traditions, I've got a piece of news for you. . . . Our religions are *ours*. Period. We have very strong reasons for keeping certain things private, whether you understand them or not." Anyone who does not respect this privacy is "complicit in cultural genocide. . . ."[183]

Despite how it may seem, writes Andy Smith of Women of All Red Nations, "the New Age movement is part of a very old story of white racism and genocide against the Indian people." Indians are seen as "cool and spiritual," while their actual condition is overlooked—everything from violated treaty rights to low life expectancy to forced sterilization. Smith alleges that New Agers understand neither Native American "struggles for survival" nor their spirituality. "They trivialize Native American practices so that these practices lose their spiritual force. They have the white privilege and power to make themselves heard. . . . Our voices are silenced, and consequently, the younger generation of Indians who are trying to find their way back to the Old Ways become hopelessly lost in this morass of consumerist spirituality." Smith calls this "spiritual abuse."[184]

Activist Winona LaDuke protests that "indigenous cultures have become commodified in the New Age movement. What is happening is that our culture is taken out of context and certain parts of it are sold or just extracted. It's like mining. . . . [T]o me, that's expropriation of our culture. It is the same as expropriating our wild rice resources or our land. And it is one of the last things that we have. It is our culture. . . . Pieces of it are taken out and moved around and it does bad things to us."[185]

Other activists, including Vine Deloria, Jr., The Traditional Elders Circle, and the National Indian Youth Council, also attack all selling of spiritual paraphernalia and practices for profit. "The exploitation of the sacred symbols of our ceremonies cause[s] pain and distress among our people, and denigrates the fundamental instructions of our cultures and teachings."[186] "True spiritual leaders do not make a profit from their teachings, whether it's through selling books, workshops, sweat lodges, or otherwise."[187] (Similar charges were levelled against both Wovoka and Sitting Bull during the heyday of the Ghost Dance.[188]) While a shaman often receives recompense for services, the person or family in want of help always applies to the shaman, is never solicited by the shaman. Hence the objection to all forms of promoting spiritual services.[189]

Native Americans who violate these traditions are especially indicted, but so too are non-Natives who sell objects and ceremonies—whether purported to be authentic or only "'based on' Indian traditions."[190]* This indictment evidently encompasses all of the dreamwork borrowers mentioned in earlier paragraphs.

It should be said that Native American cultures were and still are quite eclectic among themselves, borrowing and adapting freely. Dissemination both of the Ghost Dance and the Sun Dance demonstrate that. True, these cultures possess a degree of homogeneity among themselves which does not obtain between theirs and ours. But for us to incorporate their culture into ours is not absolutely different. In any event, there is probably no way to stop cross-cultural borrowing in a multi-cultural environment, and reason to approve it. Nevertheless, these considerations do not, from the point of view of the more vulnerable culture, answer the charges of commodification, expropriation, spiritual abuse, and cultural genocide, which have to be judged on their merits. Well-intentioned dreamworkers who cross cultural boundaries should at least weigh the unintended effects these protests allege, and all of us should sharpen our eye for outright exploitation.

The Judeo-Christian tradition. Writing for environmentalists, LaDuke acknowledges the spiritual hunger which ends in cultural expropriation and destruction, but she adds: "We must all find our own [instructions] in our own traditions. . . . You progressive people have to find your own answers in your own culture."[191] Reflecting on the books of Lynn Andrews as feminist texts, Smith writes: "A medicine woman would be more likely to advise a white woman to look into her *own* culture and find what is liberating in it." She adds that "pre-Christian European cultures are also earth-based and contain many of the same elements" as Native American cultures.[192]

But speaking personally, my birthright to pre-Christian European culture is no greater than to cultures of the Western Hemisphere—perhaps smaller,

---

* Native Americans singled out for censure include Sun Bear, the father of the activist Winona LaDuke. Non-natives singled out include authors Carlos Castaneda, Jamake Highwater, Lynn Andrews, Ruth Beebe Hill, and Hyemeyohsts Storm. The declaration of the Traditional Circle of Elders (1986) reads in part as follows: "The Traditional Circle of Elders is composed of the respected leaders, medicine people and elders of Native American communities throughout the great Turtle Island of North America and islands of the Western Hemisphere. . . . These people do not sell, trade or barter the sacred ceremonies for profit. . . . We, the Traditional Elders, again speak to the general public and announce that people of our respective nations are complaining that their ceremonies, pipes and sweatlodges are being violated by non-Native individuals and Native American individuals who purport to be 'medicine people.' This is a violation of our human rights, group rights, and a violation of our religious freedoms. The exploitation of the sacred symbols of our ceremonies cause[s] pain and distress among our people, and denigrates the fundamental instructions of our cultures and teachings. We cannot prevent people from throwing their money away on so-called 'Indian ceremonies' but we can challenge those who misuse our sacred pipes, sweatlodges and ceremonies. So now once again we demand that these violations cease."

by virtue of living on this soil; especially so, if the Mormon belief should incredibly turn out to be true, that the Indians are a lost tribe of Israel.

Thus we are steered back to the Judeo-Christian tradition itself—the very tradition which has left us without a viable dream culture (until the dream movement). Writings on the subject noticeably strain to make connections between modern dreamers and forgotten antiquarian sources. That said, the tradition does offer a resource for tying dream life to life, if approached in a vital way. Some excellent books about dreamwork have been written from a Christian perspective,[193] most by clergypersons with experience as pastoral counsellors. These works concern and in a way instill Christian symbology in dreams, but perhaps more, they represent dreaming as a conduit through which a higher power encourages the Christian ethic. Several emphasize the 'big' aspect of dreams, their community import, and even their function as "prophesy."[194]

"I have seen dreamwork open up prematurely closed political and strategic ideas," writes Taylor, who is a Unitarian Universalist minister, influential dreamworker, and currently a popular author. "I have seen 'religious' people awaken to the necessities of political and social action."[195]

Louis Savary et al. say that "God gives dreams to benefit the community,"[196] and offer guidelines for finding the social dimension. Here is a small example to show how straightforward and congenial this approach can be:

[A] woman dreamed *she was being offered the gift of a spaniel puppy. Its owner told her,* in the dream, *that if she did not take the puppy, he would have to put it to sleep. Her dream ego was in a quandary. On the one hand, spaniels were not among her favorite pets and, besides, she didn't want the responsibility of caring for a puppy since it would probably hinder her present life style. On the other hand, she didn't want to see the puppy die.*

When she looked at the dream from a social aspect ["after doing basic dreamwork on a personal level" (p. 179)], she realized that being offered the puppy ("man's best friend") symbolized an offer of friendship she had received the day before from a lonely person, and about which she had mixed feelings. The potential friend was, like the puppy, not attractive to her, yet she felt uncomfortable and selfish at the thought of rejecting the person.

When she looked at the dream from a larger community perspective, she realized that the puppy symbolized all the lonely and uncared for people in her community looking for friendship and care. The dream asked her to become conscious of her attitude toward members of the community who "were not among her favorites."[197]

Jung as myth (again). In this time and place, however, Christianity does not provide the intact mythology it once did. It is not surprising, therefore, that many (though not all) Christian dreamworkers are Jungians. (So is Joel

Covitz, author of a recent book on Jewish dream interpretation.[198]) To varying degrees they join Jung—who, though a dissenting Christian, nonetheless "explicitly declared his allegiance to Christianity"[199]—in modifying the tradition to accommodate a broad quest for mankind's common spiritual ground. In so doing, Jung sought to give mythology—not any specific one but mythology in general—a genuine bearing for us. His sanctioning of dreams borrows from all cultures, not neglecting to include Western scientific-clinical ideology. As I framed the Jungian position (ch. 3, p. 123), "we can draw on world mythologies to elucidate our own spontaneous symbolism with the guidance of a conceptual psychology."

Recall James Hillman's dictum about "the interchangeability of mythology and psychology."[200] Jung's "objective psyche" probably comes as close to a coherent, believable mythic symbol as we can hope for. The collective unconscious is given a special reality status. It, like most pantheons, has a hierarchical structure: at the top is the archetype of God, the unifying and central Self. Its power is its integrative drive, and it has the ego standing in relations of identity and polarity to it, much as Christ to God (or so it seems to me, as a non-Christian). Then, the other major functional components of the psyche: persona, shadow, animus/anima. Then, all the lesser archetypes: mother, hero, death and transfiguration, etc. Finally, the actualizations of the archetypes in myths, dreams, and human affairs.

If Freud saw a parallel between dream and culture in the quasisymptomatic repression implemented by both, Jung discovered one in their common power to mediate spiritual wholeness. Clearly, our cultural life is too fractured and in respects too moribund to be reformed by Jung's doctrine in a comprehensive way. But for the diffuse community influenced by Jung, the "Jung club,"* a sanctioned context of 'myth' connects waking and dreaming, certainly in the interpretation of dreams, and to an extent also in the actual content of dreams: call it archetypal dreaming, or incubation, or 'doctrinal compliance' (Freudians tend to have Freudian dreams, etc.), but the dream lives of Jungians are enriched and connected in ways meaningful to them, by learning the Jungian psychology.

But as Ullman correctly reflects, "[w]hat Jung did not develop was a way of actually placing dream work in the hands of the ordinary person."[201] Because Jung's star has risen during the years of the dream movement trend toward deprofessionalization, Jung is sometimes mistakenly associated with deprofessionalization.[202] Actually, Jung thought that mythic amplifications

---

* British Jungian David Roomy (1990, p. 7) mentions the "Jung club" and compares it to "the fellowship of Christians, the Buddhist *Sanga*. . . ."

require expert guidance, as does overcoming resistance to the unconscious. Only certain patients at the completion of their analyses with Jung were encouraged to continue dream interpretation on their own. Jung's is, besides, a difficult doctrine, with a certain inherent elitism. On the other hand, Ullman credits Jung with "a giant step toward making dreams potentially accessible to the nonprofessional" by allowing that dreams reveal rather than conceal. Add that in spite of Jung's own requisite of expertise, his ideas about archetypal symbolism saturate the dream movement.

Ullman's covert "social myths." If Jung's psychology offers a possible solution to the problem posed by Ullman—our lacking a sanctioned cultural context contributing to dream content—, Ullman's own response is of quite a different sort. Although, as mentioned elsewhere, he may "resonate" to it, he does not "hold to [Jung's] view of the collective unconscious and its archetypal structuring."[203] Nor does he display an inclination to hitch on to alien or defunct mythologies. Ullman's response is rather to look at dreams for those aspects which are *actually* culture-born. In this he is replying to the second challenge of Bastide's project of a remedial dream sociology.[204] With his dream groups he answers the first challenge, "the legitimization of the dream's passage into the waking world." The second calls for identifying the actual "intrusions of social structure into the dream world."[205] Such intrusions, which exist despite absence of an acknowledged and coherent mythology, Ullman figuratively (and loosely) terms "social myths."[206] These appear "inevitably and of *necessity*" in dreams.[207] Thus our dreams reflect our culture, but we could not call the result culture-pattern dreaming in the strict sense, because the cultural influences in question are not prescribed, not sought, and not usually perceived for what they are.

One aspect of the Bastide-Ullman sociological (or "neoculturalist"[208]) approach to covert social myths is to raise them to consciousness in an ad hoc way when we do dreamwork. Ullman is after those beliefs and attitudes embedded in what he calls the "social unconscious."[209] (The social unconscious is instilled by the current social surroundings, not inherited genetically as is Jung's collective unconscious.) Doing dreamwork with others, believes Ullman,[210] offers a detached perspective on the social unconscious, otherwise difficult to achieve because we exhibit "social resistance" to hard cultural truths, to go along with our resistance in the personal sphere.[211] The value of dream sharing (or enlightened therapy) in this regard is that one gains the benefit of others' social and political insights.

Ullman asserts that "the interplay of the social and the personal inevitably emerges (or should emerge) in the course of dreamwork."[212] In actuality, it emerges less often than it should. As Hillman's anthropological study of the dream movement finds, "although dreams contain a wealth of social and cultural information, these aspects are rarely explored in dreamwork settings, at least not explicitly."[213] In a comment meant to encourage optimism about the status of socially conscious dreamwork, Ullman concludes with an unintentionally pessimistic observation, which all of us should consider: "To the extent that those involved in dreamwork remain impervious to the deceptions and imperfections of the social order, the work itself will collude with the dreamer's waking collusion with that order."[214]

The efficacy of the approach Ullman recommends has to depend on the aptness of the social critique brought to it. One must have an idea what to look for. As for Ullman's own evaluation of our society, his views apparently fall between, on one hand, the rather diffuse commentaries of Bonime and other culturalists[215] who point out social, political, or economic dream meanings, and, on the other hand, Fromm's neo-Marxist critique, which Ullman admires in general terms.[216] Ullman's overview of our society is as negative as Fromm's, as can be inferred from this passage: "There are segments of society in a position to misuse power and to deny that any such misuse exists. Rationalizations buttress the denial. These deeply ingrained, taken-for-granted rationalizations form the social myths at work in a given society."[217] We should be about "dismantling" our social myths, therefore, as pernicious things comparable to illusions and neurotic distortions.[218]

Ullman broadly characterizes the perniciousness of social myths in several obviously interrelated ways, all amenable to dreamwork: in terms of "the emotional fallout from the social arrangements and institutions around us";[219] in terms of "embedded kinds of ignorance" which are socially conveyed;[220] and in terms of "power deprivation."[221]

As for "emotional fallout," he follows Fromm in thinking that specific social structures produce characteristic patterns of ill-health. He goes beyond Fromm, perhaps, in suggesting that *all* ill-health may require implicit cultural reinforcement to endure.[222] Among our characteristic patterns of ill-health —our life styles, Adler would have said—Ullman mentions impotence, dependence, aggression,[223] irrationality, and violence.[224]

As for "embedded kinds of ignorance," he singles out racial and gender stereotypes, and particularly blames the mass media for insinuating harmful role models which often show up in dreams.[225]*

---

* But not all media effects are pernicious. Perhaps it would qualify as another approach to social myth, what Dee Burton does in her book *I Dream of Woody*. She surveys dreams dreamt by fans in which Woody Allen appears, to discover what Allen means to them. Burton's most general conclusion: "More than anything else, Woody Allen stands for a search for meaning in a shallow world" (1984, p. 194). It would be interesting to repeat this survey, in light of Allen's bad publicity.

As for "power deprivation," social myths "are apt to operate to the disadvantage of minorities, women, children, older people, and the poor."[226] Along such lines, several authors have raised *feminist issues*. Emphasizing that dreams compensate (in the Jungian sense) not only personal attitudes but also cultural attitudes, Signell discusses how women can become more conscious of their internalizations of gender stereotypes by dreamwork.[227] Koch-Sheras et al. affirm that "[o]ur dreams can also reveal *cultural beliefs*. . . ."[228] Subtitled *A Dream Interpretation and Exploration Guide for Women*, their book, published in 1983, credibly "emphasizes the need for changing the environment around you in order to resolve your 'personal' problems." "In seeking solutions to our personal dilemmas through dreamwork, we need to understand the social fabric out of which these issues may arise. In turn, when we change ourselves through dreamwork, we also affect the world of the people around us. . . . Social change may be swept along by political activism such as the women's movement. However, such changes only become a reality because many individual women *live these changes in their own lives*."[229]

Existing dream books, these writers accurately point out, do not for the most part directly address women's issues, even though many were written by women.[230]

Issues these and other writers[231] approach through dreamwork include: overcoming the stereotype of the pretty homemaker; not getting unbalanced toward masculine values; affirming autonomy; overcoming "fear of taking power and assuming leadership"; learning to risk confrontation; combating the "superwoman syndrome"; taking control of child-rearing decisions and reproductive choice; enhancing "body consciousness and sexuality"; and exploring "new models for our relationships."[232] Under the heading "Competence and Confidence," "[t]he following dream example illustrates how one young girl, through a dream, glimpsed her own truth about success despite strong family messages to the contrary":

> I'm walking along a cold and lonely beach. I see a wood frame house going up ahead and only one person building it. This seems strange because my grandfather and other carpenters all work together building a house. I step inside the frame and look up at the carpenter hammering above. It is a woman! She smiles and winks at me. I feel very proud that we share a special secret between us.
> When I was eight years old I told my grandfather, a successful carpenter, that I might want to be a carpenter when I grew up. My whole family laughed at this. My mother said that women's arms aren't strong enough. My father said a woman could never be a **successful** carpenter, because the job requires logic and common sense, and women were weak in this area. My grandfather put an end to it by saying, "If women could be carpenters, why don't you see them working

at building sites?" I thought this over and decided disappointedly he must be right. That night I had this dream.

I never shared this dream with anyone, but the image of the woman working above me stayed with me for a long time and was a source of inspiration for me throughout my high school and college years.[233]

The following two examples of socially conscious dreamwork center on *racial issues*. The first is from Ullman's book with Nan Zimmerman about dream sharing groups. It concerns conflicts and alternatives confronting an upwardly mobile African-American. The second, from John Wikse's chapter in a book edited by Ullman and Claire Limmer, comes at it from the other side of the black/white divide. The first:

[This] is the dream of an ambitious young black lawyer working hard to advance himself. At the same time he feels strongly committed to "being of help to my people." Edwin's dream:

I was playing baseball with a childhood friend in a wooded area. There were two out for the home team. I looked and assessed the situation. I realized that the better team was the one that was out on the field. I felt conflicted. I wanted to be on the winning team but my friend, who was on that team, said that I would have to play in the outfield. This didn't appeal to me. I wanted to be at bat and the center of the action.

I wound up coaching a rundown between first base and home plate. I finally saw the first baseman was going to miss the ball. I encouraged the batter to go. He rounded first and was going to second.

The night before the dream Edwin had been at a meeting where he was called upon to act as a mediator between a group of black workers and their higher-ups. He realized that, as an educated black professional, he was facing choices that would test his resolve to be a leader to his people when such choices might compromise his own ambitions. . . .

"In the dream I was torn. I wanted to be part of the winning team but I knew what would happen if I did. I would find myself out in left field, socially successful perhaps but unimportant, unrecognized, unfulfilled. This is what happens to upwardly mobile blacks. They are co-opted and give up the struggle. The other choice was to do what I could for my own home team. I would have liked to be a hero and save the game by my performance at bat. This is the part of me that wants to make a grandstand play and gain recognition. In the dream I seem to have worked through to a role that will take into account my need to further develop my professional skills and, at the same time, direct those skills toward helping my team. . . ."

There were a number of more personal associations to the dream, but one in particular opened the dream up for the dreamer. He became aware that the friend in the dream who warned him of being in the outfield if he joined the winning team was a composite image of two childhood friends. One tended to play it safe and went on to a successful career in the business world. The other took risks, became alcoholic, and died quite young. He could identify with both. The dream seems to be saying that both images would have to be transformed if he was to work toward his ideals and still survive. It also pointed to a strategy that seems to work. Being on the losing side he has to take advantage of the errors of his opponent. He does this in the dream even at the risk of being "run down."[234]

The next reading is from an article concerning the "social intelligence" of dreams. Like Ullman, Wikse find in dreams a detached perspective from which interconnections of "social, individual, and political reality" become visible.[235] His dream is titled "The View from Across the Aisle":

While traveling on a Greyhound bus from Pittsburgh to Chicago I was reading a book on the Haymarket "riots" in Chicago at the end of the nineteenth century. Included were several examples of anarchist posters organizing workers to strike. Across from me was a young black man. I curled up into the seat to sleep and dreamed that *I was watching myself as I slept from his seat across the aisle. Above me as I saw myself sleeping, in the space reserved for commercial advertising, was a poster. It was composed of a series of columns of figures which computed my lifetime grade point average, from kindergarten through my Ph.D.: 3.9 was the total. Above these numbers was my signature, Jack Wikse. Someone walked over and scribbled "Jack Wis" over the poster.*

. . . The anarchist posters from my reading have been transformed into a self-advertisement of my academic achievements, a sign or signature of my persona, projected from the perspective of a stranger across the aisle. "I wonder how he sees me?" is the seed of the dream, projected by the social unconscious across the aisle of race and class and privilege. The answer is mediated by the iconography of the lifetime grade point average, simultaneously a personal and a social image (perhaps even an institutional). The dream tells me it is my signature, that is, the way that I am recognized by others. It is an image of privilege and success.

An off-kilter version of this identity is scribbled, across my self-image, a defacing of my poster-signature, "Jack Wis," something strange and feeling unfinished. When I worked with this dream I felt that the transformation of my last name into "Wis" was an ironic way of saying, "You think you're so knowledgeable and 'wise,' studying the history of the working class, such a 'wiz' studying the anarchists, but cut off from the man across the aisle." . . .

The dream confronted me with my unfinished self-image. It challenged me to integrate this perspective on my social self, pointing me to explore the relationship between race and privilege and academia, those patterns of identification that had made it a dilemma for me to cross the aisle to another part of my divided social body.[236]

Race is one of the great problem areas of our society. Yet apart from the items just quoted, there are exceedingly few references to race to be found in the dream literature,[237] let alone examples of dreamwork such as these, dealing directly with race relations,[238] or discussions of African-American dream culture. An effect of this circumstance, and a cause, is the scarcity of blacks in the dream movement. I have discussed the reasons for this situation in another publication.*

Briefly, many blacks, with pressing economic and other reality concerns, consider dreamwork a luxury they cannot afford. Dream groups, along with other growth formats, are viewed as white middle class pursuits. Even successful blacks, says black Jungian Father Charles Payne, often do not possess the mentality of leisure which such pursuits require.[239] As for potential black dreamworkers, most of them have had to struggle to achieve the status of professional, and understandably they lean toward more conventional and promising career tracks. So observes black dreamworker Loma Flowers,[240] Gayle Delaney's associate. Others choose approaches they believe address survival in a racist society more directly than does dreamwork. Bear in mind the urgency of social and economic (on top of emotional) problems often besetting blacks seeking help. When "the real world is the problem," dreams and dreamwork may seem "less relevant."[241] Black psychologists opt for approaches perceived to be more empirical and concrete.[242]

This attitude toward dreamwork belongs in the context of a general criticism of Euro-American psychology expressed by some black psychologists. They consider racism "the major impediment to psychological wellness in the Black community." Consequently, when blacks reach out for guidance or help, they have a right to expect "social and political advocacy."[243] Otherwise, "the professional's mission is oppressively one of getting the client to adjust to the status quo. . . ."[244] But nominally color-blind white psychology suppresses specifically black issues. It lacks a proactive orientation, but implicitly throws the burden of change onto blacks.[245] Many potential black participants in the dream movement expressly or intuitively share this viewpoint, articulated by black psychologists.

Another reason cited by black psychologists for why blacks are alienated from white psychology, and by extension from dreamwork, is its strong emphasis on *intra*psychic processes (see ch. 6, p. 213 passim). It is sobering to realize that Euro-American dreamwork is considered uncongenial to the psychology of African-Americans in just this aspect which might well be re-

---

* A. Shafton (1991). For that article, I interviewed a number of black psychologists and dreamworkers: Faheem C. Ashanti, William M. Banks, Carole "Ione" Bovoso, Loma Flowers, Gerald G. Jackson, Charles Payne, William D. Pierce, Loudell F. Snow (an authority, but not black, as I subsequently discovered), and E. Bruce Taub-Bynum. Of course I do not speak for them, still less for blacks in general.

garded as its particular genius, intrapsychic analysis.* Several of the black psychologists whom I interviewed, among them E. Bruce Taub-Bynum, a family therapist, framed the matter in ethnic terms. Their argument is that African-American *extra*psychic orientation is truly African in origin. They referred to the movement among black intellectuals which finds West African[246] and even Egyptian (or "Kemetic" = 'black')[247] roots for characteristics of blacks in the Americas.

"[T]he African philosophical tradition does not place heavy emphasis on the 'individual'. Indeed . . . in a sense it does not allow for individuals," W. Wade Nobles writes.[248] Gerald Jackson argues that a sense of the "primacy of the group" conveyed from Africa,[249] as much as the harsh life here, has contributed to the real-world, extrapsychic orientation of African-Americans; in contrast, Euro-American individualism lends itself to intrapsychic understandings. Moreover, to 'do your own thing' is seen as alien to Africa-based values.[250] Hence the general coolness of blacks to the human potential movement[251] and its sequels, including the dream movement.

In the thinking of certain influential black psychologists beginning in the 1970s, the intrapsychic, self-centered approach of white psychology is connected with the assumption that blacks will assimilate by overcoming their deficits vis-a-vis white middle class standards.[252] But neither progressive policies nor the ideal of color blindness recognize black mores as valuable in their own right. These thinkers insist that African-Americans derive "unique status . . . not from the negative aspects of being black in white America, but rather from the positive features of basic African philosophy. . . ."[253] That understanding is now embedded in black nationalism.

This may have little to do with dreams directly, but it bears on why it is that blacks are reluctant to bring their intimate concerns into white settings such as those where dreamwork is being done. Most African-Americans are not be aware of these intellectual perspectives, but they are sensitive to the dissonance between prevailing attitudes to black life and their own, and are alienated from anything in the arena of white mental health by a "history of misdiagnoses and stereotypes. . . ."[254]

---

* Carried to an extreme conclusion, intrapsychic analysis gives rise to John Weir's technique of transmuting everything in the dream report into a self-reference, as follows: "It doesn't matter" → "I don't matter"; "That hurts" → "I hurt me"; "That confuses me" → "I have me be confused"; and, grotesquely, "I drive the motorcycle" → "I have me be the driving part-of-me of the motor part-of-me cycle part-of-me" (J. Weir, "The personal growth laboratory," in K. Benne, L. Bradford, J. Gibb & R. Lippett, editors, *The Laboratory Method of Changing and Learning: Theory and Application*, Palo Alto: Science and Behavior, 1975, quoted by P. R. Koch-Sheras, E. A. Hollier & B. Jones 1983, pp. 61-2).

What if a dream of "social rebellion" were said to show an "upsurging of sexual impulses" instead of a desire for social change? As Robert Haskell pointed out to the Association for the Study of Dreams membership not long ago,[255] this is the sort of bias which white treatments of black dreams have in fact shown. Few dreamworkers would insist on such a reading, perhaps; yet its standpoint is uncomfortably familiar. It exemplifies the two ways that 'our' dreamwork fails to satisfy the real-world orientation of blacks: too little focus on the world and its injustice, and too much focus on intrapsychic processes.

It is interesting to notice similar complaints about one-sided intrapsychic analysis beginning to surface inside the dream movement. Mary Watkins, in the Association's journal *Dreaming*, writes: "Until recently, when images of the world clearly suffused a dream, our modes of interpretation attempted to return the dream to the realm of the personal—by interpreting a nuclear explosion as one's rage, dreams of pollution as reflecting concerns with sulliedness."[256] (In another connection, Signell notes that a woman's "emotional intensity" is sometimes interpreted away as "negative animus."[257]) Watkins depicts the situation in terms which echo both culturalism and the viewpoint of black psychologists: "American psychology has largely been created by the forces of radical individualism, often minimizing the impact of the sociocultural context. . . ."[258]

Johanna King also takes the dream community to task for its unbalanced orientation to the intrapsychic meanings of dreams. She attributes the bias to (1) our culture's legitimization of narcissism, (2) the pervasive influence of Freud's intrapsychic focus, and (3) our sheer laziness when it comes to reforming the real world. King makes the case that "many dreams are best understood in terms of the dreamer's objective life experience," and gives as illustrations dreams from personal situations of sexual abuse, and societal situations of political turbulence and oppression, including torture. The intrapsychic bias "sap[s] attention and assets from the arena of social action and reform. . . ." King suggests that "we must be willing to look at and face the ugly, disturbing, dark parts of the world, without mislabeling them as projected shadow." She calls for balance.[259]

In an encouraging development, in 1993 the *Dream Network Journal* announced a column by Bulkley, "Dreaming Life, Waking Life," dedicated to exploring "interactions between the world of our dreams and the world of our society. . . . Our dreaming lives give us powerful insights into our social world—into politics, art, religion, communal relations—and help us to work toward the healing of our social ills."[260] I understand that the inauguration of the column has had to be suspended, but not from lack of interest on the columnist's part.[261] When the *Dream Network Bulletin* (as the *Journal* was originally called) first appeared in 1982, the founder William Stimson's lead article was titled "Dreams as a Subversive Activity," and concerned dreamwork as a means of "counter-conditioning" to political-economic as well as personal errors of thought.[262] Under the present editorship of H. Roberta Ossana, the *Journal* has become a little New-Age-ish, and has lost Stimson's political edge.

The issue of race came up in connection with ad hoc dreamwork done to raise consciousness about what Ullman terms social myths. Another potential side of his sociological approach to social myths through dreams is that of revealing sociopolitical problem areas by scanning many dreams. Such an approach is a rarity. One of the very few content analyses performed to uncover "macro-level social and political processes"[263] is Yoram Bilu's survey of dreams of Jewish and Palestinian 5th-7th graders living in various locales in Israel and the West Bank. Both groups dream frequently of the other, the Palestinians somewhat more of the Jews than vice versa. Characters of the other group are largely stereotyped, and are encountered far more in aggression (90%), frequently violent aggression, than in friendliness (4%). Usually these children dream themselves as victims of adults. Generally these trends are more pronounced, the closer the contact of the dreamers with the other group and the more pressing their situation. Hence the trends are strongest among the Palestinian refugees. Camp children are "obsessively concerned" with Jews in their dreams.[264]

The Jewish dreamers are almost always targets of unprovoked aggression. Nevertheless, effective retaliations outnumber unfortunate outcomes, indicating an ability "to retain a sense of security and mastery vis-a-vis the adversaries around them,"[265] e.g.: *"Three terrorists in a car sneak into the kibbutz. They hit the sentry at the gate and a few other members, but the other kibbutzniks seize their rifles and kill two of the assailants. The third terrorist takes the dreamer's friend as a hostage but is killed by dreamer."*

The Palestinian dreamers are also targets, but they generally fail to retaliate: *"Israeli army attacks at night. The house is surrounded. Brother is put in jail, where he is severely beaten."* However, the Palestinians themselves attack without provocation in 17% of their encounter dreams: *"A policeman asks dreamer for bread. She poisons him, usurps his gun, and kills the Israeli conquerors. Eventually she becomes the governess of Arab Palestine."*[266] The last example has features of a dream type unique to the Palestinian children, of political triumph, often with religious overtones. Taken together, these three types of Palestinian aggressive dreams, Bilu concludes, "form a psychological unity": (1) "terror, panic, and helplessness," (2) "unmitigated rage and hatred, as well as an intense wish to avenge," and (3) "wish-ful-filling fantasies . . . of an ideal future."[267]

Bilu draws the unfortunate moral: "Since today's preadolescent dreamers are the politicians and soldiers of the coming decades, these firm, well-established schemes and images, if taken seriously, bode ill for the stability and persistence of the conflict." The following dream, one of a small set of similar dreams reported by the Jewish children, grasps and dramatizes the predicament for both sides:

> *Two terrorists, Bedouins in red kefiyehs, seize the dreamer. She manages to escape and run away to her home, chased by the Bedouins; there she turns around, confronts her chasers, and beats them up. They run away, but after a while become the assailants again. Now she flees, . . . "and the dream goes on with no end."*[268]

A different approach to the political psychology of dreams can be found in Carlotte Beradt's grim retrospective study of *dream life under Hitler*. Her unusual book is titled *The Third Reich of Dreams*. It will be summarized in the next pages.

Beradt makes a record of over 300 dreams which she collected as a therapist in Germany between 1933 and 1939. The dreams seem "to record seismographically the slightest effects of political events on the psyche. . . ."[269] "The Nazi official who maintained that people could lead a private life only in their sleep certainly underestimated the power of the Third Reich":[270]

> In 1934, after living one year under the Third Reich, a forty-five-year-old doctor had the following dream:
> *It was about nine o'clock in the evening. My consultations were over, and I was just stretching out on the couch to relax with a book on Matthias Grünewald* [sixteenth century Alsatian artist], *when suddenly the walls of my room and then my apartment disappeared. I looked around and discovered to my horror that as far as the eye could see no apartment had walls any more. Then I heard a loudspeaker boom, "According to the decree of the 17th of this month on the Abolition of Walls . . ."*[271]

With discomforting clarity, Beradt exposes the dreaming psyches of ordinary people—many of them opposed to the regime or ambivalent about it—in the process of being coopted, of internalizing (and even foreseeing) totalitarian techniques of control, and of becoming complicitous. An appended essay by Bruno Bettelheim explores how this is abetted by the tendency to project intrapsychic conflicts onto the political landscape.

The following sampling and commentary is taken from Shohet's review of Beradt's book:

[Beradt] demonstrates how effective the propaganda was in penetrating people's defense mechanisms, making them afraid to disobey even in their unconscious. Thus one dreamer dreamt *she was talking in her sleep in Russian so that not only would others not understand her, but she would not even understand herself. . . .*

The effectiveness of this propaganda machine, however, depended on people's ambivalence which weakened their internal resolve to resist. . . . Thus a doctor dreamt that *Storm troopers were putting up barbed wire at all hospital windows. He has sworn that he would not stand for them bringing their barbed wire into his ward. But he did put up with it as they turned his ward into a concentration camp, but he lost his job anyway. However he was called back to treat Hitler because he was the only man in the world who could. He was ashamed for feeling proud* and woke up crying. . . .

Again and again . . . the author demonstrates not only the acceptance of conditions, but the state of mind in which acceptance grows—namely the readiness to be deceived and construct alibis for oneself. Thus *one man saw Hitler as a clown and saw through his carefully calculated manipulative gestures, but ended up* in the dream *thinking Hitler wasn't so bad after all and there was no need to oppose him. . . .* Another person *is ostracized for not saying 'Heil', and even while failing to understand how she could change her attitude so quickly, she climbs onto a bus whose destination is 'Heil Hitler'. . . .*

. . . The author sees the dreams as dealing with the political realities of the moment and the dreamer's conflict with society (unlike Bettelheim who sees the conflicts as having their roots in inner conflicts evoked by social realities) and she ends with a warning of the dangers of failing to recognize threats to freedom before they loom too large. . . .[272]

Beradt also presents dreams of the most threatened targets of the regime, the Jews. In one from 1935, *a man is refused entry in "the last country on earth where Jews are still tolerated."*[273] (Dreams of borders and checkpoints must be common in this century of displaced and migrating populations.*)

Another was dreamt by a lawyer in his sixties, in the same year. Beradt writes:

[He] had always considered a person's dignity and repute as matters of great importance. . . .

Two benches were standing side by side in Tiergarten Park, one painted the usual green and the other yellow [in those days, Jews were permitted to sit only

---

* A contemporary addition to the catalog of so-called 'typical dreams' (being naked in public, unprepared for an exam, etc.) has been termed by Czech-Canadian novelist Josef Skvorecky "The exile's dream": "In that dream," Skvorecky says, *"you are in Czechoslovakia or Rumania or Hungary or wherever. You've lost your passport, you go to the airport and you hope you will somehow sneak through the control barrier. And you wake up covered in sweat. Every exile has that dream"* (J. Gill 1985).

on specially painted yellow benches] [Beradt's brackets]. *There was a trash can between them. I sat down on the trash can and hung a sign around my neck like the ones blind beggars sometimes wear—also like those the government makes "race violators" wear. It read, "I Make Room for Trash If Need Be."*

. . . [L]ong before Beckett's characters in *Endgame* were placed in trash cans, our dream author puts himself in a trash can and is even prepared to make room for trash in this, the "endgame" of his own existence.[274]

Finally, Beradt also records a small number of *dreams of resistance*, and that is a good topic with which to wind up this discussion. Beradt's most impressive example is this dream from Inge Scholl's book, *Die Weisse Rose* (The White Rose):

[It] was experienced by Sophie Scholl, the well-known student condemned to death for resistance. It occurred the night before her execution in 1943. Sitting on her cot, she gave her cellmate the following account:

"*It was a sunny day, and I was carrying a little child dressed in a long, white gown to be baptized. The path to the church led up a steep hill. But I was holding the child safely and securely in my arms. All of a sudden I found myself at the brink of a crevasse. I had just enough time to set the child down on the other side before I plunged into the abyss.*"

Attempting to explain the meaning of this simple dream, she told her cellmate, "The child represents our idea, which will triumph in spite of all obstacles. We are allowed to be its trailblazers, but we must die before it is realized."[275]

Watkins relates a resistance dream she heard at a conference sponsored by the Association for the Study of Dreams in Moscow. The conference just happened to begin on the day of the attempted anti-reform coup, on August 19, 1991:

One 25 year old [Russian] woman, a translator, dreamt that *all the small newspapers which had burgeoned under perestroika were now outlawed. In desperation she went to her kitchen crying, and began to print her own small newspaper.*[276]

During the Gulf War, the media reported that people around the country were being troubled by nightmares. Jane White Lewis, a Jungian analyst, says that her patients brought in anxious dreams with imagery from the war, dreams in which the "shadow" was projected onto the Iraqi enemy: "[T]he war images in these dreams have a purely personal significance."[277] This interpretation bespeaks an intrapsychic approach to dreams, to the exclusion of prima facie extrapsychic meaning. However, Lewis continues that the war dreams she heard have "social and collective implications." War, she says, is enabled by collective projection of the shadow onto the enemy. As long as individuals are unconscious of their own shadows, they are susceptible to being drawn into the collective projection.[278]

I will conclude with a Gulf War dream which, whatever its "personal significance," prompted the dreamer James Harrington to resist the war. It is quite a long dream, but fairly easy to follow and self-explanatory:

I am a hospital corpsman in the United States Naval Reserve being readied for mobilization in the Persian Gulf conflict. What follows is an actual dream I had on July 3, 1990. . . . It has offered me spiritual and moral courage in speaking out for the necessity of finding alternatives to war. It has served as an initiation into social action against war in the Gulf, and into manhood. . . .

In the dream, *I know of no life outside the uniform I wear. I'm a gungho "Doc," and the Navy wants me to instruct the troops in the current strategy of how to "hold the enemy."* This is not actual Navy strategy but a dream phrase describing *a core military practice. Deep inside I know that if I teach or support the Navy's strategy on holding the enemy, I will betray the very core of my spiritual being.* So, at the start of the dream *I am plunged into a crisis between my identity and my spiritual self.*

My mind asks why I can't follow this order, and the answer comes in a vision of the mirage of personalities who make up the chain of command, from petty officers to Pentagon leaders to elected officials. They all wear outward clothes of warriorship, but none have the inner qualities of warriorship to allow them to hold the enemy properly. They are all children with awesome outward power but no inner wisdom. None are worthy enough to be followed.

I refuse to present the Navy strategy on how to hold the enemy. This refusal is taken as an act of total insubordination. Even though I know of no life outside the uniform, I refuse to participate in the Navy. I have taken an oath before God to serve the Navy, but I cannot betray God in order to fulfil the oath of service.

I am depressed for weeks as I wait for the court martial, and as I contemplate what has led me to this point, I realize the value of models in our lives. I see in the military a rich array of models for people to follow. I wonder what model it is I am now following.

In the certainty of dream knowing, *I know the answer to lie in a very sick dog. This is a faithful spiritual guide dog of my past that is now so sick that a sneeze alone may kill him.* This dog has been in my dreams in the past, ever since, as a boy, I nearly drowned . . . in a river. The dog and I have a deep psychic connection.

Military doctors and nurses are desperately trying to save the dog. They know full well it is only because the dog lives that they have power over me, and the dog remains alive not because of their efforts, but because I won't let the dog go. But seeing him in such a desperate state breaks my heart, and I give the dog permission to die.

At once I am plummeted into a depth of depression previously unknown. I know that I will soon follow the dog into death.

Ten minutes before the court martial, I decide to get a haircut. I want to end things in a proper manner. I leave the base looking for a haircut and realize what

I really want is initiation. I cross the country looking for a barbershop from Hawaii to Disneyland. Places that look like barbershops end up turning out to be candyshops. Little time is left before the court martial, when I suddenly "know" the place to get a haircut is in Cambridge, Massachusetts, an old Victorian house in the middle of the great universities there. I know of this house and know of some scissors in the bathroom there.

I begin to cut my own hair and have almost finished when I notice over my left shoulder, where the dog has always been, a strong fierce presence named Ali, a Muslim. His fierceness is surpassed only by his love and loyalty to God. I smile and he smiles. I know he is the sick dog reborn a man.

The woman of the house has noticed me, and I feel awkward since I am a stranger there. I pull up my pants (which have been down while I was cutting my hair) and decide to leave the house pretending I didn't see her. She cannot stop me but she stops Ali. She points to me and tells Ali, "He is a teacher for this world and has to stay." They make arrangements. My connection to Ali is such that it is as if I am making the arrangements. This is the first time in the dream that *I realize I have a life beyond the uniform I am forsaking.*

Traveling back across the country, I look into the psyches of people. Each person is wearing a huge sombrero with a video monitor on the front. When the hats are flapped up, I can see the ideals of Star Trek playing across each person's mind. Then, at a speed that astounds me, the hats flap down and the monitors show bombers and war films reminiscent of the Vietnam era. A voice within tells me the ideals of Star Trek are everlasting and are the ideals I need to support and not those of war.

I wake to my roommate throwing me some keys and telling me to get to work. I say, "This is my work," and get up. Soon after I realize I am still asleep and decide to get up "for real." The dream is over.

. . . The dream has spoken a great truth, and I must follow it. I will need to take a stand against the military and speak for the need to find alternatives to war. The dream offers me moral courage in standing against a nation's destructive war psychosis.

(One month after the dream Iraq invaded Kuwait.)[279]

"We are social beings," writes Ullman, "and by gaining a more honest perspective about society and our role in it, we can become better social beings."[280] He specifies little of his own agenda, but his impulses are unmistakably toward reform. "We have not yet worked out a system of economic democracy without which our political democracy will be played out only by those who hold economic power."[281] He says that resocializing the dream challenges the assumptions of bureaucratic-technological society,[282] and that dream groups tend to foster social activism.[283] Such results occur as embedded, unexamined social myths are raised from social unconsciousness into "social consciousness."[284]

In one place, Ullman considers whether "social consciousness" is perhaps more than a useful abstraction. Citing theories of Trigant Burrow (1927) and Andras Angyal (1941),[285] he speculates that it has an "organismic" actuality. Ullman explores this notion of society as supraorganism little further, but the ethical and clinical implications drawn, in particular by Burrow, go to the heart of Ullman's culturalism. He summarizes Burrow: "Our thoughts and feelings have a suprapersonal dimension. There is a social consciousness which they influence and to which they are accountable. Health is an acceptance of this supraindividual or organismic state of affairs. Illness, in this sense, is its neglect in the interest of individualistic ends."

This discussion began with Adler's concept of social interest. In closing the chapter, Adler's precedence should be recalled. Take away the "organismic" speculation, then Ullman's paraphrase of Burrow sounds substantially like Adler on social interest as the foundation of health. While the healthy individual rejects "the faulty values that culture projects," as the Adlerian Mosak puts it,[286] the basis of her/his health is "the feeling of being socially embedded, the willingness to contribute to the communal life for the common weal."[287] Without pressing the point too far with regard to direct influences, and not forgetting the quirkiness of Adler's views about dreams, it is fair to say that Adler anticipated the currents of socially conscious dreamwork discussed above. Something akin to Adler's social interest, with its inherent criticism of how things are and commitment to how things might be, joins Bonime, Fromm, Reed, Shohet, Christian dreamworkers, the dream sharing communities, Signell, Koch-Sheras, Wikse, Beradt, Watkins, Lewis, Harrington, and others mentioned, notably including Montague Ullman.

□ 6 □

Gestalt

Frederick (Fritz) Perls first used the designation *Gestalt therapy* in print in 1951.[1] Trained between the wars as a psychoanalyst, he began forming his own approach in the 1940s, with his wife and collaborator Laura Posner. According to James Simkin, one of Perls's original students in the U.S., it was she who contributed much of the foundation of existential, phenomenological, and Gestalt thinking to Perls's early development and writing.[2]

Gestalt is known for the style of dreamwork Perls practiced at the Esalen Institute in California from 1964 to 1968. By then, work with dreams had become his technique of choice.[3] He had proclaimed individual therapy "obsolete,"[4] superseded by workshops where the therapist takes on participants in turn as they occupy the "hot seat" in front of the group. Before his death in 1970, he had decided that "even group therapy was obsolete"[5] and had departed to a "Gestalt kibbutz" of some thirty members.[6]

Since that heyday, so strongly flavored by the personality of Perls, the Gestalt approach has moderated.* The dream workshop format is less prevalent; in fact, most therapy is now done individually, or with families or in other modalities. Methods have become less confrontational and "abrasive," there is a gentler emphasis on self-acceptance, and more tolerance is shown for conversation about psychodynamics and other techniques not requiring role-playing.[7] Be that as it may, the abiding influence which Gestalt exerts in contemporary dreamwork, almost across the board, derives not from current practices but from Perls's original technique:

Assume that every element of the dream represents a projected part of the dreamer's personality (the 'intrapsychic' assumption discussed in chapter 5).

---

* Perls's "Gestalt prayer" (1969, p. 4) is almost embarrassingly evocative of those years: "I do my thing, and you do your thing.| I am not in this world to live up to your expectations| And you are not in this world to live up to mine.| You are you and I am I,| And if by chance we find each other, it's beautiful.| If not, it can't be helped."

213

Let the dreamer play the role of dream elements, and of her/his responses to them (thoughts, feelings, body actions). S/he should speak in first person present tense.

Hold dialogues with and/or between these *split-off* fragments of personality, with a view to integrating or *reowning* them.

This technique, accessible as it is and at least superficially simple, so easily generates novel insights and feelings of catharsis/acceptance/resolution, that Perls felt compelled to warn against its abuse as a gimmicky quick-fix cure, like other quick fixes of the late 1960s falsely promising that "if you get some breakthrough, you are cured. . . ."[8] Twenty-five years later, Gestalt authors still warn against insufficiently trained Gestalt practitioners offering shortcuts[9]—which actually testifies to the power and viability of the technique, whatever abuse it may lend itself to.

Gestaltists apart, virtually every contemporary approach to dreams owes something to Perls and his dream dialogue method. Certainly it is a staple of any eclectic approach. Diana Whitmore states the reason: "To relate to each item or object in the dream as a part of yourself . . . can be quite illuminating. I'm not convinced that this is the true meaning of our dreams but it certainly can be revealing."[10]

A Variant of Existential Psychology

To put Perls's Gestalt therapy in context, it is—whatever its special traits may be—a variant of "phenomenological-existential therapy."[11] Perls, in acknowledging debts to Buber, Tillich, Sartre, Heidegger and others,[12] said he was doing "existential psychiatry."[13] Dream movement pioneer Ann Faraday —whose popularization of Gestalt as part of her eclectic "dream power" approach is still very readable—calls Gestalt "the active component of existentialism," for its aggressive insistence on the here-and-now.[14] Gary Yontef & James Simkin describe the "constant and careful emphasis on *what* the patient does and *how* it is done," including what s/he thinks and feels, from moment to moment.[15] One of Perls's most universally adopted dreamwork techniques embodies this emphasis: he required the person telling a dream to heighten its presentness by using the present tense: 'I am running,' never 'I was running.' Gestalt work tends to recast all verbalizations as first person present tense declarative statements.*

---

* Lillie Weiss (1986, p. 73) believes it can be helpful to reduce, not increase, the immediacy of the dream in recalling it. She sometimes has a dreamer relate the dream in the third person "as though it were a story that is happening to another person. This gives the dreamer some distance

Features of Gestalt ally it to some of the Adlerian-existential-culturalist trends already discussed. Gestalt is a *social psychology*, concerned with the "Mitwelt" (with-world) of organism in environment.[16] Notwithstanding its emphasis on wholeness of self, including the credo that all dream elements signify parts of the dreamer's self, Gestalt's tenor is markedly extroverted. "Meaningful awareness is of self in the world, in dialogue with the world, and with awareness of Other—it is not an inwardly focused introspection."[17] That said, Perls was staunchly countercultural: "I believe that we live in an insane society, and that you only have the choice either to participate in this collective psychosis or to take risks and become healthy. . . . If you are centered in yourself, then you don't adjust any more."[18]

"There is no essence of human nature," say Yontef & Simkin recently, in familiar existential language; "people are endlessly remaking or rediscovering themselves."[19] All the emphasis is placed on *choice, authenticity, self-responsibility*. No doubt exaggerating for effect (exaggeration being a hallmark of his method), Perls wrote: "I haven't seen a single case of infantile trauma that wasn't a falsification. They are all lies to be hung onto to justify one's unwillingness to grow."[20] He meant, of course, not that the unhappy past is a fabrication, but that one has to assume responsibility for holding onto it, in the form of shame, resentment, etc. "This is where Freud went completely astray. . . . He thought a person does not mature *because* he has childhood traumata. It is the other way around."[21] So the therapeutic issue is not how your problem came about, but "what is it 'doing for [you]' in the here-and-now."[22] (In the final sample of dreamwork in this chapter, Perls illustrates his repudiation of psychoanalysis.)

Importantly, Perls "rejected any notion" of the *unconscious*, instead describing the personality with a notable metaphor as "a rubber ball floating and turning in the water, so that only one portion is visible at a time. The Gestalt therapist works with the portion that is visible in the context of the moment."[23]

Though Perls did not label it as 'unconscious', there is one unconscious, essential, and all-encompassing instinct or drive of crucial importance in the Gestalt conception of personality: the "innate drive to health,"[24] or to "self-actualization."[25] Here Perls's conception has much in common with Jung's Self-system. Both are animated by the same paradigm of organismic wholeness, a paradigm which likewise influenced Horney's biological "striving toward self-actualization,"[26] Medard Boss's "innate existential possibilities,"[27]

---

from the dream and helps him or her see the actions more clearly." Rosalind Cartwright makes the same suggestion (R. Cartwright & L. Lamberg 1992, p. 264).

and the entire 'human potential movement' of which Gestalt has been an important constituent.

Perls's Gestaltist slant, influenced by all of the above, derives ultimately from a theory of perception developed by Wertheimer in Germany before World War I and elaborated by Köhler and Koffka between the wars. Higher organisms, according to this theory, immediately perceive the world as forms or patterns (*Gestalten*), they do not secondarily construct these from smaller bits of sense data. The perceptual array presents itself as a unified field, one as whole as prevailing conditions allow.*

For Perls, the idea of gestalt perception melds with a broader organicism to become a homeostatic law of life: "the only law which is constant is the forming of gestalts—wholes, completeness."[28] This law also governs human personality, which is described, perhaps metaphorically, as functioning by "mental metabolism"[29] which maintains the personality as a 'good gestalt'. Life is a continuum of incomplete gestalts; as we close or complete one, the next arises. When a person is in good health, "what is of greatest concern . . . becomes Gestalt, comes into the foreground where it can be fully experienced and coped with . . . so that then it can melt into the background . . . and leave the foreground free for the next relevant Gestalt."[30] This gestalt-forming "metabolism" constitutes the drive to health or self-actualization.

Ill-health is found as there exist defects, or "holes," in the prevailing gestalt of personality. Holes are due to the "disowning" of parts of ourselves "in order to avoid pain."[31] An ongoing avoidance of these holes causes transient holes, or incompletenesses, in the perceptual gestalts which make up the continuum of awareness: we mistake reality. The attention flow becomes impeded, we confuse figure and ground, gestalts compete, we "get confused . . . split . . . fragmented."[32]

The overall aim of Gestalt work is to get us to reown our split-off parts, to fill in our holes. The therapist does this by calling attention to what we are disowning. S/he assists and corrects the flow of attention, at critical moments making us aware of what actually occupies the foreground, even when it seems a distraction or interruption. Perls called this particular technique "feeding back the experience." Here is a fragmentary example of the technique, applied with dreamwork. It and subsequent examples are from published transcripts of dreamwork sessions. The dreamer, Carl, has associated

---

* This original Gestalt psychology produced the well-known figure-ground illustration which we cannot help but see now as 'the gestalt' of two faces in silhouette, now as a vase. It is also known for Wolfgang Köhler's experiments (1921) showing that chimpanzees not only modify tools but solve the problems requiring them (e.g., joining sticks to fetch bananas) by sudden insight into a whole situation rather than by raw trial-and-error.

the *train tracks* of his dream to his mother, who, he says, controls the train of his life. He speaks as the tracks-mother:

> C: . . . I direct you. I am inanimate, I am dead, but nevertheless I structure your life force. And although you are the life, I lead you in such a way that you are not unique, you're not your own thing. . .
> F[ritz Perls]: You know something? I don't recognize your mother's voice. I think you're talking literature. So play your mother.
> C: I direct you.
> F: This is how she speaks?. . .
> C: I can't come out with the way she speaks.
> F: Now go back and tell her that.
> C: I can't revive or reconstruct how you speak, Mother.
> F: What does she answer?. . . You see, we pick up every experience and feed the experience back. . . . [T]he part that is alive.[33]

Perls has guided the dreamer away from conceptual understanding toward vital *feeling*. As singlemindedly as any existentialist, Perls rejected cerebral interpretation as "antitherapeutic."[34] Feelings are what generate insight (formation of good gestalt), and insight cures. "It's the awareness . . . of *how* you are stuck, that makes you recover, you realize the whole thing is just a nightmare, not a real thing, not reality."[35] Much of dreamwork, then, consists of getting the intellect out of the way to let feelings and awareness follow "the wisdom of the organism" in its self-regulation.[36]

Two further points about feelings. First, Perls held no brief for anxiety, that emotion which existentialists such as Rollo May (ch. 4, p. 150) esteem as honest in the face of death and other painful inevitabilities. Perls was all for "explosive" emotions, such as grief, but anxiety he dismissed as vitality gone stagnant, a sort of "stage fright" in life: "If you are in the now, you can't be anxious, because the excitement flows into ongoing spontaneous activity."[37] This facile half-truth belies the Zen-on-the-cheap side of Perls, who sometimes seemed to offer now-ness as a panacea.

Second, Perls underwent therapy with Wilhelm Reich in the 1930s. Perls was influenced by Reich's view of habitual body set as a means of emotional armoring, an influence passed on to the "feeling therapy" of Richard Corriere et al., to the "dreambody work" of Arnold Mindell, and to the "focusing" of Eugene Gendlin.[38] All aim to release energy locked in the body by neurosis. In Gestalt theory, our repressed needs take the form of "muscular contractions which prevent flowing movement and at their worst cause us to develop body symptoms and joint involvements."[39] A Perlsian session almost always features attention to how emotions are expressed through involuntary activity or suppressed through tension or desensitization. The usual approach is to exaggerate the effect: "You never overcome *anything* by resisting it. . . . Whatever it is, if you go deeply enough into it, then it will disappear; it will be assimilated."[40] So, for example: "Close your eyes and tense up. Take responsibility for tensing up. See how you tense up; which muscles tighten?"[41] Characteristic are passages such as the following, where Jack Downing, a protege of Perls, interrupts the dreamer playing the role of *a threatening building* from her nightmare to ask:

> JACK: What's your right foot doing?
> PATTY: Reaching . . . hmmm.
> JACK: Ask your right foot what it's reaching for.
> PATTY: What are you reaching for?
> PATTY as right foot: Holding her back. Keeping her from getting into that bad place again.[42]

And here is Perls, seizing upon the physicality of a dream, making its enactment the entire dreamwork:

> Beth: (harsh, grating, strong voice) In my dream, *there is a steel band, like part of a truck wheel, around my chest and I can't get out. I feel trapped in the steel ring and I keep trying to get out—*
> Fritz: Okeh. For this, I need a strong man, somebody to come up here. (man steps up) Beth, become this steel ring in your dream. Put your arms around his chest and try to keep him trapped. (she does this, and squeezes tightly) Okeh. (to man) Now **you** try to break out from this steel ring. (there is a brief, vigorous struggle and he breaks free)
> B: (discovery) But I'm not made of steel!
> F: Yah! Get the message?
> B: I really thought I could hold him![43]

Something to note about this exercise is how Perls takes up the obvious opposites in the dream. Usually such opposites either manifest themselves plainly—as do, in this instance, the confining steel band and the struggling dream-ego—, or else emerge in the course of dreamwork. Gestalt regards opposites as *poles* of a reconcilable conflict in the personality. "The concept of polarities treats opposites as parts of one whole, as *yin* and *yang*."[44] So a dream polarity is "a starting point for the potential integration of the total personality" in which maladaptive, self-alienated oppositions are resolved.[45] Playing on Freud's famous saying, Perls calls the dream "really the royal road to integration."[46]*

---

* Polarity and conflict are of course ideas which feature in many dream theories. According to Werner Wolff (1972 [1952], p. 290), it was Wilhelm Stekel (1943 [1913 and later]) who first tried to view all dreams as attempts at conflict resolution, rather than as wish-fulfillments. In Great Britain

The enactment with the steel band is atypical in that a second party was enlisted to play a role, as in psychodrama.* Usually the subject plays both conflicting roles.[47] And usually, the enactment is largely conversational, except that the person may move from one to the other of two facing chairs as s/he changes roles. Here is a more typical encounter, staged when a set of opposites had become clear after many minutes of working on a dream about *going home to see mother and father*:

> F[ritz]: All right, now let's see whether we can't get these things together. Now have an encounter between your baby dependency and brazenness. . . . Those are your two poles.
>
> J[ane]: (as brazenness) You really are a punk. You sound just like a punk. You've been around. You've been around for a long time. You've learned alot of things. You know how to be on your own. What the fuck's the matter with you? What are you crying about?
>
> Well, I like to be helpless sometimes, Jane, and I know you don't like it. I know you don't put up with it very often. But sometimes it just comes out. Like I can't work with Fritz without it coming out. I can hide it—for a long time, but—if you don't own up to me I'm gonna really, I'm gonna keep coming out and maybe you'll never grow up.

W. H. R. Rivers (1923) took a similar line. Thomas French and Erika Fromm (1964) employed a standard notion of conflict in their influential hypothesis that every dream contains a "focal conflict." A typical focal conflict: "The conscious purpose to continue with his psychoanalytic treatment *versus* [f]ear of reactivating disturbing conflicts from his 'prehistoric' past" (p. 31). They regard dreaming as a defensive reaction to the focal conflict, an attempt to keep it from reaching consciousness.

Cartwright (R. Cartwright & L. Lamberg 1992, pp. 42–3) advises us to pay close attention to "dream dimensions, distinctions that we make to define and categorize our experiences. . . . The idea of our using a system of opposites in our dreams is one I have adapted from the work of the noted anthropologist, Claude Levi-Strauss, who . . . suggested that the mind works on problems by dividing key issues into pairs and then by juggling these elements . . . until they fit the needs of the person telling the story." Typical dream dimensions: "Safety versus danger." "Pride versus shame." "Authenticity versus pretense." By and large, Cartwright sees our well-being served by gravitating to the positive side of the polarity, not by reconciling or integrating the poles.

Perls's view has more affinity with the Jungian view concerning archetypes of which we are insufficiently conscious. Discussing a dream about a mermaid, Karen Signell (1990, p. 168) writes: "An archetype which is very unconscious seems to offer only two extreme choices, as does the mermaid: to be too self-contained alone on the rock, having just emerged from a state of oneness with the sea, or else too devoted, sacrificing unduly for relationship." And commenting on a woman's dreams about unicorns (p. 74): "The unicorn in all its beauty has come into her consciousness so that she can respect its qualities and carry them forward in her life, rather than be unconsciously captivated by the unicorn and live her life in one of the two opposites it represents: in solitude or in utter vulnerability. . . ." Robert Hopcke (1990, p. 67): "the very polarity of . . . any archetypal constellation makes for a cyclic kind of self-wounding if the opposites are not discerned and made conscious within ourselves."

* For an example of dreamwork done with psychodrama, see chapter 15 (p. 493).

F: Say this again.

J: I'm gonna keep coming out and maybe you'll never grow up.

F: Say it very spitefully.

J: I'm gonna **keep** coming out and maybe you'll **never** grow up. . .

F: Okeh, be the brazenness again. . . .

[Brazen asks Baby what she wants. Baby whines that she wants to be listened to. Brazen suspiciously agrees, with threats of retaliation if Baby keeps making a fool of her by not letting her grow up. Baby protests she doesn't want to grow up, it's too hard. Brazen gives Baby some tough encouragement. Baby agrees, but insists Brazen help by not always threatening her.]

F: Say this also to the group—the same sentence. . .

J: You have to allow me to exist without threatening me and without punishing me.

F: Say this also to Raymond. (fiancé)

J: (crying) You have to allow me to exist without threatening me. . . you know that. . .

F: Got it?

J: Yes. . .

F: Okeh.[48]

In their opening declarations, Jane's "brazenness" and "baby dependency" make a good example of Perls's arch polarity, which he tagged *topdog* and *underdog*. This useful conceit holds echoes of Adler's superiority/inferiority, as well as of Freud's superego/ego and Jung's persona/shadow. Perls "called the internal authority voices 'topdogs' of the mind, trying continually yet fruitlessly to impose their will on the rest of the personality, which then behaves like an 'underdog' wanting to keep topdog's approval and at the same time trying to get its own way."[49] "[T]opdog is a preacher, a dogmatist, a perfectionist, and a bully" as well as "a hypnotist and an exaggerating hypocrite," while underdog is a "coward, victim, masochist, and dupe —but he is also a cheat. . . ."[50] "The topdog manipulates with demands and threats of catastrophe," says Perls, while "underdog manipulates with being defensive, apologetic, wheedling, playing the cry-baby, and such."[51] Either dog can show up in dreams in the conduct of the dream-ego. But often, says Rainette Fantz, topdog comes in the guise of a policeman, judge, or other authority figure, including parent, while underdog appears in characters who "possess traits which we regard antipathetically—persons who are miserly, avaricious, hostile, self-pitying."[52]

Components of topdog get into us as "introjections, those pieces of our early environment that we've swallowed whole without assimilating. . . ."[53] All societal regulations can generate topdog introjects, but especially potent are parental shalls and shall-nots. Thus our parents are in this sense present in our psyches and our dreams. Whether called unconscious or not, they and their topdog surrogates represent the past, just as underdog represents our history of repressions and adaptations.

But although the distinction between dream image as signifying "object" (e.g., historical parent) or "part of the self" is not always strictly maintained,[54] still, the basic existential posture of Gestalt is that an introject is part of our own psyche now, for which we have to take responsibility. "The aim is to reduce the power of topdog and allow underdog to express his needs openly."[55] This is the resolution to which Perls led Jane's polarity. When resolution is effected, antithetical traits tend to transform into valuable qualities. In this revealed guise, disowned parts of personality are reowned and integrated.

Projection

Perls's view of dreams—that they provide material for fixing holes in the gestalt of personality—is a compensatory view. As with Jungian compensation, dreams trend toward "self-actualization." They draw up into the light "one's nonexistence"[56]—they give the floating ball of personality a turn.

But differently from Jung, Perls betrayed some of Adler's disdain toward imagery as such, connecting it with disguise (in all but name), and with ill-health. He thought that the dream "is always a cryptic message. If it would be a straight message, you wouldn't need to dream it. Then you would be honest, which means that you would be healthy and sane."[57] Also differently from Jung, he thought that in principle the entire self is represented in every dream. "'[E]verything' (the existential difficulty, the missing part of the personality and the integrated self)" is there.[58] Hence Perls preferred working with short dreams, which are less likely to confuse us, or even with an isolated dream fragment, which is like a fragment of a holographic plate from which the entire self can be generated. Anywhere at all we enter the dream world, we find "a condensed reflection of our existence."[59]*

---

* Freud (1953 [1900]) advised scrupulous attention to all details of a dream: "Examples could be found in every analysis to show that precisely the most trivial elements of a dream are indispensable to its interpretation and that the work in hand is held up if attention is not paid to these elements until too late" (p. 513). Counterintuitively, the intensity of a dream element is unrelated to its psychic importance (p. 330).

Erik Erikson wrote in 1954 (p. 6) that only an advanced interpreter should risk overlooking something essential by picking out what s/he believes are the relevant elements. But Harold Blum, in a paper from 1976 (p. 319) on "the changing use of dreams in psychoanalytic practice", said: "Free association is also disrupted if the analyst's style is to ask for associations to each and every

The mechanism underlying the Gestalt theory of the semantics of dreams is, again, projection: an aspect or quality of one's own is put outside oneself and experienced as belonging to someone or something else. Here Perls reverses the approach of Boss, who advises treating the dream world as if it were objectively real, no more or less projection than the waking world. For Perls it is all projection.

Jung made the distinction between objective and subjective interpretation. Objective interpretation takes dream images as standing for their real-world counterparts or as symbolizing something in the real world; subjective interpretation takes them "as personified [or otherwise symbolized] features of the dreamer's own personality."[60] Subjective (intrapsychic) interpretation has a history which Heinz Lehmann traces as far as Hippocrates, who, Lehmann writes, "insisted that dream images—no matter what or whom they concerned—always referred to the dreamer's own self."[61] The point was made nicely by Ralph Waldo Emerson: "If I strike, I am struck; if I chase, I am pursued."[62]

Emil Gutheil, discussing projection in dreams ("other persons may play the role of the repressed part of our personality"), quotes Freud expressing the same point in surprisingly definite terms: "It is an experience to which

---

aspect of the dream. The compulsive attention to dream details will resemble the patient's compulsive recitation of facts and fantasies or the inundation of the analysis with dreams." Jungian Mary Ann Mattoon (1984 [1978], p. 104) attends to every element: "overlooking one detail sometimes makes nonsense of the interpretation." Robert Bosnak (1988 [1986], p. 18): "I take a dream to be a psychic organism, a living reality in spatial form. One cannot remove an organ from a human being without altering the entire body, and the same is true of a dream image." And Mary Watkins (1984 [1976]): "When we take one element *out* . . . we use the dream. We single out something that interests us and let the rest go down the drain to forgetfulness. We think we are 'giving a lot of attention to our dreams,' but we are not. We are giving a lot of attention to the part of ourselves who sucks the image for its own gain. The imaginal scene has an integrity. Each element is *absolutely* necessary for the total image." Existentialist Boss (M. Boss & B. Kenny 1987 [1978], p. 174) discourages free association because it leads away from the dream, and to that extent agrees with Perls (1969, p. 51): "What Freud called association, I call *dis*sociation, schizophrenic dissociation to avoid the experience." But Boss says that the dream's analogy to the waking life will develop from precise descriptions of all elements of the dream itself "to the last detail." Walter Bonime (1982 [1962], p. 83) recommends sticking to crucial themes during the interpretive process. Jeremy Taylor (1992a, pp. 51-5) states and illustrates that fragments of dream recall communicate everything there is to be communicated, by what he calls "Zen telegraphy." In most grassroots dreamwork formats, and in any brief psychotherapy, there is rarely time for exhaustive examination of each and every dream element. In an article on "rapid dream analysis," John Scott (1982, p. 95) says that "[w]hen over half of the dream appears clear to the therapist and patient it [the analysis] should be considered successful. One should not endeavor to interpret everything; getting caught up in too many details should be avoided. There is always filler material to give the dream continuity, to try to interpret such would be misleading."

I know no exception, that every dream represents the dreamer himself. . . . When some person other than myself appears in the dream I must assume that my personality is portrayed, through identification, in that person."[63]

Freud actually attended to this subjective, projective side of dreams less consistently than many who learned from him.[64] Wilhelm Stekel, for example, compared his own and Herbert Silberer's[65] contrast between "material" and "functional interpretation" with Jung's distinction of objective and subjective, respectively.[66] He illustrates:

> I break open a locked door, and in so doing I destroy the lock, so that the door can no longer be closed properly.
>
> Here is the "material" interpretation:
>
> The dreamer has become acquainted with a girl, a virgin. He intends to seduce her. Defloration is symbolized. . . .
>
> Here, on the other hand, is the "functional" interpretation:
>
> I am forcing my way into my own interior. To do so I must destroy something precious. The new knowledge annihilates a fiction, which has hitherto served as a safeguard (self-protection).[67]

But it is to Jung, of course, that the subjective/objective contrast owes its development. Jung felt that "just as the image of an object is composed subjectively on the one side, it is conditioned objectively on the other."[68] This quotation shows his even-handedness to the two sides; but elsewhere, his position sounds nearly as one-sided as Perls's: "One should never forget that one dreams in the first place, and almost to the exclusion of all else, of oneself."[69] Jung tended to equate objective interpretation with Freudian reductiveness, and subjective interpretation with his own constructive psychology. When in doubt, he leaned toward the subjective.[70] Moreover, because real people have "hooks" for our projections (e.g., someone else's anger attracts our projection of anger), even dreams dealing with objective aspects of our lives must be approached with an eye to their subjective meaning.[71]

The rule of thumb, contends Jungian Robert Johnson, should be that the superficially objective image is actually subjective. The husband dreaming of his wife, for example, usually "needs to stop blaming his physical wife for his conflicts with his inner wife—which turn out to be conflicts within himself."[72]*

---

* Johnson (1986, p. 68) advises us always to begin with subjective interpretation, and only later to look toward "an external situation," if indicated. But Faraday (1976 [1974]), in her "three stage method" with its borrowings from both Jung and Perls, sensibly recommends that we begin from the objective side first, to see what "literal information" a dream might contain (p. xvi); "your marriage can disintegrate while you try to understand [e.g.] what aspect of the 'inner husband' is jealous. . . " (p. 119). Mattoon (1984 [1978], p. 113ff.) thinks that Jung himself somewhat over-

In different ways, both Freud and Jung viewed projection in dreams as a case of a more general propensity to project. Projection for Freud was one among the defense mechanisms, essentially neurotic in character. Jung, of course, knew this defensive aspect, noting for example that a neurotic's life is full of conflict because s/he loads projections onto intimate relationships.[73] (However, this can serve a "positive function," notes Robert Hopcke. "Jung understood the psyche as a self-corrective system, for even those maneuvers intended unconsciously as defensive often ironically work to present in external form that which we must eventually encounter within ourselves."[74])

But Jung's more fundamental, more profound understanding was that projection is a basic law of psychic functioning. "Everything that is unconscious is projected,"[75] he wrote, and everything unknown outside us draws projections: "In the darkness of anything external to me I find, without recognizing it as such, an interior or psychic life that is my own."[76] Projection, so understood, is "a natural proclivity for unconscious activities to be experienced as objectified."[77] Consequently, it is not a defense mechanism but "an original choiceless illusion caused by unconsciousness."[78] Projection is the primitive condition of organisms, and it is only with the development of ego consciousness that projections can be withdrawn, i.e., recognized as aspects of oneself.[79]

The so-called *transference* is a special case of projection which can illustrate this difference between Freud and Jung. By Freud's ground-breaking conception of it, the therapist, by virtue of being a powerful but ambiguous figure to the patient, acts as a screen on which the patient projects, or transfers, neurotic imprints of the child-parent relationship lingering from childhood. Thus therapy is a laboratory in which, with the therapist's guidance, "the patient achieves the opportunity to see very clearly the extent to which he has developed in his family experiences a set of images and fantasies that are . . . leading to gross confusions in the pattern of his interpersonal relationships."[80]

Jung affirmed the importance of the transference in therapy,* but with this elaboration: in addition to their personal neurotic contents, patients project those archetypal predispositions which were never realized in the usual way, in childhood relationships. This enables the therapist to "bring to birth in the

---

stressed the subjective side; she offers rough guidelines for deciding when to begin by looking one way or the other.

* At the end of their first meeting, Freud asked Jung, "'And what do you think of the transference?' Jung replied that it was the 'alpha and omega of the analytic method,' whereupon Freud, visibly gratified, dismissed him with the remark: 'Then you have understood the main thing'" (C. A. Meier 1959, p. 22, quoting and paraphrasing C. G. Jung, CW 12).

psyche of his patient those aspects of the archetype that had previously existed only as potential. As a result, the patient can complete his business with
the parents," actual and archetypal.[81] This entails, not only overcoming defenses, although defenses inevitably are involved, but also and more fundamentally, increasing the "range of consciousness." For Jung, transference
participates in that scheme of withdrawing projections which "underlies the
development of consciousness in general."[82]

Existential therapists typically dispense with the transference gambit. Bonime considers the Freudian conception of transference as a mere construct,
which distracts from therapeutic actualities of the present[83]—as no doubt it
can.* Boss prefers to say that a patient's capacity for relating, her/his "field
of seeing," has been arrested at childish levels, so that parent/child-like relations recur without the analyst being, therefore, a projected substitute for the
original parents.[84]

Existentialist Perls, however, takes the notion of transference on board,
though without an unconscious to motivate it, and without concentrating on
parental issues necessarily. His Gestalt account of projection in therapy is
close to Jung in its holistic spirit of reclaiming unactualized consciousness,
if comparatively simplistic concerning what it is which gets projected and
reclaimed. Perls painted with a smaller palette: "[T]he patient uses me, the
therapist, as a projection screen, and he expects of me exactly what he can't
mobilize in himself. . . . [E]very one of us has holes in his personality. . . .
Where something should be, there is nothing." Here Perls mentions soul,
genitals, heart, legs, eye, ears, and "center": "Now these missing holes are
always visible . . . *in the patient's projection onto the therapist.* . . . We apply enough skillful frustration so that the patient is forced to find his own
way . . . and discover that *what he expects from the therapist, he can do just
as well himself.*"[85]

So for Perls, as for Jung, projection is a crucial propensity, even apart
from dreams. A way of comparing their views of the matter is to ask, what
happens when projections get withdrawn? Again, Perls's vision seems relatively simplistic. He promotes the idea that withdrawing projections is easy
for the willing. His book *Gestalt Therapy Verbatim* ends with him saying,
"Once it clicks, you are through the projection and it's all over. First you
look through a window, and suddenly you recognize that you are just look-

---

* R. D. Gillman (1980, pp. 34 and 42), for example, maintains that to dream of the analyst undisguised is to put up a defensive barrier against the transference: "The patient's dream momentarily
insists on the reality of the analyst in order to repress those memories that are reappearing as
transference feelings." On the other hand, in James Fosshage's (1987a, p. 305) "revised model the
analyst is viewed as present only when he or she actually appears in the dream."

ing into a mirror."[86] We can value and seek this experience, without agreeing that it solves as much as Perls would have it do. Not only do our experiences "swarm with these projections," said Jung, but the hard thing about withdrawing them is that it eliminates the "bridge of illusion" which enables the expression of libido, in positive as well as negative ways.[87] This poses a profound dilemma which, Jung's autobiography hints, is soluble if at all only by the triumph of wisdom over desire in old age.[88] (In Asian systems, the dilemma is solved by enlightenment.)

Perls and Jung agree that when we withdraw a projection, something of ourselves is reclaimed by consciousness. But again, the Jungian version of this seems to do more justice to the difficulty and complexity of it. Seldom if ever, explains Marie-Louise von Franz, can a withdrawn projection be entirely absorbed by consciousness—a part falls back into unconsciousness. An archetype, moreover, cannot itself actually be integrated by the ego. Even in the case of archetypal dream images, failure to recognize that they represent something *"psychically real"* but *"autonomous,"*[89] and not just split-off parts of the ego, must result either in ego inflation[90] or the reprojection of the contents.[91]

For those made uncomfortable by the language of archetypes, let it suffice to acknowledge the existence of something transpersonal in the psyche —a point of view seemingly foreign to Perls, who would appropriate everything to the ego.

Perls says that most people have a void where they should have a self[92]— just the opposite of the Buddhist formulation. Perls's goal is in a sense the opposite of Buddhism's: his is the reowning or reclaiming of everything into the 'I'; Buddhism's is 'anatta', the emptying of the 'I'. Nevertheless, Perls promises us a life of successive mini-satoris,[93] or Zen-esque moments of enlightenment, resulting as we withdraw projections, reown parts, fill holes. We escape what he nicely designates the "intermediate zone"[94] of delusion (bad gestalt), where we are not quite ourselves nor is the other allowed to be itself. We come wide awake to recognize things for what they are.

Perls's payoff of heightened here-nowness is an extremely attractive offer, and unquestionably valuable, as far as it goes; but it looks a little one-dimensional at the end of the day. Perls conveys scant appreciation for the paradoxical nature of projection, which makes it at once the most obvious but also the most abstruse concept: obvious, because we easily detect what we overcontribute to some perceptions; abstruse, because we cannot conceptualize (though we may believe we experience) that vanishing point where the bubble of illusion prolapses, projections are all withdrawn, and we contemplate reality as it really *really* is.

But Jung, as von Franz tells us, finds "a meaning here of which those in the East have always been much more conscious than we have: namely, that in the end the whole world is only a projection," and the only "conclusive ending of all projections" is death.[95] And so a characteristic Jungian description of withdrawn projection less resembles a high moment of breakthrough enlightenment, and more resembles the experience of the sage when s/he has come down from the mountain to dwell again in the ordinary world: the Tibetan sage Milarepa delights in the details of a world which he knows to be illusion[96] (ch. 14, p. 474). This comes close, I believe, to what Jung meant by a 'symbolic life', that is, living in a creative tension between inner and outer images, in such a way that projections, unavoidable though they be, have become in some sense unbound.

Robert Bosnak conveys something of the sort when he tells what happens when we contain and work through a projection instead of harmfully acting it out: "It is a matter of action that gives the tendencies of the image world their due and at the same time perceives the images in the so-called outer world and reacts to them. One then lives in a world of inspiration in which the sharp distinction between inner and outer, contemplation and action, has been diminished."[97] This seems to describe a different sort of "intermediate zone," one of heightened and sustained clarity, not the muddled, frustrating intermediate zone which Perls correctly imputes to those in the thrall of their projections.

Be this as it may, Perls's and Jung's approaches do coincide in finding dreams to be an excellent tool for the work of withdrawing projections. For Perls, paradoxically, if projection accounts for dream formation, "projecting ourselves completely" is how we go about undoing the projection.[98] He contrasts "pathological" and "creative" projection.[99] "What is pathological is always the *part*-projection." By implication, most dream experience is part-projection, because, just as with waking projection, although we experience whatever is involved as outside of ourselves, our psychological investments enshroud it and trap it in the unclear intermediate zone. By contrast, "[t]otal projection is called artistic experience. . . ."[100] Total projection is also the basis of empathy,[101] which enters crucially into the Gestalt performance art of dreamwork.

The method involves complete projection in two senses. First, we project the dream item completely outside ourselves in order to confront, observe, or ask questions of it. Second, we project ourselves completely into the item and play its role.

Downing describes the first step: "The car in my dream isn't my actual car, it is my impression, my memory trace of that automobile having attributes and opinions and attitudes coming from me, not the vehicle. My playing that little gestalt game called projection separates the imaginary machine from me, puts that aspect of me outside, out there. Now I can talk to it as separate from me. . . . So, what is involved in being able to carry this apparent paradox out is knowing that the dream figure is truly me, at the same time that I'm projecting out and pretending it-me is not me."[102] And now the second step is to switch roles and become the car or whatever; we identify with it, "projecting ourselves completely" into it.[103]

A Gestalt enactment is something like a rehearsal for a play reading, with the Gestalt guide as director. Insofar as the actor's performance is verbal, it is less often speaking-about, more often speaking-as. Tone of voice along with expression, gesture, and posture help raise the qualities of the split-off part to awareness. (When the technique of switching chairs is used, it is to facilitate a quick change of identification by breaking up the previous body set.) This injunction to experience the bodily manifestations of the split-off parts makes a difference from Jung's active imagination and other passive dream re-entry techniques (chapter 15), though Jungians and Gestaltists borrow each other's methods.[104] In fact, here in a last, extended sample of Perls at work, it can be seen how dialoguing can merge into and out of dream re-entry and continuation, if one is so inclined—as this willing and suggestible dreamer clearly is. This is the passage mentioned earlier, where Perls draws his existentialist's moral about Freudian treatment of neurosis:

June: The dream starts *in an automobile that is parked in a great cavelike underground parking lot, by a train station, and I'm a little girl. I'm only about seven years old. . . My father is sitting beside me in the car and he looks very big, very dark. There are no lights on—it's a blackout, and I know that he's taking me to the train station to put me on the train to go back to school, because I have my school uniform on, my blue middy and my blue skirt, and there's an air raid going on, so we have to sit in the car, and the bombs are falling and it's very noisy.*

(thin, small voice) I'm very frightened. Daddy, I'm very frightened. I don't want to go to the train and I don't want to go back to school. (very faintly) I just want to stay home with you and mother.

(sternly) Are you frightened of the bombs, June? Or are you frightened to go back to school? . . .

(faintly) I just don't want to go back to school, I don't like it there.

Well, I'd like you to stay home . . . but your mother doesn't want you back there. . .

(whining) But you make the rules.

I don't make the rules. I have to live with your mother.

But bombs are dropping.

Fritz: You be the pilot. . .

J: There's a great feeling of power, to fly an airplane and find someone to drops bombs on and then just—press down the button. (confidently) . . . Plop. Drop 'em. Plop. . . . (fainter) I sure as hell frighten **some** people.

F: Okeh. Be still the bomber, go to Vietnam.

J: I can—I can (breathless and trembly voice) I can fly the plane there, but I] can't drop the bombs! They're real people there. . . . I can go around in circles, I can dive low and be shot at, but I can't shoot back. . . I don't wanna shoot back.

F: So go back and throw the bombs once more on that car.

J: (almost crying, helpless voice) There's a little girl in that car. I can't do that. . . Yes, I can. . . I did. They fell all around the car.

(rocking) And I'm the car, and I'm rocked, and I'm shattered, but the inside is intact, and the people in the car are safe. They're very frightened.

F: Much ado about nothing. . . .

. . . Let's try once more. . . .

. . . Be a bomber and drop napalm bombs on the Vietnamese.

J: All right. . . I'm coming now over the edge of the land, and I have a whole cargo full of deadly napalm. Jelly stuff. Now I go lower, and lower, because this time I'm really gonna hit it, and I want to see what I hit. . . (cries, chokes) Oh, **nooo**!. . . I hit a lady, who was running with a child in her arms, and a dog behind her. . . (cries) and they **writhed in pain**!. . . and I didn't kill them. . . but they burned.

F: So find someone else to kill. . . .

. . . Doesn't matter, as long as you get the killing out of your system.

J: (cries) My mother. . . how can I kill her. (softly and intensely) I want it to hurt. . . Boy, do I want it to hurt. . . Oh! I killed her. (still crying) Into the swimming pool, all filled with acid, and she dove in. There's just nothing left. (laughs). . . (quietly) You deserved it. I should have done it a long time ago. There aren't even any bones left. She just disappeared. . . .

. . . [S]he came down to swim, she dove in. . . and she—she **burned**. And she fell to the bottom, and the flesh came away and dissolved, and the bones started to go down, and they dissolved. And then it was all clear and blue again . . . And then I sorta felt **good**. I should have done it a long time ago.

F: Say this to the group.

J: It felt good! . . . Her death felt good. I should have done it a **long** time ago.

F: Okeh. Now close your eyes. Withdraw to your seventh year of life. Become seven years old.

J: (faintly) All right. . . Seven?. . . Oh boy, am I ugly. **Very** fat. I have crooked bangs . . . because I have to cut them myself because nobody cuts them. My hair is. . . frizzy and unkempt. My nails—they're all chewed down. From my neck to my knees I'm like black—dirty!—because all I have to do is button my middy buttons to say I washed, . . . and they never undid the middy buttons to see

if you washed any further than your wrists. . . . And a bell rings, and that means
we have to go out in the hall, and we line up. (cries words) And who can I talk
to? and I don't even know—ugrh—that no one wants that child. (wails) I always
get five demerits. I never get candy or ice cream. I eat potatoes and stuff. My
grandmother sends me a box of candy, and I'm not allowed to keep it . . . and I
don't even get **any**. (burst of crying) Please can I have one to eat?—and then I
won't have any next week. (sobs) . . .

[F:] . . . Play a thirty-five-year-old woman talking to this girl. Let the **now**
girl talk to the **then** girl. . . Put her in that chair, and you sit here. You are thirty-five now.

J: (gently) You're not a **bad** girl. . . . You're just pretty dumb, and not even
that's your fault. . . . I don't care if you've got holes in your teeth from eating
chocolate. And, June, I don't care if you're fat. I don't care if you're dirty, because all those things are really very superficial.

F: Now I want you to come back to us. I'd like to just have a bit of bullshit
about this. Any idea what makes you hug this memory to your bosom so much?

J: It went on for such a **long** time.

F: Okeh, look around, what's going on here?

J: I don't know. It doesn't have the **faintest** relationship with anything that
I'm doing here and now.

F: So, I'm interested that you have to drag this girl with you, that you can't
let her go.

J: Yeah. . . Sometimes. . . I don't even feel like I'm **dragging** her. I feel
like she's—she sits there, and she like waits for an opportunity when somebody
puts me down, and—boy, then she just takes over, and I'm a child.

F: **Exactly**, exactly. Now say, "I'm waiting for an opportunity to play the
tragedy queen," or something, and so on.

J: Uh, I can; I'm not sure it's gonna fit.

F: "I play you for a soft touch."

J: I wait for an opportunity to play on your sympathy, and warmth, and understanding. . . and then if I get it, I'm very grateful, and I feel better, and I
feel thirty-five years old again. So that I can cope. But the minute I feel that I
can't cope, then I shrink, and I'm little, and I let somebody else cope with me.

F: Then you pull her out of the garbage bin?

J: (strongly) Yes, then I pull her out, I present her to myself, I accept her,
and I act her, until I find somebody who is sympathetic, gets sucked in, and then
they're kindly, and then I feel reassured, then I can pull her away.

F: Now go back to her. Talk to her. Tell her about the con game you are both
playing. . .

J: Baby, we've got a game going. I didn't even know it until just now. (laughter) I'm thirty-five years old. I'm not fat. I don't have dirty wrists. (laughter) I
can buy a box of candy and eat it whenever I want to. I have **many** people who
love me dearly. I have many people that will give me support when I need
support, so what do I need **you** for? (laughter)

F: What does she answer?

J: Ahhh, she says, You're not altogether **su-re**. You know? Ah—I'm—a **very** handy little girl to have around. (laughter) (laughs) **An acid bath for you, too!** (much laughter)

F: . . . [T]his is one of the famous traumata the Freudian analysts peddle around. . . . They think this is the **cause** of the neurosis, instead of seeing it's just a gimmick. Psychoanalysis in an illness that pretends to be a cure. You understand, it is very difficult to bring home that all that happens here takes place in fantasy. . . . There are no bombs here, there is no killing, there is no little girl, **these are only images**. Most of our whole striving in life is pure fantasy. We don't want to become what we **are**. We want to become a **concept**, a fantasy, what we **should** be like. Sometimes we have what people always call the ideal, what I call the curse, to be perfect, and then nothing that we do gives us satisfaction. There is always something we have to criticize in order to maintain the self-torture game, and you see in this dream the self-torture game taking place to quite an extent.[105]

To repeat in conclusion, Gestalt techniques are readily appropriated by eclectic dreamwork approaches. At propitious junctures—particularly when polarities are in question, as they are in most conflicts—, the dreamer can be invited to take the point of view of one or more dream elements, without it monopolizing procedures.[106]

Gestalt is also available to those working alone. While allowing that the best results may call for an experienced guide, Faraday demonstrates with her own dream how effective Gestalt can be, used privately.[107] Though Perls thought self-therapy problematical for the usual reason of resistance,[108] he did give advice for going about it:

Write down every single detail you can remember of the dream.

Then, "*become*" each in turn, and "[h]am it up. . . ."

Then, "let them have encounters between them." If you get the right opposites, they will start out in conflict but finally "come to an understanding. . . ." "Then the civil war is finished, and your energies are ready for your struggles with the world."[109]

Part III

TOPICS

"Mother, I had a story last night; it was a bear story
—and I was in it too!"

— John A. Sanford, *Dreams: God's Forgotten Language*

On a journey, ill,
  and over fields all withered, dreams
    go wandering still.

— Basho (translated by Harold G. Henderson)

□ 7 □

Catagogic/Anagogic

Freud taught that dreams form as neurotic symptoms do, by compromise between wish and censorship (chapter 2). In both dream and symptom, the energy of a wish inadmissable to consciousness finds spurious release when transformed and disguised.

It was Freud's working out of the dynamics of these parallel phenomena —dreams and symptoms—which was epochally original, but not the underlying idea of such a parallelism. That idea already had a history, which Freud recounted as background for his own presentation: clinical connections between dreams and psychoses "were a favourite topic among medical writers in earlier times and have become so again today. . . ."[1] Beyond the clinical literature, Freud cited copious references[2] concerning a more general sense of the parallelism, starting with Kant's comment in 1764 that "[t]he madman is a waking dreamer" (a notion dating at least to the prior century[3]). Mentioning among others Schopenhauer, who in 1862 "call[ed] dreams a brief madness and madness a long dream," Freud went on to synopsize various writers (particularly Maury, Spitta, and Radestock) who examined dream/-madness similarities along parameters prefiguring the contemporary cognitive study of dreams.*

Freud concluded his survey by pointing out that these previous drawings of the "indisputable analogy between dreams and insanity" convey a depreciation of dreaming as "a useless and disturbing process. . . ."[4] However, Freud's own contribution to the discussion—namely, a tenable theory (one

---

* J. Allan Hobson, who is a psychiatrist, lists features of resemblance between dreams and psychoses: "1. formed sensory perceptions (akin to hallucinations); 2. cognitive abnormalities (akin to the cognitive inconsistencies and uncertainties that characterize delirium and dementia); 3. uncritical acceptance of all such unlikely phenomena as real (akin to delusions); 4. emotional intensifications (akin to those seen in panic anxiety); and 5. amnesia (akin to that seen in organic syndromes)" (1990, pp. 217–8; see also 1988, pp. 9 and 229–30).

derived from neurosis theory but extensible to psychosis) of the causes common to the two phenomena—, while it (almost) guaranteed that dreams could no longer be dismissed as senseless, nevertheless entailed depreciations of its own. Dreams, thought Freud, are excretory, "infantile," and "completely egoistic" (as opposed to altruistic), "reveal[ing] us as ethical and moral imbeciles."[5] John Mack, who reviews psychoanalytic opinions concerning the relation between dreams and psychosis up to 1970, points out that "[i]n one his last papers, Freud referred to the dream as 'a mental disorder occurring during sleep. . . .'"[6]*

I maintained in chapter 2 that the "dream-thoughts" comprise a far bigger component of the Freudian dream than is generally conceded, indeed than Freud conceded. Including, as they can, any waking mentation whatever, the dream-thoughts bring non-neurotic substance to the dream, even "altruistic impulses," as Freud acknowledged in a footnote.[7] Another important qualification of the dream/symptom paradigm was pointed out by James Hadfield: Freud's recognition in 1932 of such a thing as "super-ego dreams"—those in which punishment for a wish occurs, rather than just a wish—opened the door to an entirely as it were un-Freudian way of regarding dreams, namely, that "they have a moral function to perform!"[8]**

But dream-thoughts and punishment dreams notwithstanding, the overall negative and reductive cast of Freud's opinion of dreams is unmistakable: they come into being like and function like symptoms.

If Freud modeled dreams and neuroses after one another (thereby, says Charles Rycroft, "obliterating the distinction between health and illness"[9]), Jung instructed us that dreams can embody the trend to health. They heal by lifting toward consciousness those matters needed to compensate the ego's distortions of the psyche's overall balance.

Following other, mostly Romantic nineteenth century precedents, Jung believed that for modern, self-alienated mankind, dreams are the principle means by which universal values reach awareness. On one hand, Jung took numinous and guiding dreams seriously. But he also believed the healing, compensatory function to be at work in dreams which are not of a manifestly improving nature. These, our more typical dreams, lift personal as well as collective matters toward consciousness. They are frequently unpleasant and confounding, especially when our shadow asserts itself.

---

* In an extended discussion of this topic, Mack (p. 235) quotes Dostoyevsky—"a dream, a nightmare, a madness"—and himself writes (p. 176): "One might conceive of a continuum between normal affective dreaming and acute psychosis, with the nightmare as an intermediate state."

** But if Perls is right about "topdog" (ch. 6, p. 220), the punitive super-ego voice in dreams is moralistic rather than moral, and ought not to be heeded.

Of such dreams it can be said that they do indeed resemble neuroses, but for an un-Freudian reason: symptoms can be compensatory, as dreams are.[10] In *Healing and Wholeness*, John Sanford quotes Jung: "A neurosis is truly removed only when it has removed the false attitude of the ego. We do not cure it—it cures us. A man is ill, but the illness is nature's attempt to heal him. From the illness itself we can learn so much for our recovery, and what the neurotic flings away as absolutely worthless contains the true gold we should never have found elsewhere."[11]

So the difference between Freud and Jung involves not the fact of comparability between dreams and symptoms, which both find, but their different assumptions about the nature of disease. The Jungian slant is suggested by Robert Johnson's characterization of neurosis as "a Low-grade Religious Experience. . . . [I]f we don't go to the spirit, the spirit comes to us as neurosis."[12] (Jung also noted the resemblance of psychosis to a dream state.[13])

However that may be, the main point to be made is that Jung, in contrast to Freud, regarded dreams as essentially curative. True, the compensatory process has certain fallibilities and limitations. Sometimes "compensation may be as off-balance and off-balancing as the initial factor for which balance is being sought."[14] I quoted Jung's prediction of a suicidal accident on the basis of a casually related dream ("He mounts upward on empty air," ch. 3, p. 110). Archetypal inflations from dreams can precipitate mental illness. And in general, dream compensation requires the collaboration of consciousness to succeed. But all and all, dreaming is an organismic self-healing process of the psyche.

Both Freud's disguised wishes and Jung's symbolic compensations stand in a complementary relation to waking. The existentialists (chapters 4-6), on the other hand, stipulate continuity between dream and waking, and hence do not find dreams inherently to be either symptomatic or curative. Rather, waking ill- or well-being becomes analogized in dreams. That said, there are certain influences the two states can have on one another, having to do with mood effects, practice effects, work on retrieved dreams, etc.; and within the overall frame of the existential continuity hypothesis can be discerned a similar if less pronounced polarity as that between Freud and Jung. At the negative, Freud-like pole, Adler thought dreams tend to reinforce the less wholesome trends of the waking life style, a view resembling that of Freudian ego psychology.* At the positive, Jung-like pole, Perls's notion of filling

---

* "The defensive qualities of the waking state are very frequently reduplicated in the pattern of the dream" (E. S. Tauber & M. R. Green 1959, p. 166). If final shape is given to impulsive material by ego censorship to ensure its tolerability to ego consciousness, then the manifest dream will

holes in the gestalt of personality with matter brought up by dreams approximates Jungian compensation; and Montague Ullman considers that "[t]herapeutic systems may ultimately be judged by . . . [how well they succeed in] distilling from the dream images the healing power that lies within them."[15]

Chapter 1 concluded by saying that compared with J. Allan Hobson and others, Freud's view of dreams appears actually positive—as it did when he set it against prevailing nineteenth century scientific opinions of dreams as being meaningless, deranged, or merely somatic. On the other hand, when compared with Jung, nineteenth century mystical ideas, etc., Freud appears starkly negative. To some this way of speaking may seem overly dualistic, but it impresses me that almost all treatments of dreams implicitly or explicitly evaluate them, and that evaluations fall naturally into polarities of negative/positive.

Whether meaningless/meaningful, symptomatic/curative, or some other, these dualities are our culture's versions of what is actually a pervasive, perhaps universal fundamental of how humans understand dreams—how we understand life. The criteria of bad and good may be shifting and convoluted (as they are in the rich dream tradition of India[16]), but the categories of valuation are almost inescapable.

Indigenous cultures typically regard dreams as always spiritually real, but as only sometimes true or good. Bad dreams deceive, bring misfortune, or draw one into sorcery,[17] and must be counteracted appropriately to forestall bad consequences.[18] In addition, dreams can be "little" or "big," the latter depending on their special images or timing, or the dreamer's high status[19] (ch. 5, p. 175).

Pharaoh's dreams were big, as we know from the story of Joseph.[20] The earliest dream papyrus spoke of "bad" and "good" dreams.[21] The Egyptians dwelt more on dreams from spiritual sources which guide, warn, and answer questions posed during dream incubation,[22] whereas the Babylonians, who likewise had temples for dreaming, were evidently preoccupied with a need to ward off demonic influences. A Babylonian prayer asks for a "true" and "favourable" dream.[23]

Homer bequeathed us the image of the two gates of sleep, one of ivory for false dreams, one of horn for true.* Later, Plato discerned both "wild-

---

exhibit the same defense mechanisms as those with which one copes with the waking world, i.e., "ego defenses" (E. Sheppard & L. J. Saul 1958, p. 237).

* When thinned, horn becomes transparent, allowing one partially to see the truth beyond; ivory remains opaque, no matter how thin. This explanation is mentioned by Erich Fromm (1951, p. 116). It comes, says Naphtali Lewis (1976, p. 22), from Porphyry's *Commentaries*, as cited by Macrobius in *Commentaries on Scipio's Dream*. Katherine West (1977, p. 80) offers this explanation: "Ivory

beast nature" and God's voice in dreams.[24] It was not until Aristotle that a nondualistic viewpoint emerged in Greece. He "reduced dreams to the activity of the senses."[25] Then, just as in our pluralistic times, the polarity was expressed by competing perspectives within the culture, rather than by an integrated received viewpoint. Aristotle's skeptical empiricism was taken up in Rome by Lucretius and Cicero;[26] while Artemidorus, drawing Near Eastern beliefs into the mix, stipulated both false dreams, which come from personal passions and imaginings, and true dreams, from our own higher faculties as well as from divine sources.[27] Macrobius had a similar set of dream types: two types were of no worth for revealing truth, three were.[28]

The Old Testament God communicated through dreams; but personal, or little dreams were false.[29] According to Jewish Jungian Joel Covitz, the biblical ambivalence about dreams persisted through Jewish history, hardening if anything into mistrust of dreams,[30*] just as it did for most Christian writers after the first few centuries.[31] From its several traditions of origin, early Christianity acquired views about physical and psychological as well as divine and demonic dream causations. Some of the church fathers emphasized the divine (Synesius[32]), some the false and demonic (Jerome[33]), but not until Gregory the Great's time (600 A.D.) did "Christians beg[i]n to doubt the importance and value of dream interpretation."[34] Thomas Aquinas (1200 A.D.) confirmed this trend. While he acknowledged the full array of causations, including divine and demonic, he strongly reinforced Aristotelian empiricism and thus set the tone for Euro-American negativity about dreams.[35] Luther's Reformation did not help. He admitted divine dreams but mistrusted most seeming instances of them. Dreams of lust, etc. give us practice confronting Satan's devices, but as for guidance, better trust waking reason.[36**] By con-

---

is *elephas* in Greek, coming from the verb *eliphairo* meaning: 'to cheat with empty hopes'. Horn is *keras* in Greek, coming from the verb *karanoo* meaning: 'to accomplish'." Homer's metaphor was reiterated in the *Aeneid* by Virgil, who implied that horn is a more honest material, while the ivory gate of false dreams is beautiful but ostentatious.

* Maimonides, the twelfth century Jewish philosopher, divided dreams into three types (J. Covitz 1990): (1) "[P]rophetic" dreams, which ceased with the fall of the temple. (2) "[O]rdinary" dreams —"one-sixteenth part prophetic"—in which God sends information about our lives and futures. (By Islamic law, the ordinary dream is 1/46th prophesy, according to H. J. Fisher 1979, p. 220.) (3) "[D]reams of sorcerers and false prophets," which are demonic and "self-induced" (pp. 13-4). "Bad" ordinary dreams are warnings from God, and they fundamentally differ from "bad" demonic dreams (p. 57). Covitz tells us that Almoli, whose sixteenth century dream book Covitz translates, was one of very few Jewish thinkers to show much trust in the positive function of ordinary dreams. And "today dreams have no religious significance at all in mainstream Judaism" (p. 4).

** This did not, however, stop Artemidorus's *Oneirocritica* from becoming "the most popular book, after the Bible, in the century following the invention of the printing press. . ." (C. S. Hall & R. L. Van de Castle 1966, p. 23).

trast, the Koran's distinction of false and true dreams developed into a classification system with a persisting influence in Islam.[37]

Selective and oversimplified though it be, this survey illustrates the pattern. Whether, bad/good, false/true, inauspicious/auspicious, invalid/valid, physical/spiritual, secular/sacred, demonic/divine, or little/big, some combination of the negative/positive polarity typifies every culture's regard for dreams. These pairs all have survivals in our times, while even the polarities most characteristic of our times, meaningless/meaningful and symptomatic/-curative, have historical antecedents—the latter pair, notably in the medical diagnostic dreams of Hippocrates as against the curative dreams incubated in temples of Asclepius and other deities (see chapters 8 and 13).

Earlier in this century, Herbert Silberer and Wilhelm Stekel introduced a pair of terms which is apt for the general duality. First Silberer spoke of *anagogic*, or upward leading dreams.[38] As Stekel later described it, the anagogic trend leads to "all the loftier aspirations, such as ethics or morality, religion and romanticism, idealism, altruism, and the sense of social community. . . ."[39] Silberer was addressing himself to Freud's reductionism, and therefore termed the opposite, downward trend "psycho-analytic," to which Freud predictably responded that "the majority of dreams . . . are insusceptible to an anagogic interpretation."[40] Then Stekel, followed by Emil Gutheil and Werner Wolff,[41] broadened the context by renaming the negative trend *catagogic*, or downward leading. The catagogic "leads to . . . the sphere of sex, criminality, asocial attitudes, anarchism, and egoism."[42]

Like Jung, and unlike Freud, Stekel emphasized that we repress our morality as well as our immorality,[43] and he characterized "the mentally sick person as the champion of a disavowed ideal. . . ."[44] Dreams "search for a compromise" between the conflicting trends.[45] At night, our repressed anagogic side finds (compensatory) expression as much as does our catagogic side.[46] Wolff calls them "necessary aspects of the same thing."[47]

Stekel's vocabulary for the two sides—"romanticism" and "idealism" opposite "sex" and "anarchy"—sound quaintly dated to us now. Nevertheless, with Silberer he has bequeathed us this useful word pair, which, as Wolff remarks, captures a "psychic polarity which has been recognized from the ancients on."[48]

Stekel, Gutheil, and Wolff supply quantities of examples of both trends, but with express preference for dreams where the anagogic trend asserts itself against that daytime repression of it which they find common in our culture.[49] Medard Boss, in an early paper, provides an example of this where the conflict is pathologically extreme. The case reminds us that the anagogic trend sometimes loses out:

A cow, which is to be slaughtered, is lowing in the stable of our tenant. I wanted to go and help the cow, but got stuck in the filth in front of the stable door. The nursemaid Anna came over from the manor and ridiculed me. I awoke in great fear and excitement.

. . . Repeatedly during her first schizophrenic episodes she was tempted to kill her mother. In the dream, however, a counter-tendency is still active: she wants to help the cow which is to be slaughtered. Tendency and counter-tendency have her paralysed. The patient gets stuck in the filth before the stable. The filth stands for the dirty stories which the nursemaid had told her. . . . [S]he is in danger of bogging down in the filth of her primitive impulses. . . .

In the 9th year of her illness, when the patient's condition had progressed to the point of constant hallucinations and incapacity to perform continuous work, she dreamt:

I crossed a swamp with Mother and Anna. Suddenly I was seized with a terrible rage against Mother, and immediately I pushed her into the swamp, cut off her legs, and pulled the skin off her body. Then I watched her drown in the swamp and had a certain feeling of satisfaction. As we decided to walk on, a large man with a knife in his hand came running after us. First he grabbed Anna and then me. He put us on the ground and then had intercourse with us. Meanwhile I was not afraid at all, and suddenly I was able to fly over a beautiful landscape.
. . .

. . . One further dream, from the 12th year of her illness, when her personality had deteriorated into silly, hebephrenic demeanor, goes as far as undisguised incest. She dreams:

There was a woman in a crouched position, with doubled up legs, and a man riding on top of her. Suddenly I sneaked into this woman, and my father was drawn into this man. He came to me and committed all kinds of sexual obscenities with me.[50]

Something exemplified by this series is that a catagogic dream is not necessarily unpleasant, nor an anagogic one pleasant. The middle dream moves from matricide to intercourse to euphoric flying. While one might conjecture that this dreamer needed to oppose a 'bad mother' or integrate an 'inner father', it is hard to ignore the appearance that what brings euphoria is impulsive and maladaptive wish-fulfillment. By contrast, the first, most anagogic of these dreams was apparently the least pleasant to have. The anxious tone of that dream is, in fact, quite characteristic of dreams Stekel considered to be anagogic. Here, from Stekel's student Gutheil, is a typical instance:

A picture of the inner moral attitude is seen in the following dream by a forty-two-year-old physician:

I was acting as a messenger boy. I was asked to carry some flowers to a man who was very wealthy. I stopped by a lunchroom. I was in a great hurry to deliver the package, but at the same time I was very hungry. I had lunch and then de-

livered the package to the man. In giving it to him, I noticed that the flowers were pressed as if they were in a book. I was much worried when I saw the flowers in that condition. The place where I met him looked like a graveyard, and I saw tombstones.

In this dream we see the patient's conflict between duty (delivery of the package) and desire to gratify his physical wants (hunger). While he is satisfying his physical desires, the flowers become spoiled. We understand this dream if we interpret the "wealthy man" who receives the flowers in the graveyard as God. It is as if the patient were worried that at the end of his days, God would ask him, "What did you do with the flowers you had to deliver to me fresh and intact?" The flowers here are a symbol of the patient's innocence. In the dream the flowers are spoiled and faded and we see in the patient's emotional reaction a distinct feeling of guilt.[51]

This dream calls to mind that dream of Freud's discussed by Wolff, where instead of entering a church he goes to a beer cellar ("He turns aside into beer cellar," ch. 2, p. 71).

One thinks first of Jung and other holists in connection with this idea that the anagogic trend often appears as superficially catagogic, whether because dreams come to grips with catagogic material, because transformation entails destruction, or because we feel aversion toward the unknown, even though it can heal us. But also most post-Freudian psychoanalysts perceive the anagogic in dreams, even in some of an unpleasant quality. For example, the Winnicottian analyst Masud Khan wrote that the "good dream" is not necessarily pleasant or cathartic, or even one the dreamer feels good about having had. Rather, a good dream entails a high level of ego capacity and forward movement.[52] In a similar manner, Thomas French considered that a certain patient's dream of *washing himself in his own shit* signified an unconscious acceptance of the analytic process and a readiness to become well. "In the analysis, telling his dirty thoughts is a kind of soap with which he can wash himself. . . . [T]he dream work has succeeded in a bit of reality testing of which the patient has not yet been capable in waking life." To that, the old-style Freudian Robert Fliess replied that this dream is nothing but an infantile fantasy of compliance to parental toilet demands, transferred to the analyst and his demand to hear the patient's dirty thoughts.[53]

Fliess was of course wrong to maintain that French's anagogic, curative reading is impossible on grounds of Freudian theory, but it is important to realize that Fliess's catagogic, symptomatic reading of this particular dream, though inherently so much less attractive to current sensibilities, is not necessarily irrelevant.

French was one of the ego-psychology Freudians who found an anagogic trend in dreams, to the extent that they exhibit constructive ego functions.

Other post-Freudians, however, came to discover virtues in the very illogic of the so-called 'primary process' of the unconscious. This development became prominent during the 1950s.

Within this group, but leaning toward the catagogic insofar as dream are concerned, was Lawrence Kubie. He regarded dreaming as a universal form of "creative art,"[54] but placed it at the lower, neurotic end of a continuum of creative-symbolic processes. What, in his view, distinguishes successful from poor creativity, and healthy from neurotic behavior, is the "flexibility" of each of the former, the "rigidity" of the latter.[55] Rigidity may be due to an excess of "reality," but equally to domination by the unconscious. Maximum flexibility comes in the intermediate, preconscious zone which reconciles reality and unconscious. Dream and symptom, as well as neurotically motivated artwork, occupy that "rigid" end of the continuum overly influenced by the unconscious. (Compare Bosnak on projection, ch. 6, p. 227.)

Within this group, but leaning toward the anagogic insofar as dream are concerned, were Edward Tauber & Maurice Green, who in their book *Prelogical Experience* took a position closer to present-day views about dreaming as an expression of virtues inherent in the unconscious: "The peculiar wisdom of the dream, inscrutable as it may appear, often transcends man's waking knowledge of himself."[56] Recently James Fosshage writes that the primary process "is no longer viewed as an unchanging primitive mode of mentation. . . ." Rather, it contributes in dreaming to "developmental, regulatory, conflict resolving, and reorganizational functions."[57]

Still in the 1950s, Erich Fromm (ch. 5, p. 167) wrote "that dreams can be the expression both of the lowest and most irrational *and* of the highest and most valuable functions of the mind."[58]

Karen Horney perceived two levels of conflict represented in dreams: one internal to the neurosis itself and fundamentally catagogic (dependency vs. resentment, desire vs. guilt, etc.), the other between the whole neurotic system and the "real self," that (quasi-Jungian) personality which emerges as the obstacle of neurosis is removed.[59] From this catagogic/anagogic conflict come dreams "in which [one] is struggling to come alive; dreams in which [one] realizes that [one] is imprisoned and wants to get out; dreams in which [one] tenderly cultivates a growing plant or in which [one] discovers a room in [the] house of which [one] did not know before."[60]

In the 1960s, the post-Freudian French, mentioned above, together with Erika (not Erich) Fromm, presented an influential theory of conflict resolution in dreams. According to the theory, dream formation can go two ways in fashioning imagery: (1) "defensive substitution," that is, repressive disguise as described by Freud, and (2) anagogic "ends-means substitution," which recasts the conflict in an imagery which buffers the dreamer from the conflict's full force, thereby enabling her/him to search for a symbolic (if still usually defensive) solution.[61]

Psychoanalyst Hanna Segal asserted that "the dream is not just an equivalent of a neurotic symptom" but also part of "working through."[62] And by the 1980s, so far had the anagogic bias taken hold, even among psychoanalysts, that Donald Meltzer is reminding his readers, not of the anagogic element, as had Segal, but of the catagogic: "But poets can be liars as well as prophets, as Plato emphasized, and we cannot look upon dreams as telling the truth, the whole truth and nothing but the truth. In so far as they tell the truth, it is the truth about how emotional experiences are dealt with in the depths of the mind, but truth is not always treasured there, for it is freighted with mental pain."[63] Meltzer emphasizes the "distinction between the truth which dreams struggle with and the lies which invade them to deal with the excesses of mental pain which inhabit the conflict."[64] Meltzer also says that dreams present us with "the great option between an optimistic and a pessimistic view, not only of our lives, but of Life."[65]

Since the 1950s, a one-sided catagogic view is very hard to find, unless it is in the nothing-butisms of Crick and a few others (ch. 1, p. 32ff.). It has virtually disappeared among those who actually work with dreams. The different approaches to dreams during these years give us variations of the catagogic/anagogic polarity.

Of learning and information processing models of dreaming, for instance, some stress the conservative assimilation of ongoing experience by "customary coping mechanisms,"[66] by a "matrix of solutions" which is as likely to be defensive or fantastic as realistic.[67] Another view stresses that dreaming "involves creative thinking, . . . taking what is given and arriving at new solutions, etc."[68]

Milton Kramer discerns both dimensions in virtually every night's set of dreams: "a *repetitive-traumatic* type in which the problem is simply restated and no progress occurs" and "a *progressive-sequential* type in which problems are stated, worked on and resolved. . . ." Kramer enlists the terminology of developmental psychologist Jean Piaget: dreams of the former type *assimilate* new experience to standing patterns (memories, complexes), while dreams of the latter type *accommodate* for new experience by changing mental patterns to cope with new conditions. Kramer's "selective affective mood regulatory theory of dreaming" states that we wake up feeling better after successful accommodative progressive-sequential dreaming.[69]

Piaget himself, it should be recorded, said dreams exhibit a "total lack of accommodation," because the dreamer is cut off from the actual world at the moment of dreaming. During dreaming, "the subject has only at his disposal . . . a mode of thought based on assimilation as such. This is symbolic thought."[70] Symbolism in general and dream symbolism in particular, "rather than offering a metaphoric reflection of otherwise inaccessible processes, is conceptualized as a [merely pre-logical] concrete fixation."[71]*

Many dream theorists who hold a less disparaging view of dreaming than Piaget make distinctions which seem to echo Piaget's important polarity of assimilation/accommodation. These include the following:

In Ullman's opinion, dreams balance "the defensive and growth potential aspects of the personality involved."

Stanley Palombo proposes that dreams engage in "defensive operations" which modulate "integrative activity and [prevent] an overload of affect that can't be dealt with."

Don Kuiken & Shelley Sikora pose "defensive" against "revelatory.

Fosshage believes that dreams both "maintain" preexisting "organization" and "develop" "new psychic configurations."

Kenneth Kelzer speaks of "reformation" and "transformation."

John McManus et al. have "conservation and stability" versus "expansion and development."

Rosalind Cartwright contrasts dreams which preserve the self "in a steady state" to those which change the self-image.

David Feinstein, explaining his and Stanley Krippner's "personal mythology" method of growth, contrasts "old-myth dreams" to "counter-myth" and "resolution dreams." The pattern of thesis/antithesis/synthesis serves the renewal of mental patterns which otherwise drag us down.

And according to Kathryn Belicki, "lifelong repetitive nightmares may represent functionally autonomous, well worn habits, mindlessly triggered by specific stimuli . . . while bizarre, original nightmares in the absence of a traumatic precipitant may well reflect the creative workings of a talented dreamer."[72]

Another contemporary version of the catagogic/anagogic polarity is presented by Roberto Assagioli's doctrine of "psychosynthesis." Depending on the level of the unconscious from which they arise, dreams can be spiritual, can do psychological housekeeping, or can be regressive. "Since we are not yet totally integrated and whole, some of the messages of the unconscious

---

* Piaget cuts the legs from under Jung's archetypal symbolism by deeming it not "congenital" but "merely infantile" (J. Piaget 1962 [1945], p. 196). As for Freudian dream symbolism, there is no need to hypothecate any mechanism of disguise, because repressed contents necessarily find symbolic means of expression simply by virtue of being repressed and of the adverse cognitive conditions of sleep (p. 203).

might be right, true and to the point; while others may be useless, meaning-less, or deceiving."[73]

Among writers who have shaped the popular dream movement, Patricia Garfield shows a healthy respect for the catagogic side of dream life. It was she who set in train the fad of lucid dreaming[74] (see chapter 14), and so the thrust of her teaching is that we ourselves can take responsibility within the dream state for giving our dreams an anagogic direction. But she does not shirk the fact that our spontaneous dream life is often dark. And she allows that Freudian interpretations give access to one level, if a low level, of what dreams can be about. When a woman weeps in a dream because "*my sister and I had to be separated*," Garfield calls it "a wish-fulfillment dream. Anx-iety over this idea is lessened by the dreamer's having no choice in the sepa-ration and feeling sorry about it."[75] This is Freudian reversal. Garfield men-tions another dreamer who becomes able to vent anger against her sister by "disguising" the sibling as someone else in her dream.[76]

Ann Faraday, the first widely heard voice of the dream movement in the 1970s, pays more extended if also more grudging respects to Freud.[77] At the same time, she employs the sort of feel-good rhetoric about dreams which has since become both more prevalent and more one-sided. Her rule is that a "dream is incorrectly interpreted if the interpretation leaves the dreamer unmoved and disappointed. Dreams come to expand, not to diminish us."[78] A horrible nightmare can be "a really loving and caring message from [the] inner self."[79] All the same, it is not clear with Faraday whether the "loving and caring" always comprise an objective feature of dreaming itself, or rath-er sometimes a strategy for coming at the dream, and at life overall. Fara-day detects a "secret saboteur" in many dreams, bent on retarding instead of fostering growth.[80] (Recently, Rosalind Cartwright also used the metaphor of sabotage.*)

Faraday's secret saboteur comes from Perls's topdog/underdog, while her growth side comes from both Perls and Jung. Another dreamworker under the same influences is Eugene Gendlin, who tells us that with his "focusing" method, every dream brings a "growth step." I mentioned Gendlin (ch. 3, p. 108) as one whose ideas seem to imply an anagogic misreading of Jung, whereby dreams come as intentionally improving "messages" (Ann Manko-witz[81]) through a "highly refined channel of communication" (Robert John-son[82]). The dream, Gendlin also says, is "sent" by "'the other side'."[83] But

---

* R. Cartwright & L. Lamberg (1992), p. 6: "Our sleeping minds search through our memory banks to find old emotional information that holds relevance to the present. What we find there may aid—or sabotage—our attempts to cope with problems we face today."

where Gendlin, like Faraday, is a little ambiguous about whether the dream itself is always benevolent, others who have popularized Jungian insights entice us more unmistakably toward an anagogically partial view. Jeremy Taylor ventures to claim that "death and the fear of death in dreams (and myth) are always associated at some level with the growth and transformation of personality and character."[84] It is not the paradoxical dynamic he points to which is dubious, but the assertion that dreams not sometimes, not usually, but *always* work that way.

"*I pushed her into the swamp*," said Boss's sick dreamer (above, p. 241), "*cut off her legs, and pulled the skin off her body*." To insist that such malevolence *necessarily* works for the good voids badness of meaning.

In fairness, all these dreamworkers influenced by Jung mean to give the catagogic its due, in the name of integration. But when anagogic forces are portrayed as utterly prepotent, then catagogic forces surrender their nature, to become mere strawmen presenting no real obstacle to inevitable psychic improvement. It is this prejudice favoring what might be termed *anastrophic expectations** of the dream to which James Hillman reacts when he adopts his catagogic rhetoric. Elaborating the metaphor of Hades, he tells us that "dreams belong to the underworld" and do not benignly occur for the sake of "more consciousness about living. . . ."[85] Therefore "[w]e can no longer turn to the dream in hopes of progress, transformation, and rebirth."[86] "The contemporary growth cult of optimistic therapies that focus on peaks, freedom, cures, and creativity is a manic defense against psychotherapy's own ground. . . ."[87] Dreams are about "death," and "[t]o go deep into a dream requires abandoning hope. . . ."[88]

W. A. Shelburne writes in a paper about Hillman: "We cannot then take the metaphor of death in a life-affirming way as being really in the service of growth and life. The dream momentum toward death is not for the service of life but for its own sake."[89] Hillman, says Shelburne, does not have a covert "growth" agenda. He means us to rediscover the reality of our souls, which are of the dream underworld, by abandoning the waking world perspective of the ego (a dreamlike illusion) when we approach our dreams.

Nonetheless, in the long run, as argued earlier (ch. 3, p. 118), Hillman restores hope for an enhancement of waking consciousness by dreams much like the enhancement which Jung offered, but the Jung who "often enough said that dreams lead us astray as much as they exhort."[90]

---

* I thought I had invented a word, but find that the *Oxford English Dictionary* lists 'anastrophe', with, however, a different meaning: "Inversion, or unusual arrangement, of the words or clauses of a sentence."

That dark or catagogic side of dream life which Jung held in mind is now sometimes being overlooked. If at one time Freudian pessimism dominated the field, we now more often find the opposite imbalance. Consider Gayle Delaney, first president of the Association for the Study of Dreams, perhaps the most popular dreamworker on the scene, and a top-notch teacher of anastrophic expectations. Adopting the metaphor of Hollywood, she tells us that "we" produce, write, and direct as well as star in our own dreams. "We" is an interior "dream maker" part of us who always acts with constructive intentionality. The dream is "very deliberately planned" to achieve certain effects on the waking mind.[91] You should not be embarrassed or worried by painful dreams; "your dream maker's main goal is to help you out. . . ."[92] The dream maker part of us exists in, or has access to, realms out of space and time which Delaney, with prudent noncommitment, calls "the subconscious, the unconscious, the inner self, the higher self or God."[93] But when she endorses the literal reality of out-of-body experiences,[94] it becomes likely that her dream maker is not just spiritually good, but is some sort of real good spirit.

Anyone who has seen or read Delaney must admire the way she has with dreams. I do not for a moment mean to question the legitimacy of her anagogic dreamwork, the tone of which is not, as a matter of fact, as Pollyanish as some of her generalizations.* For that matter, the attending, diagnosing, interpreting, or other honoring of dreams we all do is obviously intended to be anagogic (Hillman notwithstanding). But to agree that we can make the anagogic most of every dream is different from agreeing that every dream is inherently or predominantly anagogic. Robert Langs puts it: "The very paradox that tethers life to death couples the incredible wisdom of the dream with fear and anxiety—and therefore with ignorance."[95]

My own high regard for the inherent anagogic thrust of dream life should be apparent from the prominent position Jung occupies in this book. However, I follow Jung in respecting the other, catagogic side of our inner life as well. If the goal is reconciliation or transcendence of inner polarities by an integration of opposites, that is not done by underestimating the authenticity or power of half of what is to be integrated.

In the present environment, where much more attention is given to the anagogic dimension of dreaming than to the catagogic, balance requires not,

---

* For example, Delaney (1991, p. 285) shows a skeptical edge when she refutes the "conventional wisdom" that the death motif in dreams is necessarily a good thing, a "prerequisite to the rebirth of something better. . . ." She interprets a dream in which death represents the loss of something valuable, a loss which the dreamer should avoid if possible. The dream as a whole carries this anagogic message. (See also above, ch. 5, p. 192n.)

as in Jung's, Silberer's, and Stekel's days, that we establish the anagogic, but rather that, like Meltzer, we remind ourselves of the catagogic.

Accordingly, chapter 8 returns to the idea of a dream/symptom parallel. That connection is often belittled by the anagogically-minded. But if we get past seeing it as the vanguard idea of a dreary Freudianism, to view it rather as at one pole of a full rendering of dream life, it ceases to be objectionable. Certainly the symptom/cure polarity is one by which the general polarity of catagogic/anagogic gets expressed in our culture.

Freud's theory of dream formation was related in chapter 2. What chapter 8 does is to pursue the fundamental idea of a connection between dreams and symptoms in several ways, on Freudian principles and otherwise. The focus here is not so much on the theoretical likeness of dreams to symptoms as on how dreams actually correlate with the clinical picture. The emphasis will be on pathological material, interesting in its own right and also instructive for the average person who wants to sharpen perception of her/his own dreams and those of fellow dreamers.

Chapter 9, "Dream Style," first concerns the relation of such factors as personality and gender to dream style. But the chapter chiefly concentrates on the characteristics of the dreams of people suffering from various common or interesting syndromes. This material should interest lay readers as well as professionals. To recognize, for example, the dream style of clinical depression helps identifying the depressive dimension of one's own dreams.

Chapter 10, "Dream Residues," considers the onset of neurotic and psychotic symptoms from dreams, suicide attempts following dreams, and recall of the dream as a continuation of the dream process. It concludes with a section on 'acting out', which here refers to the unconscious continuation of the 'disease process' of dreaming into symbolic behavior following waking. This material heightens awareness of how all of us unconsciously 'continue' our dreams occasionally. For one example, the incidental words and demeanor of someone before sharing a dream sometimes bear a symbolic relation to the dream.

Chapter 11, "Initial and Termination Dreams," makes a transition to the concluding chapters, where the anagogic side of dreaming and dreamwork will be emphasized.

Chapter 12, "The Non-interpretation of Dreams," is a general discussion of non-interpretive approaches to dreamwork.

Chapter 13, "Incubation," confines itself to a dreamwork method particularly and historically related to the purpose of cure. Incubation, one of the hallmarks of contemporary dreamwork, involves the intention of prompting or controlling the dream process for the sake of a desired effect. Control of dreams also comes into chapter 14, "Lucidity," chapter 15, "Re-entry," and chapter 16, "The Bo Tree Principle." Derived largely from Jung's conception of the shadow, what I call the bo tree principle is a governing paradigm of dreamwork at present. The basic idea is that threatening dream symbols of our symptoms and of dark aspects of the psyche are better dealt with by approaching them than by avoiding them.

A final word about the upcoming several chapters. The way their topics are organized does not lend itself to a complete segregation along catagogic-symptomatic and anagogic-curative lines—if such were possible. Some of the sources drawn upon to illustrate symptomatic characteristics come to their dream material with anagogic orientations. Moreover, some of the conformations discussed under 'symptom' reappear under 'cure'. Thus, while on one hand the nightmare is a symptomatic dream style, on the other hand it is the natural territory of the dreamwork discussed in chapter 16. And thus, while many authors of the psychosomatic literature presuppose a neurotic, catagogic parallel between dream and symptom formation, others discern a profoundly anagogic, self-curative direction in the tandem of psychosomatic symptoms and dreams.

What should be born in mind is that any anagogic interpretation can, if one is so inclined, be transposed to a catagogic one, and vice versa. Most notoriously, wish-fulfilling disguise is a blotter which in the wrong hands can be made to absorb anything—but so can Jungian compensation be made to do.

The impression I hope to create is that when it comes down to cases, neither major orientation, catagogic or anagogic, is sufficient to the exclusion of the other. With our fallible understanding, the best course is to entertain all approaches, even if that entails some mixing and matching of theoretical perspectives. Best to assume any given dream may embody both catagogic and anagogic trends. What is more, we do not necessarily have the wisdom to know which is which.

Bearing this in mind, ponder Jungian Donald Kalsched's thoughts about "protector" and "persecutory figures" in the dreams of persons with Multiple Personality Disorder (ch. 9, p. 313ff.). Kalshed explains that protector and persecutor personalities are both often found as "alter-personalities" in these cases:

> Of particular interest to my understanding of certain patients' dreams is . . . the extraordinary intelligence of the protector personality, including the possibility that the protector may even resort to persecution of the host-personality in order to "keep it in," so to speak, and prevent it from being traumatized again in the outer or inner world. Protector personalities . . . in the guise of persecutory fig-

ures . . . may, to borrow an idea from James Grotstein (1981), attack all linking in the psyche to prevent affects and their associated images from integrating. . . .

These considerations helped me to understand the nightmare of a young female artist who, as later treatment revealed, had suffered repeated incestuous violation by her father between the ages of five and eleven. . . .

The following dream occurred about six months into her treatment after a session in which a very moving moment of warm emotional contact has occurred in the transference—a connection between us that apparently threatened to revive the associated traumatic memory of abuse by her father.

I am in my room, in bed. I hear someone open the door of our apartment, then walk in. I hear the footsteps approach my door, then it opens. A very tall man with a white ghost-like face and black holes for eyes walks in with an axe. He raises it over my neck and comes down! I wake up in terror.

Here we have an image of a violent split between mind and body. The neck, as an integrating and connecting link between the two, is severed. The patient recognized this dream as a repetitive nightmare from her childhood. She had no other associations.

. . . [S]o this murderer in her psyche (protector/persecutor) took his axe and severed the connections (links) between her body (where her traumatic memories were stored) and her mind. This figure, then, represents the patient's resistance to healing. By resistance, I do not mean what Freud originally meant by the term. Here, resistance is a defense of the whole psyche against any re-experience of affects that have previously been experienced as unbearable. These are defenses of the Self, not of the ego, and this axe-wielding figure represents the Self in its daemonic aspect.[96]

Dream and Symptom

The first section of this chapter considers the representation of neuroses and neurotic symptoms in dreams. The next section concerns body symbolism and the portrayal of physical symptoms in dreams. The final section is about the dreams of psychosomatic patients.

Representation of Neuroses and Neurotic Symptoms in Dreams

Wilhelm Stekel followed the introduction of his two volumes of collected writings about dreams with a chapter from 1913 entitled "Representation of Parapathy in Dreams" ('parapathy' means 'neurosis', and will be so rendered below):

> In many of the dreams of neurotics we find symbols of their neurosis, which is usually personified. . . .
> A highly gifted young man came under my care for severe obsessional neurosis. He had touch phobia and syphilophobia, practiced an elaborate obsessive ceremonial, confined himself to a rigidly vegetarian diet, and was incapacitated for study, so that his life had become intolerable. His first dream after beginning treatment ran as follows:
> *King Alfonso of Spain should be informed that an attempt is to be made on his life.*
> The customary interpretation that the king was a father imago would have given some meaning to the dream, but I was dissatisfied with this facile explanation. . . .
> . . . Then one day [after a year] he heard inner "voices"—the illness—saying: "Don't put me to death! Let me live! Let me live!" When he told me of this, it suddenly became clear to me who "King Alfonso" was—the personification of the neurosis. . . . [H]e told me that he was born in 1886 on May 17th, the same day as King Alfonso XIII. . . .

. . . [So] in the very night after beginning treatment, [he had dreamt] that he must be on his guard, for he [wa]s in danger of losing his beloved illness.[1]

Another example:

[O]ne of my patients had the following dream a few nights before he suddenly (and to me quite unexpectedly) broke off the treatment:

Lilly, a servant who has been with us for twenty years, a trusty creature, is dying. Dr. Stekel is leaning over the bed, and listens to her heart with a stethoscope. "It will soon be over," he says. "Oh, no," I reply. "She will go on living for a long time."

In the dream I predict the approaching end of the illness. He contradicts me, and decides to go on being ill.[2]

Stekel's catalog of common personifications of neurosis includes servants, authorities, relatives, friends, enemies, beasts, criminals, beggars, lunatics, and idiots. He also observed nonpersonal symbols of the neurosis, including cage, cross, room, old house, new house "(when the neurosis is exhibiting new symptoms)," chain, shadow, abscess, privy, skin, helmet, tight shoe, eyeglasses, crutch, and mask.[3] Emil Gutheil offered a similar list.[4]

In such dreams, the neurosis as an entity becomes symbolized; thus, the neurosis performs as a coherent actor or thing within the dream story. It appears from Stekel's account that such symbolizations might occur when the person is taking an unconscious stance toward the neurosis as a whole—in the examples, both dreamers unconsciously plan for their illnesses to endure. But certainly it is more usual for the entire dream to stand as an analog to the neurosis, rather than for the neurosis to be depicted *within* the dream. The dream then paraphrases or mirrors the neurosis, without discussing it as such. A plain example of this comes from Ernst Rosenbaum, via Gutheil:

I am sitting at a dinner table eating meat. Suddenly I notice that it is the dead body of a man that I eat.

The dreamer lives on the money his deceased father left. In spite of all the advantages this kind of life offers to him he is unhappy because he wants to prove to himself and to his family that he is a useful member of society and is able to make his own living. In the dream, he literally lives off his dead father.[5]

We are told too little to conjecture what blend of oral aggression, bad conscience, and sacramental cannibalism might be at work here; but however that may be, the dream unquestionably symbolizes the dreamer's condition of unwholesome dependency. It gives a fix on the dreamer's core problem.

David Feinstein frames the same phenomenon in the language of 'personal mythology' instead of neurosis, when he presents the dream of a woman unready to outgrow an "old" or "prevailing myth":

A forty-two-year-old woman who carried overbearing parental injunctions had the following dream the evening after she proudly announced to her therapist some progress in liberating herself from those injunctions. *I was walking down the street in a sort of run-down neighborhood when I noticed two men on motorcycles, both pretty stocky, pretty good size. One of them said "You're coming with us." I said, "No I'm not," but I felt absolute terror when he spoke to me.* Like the motorcyclists in this dream, many dream symbols reveal that the old myth is still a potent force, new attitudes and beliefs notwithstanding. These dreams maintain a psychic economy by supporting prevailing myths that are being challenged by new experiences. In such dreams, we see Piaget's process of assimilation in operation. The woman's newfound experience of independence came into conflict with the domination of her internalized parents, and the dream attempted to diminish her experience of autonomy by portraying dominating figures who invoked terror in her about acting independently of their wishes.[6]

If a dream offers an analog of issues to someone functioning more or less well, s/he probably will look upon any work pursued with the dream in the light of self-improvement, not of clinical relief of symptoms. The following dream concerns what is termed lately a 'co-dependency' problem. Whether the problem is considered clinical or not, what matters is that the dream presents a neat synopsis of the dreamer's negative pattern. It comes from Lillie Weiss's chapter "Defining a Pattern," and I have selected it partly because Weiss demonstrates with it an interesting technique for doing just that. The technique defines the pattern of this woman's dream, and the dream defines her psychological pattern:

> If the therapist [or dreamer] substitutes the words 'someone' or 'something' for every noun in the dream story, the pattern becomes much clearer. . . .
> *I am at a picnic and sitting there with Tom. We are drinking beer and I am looking for ice to cool his beer bottle, but I can't seem to find any. I want to cool his beer so that I can go running and then eat my sandwich. Before I can eat it, however, I see John and Dick who need my help. I go to help them, and then the next thing I see is that my grandmother has packed away my sandwich, and I never get to eat it.*
> Rewriting the dream with indefinite articles [*sic*] may result in the following version:
> I am somewhere with someone. I am trying to do something for him before I can go do something I want. Before I can get at something I want, however, I have to help others. When I come back, someone has put away what I want, and I stay hungry.
> . . . The above pattern may be summarized as follows: "The dreamer doesn't do what she wants until she takes care of others first. By then, it is too late for her to meet her needs, and she feels frustrated." . . . [H]er dream summarizes her basic conflict or dilemma quite accurately.[7]

Henry Reed recommends the same technique, calling the rewritten dream an "action plot."[8]

The following dream comes from a study of dreams in phobic states, by Sydney Pomer & Robert Shain. Here neither doctor nor patient doubts that serious symptoms exist. The dreamer's assorted phobias appear to be layers of symbolic processing of his underlying neurotic conflict. The dream is one more symbolic rendering of the same conflict, so that multiple parallelisms present themselves among the various phobic symptoms, the dream imagery, and the underlying disturbance:

A young physician came to treatment because of symptoms of severe anxiety, hypochondriasis, and a phobic state which markedly interfered with his personal and professional life. Although accomplished in his field, he had difficulty concentrating and was increasingly haunted by frightening homosexual preoccupations Claustrophobia was a main inhibiting feature. He would avoid entering elevators, tunnels, and closets at all costs. . . . He was concerned with fleeting physical symptoms. "I have this throbbing pain over my eye. Do you think I have a brain tumor?". . . . It was an early dream which conveyed his anxiety over heterosexuality, and, in effect, a phobia of female genitalia.

Word had gotten around the hospital that there was a cat in the pathology refrigerator which had come back to life. I thought, "That's surprising—the cat was dead when I put it away. I must have misdiagnosed it." Someone was sticking something into the cat's chest, and I was angry at whoever was doing this. The instrument looked something like a screwdriver. Then someone was sewing up the cat. At another point, one of the legs of the cat was almost off, and the cat was walking around with the leg just hanging on, dragging behind. All the time, I could feel the cat's claws on my hands.

He immediately associated to his fear of a situation in the hospital when he is asked to confirm that a patient is dead. . . . Maybe, he thinks, he will miss a sign only to have the patient return to life. He used a screwdriver to fix a radio on the evening of the dream. He loves to assemble radios, clocks, to put things together and fix them, if he can. Now the idea of resurrection comes to him. The cat has come back to life. He thought of the clawing wounds on his hands as the stigmata on Christ's hands. A frequent fantasy, he now revealed, was that analysis would find him guilty of a heinous crime and crucifixion would be the inevitable result. The wounds were a punishment he deserved for what he did to the cat. The cat was alive again, born again. Early memories surfaced: his mother telling him how he had damaged her in his difficult birth. . . . His mother had to return to the hospital for several months, while he was cared for by a nursemaid. Further, the nearly amputated leg of the cat was his mother's leg which had bled profusely when, as a small child, he kicked at her during a quarrel. Now he was able to talk of his horror at the sight of female genitalia especially during menstruation. The bleeding cat was his mother's injured genitalia. That the central issues were thinly disguised did not necessarily result in a shortening of the analytic procedure but the dream did afford the analyst the opportunity to more readily comprehend the core conflicts of the patient.[9]

Gutheil states a rule which applies in this case: "[D]reams containing the patient's disturbance often portray not only the disturbance itself but the specific pathogenic situation as well."[10] He provides abundant examples of this observation, among them an incidence of incestuous abuse. The dream scenario quite closely 'portrays' or analogizes the symptom in question:

> One of my patients, a thirty-two-year-old woman, married, described a fugue in which she left her husband and went to her father who was divorced and lived in a neighboring town. She appeared confused, dazed, and disoriented. The father called a physician who brought her out of this condition. During analysis she had the following dream:
> *I am in a sort of penthouse garden. Many people around. A glass window opens and a dwarflike creature comes up on a ladder. Offers a tumbler with a drink on a platter. I am disgusted by his looks and refuse the drink—I know it is poison. I am surprised that nobody pays attention to this intrusion. A fascination emanates from the person and it makes me drink. I am about to fall into unconsciousness when I awaken with a start.*
> This dream portrays the symptom and, as such, is capable of enlightening us about the inner mechanisms of the symptom. . . .
> . . . [O]ut of the lower recesses of the house, a sinister creature comes up, a dwarf. It offers the dreamer a drink, i.e., enjoyment, which she refuses at first, knowing it to be harmful, and then, fascinated by the creature, she accepts. It makes her lose consciousness.
> We assume that similar circumstances made her lose consciousness when she developed the state of fugue.
> The dream conveys to us a scene in which her father, on whose lap she was once sitting as a small child, had pressed his genital against her body. The dream clearly indicates the approach of the dwarf from below. . . . And then repulsion turns into acceptance. . . . The "poison," of course, can be considered to be the incestuous wish. The unconscious state into which the patient is about to succumb, indicates her desire to withdraw her defenses and to surrender to her id.[11]

With the heightened awareness about incest, a contemporary therapist would not "of course" assume that the "'poison'" the dream-ego is made to drink represent's the dreamer's "incestuous wish." A possibility of actual oral sex would have to be considered.*

---

* Nightmares and sleep disturbances are the primary indicators of ongoing sexual molestation (except perhaps in older children where sexual acting out occurs) (P. Garfield 1987, p. 93). Trends revealed in dreams of children who have suffered from sexual abuse include general regression and

Stekel began his chapter entitled "Representation of Neurotic Symptoms in Dreams" with the statement that "individual symptoms, in addition to the malady as a whole, can be recognized in dreams, so that from these we can make valid inferences regarding the precise nature of the malady. . . ."[12] It is more usual for the symptom than for the neurosis as an entity to make an appearance within the dream story. "[E]very considerable dream includes a reference to the patient's main symptoms, and thus gives a clue to his mental conflict." Here is a transparent example, "the typical dream" of a man suffering from emotionally driven sexual impotence:

> *I want to pay a visit, and arrive at a villa surrounded by a fine garden. I try to open the door, but it appears to be locked. I try to ring the bell, but with little success for the machinery is rusted. At last I produce a faint ring. An elderly woman appears at the window and says: "The door is open. Press hard on the latch." I try, but the door does not open. I feel that I should make myself ridiculous were I to call for help; and when, in the end, I decide to call, I can hardly make a sound—I suppose because I am ashamed. Then there comes up a rough fellow, obviously a butcher's delivery man, who looks at me contemptuously, presses the latch, and opens the door. I give up the idea of paying my visit, and hurry away.*

---

questioning of sexual identity, according to Stephen Catalano (1990, p. 154). Themes include "bleak emptiness" and unprotected exposure to danger. "[A] 4-year-old boy who had been sexually abused by his adolescent brother" dreamed: *"I was with my Mom in a big shopping center and we got lost from each other. I couldn't find her. There was too many people. Then I started to cry and get real scared."* He also dreamed that *he was "in the middle of the water" calling unheeded for help as he drowned.*

Histories of both sexual and physical abuse tend to cause nightmares in later life (M. A. Cuddy & K. Belicki 1992). According to psychoanalyst Robert Friedman, dream indicators of childhood sexual abuse "include overt sexual acts, or symbols such as looking for a lost object, a secret trunk, a scary unopened door, or a child who can't communicate" (R. M. Friedman 1992, pp. 17–8, citing Renee Frederickson, "Advanced clinical skills in the treatment of sexual abuse," workshop lecture, New York, 1990). Another indicator "is the reference in the manifest dream, or in glosses to the dream report, to the possibility of cover-up or 'not seeing' something that is there" (p. 18). In the incest dream from Gutheil, ":obody pays attention. . . ." Jeremy Taylor (1992a, p. 170) relates the next dream, of a female abuse amnesiac, symbolizing concealment or 'white-wash' on the verge of being penetrated: *"A disembodied close-up view of a wooden surface painted white. The paint is just beginning to blister and bubble."* Friedman also discusses a "dream indicator of hidden [childhood] trauma" in general, including sexual abuse: it is that "some seemingly unimportant detail—a specific place or realistic embellishment—is repeated in a series of manifest dreams, at first without significant associations" (op. cit., p. 16). Friedman credits this observation to Ella Sharpe (1978 [1937], p. 156), and cites Frederickson's example of a man who "dreamed repeatedly of *standing in front of a particular building*. As a child he had been abducted from that spot and sexually abused in a nearby basement." Similarly, Rosalind Cartwright (R. Cartwright & L. Lamberg 1992, p. 186) notes that "memories may come back in bits and pieces. A dream may focus on only one aspect of the experience. One woman reported this . . . dream: *All I saw were stained glass windows.* This woman

The inhibition is thrice referred to. He cannot open the door; the bell won't work properly; and he cannot call for help. This is a fine illustration of the fact that the leitmotif of a dream is usually repeated several times—for emphasis, as it were. . . . Very plainly displayed is the central idea: "I cannot."[13]

Body Symbolism, and the Portrayal of Physical Symptoms in Dreams

Body symbolism. Stekel's and Gutheil's books contain an abundance of examples of dreams representing symptoms, ranging from purely psychological symptoms, such as agoraphobia, to presumptively psychosomatic symptoms, such as asthma. But neither of these authors, curiously enough, chose to discuss dreams at the other end of this particular axis: dreams concerning medical symptoms of strictly biological origin. The subject obviously stands in the background of psychosomatics.

Accordingly, before getting into psychosomatic dreams, some pages will be devoted to dreams insofar as they are traceable to the body alone: both the body in general, and in case of specific distress or disease.

In reviewing nineteenth century physiological theories of dreaming, Freud showed some warmth for the views of Scherner (1861) and his follower Volkelt (1875).[14] Scherner, like many from Aristotle to the present, thought that the mind, when freed of waking inputs, becomes occupied by somatic stimuli, magnifying and converting these into dream images. Scherner said that the images consistently reflect the site and quality of their stimuli. "Thus he provides a kind of 'dream-book' . . . which makes it possible to deduce from the dream-images inferences as to the somatic feelings, . . . [and] the state of the organs. . . ."[15]

So, for example: "blazing furnace" = lungs functioning; "hollow boxes or baskets" = heart; house = entire body; parts of houses = body parts: ceiling = head; "row of houses" = intestines; while "muddy streets" = in-

---

had been molested at church by a priest." Similarly, Kathryn Belicki (1992a and 1992b) finds that dreams of sexual abuse victims usually depict the traumatizing events in fragments, though sometimes in recognizable form. Their dreams have dark sexual themes, as would be expected; but even more, they dream of explicit violence, often done to other figures in the dream. Their dreams are actually more violent than those of victims of physical abuse. According to Patricia Garfield (1987, p. 96), the dream villain is often the known offender, in contrast to nightmares in general, where the villain is usually a stranger.

Chapter 7 concluded with a dream preserving the dissociation and amnesia of an incest victim with Multiple Personality Disorder (D. E. Kalsched 1992, pp. 91–3). In chapter 11 (p. 365), Gayle Delaney's (1990b [1986]) account of the recovery dreams of incest victims is briefly summarized.

testinal contents.[16] These are common instances, but the imagination is free to invent others, said Scherner.[17]

What pleased Freud about Scherner in comparison to other physiological theorists (e.g., Wundt) was that, whereas these reduced dreaming to an essentially vacuous scintillation off of physiological events (as later would J. Allan Hobson & Robert McCarley [chapter 1]), "[t]he formation of dreams only begins, in Scherner's eyes, at the point which the other writers regard as its end."[18] For Scherner dreaming belongs to the creative imagination, to which organic stimulation merely provides the palette, as it were. Freud obviously would not emulate Scherner's "almost intoxicated enthusiasm"[19] for dreams, yet he considered Scherner a predecessor insofar as he understood that the dreaming mind performs genuinely meaningful transformations of somatic stimuli into imagery. Many present-day writers hold to some variant of the underlying principle.

A century after Scherner, the psychoanalyst Geza Roheim (1952) put a hyper-Freudian spin on the notion of body-to-dream-image translation. Roheim claimed to discern mankind's universal *basic dream*. Its first phase is a "regressive" return to the womb (with overtones of death), brought on by "the break with the environment."[20]* Its second phase is a "progressive" endeavor to reestablish the environment by shifting the body's erotic energies (libido) from the body to the dream scene. This double movement is most visible at sleep onset, and there is, in fact, a resemblance here to Foulkes's

---

* Another special theory along comparable lines is that of Daniel Schneider, who proclaimed that the heart is a "neurosexual tissue," and that every dream at one level consists of a "genital and cardiac image fusion" (1955, pp. 349 and 351). Compare also Bertram Lewin's notion that the "dream screen" on which dreams are projected symbolizes the maternal breast at which the infant once fell into satiated sleep, and to which every dream wishfully symbolically returns. "He argued that dreaming was a mentally dramatized form of the feeding cycle of succour and repose. . . (C. de Monchaux 1978, p. 444). The breast-screen supposedly makes an occasional appearance in its own right, in a visually empty or "blank dream" (B. D. Lewin 1946), or some variant thereof, e.g., *"my field of vision is filled by a huge butter cookie. . ."* (H. L. Levitan 1967, p. 166). Another dream reported by Harold Levitan (1981b, p. 230) for a bulemic patient has similar atributes: *"I am being overpowered by a huge navel orange . . .* (the navel reminded her of a nipple) . . . *It is about to devour me . . . I am suffocating . . . In a funny way it is as though it is overtaking the world."* According to Wayne Myers (1977, pp. 170–1), the dream screen is usually white, but can be black or dark for black dreamers, and also for white dreamers who associate maternal qualities with black women.

I am not certain what the relation is between white blank dreams and so-called "white dreams," i.e., "cases in which subjects reported to have dreamt, but could not remember any content. . ." (L. DeGennaro & C. Violani 1990, p. 7).

Charles Rycroft (1981, p. 123) connects blank dreams with "people who are abandoning a schizoid state of withdrawal and entering, or teetering on the edge of, a manic state." They "symbolize a state of ecstatic fusion with the breast. . . ." "[E]mpty dreams" are one of several dream types experienced by "susto" sufferers, according to Carl O'Nell (1976, pp. 65–6).

stages of sleep onset, with respect to the dissolution and partial reestablishment of ego functions (ch. 1, p. 28). In Roheim's psychodynamic scenario, the regressed sleeper is stimulated by imaginal proximity to mother's genitals (return to the womb) to fantasize incest. For this purpose he, or she—female as well as male—generates a "phallic double" in dream imagery.[21] Here, the phallic double takes the form of a rope:

> The dreamer is a business man of forty. He has not been in business for many years because of severe anxiety derived from the oedipus complex and the superego.
> Dream: *I am on top of a mountain. I am trying to get off the top and I could do so by getting into a shaft. But the jump from the top to the shaft is dangerous. Two strong young men help me with a rope. . . .*
> Interpretation: The top of the hill—his mother's bosom. The two helpers—his testicles. The rope—his penis. The shaft—his potential wife's (mother's) vagina.[22]

As doctrinally slanted as Roheim is, the wealth of examples he provides does alert us to pay attention to body symbolism, especially sexual symbolism, in dreams. For another example:

> The next is a characteristic masturbation dream, dreamed by a menstruating woman of about forty.
> *I am holding on to a motor car and running after it with great exertion. It is going toward a red light district on the other side of the Hudson over a bridge.*
> *Two women are in the car. I can't hold on any longer. I land near bushes on the other side.*
> The red light (besides indicating prostitution) is her menstruating vagina. The rushing motion, the car = sexual excitement. Holding on = masturbation. The two women = her two breasts. The bushes are her pubic hair. The exertion in the dream is her anxiety about masturbating which she finally stops—i.e., she lets go.[23]

Roheim's readings are based on a special psychological theory. It is of course possible to find less encumbered, more self-evident examples of body symbolism in dreams. (One excellent survey of body symbolism, especially but not exclusively for women, is contained in Patricia Garfield's *Women's Bodies, Women's Dreams*.[24]) Perhaps the most indubitable cases are those where an identifiable stimulus causes a bodily disturbance which prompts a dream image. From Bertram Lewin (1958):

> *[T]he dreamer found himself in the House of Lords. The Lords were seated not in rows but in a semicircle, the dreamer was at the center of the circle. Suddenly a very large rubber axe blade chopped down between two of the Lords on the right,* and the dreamer awoke to find an irritating fragment of food between two teeth of his lower jaw in an exactly corresponding position.[25]

Herbert Silberer's "auto-symbolic phenomena" at sleep onset (ch. 1, p. 27) include images which symbolically transform somatic sensations:

> I inhale deeply; my chest expands. The hypnagogic image shows me *lifting a table on high, with the assistance of another person.* The image is self-explanatory. The fact that there are two persons may represent the two lobes of the lung or may correspond to the ease of the act of lifting.[26]

Jean Piaget, who leaned on Silberer's research when he developed his own position on dream symbolism (ch. 7, p. 244), offered several examples from his own files of "anatomical symbols," including this one closely comparable to the House of Lords dream:

> The dentist had left a small pad of cotton wool between two molars. *The subject saw a mass of wet moss in between two rocks* just when, in his half-sleep state, he was feeling this foreign body with his tongue.[27]

In these examples, symbolization turns on the physical, spatial equivalence of body part to dream image, though to say so does not rule out an additional, psychodynamic purpose for selection of the particular images—the House of Lords, the high table, the wet moss between two rocks. The same consideration applies to a dream reported in chapter 2, told by Rosalind Cartwright about her cousin the "inveterate card player," only here, rather than turning on any physical resemblance, the body-to-image equivalence turns on wordplay, or punning:

> Her back was to an open window and a cold wind was blowing. The blanket slipped down, and her nightie up. She dreamed that *she was playing cards. Someone looking over her shoulder at her hand questioned why she was not betting more on such a good hand. She replied that she couldn't because her "assets were frozen."*[28]

Portrayal of physical symptoms. With these last two dreams, an external stimulus causes a sensation which influences the dream. In disease, by contrast, the stimulus originates internally. Francis Crick & Graeme Mitchison quip: "A doctor rarely says, 'We'd better take a sample of his dreams or he might sue us.'"[29] But one need not draw the same, skeptical lesson as they do from the observation. Modern medicine largely ignores a diagnostic aid with a long and respectable tradition. "Even as fire maketh yron like itself, so the firie inflammations of our liver, or stomach, transforms our imaginations to their analagie and likeness." Thomas Nashe in the sixteenth century enunciated this diagnostic principle of *symbolic correspondences*, which he shared with Cardano and others of that epoch.[30] They were no doubt influenced by Greek medicine. Hippocrates, Aristotle, and Galen all wrote about diagnostic, or prodromal, dreaming.* Substantially the same principle has been espoused by Scherner and others in the nineteenth century, and in the twentieth by Freud, Jung, and others. Jeremy Taylor, with his penchant for absolutes, asserts: "There is . . . always an aspect of every dream that provides an exquisitely accurate 'readout' of your physical health and the condition of your body at the moment of the dream."[31]

Ideas have differed as to the still uncertain mechanisms involved in producing symbolic correspondences. Harry Hunt describes Silberer's somatic auto-symbols as "self-referential visual depictions of physiological and muscular conditions."[32] In Hunt's view, their occurrence is not as surprising as might at first appear, if human symbolic capacities are based on cross-modal sensory translations, integrations, and synesthesias. Silberer himself noted that dreams amplify stimuli detected during sleep—a phenomenon well-documented from incorporations of external stimuli (ch. 13, p. 396ff.). Silberer wrote in 1918: "Before the actual outbreak of an illness it usually knocks so lightly at the door of our inner senses that its advent is audible only in the stillness of the night, e.g., in the period of incubation of an infection. And it is heard only as if through a microphone or seen through a microscope, thanks to the exaggerating qualities of the dream."[33]

Vasily Kasatkin theorizes that "signals of an incipient disease or malfunction . . . are too weak to excite the pain receptors, but strong enough to innervate the extremely sensitive optic area in the brain. The innervated optic cells 'conjure up' images which point rather accurately to a rising disease." Kasatkin, a Russian, asserts that dreams can help to diagnose illnesses up to "several years" before the noticeable onset of symptoms.[34]

Ernest Rossi & David Cheek have theorized that "'[t]he phenomenological experience of dreams in the languages of imagery, metaphor, symbol

---

* "The term *prodromal* refers to a symptom that appears before the outbreak of a disease that gives some clue to the nature and severity of the illness to come" (A. B. Siegel 1990, p. 213). Aristotle, in *On Divination*, said that the dream is a "token" of a commencing disease, in the same way that "roughness of the tongue [is a token] of fever. . ." (quoted by S. Resnik 1987, p. 50; brackets Resnik's). The ancient physicians, with a few exceptions, held both that the gods send "curative directives" in divine dreams (see chapter 13) and that "the soul could portray through its visions the humoral imbalances of the body." In addition to divine messages and humoral symptomatology, other dream-causing factors enumerated by Galen included food, character, current thoughts, prophesy, etc., and he warned that "it is not easy to say how these dreams are to be distinguished from those which originate in the body" (S. M. Oberhelman 1983, pp. 36–7 and 44–5, quoting Galen, *On Diagnosis from Dreams*, Oberhelman's translation). Survivals, not of the humoral theory of body functioning per se but of its characteristic readings of dream images, can still be found, and not only in less conventional authors (C. A. Cannegieter 1985, p. 48), but also in recognized authors such as Patricia Garfield, who does not hesitate to cite the authority of Hippocrates (e.g., 1991, p. 127).

and analogy is isomorphic with organic brain-body processes down to the cellular-genetic-molecular level.' Thus," comments Garfield, "these symbols can mediate mind-body communication in illness and healing."[35] More simply phrased by Garfield, prognostic dreams "are probably responses of the brain to minute bodily sensations that are magnified and dramatized during sleep."[36] In *The Healing Power of Dreams*, she lays out a typical course of dreaming, from possible forewarnings of illness or injury, through "diagnostic dreams," to return to complete wellness (if achieved).[37]

Harry Fiss likens the detection and transformation of illness in dream imagery to the figurative incorporation of subliminally registered external sensations in dreams, which are "uniquely sensitive to low-level stimuli, both internal and external."[38]

Following are a number of examples of 'symbolic correspondences' between dreams and illnesses or injuries. Dreams reflecting (1) the dreamer's conscious knowledge of a medical problem, or (2) unconscious cuing by the disorder itself, or (3) both, are reported in Louis Breger et al.'s book about dreams of presurgical patients. As related by Robert Haskell: "[S]ome of the dreams reflected illness in symbolic represented form. For example, a patient with reduced circulation in his legs dreamed of '*a half dried river bed.*' Another patient with bowel problems and scheduled for a colostomy, dreamed of '*plugged pipes.*' The symbolic representations often become quite cognitively complex."[39] Haskell discusses other examples, including this one:

> A hypoglycemic (low blood sugar) patient known to this writer was feeling tired and had been having a slight case of diarrhea. He dreamed of *a tan colored dog who defecated on the floor. The defecation looked like maple sugar. Each time the dog defecated the dog got smaller.* The clear message here is that the diarrhea was eliminating the needed glucose too quickly from his system.[40]

Edward Whitmont & Sylvia Brinton Perera supply an example of a stroke victim's prodromal dream:

> A dream containing a serious warning of bodily disruption was dreamed by a woman the day before she had a stroke. In the dream *she saw her house roof pierced by the branches of a tree torn loose in a windstorm.*[41]

Hunt provides a persuasive instance from his own experience:

> Feeling feverish and light-headed shortly after a flu shot and aware of an exhaustion in my limbs associated with a rapid, involuntary tremor, I lay on the floor, fell asleep, and *found myself in my study facing a rattlesnake. Its uplifted head was oscillating rapidly* (at what I realized on awakening was the same rate and quality of my shaking leg muscles). *Sinking to the floor, overcome by terror, I crept backward before its steady advance. Finally, I pushed a chair against it. To*

my surprise, the rattlesnake stopped its advance, and I awoke with the brief fever gone.[42]

Epileptic seizures can be associated with recurrent dreams, as documented by Arthur Epstein. Such dreams may predate seizures, as in the example below, or may commence in the same time frame, either as a prelude to or a component of the seizure. Emotionally and in imagery, the dreams have traits typical of seizure: catastrophic themes, fears of annihilation, "a sense of struggling or attacking with accompanying rage," and/or awakening with feelings of depression and depletion. An example:

> *I am way up in the sky. There is a dark background, like night. There are all kinds of stars of different colors. They are multicolored. There are moons, and I see the planet Saturn. I can tell that it is Saturn because it is turning and has a ring. I fall between these stars and moons. I fall and fall. All the time, my body is twisting this way and that. . . . I feel very frightened. My greatest fear is when I hit the earth, what will happen. I can feel myself being splattered to bits. . . . I never land. I feel as though I'm trying to grab on to something but there is nothing to really grab on to. I never really strike earth.*
>
> When it first appeared [at age 17], the dream occurred almost nightly but gradually became less frequent. . . . Immediately prior to the appearance of the dream, the patient has the thought of "fighting someone off." He notes a sensation of "tiredness" after the dream.
>
> At about age 33, the "dream" began to occur during the waking state . . . often preceded by thoughts of fighting . . . [and] "dizziness." . . .
>
> At age 38 . . . the "dream" suddenly appeared and was followed immediately by dizziness, loss of consciousness, and a generalized convulsion.

Epstein conjectures that in these cases the dreams are themselves "manifestations of abnormal cerebral discharge" directly related to the physiological pathology of the epilepsy.[43]

The next examples are from Patricia Maybruck:

> Ward, 51-year-old man winemaker: *I see what looks like an X-ray of my stomach . . . It's full of grapes and there are tiny little Italian peasant women stomping on them. One huge grape bursts.* (Woke up with bad stomach pains and later found out I have an incipient ulcer.)
>
> Maureen, during recovery from surgery: *Walking through a shopping mall, looked down and saw the seams of my dress had come apart and people were laughing.* (Woke up to see my sutures had opened and I was bleeding.)[44]

Maybruck says that pregnant women's dreams are consistent enough that pregnancy can be diagnosed from them[45] (ch. 9, p. 299). Even more striking, perhaps, are the dreams dreamt by unfortunate women who are not as yet consciously aware that they are carrying fetuses which have died. Joan

Windsor relates a mother's series of such dreams, concluding with the following dream:

> Three days before the birth, she dreamed *her baby was doing the dead-man's float and then smiled at her and waved good-bye*. She woke up crying hysterically, and requested an immediate examination. The doctors could find no heartbeat. Eventually, the baby was born dead.[46]

Robert Van de Castle reports two other such dreams. In one, *the obstetrician says the baby is too cold*; in the other, *the dreamer's own mother has placed the infant in the refrigerator, where she finds it*. Garfield, who writes about Van de Castle's reports, surmises that "the dreaming minds of these women were sensing the abnormal coldness of the fetuses they were carrying."[47] However, it is questionable that the surface body temperature of a dead fetus within the womb is detectably different from the mother's own core body temperature. Quite possibly, these women detected the condition of their babies in some other way and associated death with coldness. (Similarly, when someone with a sore throat dreams of "*a stairwell painted pink, covered with scratches*,"[48] the color pink is contributed to the dream from memory and association, not from concurrent color sensation.)

Note also that Eileen Stukane, in her book about dreams during pregnancy, records two baby-in-refrigerator dreams, but neither of them signalled a dead fetus.[49] She presents a number of prodromal miscarriage dreams, together with a caution that most dreams which appear to alert women to dangers to their pregnancies are in actuality false alarms.[50]

Garfield's book is the best comprehensive survey of images of illness in dreams. It is loaded with examples of symbolic correspondences, both prodromal and concerning established disorders, or 'pathognomic' (defined by Webster's as "characteristic of a particular disease"). For example, someone with hemorrhoids dreamt of being "*impaled on a stick in the anus*." Someone with broken right ribs dreamt of *the collapse of a right hand bannister*. After a hysterectomy, a woman symbolized her distress as *a jagged car fender coming painfully out of her vagina*.[51] Garfield lists typical dream motifs for lung disorders, arthritic disorders, dental problems, and most other common ailments.

A number of "Garfield's Dream Aphorisms" actually go to illustrate that motifs which *may* correspond symbolically to physical symptoms are really more likely to relate to psychological matters. For example: "Freezing rain, frost, ice, or snow, | Body circulation slow." "Arid earth, plants wilt and die, | Body tissues overdry." Water = too much body fluid. Dryness = too little. Obstacles = blockages. Repugnant images = toxins.[52] Garfield does remind readers that dream images such as these may have a psychological meaning apart from or along with a medical meaning.[53] Yet in advocating her subject, she encourages more confidence in dreams for this purpose than seems strictly warranted. "Better to take action and be well," she advises, "than ignore a dream warning and fall ill." Speaking for myself, if I were to follow that advice for all the motifs she lists, I would never cease worrying about my health.

From these relatively straightforward demonstrations of symbolic correspondences between disease symptoms and dream images, we turn to Jung and the suggestion that correspondences may be mediated by archetypes of the collective unconscious. In the example to follow, Jung proves to have performed medical diagnoses from dreams as virtuosic as his psychological diagnoses, such as when he foresaw the fall of the ecstatic mountaineer who dreamt "He mounts upward on empty air" (ch. 3, p. 110). Here is Russell Lockhart's account of an impressive medical diagnosis by Jung:

> In 1933, Dr. T. M. Davie submitted a patient's dream to Jung for interpretation. No other information about the patient was provided. . . .
> *Someone beside me kept asking me something about oiling some machinery. Milk was suggested as the best lubricant. Apparently I thought that oozy slime was preferable. Then, a pond was drained and amid the slime there were two extinct animals. One was a minute mastodon. I forgot what the other one was.*
> Jung told Davie the dream indicated an organic condition and that the drainage of the pond referred to the damming up of cerebrospinal fluid. Dr. Davie was very impressed with Jung's diagnosis and concluded his own published report of the case with these words:
> > "Dreams . . . do not merely provide information on the psychological situation, but may disclose the presence of organic disorder and even denote its precise location."
> When later asked how he arrived at such a diagnosis, Jung told his medical audience at Tavistock:
> > . . . why I must take that dream as an organic symptom would start such an argument that you would accuse me of the most terrible obscurantism. . . . I should have to give you a course of about four semesters about symbology first so that you could appreciate what I said.

Lockhart next takes it upon himself to provide the explanation from which Jung demurred. Of course there is no telling if Jung would have endorsed Lockhart's amplification. Certainly it does not lack the promised "obscurantism," but Jung could well have arrived at his diagnosis by another route. However, Lockhart's speculation is valuable in its own right as a sample of the approach:

[T]he Latin word for slime is 'pituita'.

From this word comes pituitary. The slimy colloidal secretions of the pituitary gland . . . flow into the third ventricle . . . through which the cerebrospinal fluid also flows. The cerebrospinal fluid has the function of lubricating these cavities and provides a mechanical barrier against shock to the brain. . . . If cut off or blocked, the effect, as in a real aqueduct, is a drainage of the cerebrospinal pool downstream.

Milk is suggested as a lubricant. This detail of the dream is understandable in connection with the image of the mastodon. . . . The element 'odon' refers to "teeth" and comes from the Latin 'odontia'. The 'mast' element comes from the Greek word 'mastos', meaning breast. So, a mastodon is an animal that has "breast teeth," and in fact was given this name because of the nipple-like projections on its rounded teeth. . . . And, now, those of you who know brain anatomy will immediately think of the "mammillary bodies," those breast-shaped structures of the hypothalamus lying at the base of the third ventricle with nipple-like projections protruding at the base of the brain.

There is much more to this dream, but already we see a drainage of fluid Jung felt to be the cerebrospinal fluid, an oozy slime that could refer to the secretions of the pituitary, and a mastodon whose etymology is related to breast, and therefore, to milk symbolism—all elements physically related to the third ventricle. . . . Perhaps in this dream the two extinct animals are images of the hypothalamus and the pituitary that lie beneath the cerebrospinal pond. The case was medically diagnosed as a neurological disturbance of the third ventricle.[54]

Meredith Sabini tabulates that Jung discussed medical dreams nine times in his *Collected Works* and *Letters*.[55] The case most often cited is his forecast of the death of a 17-year-old girl "in the first stages of progressive muscular atrophy," on the basis of a pair of "gruesome" dreams depicting *the death by suicide of her mother* and *of a horse*. "[T]he unconscious life" and "the animal life" of the girl were self-destructing—such Jung understood to be the message of these archetypal fatalities "to the conscious mind of the dreamer and to anybody who has ears to hear."[56]

Marie-Louise von Franz, in *On Dreams and Death*, relates a comparable story of a death foreshadowed by that of a dream horse, and her interpretation is similarly but even more explicitly couched in terms of a compensatory function. The dream was dreamt by a 61-year-old cavalry officer, four weeks prior to his "unexpected death from heart failure":

> He was once again in the officer's school where he had acquired the rank of lieutenant thirty years before. An old corporal of whom he thought highly at that time and who in reality had the meaningful name of "Adam," appeared and said to him, "Mr. Lieutenant, I must show you something." He led the lieutenant down into the cellar of the barracks and opened the door—made of lead! The dreamer recoiled with a shudder. In front of him the carcass of

a horse lay on its back, completely decomposed and emanating an awful corpse smell.

The simple "mortal Adam" shows the dreamer what is awaiting him, namely the decomposition in death of his animal body, that is, the horse. By means of the shock produced by the dream, the unconscious meant to detach the dreamer from his body, as if to say, "Not you, yourself, but your horse will die." For a cavalry man the horse is, to a special degree, a symbol for that instinctive part of his physical nature which "carries" him. Adam, the universal "simple" man (anthropos) in the dreamer (an image of the Self), knows about the body's impending decomposition and tries to prepare the dreamer for it.[57]

Von Franz's officer suffered from heart disease. The dream is presented, however, as reflecting not that specific disorder but his general clinical outlook. Perhaps it is also the general outlook which is reflected in the dreams of heart patients studied by Alfred Ziegler, whose 1980 report Sabini cites to illustrate her contention that the destiny of buildings is particularly telling in the dreams of those ill from (nonspecific) physical causes. She states:

The patient found herself in a marshy area surrounded by high steep crags. All around her was water and loam. Suddenly she was transplanted to a three story house standing on a high rock. But the house began to sink and she landed in the cellar; she could not find her way out of it. She was seized by panic because she began to sink even deeper into the mire which lay on the floor. She awoke terrified and gasping for air! . . . It is as if her whole earthly existence, as symbolized by the house, is being swallowed back into the primordial slime. . . .

. . . [T]he severity of the physical disorder is paralleled in the dreams by the severity of dis-order in the dreamer's earthly house or structure. At its most severe, when the life process is in danger or ending, the whole house may "go under."

This dream, taken with others Sabini cites which correspond to less severe conditions, illustrates her rule of thumb about buildings. But Ziegler, as Sabini further relates, draws a more specific connection between heart disease and a type of dream exemplified by the one above:

Ziegler said that this dream contained all the elements he found to be typical in a sample of 26 dreams from 16 clinic patients in the latter stages of heart disease. Several aspects of their dreams distinguished them from the dreams of a non-cardiac control group. The intensity and frequency of severe anxiety, reaching proportions of terror, was one of these factors. And these anxieties were linked with three particular motifs: sinking into water, marshes, and the like; being hard pressed from all sides; and being exposed to attack. The other significant element was that all forms of aggressiveness—healthy protest, anger in the service of the self, action to ward off threats—were missing in the heart patients' dreams. In other words, the dreamers seemed to be caught in a grave situation where they were completely helpless to save themselves, and there was no intervention on their behalf.[58]

Ziegler terms the dream type *aporetic*, from a Greek word meaning "to be at a loss," or "impassible." As Sabini notes, Jung based his prognosis of death in the case of the two "gruesome" dreams of suicide upon this very absence of any solution. Jung generalized that "[i]t is dangerous when there is no trace of a way out." His sense of "a way out" was generous, however: "A solution could be, for example, that the dreamer awakens with the feeling, Ah, it is only a nightmare. Another type of solution lies in the fact that the danger does not reach the dreamer at all because he wakes up beforehand. As a rule, one can see some ray of hope."[59] Also notice that in commenting on the dream "Extinct animals in a drained pond," Jung remarked: "It is notorious that one often dreams of one's own death, and that is no serious matter. When it is really a question of death, the dream speaks another language."[60]* And Jungians Whitmont & Perera give this advice: "It is important . . . to keep in mind that ominous motifs are to be treated as warnings but never as definite predictions. . . . Moreover, no dream ever tells a final or unalterable story." However, they add: "Only in rare circumstances do they indicate finalities."[61]

Since Jung's prognosis of death from dreams of suicide involved a case of multiple sclerosis (in Sabini's judgment), it appears that Ziegler's "aporetic" quality is not specifically linked to heart patients' dreams. But possibly the conjunction of dream features—"sinking into water," etc.—is linked to the heart.

Garfield offers a somewhat different list of typical dream motifs associated with heart disorders: "Dreamer or other character is hurt in accident, war, or fight. Wounds typically appear in left arm, heart area or neck. Pain in heart, left arm, or neck often accompany [sic] the wound. Squeezing or clutching pressure on heart, chest, and/or neck. Sense of heavy weight falling on chest. Sense of strangulation, of suffocation, or difficulty breathing

---

* Surveying college students' dream diaries collected for another purpose, Deirdre Barrett (1987) found that ½% of dreams were of dying and that these came from 3% of the subjects. Interestingly, dreams of actually dying and being dead were striking for being pleasant (84%) or neutral (14%), whereas dreams of *almost* dying were overwhelmingly unpleasant (94%). Another study which asked students if they had *ever* dreamed of dying found that 11% had. Their dreams had the same characteristics.

Barrett found two kinds of death dreams. The first kind, comprising almost ⅔ of the total, mostly concerns what happens after death. The dream-ego is likely to leave the physical dream-body. These dreams, Barrett supposes, concern afterlife themes or else represent archetypal treatments of psychic transformation. The second kind, just over ⅓ of the total, ends with dream death, and these Barrett supposes to concern Elizabeth Kubler-Ross's "acceptance stage of death" (p. 2).

or of stagnant air. An impression of an explosion, as with shots or bombs. References to death, blood, pain. Effortful behavior with sense of urgency and/or fear. Objects capable of clutching or squeezing."[62]

The next examples are from Haskell, citing H. A. Savitz, and from Raymond Rainville. The first dream is diagnostic; the second is associated with a chronic disorder:

[A man] complained of a fluttering feeling in his stomach. After returning from a vacation in Bermuda, he dreamed that *he fell from a wharf into the water between the wharf piles. A yacht was moored alongside. The yacht squeezed him onto the pier structures.* On the basis of this dream Savitz administered an EEG [*sic*] and found . . . a myocardial infarction.[63]

[This dream was] reported by a 37-year-old man awaiting a heart transplant. This man suffered from chronic cardiac insufficiency, severe chest pains, and nightmares, all of which occurred more than once. After he awoke from these dreams, he suffered serious chest pains, was compelled to assume a sitting-up posture, and take medication. . . .

I am watching a small hamster crouched in the corner of a cage. A strong man's hand grabs the animal and places it in his palm. Very slowly and deliberately the thumb comes around the animal's chest and the index finger around the animal's neck. I know the hand is going to squeeze him to death and I try not to watch. But then the animal wheezes and coughs and I have to look back at it. As it starts to struggle and its paws are flailing, my own hands grasp the wrist of the hand. It is then that I realize that it takes both my hands to get around the wrist. I feel like a child to a giant. I am pulling myself up by the wrist when I wake up sweating and in pain.[64]

Something not unrelated to Ziegler's aporetic motif is reported by Robert Smith. Smith looked "retrospectively" at dreams from seriously ill patients, mostly heart patients, to see what if any dream motifs might have predicted their condition. He found *traumatic dreams*: for men, the motif was death, and for women, though less consistently, the motif was separation.[65] Next, he looked at the current dream motifs of long-term patients not manifesting acute symptoms. He found that the same motifs correlate with underlying disease severity.[66] Smith concludes that there must be some "physicochemical interaction with the dreaming process," which serves "some warning and adaptive function."[67]

But again, it is the general prognosis which is represented by the motif, not the heart symptom per se; and not even physical illness per se, but illness's threat to ego integrity—Smith compares his sample to death dreams following severe psychological trauma, reported by Kardiner.[68] Smith holds that "traumatic dreams" arise with "severe underlying dysfunctions of the dreamer, whether biological, psychological, or both. . . . [T]he more traumatic the references, the more severe the dysfunction."[69]*

Smith looks for a possible explanation for the gender difference in motifs (death vs. separation): "There is some evidence that men as a group respond in more individualistic, aggressive ways than women, who, as a group, respond in more interpersonal, other-directed ways. Such data are compatible with death and separation as markers of serious distress in men and women, respectively."[70]

The interesting thing is that the dreaming mind gets alerted to the threat in anticipation of acute symptoms. "In these two studies," comments David Koulack, the patients "evidently were not consciously aware of the degree of severity of their illness. However, it was precisely the severity of their illness that seemed to be responsible for the alteration of dream content."[71]

Smith also found that the worst clinical outcomes tend to ensue after an absence of any recent dream recall. When the threat to life becomes critical, he suggests, dream recall is aborted in "a last-ditch protective measure," as Harold Levitan calls it.[72]

This section on dreams traceable to bodily disease will conclude with several examples of an interesting variant: dreams which contain explicit verbal references to symptoms. This is one subtype in a classification of dream images of illness made by Sabini. Her classification embraces dreams related to: diseases arising purely somatically; those of the standard psychosomatic type, that is, where psychological issues get transferred to the body strictly in service of repression; and diseases where, as she believes, dream and disease cooperate to bring psychological or spiritual healing to the ill person.

Sabini begins with two general categories: (1) dreams which figure the illness symbolically, and (2) those which present the illness without symbolic transformations. This is a general distinction which can be applied—and was already applied by Artemidorus[73]—to dreams on any topic.

(1) Symbolic presentations commonly include the following:

Vegetative imagery, which concerns "deep connection with the chemical somatic processes."

Animals, which "stand for general psychophysical libido as well as for specific instincts and bodily functions."

---

* In the *aftermath* of cardiac arrest, survivors, who typically afterwards defend against fear and profess themselves "calm and tranquil," experience "dreams of violence and violent death" (R. G. Druss & D. S. Kornfeld 1967, p. 293). Interestingly, such nightmares are the only psychological manifestation distinguishing them from emergency coronary thrombosis patients who do *not* undergo cardiac arrest. The dreams may reflect the experiences of being "'dead' and returned to life," or the violence of emergency resuscitation (p. 291).

Inanimate things—often buildings, vehicles, and machinery—which pose analogies to the body.

(2) Nonsymbolic presentations include the following:

Direct imaging of the symptom. Sabini generalizes that it is important for the psychological aspect of the illness whether the symptom is pictured in its actual place, or displaced; and whether in the dream-ego's body or transferred to someone else.

Parental figures. When appearing in conjunction with symptoms, these often refer to archetypal aspects—issues of origin, etc.—, or to familial issues in the genesis of the disease.

Verbal reference to the symptoms. This subtype, of which examples will now be offered, may occur when there is a "movement of psychic contents toward consciousness" or "an urgent need to enlighten consciousness about the condition."[74]

The well known surgeon Bernard Siegel routinely solicits dream material as a diagnostic aid. He explains:

> The body is not a machine, but is a vibrant system of physical and electrical energy whose tissues and organs have their own frequencies and cycles, their own rhythms. . . .
>
> . . . Disease states represent an alteration in the pattern and if one "listens," the symptoms present themselves. For some, these symptoms or this awareness is through physical signs, but for many, the message comes via dreams, intuition and the unconscious.
>
> As a practicing surgeon, I became aware that patients knew their diagnoses. The mind literally knew what was going on in the body. When I shared my beliefs and was open, the patients began to share with me their knowledge of future events and the outcome of their diseases and treatments. Now, I routinely ask for dream material and for drawings. . . .
>
> Dream #1 Patient with breast cancer reported dream in which *her head was shaved and the word cancer written on it*. She awakened with the knowledge that she had brain metastases. No physical signs or symptoms until three weeks passed and diagnosis confirmed. . . .
>
> Dream #3 (Personal dream at a time in which I had symptoms possibly due to cancer.) *A group was present* in dream. *Others had cancer but I was pointed out as not having it.* I awoke with the knowledge that I did not have cancer, which was verified by later tests.

Siegel's "Dream #2" crosses Sabini's categories of verbal reference, animal symbolization, and parental figure:

> Patient had dream in which *shellfish opens and worm presents itself. An old woman points and says, "That's what's wrong with you."* The patient, a nurse,

sick with an undiagnosed illness awakens with the knowledge that hepatitis is her diagnosis. Confirmed by physician later.[75]*

Windsor, in her book *Dreams and Healing*, gives these examples from her personal experience:

[A] minor pain made its appearance across the small of my back. I could not recall how I hurt myself but began applying heat and massage to alleviate the condition. As if to assure me that no major disaster loomed on the horizon, on March 27th as I awoke, I received the following sentence of explanation and vote of confidence in my choice of treatment.
"You hurt your back picking up the brown suitcase. You'll be ok."
Another message received May 29th, 1984, stated in no uncertain terms what my sedentary work life was accomplishing with regard to my circulatory system.
"Your blood does not circulate well. You need to jog."[76]

Garfield also gives an example from experience. After her broken wrist had been misdiagnosed as a sprain, she dreamt that *she has "a revelation" as a man* (her doctor was a man) *makes a diagram: "Don't you realize?! That's my broken arm!"* Another dreamer in Garfield's book has her pregnancy announced to her: *"O by the way, you're pregnant."*[77]

Still another dream from Garfield's book directly involves recovery. After forty years of recurring migraines, a woman dreamt that *a man "laid his hand on her forehead and said that she would never again, as long as she lived, have another one of those headaches."* And she did not. Under the heading "Dreaming Oneself Well," Garfield comments: "Strange as it may seem, healing sometimes occurs *within* a dream state."[78] That construction of the episode is as legitimate as another; however, might not the dreamer simply have detected a change in her physical (or psychological) condition, just as dreamers entering an illness sometimes do?

Deirdre Barrett records a subject's explicit diagnostic dream, deliberately induced by a dream incubation procedure (ch. 13, p. 417) for the purpose of finding the solution to a medical problem:

Problem: I've been having major problems with my menstrual cycle and my doctor can't figure out what is wrong. Dream: *my doctor told me I was having a reaction from being on a diet and exercising more than I ever have.* In the dream,

---

* See also B. Siegel, *Love, Medicine and Miracles*, New York: Harper & Row, pp. 113–4, 1986, quoted by P. Garfield (1991), p. 106 and by R. Cartwright & L. Lamberg (1992), p. 163. Also reported in *Dream Network Bulletin* 2(2), 1983, quoted by G. Delaney (1990b [1986]), pp. 4–5. Compare this comment by Jung: "The crab, which possesses only a sympathetic system . . . is therefore an abdominal image" ("Le rêve," *Revue de Psychologie Analytique* 2, 1971, quoted by S. Resnik 1987, p. 63).

my doctor gave me medicine to correct this and I would be fine if I took this medicine. In waking life, he did ask about diet and I didn't tell him how much I'm dieting: he's never asked about exercise. I guess I should tell him about the diet and exercise, huh?[79]

Following this look at dreams imaging the body and its diseases, we will return to dreams of psychological symptoms, but those which take a somatic form, i.e., psychosomatic symptoms. As a bridge to that section, here from Sabini is a dream which makes direct verbal reference to symptoms so as to self-diagnose them as psychosomatic:

On occasion . . . there are dreams which give a simple and direct answer about whether a condition is psychogenic or organic. The following is such a dream from a woman who had been experiencing mild but disruptive symptoms of stomach upset, sleep disturbance, and tiredness for several weeks:

I dreamed that the strange feelings and physical difficulties of this period were due to the fact that I was passing through a transition now that I had avoided years earlier by getting married at the end of college.

The woman was in analysis at the time and understood what particular transition the dream referred to. This dream shows that physical symptoms can be a natural accompaniment to personal development and not necessarily a manifestation of pathology. In this case, the physical symptoms paralleled a process in the psyche, and when it ran its course, they subsided.[80]

Dreams and Psychosomatic Symptoms

The term 'psychosomatic' in a broad sense covers all mind-body interrelationships, including the dream/symptom connections just discussed, where symptoms are presumed somatic in origin. In a narrower sense, of interest now, 'psychosomatic' means that psychological factors in some way cause the somatic disorders, hence the symptoms are simultaneously somatic and psychological. The sense of the term which pertains to a given case is sometimes obvious, but sometimes not, and it should be held as a caution when reading in this field that judgments about psychological causations are often presumptive, perhaps unavoidably so. In some cases the causal connection is compelling, while in others it is not well explained how dreams claimed as psychosomatically related differ from simple disease dreams. After all, once the physical disease process in underway, the dreaming mind can pick up the same information directly from the body as in the case of straightforward diseases.

An issue of psychosomatics with a bearing on dream interpretation is the siting or targeting of the conversion to somatic symptom. H. Warnes & A.

Finkelstein (1971) state the classic understanding: "The leap from psyche to soma is possibly due to specific organ predisposition or vulnerability."[81] In other words, the psychosomatic disease process acts like a predator taking the weakest member of a herd. In this event there is no primary psychological significance in the selection. Nor is there, in the event of what Wilfred Bion termed "somatopsychosis," a chaotic somaticization of a psychic problem in a cluster of unrelated symptoms.[82]

But many psychosomatic conditions evidently get unconsciously selected for a specific symbolic reason, comparably to the generation of dream symbols; and they have counterparts in the dreams of these patients. If the process is anagogic, then the symptom may be regarded as pleading or demanding that attention be drawn in a certain constructive direction (see, e.g., the dream "Evil incarnated in a giant" below). If catagogic, then the symptom arises as a result of repression. Thus, for example, Gutheil comments on the case of an envious sister with hysterical epilepsy. Some of her dreams symbolize the symptom, e.g., as *a mute paralysis*: symptom and dream comprise collateral symbolic expressions of a single psychological complex. A further dream, in which *the envied sister drowns*, reveals the underlying conflict. Gutheil says: "Whenever this antimoral drive [to kill her sister] threatens to break through, the patient drowns it in her epileptic attack."[83]

A scheme for symptom siting which combines organ predisposition with psychological symbolism was offered by Warnes in 1982: specific parts and processes of the body become sensitized and vulnerable as a consequence of vicissitudes in the formation of the body image during early development. Warnes writes that "[b]ody image, the self and significant objects interact with each other and can symbolize one another. Their boundaries are fluid." Especially important is the mother "object," in regard to problems of "fusion and confusion between the patient's body and the mother's fantasized body. . . ." "The 'matrix' of disturbed bodily experiences inscribed in the preverbal somatic memory which has not been psychologically processed appears to predispose and facilitate the onset of [psychosomatic] symptoms later in life."[84]

Warnes's accompanying "clinical vignettes" unfortunately do not well illustrate this somewhat jargony scheme. Warnes's article is good, however, as a presentation of the "consensus" which, he says, exists concerning the profile of the "'typical' psychosomatic character."

Warnes describes a person who has reacted to developmental problems involving ego boundaries and identity formation by constructing a powerful barrier against impulses and feelings.[85] "Psychosomatic symptoms are a substitute for massive anxiety, depression, rage, guilt and fear."[86] While there are certainly many exceptions, the "character armor" of the psychosomatic person is likely to appear as follows: "superadaptation to external reality," or "pseudonormality," interestingly characterized by absence of other neurotic features; "overconcern for facts and things," with "pragmatic use of language" and impoverished fantasy life; stiff posture, and "diminished affective response and remoteness in relationships."[87]

Levitan, who has done a valuable series of concise papers investigating the dreams typical of different psychological syndromes, gives one account of how the psychosomatic personality profile shows up in dreams. He claims to have observed certain types of dreams which occur quite regularly and regardless of specific medical diagnosis; this observation "supports the concept of a commonality of mental structure" for most or all psychosomatic persons.[88] Whereas during waking hours their impulses are stifled, in dream life these people lack normal defenses against impulses. This "failure of the defensive functions of the ego" comes out as failure to convert impulses into symbolic forms. This is a trait of dream style consistent with "their excessively reality-oriented way of thinking during the day." Thus one group of psychosomatic dreams contains episodes of frank sadism, masochism, and/or incest. To illustrate masochism, Levitan tells a dream dreamt after a man received catastrophic financial news, and just before a coronary. The dream is from an article by Daniel Schneider, where it appeared as follows:

> I am a great violinist—one of the world's greatest—and am about to give a concert in our Town Hall with its sumptuous red plush.
>
> The evening arrives. The auditorium begins to fill up with every celebrity near and far, in formal clothes, the rich and the powerful, bedecked and glittering with diamonds and jewels.
>
> The concert piano with my violin in its case resting on top is in center stage. My accompanist and I are in the wings waiting for the audience to become quiet as the lights dim a little. There is a hush. My accompanist goes out on stage, bows to a small ripple of applause, sits down at the piano, flicking his tails behind him on the piano bench and spreading his fingers out over the keyboard, poised at the ready.
>
> Then I come out to tremendous applause. I bow and the hush deepens as I turn toward my violin case and take out—not a violin but a gangster-style submachine gun, and swiftly I put the muzzle to my mouth and—rat-a-tat-tat—I blow my brains out. . . . I am aware that I fall.[89]*

---

* Levitan (1981a, p. 6) comments: "The positive tone which exists in the first part of this dream . . . masked awareness of the developing onslaught to such a degree that the dreamer had no opportunity to modify the onslaught or, failing that, to awaken prior to the denouement. I want to stress that in a large percentage of dreams in this category the traumatic events pass beyond the point of

To illustrate unsymbolized incestuous wishes associated with psychosomatics, Levitan tells this dream:

> Mr. C., a middle-aged executive with asthma, reported the following dream shortly after noticing the onset of his daughter's pubescence:
> *I am with my daughter... she wants to have sex... we walk around the block trying to find a secluded place... everywhere is too public... finally we hide in a clump of bushes... and have sexual intercourse there...*[90]*

Notice that although these dreams are dominated by powerful impulses, appropriate emotional tones appear to be missing or muted.

In a further variety of psychosomatic dream, appropriate emotion does occur as a feature of the dream story, only it is projected outside the dream-ego. This dream type, which Levitan says displays a relatively better level of ego functioning, contains during dreaming the same incapacity to experience negative emotion as is typical of the psychosomatic personality awake. Here is Levitan's interesting example:

> Miss S. is a 60-year-old secretary with rheumatoid arthritis. Her unawareness of her own feelings is astonishing. For example, she sought ophthalmological consultation for the complaint of "wet eyes" without any recognition of the fact that her eyes were wet because she was crying.
>
> In the midst of our therapy her mother died. Though she was deeply attached to her mother she was aware of few signs of sadness. The following dream which occurred very shortly after her mother's death illustrates the process by means of which she was able to avoid awareness of her grief:
> *We were all at mother's funeral... Suddenly my brother Jack burst into tears ... I never saw anybody cry so hard... I felt very sorry for him...*

---

threat to the point of consummation."

Schneider himself (D. E. Schneider 1973) uses this dream to illustrate that some heart attacks are associated with "what he calls 'shock-dreams.'" Schneider is advancing a somewhat abstruse theory, which I will let Haskell (1985c, p. 111) summarize, as follows: "Schneider . . . hypothesizes a 'paraconscious' monitoring process in the frontal lobes that regulates excitatory and calming effects. In addition, he suggests that what he calls the paraconscious constructs certain dreams, and will construct an anginal dream quite differently from a thrombosis dream. It is his contention that a study of dreams will yield prediction of disease." I am not clear whether Schneider thinks these dreams only reflect or monitor the physical state, or whether the dream "shock"—as in Levitan's discussion of it—helps to cause the attack. The latter is implied by Schneider's (p. 364) interpretation of this dream, which emphasizes its raging sadism as well as masochism. He writes that the essence of the dream is "its very ugly, very repulsive design to shock both the rich and the brilliant who may have succeeded by whatever means, while he has failed. . . . [E]ach and every person in his dream-audience [is] crucified by the indelible memory of how utterly exploded into bloody meaningless fragments the soul of a man may be."

* In another paper, Levitan (1981b, p. 228) finds that bulemic women also have "frankly incestuous" and violently sadistic or masochistic dreams.

Though she noted during the dream how sorry she felt for her brother whose suffering was intense, it is clear that her grief on behalf of his grief was easier to bear than would have been her own grief at first hand.

On awakening from this dream her pillow was wet. This dream sequence serves to emphasize how wide may be the split between the mental and physiological components of emotion: while she was an observer in the process of watching someone else cry, her own body was actively shedding tears.[91]

Alan Siegel also records an example of grief projected onto a dream character, but by an essentially healthy dreamer. Here, the projection was part of a healthy process of coming to terms with grief.[92]

Levitan concludes his paper with the speculation that dreams may play an active role in the genesis of some psychosomatic disorders—may, in fact, be the "Achilles heel" of some patients with stress-induced diseases. He reasons that repeatedly undergoing nighttime "traumatic events" brings "an abnormally intense physiological response" which eventually disturbs normal body functioning.[93]

In that connection, Ernest Hartmann notes that the predawn hours claim many fatalities in hospitals. He relates aggravation of a range of somatic as well as psychosomatic illnesses to the heightened arousal of the dream state (but not necessarily to specific dream content).[94] This connection is so well established that coronary patients in intensive care are routinely medicated to suppress REM sleep.[95*] And Haskell advises physicians to be aware of the possible harmful effects of REM rebound following withdrawal of medicines which suppress REM.[96] Among physiological accompaniments of REM that might have an impact on illness he includes shifts in hormone level and kidney functioning.[97]

"Since ancient times," write Rossi & Cheek, "it has been known that unpleasant thoughts and ideas may have profound disturbing effects upon the body and its functions." "[D]aytime stresses may be troublesome, but they are not as troublesome as what the unconscious mind does with these experiences at night." Especially potent are "the disturbing thoughts and emotions associated with terrifying dreams; hence there is a definitely conceivable possibility of actual physical harm resulting from a dream."

---

* "During REM sleep, sympathetic-nerve activity increases above the levels recorded during wakefulness, and the values for blood pressure and heart rate return to those recorded during wakefulness. Momentary restoration of muscle tone during REM sleep (REM twitch) is frequently associated with cessation of sympathetic-nerve discharge and increase in blood pressure." These fluctuations may act as a "triggering mechanism for thrombotic events. . ." (V. K. Somers, M. E. Dyken, A. L. Mark & F. M. Abboud 1993, pp. 305-7). But nocturnal angina is more likely to occur during NREM than REM (P. M. A. Calverley & C. M. Shapiro 1993, p. 1403).

Rossi & Cheek judge that "[o]nly 10% of damaging dreams are recalled on awakening; the rest are repressed."[98] Some dreams of this sort can be retrieved under hypnosis:

> A 32-year-old divorced . . . woman was visiting with friends while recuperating from a conization performed . . . eight days earlier. She felt well and had been free from vaginal bleeding after the third postoperative day. However, on the eighth postoperative day, after an uneventful visit and quiet chat with her friends, she took a nap at 3:00 p.m. and awakened at 4:00 p.m. because of profuse vaginal bleeding. There were no cramps, and this was not the time for her expected period. . . .
>
> The patient stated that the operation had been performed to remove tissues containing intraepithelial carcinoma diagnosed on smear and biopsy. Her gynecologist had announced that it was all out and that tissue examination corroborated the conclusion that this was not malignant. . . .
>
> . . . [Under hypnosis, the patient retrieved her forgotten dream:] "I'm asleep. I'm dreaming that *I have cancer. I am dying of cancer.* I'm feeling restless. As I turn over I can feel the blood starting to come from me." . . .
>
> . . . [Following therapeutic reassurance while hypnotized, s]he had no further bleeding and reported three days later by letter that there had been no bleeding after the flight home.[99]

Cheek, an obstetrician, asserts that disturbing dreams and/or other nocturnal mentation may precipitate premature labor and miscarriages. He advises that timely intervention to help the woman understand her dream can sometimes save the baby by reducing hemorrhaging and contractions.[100] Cheek does not discuss the possibility that the disturbing dream is itself a response to somatic events already in progress. But as Koulack comments in connection with studies of asthma and ulcers, "these results can just as easily be interpreted as reflecting a somatic state rather than causing a somatic response. It is really a chicken or egg question."[101] Similarly, Rainville observes that the dream accompanying an ulcer attack may have been "a warning, a cause, or simply a parallel experience. . . ."[102]

In connection with ulcers, a fact worth noting is that patients frequently show increased gastric secretions during REM sleep. Dreams may thus possibly mediate or cause aggravation of the disease.[103*] Compare this with the onset of angina pectoris during REM. Warnes & Finkelstein cite articles to

---

* Later, Anthony Kales changed his opinion and stated that the surplus of gastric secretions is *not* related to dream content. Haskell does not see how the effect of dream content can be extricated and disproven (1985c, p. 111, citing A. Kales & J. D. Kales, "Sleep disorders: recent findings in the diagnosis and treatment of disturbed sleep," *New England Journal of Medicine* 290, pp. 487–99, 1974).

the effect that shifts in blood pressure precipitate the angina; and M. Andrisani blames anxiety dreams for the pressure shift.[104]

In the above instances, the dream acts essentially as a general stressor. Alternatively, Anna Potamianou relies on classical Freudian energy dynamics when she theorizes that dreams "bind drive excitations," and that in certain individuals, failure of this function leads to somatization of the energy. She identifies inadequate dreams as those which are "repetitive," those with "poor symbolization," and those with "no narrative" dramatizing and elaborating the underlying conflict.[105]

There are apparently also cases where a dream plays an instrumental psychodynamic role in the emergence of a bodily symptom. If the dream fails in symbolic management of inadmissible thoughts and feelings, it may mediate their conversion into a symptom. (This corresponds to the mediative role of dreams in the development of psychological symptoms, to be illustrated in chapter 10.) An example is provided by medical anthropologist Loudell Snow, when discussing sorcery and hexing in African-American folk medical beliefs and practices:

> There can be no doubt that the death of her mother [by sorcery] has been a powerful influence in Bernita's life; she learned at an early age that love and sexuality are inextricably blended with danger, aggression and control. . . .
>
> It is apparently one of . . . [her] lovers who was responsible for her own unnatural illness. How did it happen? . . . [To Bernita's understanding, her hexing was accomplished in a dream]:
>
> So, what had happened to me in a **dream**—I **dreamed** that *there was a stream of water comin' through my window, comin' all way. It was a stream of water comin' through the house.* O.K., so within my dream *I said, "I'm gonna throw out* (a fishing line) *here in this beautiful stream; I know somethin' comin' through this is gonna bite. I'ma catch me a big nice fish in here!"* So, *I threw out there* (imitating casting her line) *in this stream and something ran up there, and I snatched* (it out) *but it didn't do anything. So I said, "Oh, no, I'm gonna bait up and throw out here again—because I know there's something out there in all that pretty water, running water—I'm gon' catch me a big, nice fish!"* So *I baited up and I threw out there again in that beautiful stream, and when I threw out there in that beautiful stream, oh, something just grabbed that cork and it just gone with it and I just snatched up* (imitating pulling the line from the stream)—*and when I snatched up, I snatched so hard 'til that's when that pain hit me in my side. . . .*
>
> . . . [T]he pain was apparently a divine sign that something was terribly wrong, though at first she did not recognize it:
>
> So the Lord was lettin' me know there was something wrong. **But,** I didn't realize what had happened, so I **did** go to a doctor. . . . So the doctor, oh, he give me every kind of medicine he thought it could cure me. . . . [But] I was

gettin' worser still. . . . So, I laid there and I prayed and I asked God, I said, "Oh, God, I know You's able; **tell** me what to do about this!"

The Lord recommended that she begin by seeing what she happened to have around the house—she would need nine different things—and then boil them up into a tea. . . . She found a rusty nail and some peach leaves in the yard and then went into the kitchen to round out her prescription. . . .

The Lord said some other things for her to do as well, however. He reminded her that it was her own folly for leaving personal items—in this case, shoes—out in the yard where anyone could get to them and use them in sorcery. He also directed her in the purchase of sulphur and salt. . . .

. . . And so the Lord said, "Take those three shoes, and your shoes, and everybody else shoes that you find out there and put those shoes on the fire and **burn them!**" . . . [And] He said, "Put that box of sulphur on there and let it **burn!**" So I did that. And the Lord told me, said, "Well, now **this**, you will be free. You'll be all right." And I was. . . .

I was so intrigued by all of this that it was not until I got home that it occurred to me that I did not know what—if anything—she had caught from the beautiful stream flowing through her bedroom! I could scarcely wait . . . [to] ask her about it. She had been hoping for a "big nice fish" but what she landed, it seems obvious, symbolically expresses her ambivalence about her own sexuality—and how it can be used by a man to control a woman:

. . . *[It was a] fish eel.* . . . *Round and long.* . . . *[W]hen I snatched up **he*** (italics mine [Snow's]) *was so heavy 'til it put that pressure on my side to cause my side to go hurtin'.* . . . *[It] just a long black something.* . . . I woke up; because I was hurtin' just that **bad,** I **had** to wake up! (The pain) came **right** in the dream; when I woke up I couldn't move anymore.[106]

In a paper entitled "Dreams Which Culminate in Migraine Headaches," Levitan considers the immediate, psychodynamic impact of specific dreams on the symptom which comes as their sequel. Usually, although not invariably, nocturnal migraine attacks awaken the sufferer during or shortly after a REMP.[107] The typical preceding dream contains strong, "persistent negative affect"—frustration, and loss, but especially terror—accompanied by a threat to physical safety.[108*] Levitan assumes there to be a psychological trigger in the dream; however, he allows that a state of physiological readiness must also exist, since similar dream affects and actions in the same dreamers sometimes do not bring migraines. But a notable fact argues that a symbolic psychological factor is at work: an unexecuted threat to physical safety in the dream, and not a threat executed, is what seems to trigger the symptom.

---

* Although Levitan does not comment on it, the migraine syndrome appears to be an exception with respect to the poor capacity for experiencing negative affects, even in dreams, which he elsewhere (1981a) purports to exist in the psychosomatic personality.

As Levitan's remarks on the following premigraine dream of not completed threat with terror show, one can observe horrendous dreams of physical destruction of the head which do not induce migraines in the same dreamer—though such dreams do surely bear a symbolic relationship to the dreamer's proneness for that symptom:

> *Nazi officers are in my house searching for money ... I told my mother to give them the money or they would kill us ... one Nazi officer started throwing metal objects shaped like stars at me ... another officer said 'You can't kill her that way'... then he took out a revolver and shot me. I was very frightened ... I heard the gun go off ...* but I woke up before the bullet hit me ... my head was throbbing with a headache ...

> This dream of terror recalled many frightening situations from the period of the patient's childhood during which the Nazis occupied her house. Though she had witnessed many shootings in cold [blood] during this period she had never been directly threatened herself. . . .

> . . . It is important to note that she had many other dreams in which the action progressed even further. Some of these dreams contained scenes in which, for example, a bullet penetrated her body or even blew off her head. However, these extremely traumatic dreams did not culminate in migraine.[109]

It should be noted here that a premigraine dream reported by Warnes & Finkelstein contains the expected negative affect, again terror, but appears not to conform to Levitan's specification about the non-completion of threat:

> Female aged 17. Dream: *A man broke in through her bedroom windows. She tried to escape to the bathroom but at that point the man shot her in the left side of her head. She was "scared to death"* and woke up with a "terrible" left hemicrania.[110]

Gutheil's specimens of migraine dreams also include one with a completed threat to the dreamer's head, as well as a few where someone else's head receives injury.[111] It may be that Levitan has identified what is no more than a tendency, or that the force of the non-psychological medical component of the migraine makes a difference in cases.

Gutheil's treatment of migraine dreams is of a vintage with rather a different flavor from Levitan's. Of Gutheil's dream specimens (some but not all of which immediately precede headaches), most do contain strong negative affects as expected by Levitan. But few exhibit Levitan's threat motif, most of them revolving instead around themes of overt and covert sexuality; and while terror is not absent, most of these dreams contain instead feelings of repulsion or disgust. The dream material is quite varied, but here is one example:

I have eaten a living animal. A white mouse or a white rat. When I came to the face, I thought of hurting the animal and felt disgusted.[112]

In most cases, Gutheil thinks, the migraine constitutes a somatization of unacceptable erotic feelings on the part of persons with "far-reaching moral regressions and some atavistic trends. . . ."[113] Their dreams contain "peculiar cannibalistic, necrophilic, and mysophilic features." Mysophilia is attraction to filth, including eating feces. One dreamer *feels disgust when she discovers that she has had diarrhea over her groceries instead of into a bucket, while talking to a shoemaker.*[114] Gutheil notes that nausea is a common secondary symptom of migraine. Disgust in the dream, as well as headache and nausea awake, are "a curtain behind which the tabooed thoughts and affects can be carried on. . . ."[115]

In the dreams of one migraine patient discussed at length by Gutheil, an incest theme breaks through explicitly. Levitan also lists incest as a variant characteristic of migraine dreams. In addition to that, he describes "a special category of dreams containing outsized creatures"[116] which has no counterpart in Gutheil or Warnes. Here is one dream of that type, belonging to the same 45-year-old woman who dreamt "A Nazi shoots at her":

> ... *on the other side of the door is a black, furry animal with enormous devilish eyes ... it keeps growing and growing until it becomes a huge blob ... it tries to block the door so I couldn't get out ...* I woke up screaming with a migraine
> ...
> ... Lippman (1954) considers them [i.e., dreams of outsized creatures] to be diagnostic of the migraine even if they are unaccompanied by headache. He points to the presence of size-change phenomena in *Alice in Wonderland* written by Lewis Carroll, who was a migraineur. In contrast to the types of dreams discussed earlier which appear to precipitate the migraine attack, dreams containing size-change phenomena indicate that the migraine attack is already under way.[117]*

Garfield's list of migraine dream motifs does not include outsized creatures, incest themes, or disgust, but does include head injuries, as well as "distorted or detached heads," head bandages or headgear which is tight or obstructs vision, reduced visual field, "odd visual patterns," dizziness and falling, "unpleasant jarring or pounding," and objects the sufferer associates with headache.[118]

We turn briefly now to miscellaneous other common psychosomatic syndromes and their associated dreams. One early Freudian researcher in this area was Franz Alexander. Beginning in the 1920s, he studied peptic ulcers

---

* Jung thought that generally animals of unusual size indicate "an organic factor" (C. G. Jung, "Le rêve," *Revue de Psychologie Analytique* 2, 1971, quoted by S. Resnik 1987, p. 63).

among other disorders, finding that the dreams of patients "showed intense intaking tendencies, both passive-receiving and aggressive":

> An example of an inhibited receptive dream—*I am about to have dinner. There is not enough food.*[119]

This specimen, quoted in the introductory remarks of Warnes & Finkelstein, is actually quite different from the peptic ulcer dream which they themselves present as typical:

> Male aged 85. Dream: *His house was burning. He shouted for help but nobody came to rescue him.* Terrified he woke up.[120]

This dream has a transparent relation to the symptom, and could well be a reaction to it; but the text implies that the dream was dreamt before "acute onset" or "exacerbation." However, it was probably a recurring condition. Of the four other ulcer or pre-ulcer dreams they present, one involves food and one the mouth, but all involve images of physical trauma, at various removes from the actual symptom site. Here are edited segments of these four dreams:

> *His left leg was amputated.*
> *He was attacked, clawed and scratched by cats.*
> *The patient saw himself tearing out his teeth one my one and breaking them between his fingers which were full of blood.*
> *He was eating pizza and his stomach "broke open."*[121]

Bronchial asthma is another disease often thought to be psychosomatic. Sleep, but especially REM sleep, is associated with constriction of the airways in asthmatics.[122] In patients with nocturnal asthma attacks, "changes in breathing" occur during "dreams, particularly emotional ones."[123] Alexander, in collaboration with Thomas French, studied asthma in connection to dreams. They interpreted asthma as a flare-up of unresolved childhood conflict involving fears of losing mother, usually due to forbidden oedipal desires[124]—in short, the asthma attack is "a cry for the mother."[125] Dreams of asthmatics are said by Alexander to contain "frequent intrauterine fantasies, themes of pregnancy, abortion and birth and a specific wish to be liberated from mother and/or to regress into her."[126] Most of Stekel's and Gutheil's samplings of asthmatic dreams (not necessarily dreamt prior to bouts) arguably follow this pattern,[127] as do the two examples of preasthmatic dreams in Warnes & Finkelstein. Here is the first:

> Female aged 62. Dream: *Her mother brought her two glasses of water and rinsed her face and lips telling her not to worry because she will get well. Felt helpless, unhappy* and woke up crying. Soon after developed her asthma.[128]

The second dream is directly connected with the onset of the symptom:

> Female aged 22. Dream: *"A man was trying to kill me. He invented a machine to kill people by suffocating them by holding them under water for three minutes. It was very dangerous and he had to be stopped. There were eight women in the room. I felt very mad at you* [the doctor] *because you left me there. I woke up wheezing."*[129]

James Wood et al. find that nightmare frequency is three times greater for asthmatics than for controls, and that it is also, interestingly, three times greater than for persons with chronic obstructive airways disease (COAD, or bronchitis). Since asthma and COAD sufferers score equally high for other anxiety disorders (particularly panic attacks), there appears to be a special connection between asthma and nightmares.[130] These authors remain uncertain what that connection is. But as to the possibility that the asthma attack triggers the subsequent nightmare, they note that sleep apnea patients, who likewise undergo a measure of suffocation, seldom have nightmares.[131] Thus they seem to lean toward the option that the nightmare itself somehow triggers the attack.

Levitan compares dreams preceding bouts of asthma to those preceding migraines. In both, the dreamer is frequently a victim of aggressive attack. But whereas in about a quarter of preasthmatic dreams the dreamer her/himself perpetrates the aggression, s/he did so in none of the premigraine sample, a difference for which Levitan has no explanation.[132] One of Warnes & Finkelstein's premigraine dreams conforms to this pattern, the one quoted, "She is shot in the head"; in the other, it is *the dreamer* who *shoots her husband*, but *"by accident."*[133] Gutheil also mentions one where *a brother accidentally splits his sister's head.*[134]

Hypertension is another syndrome where aggressive drives are considered a factor. Hypertensives score high on Leon Saul & Edith Sheppard's "Hostility" scale for dreams (but in appearance the scale, which descends from "Death of a person" through injury and damage to "Minor impairment of an object," is more straightforwardly a measure of integrity than of hostility[135]). The dreams of hypertensives "during the hypertensive crisis" show the dreamer caught in insoluble crisis situations.[136]

This chapter will conclude with three longer clinical excerpts. The first concerns a case of multiple sclerosis. It is drawn, once again, from Sabini, who here quotes and reflects upon a report by James Kirsch from 1949. The dream belongs to Sabini's category where medical symptoms are represented by animal imagery. And it is a textbook case of the role of repression in the etiology of psychosomatic disease. Here the psychological preconditioning of the disease process finds figurative representation in the dream action:

[A] woman with multiple sclerosis seen for psychiatric evaluation [dreamed]: *She was trying to kill a big tarantula. She stepped on it again and again, but it seemed impossible to kill this animal. At last, she succeeded in stepping in such a way on the tarantula that its legs were stretched out in complete paralysis.*

The dream image and the physical symptom are virtually identical: the appendages of the woman and of the spider were stretched out and paralyzed. He [Kirsch] commented that the dream . . . "represented a view from within of the patient's own organic illness. The tarantula is a frequent symbol of the instincts, especially in its aspect of functioning like the autonomic nervous system." Stepping on the spider would indicate a severe repression of the instincts, and evidence of this came out [during] interview; the woman revealed that she had "begun to repress her feminine instincts after she discovered that her husband had an affair with another woman." She had "borne this situation in silence," i.e., as if paralyzed. Kirsch concluded that although the dream and the illness might be coincidental, "to the psychotherapist, this dream appears, however, as most significant, and as a concise description of the psychological condition that led to this organic illness."

This is an especially clear example of the parallel between the physical symptom and the dream image. There is an imagistic correspondence—of being splayed out, paralyzed—and also a correspondence between the phylogenetic level of the animal and the physiological level of the symptom. It is important that nothing seems to be inherently wrong with the spider, and thus perhaps there is no reason to suspect an initially organic disease. Nor has the spider done anything to frighten or harm the woman. Rather, as Kirsch concluded, the somatic condition seems to have been brought about through the destructive attitude of the patient herself. The ending of the dream suggests a poor prognosis: although the animal is not dead—which would mean a fatal outcome—it remains completely paralyzed; there is no hint of its recovery or of the woman's concern over the situation.[137]

The next case is from Ziegler, whose ideas about the hopeless "aporetic" dreams of terminal heart patients were discussed above. Here he finds evidence of an anagogic psychological process at work simultaneously in heart disease and dream. A man suffered a cardiac infarct during sleep, and evidently the dream coincided in real time with the infarct. The whole dream and Ziegler's text are too long to quote in full, but here are the main points of correspondence between dream and physical symptoms.

Dream: "*I could feel the bullets going through my heart, and saw the blood flowing out of the wounds. A fierce pain overcame me, made me faint, and I saw myself as if another person, collapsing in death.*"

Symptom: The dream reflects "well-known and typical sensations associated with angina due to infarction of the heart. . . . The patient then experiences himself as two people, for he observes his own body collapsing in death. This form of depersonalization has been described by other patients who have endured a similar attack as 'breaking up into body and spirit'."

Dream: (Scene change) *The dream-ego aggressively unmasks and kills a variety of* what Ziegler takes to be personal shadow *figures.*

Symptom: Infarct patients, "following the attack of pain, find themselves in a state of alarm which compels them to further activity."

Dream: *The dream-ego is approached and attacked by "the spirit of evil incarnated in a gigantic human form. I remained like one paralysed, rooted to the spot. The giant . . . started to strangle me. I called to God for help, and the giant's strangling grip loosened. Yellow-green foam came from his mouth and his teeth became visible. But he would not let up. Finally I called: 'Jesus', and immediately, as if a bomb had exploded, the whole phenomenon dissolved into air.* At that moment, I awoke, covered in cold sweat."

Symptom: "Physically, this corresponds to increasing nausea with unsuccessful vomiting, which together with his waking in a cold sweat easily fits within the framework of vagal collapse. The protrusion of the teeth, and the fact that the attack is made by strangulation, can equally be coordinated with clinical observations. . . . The final victory of life over death through uttering the Saviour's name is a dream image which co-exists with the patient's return to consciousness."

Ziegler continues with his surmise of a psychological process carried forward simultaneously by dream and disease. He decides not to attempt psychotherapy because the dream image of the evil giant suggested "an invasion from the collective unconscious" too powerful for the patient to integrate. However, Ziegler asks "whether the infarct in itself did not constitute a kind of therapy. When I got to know the patient in the hospital, he was in an almost serene state of mind . . . no longer assailed by his, as he called it, wild character to dominate. . . . There were no traces of fatigue, tension, depression, or the outbursts of rage mentioned in the old case history. Had nature tried to put an end to his mental sufferings by tackling the collective shadow at the cost of an irreversible physical defect, in this case a scar in the heart?"[138]

The last case is again from one of Sabini's rewarding articles, this one written with Valerie Maffly. In chapter 3 (p. 121), I mentioned their account of a cancer patient, whose unconscious individuation process outpaced his ego's capacity to absorb so much challenging material being raised all in a rush at the end of his life. The article contains many suggestions concerning the relation between dream content and a psychological 'cancer pattern' considered by some as predisposing to cancer. In that pattern, an ego-impairing early loss or trauma occurs through separation, death, or the emotional withdrawal of an important other. The resultant anger is repressed and turned inward. Overcompensatory 'strength' develops, together with a tendency to be the responsible one and to sacrifice for others. Outward conformity combines with secretiveness. Then 6 months to several years prior to diagnosis of cancer, the person experiences a new difficulty which resonates with the childhood trauma: death, divorce, children leaving home, retirement, etc. Sabini carefully makes "no implication that this pattern appears in cases of environmental cancers, childhood cancers, or in the very aged."[139]

One type of dream, Sabini finds, often occurs before the cancer becomes apparent:

> Cancer can be seen as a 'growth' process that lives wholly in the body; the impetus for growth has existed in the psyche but has been impeded, or deflected . . . taking place incorrectly in the body rather than in the whole being[.]
>
> We believe there is evidence that prior to the onset of cancer, development has been hindered for some time. There is, for example, . . . the frequency of recurrent dreams among cancer patients. . . . Such dreams mean that a core issue has needed attention for some time. The recurrent dreams we have heard are of one particular type: they allude to the dreamer's being stuck in his or her 'journey of life', for example, being on a train and not getting anywhere, or having their motor car continually go off the road: in sum, being stuck in a helpless and hopeless position.
>
> During the initial interview David reported having had the following recurrent dream for two, or perhaps as long as ten, years:
>
> *I am trying to arrive at a destination—usually a city—to keep an appointment. I never get there and I agonize over long periods of time. The modes of conveyance—usually trains like the New York City subway—turn out to be going in the wrong direction, or I have taken the wrong train, or connections are missed, or mysteriously I am not on the train on which I started, etc.* This travel theme I have learned to recognize as my symbol of not achieving my goal. The dream exhausts me.

For a long time, then, David has been unable to move along the track of his life. Two years ago his daughter killed herself; we do not know what happened ten years ago.[140]

Toward the end of this case study, Sabini reflects: "Whether cancer is the agency by which growth is initiated, or whether it marks the irretrievable somaticisation of a growth process can only be determined with each individual case."[141]

Dream Styles

Continuing in the vein of relating dreams to symptoms, the bulk of this chapter concerns the traits of dreams in people suffering from several common or intriguing psychological syndromes. Harold Levitan has laid down the premise that "each syndrome possesses a type of dream which is as characteristic for it as are the stereotyped phenomena of waking life."[1] Things may not be as clear cut as that, but sufficient connections have been drawn to make for interesting reading; and any dreamer can profit from trying to identify dimensions of her/his own dream life on this grid.

What Levitan calls dream "type" in relation to syndromes is an aspect of the general topic of dream style, at issue whenever a content analysis of any kind is made.* Thus it is the style of older Asian Indian children to continue to have "purely pleasant dreams" at an age when U.S. children have ceased having such dreams almost completely[2]—a disquieting fact. Thus sociable Freud had more populous dreams than solitary Jung,[3] and Harry Hunt has shown how the dream styles of both men are reflected in the different emphases of their theories[4] (ch. 3, p. 114). So from the level of whole cultures to that of individual personalities, we notice distinct dream styles,** and

---

* Concerning recent anthropological objections to cross-cultural applications of content analysis, see chapter 5, p. 173.

** There is surprisingly little literature which tackles the relation of personality to dream style in a comprehensive way. Certain dream attributes, such as lucidity (see chapter 14) and recall (if that is a dream attribute), have been correlated to attributes of personality. And looked at in one light, almost everything to do with dream content variables can be said to pertain to personality, so the subject is virtually as big as that of dream experience itself. Certain work, for instance Harold Levitan's article (1981a) on "psychosomatic patients" (chapter 8) or Ernest Hartmann's (1984 and elsewhere) hypothesis of thick/thin "boundaries" as a variable affecting susceptibility to nightmares (see below), concern the dream styles of specific personality types. Some such studies fail by aiming to establish correlations which are too detailed (J. F. Rychlak & J. M. Brams 1963) or too exclusive (M. Kramer 1970, p. 151), but it may be interesting briefly to scan a few examples. (It should be

indeed we find stylistic distinctions within one individual as well, when we consider dreams from different functions of the psyche, or simply from different life circumstances. Thus within our culture the widowed, divorced, and separated dream "more often of the family members of a marital family" than do either the single *or* those currently married.[5]

Before taking up the syndromes, we will first look at two other variables affecting dream style: gender, which affects everyone, and blindness, which affects relatively few. Frankly, little really justifies discussion of these particular topics of style instead of others here, beyond personal curiosity on my part. As for gender differences, they interest just about everyone. As for the dream style of the blind, it is interesting along the lines of 'There but for the grace of God,' but also, it challenges some of our unconsidered assumptions about dream experience.

Gender

Samenesses. As background for gender differences, we will first look at some highlights of gender sameness. We can start with children's dreams, where sleep lab studies by David Foulkes provide the best information.[6]

---

borne in mind that the majority of dreamers studied are from the U.S., most of them white, many of them college students, and more male than female except when gender is the variable.)

In an article questioning the common assumption that poor recall of dreams is due to repression, David Cohen (1974, pp. 53–4) also suggests that the pre-sleep mood of *anxiety-prone* people is more likely to reappear in their dreams than that of *repressors*. They also dream more of the past (worrying, blaming) and the future (fantasizing) than do repressors, who are "better-adjusted" to the here-and-now.

Ursula Niederer (1990) says that *anxious children* tend in their dreams of animals to dream of household pets, whereas *less anxious children* dream more of "indigenous undomesticated animals" (deer, bear, etc.). She supposes that the anxious child has less aggression, so projects onto affiliative animals.

Dreamers are quite consistent in the levels of thinking and explicit feeling in their dreams, and those levels correlate with waking *"psychological differentiation"* (measured by the detail and gender differentiation of figure drawings) (M. Hendricks & R. D. Cartwright 1978).

Robert Hicks, Cheryl Chancellor & Tim Clark (1987) find that *type A* personalities report more disturbing dreams than do *type B*. They attribute the difference to type A's more "persistent. . . struggle with stressful events. . . ."

In his study of sleep onset, David Foulkes (D. Foulkes, P. S. Spear & J. D. Symonds 1966, pp. 280–4) finds that *hypnagogic dreamers* are "less anxious and constricted," more poised, more self-accepting, and less conforming. *Hypnagogic non-dreamers*, Foulkes says, have characteristics of the "'authoritarian personality' . . . (rigidity, conventionality, intolerance . . .)."

Samuel Meer (1955, p. 74) reports that *authoritarian* personalities repeat a major waking trait in their dreams, namely "uncritical acceptance of the ingroup and moral condemnation of the outgroup," as assessed by patterns of friendship and aggression in dreams.

At *age 3–5*, children's dream reports are very brief. They concern body states, such as hunger (or sleep itself). Animal characters predominate, usually the familiar and domestic species, placed in "homelike contexts," and "relatively statically portrayed." Features missing include: a storyline; an active dream-ego; much physical activity; known characters other than the immediate family; strangers; interpersonal interactions; and feelings of any sort.

Age 5–7 brings an increase in dream length and other adult-like features: physical movement including locomotion; a shift from body states to social events; more human characters (but animals are still common); "primitive storylines"; and wholly imaginary human characters. However, there still is not a fully participating dream-ego. Foulkes believes it is cognitively easier to "watch" a scene than it is to dream an active self-portrayal.

At *age 7–9* dreams approach adult length. Qualitative improvements occur in physical mobility, "thematic coherence," "narrative quality, self-representation, and character 'psychology.'" There is a further reduction of animal characters and an increase of social interactions, usually friendly. The most commonly reported feeling is happiness, belonging, "almost invariantly, to the self." But feelings and thoughts are now ascribed to other characters.

Age 9–13 brings consolidation of improvements. But there is still relatively little feeling tone in comparison to adult dreams. Fear and anger become more common, though happiness still predominates.

Adolescence (13–15) brings fewer developments than might be anticipated. Dreams become somewhat more "abstract," with less physical activity and attention to body state, more speech, perception, and thought. Unknown

---

Creative people dream of varied and unusual settings, whereas a high percentage of *non-creative* people's dreams are set at home. So find W. H. Sylvia, P. M. Clark & L. J. Monroe (1978).

Writing on dream *color* preferences and personality, Richard Suinn (1967, p. 27) cites connections found between blue and calm, red and excitability (Y. Tatibana, *Tohuka Psychologica Folia* 6, 1938), and black-and-white and introversion (R. Fortier, *A Study of the Relationship of the Response to Color and Some Personality Functions*, Ph.D. dissertation, Western Reserve University, 1952).

Suinn himself, working in the frame of *Jungian personality typology* (C. G. Jung [1921], CW 6; I. B. Myers with P. B. Myers 1985 [1980]), states (p. 27) that "color dreaming [i]s significantly correlated with being a sensation, feeling, or introvertive type for males, and a feeling or intuition type for females." Generally, he believes, heightened color dreaming could reflect sensitivity to either outer or inner reality. Surprisingly little has been written about dream style and the typology. Douglas Cann & Don Donderi (1986) investigate typology as a variable affecting recall of archetypal content. Introverts recall more "everyday" dreams than do extraverts, but both recall archetypal dreams equally. Intuitive types recall more archetypal dreams than do sensation types. Patricia Maybruck (1991, p. 82ff.) devotes some pages to the question, but unfortunately distorts the typology by essentially reducing Jung's four functions to two.

characters increase, as does aggression.[7] There is some retrogression in active self-representation, evidently due to adolescent confusions. But whereas younger children portray themselves as they "really" are, at this age they can dream themselves other traits, suggesting "a mental world in which the conscious self is less constrained by objective reality, yet is better able to redress or compensate for that reality."[8]

Calvin Hall—whose application of content analysis to dreams (ch. 3, p. 94) either generated or inspired the generation of most of the information in this discussion—had painted children's dreams as containing more aggression, particularly physical aggression, than adult dreams, as well as more misfortunes, and also more anxiety, usually as a result of obvious threats.[9] Foulkes explicitly refutes this picture, denying "that children's dreams are especially 'dreadful'. . . ."[10]* This discrepancy of views is almost certainly due to the fact that Foulkes collected dreams in the sleep lab, whereas Hall worked with spontaneously recalled home dreams. Foulkes's picture probably corresponds better to the objective situation, Hall's, to an awake child's subjective sense about dreaming.**

Coming now to dreams of *adults*, Milton Kramer summarizes the "typical content characteristics"[11]*** of an average dream: "[T]he dream usually con-

---

* In the same place, Foulkes (1979, pp. 147–8) also levels his aim at Freud and at Jung. As to Freud, Foulkes disputes "that children's dreams are more manifestly wish-fulfilling than those of adults. . . . Plot resolutions in [children's] dreams tend to be realistic and appropriate, rather than grandiosely self-serving." As to Jung, Foulkes denies "that children's dreams employ archetypal or other exotic forms of symbolism beyond the reach of the child's direct experience.... The most common plot sequences in the child's dream involve everyday forms of social interaction, with a particularly strong emphasis on play activity."

** B. Elkan (*Developmental Differences in the Manifest Content of Children's Reported Dreams*, Ph.D. dissertation, Columbia University, 1969) showed that the preoccupations found in the manifest dreams of children of different ages correspond to Erik Erikson's eight stages of psychosocial development ("Identity and the life cycle," *Psychological Issues* 1, pp. 18–171, 1959). L. T. Mack (*Developmental Differences in the Manifest Content of the Dreams of Normal and Disturbed Children*, Ph.D. dissertation, Columbia University, 1974) showed that disturbed adolescents' dreams rate below age level on Erikson's timetable. Neither Mack nor Stephen Catalano (1990, p. 46 passim) could confirm a significant difference between dreams of disturbed and normal 8–9-year-olds on Erikson's timetable. As for adolescents, Catalano's discussion is convincing in showing that dreams of disturbed adolescents exhibit fewer age-appropriate concerns than those of normals, but he fails to clarify how delayed development affects dream formation. His examples indicate that a disturbed adolescent does not simply have dreams appropriate for a normal preadolescent.

*** Kramer's "typical" characteristics are not those of so-called "typical dreams," of falling, finding money, etc., which actually occur relatively seldom (D. G. Schwartz, L. N. Weinstein & A. M. Arkin 1978, p. 148). L. Gahagan found women higher in typical dreams of "being pursued by a person; examination; frustrated effort; being inappropriately dressed; a person now alive as dead; being a child again." Men scored higher in "dying or being killed; being a historical, legendary, or literary character; being nude; and flying, soaring, or floating in the air" (C. Winget & M. Kramer 1979,

tains two characters in addition to the dreamer, occurs in a building, and is more passive than active, more hostile than friendly, and more unpleasant than pleasant." Most striking is the fact that negative emotions predominate over positive, with "apprehension" the single most common emotion.

Dream Emotion	Women	Men
Apprehension	37%	34%
Confusion	18%	21%
Anger	13%	16%
Sadness	13%	9%
Happiness	19%	19%

"This, above all, is what dreams are," writes Hall, "an authentic record of a mind made anxious by conflict."[12] A recent study by Tore Nielsen et al. concurs that "positive emotions in dreams [a]re relatively infrequent when compared . . . with negative emotions. . . ."[13]* Along with negative emotion goes misfortune: there is 6 times as much misfortune as good fortune.[14]

As for characters, the dream-ego is alone in only 15% of dreams.[15] Well over 90% of characters in adult dreams are also adult.[16] And as for settings, many dreams take place in dwellings, usually not the dreamer's actual one (33%); in conveyances (15%); and in recreational settings (10%).[17]

Coming now to dreams of *the aging and elderly*.[18] With aging, the active participation of the dream-ego decreases; aggression decreases; bizarreness decreases slightly; and not surprisingly, dreams increasingly look backward in time; and death anxiety and other death themes increase.

A paper by Martin Barad et al. in 1961 pioneered in studying dreams of those over 65. Barad's subjects lived in a home for the aged, and most had reached some stage of organic deterioration. "Almost without exception initial dreams revealed a preoccupation with loss of resources. The dreamer is represented as weakened, lost, frequently unable to complete an action, frustrated, vulnerable, and threatened by a loss of his previous control over himself and his milieu. The environment is pictured as threatening and aggressive, or as confusing, incomplete, and fragmented, perhaps a projection of his own damaged self-concept."[19]

---

pp. 208–9, citing L. Gahagan, "Sex differences in recall of stereotyped dreams, sleep-talking, and sleep-walking," *Journal of Genetic Psychology* 48, pp. 227–36, 1936).

* Against the consensus, J. Allan Hobson (1989, p. 165) says that in dreams there is "a shift to more positive emotions."

But with a different group, composed of "relatively self-sufficient persons deeply engaged in living and running their lives," the same authors (as have others since[20]) determined that "[t]he theme of loss and repair was not a major component. . . . Their dreams were more richly elaborated, detailed, and varied. The dreamer often saw himself as active in pursuit of a goal. . . ."[21]

Dreams of "lost resources" in the elderly possibly correlate with incipient brain atrophy.[22]

Differences. Foulkes reports no gender differences before 7. From that age until 11, a single difference emerges: dreamers show more interest in characters of their own sex who are peers. At age 11, other differences appear. These are not well charted yet, but one which stands out is the higher level of aggression in boys' dreams.[23]

Raymond Rainville detects that difference at an earlier age. Beginning at 5–7, he writes, girls' dreams are more pleasant, while boys' dreams "deal with more hostile and aggressive themes. . . ." Age 7–9 brings a further decrease in aggression for girls, and a decrease in "warm, affectionate behavior" for boys. "The dreams of girls are largely populated by women and girls who are friendly and cooperative. Boys' dreams are populated by men and boys who are hostile and competitive." Then in preadolescence, boys' dreams become increasingly active and set outdoors and away from home. In contrast to this, girls' dreams become more verbal, with more indoor and home settings. These differences "add to the increasingly unpleasant nature of boys' dreams, as well as to the stability and relative pleasantness of girls' dreams."[24]

Of preadolescents, Swiss researcher Ursula Niederer reports that boys endeavor to dominate and they show more anger in their dreams, while girls "participat[e] more without dominating" and show both more fear and more positive emotions.[25]

Coming now to adult gender differences.* First of all women *recall* more dreams than men. One experiment indicates that "stress increases recall in females and decreases recall in male."[26] Roseanne Armitage concludes that women and men have different styles of processing emotional information.

The table above shows dream *emotions* of the genders to be very similar. Perhaps, Hall suggests, women are marginally readier to see happiness in others, and to experience their own sadness (overall, 85% of emotions be-

---

* Unless otherwise indicated, information on gender differences comes from the following sources: A. F. Paolino (1964); C. S. Hall & R. L. Van de Castle (1965) and (1966); B. Brenneis (1970); M. Kramer (1970); C. Winget, M. Kramer & R. M. Whitman (1972); C. S. Hall & B. Domhoff (1974 [1968]); C. W. O'Nell (1976); C. Winget & M. Kramer (1979); P. R. Koch-Sheras & A. Hollier (1985); R. E. Rainville (1988); R. L. Van de Castle (1990).

long to the dream-ego). Moreover, although the spectrum of emotions is the same for the genders, more emotions are reported by women.

Jeremy Taylor thinks the reason women also report (but do not necessarily dream) more *color* may be that our culture teaches women to pay more attention to what color symbolizes, emotion, as well as to color itself.[27] Sensitivity to emotion may account for the recall difference as well.

Cultural influence is also apparently reflected in the *objects* dreamt of. Women dream more than men of clothing and adornments. They tend to associate their bodies symbolically with things put on and with houses, says Patricia Garfield, whereas men tend to use vehicles.[28] These are of course only tendencies. In general, women dream of more objects of all kinds, 5.3 per dream, compared to 4.8 for men.

Women's dreams also have more *characters*, 2.8 per dream as compared to 2.4 for men. Women's characters are about equally male and female; by contrast, men dream of more males than of females. (Ernest Hartmann has characterized this as the "one consistent" gender difference.[29]*) Women generally dream more of familiars than unfamiliars, and especially of familiar females. And women have considerably more friendly interactions than men, who dream more of unfamiliars than familiars, and especially of unfamiliar males.

In keeping with these data, women's dreams contain more *home and family motifs*—parents, babies, pregnancy, contraception, marriage, and shopping (in connection with marriage), etc.—as well as more "themes of intimacy and fear of loss of loved ones."[30]

Also in keeping, women's dream *settings* tend to be indoors and within boundaries and enclosures more often than men's, who prefer strange surroundings and open spaces.

With respect to number of characters, friendly interactions, and indoor settings, the dream profile of male homosexuals is closer to that of women than to that of men.[31]

---

* Kenneth Rubenstein (1990, p. 137ff.) discusses various explanations which have been offered for the different sex ratios of characters in women's and men's dreams, e.g., the different dynamics of the oedipus complex for girls and boys (C. Hall, "A ubiquitous sex difference in dreams revisited," *Journal of Personality and Social Psychology* 46, pp. 1109–17, 1984); the gender contacts women and men make in their daily lives (S. Urbina & A. Grey, "Cultural and sex differences in the sex distribution of dream characters," *Journal of Cross-Cultural Psychology* 6, pp. 358–64, 1975); and differential interest in the activities pursued by the genders (J. Wood, D. Sebba & R. Griswold, "Stereotyped masculine interests as related to the sex of dream characters," *Sleep Research* 18, p. 113, 1989). Robert Dentan (1986, p. 325) puts it that the trait "may reflect patriarchal social arrangements."

The impact of changing gender roles is discussed further at the end of this section.

A noteworthy gender difference involves *nightmares*. Women, at least up until age 50,[32] have twice as many as men, have more distressing ones, and complain of them three times as often.[33] However, these differences fades when abuse during childhood, especially sexual abuse, is taken into account as a cause.[34] Consistently with this, no difference of nightmare frequency is noted in very young girls and boys.[35]

Sleep lab researchers often prefer male subjects because the *menstrual cycle*[36] has effects on women's dreams which are not altogether predictable. Here is a digest of various findings about those effects.

Estrogen increases total REM time per night.[37] Some women have a peak of REM time in mid-cycle, but for most, dream frequency builds following ovulation, then drops during menstruation.[38] Dream intensity is also highest in the premenstrual week.[39] This pattern is accentuated in women prone to menstrual tension.[40]

Women rate their dreams more unpleasant during whatever part of their periods they feel most depressed.[41] Those with longer periods have dreams with more anger and apprehension.[42] Anxious and hostile dream content increases with the degree of menstrual distress; and the variability of distress may account for some inconsistencies in other findings concerning women.[43] Jayne Gackenbach says that menstrual dreams are "more positively emotional,"[44] but dreams of misfortune are found by Robert Van de Castle to peak during the initial days of menstrual flow;[45] another study reports "more self-focused, less object-directed contents, e.g., anxiety, depression, oral wishes, and efforts at self-soothing . . . prevalent in the premenstrual and menstrual phases," as compared to "object-directed themes, e.g., love, anger, fear," when gonadal hormone levels are high.[46]

Women tend to show friendliness toward men in their dreams during ovulation, but toward other women during menstruation[47]—"although others, especially males, may not be as friendly toward her" during menstruation.[48] Sexual content is said to increase prior to ovulation[49] (but is also said to increase during menstruation;[50] at the latter time, sex partners are more likely to be known to the dreamer[51]). Dreams of menstruating women also contain more references to babies, children, and mothers, as well as to "enclosed spaces, such as rooms, and to anatomy. . . ."[52]

Menstrual dreams are "less visual . . . and more transpersonal." "Intensified" dreams—nightmares, archetypal dreams, and lucid dreams—are more likely than at other times.[53]

Garfield has written a comprehensive chapter on this subject.[54] The reader is referred to her descriptions of dream motifs typical of the seven phases into which she breaks the menstrual cycle. Here is a sample:

A huge red purse is suspended from a pole that is carried by two men, who support it between them on their shoulders. The purse is so large and heavy it requires the two to carry it. I wake up knowing that my period will start today. . . .

Women who are sensitive to their dream imagery learn to recognize where they are in their menstrual cycle from the pictures in their dreams. . . .

. . . Many objects that are shaped like a receptacle, with an opening capable of enclosing contents, may represent the womb in dreams. Other symbols—such as the two men required to support the purse—relate to the dreamer's individual circumstances. In her case, this dreamer had two lovers; between the two men in her life, her femininity hung suspended. The pole was probably the dreamer's symbol for the phallus. . . . The heaviness of the dreamer's purse referred to the heaviness in her womb that was about to shed its accumulated monthly blood.[55]

Garfield also has a chapter on *pregnancy* dreams.[56] She says that women may dream more while pregnant than at any other time, which she attributes to high hormonal levels. Eileen Stukane, who was first to bring out a book about pregnancy dreams (with the assistance and guidance of Robert Van de Castle), thinks that the disruption of sleep patterns by pregnancy is partially responsible for increased recall.[57] Patricia Maybruck agrees, but connects hormones to the fact that dreams of pregnant women are "frequently vivid and rich in detail, bizarre, and often nightmarish."[58] She finds that 40% of dreams during pregnancy are frightening, a circumstance she additionally attributes to factors which induce anxiety about pregnancy in our culture.[59]* But here is the lovely dream with which Stukane opens her book, a dream announcing pregnancy to a delighted mother-to-be:

"In the dream *I open my eyes,*" she said as she widened her gaze, "*and everything is black and empty. I'm staring at a dark, starless sky. Slowly I look over my right shoulder*"—she turned her head—"*and a huge, full moon overwhelms my vision. I can't see anything else, but I'm not concerned. The moon gives off a glowing aliveness. I absorb a feeling of complete benevolence from this moon, and I face it head-on.*

"*Looking again, I see that there's a smaller moon racing within the large moon. Clouds are crossing back and forth in front of the little moon. Together the two moons produce a sense of total innocence and wonder. I accept the clairvoyance, the inner light, the brightness that exist. I am not surprised.*"

When the dream ended, the woman, whom I'll call Cheryl, jostled her [sleeping] husband and told him, "I'm pregnant, and it's a girl." . . .

---

* The fact that Englishwomen have more anxiety dreams about pregnancy than do black Jamaican women, even though birth is more dangerous for the latter, has been attributed to a more positive attitude toward female natural functions in "peasant cultures" (S. Kitzinger 1980 [1978], p. 79).

Cheryl and her husband hadn't been trying to conceive a child. . . . She had a daughter, who is now twelve years old.[60]

Maybruck discovers that "[t]here is remarkable consistency in the actual components of most expectant women's dreams."[61] Common motifs noticed by Stukane, Maybruck, Garfield and others who have investigated this subject include animals, of progressively greater size and phylogenetic proximity to humans, reflecting fetal development over the trimesters. Buildings, of progressively greater size, correspond to changes in the uterus or body. Dreams of the first trimester commonly concern fertility, without much direct reference to pregnancy. Further motifs and themes include the body itself; lush vegetation (i.e., fertility); water; windows; babies; the mother of the dreamer; dependence/independence; threats; personal history; shopping centers; and, toward term: journeys; the body image and sexuality; and realistic dreams concerning pregnancy, delivery, and the child's care and wellbeing.[62] Here, from Maybruck, is a dream exhibiting some of these typical features. It was dreamt during the fourth month of pregnancy:

> *I am swimming in the ocean, trying to get to the shore. There's a strong undertow that keeps me from going very far but I'm not worried. The water feels pleasantly warm and I'm only a few yards from a house which is built right out into the water. Somehow I know I'll get to the house eventually. It's a big two story shingled house, and I can see every detail—even the nail heads in the shingles. Then I notice my mother* (who I haven't actually seen for several years) *looking out one of the windows. She's smiling and waving to me. Next I notice the water around me is full of turtles of all kinds! Most are huge and they're swimming right along beside me.* Then I woke up, feeling quite puzzled about this weird dream.[63]

Alan Siegel has studied the dreams of expectant fathers, and found that their dreams are similar to those of expectant mothers. Themes and motifs common to both include anxiety over birth defects; the sex of the baby; giving birth to animals; precocious walking-talking newborns; fertility/virility; and "fetal identification" (floating in water, etc.).[64] Siegel regards these paternal dreams in the light of the 'couvade syndrome', in which men mimic physical signs of pregnancy, such as nausea, food craving, etc. (Ninety percent of expectant fathers have at least one couvade symptom, and as many as 30% have multiple symptoms.[65]) A theme more confined to expectant fathers is that of being left out. Stukane thinks the couvade syndrome may be a compensation for feeling excluded.[66]

Here is an expectant father's dream, a Chagall-like dream which makes a sort of set with the dream of "Two moons." The source is again Stukane, but included are comments by Siegel, upon whom she draws heavily:

Roger, a forty-three-year-old expectant father, had this dream about four weeks into his wife's pregnancy: *There are small creatures with twenty teeth each. They're like rats, but a little bigger than rats. Two of them are fighting with each other. Then the dream changes. I walk across a flat rooftop to get something for Amy* (his wife). *I see a beautiful face in the moonlight, as though I'm seeing it through music. Amy's window is above the roof. I have a blanket. I jump and dance in the moonlight on the roof. I hear a song, 'You Are So Beautiful to Me,' and a strong wind picks me up and carries me through the window.*

"This dream shows the volatility of men's feelings," said Dr. Siegel when he heard the dream described. "Men at this time are going from being aggressive to being ecstatic. . . .

". . . The phases of the moon are often associated with a woman's fertility, and here he is in the moonlight, being swept up through her into her. He's fertilizing in a more literal sense."[67]

Returning once again to general differences between men's and women's dreams. Men have more *interactions*, and those they have are more intense. Especially there is more overt *hostility* in men's dreams (regardless of culture). Aggression in women's dreams tends to be verbal but in men's to be physical, with four times as many weapons. Men's aggression tends to take place with strange males of the same age; women's, with familiars who are older and, by a small margin, also more often male than female. Both genders are frequent recipients of aggression, but men also fight back and initiate more aggression than women do. These differences increase with age.

Men are more *doers* in their dreams, women more receivers. Men have more references to sports, money, occupation-vocation, and "achievement striving with success." At the same time, men's dreams also show *castration anxiety*.[68] As dream-egos men undergo more *misfortune* than do their other dream characters, whereas for women the ratio is about equal.

Young men, observes Rainville, frequently dream about *male bonding*. He finds "father/son dreams, combat dreams," including sports, "and expeditionary dreams." In combat dreams, "[t]he dreamers are always contentedly part of a hierarchy. This is in sharp contrast to male dreamers' reactions to dominance in sex dreams. . . . Expeditionary dreams contain all the same elements as combat dreams except for direct competition with an enemy."[69]

Men dream more of *vehicles and travel*, in keeping with a penchant for *strange and open places*.

Men's dreams have more *animals*, which tend to be birds, reptiles and other non-mammals. Women dream more of mammals, and are more likely to picture aggressors as animals than are men.

Finally, men have more dreams about *sex* than do women. Overtly sexual dreams commence younger in males.[70] In middle age, an average of 30% of women's dreams contain explicitly sexual content, of men's, slightly more. Fathers dream of incest with daughters five times more than mothers do of incest with sons. Men are also more likely to dream of sex with unfamiliar partners. Especially young men's dreams are more impersonal, emphasizing genital arousal and autoeroticism, and having more homoeroticism. Women tend to have dream sex with known men, especially their real-life partners, or otherwise feel guilt. Their dream sex emphasizes "interpersonal relations and activity, expression, and feelings."[71] Women's sexual dreams also tend to be more symbolic than do men's (though women become more explicit around the time of ovulation).[72] Nonetheless, at least in lucid dreams women experience orgasm "much more frequently" than do men.[73]

It has of course been wondered whether certain of the gender differences in dreams might reflect differences in gender role assigned by our culture. Hall expected so when, in 1980, he ran tests on college students to compare against his original 1950 results.[74] To his surprise, Hall found no changes whatever in comparative features, despite the sexual revolution and other intervening changes in society. Women and men of 1980 both dreamt less of sexual encounters and clothing; and there were a few other slight changes in degree, such as that women had become less friendly overall. But all of the general differences or lack of them remained unchanged. Hall lists the possibilities: either thirty years is too little time for social changes to show up in dreams; or there have not really been the changes we imagine; or else content features reflect human nature deeper than social influences.

One recent study confirmed Hall's unexpected results. Women of 1990 score more or less identically to women of 1950, notably on two of the most consistent gender differences, sex ratio and settings: women dream equally of women and of men (while men dream more of men); and women dream more of indoor settings (while men dream more of outdoor settings).[75]

However, other studies do detect some of the anticipated effects of social change. Scores of a sample of young California women taken in about 1990 differed from Hall's 1950 sample in few, but possibly in socially significant ways: they reported more dream emotion, and they showed more aggression (verbal included) and received more aggression from other women than the 1950 women. These trends implicate 'liberation', although the absence of changes in settings, characters, and sexuality does not.[76*] But another survey finds that women's dreams have acquired more out-of-home locations and occupational concerns, as well as more aggression.[77] A comparison of working and homemaking mothers finds that the working mothers dream of more

---

* A subset of Asian-American women conformed to the 1950 scores.

male characters (though fewer than men dream of), and of fewer residential settings (though not fewer indoor settings). Other dream traits in which the working mothers lean in the supposed male direction include more strangers and more negative emotions.[78] A study of Swiss adults finds hardly any gender difference in indoor/outdoor settings, with women actually having more unfamiliar settings.[79] (Another study finds men's sex ratio in dreams moving in the expected female direction of equality.[80]) The Swiss study finds other gender differences in the expected direction, but reduced.

Kramer et al. still find the sex ratio difference in university women and men, but in many other respects their dreams are converging.[81] "They say that 'the contemporary sexual revolution has had some psychological impact on dream imagery.'" Natalie Rinfret et al. add: "These findings suggest that as women adopt roles traditionally assigned to men, gender-typed dream imagery may be decreasing."[82] And Stanley Krippner & Kenneth Rubenstein detect "no differences between men's and women's dreams in the amount of aggression, friendliness, sexuality, male characters, weapons, or clothes. However, women's dreams still ha[ve] a higher number of family members, babies, children, and indoor settings. . . ." They ascribe the new pattern to the mix of women's liberation with the biological role of mother.[83] Rinfret et al. report that working mothers have more "male-typed" imagery in their dreams than do female students. The students, they believe, are still under the influence of gender-role socialization, which is counteracted in the mothers by entering the workplace.[84] Garfield notes that U.S. women now "seem to dream of more varied sexual acts with diverse partners."[85] (She adds that AIDS may be halting this particular change.) Phyllis Koch-Sheras et al. say that women's dreams show less concern with marriage, and that women are more likely to dream of homosexuality.[86]

Further studies will be needed to clarify to what extent Hall's gender differences do run deeper than social influences.

Blindness

Because dreams seem to most sighted people to be fundamentally visual,[*] one is curious about the effect of blindness on dreaming. It is mostly thought that the congenitally blind have no visual experience, awake or dreaming,

---

[*] There are a few exceptional sighted people whose dreams are fundamentally nonvisual. Linda Magallón (1989, p. 7) discusses a mathematics instructor who has "mental dreams" lacking "motion picture" image attributes, though she does receive patterns, some of them constituting mathematical formulae. As described, these dreams seem to be as unlike dreams of the blind as of the sighted.

nor do those blind by age 5, with rare exceptions.[87] But Stevie Wonder, who was born blind, told Rainville that he "sees music in color." A psychologist himself blinded at 25, Rainville does not altogether rule out the possibility of visual dreaming and other visual experience in the early-blind. They may possess "unsocialized visual intelligence,"[88] but simply lack the consensual vocabulary with which to talk about it.[89] So it is hard to know what someone like Wonder means.

The early-blind do have REM, though reduced in amplitude.[90] On the assumption that they do not dream visually, this shows that REM does not in itself imply visual dreaming.[91] Dreams of the early-blind also have the usual characteristics in relation to REM and NREM sleep stages.[92] So the one outstanding peculiarity of their dreams is absence of the visual.

Among those of us with senses intact, the rank order of sensory modes in dreams is sight > sound > balance/motion, followed by taste, smell, touch and temperature in uncertain order.[93] (Pain is exceedingly rare.[94])

In dreams of the early-blind, sound takes first place, with conversation prominent; and touch joins with balance/motion as the modes of next importance.[95] Otherwise, early-blind dreams remain substantially unaffected.

Rainville attributes the fact that blind children have more nightmares than do sighted children to the prevalence of different senses in their dreams. Vision he terms an "allocentric" sense, that is, the information it conveys is ordinarily perceived as external to us. Hearing is only slightly less allocentric, but the other, "autocentric" senses common in dreams of the blind—touch, smell, etc.—are more easily perceived as proximate or internal. The blind, therefore, less readily distance negative dream feelings by processing them into externalized imagery.[96]* Rainville compares two dreams:

> The first of these was dreamt by a sighted 9-year-old girl. . . .
>
> *I was in the woods behind the school. I could hear something following me so I climbed up a tree and sat in the crook between two big branches. Then I saw a giant cat, tiger or leopard. He was mostly black with orange-gold spots. He was sniffing at my trail. He came right up to the trunk of the tree, sniffed, and kept walking. I didn't move a muscle. I could see its clear green eyes, but it never saw me. . . .*
>
> Contrast a similar animal nightmare . . . [of] a congenitally blind girl, age 10. . . .
>
> *I was walking back to my house from the garden. It seemed to be very early morning. There was a heavy dew on the grass and moisture like before the sun*

---

* By Rainville's scheme, the preeminence of sound in dreams of the early-blind should allow for projection in that sense mode. However, for whatever reason, auditory sensations commonly feature in the fearful dreams of the sighted (D. Kuiken & S. Sikora 1990), so presumably that sense mode offers little relief to the blind.

rises. I was carrying things in my right arm, I think squash and tomatoes. Then I heard it coming toward me, a very large animal, its head waist-high to me. I dropped the vegetables and reached out slowly. It sniffed at my fingers and 'though I was terrified, I knew I shouldn't make any jerky motions. Its tongue, twice the width of my hand, licked my fingers curiously. My head slowly entered into its mouth, being pulled in by its raspy tongue. Its upper jaw had razor-like teeth, three or four rows deep. It was just inspecting me, tasting and smelling my flesh. I felt its nose and lips and knew I could do nothing to defend myself if it decided to bite me. It purred more and more threateningly and was beginning to nudge me backwards when I woke up.[97]*

The blind girl's dream illustrates an important point made by Nancy Kerr et al.: "Sighted students of dreaming often seem to be prone to thinking that visualizing must play some privileged role in dream generation. . . . But, in general, dreams never are simply simulations of seeing; they are simulations of living. . . . In the absence of the visual-imaginal component, the other systems apparently are in no substantial way impeded."[98] Another illustration is the following dream of a 13-year-old girl, blind from birth. The source is an article by H. Robert Blank:

Mrs. Jones was in an elevator going up in a high building. The elevator got stuck just before it reached the eighth floor. Was that funny! I woke up scared. . . . Asked how she knew it was Mrs. Jones who was in the elevator with her, Mary replied, "I just knew it, I know what an elevator is like." Asked to be more specific about her recognitions, she said, "I don't have to see it; I can hear it and feel it" (patient carves out an elevator shaft in the air with both hands), "I just know what it is." She then described the "funny" feeling, i.e., anxiety expressed chiefly by abdominal sensations. In questioning her about another dream, Mary had stated, "Naturally I couldn't see him, but I can smell him a mile away."[99]

The critical age for retaining visual dreams is 5–7: some blinded during those years do, some do not dream visually later, whereas those blinded after 7 continue to dream essentially as do the sighted, though sometimes with deterioration of the visual mode if blind before 10.[100] The late-blind not only dream visually, but "see" in detail people and scenes never actually seen or conceived of before blindness, thus demonstrating the independence of visual imagination from current visual perception.[101]

Blindness has actually been connected with remarkably few of the standard content analysis dream variables. Dreams of the blind are more conversational, are more concerned with the human body, and have more indoors

---

* But see the dream "She falls into monster's jaws" (ch. 12, p. 387), where running up a tree is of no avail to a sighted girl's dream-ego.

and fewer unknown settings than dreams of the sighted.[102] But in spite of the last trait, the late-blind have a proclivity to a kind of "grand" spatial imagery less common in dreams of the sighted. In one such dream mentioned by Rainville, a man dreams that *he and his wife are in a glass bubble on the moon.*[103] In another, *the dreamer drifts "aimlessly in space between the earth and the sun.* "[104] And below is another example, a sad and amusing dream borrowed by Rainville from Donald Kirtley:

> *I am God—a tremendous giant—just sauntering through the vast stretches of infinite space. Suddenly, the earth looms up before me. It is about the size of a volleyball in relation to me. I look down at it and see that man with all his corrupt and petty doings has befouled my creation. He engulfs the entire globe, like a swarm of bacteria, putrefying everything he touches. I decide the earth has lasted long enough. With man on it, even the things that are good can't survive. His soul is a cesspool of egoism and hate. He is just a germ with a big brain, and the planet reeks irremediably with the stench of him. So, I take my godly penis in hand, like some giant redwood from heaven, and with one mighty swing of it, slap the earth out of orbit—to send it tumbling off into the dark void, never to be heard from again. . . .*

The earth may be an orb which represents his own eye, and the godly phallus represents the arrow which in real life blinded him. The godly contempt for man would represent an attitude about himself as the victim of godly whims.[105]

Rainville discusses the two major ways people respond to new blindness: overcompensation, and the "catastrophic pattern."[106] Overcompensators are those who try to continue emotionally and actively as though little affected. They tend to have dreams of denial, which include "reminiscent dreams" set prior to blindness, and "undoing dreams" where the events leading to blindness are modified and the consequence rescinded. They also have compensatory dreams, in the Jungian sense, showing the possible consequences of denial, as well as (Jungian) compensatory "reversal dreams" which help them to "recognize their adjustmental excesses"—dreams in which they can see, while everyone else is blind. Possibly a dream recounted by Rex Furness, a blind writer, falls into the last category. Furness explains that in most of his dreams he knows he is really blind, although he "sees":

> *I was in my old college laboratory when I saw a young lady, unfortunately blind, so I thought, in obvious difficulties as regards her whereabouts. I immediately went to help her, and led her through the intricacies of the passages, but all the time I knew I was blind, and could think how strange it was that I could act as escort. . . .*

Those of us who become blind in adulthood seem to have four distinct types of dreams—namely, those in which we "see" perfectly, those in which we "see" but are conscious all the time of being blind, those in which objects are blurred, and those in which impressions come to us, as in waking hours, through the intermediary of senses other than sight. It is the experience of some that dreams of the fourth class gradually take first place as time passes and the stock of remembered images gradually fails.[107]

Losing the capacity to visualize, stresses Rainville, is the worst thing that can happen. Ongoing visual dreaming helps the blind person when awake to employ visual imagination, so important for orienting.[108] "The capacity to imagine the visual environment and to orient in it by looking in the direction of imaginary things helps to orient the other senses. . . ." Hence visual dreaming is critical for people in Rainville's second category of response to new blindness, the catastrophic pattern. Such people frequently develop "a darkness response . . . a constant state of awareness which reiterates, 'I can't see.'" "A dream with clear visual imagery can be the breakthrough which subjectively convinces the blind person that the darkness experience was in fact a visual response to fear, and it need not be a constant companion."[109]

Early *deafness*, not unexpectedly, causes enhancement of the visual mode in dreams. Dreams of those deaf before 5 are of greater color and more vividness and depth than dreams of those deaf after 5 and normal hearers. And the deaf remember their dreams well. A high percentage recall dreams every night.[110] As for the *blind-deaf*, apart from Helen Keller's somewhat literary dream descriptions, which are difficult to sort out as to their sensory modalities,[111] there is this account, from Sandra Shulman's book on nightmares:

> A young girl, born deaf and blind, would awake abruptly from nightmares, feeling her blood rushing about and her heart beating rapidly. She described a frightening dream as *hard, heavy and thick*—adjectives that the sighted and hearing would least employ to relate their nightmares.[112]

Syndromes

We turn now to the dream styles associated with several psychiatric syndromes. Here will be discussed: nightmares (and night terrors); dreams of multiple personalities; and the dream styles associated with depression and schizophrenia.

Nightmares and Night Terrors. Certain sleep disorders are known to be associated with qualities of the dreams and/or REM patterns of sufferers.*

---

* *REM sleep behavior disorder* consists of loss of atonia, the normal inability to move during REM sleep, with "elaborate motor activity associated with dream mentation. . . . Dream content may become vivid, unpleasant, violent, or action-filled. . ." (M. J. Thorpy 1990, pp. 177–8).

But nightmare is the only REM dream condition listed as a sleep disorder in its own right in *The International Classification of Sleep Disorders*.[113]

Thanks in large part to the writings of Ernest Hartmann, a distinction is recognized between nightmares and night (or sleep) terrors. Hartmann credits the distinction to Richard Broughton and Charles Fisher.[114] In the case of night terror, the sleeper suddenly starts with a scream of fear out of stage 3 or 4 sleep, not stage 1 REM. Usually this happens 1–2 hours after sleep onset. S/he often sits up and sometimes tries to escape or ward off an attack. If awakened, the person will probably be confused as to what is happening. Night terror is an arousal disorder—the unusual arousal from deep sleep *is* the night terror. Sufferers, according to Hartmann, know subjectively that they are not dreaming;[115] however, terrors are sometimes accompanied by vivid transient images, most famously of something sitting on one's chest, with sensations of choking or claustrophobia.

Typically, terrors occur in children and disappear with adolescence.

Nightmares, in contrast, are fearful dreams, usually occurring in the 3rd or 4th REMP of the night. They have no clear demarcation from dreams in general, unless it is that they are frightening enough to cause waking. Hartmann calls these "nightmares proper." (But do not expect consistency in the

---

Sleep paralysis "consists of a period of inability to perform voluntary movements either at sleep onset . . . or upon awakening either during the night or in the morning. . . . At times dreamlike mentation is also experienced, especially if the paralyzed person becomes drowsy or light sleep occurs during an attack" (ibid., p. 166).

Chronic alcoholism produces insomnia or somnolescence accompanying REM suppression, with a huge REM rebound following alcohol withdrawal in the form of delirium tremens, an effect comparable to that resulting from sleep deprivation (R. Greenberg & C. Pearlman 1967). REM rebound also occurs with withdrawal from various drugs, often producing vivid and frightening dreams (P. Garfield 1991, p. 60). Intoxication itself can also produce vivid, intense dreams regardless of REM effects (S. J. Wolin & N. K. Mello 1973). Psychological features of dreams noticed in alcoholics include more oral content (C. S. Hall 1966b, p. 136); more sexual and aggressive content, especially in those whose waking behavior is inhibited by alcohol (S. J. Wolin & N. K. Mello 1973); fewer dreams of their children, and more of strangers; more fear and unhappiness (E. M. Scott 1968, pp. 1316–7); and alcoholics cast themselves as victims (R. A. Moore 1962, p. 587). The Russian Vasily Kasatkin finds that if alcoholics "continue to imbibe in their dreams, the prognosis for abstention is poor" (S. Krippner & J. Dillard 1988, p. 162, citing V. Kasatkin 1984). And Harry Fiss observes that after a week of detoxification, alcoholics who dream more and dream conflictual dreams about drinking have more craving for alcohol when awake than those who dream less and dream pleasantly of drinking (1993, pp. 399–401, citing H. Fiss, "Dream content and response to withdrawal from alcohol," *Sleep Research* 9, p. 152, 1980). Fiss equates craving with likelihood of relapse, but does not discuss his subjects' actual recovery outcomes. However, his implication and Kasatkin's conclusion are contrary to an often-cited finding by Sei Choi (1973), that dreams of drinking are a good prognostic sign among alcoholics under treatment; and Fiss and Kasatkin also contradict the general experience in Alcoholics Anonymous, that such dreams are 'first step' dreams, which serve to remind one in recovery of powerlessness over alcohol (N. K. Denzin 1988, pp. 136–8; N. Piaget, no

literature. For example, Montague Ullman uses the expression "true night-mare" to refer to night terror.[116])

Most nightmares, except in the case of those induced by trauma, do not reproduce life events or repeat previous nightmares in detailed manifest content. Few are explicitly sexual. The dream-ego rarely perpetrates violence in them, but is often attacked or chased. Perhaps surprisingly, nightmares, even "worst" ones, are no more bizarre than other dreams.[117]

There are two peaks in the lifespan for the occurrence of nightmares: one before age 5, when occasional nightmares are commonplace, the other in adolescence. Nightmares decrease with age. Perhaps one per year is average for adults. About 5% of adults (but about 60% of Vietnam combat vets[118]) have them frequently, while 50% of adults have no nightmares at all.[119] One recent study, however, finds that close to 50% of college students have at least one nightmare every 2 weeks.[120]

Hartmann believes that nightmares begin to occur as early as dreaming does, during the latter part of the first year, that is, before the child has verbal skills to report the fact. He proposes further that the causative anxiety-provoking experience is the disturbing realization that strangers exist in the world. This can begin to occur at 8 months:

---

date). Also, P. Hajek & M. Belcher (1991) find that smokers who relapse in their dreams while trying to quit have a better chance of remaining abstinent. (See also ch. 3, p. 101n.)

Enuresis (bedwetting) and REM dreaming, it was thought after the initial sleep lab studies, rarely occur in conjunction (C. M. Pierce, R. M. Whitman, J. W. Maas & M. L. Gay 1961; C. M. Pierce 1963). It was believed that bedwetters universally incorporate the sensory experience into subsequent dreaming. These subjects typically had only two REMPs per night, alternating with wetting episodes, the first of which often took place early in the night when one would normally have the first REMP, which was delayed as much as 2 hours or more. Along similar lines, it was proposed that enuresis is an arousal disorder, a parasomnia like sleepwalking (R. Broughton & H. Gastaut, "Recent sleep research on enuresis nocturna, sleep walking, sleep terrors and confusional arousals," in P. Levin & W. Loella, editors, *Sleep 1974*, Basel: Karger, 1975), at least when found in psychiatrically normal children (E. R. Ritvo, E. M. Ornitz, F. Gottlief, A. F. Poussaint, B. J. Maron, K. S. Ditman & K. A. Blinn, "Arousal and non-arousal enuretic events," *American Journal of Psychiatry* 126, pp. 77–84, 1969). Subsequent studies indicated that enuresis is not an arousal disorder, and that episodes occur randomly distributed among the sleep stages in both disturbed and non-disturbed children; but these studies disagreed whether episodes tend to concentrate in the first third of the sleep night or not (A. Kales, J. D. Kales, A. Jacobson, F. J. Humphrey II & C. R. Soldatos 1977; E. J. Mikkelsen & J. L. Rapoport 1980; E. J. Mikkelsen, J. L. Rapoport, L. Nee, C. Gruenau, W. Mendelson & J. C. Gillin 1980; J. L. Rapoport, E. J. Mikkelsen, A. Zavadil, L. Nee, C. Gruenau, W. Mendelson & J. C. Gillin 1980). A recent study suggests "there may be different kinds of enuretic patients who can be classified according to the time of night and the sleep stage during which the enuretic episode occurs" (G. Nino-Murcia & S. A. Keenan 1987, pp. 258–9). These various studies agree that bedwetting is sometimes associated with medical pathology (pp. 255–8) or with delayed development and behavioral disturbances.

[S]tranger anxiety . . . [is] the first well-recognized childhood anxiety, which develops when the child realizes that the adult up there is **not** mother—that the large looming face above him is the "wrong face." . . . We cannot ask the nine-month-old dreamers, but I have been impressed with the frequency of stranger-anxiety themes in remembered early childhood nightmares and in the nightmares of adults as well:

Her face changed and she looked horrible, like a monster.
The face became larger and larger. I didn't know who it was; I screamed.
It wasn't my friend at the door, but this monster with a knife.
It wasn't my real husband I was with but an android creature who had taken his place.

This last theme, of course, has also invaded science fiction and horror literature, but its seed required no galactic winds to reach us; it was planted in the cracks of our developing minds when we were nine months old.[121]

Hartmann suspects lack of maternal support before age 2 to be a common developmental attribute of the nightmare-prone.[122] Among adults, he adds, nightmares are most likely to occur in circumstances that evoke feelings of helplessness reminiscent of early childhood.[123] This is not inconsistent with the finding of Karen Dunn & Deirdre Barrett, that people subject to nightmares get them usually when under "significant, long-term stress," but not from "minor, shorter-term 'hassles'"—though recent frights, including from movies, can act as triggers.[124]

Whereas night terror sufferers do not have any special personality profile, Hartmann finds that nightmare sufferers do.[125] They tend: to remember their childhoods unusually well; to have been sensitive as children, but to have undergone no unusual traumas (recall, however, that Alan Moffitt ascribes the higher nightmare rate of women to abuse in childhood[126]); to have relatives with psychiatric histories; to have had some bad drug experience; to have contemplated or attempted suicide; to get quickly involved in stormy relationships leading to painful separations; to have fluid, non-stereotyped sexual identities. Dunn & Barrett add that they have "heightened death concerns."[127] In general—and this is the key—, they have *thin boundaries*. But whereas most people with boundary deficits also put up strong boundary defenses, the defense mechanisms of these people are also poorly developed. In dreams, charged material enters without well-developed dream defenses.

Besides having more nightmares, people with thin boundaries recall more dreams than do thick boundary people,* and their dreams are more vivid and

---

* A. Moffitt, R. Hoffmann & S. Galloway (1990) failed to confirm that thick boundaries correlate with poor recall. Their analysis did find reduced recall to be associated with a medley of traits comprising a "reality" orientation, which they termed "tough-mindedness" (p. 70). "Consistent" re-

emotional, and involve more interaction with characters.[128] Awake, they are not unusually anxious,[129] fearful, aggressive, or helpless. They are not especially maladjusted or neurotic,[130] but they are vulnerable to schizophrenia. Having thin boundaries, Hartmann proposes, is a unifying characteristic of nightmare, creativity, and madness. Others have also pointed to the likeness of madness to nightmare, especially in the experience of overwhelming terror and helplessness before an external danger.[131] Nightmares are, in fact, common near the onset of psychosis. Hartmann finds that his patients also share "artistic tendencies" with schizophrenics.[132] But this observation has been challenged by Ross Levin.[133] Agreeing that schizophrenics and nightmare sufferers both have "porous" boundaries, and thus have access to the "primary process" which is associated with creativity, he and his associates tested to see if nightmare sufferers actually score high for creativity. Finding they do not, Levin concludes that nightmare sufferers are poor at *controlling* the primary process, and control seems to be a crucial ingredient of creativity. Others have similarly questioned the creativity of schizophrenics.[134]

The expression 'nightmare sufferers' has been used. But Kathryn Belicki & Marion Cuddy have recently pointed out that "it is possible to have, but not suffer from nightmares."[135] Nightmare frequency does not necessarily imply nightmare distress, and some people come to therapy wishing to understand but not eliminate them. Nevertheless, other people would gladly be rid of their nightmares, and in later chapters some approaches to nightmare relief will be discussed.

Posttraumatic nightmares. Various 'bad dream' phenomena do not fit into the categories of night terror and nightmare neatly: cases where the two occur together; certain manifestations of narcolepsy (pathological sleepiness); hypnagogic (sleep onset) nightmares; and most notably, posttraumatic nightmares, much publicized for their occurrence in Vietnam vets with posttraumatic stress disorder (PTSD).

Posttraumatic nightmares can occur after any severe trauma (fire, abuse, surgery, combat, etc.), and persist for days or years. Like other nightmares, PTSD nightmares present well developed imagery which is understood subjectively to be a dream; but like night terrors, they often come early in the night, occur outside of stage 1 REM sleep, awaken the dreamer screaming, and display other signatures of an arousal disorder. Hartmann provisionally classifies PTSD nightmares as a third phenomenon.[136] Their most conspicu-

---

callers they found to be imaginative, creative, and flexible (p. 69), which accords with other findings, e.g., of "higher cognitive flexibility and more divergent information processing among high dream recallers" (T. Fitch & R. Armitage 1989, p. 869).

ous feature is the literal or just slightly altered reliving of the terrible event, dream after dream. Rosalind Cartwright notes, however, that in the case of childhood sexual abuse the nightmares "are less likely to be exact literal re-enactments . . . , perhaps because the sexual abuse often occurs before language and memory skills crystallize."[137] Such persons can experience recurrent nightmares which render the trauma cryptically, without ever literally replaying it.[138] Moreover, even PTSD combat nightmares can substantially depart from the traumatizing events.[139]*

In a small percentage of cases of PTSD, onset of the first nightmares is delayed, even for many years.[140] But in a typical case, the initial nightmares closely follow the trauma. They then dissipate, only to resume—sometimes years later—when triggered by a new loss (death, divorce, etc.). Intrusive thoughts and waking flashbacks, to which the near-literal dreams have obvious affinities, may occur as well.

Among combat vets, says Cartwright, "[t]hose who proved most susceptible were those who'd had experiences earlier in life that resonated emotionally with their war experiences.** The war, in turn, heightened their sensitivity to later traumas."[141] The vulnerable tend to have been younger, and to have formed very close attachments with one or more buddies whom they witnessed maimed or killed. (Note, however, the observation of Judith Herman, whose main work is with incest survivors, that it is the *perpetrators* of combat atrocities who are most at risk of PTSD.[142]***) Of those who witnessed buddies harmed, Hartmann believes that they were "involved [in] a temporary merging, or confusion of boundaries" reminiscent of adolescent identity formation—catastrophically interrupted, in the event.[143] They were not, however, predisposed as a group by the structural boundary vulnerabilities and weak defenses found in those prone to ordinary nightmares.

---

* A claim by Melvin Lansky & Carol Bley (1993, p. 22) that PTSD nightmares always vary from the instigating events in significant details is probably colored by the facts that their subjects all exhibited "severe character pathology," and that they did not see their subjects until well after the onset of their nightmares.

** John Mack (1989 [1970], pp. 219–20) had earlier said much the same. But Mack discerns a similar dynamic in the generation of ordinary nightmares (p. 212): "[I]n the regressive sleep-dream situation, the current danger becomes linked with earlier dangers, the current anxiety with earlier anxieties, . . . especially in the second year of life when abandonment and loss of love are such critical dangers for the child."

*** Along the same line, Harry Wilmer found in a sample of combat veterans that "[d]reams of *killing others* were more frequent and more disturbing than dreams of being wounded or killed oneself" (1986a, pp. 128–9). "[T]he most stressful dreams the veterans had were not of their own danger . . . but of seeing others, particularly buddies, and next the children, and then women, being killed and slaughtered" (1986b, pp. 57–8). Mack (1989 [1970], p. 46) mentions his clinical experience with young murderers who consequently suffer from PTSD nightmares.

When PTSD nightmares ameliorate, they tend to do so by merging into ordinary dreaming as untrue-to-fact, dreamlike imagery intrudes:

> *I was with some friends at this place we used to have near New York. Some kind of a party; and then those guys came in who looked like the guys who attacked me last month, except in th[is] dream they were wearing these funny old-fashioned suits. I was kind of scared, but I kept talking to my girlfriend, and ignored them.* . . .[144]

Dreams like this, which undo the traumatic event instead of repeating it, are associated with recovery.[145] But again, as Harry Wilmer points out, combat nightmares containing dreamlike, unreal elements can be as repetitious and as frightening as literal replay dreams: *"There is a stink of dead bodies. I am burying the dead—just the heads with big holes in them."* The dreamer of another such dream commented: "I can't sleep, I'm afraid I'm going to have this dream which I've had over and over again. It never really happened. It's not even a realistic dream. The only thing that ever changes is the faces. Everything else is always exactly the same."[146]

Unfortunately, the treatment outlook for PTSD nightmares is rather poor. Whereas open talk and other interventions which integrate the bad dreams and their references work relatively well with ordinary nightmares, chronic PTSD nightmares are less (though not always[147]) unresponsive. There is no consensus as to the best treatment, whether group work such as psychodrama, desensitization, drugs, etc. Often the best to be hoped for may be to get the sufferer to accept the condition.[148] "There are World War II veterans and survivors of the holocaust who have continued suffering posttraumatic nightmares since the 1940s."[149]*

Multiple Personality Disorder (MPD). MPD can also be seen as a stress disorder. Herman discerns a spectrum of stress reactions, some less severe than PTSD, and others such as MPD more severe.[150] Variables include the age of occurrence and the severity and perseverance of the trauma(s).

An early case study of a split personality by M. Prince (1906) concluded that "during sleep these personalities reverted to a common consciousness

---

* Wilmer (1986b, p. 48) asks: "Could it be that the war nightmare, which is the exact replication of a catastrophic trauma, is the archetypal dream of war?" "The war nightmares are symbolic of our national [Vietnam War] nightmare, which is just beginning to go away. But it will not fully go away, and so we run a high risk of repeating it in another war . . . unless we face that nightmare horror. . ." (p. 52). I suggest that The Vietnam War, and other recent U.S. wars, reveal the return of horror and guilt repressed for a different set of reasons (near universal idealization of the conflict) after World War II, a repression which manifested itself initially in the Cold War mindset and McCarthyism. Then the Vietnam antiwar movement was a reaction, on the part of the first post-WWII generation, against that repression belonging to their parents.

and became one and the same; that is, the dreams were common to both."[151] More recent research indicates that typically "the same splits in the ego continue through the night and affect mental life during sleep as well as during waking." But taking the dreams of MPs one by one, Stephen Marmer can find nothing especially characteristic of them.[152]

Al Carlisle, however, does find special characteristics of MPD dreams. First, alternate personalities may appear as dream characters.[153] This calls to mind the representation of so-called split-off parts of the psyche in everyone's dreams (chapter 6). Ordinary dreamers usually have dream characters, character types, or animals—or inanimates, for that matter—who show up regularly representing psychic components or complexes. "In our dreams we all have the potential of being multiple personalities," writes psychoanalyst Marianne Goldberger, "and, like individuals with actual multiple personalities, we do not recognize that we inhabit those other people."[154] The great difference is that these components do not ordinarily invade and occupy the waking ego.

Carlisle's second MPD dream characteristic is that different personalities "may have the same dream from different points of view." This brings to mind Freud's observation that episodes of anyone's dream may represent the same material from different viewpoints.[155] Also, sometimes a shift of viewpoint happens within a single dream scenario and is quite literal and graphic. Recall the episodic dream "Evil incarnated in a giant," which coincided with a cardiac infarct (ch. 8, p. 287). In the opening episode, the man dreamt: *"I could feel the bullets going through my heart, and saw the blood flowing out of the wounds. A fierce pain overcame me, made me faint, and I saw myself as if another person, collapsing in death."* Alfred Ziegler adds: "This form of depersonalization has been described by other patients who have endured a similar attack as 'breaking up into body and spirit'."[156]

Dreams of falling sometimes involve shifts of perspective. In the dream "He falls from a turret toward a moat" (ch. 4, p. 152), *the dream-ego first observes a man in an elevated position from below, then abruptly becomes that man falling.* A dream related by Hervey de Saint-Denys, a lucid dream, makes the opposite and I suspect more usual shift, from the viewpoint of the faller to that of the observer (no longer lucid, in this case):

I waited for nearly a month—one needs perseverance. Finally one night I dreamed *I was walking down the street. All the images of my dream were quite clear, but nevertheless I knew that I was not awake; and I suddenly remembered the experiment I wished to make [of trying to experience something in a dream that he had never experienced awake]. Immediately I climbed to the top story of a house which seemed very high; I saw an open window and, a long way below, the court-*

*yard; I paused to admire the perfection of this sleeping illusion, and then, before
it could change, I launched myself into the abyss, full of anxious curiosity.* . . .
*Instantly losing all memory of what had gone before, I found myself in the square
in front of the cathedral, among a curious crowd which had gathered round a
dead man. They told me that the man had thrown himself from the cathedral tower, and I saw his body being carried away on a stretcher.*[157]

I personally once recalled two dreams from separate REMPs of one night,
in the first of which *I was in a high place and afraid of falling*, while in the
second *I was watching someone fall.* One thinks also of out-of-body experiences, often associated with traumatic dangers. Another related phenomenon
is what Rainville calls "dreams of multiple self-representation," which can
occur "when a person is conscious of undergoing change, particularly body
change":

> The following dream was taken from a high school freshman who was recently
> informed that he had been accepted on the football team for the following school
> year. . . .
>
> *I was in this dream three times and no matter which of me I was, I could still
> see the other two. The three of us were walking to school. On my right was me
> in a football jersey. I wasn't wearing pads, but I was taller and bigger than the
> other two. On my left was me as I was in junior high school. I had much short-
> er hair and a t-shirt with a goofy saying on it. I couldn't really see the me in
> the middle, but that was who I was most of the time. When I was inside the one
> on the right, I knew they were looking up to me and I liked it. I kind of ignored
> them and was setting a pace which would keep them jumping. When I was in-
> side the one on the left, I realized I had a big scar on my elbow. I felt sad and
> wanted to go back home, but I knew they wouldn't let me and I was afraid to
> cry.* I felt very excited when I woke up.
>
> Multiple self-representations normally begin at this age, but they have been
> reported in younger children who have undergone serious physical disfigure-
> ments. They have also been reported in the terminally ill of all ages.[158]

All of these dual perspective and multiple self-representative dreams and
dream sets exhibit substantial continuity in the dream-ego, a difference from
MPD dreams—there, the dream-ego is occupied by discrete identities in different dreams or dream parts.

A third characteristic of MPD dreams noticed by Carlisle is that "[s]ome
inner entities report having an influence on dream content."[159] The ability
claimed by fractional personalities to "create dreams in order to communicate with the host personality" is a conspicuous feature in the case study of
MPD presented by Roy Salley.[160] The phenomenon of multiple personality
is so intriguing, and this case so revealing, that Salley's study will be quoted
at length:

Personality fragmentation usually occurs in future multiple personalities between the ages of 4 and 8 years as a result of severe abuse and trauma. Typically, several personalities are developed that frequently have no or limited access to the memories and experiences of other personalities. The host personality often has no knowledge of the other personalities and experiences blackouts when others emerge.[161] Some multiples have internal self-helper (ISH) personalities that are aware of the multiple organization and can function as therapeutic allies in the treatment.[162] Each personality usually organizes around a predominant affect or function (rage, sex, rational thinking . . . , etc.). . . .

Frank is a 37-year-old white man with multiple personality. His biological father was incarcerated when he was born. Frank lived with his maternal grandparents soon after his birth. The multiple organization began at the age of 6 years when he was sent to his biological mother's home. His mother had remarried an alcoholic who abused Frank physically and emotionally. A history of blackouts, amnesia for certain actions, fugues, abrupt personality changes, and hysterical conversions has been well documented . . . back to Frank's late teens. . . . This patient had a long history of appearing on hospital grounds in a state of seizure with no memory for person, situation, or past. . . . His life since his late teens has been an almost constant pattern of hospitalizations and fugues that have taken him all over the country. . . .

Early in treatment, before . . . [MPD was diagnosed, hypnotherapy] was used to attempt to uncover lost memory. An ISH was discovered . . . who identified himself as Self, a protector of Frank. Self, in somnambulistic trance, explained that the seizures resulted from a struggle between Frank and Self at those times when Frank would resist regaining consciousness after a blackout and Self would attempt to force him to be conscious. Self stated that his only line of communication with Frank was through dreams and that he would create a dream that would explain to Frank the functions of the seizures. Out of trance, Frank, as was typical, had no memory of what had occurred in hypnosis. That night Frank dreamt that *he was standing on a pedestal and two voices were shouting at him; one voice shouted "Yes!" and the other "No!" The vibrations from the shouting were so intense that the pedestal began to shake and split open, whereupon he fell to the ground shaking.* Free association . . . led Frank to relate the shaking to his seizures and the screaming to internal conflict and his resistance to regaining consciousness after a blackout. In the two years since he had this dream, he has experienced no recurrence of the hysterical seizures. . . .

Dreams were used in the above fashion throughout this man's treatment. Soon after the seizure dream, Frank reported a dream of *standing outside a crowd. The people in the crowd were shouting for Frank to do things for them. One person stood between Frank and the crowd throwing the crowd members aside and shouting, "Leave Frank alone! You'll take everything he's got and I won't let you!" Frank's defender is attacked and bleeding; together they run from the crowd.*

Interpretation of this dream led Frank to view Self as the dream defender. Self then revealed for the first time that Frank had multiple personalities. The crowd in the dream represented the angry personalities. Self described the nature of many of the personalities and said that they were enraged at Self for exposing their cover (seen in the dream as Self fighting the crowd). Therapy then focused on getting to know the personalities one at a time through trance. Most . . . knew of only two or three of the others, and each believed he (or she) lived in his (or her) own different physical body; most denied the multiple personality diagnosis. . . .

Frank reported, at this point, a dream of *standing on a street corner and being picked up in a Model T Ford. The Ford then deposited him at another street corner. The car returned, dropping off one more person at a time until the street corner was filled with a crowd arguing and fighting with one another.* In this dream, Frank saw the car as hypnosis, the vehicle through which he was gaining insight. Through trance, each personality was becoming aware of the other[s] . . . with much resultant arguing. In fact, Frank was complaining of increasing anxiety and almost constant internal bickering. This dream served as a clue to . . . allow time for the consolidation of new information. Eventually, 13 clearly defined personalities were uncovered, all of whom organized between the age of 6 years and Frank's late teenage years. . . .

The next three dreams were important in understanding the roles of the two child personalities in Frank. Tinker was an extremely frightened child who remained huddled in a fetal position most of the time. In the first dream . . . , *Frank saw himself as a little boy in the woods running, horrified. He was being chased by something that was closing in on him.* He awoke screaming. Free association to this dream led to uncovering a repressed memory of a beating by his stepfather that occurred in a forest. . . .

Another dream pictured *a 10- to 12-year-old boy running through the woods, happy and carefree.* This dream revealed the function of Ty, . . . created when Frank's family moved to a house surrounded by woods. Tinker was phobic of forests after his stepfather's beating. Ty's function was to enjoy the woods so Frank could tolerate his new home.

In the final dream of this series, *an image of a spinning Ferris wheel appeared. Large faces of four of the most dominant personalities replaced some of the seats. Tinker's face was at the hub of the wheel.* Interpretation of this dream indicated that Tinker, the frightened core of Frank, was the reason for the creation of all of the personalities. Their function was to protect this terrified aspect. . . .

At one point in therapy, hospitalization and . . . restraints were periodically necessary when Ernest, a violently angry personality, attempted to kill the others in order to stop the uncovering of painful memories. . . . Lawrence, another ISH like Self, reported that Frank was to use his dreams to help remember some of Ernest's past actions. Lawrence stated that he and Self were preparing dreams for this purpose. A dream was then remembered of *Frank attending a party with 12 people. The party was to be at a church. The dream ended with Frank standing at the church door, thinking, "You shouldn't party at a church."* Frank associated the 12 people with his other 12 personalities. Free association . . . led to Frank's sudden memory of actions Ernest had performed as a teenager. Ernest had organized a band of teenagers who systematically vandalized the sanctuaries of a series of churches.

Regaining this memory through dream-work was critical in helping Frank and the other personalities to understand the deceit and destructiveness of Ernest. At the time . . . , Ernest was the most powerful personality and many of the personalities had been aligned with him. Uncovering this material . . . disrupted that unhealthy balance of power. Several of the personalities realigned themselves away from Ernest . . . and assimilated.

As Ernest lost power and credibility, he became more destructive. Repeated attempts at fusion and cooperation proved futile. Ernest was then hypnotically destroyed after he made several attempts to kill Frank. The removal of Ernest led to rapid improvement in functioning. . . .

[Work continued with members of Ernest's "gang."] Ernest has not reappeared in over 2 years. Fusion of the remaining personalities was completed. After several months, the fusion disintegrated when Frank was mugged and stabbed. The gang reappeared, causing further blackouts and confusion. Hypnotic elimination of the gang was performed. Psychotherapy is continuing with this patient.[163]*

Depression.   At the beginning of this chapter Levitan's belief was quoted, that "each syndrome possesses a type of dream which is as characteristic for it as are the stereotyped phenomena of waking life."[164] In apparent contrast to this opinion, there seems to be a consensus, endorsed by Hartmann, that "manifest dream content does not provide one of the more useful diagnostic tests for schizophrenia, depression, or any other mental illness."[165] And Kramer, a leading researcher of this very question, in whose articles one does in fact find dream profiles of depressives and schizophrenics, nevertheless states (with Thomas Roth) that, in view of the small quantity of studies in this field, "[i]t seems highly unlikely . . . that a meaningful characterization of the dream life of any psychopathologic group could be developed."[166]

Even experienced clinicians do actually have difficulty telling the dreams of psychotics from those of normal people, when shown random, unlabelled samples.[167]

But the conflict between these perspectives is less sharp than at first appears. Syndromes may indeed have typical dreams—if less distinctive ones than Levitan asserts. The problem Hartmann and Kramer see arises from the fact that any given dream of, for instance, a schizophrenic, is likely not to be a 'typical' schizophrenic dream, while at the same time such a 'typical'

---

* A preliminary report by Salley (1985) on the case of Frank named him John! In another article (1991, p. 154), Salley reflects that MPD dreams give the lie to Hobson's activation-synthesis hypothesis (ch. 1. p. 34): "In all of the cases presented, dreaming was not a byproduct of biologically driven hindbrain jolts to the cortex but a systematically and meaningfully created communication device across split off aspects of personality structure." (See also ch. 1, p. 37.)

dream may well be dreamt by someone who is not schizophrenic. Dreams do not all run conveniently to type.

Nevertheless, the typification of syndromes by their dream styles is not a wasted effort. In the case of MPD just quoted, it is true that none of the dreams actually yielded the diagnosis—one can dream of fractious crowds without being a multiple personality. But put together with the life history, the dream material proved most useful. Similarly, clinicians familiar with the dream styles (and the sleep styles[168]) of other syndromes possess a helpful tool.

Just as important, we who follow our own dreams and those of familiars can use such information, with discretion—not to render clinical diagnoses, but to discern, say, a depressive trend of mood which has gone unnoticed.

In reports on the dreams of depressives one finds a diagnostic subclassification,—if one not always identifiably maintained—, between the severely or psychotically depressed and those who are variously called "neurotically depressed," "depression-prone," "moderately depressed non-patient individuals,"[169] and so on. We will consider first the dreams of the latter group, to be termed for convenience 'moderately depressed'.

Moderate depression. The first noteable thing about the dream style of the moderately depressed is that their remembered dreams are shorter than those of the not-depressed. Cartwright's research on people in the midst of divorce is interesting in this connection.[170] Generally speaking, their dreams become longer; but not if they are depressed. Cartwright concludes that in depression the coping function of dreams is partially disrupted. Significantly, the roles of "wife," "separated or ex-wife," and "alone" figure prominently in the dreams of the not-depressed women, but not of the depressed. This indicates in another way that the depressed do not come to grips with things in their dreams. People who dream about what is stressing them, and who experience appropriate emotions in dreams, work through their difficulties better than those who do not so dream, in that way either avoiding or overcoming depression. Cartwright aligns these results with those of studies on dream responses to artificially induced stress, the stress of surgery, and that of childbirth.[171] Also, students who have "test-anxiety dreams" get better grades than those who do not.[172] An exception to the rule may be "very severe, or very long term trauma," which may best be contended with by "walling off," in Hartmann's phrase.[173]*

---

* Cartwright (1991, p. 9) also comments that in the case of posttraumatic stress disorder there do not exist sufficient memories to which severe trauma can be likened by a "positive previous coping strategy," so that avoidance may work better in such cases. In their article titled "Dreams that

In tone, dreams of the moderately depressed are typically "unhappy" and "barren."[174] They usually end the night with a dream governed by negative emotions.[175] Their dreams have a reduced number of characters, especially of strangers. Instead, dream personnel tend to be natal family members and others from the past. The sense is of individuals whose energy, withdrawn from "external objects" and muted, "adheres to objects associated with the past and dependency."[176]

In his portrait of moderate depression and associated dream life, Walter Bonime sharpens the description of dependency as being an unwillingness to take responsibility for one's own life. He illustrates with a dream where the dependency has become transferred to himself as therapist. The dreamer is a housewife and mother in her mid-thirties:

> She came to a session depressed. . . .
> After she had talked extensively about what an awful "bitch" she felt she was, how unwilling she was to do anything for anybody, how unhappy she was, I reminded her of her demonstrated capacity to enjoy life and make others feel good. "But," I added, "as we've seen so many times, you get sore as hell because this happiness doesn't come to you without your having to work for it."
> At this moment the patient said, "I had a dream. *I had a sort of screened-in porch, something that we had seen in a magazine for attaching to a house. A neighbor was saying to me, 'It's no good. It has hydrogen and it will burn.' Then it is burning and I call the fire department, but right while I'm on the phone the fire starts going out and I say, 'Never mind, I'll call again if it's necessary.'*
> "*Then a neighbor comes with a pot of water to throw on the small flame that's left. I say, 'Thanks, never mind,' but she says, 'It's perfectly all right. Let me do it for you,' and she throws the water on the flame. I was so pleased that someone else was doing it for me.* That's what I thought of when you said, I don't want to work for my own happiness. **I want to be happy but I want you to do it.** I don't want to have to change, I don't want to have to work for it my-

---

poison sleep," Peretz Lavie & Hanna Kaminer (1991) compare dreams of well- and poorly-adjusted holocaust survivors. Both have a very low recall rate from REM sleep, but surprisingly, the well-adjusted have an even lower rate (34%) than the poorly-adjusted (50%). The same direction of difference is found in dream length and other features. Dreams of the poorly-adjusted exhibit all-too-appropriate anxiety and fear (p. 17): "*I saw some Germans, many Germans. They were making selections. It was in Auschwitz. I was there, they dragged me out of the train. Nobody knew where to go. Then I felt great fear since they started sorting us. They told me where to stand, but that was the side of the gas chambers, I ran to the other side. But they told me the same thing and I ran back again. A German soldier caught me and started to beat me and took me back there. He had a big dog, I was very afraid, I can see the dog . . .* and then you woke me up." But the well-adjusted appear to suppress their memory of the past and, like most people, dream more of the present. The authors suppose that suppression of the traumatic past and of the dreams recalling it serves an adaptive function.

self. **I want to yell and scream and fume** and be a prima donna. I want to spit venom and not have anyone interfere."[177]

Besides dependency, Bonime lists several other traits of the moderately depressed personality, and illustrates them with dream material: manipulativeness (the engineering of dependency), coupled with resentment and defiance of coercion (the denial of dependency); the withholding of gratification from others ("they sullenly maintain their grievance at having been deprived of a nurturant childhood"); anxiety; and a "core of anger."[178]

A trait not explicitly mentioned by Bonime, but frequently attributed to moderate depression,[179] is masochism, something explored by Aaron Beck & Clyde Ward in an often-cited paper from 1961. "Neurotically depressed" persons, they say, are regularly "recipient[s] of a painful experience, such as being disappointed, rejected, or injured" in their dreams. In this way they exhibit a masochistic "need to inflict suffering on the self."[180] Beck & Ward observe a correlation between "the degree of depression and the incidence of masochistic dreams."[181] Cartwright finds the same correlation for the motif of self-reproach and self-blame.[182] A typical depressed man's dream of self-blame: "*Some men were threatening to rape my girlfriend. We were out in the desert and it was my fault for exposing her that way.*"[183]

Beck & Ward spell out some correspondences between typical masochistic dream themes and the waking behavior of the depressed: "[D]reams of being reproached, rejected, or punished, may be compared with the depressive's verbalized self-reproaches and self-criticisms and his belief that he is deserving of punishment. . . . [Dreams] of trying to attain some goal and being consistently thwarted . . . [suggest] the depressive's constantly setting up barriers against any goal-directed activity . . . [and] a general attitude of indecisiveness and ambivalence. The dream of being injured or dead, which is also characteristic of depressives, may correspond to the depressive's conscious self-destructive urges."[184]

However, because such dreams are also dreamt by those who are neither depressed nor masochistic, as well as by masochists who are not depressed, the masochistic dream "may more properly be regarded as related to certain personality characteristics of individuals who may develop depressions."[185]

Also, Cartwright points out that the major studies finding masochism as a trait of depression have had a large preponderance of female subjects. "It has been observed by many authors . . . that the traditional female sex role is comprised of personality traits, such as dependency, helplessness, negative self-evaluation, and submissiveness, that when exaggerated in strength, resemble the psychological characteristics of depression." Cartwright's research reveals that a tendency to experience dreams in which the dream-ego fails or is deprived, attacked, or excluded "is more characteristic of women than men, even in the presence of a mood disorder."[186]

Deep depression. Coming now to 'psychotic', 'endogenous', or what will here be called deep depression. Not only are recalled dreams of the deeply depressed shorter than usual, as with the moderately depressed, but recall overall is greatly reduced compared both to the latter group and to the not-depressed.[187]* Even with laboratory awakenings from REM sleep, the deeply depressed recall dreams only about half the time, compared to about 70% for schizophrenics[188] and 85% (or higher) for normals.[189]

REM characteristics of depression, but especially of deep depression, are as follows. The first REMP comes sooner than normal (as little as 10 minutes after sleep onset). This decrease of latency, as it is called, is more pronounced in older subjects. (Where it occurs with other syndromes—borderline personality, eating disorders, and perhaps schizophrenia—a decrease in REM latency points to possible concomitant depression.[190]) The first REMP lasts longer than usual (may be the longest of the night); the eye movements themselves are augmented; and EEG phasic activity is increased. There are other irregularities. The deeply depressed have most of their REM time in the first half of the night; have an increased percentage of total sleep time in REM, with reduced amounts of stage 3 and 4 sleep (even no stage 4 at all); and are prone to periodic awakenings.[191] "What is worse," commiserates Cartwright, "the night also ends too soon, often at 2, 3, or 4 A.M."[192] She summarizes: "It looks as though [some] people with depression skip the restful first half of the night, start in the middle, and then awaken after only three or four hours' sleep."[193]

With respect to REM profile, it appears there is no qualitative difference between moderate and deep depression. This would seem to be corroborated by the fact that Kramer's profile of anxious people is quite similar: "anxious people take longer to fall asleep, wake up more often, sleep less, have less deep sleep and REM sleep, but enter dreaming sleep earlier; and . . . the intensity of anxiety is related to the intensity of these sleep disturbances."[194]

Cartwright observes that depressed people with the abnormal REM profile actually recover faster than those without it. Their earlier-than-normal dreams feature the ostensible cause of their bad feelings (in Cartwright's divorce study, the spouse), and move the dreamers toward responsibility for their own well-being. These early dreams are more emotional, bizarre, and rich in image and story than dreams at normal times.[195]

---

* In Kramer's opinion (1970, p. 150), the brevity of dream reports from the depressed to some extent probably reflects difficulty communicating rather than dream experience per se.

In apparent conflict with Cartwright's observation, it has been surmised that the benefit of antidepressant drugs derives from suppression of REM.[196] Indeed, REM sleep deprivation has been found as effective in relieving depression as antidepressant drugs.[197]*

As for content characteristics, dreams in deep depression are said to be "barren,"[198] and "sparse in content."[199] Frequently the dream-ego finds itself alone,[200] or, when with others, usually with individuals (about 80% of the time) rather than with groups (20%) (for schizophrenics the percentages are 60% individuals, 40% groups).[201] As with the moderately depressed, family members predominate among dream characters.[202]

Depression can be associated with an increase in nightmares.[203] And just as masochism in seen in dreams from moderate depression, so dreams from deep depression score high on themes of "helplessness/hopelessness,"[204] and the dream-ego is more passive than other dream characters.[205] It is surprising, therefore, that Kramer finds hostility about equally directed at and from the dream-ego, a ratio comparable to that in dreams of normals.[206]

Another confusing item: in contrast with his finding of themes of "helplessness/hopelessness," just mentioned, elsewhere Kramer remarks on the "paucity of depressive content in the dreams of the depressed."[207] He points out the very high percentage, nearly 50%, of friendly interactions in dreams from deep depression, which is much higher than in dreams from the general population.[208] And he comments on a particular type of pleasant dream commonly found in deep depression: the dream of "escape." Having set up what he thought would be a compatible combined category of "escape and suicide" to look for, he found no examples whatever of the suicide motif,[209] whereas very nearly half the dreams collected contained "escape" in a simple, sometimes repetitious, and not unpleasant form, notably "going home and going on trips":

A typical escape dream is illustrated by the following dream from a 49-year-old, married depressed male: *I was with my father on the train. I was glad and happy to be with him.*[210]

---

* S. Krippner & J. Dillard (p. 91) comment: "Vogel reasoned that in depressed people, the mechanisms which mediate pleasure, appetite and motor behavior might be active during dreaming and inactive during waking. Depressed people, if Vogel is right, are dreaming their waking lives away!" An alternative explanation for the good effect of REM deprivation on depression, based on information processing rather than drive, is that REM deprivation partially disconnects the person from difficult memories and restores her/him to the present (R. Greenberg, C. Pearlman, W. R. Schwartz & H. Y. Grossman 1983, p. 381). This theory conflicts with Cartwright's position.
An anonymous peer reviewer of this book who sounds like s/he knows what s/he is talking about asserts that REM deprivation becomes ineffective against depression after 2–4 days.

Quite possibly the discrepancies in these accounts of dreams from deep depression—"helplessness/hopelessness" and "barren" on one hand, "pleasant" and "friendly" on the other—can be rationalized along lines suggested by Jean Miller. She contrasts the dream of those in the bottom of deep depression with those on the way to improvement. The dreams of her improving patients have in common with dreams of the moderately depressed (as described by Bonime and by Beck & Ward) the themes of harm, especially in the form of coercion, of thwarted effort, of dependency, and of death, all with overtones of anxiety. In contrast, Miller's dreams from the bottom of depression have the traits previously noted: pleasant and friendly, with the theme of escape. Presumably, then, reports about hopeless or barren dreams from patients in deep depression may actually concern dreamers on the way to improvement, that is, moderately depressed patients. Here are passages from Miller's paper:

Dreams in Deep Depression.— . . . The 16 patients produced a total of 22 dreams. Seventeen were clearly pleasant or bland. Three were pleasant but contained some evidence of a conflict and were therefore called intermediate. Two were unpleasant.

. . . [Seventeen] dreams showed an absence of conflict, threat of harm from other people or the environment and an absence of inner conflict, danger, or worry. The following descriptive reports are based on the first dream from each of the 16 patients. . . . Most dreams were positively happy, for example:

No. 1.—*I was by myself with beautiful girls in Venice—in a coffee house. They were dancing there. There was a lot of entertainment. Then suddenly the man from the gondolas came in and said, "Now we are ready to go around the city in a gondola." I had a beautiful girl with me.*

No. 2.—I had a pleasant one last night. *I gave someone a gift. I can't remember who. Then we were going out in the car. We had to wait to get into the stream of traffic—like on a big thoroughfare. I was happy in it.*

Three dreams were more neutral or bland, e.g.,

No. 3.—*I had moved into a new apartment with two screened porches and I was thinking about changing the color scheme in one of them to orange and aqua.*

Two dreams of the first sixteen were judged to be intermediate. The dreamers said they were happy, but there is explicit conflict present. For example, the patient said he felt "very hilarious" in this dream:

No. 4.—*While living at a previous apartment, I was returning home with a friend of my wife, Aunt Sophie, and before entering my home, I opened the door and told my wife we had company and was it all right to come in—was the house tidy? My wife responded, "No," and started to run into the living room to tidy up. I pulled the door closed so Sophie could not go in. We both started to laugh in the hall at my wife's shortcomings in housework.*

In answer to the questions about how they felt during the dream, all patients gave replies such as "good" or "happy," or "normal." These statements contrast with the answers to the next question. "How did you feel after you awoke this morning?" Almost all patients answered "bad," i.e., statements similar to their usual expressions of mood. Of the first 16 dreams, 9 were short, generalized statements. Seven were somewhat longer, as in No. 1. . . .

Dreams in Improving Patients.—These dreams showed a marked difference from those just described. Almost all were troubled and troubling. The 13 improving patients produced a total of 21 dreams. Nineteen were disturbing. Only 2 had the happy quality of the earlier dreams.

In examining these dreams, we will use the first dream reported after improvement by each patient. Twelve were troubled. Analysis of these dreams revealed that certain forms of conflict predominated. There were 2 short dreams of death and 9 dreams of interaction between two or more people. In 5 of the latter, the dreamer was either experiencing or complaining about another person's harming her.

This was the most common dream. . . . In addition, one particular type of harm is most frequent: . . . the forceful coercion of the dreamer by another person. An example is:

No. 5.—*My husband was in a boat fishing and had the outboard motor running. I wanted to get in the boat also but he insisted I stay on the shore and wait while he fished. I decided my fishing license had expired so I wouldn't be able to fish anyway so it was safer to stay on the shore.*

. . . Physical harm did not occur to the improving depressed patients in any of their dreams. In 2 dreams, both fragmentary, it occurred to other people. . . .

Two dreams portrayed the dreamer either worrying about her own ability to perform at a task or failing at it. . . .

. . . [Sometimes she is] stopped from carrying out her activity. . . .

The 3 dreams in which the predominant content was death showed two notable points. They occur proportionally more often . . . and they were all brief scenes in which death is already accomplished and complete . . . :

No. 7.—I dreamed that *I was at my own funeral. It was a black coffin and very simple and shut.* . . .

In answer to the question about feelings in the dream, the majority of the improving patients gave some distressing feeling such as "terrible," "anxious," "angry," or "sad." By contrast with the deeply depressed patients, several of the improving patients said that they felt better when they awoke and that they were "glad it was only a dream." Of the 13 later dreams, 7 were short and 6 were of moderate length.[211]

Schizophrenia. Schizophrenia is a "thought disorder" involving impaired reality contact, disturbed body image, and difficulty with all relationships. Emotional expression tends to be "impulsive" and "inappropriate." "[T]he programs which organize the dream-stream material, the inner responses of feelings and fantasies, are not turned off while the necessary work of relating to the external world is done."[212] Common are delusions (ungrounded beliefs) and hallucinations (ungrounded perceptions). Also common are preoccupation with dreams, often with a magical belief in their prophetic power, and a compulsion to interpret them.[213]

The schizophrenic's disordered thought process is said to persist in sleep, where the dream "is often experienced as a strange, sinister, sometimes badly articulated ensemble"[214] with rapid scene changes.[215] You might expect, therefore, that schizophrenics would have highly idiosyncratic dreams. But actually, judges find it easier to sort the dreams of a group of healthy people by individual than those of a group of schizophrenics, which more resemble one another.[216]

Here are a few miscellaneous points about content features (others will be presented and debated as the section proceeds). We know that, in contrast to the deeply depressed with their escape dreams, for most dreamers happy dreams are relatively scarce. So it is surprising that Patricia Carrington finds that *acute* schizophrenics have somewhat more dreams with "gratifying content" (12%) than do normals (6%); however, in keeping with their disorder, gratifying scenes are generally "unrealistic, precipitate, and magical," with "implausible changes of mood."[217] But studying long-term *chronic* patients, Tereo Okuma finds more unpleasant dreams and, again surprisingly, fewer dreams with no emotion than for normals.[218] Kramer reports that dreams of schizophrenics show elevated aggression, along with apprehension and anxiety. In contrast to depressed dreams, where aggression is equally expressed by the dream-ego and by others, in schizophrenic dreams the dream-ego is usually the target.[219]

As mentioned earlier, schizophrenics dream themselves in groups more often than do the depressed. Kramer characterizes their dreams as populated by strangers, with few meaningful others.[220] Again perhaps because his subjects are chronic, Okuma reports no more strangers than in dreams of normals, and actually more family members (23%) than for normals (10%),[221] though not more than for the depressed. S. Chang earlier had noted family members to be the focus of chronic but not acute schizophrenic dreaming.[222] It is also the case that schizophrenics have "more aggression with familiar characters" than do other dreamers.[223]

A suggestive idea about schizophrenia advanced by Cartwright and others is that hallucinations and other bizarre waking mentation are "misplaced" dreams that have "leaked" or "escaped" into waking life.[224] The REM profile of schizophrenia is not settled[225] (there are many more sleep studies of depression than of schizophrenia[226]). But it has been found that during onset or worsening phases of the disease, REM time is reduced below normal levels. And although chronic, stabilized patients do have a normal proportion of REM time,[227] neither acute nor chronic patients show the usual rebound effect of increased REM time which is shown by normal dreamers when experimentally deprived of REM sleep.[228] Cartwright thinks the explanation is that the "normal quota of dream-like experiences" gets "distributed" and in effect dissipated into waking, and also into NREM sleep.[229] Even when, as with chronic patients, the physiological REM process proceeds more or less normally, it does so autonomously, apart from adaptive dreaming—that is, REM time and the dreams occupying it have become divorced from adaptive functions such as problem-solving and conflict resolution.[230] By this reckoning, the fact that chronic schizophrenics may enter REM sleep a little sooner after falling asleep than do normals[231] would seem to have no relation to any urgent need to dream.

That dreaming leaks away into states other than REM sleep explains to Cartwright why REM dreams collected from schizophrenics in the lab are undeveloped, bland, and dull. William Dement wrote of this in 1955:

> [H]alf of the chronic schizophrenics frequently reported dreams of isolated, inanimate objects, apparently hanging in space, with no overt action whatsoever. . . .
> Q.—Were you dreaming?
> A.—Yes.
> Q.—What about?
> A.—*There was ah- ah- a trunk and curtain rods.*
> Q.—A trunk and curtain rods?
> A.—Yes.
> Q.—What else?
> A.—Nothing.
> Q.—You mean there was nothing but just a trunk and curtain rods? No people?
> A.—Yes.
> Q.—Were you in it?
> A.—I don't think so. I saw them. . . .
> . . . That these peculiar dream reports were probably not just the result of a deteriorated ability to communicate was brought out by the fact that the same patients described other dreams which seemed quite normal and were also able to communicate fairly adequately in the waking state.[232]

Such dreams bring to mind the isolated, static images of certain NREM dreams (ch. 1, p. 24). Other examples from Dement include *a hat, a shelf, a ripped coat,* and *a suitcase.* Earlier observers, without benefit of sleep lab procedures, had already remarked on a "lack of content"[233] in many schizophrenic dreams. Confirming Dement, W. Biddle records such dreams as "*a wash rag, a dilapidated house* or *an empty field*," and says that dreams become more developed as the patient improves and hallucinations diminish.[234]

Dement's dreamers and probably these others were chronic cases. Cartwright cites this evidence in support of her idea that dreaming partially escapes from REM sleep in schizophrenia, and she further adduces acute cases of her own:

> Only half of the reports from their REM awakenings had the qualities of a dream—that is, visual images which were accepted at the time as real. Despite the fact that half of these reports were "dreams," many of these were not at all bizarre, but really quite realistic. In fact, two-thirds of the patients' REM reports were everydayish in quality as opposed to less than half of those from the normals. . . .
>
> . . . Most of the patients' dreams were of home, work, and the hospital without much story development or abrupt change in time or place. The theme was usually a single statement: *I was at work, thinking about the good times I had there*; *I was in my room at home, feeling afraid*; *I saw a pass. I wondered whether my doctor would sign a pass for me to go on the picnic.* These were not elaborated in terms of characters or plot, although there was usually at least one visual image involved.[235]

Dream realism is not always unelaborate, however. John Kafka mentions a patient who, in dreams about his past, found departures from literal reality as unusual as most of us find instances of it. Another patient could maintain a realistic thought process for five or ten minutes after abrupt awakenings, only to relapse then into delusion. Kafka affirms Freud's observation, "that ordinary reality br[eaks] through into dreams in the same way in which material related to 'instinct' br[eaks] into the dreams of the nonpsychotic individual."[236]

The circumstance that REM mentation is sometimes static and/or realistic while the waking state is sometimes invaded by hallucinations and delusions must contribute to the inability schizophrenics are said to experience telling whether something is happening in dream, in fantasy, or in waking actuality.[237] John Frosch relates:

> One of my borderline patients agitatedly reported a dream in which *her mother was lying on top of her, having intercourse with her.* What troubled her was that the sensation was so vivid that she was not sure that it had not happened and kept wavering about the reality of the experience. Another acutely psychotic patient came into the hospital in a panic, thinking that he had murdered his brother-in-law. It turned out that he had had a dream of *choking his brother-in-law to death.* The feeling in his hand was so real that he began to wonder whether he had really committed the deed and rushed into the hospital in a panic.[238]

The confusion runs both ways, that is, not only is dreaming mistaken for reality but reality is mistaken for dreaming. Kafka tells this anecdote:

> [A] patient, . . . who lived most of his life outside a hospital, found that he had made all kinds of commitments, had pledged charitable contributions, and had accepted invitations when he had actually answered the telephone, but had believed that he was dreaming the whole thing. By the time I started working with him, he had already developed a method to circumvent this problem. Since he did not know if he was awake or dreaming—he had multiple dreams within dreams—and since "pinching himself" didn't do the trick, he had learned to always ask, "What is your number? I'll call you back."[239]*

John Mack tells the case history of a man who had difficulty telling (a) nightmares from (b) actual lethal threats in his waking life from (c) psychotic hallucinations.[240]

It ought to be pointed out that there are profoundly psychotic individuals so alienated from reality that they cannot contemplate any such distinctions. In commenting on the "rather banal character" of a category of schizophrenic dreams, Medard Boss tells of a certain woman for whom the mere touch of authenticity in a dream was overwhelmingly distressing:

> [She] dreamt *she is lying in the hospital. A nurse comes in and straightens the patient's pillow. This scares her so boundlessly* that she awakes with trembling and screams for help. . . . The patient was frightened because the dream scene had appeared with long forgotten realism and feeling tone, while for many years past she had lived in severe autism which made the outside world appear as in a shadow. . . . This type of patient cannot bear the attempt of their affective tendencies to reestablish a deeper object relationship in the dream. . . .[241]

As the dreams of lesbian incest and brother-in-law murder excerpted from Frosch show, not all schizophrenic dreams have a banal, everydayish quality or treat isolated, static objects. Boss stipulates a further category, one which fits Frosch's samples: dreams displaying undisguised impulses. This characteristic progresses with the disease. A series from Boss exhibiting the progression was already quoted in chapter 7 (p. 241): an early dream had *the dreamer pitying a cow before slaughter*; in a later dream, *she mutilates and murders her mother as prelude to being raped*.

Boss considers uncensored dreams to be diagnostic indicators when they occur early in the disease, at which time they usually conflict to an extreme

---

* I cannot resist recalling here from memory the anecdote Max Bröd told in his biography of the better-known Kafka. Franz Kafka and Bröd were trying to tiptoe through a room without disturbing Bröd's dozing father. When the father stirred and looked up at Kafka, the writer said, "Please look upon me as a dream."

with the dreamer's conscious attitudes,[242] as in the case of Frosch's appalled brother-in-law who rushed himself to the hospital. But such dreams are more in evidence with deterioration over time:

> A young man, still healthy and successfully studying, had the following repeated dream around the age of 20:
> *I am building a beautiful house which has two balconies, decorated with beautiful flowers. Then a rich gentleman appears who wants to buy the house from me. I only give it to him when he pays me a million dollars for it.*
> . . . [This dream recurred in progressively more uncensored forms until four years later when,] considerably into his psychosis, he dreamt:
> *I am lying in bed with a beautiful woman. The woman's husband enters and wants to murder me. However, I strangle him and throw him out of the window. I do the same to the numerous policemen who want to capture me. In the end I go downstairs to the front of the house and cut the limbs and heads off all the corpses. All this filled me with an inordinate greed.*[243]

While not apparent in this instance, it has been noted that affect may be flattened in such primitive uncensored dreams.[244]

That lack of censorship is a reliable enough sign of early schizophrenia to be a diagnostic aid at that stage, as Boss suggests, has been disputed by George Richardson & Robert Moore. They ran a test using psychiatric first admissions, half schizophrenics, half not. A panel of professionals had to diagnose the admissions as schizophrenic or not, solely from the evidence of their dreams. The experts chose only a little above 50% correct, and they actually did much better picking the nonschizophrenic dreams (67% correct) than the schizophrenic (45%). What is significant: many wrong choices were based on the expectation that schizophrenic dreams would possess the very characteristic in question, undisguised sexuality and aggressiveness.

On the other hand, "bizarreness, uncanniness, unreality, strangeness, or a cosmic quality," though by no means present in all of the schizophrenic dreams, was the criterion by which the judges most successfully differentiated the two groups (along with flat affect and infrequent scene changes).[245] Other investigators have also found bizarreness, implausibility, or distance from daily reality to be relatively common in dreams of schizophrenics.[246] Both Carrington and Kramer look upon bizarreness as a facet of the waking thought disorder which continues into sleep.[247]

The situation is obviously not straightforwardly clear. The attribution of bizarreness is just the opposite of Cartwright's picture of the situation, by which the normal bizarreness of REM dreams becomes dissipated outside of REM sleep (especially in hallucinations), leaving REM dreams relatively realistic and featureless. Her own tests show that acute schizophrenics have less bizarre dreams than normal people, and even show that those normal people with the less schizoid personalities have the more bizarre dreams.[248] Some other studies confirm Cartwright's picture,[249] including one by Calvin Hall, where he performed a content analysis on Richardson & Moore's sample of supposedly bizarre acute schizophrenic dreams. He found them actually no more bizarre than the dreams of other hospital patients or of college students.[250] As for chronic patients, Okuma found their dreams less bizarre than those of normals.[251]

A number of factors have been raised as possibly confounding the results, in both directions. On one hand, non-bizarreness may be exaggerated by the brevity of dream reports collected from schizophrenics, brevity being a feature found for both acute[252] and chronic[253] patients. Short dream reports tend to appear less bizarre.[254] On the other hand, bizarreness may be magnified by the practice of collecting dreams, not from REM awakenings but during the day (Carrington; Richardson & Moore; Langs), leaving the possibility that dream material gets conflated with disordered waking thoughts.[255] Another issue is medication. While "blandness and sterility of content" may be a drug effect, it is also possible that compensatory bizarreness crops up in dreams when waking bizarreness is suppressed by drugs. Cartwright considers both possibilities, favoring the latter.[256]

Cartwright raises the point about medication, as well as the matter of delayed daytime collection of dream samples, in the course of explaining how Carrington's findings of bizarreness and certain other extreme features can be so different from her own findings. However that may be, Carrington's is one of the most interesting papers on the subject. Whether or not drug effects and waking conflation give a slant to her dream sample, Carrington at the least reveals the waking recollections acute schizophrenics communicate about their own dream experiences.

"In general," summarizes Carrington, "the dreams of schizophrenic subjects represent a state of emergency or stress. Schizophrenic subjects tended to view their dream environment and the persons depicted in it as overwhelmingly threatening. Their dreams were replete with mutilation imagery and morbid themes. They were more aggressive, more bizarre, and more often reflective of ego dyscontrol. . . . The impression was that the sleeping schizophrenic subject was struggling, often futilely, with massive disruptive forces in her personality."[257] Carrington concludes that schizophrenics preserve the personality traits of their illness in their dream life.

Two of her specific findings have already been mentioned: *bizarreness*, and a certain incidence of *implausible gratifications*. Another she calls *dyscontrol*: dreams where the ego is out of control. Over a third of these actu-

ally depict "loss of sanity, variously described as 'craziness,' 'catatonic stu-
por,' 'going berserk,' and the like."[258] The other features of schizophrenic
dreams defined by Carrington are *aggression, environmental threat, human
physical deficit states*, and *morbidity*.[259]

First, *aggression*. Carrington's schizophrenic women dream relatively often of physical aggression aimed at the dream-ego. Half these attacks were
life threatening, and some fatal. The other half "often seemed to *imply* danger to life," e.g., "sexual assaults, rapes, . . . [and] someone throwing a jar
of spiders over the dreamer." And whereas nonschizophrenics when they attack others most often do so verbally, and sometimes refrain from acting on
their anger altogether, Carrington's schizophrenics expressed dream anger
through impulsive physical attacks which were never restrained.

Next, *environmental threat*. Impersonal threats proved to be frequent, unmitigated, and irresistible. They often culminated in "[h]elpless surrender"
or "entrapment . . . with no escape in sight," whereas "mildly threatening or
inconvenient occurrences . . . were entirely absent":

> [T]he disasters tended to be overwhelming and ruthlessly demolishing in nature.
> *A volleyball hits a girl and pulverizes her into a million pieces*; *an alligator eats
> the dreamer alive*; *a dreamer's head is pressed into quicksand*; nuclear wars and
> world destructive cataclysms are common.[260]

Dreams "of a complete and malignant world- and self-dissolution," it has
been said, occur only with schizophrenia.[261] But such dreams have also been
noticed to occur without psychosis, e.g., with movement toward a drastic
reorganization of the personality.[262]

Next *human physical deficit states*, or *mutilation imagery*. Carrington's
*non*schizophrenic subjects dreamt of such deficits as blindness, stuttering,
illness, stupidity, and lameness. These "did not involve bizarre or jarring
dismemberment of persons or the rendering asunder of living creatures." In
nonpsychotic dreams such images occasionally do occur. However:

> [A] large proportion of the schizophrenic group deficit dreams contained outright
> mutilation imagery, often savage and brutal. For example, . . . *a penis is torn off
> leaving a big hole "with blood oozing out and pus"*; *a dreamer burns her arm
> which then falls off exposing raw veins and bloody flesh*; *a woman kills her hus-
> band and stuffs parts of his body into camels' heads*; *a girl kills and throws dis-
> sected body parts down the toilet*; *cut-up pieces of people are hung on racks with
> blood oozing and mingling with the sawdust on the floor*, etc.
> The following schizophrenic group dream is typical: *I was decapitated. My
> ribs were picked clean, no skin, no muscle. My body was cut in half. I was just
> a pile of bones. They didn't know who I was, but I still knew who I was. I want-
> ed to pull myself together but I couldn't.*[263]

The last items brings to mind shamanic dreams of dismemberment, but with the radical difference, noted in chapter 5 (p. 177n), that the schizophrenic fails to become reassembled. Moreover, shamans who have been examined with this similarity in view have proven neither psychotic nor neurotic, and may even be healthier than others in their groups.[264]

Lastly, *morbidity*. Carrington treats this quality, noticeable in many samples already given, under bizarreness; but it strikes me as being worthy of separate mention:

> Morbid dreams appeared as a peculiarly schizophrenic manifestation in this study. These "morbid" dreams . . . were often repugnant. They included *a man sweeping up a girl's bones and throwing them into a sanitation truck, dead flesh decaying in layers, the dreamer lying down in a coffin from which her dead parents had just risen*, and *the dreamer raking up a huge ten-foot piece of decaying feces which was wrapped in a white sheet*. . . .[265]

To recapitulate this section on schizophrenic dream style: bland dreams are said to be dreamt by both chronic[266] and acute[267] patients, but so are horrific dreams said to be dreamt by chronic[268] and acute[269] patients. Chronics are said to dream realistically[270] and bizarrely,[271] but acutes are also said to dream both realistically[272] and bizarrely.[273] Bizarreness is detected in lab-collected dreams[274] and day-collected dreams,[275] but realism is also detected in lab-[276] and day-collected dreams.[277] So it does not appear feasible to extract a unified characterization of schizophrenic dream style from this diverse material. Personally, I take away a certain complex impression of the style, and I trust that you the reader have formed your own.

I should add that there are certain occasional peculiarities which have not been introduced, to avoid further complicating the picture.[278]

Also, nothing has been said about differential diagnosis within the broad category of schizophrenia, largely because authors do not consistently identify their dreamers in this regard. As far as it goes, here is Kramer's sketch: "Hebephrenics* are described as having either coarsely sexual dreams or else dreams free of sex; dreams of catatonics are characterized as hostile, aggressive, sexual, and omnipotent; paranoids as homosexual and narcissistic,"[279] with the direction of hostility overwhelmingly toward the dream-ego.[280]

Finally, bear in mind that, except for deteriorated cases, many dreams of schizophrenics are indistinguishable from those of other people.

---

* Hebephrenia is "a chronic form of schizophrenia which is characterized by immature, silly behavior" (R. E. Rainville 1988, p. 185).

□ 10 □

Dream Residues

Walter Bonime, Fritz Perls, Strephon Williams, Jeremy Taylor, Arnold Mindell, and Eugene Gendlin recommend applying dreamwork techniques to passages of waking life, when appropriate.[1] The premise of this advice is that dream*like* symbolic processes occur in waking. We know this from our understanding of everything from slips of the tongue, to transference in psychotherapy, to creativity, to living in the mythic dimension of life in a constructive way.[2]

The present chapter will consider only a small segment of this very large question of waking as dream or dreamlike. Its topic is the perpetuation of the symbolic process of actual dreams into subsequent waking thought, feeling, and action.

In her stimulating book *Waking Dreams*, Mary Watkins employs the term *dream residue* to designate such persistences of dreams into the day.[3] She is, of course, playing on Freud's term 'day residue', "the event of the previous day which set it [the dream] in motion."[4] Watkins says that dream residues frequently give form to waking: "[T]he concrete events [of the day] are as likely to reflect the imaginal movement [of a dream] as the other way around. . . . As he goes through the day the dreamer could note the 'residue of the dream' in his dayworld. . . . [T]he relating of the day and the dream world . . . circles back and forth, never getting far from the experience of the imaginal."[5]

Watkins's example accompanying this statement describes the disturbing shadow cast on the day by a dream, but in general she focuses on constructive effects. For the most part this chapter, however, looks at the catagogic side of the dream-to-waking connection. It considers unhealthy behaviors in some way triggered, facilitated, led up to by specific foregoing dreams.

This particular range of phenomena had attention called to it in 1961 by Alan Leveton.[6] Fifteen years before Watkins, he made essentially the same play on Freud's term. Leveton called persistences of dreams into the day the *night residue*. His explanation of the phenomenon was basically Freudian: just as unconscious energy attaches to a day residue in the formation of the dream, so in the formation of waking consciousness some aspect of the manifest dream, possibly a trivial one, can serve as a "point of attachment" for unconscious energy which has been uncapped during the night and then not completely re-repressed.*

Explanations in terms of unconscious energy dynamics will not serve for all cases. However, the range of phenomena Leveton observed is very nearly the same as that to be discussed below. First will be considered the onset of neurotic symptoms from dreams; next, the onset of psychotic symptoms after dreams; then, suicide attempts following dreams. Then come subjects of more obvious application for the average interpreter: dream recall as a function of the symbolic process underlying the dream; and the 'acting out' of foregoing dreams while awake.

Onset of Neurotic Symptoms from Dreams

Psychosomatic symptoms. As brought out in chapter 8, dreams and psychosomatic symptoms often constitute a matched set of symbolic processes. Additionally, several ways were mentioned in which dreams may relate instrumentally to subsequent symptoms. (1) Dream content, or the mere dream state itself, acts as a stressor on the body, increasing, for example, stomach secretions leading to an attack of ulcers. It would seem that there is nothing necessarily neurotic about this process, although it is easy to imagine how neurosis might become involved. Moreover, the connection does not necessarily hinge upon the symbolic affinity between dream content and symptom. (2) In some cases, for example, dreams of physical threat and terror before migraines, it is not clear whether the dream triggers the medical condition, or the condition the dream. (3) In other cases, for example, asthma as Franz Alexander interpreted it, the dream definitely contains specific psychological content which triggers the condition. There occurs a symbolic somatization of inadmissible thoughts and feelings which the dream fails to manage. Thus Alexander conjectured that an asthma attack symbolically stifles the cry for

---

* Robert Langs's term *recall residue* (1971 and 1988) has a different meaning. Recall residues are day events which jog the recall of a previously unremembered dream. Prior to dreaming, Langs notes, the acquisition of day residues is not always passive; the unconscious goes looking for experiences which hook it. Similarly, recall residues "may be sought out by the ego in its effort to recall dreams as part of its constant endeavor to work through and resolve ongoing conflicts. . ." (1971, p. 508). Recall residues may also be thrust upon one by events.

mother detectable in the foregoing dream. This is more or less the sort of connection briefly to be looked at further here.

"We dream ourselves into illness quite as often as out of it."[7] Lawrence Kubie's remark may exaggerate the catagogic trend of dreams, but there are sufficient examples to be found, particularly in the less recent literature. Besides examples of dreams preceding symptoms in chapter 8, there are others where the dream/symptom relationship is patently obvious. Leveton's first illustration of "night residue" is Féré's case of hysterical paralysis from the 1880s, also mentioned by Freud.[8] A 14-year-old girl dreamt recurrently of *running away from men trying to stab her*. Her legs after successive awakenings felt progressively weaker, and she began to have daydreams with the same theme, until finally dreams and daydreams stopped when she awoke paralysed. "[I]t would not be correct to say that the dream 'caused' the paralysis," says Leveton, "but rather that the failure of waking re-repression to handle what emerged in sleep left a residue that threatened the now awake individual and had to be dealt with by other mechanisms of defense."

Leo Bartemeier, in a paper from 1950 titled "Illness Following Dreams," reports a case where the symptom is explicitly predicted in the dream:

> During the analysis of a young woman who had always been successful in her intellectual rivalry with her twin brother and who was strongly identified with her very intelligent father, the following incident took place: She stated, "I dreamed that *I was in your office lying on the couch. You said in a stern, cold voice, 'You had better tell me all about it.' I quickly asked, 'Tell you about what?' I felt angry, confused and sullen. I didn't know what 'it' was, so I didn't know what to talk about. After a period of silence, you said, 'You know what will happen if you don't say anything, don't you?' I didn't reply, but lay wondering what would happen. Then it came to me that, of course, I would have some sort of skin trouble—and on my arm. The dream ended without my saying anything about this to you.*" While the patient was having her breakfast, she noticed an itching on her left wrist which she first thought was a mosquito bite. As it persisted, she discovered a lesion about an inch in diameter and three smaller ones directly behind it. By nine o'clock she was in the office of her family physician. . . . As she was leaving his office she first recalled her dream of the night. The lesions disappeared after two days. Nothing was learned of this transference problem until later. At the time the patient said . . . that in the dream it was as though she were saying, "Rather than tell you about it, I will suffer skin trouble. . . ." Some months later, during the last hour before the treatment had to be interrupted because of my departure from the city, she repeatedly had the feeling she was forgetting something, and before the hour ended she had developed a number of noticeably large skin lesions on her face and neck. She subsequently wrote me and enclosed her cheque for the analytic fee. In her letter she said she had intended to write the cheque the day before the analytic hour, then forgot and made it out just

before the hour began. She next remembered it in the office of her family physician, to whom she had gone after leaving me. This, she said, is what she had forgotten during her analytic hour, and she added that as soon as she recalled it her skin lesions disappeared. The underlying factor with which both the dream and the acute reactions were trying to . . . [deal was an] aspect of the transference relationship. She had frequently belittled me during her analysis as her father had treated her during her childhood. Following the divorce of her parents during her twelfth year, her father sometimes failed to send the monthly cheque for the family's support, and she was delegated by her mother to visit him and ask him for it. On some of these occasions he would refuse her request. The reenactment of these scenes during the analysis with herself in the role of her father was on these occasions carefully concealed from the material of her analytic hours. In this instance, the dream foretold what was to come later.[9]

Bartemeier does not suggest why the woman developed skin lesions rather than some other symptom, i.e., whether the skin had a symbolic value for her or was only her vulnerable, predisposed organ. Either way, a dynamic connection between dream and subsequent symptom is obvious enough.

Nonsomatic neurotic symptoms. Several of the papers in Harold Levitan's series on dream/symptom connections, featured in chapter 8, concern the formation of classic neurotic symptoms. One case involves the onset of a compulsive neurosis following a dream at age 9. Briefly:

The patient, . . . an unemployed salesman, sought therapy in his late twenties at which time his long-standing compulsions had finally paralysed his life. He was required to perform each ablution again and again because he was uncertain as to whether it had been performed properly the previous time. . . . [His other compulsions are described.] [H]e was able to leave his apartment only with the greatest difficulty. Often we were forced to conduct our psychotherapy over the telephone.

The compulsions had been present since childhood. He related their onset to the aftermath of a terrifying dream which occurred at age 9. In this dream *he visualized himself as a skeleton.* He felt that his death in the dream had been ordained as a punishment for the sadistic acts he had been inflicting on the neighborhood animals. He awoke from the dream in a very anxious state. From that moment he was terribly afraid of the world outside his own house.[10]

It seems the child received an anagogic dream message beyond his capacity to process. Rather than reform, he became fixated in compulsive behaviors and went right ahead setting fire to cats. Thus the dream and the compulsion it triggered were successive attempts to manage the dreamer's conflict. In later years his antisocial spells came to alternate with periods of compulsion. At the time he sought treatment, he was actually highly placed in the Society for the Prevention of Cruelty to Animals.

Another of Levitan's papers concerns the development of phobic symptoms from dreams. Levitan ventures the hypothesis that the displacement of impulses onto unconnected symbolic contexts, typical of phobia and often difficult to account for, may commonly originate in dream symbolism. His patient is an agoraphobic, who dreads leaving the house except in company with her husband. The case report is quite complex, but here are the most relevant features. When she was a child, her father had been "simultaneously provocative and restrictive."[11] He would wrestle vigorously with her, then tie her hands outside the bedding to prevent masturbation. She had been given to masturbation from an early age, especially since the birth of a sister at age 4. In puberty, World War II caused her father to be absent for many years, but she blamed his disappearance on her masturbatory activity. Her phobias had begun shortly after the premature birth of her own second child. Labor had commenced just after injudicious masturbation, while her husband was away on business.

Levitan states that a forbidden incestuous fantasy, closely connected with the bedtime wrestling episodes of childhood, has been displaced onto the experience of normal motion and its cessation outside the house. "Walking is anxiety-producing, but having to stop for a red light or to stand in a queue is even worse." He conjectures that the conversion of a normal activity into a phobia first took form in a dream. He cannot retrieve the original dream, but finds its type in other, later dreams with a common theme: the very activity feared during the day becomes sexualized. Here is one such dream:

I am supposed to catch a train to go to my parents' house but somehow I never make it . . . Then I am in another place making love to my husband . . . the scene blanks out and I experience an orgasm . . . Then I am walking up Broadway attempting again to get to my parents' house but there are numerous road-blocks and obstacles which keep stopping me . . . as I am forced to stop at each obstacle I experience an orgasm.

She immediately associated to the obstacles the access of anxiety she feels at having to stop while walking. . . . [Phobia for restraint] seems somehow to be related to sudden release of sexual feeling. . . .

There is then, according to my construction, a series of steps leading from the return of the repressed sexual fantasy to the development of anxiety in the phobic situation. Firstly, there is the return in the dream of the specific sexual fantasy in association with strong sexual drive. The dream ego is able to displace the original content of the fantasy onto a previously neutral situation but it cannot control the sexual drive itself. The sexual drive is thereafter associated with the new situation. The next morning there is carry-over of preoccupation with the sexualized situation which is however now feared because of the naturally occurring enhancement of ego function at that time.[12]

Onset of Psychotic Symptoms after Dreams

Where he referred to Féré's case of "a dream which resulted in a hysterical paralysis," Freud also called attention to insanities which appear to arise within or following dreams. He mentioned schizophrenias, paranoias, and depressions.[13] Another of Bartemeier's cases provides an illustration where depression is involved:

> A young woman dreamed that *her girlfriend had been murdered and that she and her mother were dismembering the corpse and packing the parts into a trunk to conceal the crime. They were in a great hurry because of their fear of detection by the police.* When the patient awoke from the dream she told her mother she felt ill and she did not go to her employment. She wanted to remain in her room, was fearful of noises, became depressed and increasingly agitated, spoke of suicide and was admitted to the hospital forty-eight hours later. The clinical picture was agitated depression. She said "it all began with that terrible dream." The girl who was murdered in the dream was one of whom the patient had been fond but whom she began to hate when her mother manifested a preference for her over the patient. The history disclosed that these recent events had activated her infantile situation with her mother and her younger sister. Her hatred in this situation had been repressed, and when a similar rivalry again appeared, the dream and the psychosis were the last means of attempting a solution of this problem which had been activated some time before.[14]

As for schizophrenia, John Frosch presents several cases, among them this one where an archetypal dream is involved in a recurrence of delusions:

> At the beginning of her illness, a psychotic patient expressed some end-of-the-world ideas as well as delusions of persecution. In the course of her illness, these recurred in florid form, and as she improved eventually disappeared. Sometime afterward, following a whole series of disturbing events with a beginning resurgence of anxiety, withdrawal, and agitated behavior, she reported the following dream:
> *There is a beautiful tree with lovely golden leaves.* (The patient as well as her mother had blonde hair.) *The bark begins to peel off this tree and the tree begins to rot inside and gradually the earth begins to seep up into the tree, the branches, and the leaves. The leaves turn brown and the tree begins to pulsate and throb and it turns into the beating of waves and water and the waves have sharp spikes.*
> It was immediately after this that the patient had a recurrence of her psychosis in which world destruction delusions were prominent. . . . [E]go disintegration or world-destruction dreams . . . should be evaluated within the framework of the existing psychic state. For instance, they may occur in connection with physical illness, fevers, and many other similar conditions.[15]

In keeping with Frosch's concluding observation, note that this "end-of-the-world" variant—rot in the tree of life—is not only typical of the dire imagery often associated with schizophrenia, but is reminiscent as well of the 'aporetic', no-way-out dreams sometimes associated with critical physical illnesses (ch. 8, p. 270). Also, recall that fundamental personality reorganization can occasion similar dreams.

Henry Seidenberg writes about a dream of death which preceded a psychotic breakdown. He suggests that a dream of watching oneself dying or lying dead is less alarming than one where the dream-ego experiences itself dying without any distancing. The example: "*I am in an auto crash. I feel myself dying.* Then I awoke."[16]

A variant of violent ego-destruction dreams occasionally mentioned in relation to schizophrenic symptoms is that where the dream-ego ends up irreparably splattered or exploded in pieces. Levitan proposes that such dreams may involve unconscious "re-enactment" of an actual trauma in the dreamer's recent or remote life history, if the following circumstances existed: the event happened without complete awareness, that is, while the ego was unprepared to assimilate it (e.g., during infancy, seizure, anesthesia); but the event registered a fear of imminent death in the dreamer's memory. Though this configuration presumably does not account for all dreams with this motif, Levitan's cases are intriguing. For example:

> Mrs. M. was a 30-year-old woman being treated for frigidity and associated marital problems at the time she reported the following dream:
>
> *I see a group of Catholic boys coming towards me with dynamite. I am apprehensive ... they throw the dynamite at me, and it explodes. I disintegrate into a thousand pieces.*
>
> She awoke the morning after this dream with symptoms of depersonalization including a persistent feeling of dreaminess and a sense as if the world were not real.
>
> She associated to this dream an abortion under general anaesthesia which she had undergone some 10 years earlier. She remembered nothing of the experience of the operation after the anaesthetic mask was placed on her face. . . .
>
> . . . [A] long period of time elapsed between the occurrence of the presumed original traumatic event and its reappearance in the dream. Mrs. M.'s frigidity had begun following the abortion about which she felt extremely guilty. On the day prior to the dream, her husband had inflicted a fresh trauma upon her when he became especially abusive about the abortion which had occurred before their marriage. Her associations to the dream indicated that the death by explosion epitomized for her the punishment she felt she deserved. She is a devout Catholic and placed special emphasis on the fact that the boys in the dream who threw the dynamite were Catholic.[17]

In another of Levitan's cases, depersonalization came about as a consequence of repression of unbearable emotion. The near-death of a 52-year-old
woman's son fifteen years earlier had set off a train of recurring mental illnesses. Now the original trauma threatened to represent itself in a dream,
but the dream interrupted the intolerable emotion with an image in its way
as drastic as a bomb explosion:

> *I am with Pete's old girl friend and a strange man. I said in a cold voice with-
> out emotion, "Pete is dead." They were upset.—Then I am*
>
> *looking through a stack of pictures. At the last picture of Pete I feel overwhelming
> grief. . . . The worst feeling I've ever had.—Then suddenly, clump!*
>
> *Something like a steel case falls over me or over my heart and there is no more
> grief and no more feeling.*

For five days after the dream she was apathetic and manifested many symptoms
of depersonalization including inability to feel her hands, a sense of "not being
with it," and a deep fatigue.[18]

A usual feature of severe schizophrenia is depersonalization of the body-
image, in association with delusions. Leveton relates a case where on more
than one occasion the same recurrent dream ushered in a delusional state.
Each time this happened, the dreamer, a 26-year-old man, progressed into
confusion of waking and dreaming as the content of his dream invaded waking. In contrast to the repression of feelings accomplished within the dream
by the dropping of a steel barrier in Levitan's case, Leveton understands the
following dreams to involve a failure of repression:

> "I seem to be more nervous today. For the past three nights I've had the
> same dream over and over again. The one with *the devil trying to take over my
> body*. It's the same one I had before I got sick the last time.
>
> "So far the mental illness is just in my dreams, but it's getting more real and
> I've been relieved to wake up and find out that I've been dreaming.
>
> "The dreams get more and more real. I begin to feel pain in my dreams, my
> body is right there. Then the mental illness just takes me right over. The first
> thing I notice is that I'm having trouble waking up from my dreams, my body
> will still hurt where the devils poke me. Then all of a sudden, one night I just
> lose all track of time and I can't tell night from day because the dream just goes
> on all the time. I can't wake up at all. Sleeping or waking, it's all the same. . . .
>
> "As I get better each time, there are periods without dreams and I know that
> I'm awake and that there is a difference between day and night. Finally all the
> mental illness is in the dream only."

The patient again complained of increasing tension and fears of going to
sleep. He was more disturbed in the morning, and within two days was again

It is clear that we cannot say that dreams "caused" the psychosis in this patient. Disturbed sleep and disturbing dreams were the reflections, rather than the cause, of the eventual development of a psychosis. However, as a shift in the balance between the force of the drives and repression occurred, sleep became a dangerous time of relaxation of repressive forces. . . .[19]

Of the foregoing cases, some illustrate the first onset of a psychosis, and others concern episodes of relapse. In some, the dream imagery becomes directly involved in the symptom, while in others the connection is more indirect. In no case can the dream be said to "cause" the insanity in the sense that if you have such-and-such a dream, it makes you go crazy; but dreams do sometimes appear to have an instrumental function in the psychological sequence leading to psychosis. The examples given above seem variously to entail a failure to manage severe conflict, a violent repression of feelings, and/or an involvement of the dream with loss of adaptive ego controls.

One thing all of the examples given thus far definitely have in common is that in all, the dream in question closely precedes the onset of the symptom. There are other cases where more time elapses between the dream and the symptom said to be related to the dream, as in a psychotic relapse mentioned by Bernard Shulman:

> A patient dreamt that *he fell off a cliff and drifted slowly to the bottom without hurting himself. He then got to his feet and walked through a door in the side of the cliff. The door closed after him* and the dream ended. A week later he became psychotic.[20]

One can conjecture that this dream constituted a preliminary giving-in to illness, i.e., that it was entailed in the disease process in the manner of earlier examples. One can also see here a compensatory warning which eventually failed in effect. The theoretical possibilities are many. The dream may simply have mirrored the underlying condition. Such a reading would agree with the opinion of Boss in his discussion of dreams of this type, which he terms *endoscopic*, meaning that some part of the mind is able to look inside, observe the true psychological state, and epitomize it in a dream. (Dreams of this sort have also been called *self-state* dreams.*) After emphasizing that

---

* Self-state dreams feature in self psychology, Heinz Kohut's contribution to psychoanalytic theory (*The Analysis of the Self*, New York: International Universities, 1971; *The Restoration of the Self*, New York: International Universities, 1977; *How Does Analysis Cure?* Chicago: University of Chicago, 1984; for a summary, see H. Kohut & E. S. Wolf 1978). Self psychology considers that a person is at least as likely to suffer "deficit" and "arrest" as "conflict" and "repression." It gives "precedence to . . . preoedipal events," and it emphasizes environmental and cultural factors (A. M. Cooper 1983, p. 5). The state of the self is described in terms of "cohesion" (or "coherence"), of "vitality" (or "vigour"), and of "harmony" (Kohut & Wolf, op. cit., p. 414). Kohut posited a "bi-

"endoscopic dreams are by no means confined to schizophrenics," Boss presents several interesting examples. His position is not that such dreams are involved in the generation of psychosis, but that they are valuable prognostic aids:

[W]e offer the case of a young man, just before his final examinations, who intended to emigrate to America. He dreams, *he is already on his voyage to America; but the ship springs a leak, sinks, and he feels the water close above him. He begins to lose consciousness* in the dream. *He can still see a few air bubbles rise from his mouth, and he knows that he has died.* Here ends the dream, but it left a profound impression on him. Four weeks later the patient had to be hospitalized because of a catatonic twilight condition.

The following dreams are even more explicit. A female patient *observed an eclipse of the sun* in her dream. *There was a weak twilight everywhere. Next she saw herself in the midst of a crowded street. A great number of people and cars were going backwards and towards her. Every time they came quite close to her, they avoided her and rushed past the patient with ever increasing rapidity. She became dizzy and fainted. Suddenly she found herself in a homely peasant room in which a petroleum lamp spread a warm light.* Fourteen days after this impressive dream the patient went through a mild, two day long, schizophrenic disorien-

---

polar self," with "self-assertive ambitions" at one end, "attained ideals and values" at the other, and a "tension-arc" of basic talents and skills between them (R. S. Wallerstein 1983, pp. 20 and 38). "He later (1984) conceived of a tripolar self, adding the intermediate area of talents and skills to the already existing poles" (S. Sand & R. Levin 1992, p. 181). Corresponding respectively to these three poles are the basic needs of the self: *mirroring* (from "those who respond and confirm the child's innate sense of vigour, greatness, and perfection"); *idealizing* (from "those to whom the child can look up and with whom he can merge as an image of calmness, infallibility and omnipotence") (Kohut & Wolf, op. cit., p. 414); and *twinship* (from those "available for the reassuring experience of essential alikeness") (Kohut, p. 193, 1984, quoted by Sand & Levin, op. cit., p. 189).

The primary function of self-state dreams is "tension regulation" (P. H. Ornstein 1987, p. 101). Ornstein says that "Kohut did not offer us a comprehensive dream theory of his own. . ." (p. 103). But he did describe the self-state dream, which gives "direct representation of structures and endopsychic perceptions in the manifest dream" (J. W. Slap & E. E. Trunnell 1987, p. 257). These life-analog type dreams do not yield profitably to free association, because they are portrayals of an overall state (S. Eisenstein 1980, p. 325).

Self-state dreams are conspicuous in persons with narcissistic personality disorder. Kohut views narcissism as developmentally normal, but also as the prototypical pathology of our culture (Wallerstein, op. cit., pp. 43 and 21). This situation perhaps explains the fact that some self psychologists insist that not all dreams are self-state dreams, saying that most dreams are about conflict or combine self-state and conflictual dimensions (P. Tolpin 1983, p. 255), while others say that "the dream always presents various aspects of the self-experience to the dreamer's attention. . . . In this broader sense, then, all dreams are 'self-state' dreams. . ." (Ornstein, op. cit., pp. 101 and 103). Probably the more clearcut instances occur near the edge of serious disorder (Eisenstein, op. cit., p. 325), as an adaptive reaction "to a disturbing change in the condition of the self—manic overstimulation, or a seriously depressive drop in self-esteem, or to the threat of the dissolution of the self" (Kohut, *The Restoration of the Self*, quoted by S. L. Warner 1987, p. 102). "The very act of portraying these

tation. However, she was able to pull herself together, and became possibly somewhat more relaxed, affectively, than she had been before, just as she anticipated in her dream. Four years later the same female patient dreamt for several nights in a row, that *a little black cat was swimming in a large lake. The cat struggled to keep from drowning, but sank nonetheless.* The patient knew very well that the cat was herself. One day, this dream series stopped, and shortly thereafter the patient sank into a catatonia which lasted several weeks.

Another patient, who reported this dream as the most impressive one of her whole life, dreamt that *she was slowly sinking to the bottom of the ocean. She fell in the middle of a large heap of grinning skulls. Her body disintegrated, and suddenly she knew that she had turned into one of these death-heads. For hours and hours, bubbles would rise out of this skull. Meanwhile she knew long in advance that she would be dead when the last bubble was rising. Time moved with painful slowness in the dream, until finally the last bubble had risen and the dreamer died.* One month after this dream the patient entered a schizophrenia for which there is no hope of any remission. . . .[21]

In each of these dreams, the looming illness is portrayed symbolically—in the three dreams with dire clinical outcomes, the symbol is death by drowning, which is certainly aporetic (no way out). The dreamer drowns in her/his own unconscious, or own illness. There also occur less usual dreams where the symptom is portrayed and/or referred to literally (as happens occasionally with physical illness: ch. 8, p. 273ff.). John Mack speaks of a dreamer who, "before the onset of his second illness [psychosis], dreamed that *his previous illness had returned*. . . ."[22]

Boss's cases involve lapses up to a month from dream to illness, during which time the disease process was presumably advancing. Obviously, the longer the delay, the more difficult it becomes to conceive of any dynamic connection. The connection becomes all the more problematical, though not inconceivable, when the delay lasts years. Heinz Lehmann speaks of "premonitory and 'prophetic' dreams which foreshadow the development of a destructive mental illness years before the illness becomes evident. Boss gives a number of examples of patients who developed acute schizophrenia in their twenties but who had had, since their seventh or eighth year of life, recur-

---

vicissitudes in the dream constitutes at attempt to deal with the psychological danger by covering frightening nameless processes with nameable visual imagery" (Kohut, ibid., quoted by Eisenstein, op. cit., p. 325). The self-state dream restores self-esteem (J. L. Fosshage 1987b, p. 30) and "maintain[s] a continuity or cohesiveness of one's sense of self" (R. Greenberg 1987a, pp. 55-6). So a self-state dream is "simultaneously a portrayal of an internal loss of balance as well as an effort to reestablish this lost balance" (Ornstein, op. cit., p. 91).

H. Fiss (1986) discusses sleep lab findings about dreaming "in terms of its contribution to the development, maintenance, and restoration of the self."

ring dreams of *the world turning into stone* or *into skeletons* or *being engulf-ed by horrifying emptiness.*"[23]

Further, we can look at a case where the psychosis foreshadowed in the dream never actually developed, and therefore we only have the interpreter's judgment that the dream did in fact portend such an outcome. The case is Jung's, and is interesting on several grounds. It shows Jung maneuvering to avert the onset of a potential psychosis. It also demonstrates once again that for Jung, the raising of the unconscious to consciousness was not a panacea, nor was the dream a silver bullet. And lastly, the dream itself is, in Jung's word, "impressive."

Jung told the story of a person of "emphatic normality," a physician who came to Jung for training as an analyst. When informed that he must, there-fore, undergo an analysis himself, the man claimed to have no psychological problems. He also said he had no dreams, but two weeks into the analysis, he produced one which symbolically represented his arrival in Zurich to un-dertake the training:

He dreamt that *he was traveling by railroad. The train had a two-hour stop in a certain city. Since he did not know the city and wanted to see something of it, he set out toward the city center. There he found a medieval building, probably the town hall, and went into it. He wandered down long corridors and came upon handsome rooms, their walls lined with old paintings and fine tapestries. Precious old objects stood about. Suddenly he saw that it had grown darker, and the sun had set. He thought, I must get back to the railroad station. At this moment he discovered that he was lost, and no longer knew where the exit was. He started in alarm, and simultaneously realized that he had not met a single person in this building. He began to feel uneasy, and quickened his pace, hoping to run into someone. But he met no one. Then he came to a large door, and thought with re-lief: That is the exit. He opened the door and discovered that he had stumbled upon a gigantic room. It was so huge and dark that he could not even see the op-posite wall. Profoundly alarmed, the dreamer ran across the great, empty room, hoping to find the exit on the other side. Then he saw—precisely in the middle of the room—something white on the floor. As he approached he discovered that it was an idiot child of about two years old. It was sitting on a chamber pot and had smeared itself with feces.* At that moment he awoke with a cry, in a state of panic.

I knew all I needed to know—here was a latent psychosis! I must say I sweat-ed as I tried to lead him out of that dream. I had to represent it to him as some-thing quite innocuous, and gloss over all the perilous details. . . .

. . . I had caught him in the nick of time, for the latent psychosis was within a hair's breadth of breaking out and becoming manifest. This had to be prevent-ed. Finally, with the aid of one of his other dreams, I succeeded in finding an acceptable pretext for ending the training analysis. We were both of us very glad to stop. I had not informed him of my diagnosis, but he had probably become aware that he was on the verge of a fatal panic, for he had a dream in which *he was being pursued by a dangerous maniac*. Immediately afterward he returned home. He never again stirred up the unconscious. His emphatic normality reflected a personality which would not have been developed but simply shattered by a confrontation with the unconscious. These latent psychoses are the 'bêtes noires' of psychotherapists, since they are often very difficult to recognize.[24]

This dream did not induce a psychosis, but would have helped to do so if the dreamer had been pushed further in the direction the dream was tending. Edward Whitmont & Sylvia Perera comment: "As Jung remarked, the idiot child smeared with feces is not, as such, pathognomic. It could represent a two-year-old partial personality of the dreamer that needs integration. But the child's placement in the center of a gloomy, huge, uninhabited space at the center of the town, the uncanny atmosphere and the dream-ego's dramatic realization of the sun's setting and his own lostness and loneliness . . . justify Jung's assumption of a latent psychosis. . . . Always, in the face of such material, the therapist is faced with clinical decisions about the client's ability to bear the pain and conflict necessary for analytic work. If the ego is too fearful, rigid, brittle, chaotic, fused, unboundaried, it may not be able to undertake a dialogue with the unconscious without somatizing or cracking into psychosis."[25]

Robert Friedman, commenting on the same dream, adds that the "unmediated opposition to consciousness" conveyed by the central image warns of "the impossibility of any deep collaborative exploration":

> The same diagnostic principle applies to the following case of a teenage girl whom I briefly saw one summer to prepare her for out-of-town college. She presented as overtly adult, but felt stupid, and was almost morbidly shy—all traits congruent with her family and Catholic school upbringing. She responded quickly to a supportive approach, but my naive suggestion to speak up more assertively to her father elicited a strange dream [one of a sequence of dreams]: . . . *We had a puppy, a rabbit, and a cat. When my mother went out I killed them by twisting their necks. I thought nothing of it, and when my mother returned I changed back to my normal self.* With some prompting the patient could provide a number of personal associations, but it is the sudden eruption into the manifest dream of violent, sadistic imagery, all absolutely ego-alien, which makes the diagnosis now look so ominous. The patient then had an even more dire dream: *The white of my eye starts to turn to jelly. I think I'll stay this way forever.* . . . [This young woman was eventually] hospitalized for several years in a state of delusional melancholia.[26]

Suicide Attempts Following Dreams

David Raphling asked survivors of suicide attempts to tell him the dreams which preceded their attempts. He compares this sample with dreams from persons in acute psychiatric crisis, equally distressed but not suicidal. The comparison points to two content themes as being especially prevalent in the dreams of presuicidals. One is "*violence* or *destruction*":

This was denoted by references to actual or threatened killing, dying or being killed in addition to actual or threatened injury or to mutilation of men or animals. . . .
. . . *There was this man who was insane who was trying to kill me. Every place I ran he was trapping me.*

The example immediately prompts the caveat that *no* dream, taken out of context, should be viewed as a sure indicator of imminent suicide or of anything else. We just saw Jung make a different reading of a matching dream ("Pursued by dangerous maniac"), and no doubt many readers who are neither presuicidal nor prepsychotic have dreamt about insane killers. At the same time, it is worthwhile to know that the general theme of violence or destruction crops up before suicide attempts.

Raphling's other theme overlaps the first: "explicit references to *actual or threatened death, or dead persons.*" One of the examples contains *a violent death by drowning which the dream-ego watches helplessly.* But the other, a dream about a person really dead, is of quite a different quality:

I dreamt of *my aunt. I seen her standing right there looking at me with that smile and saying like she always did, "Hello sweets, you're my sweetheart, you're my special girl." She was like a mother to me. I was crying in the dream. I felt that she had come back, that she hadn't died.*[27]

Raphling stipulates "explicit references" to death or the dead, but death may also appear symbolized in presuicidal dreams, as in a dream Friedman uses to illustrate presuicidal idealization of death:

There is one type of suicide patient whose final dreams may actually represent death in highly idealized images: In these cases the patient has reached a point of absolute pessimism and then resigned himself to suicide as a longed-for solution. Death may now assume the unconscious meaning of reunion or merger with loved ones, with possible implications of rebirth, or romantic overtones.
. . . [A] woman treated by Herbert Hendin . . . attempted suicide after many unhappy love affairs by jumping under a subway train. She dreamed "*She was in a tunnel walking to the light at the end. When she got there she saw a couple standing over a manger.*" Her associations were to the birth process, the Holy

in a tunnel walking to the light at the end. When she got there she saw a couple standing over a manger." Her associations were to the birth process, the Holy Manger, and to a happy reunion with her father who had actually deserted the family in her adolescence.[28]

Robert Litman's 1980 chapter on the subject of presuicidal dreams agrees that the themes noticed by Raphling often present themselves prior to suicide attempts. Litman properly emphasizes that violence, destruction, death, and dead people usually signal, not suicide, but an orientation toward change. However, one should be especially alert, he advises, for cues that death is viewed as an attractive alternative, as in the dream just quoted. Also, death and violence dreams become more concerning as they increase in frequency and intensity, and the same can be said when dream feeling tone becomes increasingly depressed or anxious, or when "the expressed attitude [is] one of giving up or surrendering. . . ."[29]

Litman adds several additional presuicidal themes. One, "being trapped and struggling unsuccessfully,"[30] fits Raphling's example of the insane killer —"*Every place I ran he was trapping me.*" Friedman also lists "extreme entrapment," adding "estrangement from life, and final giving up."[31] Another theme of Litman's is leave-taking: "When the suicide plan has matured, the final decision is often signalled by peaceful dreams of taking leave."[32]

A presuicidal dream discussed years earlier by Emil Gutheil, dreamt the night preceding a serious attempt, appears to blend certain of these themes: dead people, being trapped, surrender, and peaceful leave-taking:

[The dreamer] is a forty-nine-year-old, unmarried woman suffering from menopausal depression.

. . . *With a childhood friend, Mary, now dead, I make a trip to the mountains. It is winter. We are walking together for some time. The landscape is in snow and ice. For some reason our ways separate. She stops while I walk on. But soon I see, there is nothing ahead.* (The patient reported this dream in German. She said '*Es geht nicht weiter. . . .*' This sentence can be translated also as '*It's no use. . . .*') *I must go back. The road is very difficult. I can't go on. . . . Suddenly, I see on the other side of a ravine something like a peaceful summer landscape. I grow weaker and weaker. I hold on to my pointed cane which I am using as a crutch, but then I let myself go . . .* and awaken. . . .

. . . [She] always secretly envied her friend [Mary] for her ability to enjoy life without scruples. Entering the change of life she is now reminded in a most definite manner that her own past life was but a series of missed opportunities and unfulfilled hopes. . . .

. . . [W]e must accept the proposition that dreams are indeed capable of easing the individual into accepting death as a solution.[33]

ing act, but only in a symbolic way: the woman subsequently took poison and cut her wrists. But "under certain circumstances . . . the manifest content of the dream expresses what the person has in mind with very little disguise." This alternative again calls to mind Meredith Sabini's categories of dreams about physical illness, the symbolic, and the literal. Litman gives an example of the literal in connection with suicide:

> An eighteen-year-old woman attempted suicide by driving her car over a cliff. The car was totally wrecked and she escaped with bruises, black eyes, and a broken shoulder. She said that the car wreck was deliberate. "I dreamed the night before that *I drove the car over that particular cliff and it killed me.*" She felt that she could no longer tolerate living. . . .[34]

It should be emphasized again that dream literalness is a fairly commonplace option to symbolization. Literalness is not confined to circumstances of pathology, much less to catagogic trends. Compare another preparatory dream, this one from Doryann Lebe:

> [An] eleven-year-old boy worried because he did not understand a math concept and feared he would get behind in school. He dreamed *he understood the math and could do all his work perfectly.* The next day, he surprised himself in school by knowing all his math and by not being nervous.[35]

Finally on presuicidal dreams, an observation has been made about mental patients which is comparable to Robert Smith's observation about heart patients (ch. 8, p. 272). The worst clinical outcomes for the latter tend to follow absence of any recent dream recall. Similarly, T. Detre et al. found that "a statement by the patient that he had ceased to dream was positively correlated with attempts at suicide."[36]

Dream Recall as Dream Continuation

About 15% of us say we never recall dreams. About 5% remember more than one a night. On average, we recall two or three a week.[37] It used to be widely held, under the influence of Freud, that normal amnesia for dreams is due to repression, and that the same repressive forces selectively distort the remembered dream, this being the last stage of disguise.[38] Persons who forget their dreams have been thought to be repression-prone, or to be inhibited, conformist, overly imperturbable, overly rational, etc.[39]

It is now understood that many other factors bear on dream recall. David Koulack sums up his review of the literature: "If repression does indeed take place it is only one of many factors making dream recall under normal circumstances an extremely elusive process."[40]

Foremost among the other factors is probably that the *states* of dreaming and waking are alien to each other, therefore difficult to transit with continuity. Freud himself explicitly rejected[41] this venerable observation.[42] Dreams have been considered variously as too primitive, too advanced, or simply as too different, cognitively and neurophysiologically, easily to be assimilated to waking.[43] The difference of states bears on the facts that recall is frustrated by leaving the sleep state gradually instead of abruptly,[44] and/or by letting the mind drift away from the dream even briefly,[45] as most of us only too well know. One reason the deaf are good recallers may be that ambient sounds do not distract them.[46]

High dream recall correlates positively with good visual recall. Good recall for numbers also correlates with good dream recall—but not being good at math, oddly enough, which correlates with low dream recall.[47] Good verbal recall does not correlate with high dream recall, either.

Dream recall is aided by the memorability of one's dreams, sometimes called "salience"[48]—their interest, good organization, vividness, and intensity. But too much intensity dampens recall.[49]*

Those whose sleep contains a high proportion of REM-time are favored.[50] Those who tend to awaken from NREM instead of REM are disfavored.[51]

Motivation is a factor in dream recall, but not one influential enough to account for individual differences. Despite assertions by many dreamworkers (ch. 13, p. 415n), striving to become a better recaller will not necessarily succeed.[52] One study finds little correlation between attitude about dreams and spontaneous rate of dream recall.[53]

Circumstantially, "life stress" enhances recall.[54] That it does so in both high and low recallers is construed by David Cohen as a refutation of the repression hypothesis. He reasons that if people are regularly low recallers because they employ the defense of repression, stress should cause them to recall even less well, and not better.[55]

Miscellaneous factors said to correlate with high recall include high IQ, introversion, hypnotizability,[56] and "more organized and structured" brain wave activity.[57] Miscellaneous factors disfavoring recall range from not being oriented toward imagery[58] to being left-handed.[59]

But all told, personality factors—being a repressor among them—turn out not to account for much of the individual differences found in recall habits.[60] Under the former way of thinking, every manifestation of memory surround-

---

* Concerning intensity, Langs (1988, p. 45) raises the idea that the function of the Freudian disguise mechanisms is not actually to disguise, but to modulate the intensity of painful contents, bringing them within the range of emotional tolerability.

ing dreams became interpretable. Bertram Lewin stated in 1946 that "forgetting or remembering a dream belongs to the dream content itself, and may be analysed as a manifest dream element."[61] Taken as universal, this rule is no longer tenable.

Nevertheless, forgetting due to repression does, no doubt, account for a certain amount of dream amnesia, as demonstrated in a recent experiment by Deirdre Barrett. She had her subjects perform an extraneous task before recording their dreams in the morning. Recall by "repressors" deteriorated more than that of others, implying some interaction between effects of personality and of state-specificity.[62] Moreover, clinicians observe a connection between dream amnesia and resistance to treatment.[63] In Barrett's opinion, repression less affects gross recall than recall for significant details.

The former way of thinking about dream recall had another aspect: that how and when a dream is *remembered*—including a dreamer's *recall style**
—also belongs to the interpretable dream content. And once again, while the rule should not be invoked indiscriminately, it also does point to something genuine. Following are several examples of these phenomena, where either forgetting or remembering a dream acts as a sort of extension of the dream itself into waking. Here is one of Freud's examples:

> A young man had a very clear dream which reminded him of some phantasies of his boyhood that had remained conscious. He dreamt that *it was evening and that he was in a hotel at a summer resort. He mistook the number of his room and went into one in which an elderly lady and her two daughters were undressing and going to bed.* He proceeded: *"Here there are some gaps in the dream; there's something missing. Finally there was a man in the room who tried to throw me out, and I had to have a struggle with him."* He made vain endeavors to recall the gist and drift of the boyish phantasy to which the dream was evidently alluding; until at last the truth emerged that what he was in search of was already in his possession in his remark about the obscure part of the dream. The "gaps" were the genital apertures of the women who were going to bed; and "there's something missing" described the principal feature of the female genitalia. When he was young he had had a consuming curiosity to see a woman's gen-

---

* Leon Altman (1969) has written about recall style as a reflection of character traits and dominant defenses. *Compartmentalizers*, he maintains, tend to bring a "fragment of a dream" to therapy. *People who leave things unfinished* bring a "smattering of dreams." *Those who strip things of meaning* say, "I can't make anything of it. . ." (p. 37). *Narcissistic personalities* try to charm with the dream. They want admiration for it, but not to deal with it. *Passive personalities* give the dream like a gift to the analyst and wait for her/him to do the work. *Obsessives* produce excessive associations to isolated fragments, until the dream itself is lost sight of (p. 72). *Compulsives* present "[i]nterminable dreams" comparable to compulsive behaviors which "prevent eruptions of disturbing thoughts and feelings" (p. 69).

itals and had been inclined to hold to the infantile sexual theory according to which women have male organs.[64]

From Mark Kanzer:

[T]he patient dreamed *something about his girl friend*—he could recall no other details—and also had the thought, "I must tell this to the analyst." In its more positive form, this meant, "I must tell the analyst that I have given up my dreams about my girl friend." Freud, in a similar way, described the forgetting of a name in a dream as meaning "I should not dream of that."[65]

And from Werner Wolff, an apparently lucid dream:

Sometimes a dreamer has recurrent dreams but cannot remember them. "I have a recurrent dream in which *I am always surprised to find myself dreaming* when I am dreaming it, but when I wake up I never can remember what it is." This is the theme of the lost memory itself, which some dreamers have, the dream of amnesia of an important period in life.[66]

One last point about dream recall as dream continuation. Many interpreters consider that associations—those that arise by Freud's method of free association or by any other means—are in effect continuations of the dream, "dream residues," in Watkins's phrase. We are told to "treat everything that surrounds the reported dream,"[67] feelings as well as concepts and images,[68] as associations having "a symbolical value"[69] which should be interpreted as part of the dream.

A dream mentioned by Wilhelm Stekel in another connection provides a graphic example of an association which continues the dream:

A miner, aged 39, suffering from anxiety states, opens the treatment with a simple dream. . . .

"*I go to see the film* **Africa Speaks.** *I see savage lions and tigers.* Awaking with a dull sense of uneasiness, I have palpitation and an attack of anxiety."

He actually saw the film during the day before the night on which he dreamed this dream. One scene in it distressed him greatly. A negro was torn to pieces by a lion, and he wondered whether the man had not been deliberately exposed to danger, in order to get an interesting picture.

. . . Wild beasts might symbolize his own passions, his sadistic trends. . . .

But what is signified by the association that the negro was deliberately exposed to danger? . . . Three weeks later, in the course of the analysis, he related something that had happened to him ten years before. In the mine his task was to release a truck down an incline upon receipt of a signal that the line was clear. The signal was passed along by relays, a youngster within call of him being the last transmitter. This boy thought it a fine joke, from time to time, to give the signal "on his own," and then to revoke it before the truck was released, shouting "Fooled again!" But he played this trick once too often, for the miner released the truck in response to a false signal, and the practical joker was run over and killed. Often the miner was troubled by self-reproach, thinking he had perhaps released the truck deliberately in response to what he knew to be a false signal, wishing to pay the boy out. Soon after the disaster, he began to suffer from anxiety states—without realizing there was any connection between his self-incrimination and the illness. The negro who was torn to pieces by the lion [the association] was an image of or substitute for the boy lacerated by the truck.[70]

Acting Out

The term 'acting out' refers to impulsive outbursts of behavior. It may refer to a healthy release of something previously inhibited. But usually it relates to inappropriate actions dictated by unconscious patterns. The term often implies that the actor forces other people unwittingly to play roles assigned for them by the actor's complex. It points as well to a failure to contain energy which would better be held inside.

In a paper on "Dreams and Acting Out," León Grinberg considers acting out to be a functional alternative to dreaming: if pent-up energies and fantasies do not get "evacuated" by a dream when they need to, they get acted out instead. Acting out is "a dream that could not be dreamed."[71]

But Lewin, with a different take on the matter, considered whether psychotic and neurotic manifestations might not be replays in waking of actual dreams[72]—dreams that could not stop. Lewin's is the general sense in which acting out will be understood in relation to dreams in this section.

Frosch relates a patent and extreme example, that of a psychotic woman who went out and became a prostitute for two weeks after dreaming of *becoming a prostitute*.[73] But in fact mild and even trivial forms of acting out of dreams may occur quite often, and probably most often without our realizing the connections, or even remembering the influential dreams. The examples to follow obviously have to involve remembered dreams. They also involve neurotics in therapy, only because the reports on this phenomenon have been written by therapists who observed it in their patients. But I feel sure that many people sensitive to their dream lives have noticed themselves acting out a dream.

In examples published by Richard Sterba in 1946, acting out of a dream occurs in the course of a therapy session, prior to the telling of the dream. With that sequence of events, said Sterba, "acting out functions as a preceding dream association":

A patient who lived near my office came to the hour without the spectacles he always wears. He stated he forgot to take them when he left home and that he did not bother to go back for them since he was a little late and could walk the short distance without spectacles. He had never before forgotten his spectacles during two years of analysis. It then occurred to him that he had had a dream the preceding night. He dreamed that *he started an argument with another man, and before getting into a fist fight he was taking off his spectacles in order to prevent his eyes from being injured by glass particles if the man should strike back.* Acting out in the form of forgetting the glasses and the dream explain each other to a great extent. The other man in the dream is the analyst, and the aggression of the dream is acted out at least to the extent of coming to the appointment without them. This symptomatic behavior is closely associated with the dream, making possible an interpretation of the dream before further associations are produced.[74]

Whitmont & Perera also relate a clinical episode where the acting out is prelude to the relevant dream report:

[A] relatively new analysand . . . walked into her therapist's office without shutting the door to the waiting room behind her, as she had done previously. This time she left it wide ajar. As the session developed, she raised the problem of her 'fear of success' and its effect in always hampering her life and relationships. She then suddenly remembered she had had a 'rather trivial dream':
I am in my childhood room, and the door is wide open.
The connection with the previously noted behavioral event struck the therapist immediately. In discussing the context of the open door of her childhood room, it developed that she was never allowed to close it, for this was taken as a sign of unsociability. To the dreamer, however, leaving the door open felt like the denial of her privacy, and the threat of impingement. She found it impossible to focus on 'doing her own thing.' While eventually she learned to accept the requirement and even developed the habit of leaving doors open behind her, both literally as well as figuratively, she felt nothing could be claimed as her own. . . . Things were always left 'open-ended,' widely ajar. Hence, her projects and thoughts and relationships felt inadequately closed and were prematurely abandoned. The open door, not the fear of success, was the issue. And in this the 'trivial' dream as well as the 'trivial' event in entering the office cooperated in elaborating it, serially and synchronistically.[75]

Nathan Roth, on the other hand, wrote in 1958 about dreams acted out after, not before, being told during a therapy session. He connected acting out in that sequence with the dreamer's resistance to interpreting the dream during the session. Stating the case no doubt too categorically, he said that the patient will leave and act out whatever portions of the dream remained unanalysed due to resistance, barring only acts strongly prohibited by the super-ego, as in post-hypnotic suggestion.[76] This is a painful experience for the person, who "describes it as 'feeling like an automaton', 'being out of control of one's own life', 'sleepwalking', etc." He illustrated:

The patient was a male in his late thirties who had entered psychoanalysis with complaints of not being able to win and hold friends. . . . [His] disorders were the result of his peculiar defenses against his oedipal strivings, which took the form of putting distance between himself and his father and wanting to know nothing about his father's activities lest he reveal an interest in the latter's sexual life. . . . His painful isolation from his father revealed itself in the transference as a lament that he could not promote the friendly relationship with the analyst that he desired. He repeated with his adolescent son the same aloof and cold state of detachment that he had had with his own father. . . . [H]e had the following dream.

He is playing golf with his twin cousins and drives a ball a tremendously long distance, about four hundred yards. As he drives the ball he thinks he is going to have a good season at golf this year and, as he watches the ball in its flight, he thinks so long a drive is impossible and yet there it is. The ball makes straight for the hole but, just before reaching it, hits the frame of a door which stands upright on the green without a door in it. One of the cousins says, "Too bad it hit the doorframe," implying that otherwise the patient would have made a hole in one.

The doorframe was first associated to the fact that the patient's son, who was very worried about his short stature, continually measured his height against the doorframe to see if he was growing taller. In the patient's mind the son's shortness represented the stunting of sexual development which the patient was inflicting on him. The doorframe also referred to the door to the analyst's . . . office, which was troublesome to the patient because every time it opened he was confronted with his feared desire to become friendly with the analyst. . . .

During the course of the session the patient showed great resistance to the analysis of the transference significances of the dream. He became fearful lest he or any member of his family become ill, since he could not feel confident that he could get the aid of a physician, a projection of his unwillingness to take help from the analyst. . . . As the patient talked he gave the analyst the convincing impression that he would strike some part of his body against the doorframe as he left the room at the end of the hour. This did not happen, . . . [but w]hile waiting for the patient at the next session, the analyst heard a loud crash at the closed door. On opening it the analyst found that, in hanging up his coat in the waiting room, the patient had overturned the coat rack and sent it falling against the door of the consulting room. . . . [This] suffices to illustrate an acting out of the manifest content of a dream whose interpretation is prevented by resistance.[77]

John Mack relates another instance of acting out following a dream told and scrutinized in therapy. In his 1970 book on nightmares, the episode illutrates the occurrence of nightmares "at times of important change in the lives of normal adults. . . ." In this instance, the dream almost literally foretells the act, and both provide the same unhappy solution to the dreamer's conflict:

[A] thirty-two-year-old research physician . . . had a severe anxiety dream several days before he was to present a paper before an important scientific meeting. In the dream, *he was sitting in the audience in the hall where his paper was to be given; a speaker on the platform had just finished delivering a paper. He heard the chairman, a senior researcher whose criticism he feared and who he had thought might discuss the paper, announce that the next paper would be his. He felt taken by surprise and realized with horror that he had left his slides and manuscript at home. At first he thought to himself, "Well, I've given this often enough. I can give it off the cuff without my slides." But then the feeling of horror returned, and he thought, "They'll never believe me. I can't prove it. What'll I do? My moment has come, and I've fluffed it."* He woke up in a sweat, with tremendous gratitude and relief that the dream had not been true.

His first association was that without his slides he would have no defense against the belittling, cutting comments of the senior man. In reality, he had especially resented this particular colleague, whom he regarded as a mean person and undeserving of his renowned position. The young doctor was coming into his own as a research scientist, leaving the status of a promising but untried young man to become a respected worker in his own right. This was the direction of his ambition, and he welcomed the shift but he also feared punishment for the hostility that underlay his competitive attitude toward his senior colleague. Familiar oedipal conflicts and castration anxiety could be uncovered with further analysis of the dream, but its most immediate significance derives from the struggle of the young man to master the important changes occurring in regard to his position and status. A postscript to the dream demonstrated vividly the internal conflict over ambitious strivings that this man was experiencing. He remembered to bring the slides to the meeting, but forgot to prepare his statistics, despite a reminder by one of his coworkers.[78]

The following dream is reported by Vamik Volkan & Tajammul Bhatti in a psychoanalytically oriented case study of a transsexual man preparing to undergo sex change surgery. This is the same dreamer whose compensatory dream about the pending change was quoted in chapter 3 (p. 103). The present dream also appears compensatory. We can follow the central symbol (Kirk Douglas = dreamer's penis) from day residue to dream to dream residue, and it appears that the compensatory function of the dream persists into the dream residue:

In spite of the obsessive declarations of these persons that they belong to the opposite sex, their dreams disclose opposing desires and other conflicts that are actively struggling to come into the patient's awareness. . . .

. . . During . . . his interview, he explored his fantasies about what would happen to his penis; he had seen a mud puddle on the way to our meeting, and the notion of the penis being thrown into the puddle crossed his mind. That night he dreamed of *standing outdoors with Kirk Douglas* (the movie actor), *who was wearing a western costume with a cowboy hat.* The dream concerned his struggle to separate himself from the manly actor. *He invited Douglas to accompany him, but met with refusal. "He was bitter about something and couldn't come. I started to walk away but turned after a short distance to see him hitching a ride on a truck. When the truck started off, however, he lost his balance and fell into a mud puddle a few feet in front of me." The patient tried to rescue him.*

The dream was interpreted to the patient as indicating his conflict of ideas about surrendering or not surrendering his penis. . . .

The next day he reported something that had occurred after his interview. He had gone to a movie theater and purchased a ticket, which he managed to lose in his purse. The search for it delayed his entrance to the theater to the point that he became embarrassed and hesitant about going in. We asked what was showing. "Why," he said, "it was 'At the End of the Rainbow,' starring Kirk Douglas." On the conscious level, he had until then been unaware of the connection between his activities and his dream. He had simply seen the movie advertised, and decided, without thinking of Kirk Douglas, to see it. It seems likely that he had seen the advertisement before his dream, and that it constituted day residue within it, along with the mud puddle. Thus he became aware of his investment in his penis; although in actuality he avoided looking at it, he wanted to see it on the screen.[79]

Harvey Kelman in 1975 called the "actualization of the manifest content of dreams" the "day precipitate."[80] He observed in his practice that dreams may precipitate out (become actualized) before, or during, or after a therapy session.

In the following example, the acting out occurred substantially before the session and was unrelated to it. Thus like most occurrences of acting out of a dream in daily experience, the "day precipitate" had nothing to do with therapy per se. It also involved a certain transformation of the dream blueprint, as do most instances of acting out, presumably to accommodate the material presented for symbolization by life. The dream in this case was a simple, rather typical flying dream:

This patient flopped wearily on the couch and exclaimed, "I'm landing with a thud." She went on to explain. "Today I took off from work to get my husband an anniversary present. Because of that I've been rushed all day. The funny thing was that when I was trying to get back to my office I got lost on some streets I thought I knew pretty well. I kept making wrong turns and ending up in wrong places. I got back to work later than I'd planned so I snuck back in so it wouldn't be obvious that I'd left. I hoped my shopping would be quick but it turned out to be quite a chore."

Later in the session she reported her dream of the previous night:

I was a little creature that could levitate. I was levitating around trying to get back somewhere without getting caught. People wanted to catch me because they

*thought I was such an unusual little creature. I had the feeling in the dream of
exerting some kind of effort, some kind of pressure in order to levitate.*

A few substitutions of terms (most notably [of] "take off" for "levitate"—the
patient, after all, "landed" on her analyst's couch) convincingly established the
patient's shopping excursion as the day precipitate of her dream. There was a
striking parallelism of content between the two, e.g. "levitate" = "take off";
"trying to get back"; fear of getting caught; "a chore" = "effort in order to levitate."[81]

In her chapter on this subject from 1980, Lebe suggests that acting out
of dreams can have an anagogic aspect. Such was the case with the compensatory acting out by the transsexual surgery candidate, quoted above. Lebe
notes that if a dream concerns preverbal childhood material, then acting out
may be the dreamer's best or only way to form associations. Alternatively,
the act may more than associate to the dream, it may continue and even resolve the dream.[82] A woman patient of Lebe's dreamt:

*I saw my old thesis professor. I kissed him goodbye and went across the street.
There were two crosswalks. At first, I resented the crosswalks. Then I realized they
were there for my own protection. I crossed in a crosswalk.*

While she related the dream, she ate a peppermint lifesaver and offered me
one. She immediately realized these were the kind her favorite grandfather had
given her as a child. This behavior was preconscious, immediately accessible to
consciousness. She often chewed gum or hard candy in the sessions, but always
sugarless because she would not allow herself the calories. This was the first time
in six years she had even allowed herself the comfort of sugar candies. This behavior immediately made the dream clear to us. She could now protect and give
to herself. She could see a crosswalk as a protection, rather than a limitation. She
had been talking about termination [of therapy] for several months, but had not
felt ready to set a date. Now we both knew she could be her own lifesaver and
protector. Shortly afterwards, we set a termination date. This is an example of
how behavior during the narration of the dream makes the dream immediately
understandable. It is only slightly different from Richard Sterba's (1946) examples where the acting out closely precedes the narration of the dream. However,
in this case, the action was preconscious, then immediately conscious and functioned as a further association and resolution to the dream.[83]

This example illustrates that acting out is not limited to catagogic manifestations, but may contribute to anagogic processes. Lebe makes a point of
emphasizing that the eating of the sugar lifesaver began by being very close
to a conscious symbolic act, and that it quickly became conscious, allowing
the lifesaver to be savored. Here acting out borders on the popular dreamwork technique of deliberately actualizing/concretizing/ritualizing a helpful
dream symbol, in order to enhance its positive impact.

Jung sometimes made pictures of his important dream symbols. The technique has been extended to include dream actualizations in any art form one prefers. Williams for one devotes a section to this subject, discussing poetry, dance, music, etc.[84] And in another section he also discusses "tasks" which can be generated from dreams, in order to root the constructive meaning of the dream in one's waking life. Williams's tasks are mostly of a concrete nature: "A man wrote a letter of reconciliation to a former guide and teacher based on having a reconciling dream. He also included the dream in the letter." One task he mentions is more encompassing:

> An older woman, who dreamed of *being on a train with two suitcases and four suitcases worth of stuff,* cut down on her outer life commitments, more appropriate to her advancing age. She received a new dream in which *she packed only two suitcases of stuff into two suitcases.*[85]

By giving her dream a symbolic continuation,—by repacking her life—, this woman did not so much act *out* the dream as act *on* it.

Of four chapters explaining his four-stage dreamwork technique, Robert Johnson devotes the fourth and longest to "Rituals," or "acting consciously to honor dreams. This step requires a *physical act* that will affirm the message of the dream," an act which may be either "practical" or "symbolic."[86] But later in the book, he observes that the boundary between *acting on* and *acting out* can be a tricky one. Here he is discussing rituals as the last step of "active imagination," Jung's pioneering creative visualization technique (ch. 15, p. 487), rather than dreamwork per se, but the same considerations apply. He warns: "You must not *act out.* . . . Active imagination [or dreamwork] presents opportunities for this, because it draws up so much fantasy material. . . . To incarnate your imagination [or dream], during this fourth step, does not mean to act out your fantasies in a literal way. It means, rather, to take the *essence* that you have distilled from it—the meaning, insight, or basic principle that you have derived from the experience—and incarnate it. . . . You can get into trouble and cause harm if you fail to make this distinction. You must not take this . . . as license to act out your fantasies in their raw, literal form."[87] Here is an example of a ritual act, from Johnson:

> One of the best rituals that I remember was done by a young college student who was analyzing with me. He dreamed that *he was out in a shopping center on Saturday night. He went from place to place, and everything went badly for him. He found "junk food" that made him sick, superficial acquaintanceships, things to buy that left him unsatisfied.*
> . . . His interpretation was that the dream referred to his "Saturday night syndrome." This consisted of "going out with the guys," drinking a lot, eating unhealthy food, getting into adventures and acquaintanceships that felt empty after-

wards. He decided, in light of his dream, that this kind of socializing . . . was not healthy for him. . . .

I asked him: "What did you do about your dream? . . ."

He decided that the essence of the dream was captured in the phrase, "junk food." In his dream he experienced the junk food of human relationship and collectivity. Like junk food, it gave him no nourishment in his inner life, his feeling life, or even in human relatedness. So he created this ritual for his dream:

He went to a hamburger stand and bought the biggest deluxe cheeseburger and an order of fries. He got a shovel and took the junk food to his backyard. He dug a hole and buried the cheeseburger and fries with high, solemn ceremony. . . . He ritually affirmed his intention to give up the superficial and destructive involvements that the dream had called to his attention.

This dream and this ritual . . . cured him of seeking nourishment where it could not be found. . . .[88]

To exit this chapter, here is a case where the dreamer takes an obvious indication from the dream of how to "act it out." From Jill Morris:

I am in a beautiful, wooded area of Germany, with a lovely bicycle path running through it. I find a bicycle and decide to ride it through the forest. Everyone tells me not to do this because I don't know how to ride a bicycle, but I insist on doing it anyway. I hop on the bike and start riding; I'm amazed at how easy it is. I ride along the path and the woods around me are beautiful. I have a great time.

In real life, the dreamer had never learned to ride a bicycle because her parents had been overprotective. . . . There was always an implicit assumption that she would fail at anything she tried. She had this dream a few months before the alimony from her divorce ended; she was embarking on a new career and preparing to support herself for the first time in her life. . . .

When she awoke from the dream, she instantly recognized that the bicycling represented all the instilled assumptions about what she was incapable of doing. . . . She decided to confront her current fears by overcoming this symbolic one: she would learn to ride a bicycle. . . . Overcoming this block gave her renewed confidence in tackling all the other things she'd been told she couldn't do.[89]

□ 11 □

Initial and Termination Dreams

Introduction

As proposed in chapter 7, the foregoing several chapters have mostly focused on catagogic aspects of dreams. That side of things having been given its due, this and the following chapters shift focus to certain anagogic (helpful, progressive, uplifting, salubrious) aspects. Much along those lines has been discussed already, of course, and some of it in detail. For example:

• Information processing theories say dreams do just that, a minimal and largely inconspicuous, if nevertheless inherently constructive function.

• Even reductive Freud recognized that constructive thinking could be advanced in dreams, and he eventually conceded a place in dreams for morality (super-ego). Neo-Freudians have emphasized that dreams can build ego capacity, as well as enlist the creative energies of the 'primary process'.

• Jung taught that dreams inherently promote self-healing. Their compensatory, prospective functions confirm or disfirm our course of life. Dreams encourage, remind, admonish. They connect conscious to unconscious, particular to universal, personal to transpersonal. It is fair to say that Jung established the moral and spiritual foundations of most contemporary schools of dreamwork.

• Other anagogic aspects of dreams already mentioned in one connection or another include the following. Dreams amuse and entertain. They affect mood for the better (or not). They inform us, about our inner selves, about our surroundings, and even about the larger world, if we have 'big' dreams. They work to solve problems. They help resolve conflicts. They provide a means of practice and preparation for waking challenges. They contain medical diagnostic information, and may assist the cure. If appreciated as such, they provide a vehicle of communication and social bonding.

The goodness, the 'wisdom' of the dream is obviously a huge subject, for which the encyclopedia has yet to be written (and this will not be it). Really there are as many ways to divide the field as there are authors who have attempted to do so. For example, Gayle Delaney in a recent book[1] recognizes six types of helpful dreams, defined "according to the kind of insight they offer." Her categories will be seen to overlap some already listed:

(1) "Emphasis dreams" underscore something we already know.

(2) "Reconceptualization dreams" give a fresh turn to an issue we are already aware of.

(3) "Confrontation dreams bring dreamers face-to-face with realities they are unwilling to admit."

(4) "Discovery dreams present dreamers with an entirely new perspective on themselves. . . ." The above four categories are adapted from Delaney's associate Loma Flowers[2] (see p. 4**), and Delaney adds:

(5) "Integration dreams show . . . the incorporation of recently gained insight."

(6) "Solution dreams" offer practical solutions to problems.

This is just one of many categorizations scattered through the literature. As pointed out in the introduction, it is easy to designate different types and sub-types of dreams, in order to highlight particular interests. So, for example (and more or less at random), Joan Windsor speaks of dreams of guidance for the sake of a second person,[3] even dreams of medical diagnosis and prescription for another's sake[4]** (reminiscent of Edgar Cayce[5] and shamanic curative dreaming in general**). Patricia Garfield presents what could

---

* In connection with his belief that psi evolved from mother-infant intra- and post-uterine communication, Montague Ullman (1986b, p. 388) gives an example of an apparently psychic diagnostic dream dreamt by a daughter about her mother. She dreamt of *being inside her mother's womb, and there she sees a mass* of which the mother was, in actuality, still unaware.

** A people whose dreaming for others is especially pronounced is the Yolmo of Nepal, studied by Robert Desjarlais (1991). "If a Yolmo experiences a 'bad dream' foreseeing illness, it may bear consequences for another. If a tree falls in a dream or many men are seen cutting wood, a close relative will die [etc.]. . . The 'bad' dreams visited upon shamans never refer to themselves but to their patients" (p. 216).

From research among Arab Muslims of Morocco, Vincent Crapanzano (1975, p. 149) reports: "Dreams can be indicative of an action that is to be taken not by the dreamer but by someone the dreamer knows." He gives an example, then adds: "There are, in fact, diviners who specialize in dreaming of actions to be taken by those who consult them. Moha, who is said to be married to . . . [a female *jinn*], lives near a river [a common residence of *jinns*] and is consulted by the sick. Men bring him a thread from their turbans; women a thread from their scarves. He places the thread under his right cheek before going to bed and dreams of . . . [the *jinn*], who tells him what is wrong with the patient and what cure to follow."

Humphrey Fisher (1979, p. 230) mentions dreaming for others by specialists as a practice in contemporary Muslim black Africa, where certain clerics perform this service for Muslims and non-Muslims alike. This is also a Yoruba practice, which can be found among those who have adopted Yoruban religion in the U.S. (Songadina Ifatunji, personal communication, 1993).

be labelled a 'permission' dream—*a woman's dead husband gives her permission to fall in love with a new man.*[6] Another might be termed an 'emotional healing' dream—*a sore from poison ivy drains clean.*[7] Stanley Krippner & Joseph Dillard praise "breakthrough dreaming," a term they attribute to Joseph Hart and his associates, and which also happens to be the title of Delaney's 1991 book.[8]* Here is a prototype from Krippner & Dillard of this not uncommon dream type, a breakthrough dream:

> Hannah dreamed *she was driving up a hill in a police car. There was a ceiling at the top of the hill and she felt it marked the limits to how far she could go. Suddenly, her car turned into a rocket ship and blasted through the ceiling into space.* After working on the dream, Hannah concluded that the police car represented her carefully regimented life in which she obeyed all the traditional "rules." The ceiling was a self-imposed limit, but one she could break through if she altered her vehicle, that is, if she broke some of the rules which may no longer have applied to her.[9]

Garfield relates a comparable dream, which she expounds in terms of getting past inhibitions. *The dreamer breaks through a crystal shell.*[10]

Dreams are sometimes discussed in connection with recovery from specific psychological difficulties. Delaney has reported, for example, about a pattern of development in the recovery dreams of incest victims who have repressed all memory of the abuse. The early dreams "portray the current boyfriend or husband as a former boyfriend or former husband who was neglectful and domineering, abusive, or manipulative in the same ways as the current partner"[11]—or else, as the opposite but boring type. As the client acknowledges patterns in her choice of partners, her dreams begin to expose

---

Loudell Snow (1993, pp. 190–1) describes dreaming for others in the medical folk beliefs of U.S. blacks: "The message that someone is pregnant is often delivered via a dream and the pregnancy may be that of oneself, a family member, or friend. Fish are a common theme of these dream-messages. . . . Thirty-nine-year old Jackie Forde laughed as she reported that her mother had called from Mississippi to see if she was pregnant again. 'At my age!' In fact her mother had called *all* her grown daughters with the same question. The older woman had been dreaming of *sitting on her front porch and fishing in a small puddle in the yard.* Her mother would no doubt continue to check with all the female members of the clan until she located a pregnant woman, said Jackie. And that would 'prove' the old belief once again. (East Lansing, Michigan; 1987)."

* Another book about breakthrough dreaming, targeted at critical life turning points (marriage, illness, grief, etc.), is Alan Siegel's *Dreams That Can Change Your Life* (1990), which goes quite a way to substantiating that "there are amazing patterns unique to each major type of turning point" (p. 16). In Jungian terms, archetypal images appear at life's transitions. These images pertain to the particular transformation at hand, but include as well "transformation symbolism" common to all transitions (C. G. Jung, "The concept of the collective unconscious" [1936], CW 9-I, quoted by M. Welman & P. A. Faber 1992, p. 62).

similarities to the abusive family member. Now, and sometimes throughout therapy, dreams occur of pathetic kittens or puppies, and/or of being chased by an armed man. As she begins to retrieve actual memories of the events, dreams point to the negative traits of the abuser, who often had been idealized previously. Finally, dreams deal with the actual incest, but apparently usually in symbolized form only.

Recovery from addiction is another timely topic. Both the *Association for the Study of Dreams Newsletter* and *Dream Network Journal* have devoted issues to the subject.[12] In the former, Reed Morrison offers a Jungian map of typical dreams for persons making a sort of hero's journey of recovery from chemical dependency:

"*The Dark Night*"—the bottoming addict dreams of death and terror.

"*Pandora's Box*"—abstinence brings REM rebound dreaming on "themes of alienation, violence, mutilation, bizarre sexuality, and persecution"[13] (up to 45 days).

"*The Dragon Fight*"—s/he dreams of struggle, symbolizing the internal struggle for control of self (20-90 days).

"*Rebirth*" (30-120 days):

In this stage the dreamer may find an island of relief and calm, what AA calls the "pink cloud" [or honeymoon] phase of recovery. Often s/he establishes a relationship with a "Higher Power". . . . Dreams often describe new living spaces, rescue, ownership, and positive self-identification.

I'm moving my office to a new floor higher up in the building. I'm aware that I'm in the present. I'm being offered drugs but I'm refusing them. I have a new and good feeling. I feel good and don't feel alone anymore.[14]

"*The Descent*"—with dissonant and guilty dreams the addict revisits unresolved issues (60-150 days).

And lastly, "*The Return*"—themes of "Rebirth" recur, together with archetypal symbols of wholeness. Henceforth the recovering addict continues to cycle between "Descent" and "Return."

Linda Schierse Leonard divides the trajectory of addiction and recovery into three phases, "Flight," "Fall," and "Creation." She discerns nineteen archetypes prominent in the dreams of addicts during those phases.[15]

A more ambitious recovery is addressed, among other places, in a recent issue of *Dream Network Journal* devoted largely to dreams for "Healing the Earth." Kelly Bulkley envisions a transformation of values through dreamwork which is to have a planetary synergistic effect ("all life is *interconnected*").[16] The editor, Roberta Ossana, reports on a call for a collective incubation of dreams for the Earth on the winter solstice.[17] Like the dreaming for peace project mentioned in chapter 5 (p. 182), this sort of well-intentioned effort can only do good.

But expectations need to be leavened with the sort of skepticism which Delaney expressed when interviewed in an earlier issue of the same journal: "Dreams will not get us there on time; it's going to take much too long. . . . So I keep hearing these great new things that dreams are going to do for the world, but I don't think we can hope for some global dream response... and when we say that, we make ourselves look very foolish."[18]

There are a couple of major anagogic types of dreams which will only be mentioned here in passing. One is creative dreaming, creative in the sense of leading to a product, such as an invention (an historical example is the sewing machine), a theoretical concept (the benzine ring), a story plot (*Dr. Jekyll and Mr. Hyde*), and so forth. This intriguing type of problem-solving is a perennial theme in dream books, precisely because it offers appealing evidence of the benefits of dreaming. Krippner & Dillard's book contains a recent and thorough survey of the subject. My favorite example of theirs tells of a woman whose creativity had ostensibly remained repressed since childhood. Nonetheless, perhaps in compensation, she composed poetry in her dreams and recited it aloud from sleep. Her roommate wrote down the verses as spoken—fortunately, since the poet had no morning recall of her sleep experience.[19]

Also to be mentioned only in passing are psychic (psi) dreams: telepathic, precognitive, prophetic, or warning dreams. The term "anomalous dreams" is sometimes preferred, since it lets one refer to the phenomena in question without prejudging their causes.[20] Again, a great many dream books contain anecdotal reports. The most thorough and best documented studies of this matter are those conducted by a team headed by Montague Ullman.[21]

The balance of this book pursues the exploration of anagogic dreams in several directions. This chapter will now look at dreams occurring during psychotherapy and directly concerning the psychological cure. These include both 'initial' dreams, already mentioned, and 'termination' dreams.

Chapter 12 will pose the question whether it is necessary to analyze or interpret dreams at all, in order to reap their benefits. Fashion is beginning to favor non-interpretive approaches.

Following chapters will consider means of controlling dreams to augment their anagogic value. We can attempt to control dreams *prior to their being dreamt*: this is dream *incubation* (chapter 13), a special case of which is the incubation of lucid dreams. *Lucidity* (chapter 14) is a state in which dreams can be controlled *in progress*. That chapter gives a general description of lucid dreaming, including the other ways in which lucid dreams are held to be good dreams. Dreams can also be controlled *after they have been dreamt*, in a sense, by dream *re-entry* (chapter 15).

Finally, chapter 16 will describe the prevailing paradigm for the optimal changes to make in bad dreams to turn them into good ones.

Initial Dreams

Dreams at the very beginning of therapy (or upon joining a dream group) sometimes contain important indications about what is to follow. "[T]he first dream often embodies the chief complaint of the unconscious."[22] An example is the dream of "Savage lions and tigers" related in chapter 10 (p. 353), which pointed to the patient's traumatic guilt about a mining accident.

Sometimes initial dreams "seem to embody both a diagnosis of the problem and a prognosis for its cure."[23] And many of them allude to the therapy itself, giving intimations of the client's posture toward the therapist and of the likely success or failure of treatment. When resistance predominates, the dream is catagogic—just because someone enters therapy does not mean that the psyche is bound to mend:

> [Leon] Saul . . . considered the manifest dream to be a frequently accurate prognostic sign of future behaviour in the analysis. In one case he reported, a patient early in analysis dreamt that *she took a trip with a free ticket.* This patient soon left the analysis and she never paid her bill.[24]

In contrast, the following dreamer, while in conscious resistance to therapy, had a compensatory initial dream suggesting that she should indeed undergo treatment. From Lillie Weiss:

> Sometimes clients may have dreams about the need for psychotherapy without being aware of it, as in the case of a woman who came for treatment at the insistence of her friend. Linda was a capable, self-sufficient woman who had always handled her problems by herself. In recent months, following a trip to her childhood home, she had become increasingly depressed and could not understand the reason for her depression or why she could not handle it on her own. She was filled with doubt about a decision she had to make and had finally made up her mind prior to coming in for treatment. She had resolved the conflict in her mind but decided to come for one session anyway, since she had already made an appointment. We had a pleasant meeting, talking about the crisis she had recently experienced and about the decision she had made. She related that she did not see a need for further therapy at this time, since she had already made a decision. The door was left open for her to come at a future date should she want to do so, with the suggestion that she bring in her dreams if and when she came again. At this point, she related a dream she had had that same morning:

I am riding on my bicycle on the way back from a social event on a path I had driven on before. On the way back, the ground was overturned, and I fell in a hole. Workmen picked me up, but my bicycle was still in the hole. We were going to get the trouble-shooter to get my bicycle out. I was still hanging, being held up by the workmen.

We interpreted the dream together. She is traveling on a familiar path (life), which has always been smooth in the past, but now "the ground is falling out from under her." Her inner drive (her "wheels") that had kept her going in the past is not functioning now. This refers to her depression. Her work ("workmen") has been holding her up (she had in fact been spending increasing time at work, which had been sustaining her) until she can get a "troubleshooter" who can help her get on with life.

"What is a troubleshooter?" she was asked.

"Someone who solves problems."

"And who would help you solve the problem of getting back on with your life?"

She smiled, "A therapist."

The dream was indeed a message for her that she needed therapy. Although she had outwardly made a decision and consciously felt she had resolved her problem, she had not resolved the unconscious conflicts underlying her decision. Linda in fact returned for psychotherapy a year later, following a similar crisis, again precipitated by a trip to her childhood home.[25]

A well-known example of predictive initial dreaming is the trio of initial dreams related by Jung. The dreamer was a woman who attempted treatment with two other analysts before reaching Jung. In a discussion of "prospective dreaming," Mary Ann Mattoon provides an edited composite of different versions of this series written by Jung, beginning with the initial dream from the woman's first analysis:

I have to cross the frontier into another country, but cannot find the customs house where I should go to declare what I carry with me, and nobody can tell me where it is. That dream gave her the feeling that she would never be able to find the proper relation to her analyst; but because she had feelings of inferiority and did not trust her judgment, she remained with him . . . for two months although the treatment proved unsuccessful, and then she left. Then she went to another analyst. Again she dreamed: *I have to cross the frontier, but the night is pitch-black and I cannot find the customs house. After a long search I see a tiny light far off in the distance. Somebody says that the customs house is over there. But in order to get there, I have to pass through a valley and a dark wood in which I lose my way. I am afraid to go on, but nevertheless I go through it, and then I notice that someone is near me. Suddenly he clings to me in the darkness like a madman. I try to shake myself free, but that somebody clings to me still more, and I suddenly discover that it is my analyst.*

This treatment, too, was broken off after a few weeks because the analyst unconsciously identified himself with the patient and the result was complete loss of orientation on both sides.

The third dream took place under my treatment: *I have to cross the Swiss frontier. It is day and I see the customs house. I cross the frontier and go into the customs house, and there stands a Swiss customs official. A woman goes in front of me and he lets that woman pass, and then my turn comes. I have only a handbag with me and think I have nothing to declare. But the official looks at me and says, "What have you got in your bag?" I say, "Oh, nothing at all," and open it. He puts his hand in and, to my astonishment, pulls out something that grows bigger and bigger, until it is two complete beds.* Her problem was that she had a resistance against marriage: she was engaged and would not marry for certain reasons, and those beds were the marriage-beds. I pulled that complex out of her and made her realize the problem, and soon after she married.[26]

The patient's resistance to the earlier therapists appears to have been well-founded, and her dreams, therefore, to have been constructive even though resistant. The third dream portrays her trust in her new therapist, to whom the dream finally also presents "the specific problem with which she would have to deal."[27]

Minor differences exist among therapists as to which dream is actually to be considered 'the' initial dream. Some Jungians deem it to be the first dream exhibiting strong archetypal themes, but Jungian Hans Dieckmann defines it more commonsensically as "the first dream which occurs after the first personal contact with the analyst."[28] Wilhelm Stekel notes, however, that first dreams sometimes only express a client's understandable uncertainty and reluctance in the circumstances, and have no real bearing on the therapy to follow; in that case, the second dream becomes in effect the initial dream. He gives the example of a first dream of passing resistance—"*I want to enter a dark cave, and shudder at the thought that I shall not be able to find my way out again*"—followed by a second dream, filling three pages of text, which "gives us a complete picture of the situation."[29]

Similarly, Joseph Henderson says that the "initial" dream is not always the first in therapy, but may have occurred earlier or follow later: it is the earliest dream thought to be especially revelatory or prognostic.[30] Nevertheless, it is prudent to bear the chronologically first dream in mind, even if it does not seem especially revealing at the time: "More often than otherwise," remarks Leon Altman, "the meaning of an early dream becomes plain only months or even years after we hear it."[31] Such was the case with the initial dream of Christopher, the subject of Robert Bosnak's eloquent book *Dreaming with an AIDS Patient*, who entered therapy without knowing he had the disease:

Visit Aunt Lib. I have to cross to the other side. . . .

"I hardly knew her. I couldn't tell you anything about her. She was some friend of Ethel's. My grandmother [who had raised him]. But maybe it has something to do with liberation. Women's lib. Maybe it means that I can be liberated from being gay. Because I have to cross over to the other side, to the straight side." . . .

[Weeks later, Christopher discovers and announces by telephone that he has AIDS.] We have never talked about AIDS. . . . We must both have been terribly resistant against considering it. Suddenly all the resistances come into focus. My desire not to take him [on as a patient]; his mysterious urgency to leave the gay world; his need to stay away from his feelings. AIDS casts a long and frightening shadow ahead. His initial dream—"I have to cross to the other side"—now shines in an altogether different light. I feel a sudden pang of loss and weep as I hang up. . . .

. . . [Yet later, the dream acquires an additional interpretation.] As long as Christopher's femininity is locked in the struggle between effeminacy and the hatred of queens, it is torn to shreds. . . . Now the love for glamorous external beauty has changed in favor of an appreciation of inner beauty. . . . This is the liberation of the inner woman from the shackles of identification with his self-image. Christopher has indeed crossed to the other side to visit Aunt Lib.[32]

In another book, Bosnak remarks that the so-called initial dream can actually be a cluster of dreams. Moreover, an "initial" dream may occur at any point where a new beginning is being made.[33]

Termination Dreams (and Curative Fantasies)

Termination dreams are those which signal to the therapist, and possibly to the dreamer, that the time approaches to bring a successful course of therapy to a close. The client is cured.

Imaginings about cure naturally arise in the client's mind earlier in therapy. As Roy Whitman advises in "The Dream as a Curative Fantasy," "it behooves every therapist to pay careful attention to them if he is going to provide more than nonspecific therapeutic leverage. . . ."[34] Dreams, Whitman finds, offer the most concise reports on the client's frame of mind about the progress s/he is making. Whitman presents a hierarchy of types of fantasies expressed in dreams, from those with no basis in reality to the fully justified "curative fantasy" proper, which in substance is a termination dream.

With "infantile fantasy," the client expects the therapist to "wave a magic wand" or to transfer magic powers by parenting, bedding, or wedding the client. The "reparative fantasy" involves a less unrealistic relationship to the therapist, but still does not conceive of fundamental change:

[A] male graduate student after a number of months of analysis with very little headway in resolving his severe depression presented the following dream:

I had a large black lesion on my forearm. You were going to cauterize it with silver nitrate. It was amazing. It started to become gray and then lighter and lighter and gradually disappeared. I was very impressed by your skill in applying the cotton swab to the lesion. The lesion was about the size of a silver dollar.

This was a patient who resisted psychoanalysis, could see no merit in depth investigation into his current and past life, and insisted that the analyst give him antidepressant medication.[35]

A "pseudocurative fantasy" may come to a client who has accomplished some good work but resists going farther or deeper:

I was driving along a road and there were two farmhouses. One was a small one and one was a large one in the background. I drove up to the small one and found out that it had been completely redone inside and outside. I was very pleased. The patient associated to how much he had accomplished in his analysis in redoing aspects of himself. . . . [But] the large farmhouse was completely untouched and unmentioned in the patient's associations and . . . this paralleled the patient's unwillingness to go into large areas of his personality which were probably even more germane to his illness than the area he had redone.[36]

Whitman's full "curative fantasy" has three characteristics or stages (resembling an initiation ritual): interpersonal interaction and/or emotional response; something conveyed to the dream-ego by this relationship; and "the return of the patient to his or her former life and other relationships, now changed in some significant way." After several years in analysis, a patient dreamt this straightforward dream:

My husband brought me to your office and sat waiting for me in the waiting room. Instead of your office it was a large dance floor. You chose me to dance among a number of other women, just a few of whom I recognized. At first we started to dance with you leading, holding each other's hand, much as one dances with a small child. As we continued to dance I watched the way you did it, and you led me in subtle ways by pushing or inclining your head, and gradually I moved closer to you and we danced more the way that a man and woman do. At one point we danced by the waiting room and I was afraid that my husband would see me through the glass door. This made me uncomfortable. Soon the dance was over and you brought me back to the waiting room. My husband and I left together.

. . . [T]he patient interacts with the therapist in an emotionally charged way (dancing). The patient learns via identification, teaching, interaction, and perhaps even insight. The end product of these four modes of communication is indicated by her changing from a little girl to a woman in the course of the dancing, and finally and importantly, she is returned to her husband.[37]

Whitman allows that all three stages of the curative fantasy may not be conspicuous in every instance, but contends that their presence may be "inferred." These stages—interaction, education/transformation, and return—might be born in mind while reading the following dreams, all identified by those who recorded them as termination dreams. First, from Thomas Kirsch:

> [An] example concerns a woman, married, in her middle thirties, with a successful career as a book editor. In addition to being quite isolated interpersonally, she had phobic symptomatology, such as not being able to be in crowds, stores and so on. In the early phases of treatment she had several dreams in which *she tried to meet me, but something would be wrong, such as the time or the place of the meeting.* . . . In thus failing to make a connection with me in the dreams, she was unable to make a connection to herself as symbolized by me. . . .
>
> . . . [Several years along in therapy, s]he dreamed that *I was visiting her home and she was showing me her kitchen. Afterwards we walked through the hallway into the living-room and then I walked out.* After all those early dreams in which we did not connect, she had finally brought the symbolic me into her house. I suggested that it was time to terminate therapy and, after her initial surprise, she concurred.[38]

Jesse Cavenar & Jean Spaulding talk about a depressive woman, married and in her thirties, who after three years of therapy experienced the following dreams. I presume that her therapist was female:

> *Two women were washing clothes outdoors in a large black washpot. They finished the wash and dumped the water which had bluing in it into a nearby stream. I watched the blue water disappear downstream and I had the feeling it was gone forever. It was a good feeling to see it disappear.*
>
> The patient felt this dream signified that her depression had been worked through and was gone forever. She raised the question . . . whether it would be appropriate to consider termination since things were going well for her. The following week she reported another dream:
>
> *I was walking downtown at dusk; I had an intense feeling of being all alone. I passed a store front with a large glass window which was cracked part way up. But somebody had put a bolt through the window so that it wouldn't crack any further. As I stood there looking at it, my husband walked up and took my hand. I felt good then and not alone. We walked off together, holding hands, and I felt happy.*
>
> The patient interpreted this dream to mean that the cracked window which had been bolted was the work which had been done in therapy to stop her feeling of depression. Her feelings toward her husband had changed in the treatment to permit him now to occupy a significant position in her life and to help her with negative feelings.
>
> . . . [A] date was set and therapy went to a successful conclusion. . . .

Such dreams may . . . be used in the service of resistance. Our experience suggests that the psychotherapist should wait a reasonable period . . . to judge whether the dreams are defensive or are, in fact, termination signal dreams.[39]

Lastly, here is an extract from near the conclusion of Ann Mankowitz's book *Change of Life*, a Jungian case study which focuses on the dreams of a woman undergoing menopause:

The ambivalent attitudes of impending separation (from me) began to show themselves in our sessions, until one day . . . [Mankowitz's client Rachel] came with a "final" dream:

I am my mature self, sitting in an armchair in a spacious room of what seems to be a club. There are other chairs around, forming a circle. Opposite me is sitting Angela, my oldest and best friend. We are talking and at ease with each other. A group of men enters; they remain standing and talking among themselves. One of them comes toward us, smiling. It is Jamie McDonald, an old friend of mine from college, who became an actor. I haven't met him since university. He looks as he used to, about twenty-two years old. We are happy to see each other. It appears I have had a wonderful idea for a project, per-haps a play or performance of some kind. Jamie is delighted with it and the other men move toward us and are friendly and congratulatory. I am surpris-ed, they seem to know more about it than I do. Then I remember that I have not introduced Angela and she may feel left out. But she is not at all offended, calmly smiling and taking part in the general conversation, sharing the atmo-sphere of pleasure and appreciation. . . .

Rachel . . . regarded Angela as representing in the dream a sort of alter ego: a mature woman like herself, but with opposite qualities; focused on work and not on family; free where she was dependent; insecure where she was protected. Their being together and talking comfortably in the dream suggested to Rachel a reconciliation of opposites within herself, an expression of her psychological integration.

The setting of the armchairs in the club atmosphere meant to Rachel the "club of women" or sisterhood in which she now felt like a fully paid-up member. This was the feeling of "belonging" to something almost impersonal, larger than one-self or family. . . .

The figure of Jamie McDonald produced interesting associations. The group of men with whom he came into the room seemed to Rachel to be that aspect of her animus which represented the collective masculine world outside the home and family. But what did Jamie himself mean, presented so vividly by her uncon-scious after thirty years of no contact?

She remembered that Jamie had acted even at college. . . . As she described his activities, she became aware of all the "masculine" associations to the words she was using. He was an "actor, acted, was active," "was prominent," "played the leading man." Furthermore, he had once urged Rachel to take part in a play he was producing. Although interested in drama she had never much wanted to act, but allowed herself to be persuaded by Jamie to go to an audition. She failed to get the part, and afterward Jamie gave her his opinion of why this had happened. He told her that she had spoken her audition piece with feeling and intelligence, but that somehow it was too small and private to come over to the audience. She lacked **projection**. If the decision was solely his, he would have given her the part and taught her how to project herself, how to magnify the small sensitive performance so that it forced itself upon the audience's attention. Rachel, a little dashed by the whole experience, felt sure he would not have been able to produce this transformation, and was relieved to be able to retire into backstage obscurity. However, the incident had lingered in her mind as a piece of potential self-knowledge which she was unable at that time to understand fully or to apply.

Now it seemed the dream was telling her that the transformation had happened. She **was** capable of "projecting" her personality outward. Her "project" was apparently highly acceptable. . . .

There was yet another dimension to the dream. The two women in armchairs reminded Rachel of her analytical sessions, during which she and I sat talking in comfortable chairs facing each other. I was now, in contrast to the former image of the faceless servant, a friend and equal in "the club of women." The change in the nature of our relationship is also reflected in Rachel's anxiety in the dream about neglecting the Angela-me figure, and the reassurance that she (Angela-me) was in fact getting on perfectly well with her own conversation and was not feeling rejected.

This told me that Rachel sensed that she could now get on in the world without me, and had needed to reassure herself that I would be all right without **her**. The ending of an analysis is indeed a delicate process which, like other separations, needs time and sensitivity to accomplish without trauma. I was grateful for the signs of Rachel's awareness of both her strength and mine, and of her readiness for our separation in an ambience of mutual caring and respect. Rachel's analysis came to an end some six weeks later.[40]

The Non-interpretation of Dreams

To benefit from dreams, is it necessary—is it even advisable—to interpret them? If by 'interpret' is meant pronouncement of an interpretation by therapist or other expert, then certainly not. Possibly in the earliest days of the psychoanalytic 'talking cure', the delivery of information about the causes of dreams and symptoms was counted on to work. But anyone can recognize the advantage of the dreamer arriving by her/his own visceral processes to a place where comprehension of the dream becomes fruitful, whether or not s/he is more or less skillfully guided to that place by an expert or support group. This is just psychological common sense.

A different question is whether verbal insight into dream meaning actually does contribute substantially to well-being. It would also seem to make common sense that cognitive interpretation can help one along toward visceral understanding and systemic change. But opinions differ greatly as to the value of understanding at the verbal, ideational level.

Certain practitioners who do interpretive work also respect the benefits which often ensue incidentally from dream-telling without any interpretation. Discussing posttraumatic stress disorder nightmares (ch. 9, p. 311), Harry Wilmer advises: "Inexperienced people who are not trained in dream analysis should not dive into these troubled, dangerous waters, but should know that listening itself, without *any* interpretation, allows the dreamer to retell his story, and in the process, possibly change his attitude and dreams."[1] And Henry Beck, discussing dreams in family therapy, observes:

> The telling of a dream may be therapeutic without the dream either being understood or interpreted. The unconscious meaning or communication seems to be directly communicated. The four-year-old son of a family refused to go to the toilet because he said the weatherman was there to attack him. Several weeks after he began this behavior he reported having a dream in which *the toilet was too tall for him to sit on*. The mother then reported that she often had had the dream

that *she had to go to the toilet but could not because it was eight feet tall.* The father then reported that as a child he often retained his feces. The son's symptoms disappeared that day. The dream had served as a vehicle for this improvement without its interpretation.[2]

Some recent dreamworkers take a stronger position, saying that dreams are part of a natural imagistic healing process which, while it can be developed, develops best when the cogitating mind stays out of the way.

Such is, of course, contrary to the classic psychoanalytic position, which holds dream, symptom, and free association all to be of the same unwholesome cloth. That position was upheld in a panel discussion in the mid-1970s by Harold Blum, against other psychoanalysts whose views were changing: "Since the dream is an archaic process of hallucinatory wish-fulfillment and not a mode of mastery or ego expansion, the dream experience itself without interpretation does not resolve neurosis. . . . The emphasis by some on the sharing of an ineffable dream experience seem[s] . . . to shift the focus away from understanding and resolving . . . conflict towards a mystical, existential approach which hopes to provide self-actualization and identity without verbal insight."[3]

Research by Mary-Therese Dombeck published in 1991 demonstrates that mainstream psychotherapists still for the most part would not even consider using dreams with a client who was not "psychologically minded," "insight oriented."[4] It is not that Dombeck's therapists were committed Freudians, for they were not. Rather, they appeared to be caught in the inertia of the Freudian dreamwork tradition, and to be unconversant with alternatives.

In a book with the significant title of *Dreams are Wiser than Men*, editor Richard Russo censures the traditional line: "Modern psychology was not built upon dreams. When Freud laid the foundations of psychoanalysis, it was the *interpretation* of dreams that he proclaimed the 'royal road' to the unconscious. In other words, the dream, though worthy of study, was not as important as what could be done with it afterwards. This bias is a comfortable one for the waking ego, and pervades most types of dreamwork to this day. . . . The mystery and beauty of the dream are lost."[5]

However, not everyone who, in Russo's phrase, does something with the dream afterwards does so out of belief in the dream's inherent poverty. The mystery and beauty were certainly not lost on the interpreter's interpreter, Jung. The compensatory function of dreams may operate without conscious understanding; but "Jung saw the compensation as even more effective when the dream is understood through a valid interpretation."[6] The interpretation boosts natural self-healing. James Hadfield, influenced by Jung, compares dream interpretation to art appreciation: conscious reasoning enhances intuitive grasp.[7] Jungians Jean & Wallace Clift say that transformation effected through dreams requires both experiencing, for energy, and interpretation, for meaning.[8] Max Zeller shows that analytic work prepares the way for the spontaneous transformations which later dreams sometimes release.[9]

Some existential dreamworkers balk at the word, but they also do dream interpretation. Medard Boss (chapter 4) thought that the dreamer should re-involve her/himself in the dream experientially and intuitively, while at the same time maintaining a certain detachment in order to conceptualize waking analogies to the dream. Fritz Perls (chapter 6) strongly rejected merely conceptual dreamwork, but all the same his method of working with images and feelings generates insight, and it is insight which heals. Perls may have set the precedent for the many dreamworkers who disdain to use the term 'interpretation' on account of its old association to the talking cure, even though their methods actually do achieve interpretation in a real sense.

Montague Ullman takes this stance. So does Robin Shohet: "Many of the newer psychotherapies which broadly go under the heading of Humanistic Psychology do *not* interpret but allow the meaning to come from the dreamer. These therapies focus on re-experiencing the feelings and images of the dream as fully as possible. In this way, by working with the feelings, meaning will spontaneously arise and connections will be made that come from the dreamer himself."[10] So meaning—interpretation—is reached through feelings as well as talk, and, importantly, the arbiter of correctness is not an expert but the dreamer and her/his own "click"[11] (or: aha; that's it; yes; pop; touché; gotcha; flash; spark; light of day; spontaneous assent; satisfying certainty; feeling of fit; rightness; tingle; felt shift; gut reaction; inner sense of satisfaction; still small voice within; satori).[12]*

---

* Dissent from or qualification of the reliability of 'clicks' should be noted. "This intuitive 'click' is criticized by Hillman as merely reflecting the ego's wishes" (W. A. Shelburne 1984, p. 54, citing James Hillman 1979). Mary Ann Mattoon (1984 [1978], p. 178) writes that the absence of a "click" does not necessarily invalidate an interpretation, for the dreamer may be resisting or misunderstanding. From similar considerations, John A. Scott, Sr. (1982, p. 91) holds that the therapist's "feel" should be relied upon, not the dreamer's. But Caroline Stevens (1990, p. 98) comments that analyst and analysand may be in unconscious collusion. "A good feeling in the room is not enough here." Patricia Berry (1974, p. 60) argues that all sorts of unreliable psychological transactions can elicit a "click," including "charlatanism, syntonic transference, neurosis, hysterical suggestion, doctrinal compliance, religious conversion, and political brainwashing." J. A. Hadfield (1954) simply remarks that a dreamer's 'aha' is no more reliable than a scientist's "brainstorm," which typically leads into a dead end.

Less severely, Alan Siegel (1990, p. 12) stresses "the value of persevering beyond the first flash of insight and discovering deeper layers of meaning in a dream." Jeremy Taylor (1992a, pp. 152–5) notices that ahas of introverts, who *"require solitude* to evaluate the value, meaning, and even the *reality* of their experiences," may not rise to consciousness until after a session of group work.

Alvin Mahrer, whose rather eccentric "experiential approach" contains elements of Perls's Gestalt, Boss's existentialism, Corriere's feeling therapy, and Gendlin's focusing, maintains that we usually cannot really know what a dream is about, much less partake of the personality transformation it offers, simply by understanding meaning—we have to experience the dream and its energy immediately. Eventually, Mahrer tells us we require his "explicit methods" in order to convert understanding into transformation.[13]

A better-known case in point is Gayle Delaney and her effective "interview" technique, an eclectic existential approach in a readily applicable format. In keeping with the trend, Delaney professes to teach her readers and students how to become "a dream interviewer rather than an interpreter."[14] All the same, the terms 'interpretation' and even 'analysis' do crop up in her language. What Delaney actually intends is to discourage "formulaic" and "premature" interpretations.[15]

The method requires the interviewer—self or other—to ask questions as if s/he were an alien from another planet, "curious to discover what life is like seen through the eyes of the dreamer."[16] This approach, observes Erik Craig, is existential-phenomenological. It aims to "bracket out what doesn't show in the thing itself," in order to minimize the influence of theoretical and other preconceptions.[17]* The dreamer's descriptions of the various dream elements are "fed back" or "recapitulated" by the interviewer, who goes on to ask questions which prompt the dreamer to "bridge" (associate) to waking life. Dream elements "usually need only be well described before the dreamer can see them as powerful metaphors."[18] Finally, the interviewer asks the dreamer to connect up the descriptions and bridges in a pattern related to the structure of the dream. Delaney's full account of the technique details ten stages, but they all involve these four fundamental operations of description, recapitulation, bridge, and summary.

Lest there be any doubt whether this is dream interpretation, the following passage shows that Delaney slides into interpretation, even in the narrow

---

A 'click' is not necessarily toned positively, as indicated by a remark by Clyde Reid (1983, pp. 16–7): "One way you know a dream interpretation has hit its mark is when some energy moves in you as a result of it. If your solar plexus tightens up, your body jumps, or you feel dizzy, you know something important is happening." Taylor (op. cit., p. 136) has discerned a "'negative aha' that says, in effect, 'No, that's totally wrong, but it's so far from the mark that it makes me realize what *is* true!'"

* Patricia Garfield's (1991, p. 78) variant of the questioning alien is, "How would you describe a particular object, animal, or person to a child who does not know them?" She attributes the technique to Jung (*Modern Man in Search of a Soul*, New York: Harcourt Brace Jovanovich, pp. 13–4, 1933; see also 1984 [1938], p. 535). According to Delaney, Garfield learned the technique from her in 1977 (personal communication, 1993).

and prohibited sense (and who does not, I wonder?). One of the settings of
the dream is a *"huge sports arena."* Delaney is already several alien queries
into the interview when she asks, "What is a sports arena, and what was the
one in your dream like?" The dreamer answers, "A sports arena? Well . . . a
place for sports events. The dream one was very big." Delaney now follows
her interpretive hunch by asking: "I wonder if the sports arena might represent your professional activities since it was so big? That's the kind used for
'pro' sports, right?" And indeed, "Yes, that would fit."[19]*

Quite a few practitioners employ techniques less exclusively verbal than
Delaney's, but still intended to arrive eventually at insight—insight facilitated and deepened, however, by the nonverbal, superficially 'non-interpretive'
preparations. Following are some representative examples.

One such technique is Harold Ellis's "Dream Drama," which has obvious
affinities with psychodrama. Psychodrama, however, usually does not work
with dreams, and is, moreover, a clinical modality and not a "growth" technique, as is dream drama.[20]** First, here is a short example. While somewhat
atypical because the dreamer aborts the process when the drift of the interpretation becomes painfully evident, the example is good for illustrating how
dramatization facilitates discovery:

> Gerry was . . . new to the group, and was not really interested in dreams. A very
> few years before, he had separated from his wife and young daughter, and moved
> far away from them to New York. . . . [H]e figured Dream Drama might be an
> amusing way to spend an evening. . . . In our warmup go-around, he contributed
> the following:
>
> Gerry's Dream. *My ex-wife is driving our car. Someone else is in front and
> also alongside me. I'm in the back seat. It's boring. I don't know where we're
> going or why I'm here.*
>
> . . . He had no associations or context to offer, and seemed amusedly aloof.
> Perhaps, we suggested, Dream Drama might open a door. Gerry agreed to it.
>
> The Dream Drama. Gerry said he'd take the role of himself, and preferred
> that someone else take over the direction. The car was quickly constructed out
> of large pillows; a round metal tray was the steering wheel. The woman driver
> and a man sat down in front, and a woman and Gerry took their positions in
> back. Since Gerry had no directions to offer, the car drove through countryside;
> the riders swayed gently, talking quietly about scenery, the lunch they expected

---

* In 1993 (personal communication), Delaney calls this "among the worst (i.e. most suggestive-
intrusive) of my work . . . —I hope I'm cleaner now."

** However, Helmut Barz (1990) gives an account of psychodrama dreamwork in a stable group
of 10–12, conducted by professionals (for an example of the work, see chapter 15, p. 494). It is
Barz's opinion that "there remains an uninterpretable remnant that, perhaps precisely because of its
feeling-induced unfathomability, represents the most important message of the dream" (pp. 170–1).

to have at the restaurant, and how restful it was to be together. Gerry abruptly changed to a kneeling position.

When the Director asked why . . . , he said there was something bumpy under the seat. The driver stopped the car; the enactors quietly turned around. They looked very concerned. Gerry looked uncomfortable and puzzled by their change. The rest of the group gathered slowly around Gerry. The Director, in a serious, low voice, asked Gerry to look under the pillow. Gerry's face turned ashen. Then he said it was his daughter.

Gerry ended the work there. . . .[21]

The following is from an outline by Ellis of a full dream drama session. A dream is reported, clarified, and given a provisional title. Next the dreamer selects a "Director," and the others take roles. Roles include characters, objects, and even moods or ambiences:

> The entire dream is portrayed, usually twice, and often with help from the use of sounds, drum rhythm, colors, and props, and sometimes masks. "Excess" group members comprise the "Chorus."
>
> By each person's empathetically "living" a dream element, the group attempts to "own" and understand the dream's context. As we proceed we call the Dreamer's attention to his or her spontaneous nonverbal expressions. . . .
>
> The first, detailed, slowly-paced enactment remains faithful to the dream report and is helpful in understanding its message about the Dreamer's current waking life. It also brings to light memory gaps, blockages within the visual dreamscape, . . . feelings, and discrepancies embodied in the dream narrative.
>
> A second, more active run-through engages the . . . entire group, and . . . opens up unanticipated memories and meanings. These two run-throughs comprise the **Current Life Action.** . . .
>
> . . . [A]t this point or in a third run-thru [sic], we may purposefully re-enact the dream **unfaithfully**, by changing scenes and outcomes, as a rehearsal for possible changes in the Dreamer's waking lifestyle. We call this an **Amendment Action**, and it is about as close as we may get to purposeful therapy. . . .
>
> Following either of the Actions, Dream Drama group members provide the Dreamer with **Feelback**. In this phase dream enactors and Chorus tell of the feelings and thoughts they themselves experienced during the drama. . . . Finally the Dreamer gives a new title to the dream . . . [which] gives one indication of what the Dreamer has gained from the drama.[22]

Another non-analytical but interpretive method is Fariba Bogzaran's "Expressive Dream Art," a process which utilizes visual and plastic media as well as other media the dreamer might prefer. Precedence for dreamwork with art should belong, if not to William Blake, then probably once again to Jung. In certains periods in his life Jung devoted much time to painting his dreams, both for the sake of integrating their energies and of fathoming their meanings.* Bogzaran writes: "Expressive arts techniques . . . become an outside agent in helping the dreamer to discover the inward journey of the self interpreting the dream."[23] The core of her method is a four-step process:

"Abstraction": without trying to understand them yet, the feeling tones of the dream (not the images) are non-imagistically expressed through colors, sounds, movements, or "short sentences."

"Chaos": the dreamer gives "indiscriminate expression to all the images and feelings" by such means as mosaics and collages.[24]

"Integration": the strongest images from the Chaos step are singled out for expression in any medium, which leads to "a gradual integration of the meaning of the dream. In this step, the dreamer might reach the 'Aha'—an insight to the dream—and realize the hidden meaning. . . . This illumination might be an immediate understanding of the dream or a gradual lucid entering into the world of the psyche."[25] The last phrase suggests that the process can lead to waking dreams or fantasies which, presumably, become subjects for further artistic expression.

"Reflection": "[H]aving had the 'Aha!' experience . . . Reflection offers time to sit with the realization and re-examine the change it implies."[26]

Phyllis Koch-Sheras et al. include in their smorgasbord of methods a suggestion to sketch our dreams. This technique is simpler and less immersive than Bogzaran's. Sketching a dream the sort of thing one can easily do in a minute whenever it might help:

> The following dream and drawing show dramatically how much insight can be gained with just a simple drawing. The dreamer was trying to conceive a child and had asked her dreams to point out any childbearing or childrearing issues that she may have overlooked.
>
> MA BELL
>
> *There is a wide hole in the ground with a railing around it. We see a giant bell made of gold inside the hole. It rings with a perfectly beautiful tone. I turn to one of the people gathered there and say, 'This is a great work of art!' He replies, 'Undoubtedly a great deal of labor went into it.' I think about 'The Hunchback of Notre Dame' and wonder how much sorrow and blood went into its making and feel very sad. Next, a little child runs up and climbs on the rail. I tell him to get back, or he might fall in.*

"The theme of childrearing was obvious to me from the child and the clue words 'dame' and 'labor'. I drew the dream to discover the meaning of the bell. Half-

---

* Paul Robbins (1988, p. 105) attributes the idea of drawing dreams to Freud. If Freud ever did use dream drawing in therapy, it would presumably have been as Robbins does, as an adjunct to more conventional interpretation, to emphasize feelings or motifs, or to amplify details.

way through drawing the bell, I stopped—what I had drawn was unmistakably a breast, and I was trying to keep the child away from it! I hadn't given any thought to the fact that my breasts would probably lose some of their 'beautiful tone' in the process of breast-feeding. The dream compelled me to thoroughly re-examine my sense of physical attractiveness in regard to childrearing."[27]

Jill Morris discusses dream drawing as a useful technique for nonprofessional partner dreamworking and for psychotherapy: "[T]he pictured image can unveil something that the mental image does not convey. For example, . . . [a man with AIDS] *thought* of the [dream] image of the nun; it became an onion only when he drew it, leading him to the association of cancer [Kaposi's sarcoma]."[28]

In addition to such non-interpretive preliminaries to interpretation, certain dreamworkers emphasize non-interpretive sequels to it. This was mentioned in chapter 10, in connection with Robert Johnson's contrast between acting *out* (neurotic) and acting *on* a dream.[29] First comes the interpretation: "An adequate dream interpretation should sum up the meaning of your dream in a nutshell. It should also provide a specific application of the dream's message to your personal life. . . ."[30] Next, the dream is honored by a "ritual": "The ritual is a physical representation of the inner attitude change that the dream called for. . . ."[31] Johnson's example quoted in chapter 10 (p. 360) is the young man who buried junk food to symbolize riddance to his psychologically unnourishing life style.

The example was also given, from Strephon Williams, of a woman 'actualizing' her dream by reducing her commitments after she dreamed about overstuffed suitcases. Williams cites his "golden rule": "*To get to the meaning of dreams, actualize them rather than interpret them.*"[32] By actualizing, he means both reexperiencing the dream awake, and being certain that the dream has an awake-world consequence. The latter may take the form of ritual, artistic expression, and/or life change. He allows that interpretation is necessary, only he aims to redress the analytic emphasis of our culture.[33] "It is our fundamental premise that we gain more from dreams by doing things in response to them than we do from simply interpreting them."[34]

For Williams, artistic expression of dream material "is an intermediate step in the whole process of integration." "Once the symbol is manifested in an art form, it is 'out there' and available for us to experience and re-experience until we have consciously integrated the energy back inside ourselves by withdrawing the projection."[35] For Janice Baylis, similarly, "the energy of dream images . . . can be better integrated consciously if it is rendered in some fashion."[36] It is implicit in such thinking that we benefit from 'rendering', even if we never conceptualize what the dream image 'means'.

Jung, however—he, the patron of these dreamworkers—, cautioned against oversimplistic enactments: "Socrates was a terrible rationalist, insupportable, so his daemon said to him [in a dream]: *Socrates, thou shouldst make more music.* And dear old Socrates bought a flute and played horrible things! Of course the daemon meant: 'Do practice more feeling, don't be so damned rational all day long.'"[37]* Many Jungians would surely say that playing even bad music might symbolically accomplish what Socrates's unconscious was driving at, but Jung more often than not insisted that the conscious ego must recognize the meaning of its actions in such cases.

It should be clear that the interpretive-analytic element is not, in much of dreamwork, an absolutely yes or no matter. Many who employ ostensibly non-interpretive means are not anti-interpretation. We come now, however, to more strictly non-interpretive methods.

One place where explicit interpretation is generally discouraged, and also deemed unnecessary, is in dreamwork with children. (British psychoanalyst Melanie Klein is an exception.[38]). Jill Gregory writes about her work with fourth graders:

> These photos are from one day that I brought my giant costume box and let the students briefly tell the dream and introduce themselves as the dream character. The girl wearing the long dress and pointed hat is Samantha. She is being *a large bluebird who bosses her and clings to her* in her dreams two to three times a week . . . *[and who] was becoming increasingly negative, to the point of attacking Samantha.* During the course, I did re-entry and re-imaging dreamwork on a one-to-one basis for a few days with each of the children who wanted it. Samantha found ways to get that bird to sit and listen to her. She set some basic limits for the bird in terms of what she was willing to do for it, and . . . found another friend for the bluebird so it didn't come to her for all of its needs. In fact, she even imaged wings for the bird which the bird told her was what it needed most. Although the bluebird was still a frequent symbol in her dreams, by the end of the course Samantha had a more positive relationship. Sometimes the bluebird would fly away and she would miss it.
>
> . . . [T]he approach of simply solving . . . dream situations and helping our dream characters—a technique developed by Ann Wiseman and Paula Phelan—
> . . . works wonders . . . without anyone needing to know who that bluebird represents in her real life, not even Samantha. Her waking life and her dream life will improve without those correlations ever being drawn.[39]

---

* This was a recurring dream which Socrates had always taken as a confirming dream, telling him to continue practicing philosophy. But under sentence of death, he though perhaps he had better try taking the message at face value, so he composed some hymns and other verses (M. A. Jowett 1937 [1892], para's 60-1).

Following is a sample of Ann Sayre Wiseman's work with children, from a chapter titled "Children Empowering Themselves." Working in schools, she had children in small groups draw their nightmares:

As the drawings were completed the child told the story of the dream, which I tape recorded. Then together we discussed what would have to happen to put them in a better position of power rather than be the victim in the dream. . . .

. . . As they imagined an alternative position, they could experience it by closing their eyes and visualizing the empowered scene. If it felt right, they drew the solution into their dream drawing. Drawing the solution is like rehearsing a real option. . . .

(Molly, age 5)

I dreamed that my house was on fire. My dad was away at work, and my mom was out at the store. I woke up so scared I was petrified. I thought my cat and I would just burn up and I'd wake up dead. [Molly has drawn a house in flames, with a face in a downstairs window.] . . .

Guide: What is that little face in the window saying?

Molly: It's real scary to be inside a burning house.

Guide: How will you save that little girl?

Molly: I'd have to get her out of the house, but I'm not allowed to leave the house without my parents and my dad is at work and my mom is shopping.

Guide: Close your eyes and ask that little girl what you should do.

Molly: She says get out.

Guide: Good idea ... can you get her out? If so draw yourself outside of the house?

Molly: (draws herself outside the house) I'm on the street but I can't do anything.

Guide: Why not?

Molly: Because I'm not allowed to cross the street, and my mom is across the street at the store.

Guide: What are you going to do in an emergency ... watch your house burn up, or get some help? Close your eyes again and see that little girl getting help.

Molly: She found a policeman. I'll draw a policeman; he can help me cross the street.

Guide: It certainly looks like an emergency ... Now what?

Molly: Now I can run and get my mom in the store.

Guide: Close your eyes and see yourself doing that. What do you see?

Molly: I can't get in the store.

Guide: Why?

Molly: Because the knob is too high for me to reach.

Guide: What will you do? Close your eyes again and see her getting in.

Molly: She got a box to stand on.

Guide: Good idea ... draw that.

Molly: It worked. I got a box and opened the door. I found my mom ... she was upstairs. (Molly writes "Hi, Mom" into her picture.)

Guide: Now what ... is that the end?

Molly: My cat is in the house. "Mommy, Mommy, call the fireman, the house is on fire and the cat will burn up ... quick, quick ..."

Guide: It looks like you're not so helpless after all ...[40]

Katherine West warns strongly against analysis of children's dreams. "In the child, unconscious material can be overwhelming if there is an attempt to be analytical about its imagery."[41] She might have added, analysis simply does not work well. West recommends the usual variety of techniques for externalizing the dream imagery, including painting, dance, imaginary conversations, and drama:

[A] bright, highly articulate and confident young lady of eleven shared a particularly horrendous monster dream which sent chills down the backs of us all. . . .

> I dreamed *my family and I were in a big house and I was carrying my little brother in my arms. All of a sudden the house started to cave in. Me and my little brother ran out, but he got hit on the head and was dead. I did not know this. Everyone else in the house was crushed. A cop car started coming. They said we would have to go to a home because my parents were dead. I said: "No," and started running with my dead little brother in my arms. We were out in a barren wasteland. I looked back and saw instead of policemen in the car, they were demons. They were great big and horrid and all red. I started running and then my own brother turned into one of those demons. I dropped him and ran up a tree. They all came up after me and started tearing at me, so I jumped down. There was a pit below, and it was full of fire. I jumped in and started to burn up, so I climbed up the sides until I got to a big pool of ice water and jumped in there. But then a big monster rose up and started to pull me in. I had a knife that I reached for and started stabbing him. He was mad, so I got up on a tree branch and hung there out of his reach. But the branch broke, and I fell right into his jaws!*

We all sat stunned at first, then various children asked her to elaborate upon certain parts. I suggested we attempt a dramatization of the dream, and lo and behold, a spontaneous cast of characters rose to the occasion. A six-year-old became the baby brother; others became the demons with an active eleven-year-old becoming the monster. But as the re-enactment began to unfold, a curious thing happened. Right about the time the young lady was finding the stabbing pointless and was preparing to make for the tree, the demons broke script and had an uprising among themselves, turning on the monster. What a beating the poor monster took. . . . The young lady was delighted; and with her friends to the rescue, the dream had released its fearsome hold on her. And needless to say, a lot of energy had been dissipated, for the action had become intense in places. . . .

Notice that . . . the child did not in any way analyze the fearsome symbol. This would be just the opposite were we working with adults, but . . . such introspection with children, particularly the younger ones, might well lead to morbid self-interest. What is far more important is to honor the concern, give it form and encourage the child either to befriend it or take power over it such that it ceases to be the manipulative force it once was.[42]

Not everyone shares West's assumption, that adult dreamwork should include analysis of symbols. Others rely on imaginal experience for adults, as for children. This tendency is nowhere more pronounced than in the treatment of nightmares. Conventional dreamwork often accomplishes little with nightmares of victims of abuse[43] and other severe traumas. Commenting on the success of non-interpretive approaches, Kathy Belicki & Marion Cuddy say: "We have in our own experience been frankly astonished (as have our clients) at how swiftly a life-long problem with nightmares can disappear."[44]

Jung's contribution to healing through imagery should not be underestimated, despite his balanced views—nor should it be overestimated, despite the views of neo-Jungian James Hillman, who on one occasion compared the dream to a Zen riddle: "If you can literalize a meaning, 'interpret' a dream, you are off the track, lost your Koan."[45]

Jung aside, most of the impetus for healing through imagery originated in fields other than dreamwork. In her book *Waking Dreams*, Mary Watkins traces modern Western imagery modalities to Pierre Janet, an older contemporary of Freud who published in the 1880s and 1890s. Through hypnosis and other techniques, Janet entered into the imaginal experiences of his patients, such as memories of trauma, to restructure them in a positive direction. "This was accomplished through the media of fantasy, not interpretation."[46] Following Janet, imagery therapies underwent steady development in Europe while being largely ignored in the U.S. until relatively recently. Nowadays, of course, guided imagery books and tapes can be found at the corner drugstore.

In these European therapies, says Watkins, interpretation "is not believed to be sufficient, nor usually necessary, for a 'cure.' . . . Although one can see and analyze the similarities between daily life and the imaginal, the connection between the two is assumed from the beginning. Free movement on one level affects the way one moves on the other. . . . [Image work] is felt to be a more direct way of influencing one's being-in-the-world. Resistances . . . take a symbolic form which can be worked through on that level."[47]

Watkins sketches this movement from Janet to Binet's "provoked introspection," Happich's "emergent images," Kretschmer's "meditative techniques for psychotherapy," Schultz and Luthe's "progressive visualizations,"

Frank's "cathartic method," Guillerey's "directed revery," and others,[48] to Robert Desoille's "directed daydreams," the best-known of these therapies in the U.S.

Influenced by Jung, Desoille meant his clients to draw upon the collective unconscious as they repeatedly entered "six archetypal imaginary situations (for example, descent into the ocean or a cave, meeting with a dragon) until the anxiety-provoking images which appeared were drained of their painful affective charge."[49] Desoille also helped clients to establish new and adaptive patterns of imagery, and hence behavior, by borrowing imaginary solutions from myths and other sources.[50] There is a double purpose here: first, symbolic resolutions of psychological conflicts; second, the evocation of images with autonomous curative powers. Of the latter, Eliade says: "Now, the type of 'waking dream' that Desoille most frequently requires . . . is precisely that of ascending a staircase or climbing a mountain . . . symbols which comprise, in their own structure, the ideas of 'passage' and of 'ontological mutation'. . . . [C]ertain symbols which are religious . . . [bring] a psychological improvement and [lead] ultimately to a recovery."[51]

Watkins[52] follows this movement further, to Leuner's "guided affective imagery," or "symboldrama," and to Virel and Frétigny's "oneirodrama," as well as to Roberto Assagioli's "psychosynthesis,"[53] better-known in the U.S.,* where it was developed in connection with dream therapy by Ernest Rossi (who was also an early advocate in this country of lucid dreaming).[54] Jerome Singer[55] discusses influences of image therapies in the U.S., on psychodrama (the Morenos), Gestalt (Perls), transactional analysis (Berne), and more recently on various behavior modification therapies. A very interesting development is the use of imagery for treatment of disease.[56]

This whole movement has helped to sway the dream movement toward non-interpretive work. As pointed out already, many dreamworkers employ and recommend non-interpretive maneuvers, without excluding or even posing an explicit or rigorous contrast to interpretive work. An instance of this is Koch-Sheras et al., from whose book *Dream On* the use of dream drawing ("Ma Bell") was quoted. They discuss a range of other techniques. We should make objects inspired by our dreams, including a "dream shield" on

---

* Of Assagioli, whom Jung introduced to Freud in 1909 as the first Italian adherent of psychoanalysis (McGuire 1974, p. 241), James Gollnick (1987, p. 116) writes: "Assagioli recommends a number of techniques to promote contact with a person's spiritual center. Dream interpretation is only one of the many techniques he uses to explore the unconscious and spiritual potential. Generally Assagioli prefers meditation, initiated symbol projection and inner dialogue because they are faster and more systematic than dream interpretation since they do not rely completely on what emerges of its own accord from the unconscious."

the Native American model, for integration and contemplation;[57]* we should act out and view enactments of our dreams, for new perspectives; dance our dreams, to intensify contact with their emotional substance; play with our dreams—preparing dream foods, making dream jewelry, and so on. In sum, we should "paint, dance, share, smell, fantasize, wear, or eat them!"[58]

But some dreamworkers have a larger agenda for the salubrious image, believing that the best (though obviously not the only) therapy and growth work with dreams is accomplished by changing or controlling dream imagery. This is the principle underlying the famous "Senoi" approach. In Kilton Stewart's account of the Malaysian tribal people, they thought they could resolve psychological conflicts by shaping their dreams.[59] Whatever the reality of the Senoi, the principle attributed to them has been deemed "effective"[60] and has penetrated U.S. dreamwork. Williams epitomizes this positive way of understanding the continuity hypothesis: "As in the dream so in life. To change your life change your dreams."[61] Also Rosalind Cartwright remarks: "The conventional wisdom is that most of us recover from a crisis by changing our waking lives, not our dreams. Can it work the other way around? . . . 'Yes!'"[62] (The contrary understanding states: "When dreamers' personalities change, dreams change also."[63] No doubt it works both ways.)

Besides symbolic conflict resolution, the benefits supposed to come from dream control are said to include desensitization to feared stimuli, and reinforcement of the ego through successful and courageous dream behavior.[64] In fact, most of the benefits of dreams mentioned elsewhere—practice, entertainment, etc.—are thought to be enhanced by control. (Jung's compensatory function has to be excluded.) Proponents of this viewpoint cite psychological studies showing that "success, good fortune and positive emotions in dreams [a]re positively correlated with more adaptive scores across all psychological well-being measures. . . ." The implication is "that dream outcomes are related to waking functioning"—and that, therefore, we should "improve" our dreams.[65]

Patricia Garfield, whose book *Creative Dreaming* in 1974 gave impetus to this tendency, makes the argument: "Let us assume that dream images re-

---

* Koch-Sheras et al. (1983, p. 71) quote Henry Reed ("Dream shields: II—the four directions," *Sundance Community Dream Journal* 1, pp. 184–9, 1977): "By collecting symbols from different dreams, you can rise above the vision of a single dream and begin to see the story of your symbolic life as a whole. Also, the visual nature of the dream shield provides a potent focus for contemplation and further opportunity for you to be moved by the consciousness-transforming energies of your dream symbols." David Feinstein & Stanley Krippner (1988) also provide instructions for making dream shields with images from dreams and other sources. Cf. Garfield's (1989 [1979]) instructions for creating a dream mandala, formed on a Tibetan rather than Native American model.

present internalized ideas . . . [and] that dream action represents the dreamer's way of interacting with himself and his environment. If these assumptions are true, then, *change in dream events can change the dreamer's ideas about himself and the world [and] waking life behavior will change, too. . . .* [But] if we simply 'understand' our attitudes as expressed in our dreams, we may or may not be able to change our waking behavior."[66] But while interpretation of the dream may not be needful, consciousness of the dream is: "Of course, you need to be aware. Otherwise, unconscious and tipsy, you'll forget who was there [at the nightly dream "party"], what you did, and lose your gifts before you reach home."[67]*

The condition of (a) being highly conscious of the dream, and (b) modifying it without interpreting it, corresponds most fully to the potentials of lucid dreaming. Jayne Gackenbach alludes to the waking imagery techniques of therapy sketched above, when she makes this claim for the still greater efficacy of lucid dream control: "The basis of healing through lucid dreaming is to facilitate the person's self-healing mechanisms by means of intentional imagery while sleeping as dreamed imagery attains a higher 'reality' sense than waking imagery."[68] About such dreaming, Stephen LaBerge comments: "Interpretation may cast an interesting sidelight on the matter, but . . . an entirely optional one."[69] (He makes a provisional exception of "chronically maladjusted personalities."[70]) Moreover, according to Peter Fellows the beneficial effect of symbolic resolution of a conflict while lucid will result, even if one's interpretation of the dream is incorrect.[71] Fellows provides this example of the waking benefit of a symbolic resolution achieved by controlling a lucid dream:

---

* More recently (1991), Garfield has written about medical healing brought about by dreams and has advocated dream control for the sake of it. "The most dramatic case is one in which a full recovery occurred during the dream. A woman whose arm had been paralyzed for some time dreamed that *her pet dog had been attacked; she began to beat the attacking animal* in her dream *with her paralyzed arm.* When she awoke, she was astonished to discover that her paralysis had vanished. . ." (p. 70, citing R. E. Haskell 1985c, p. 112, who cites G. Solovey & A. Milechnin, "Hypnotic phenomena, suggestion, and oneiric activity," *American Journal of Clinical Hypnosis* 2, pp. 122–37, 1960). Garfield goes on to extol the possibilities of healing through dream control: "If moving a paralyzed arm in a dream precedes the restoration of its waking function, let us teach paralyzed patients to use their limbs in their dreams! The possibilities of deliberate and lucid dreaming for improving healthy functioning are monumental" (p. 71).

There is probably much merit in what Garfield says. But notice that while she assumes that in dreams which reveal *symptoms,* the dreaming mind detects an existing condition, when it comes to this dream of *cure* she does not even mention the possibility that the dreaming mind detected, but did not help to bring about, an improvement in medical condition. It is also striking that despite the above claims, there are no examples in her large book of her clients, interviewees, or self having comparable experiences, either spontaneously or by dream control.

Perhaps the most common of the "invisible force" dreams are those in which the dreamer cannot move or cannot run fast enough. I had a dream of this ilk as I was experiencing writer's block with this material you are now reading. It seemed that in this dream *I was walking through endless corridors, pursued by some unseen enemy. At one point, I came upon a table with an assortment of weapons upon it. None of the weapons was in a usable form; they sat in various stages of completion, their craftsman-maker nowhere to be found. Quickly, the enemy was upon me. I tried to run away but found that I could not move. Indeed, it seemed that the more I exerted myself, the closer I drew to my nemesis.*

At this point, instead of awakening, I became lucid, which is itself a kind of awakening. *I purposefully became calm, reminding myself that this experience was of my own creation. Then, in a manner rather difficult to describe, I organized my scattered mind into one clear intention: to simply walk ahead. There was with this thought a corresponding sensation of clarity and rightness.* Upon awakening, I was free of my writer's block, and have been able to call back the same sensations and use them in the waking state to enhance my effectiveness.[72]

As pointed out previously, dream control (guidance, change) can be exercised before and after dreaming a dream, as well as while dreaming. These three phases of control will be taken up in the next three chapters, under the headings of incubation (before), lucidity (during), and re-entry (after). Discussions of those topics will be general, that is, not confined to the issue of control, nor for that matter to non-interpretive applications. Since control of the dream is most literal and apparent in lucidity, it is in that chapter that the pros and cons of control will be raised. A concluding chapter will talk about the pattern of changes widely recommended for optimizing the healing benefit of dreams.

□ 13 □

Incubation

Incubation, a "Natural Tendency"

In the ancient Egyptian and Mediterranean worlds, a dream incubation was "a ritual invoking of dreams, usually for medical purposes, by sleeping in the temple of a particular god or hero."[1] By extension, the term now refers not only to comparable practices in other cultures, but to any intention or preparation to dream, especially to dream on a given theme or for a specific purpose. With incubation, something done awake changes the dream to follow; then the changed dream in some way changes waking—by healing, bringing insight, etc.

As Johanna King points out, incubation is just a special case of dreaming about what is on our minds already.[2] David Koulack mentions this example:

> Some years ago, I was doing a study involving multiple awakenings during the course of the night. I wasn't concerned with dream content but wished to keep the subjects up for a short period of time after each awakening. To do this, I decided to have the subjects relate their dreams.
>
> The first subject was going to an adoption agency directly from the laboratory to pick up his second adopted child. That night he had the following dreams:
>
> a) Yes. *We had taken the horses out to round up the cows.* No! no! Scratch that. I know what it was. *Er, another fella and I were out collecting semen from this bull for artificial insemination.* That's what it was.
>
> b) *Well we were looking for tricycles. Er, it seems as if we were looking at some special kind of tricycle, er, maybe it was one of those tractor peddle types.* . . .
>
> . . . The dreams . . . are apparently related to conception and children. . . .
>
> Yet, interestingly enough, . . . [the subject] spontaneously remarked on these dreams in the morning, and . . . wondered aloud about their possible meanings. Here we apparently have instances of dream material which is disguised only by virtue of the dreamer['s] inability or lack of desire to make connections . . . [to] waking experiences.[3]

393

Stanley Krippner & Joseph Dillard spell out the first assumption "behind dream incubation: 1. Any action, feeling, or thought you experience during the day may affect your dreams that night."[4] The purpose of incubation, say Phyllis Koch-Sheras et al., is to "make this natural tendency work for you. . . ." "Whenever you concentrate intensively on a single issue or problem just before going to bed, you are likely to set the dream incubation process in motion and continue to work on the issue in your dreams that night."[5]

Thus it is that "[t]he tendency for young women to dream about future lovers is ritualized in folk customs throughout the world." Patricia Garfield relates that "[i]n France, adolescent girls chant a rhyme to the full moon in spring. When she is ready for bed, the girl backs into it, still focusing her eyes on the moon, in order to go to sleep and dream of her beloved."[6] Scott Cunningham describes comparable incubations from Greece and England, and this one from Scotland: "Roast a salted herring, eat it without any other food, speak to no one and drink nothing before going to bed. A person will appear in the dream and offer the dreamer a glass of water. The person is the dreamer's future husband."[7]

"If we believe in the ability of dreams to discuss waking-life problems," Jack Maguire exhorts us, "and if we develop a sense of how our dreams in general go about doing this, it's not difficult at all to proceed one step further and prepare our dreaming mind to address the material we want it to address."[8]

Before describing some ancient and modern incubation practices, several pages will be given to discussing further the "natural tendency" to incubate, particularly as it shows up in observations by psychologists of effects of pre-sleep experience on dream content and mood.

Day residues. Freud's observations were discussed in chapter 2 (p. 60 passim): the "manifest" imagery of every dream contains direct references to waking experience. These day residues, he believed, always come from the "dream-day" itself,[9] and are virtually always trivial. But "[latent] dream-thoughts are dominated by the same material that has [consciously or unconsciously] occupied us during the day. . . ."[10] When the dream-thoughts get linked with the energy of forbidden wishes, they must be disguised. Energy from the important is displaced to the trivial day residues, which represent it in disguised form.

For Jung, a dream is virtually always related to recent consciousness by way of compensation. For existentialists, it is related by way of analogy. At an extreme from Freud are the "Feeling" therapists, Richard Corriere et al., who believe that a healthy person's dreams come close to being unadorned and undistorted representations of current waking existence in its most important and conscious aspects, and that such agreement is the dream's natural function.[11] Without fully endorsing this other extreme view of how day affects dream, it is correct to say that a firm belief in scrutable connections between waking and dreaming can only encourage such connections. If we expect to dream recognizably about our lives—whether directly or symbolically—, our day and night worlds do seem to converge, at least in part.

As for Freud's belief in the triviality of day residues, nineteenth century authors before Freud—Hildebrandt, Strümpell, Ellis, and Binz—had already remarked about a tendency for trivial recent memories, more than significant ones, to show up in dreams,[12] and there is some evidence to support the observation, as follows:

It is said that the psychoanalyst, a figure of obvious importance for a patient, appears in a mere 9% of patient dreams. (The claim that s/he appears disguised in 80% more is probably biased.)[13]

Similarly, David Foulkes notes that school settings are conspicuously underrepresented in the dreams of 5- and 6-year-olds, for whom leaving home and going to school is a "momentous (and occasionally traumatic) change." He concludes that "motivational dynamics" complicate reflection of the day world in dreams.[14*]

Experiments show that unconsciously perceived (subliminal) images are more likely to turn up in dreams than consciously perceived ones. (Charles Fisher's explanation is compatible with Freudian dream theory: the unconscious percept gets attached to repressed unconscious material and becomes its vehicle of expression.)[15**]

And lastly, a study by Ernest Hartmann confirms that most day residue items are, in fact, "unimportant."[16]

As for Freud's belief that day residues always come from the dream-day itself, Hartmann found that "most waking event items . . . occurred after 6 p.m." However, "[m]aterial thought about just prior to sleep never appeared in dreams."[17] This last finding is an interesting and surprising indication, but it cannot be a law, as anyone can testify who has successfully incubated a

---

* In a study of London school children age 5–7 originally published in 1931, "[o]nly 1 percent of the dreams referred to school activities, and these involved playground activities" (D. Beaudet 1990, p. 133, citing C. W. Kimmins, "Children's dreams," in S. G. M. Lee & A. R. Mayer, editors, *Dreams and Dreaming*, Middlesex: Penguin, 1973). One psychologist in the 1960s found that "[t]he object of fear in the child's waking life will show up in the child's dreams a year or so later" (D. Beaudet 1990, p. 132, citing L. B. Ames, "Sleep and dreams in childhood," in E. Harms, editor, *Problems of Sleep and Dreaming in Childhood*, New York: Pergamon, 1964).

** Fisher's work is described by E. S. Tauber & M. R. Green (1959), p. 83ff. See also Freud's (1953 [1900], p. 181) description of Pötzl's original tachistoscopic experiments with dreams, in a footnote added in 1919, and H. Shevrin (1986).

dream, or for that matter worried themselves to sleep over something about which they then dreamt. Moreover, Hartmann's finding is contradicted by researchers who observe instead that thoughts from just before sleep tend to be directly or symbolically related to REM dreams which follow.[18] This and other considerations also weigh against the triviality of day residues.

It seems evident that both trivial and significant events and concerns find their ways into our dreams.

Some other qualifications should be noted concerning the recency of waking life events referred to by dreams. First, during a typical night's sleep, there is, according to Lawrence Scrima, a movement from (1) material associated with current life, early in sleep, to (2) memories of the more distant past, during the middle of the night, then back to (3) the recent past, toward morning.[19] Sleep onset dreams are particularly rich in references to recent life episodes.[20]

Second, while it is true that significant events show up in dreams of the same night twice as often as on the following two nights,[21*] there appears also to be a lag effect. This was first observed by Michel Jouvet. He noticed that his physical environment, when it did not appear in his own same night dreams, might show up 7–8 days later.[22] Pursuing this suggestion, Tore Nielsen & Russell Powell have discerned a peak of incorporation 6–7 days after events, with indications of a further peak at 12 days. They suppose that the "dream-lag" effect may reflect a periodicity inherent in the consolidation of learning.[23**]

Of course waking experiences do show up in dreams long after the event. Rosalind Cartwright relates an anecdote about an experiment where her staff showed subjects a pornographic film. "One of the male staff members, who claimed he had an ample and satisfactory sex life, reported that two weeks after seeing the movie he dreamed a complete rerun."[24]

Incorporation studies. 'Incorporation' experiments such as Cartwright's examine the influence of selected stimuli administered just prior to sleep on dreams which follow. Foulkes & Allan Rechtschaffen used episodes of a TV Western: to one group, they showed an episode with violence and sex, to

---

* However, T. A. Nielsen & R. A. Powell (1989, p. 561) also note a study in which erotic films were incorporated more on the second than the first night (citing R. D. Cartwright, N. Bernick, G. Borowitz & A. Kling, "Effect of an erotic film on the sleep and dreams of young me," *Archives of General Psychiatry* 20, pp. 262–71, 1969).

** Carlyle Smith (1993) refers to these findings (p. 358) in connection with his own, that when animals (rats) are given difficult learning tasks, REM increases not only just after training but also during "REM windows" coming "many hours and days [up to a week] after the end of training as well" (p. 341).

another group, a neutral episode. The violent-sexual episode elicited REM (though not NREM) dreams which were comparatively longer, more imaginative, more vivid, and more emotional, but not more violent, bizarre, sexual, or unpleasant. The two episodes, however, produced equal numbers of clear-cut incorporations—very few, in both cases. Even "uncertain" or symbolized incorporations seemed minimal.[25]

But a later study of male subjects by Donald Goodenough et al. imposed more highly "stressful" or "charged" stimulus films. One film showed an Australian "subincision rite" involving bloody mutilation of male genitals. The other showed "the birth of a baby with the aid of a Malstrom Vacuum Extractor . . .":

> Among the scenes the subjects saw was the insertion of the cup of the extractor into the vagina, the rhythmic pulling on the wire attached to the cup in time with the contractions, the episiotomy [incision of the vulva], and the sudden appearance of the baby. After this film, one subject had the following dream:
>
> > At the moment you woke me up *I was flying around in the airplane looking out, sort of, like looking out well, not through a window exactly, looking out through a, a like a hole. Well anyhow I could see part of the airplane where the wing is attached, the body of the plane. And just above me and to my left was a hole, and through the hole was protruding a coil of wire, and there was a man holding a ... the end of the wire ... big wire, he had his finger through the end of it. One loop at the end of it pulling it, it was attached ... the other part of the wire was attached to a door, and when he pulled the wire, the door would go up and down and the wire ... his hand would pull the wire and would cause him, the door would go up, he'd let it go back in, the door would go down, and uh, it was sort of a troop carrier plane, people, parachutists, jumping out of the airplane.*
>
> So in this dream, we have an instance of a rather clear representation of some of the images from the film along with the symbolic representation of the birth by the people jumping out of the plane.[26]*

In this study, the amount of incorporation correlated with the individual's degree of arousal while he watched the film.[27] Generally speaking (and contrary to Freud's belief about day residues), emotionally important events are more likely to be incorporated than indifferent ones.[28] The same may be said of stressful stimuli.[29] But note that negative presleep stimuli are less likely to be incorporated *directly* than are positive stimuli.[30]

The general result of incorporation experiments is that incorporations are always possible, but seldom reliable. Cartwright's experience tells her that

---

* Koulack (1991, p. 68) mentions that in another dream of the same night, this dreamer dreamt of bees pollinating flowers, of gloves, and of the experimental situation.

"the theme of the dreams following experimental manipulations is typically something other than that which was intended by the experimenter. . . ."[31] Much more reliable than incorporations of content, actually, are mood incorporations. Koulack comments on the Goodenough experiment: "Basically, the mood in the dreams reflected the waking mood after seeing the film."[32] Likewise, presleep stress has been said to cause "unpleasant" dreams,[33] and grim photos to elicit negatively toned dreams.[34]

Cartwright supposes that the quantity of incorporation depends upon the quantity of unresolved psychological material elicited by the stimulus.[35] This is presumably why negative stimuli have more effect on dream mood than do positive stimuli.[36] As mentioned elsewhere, Cartwright believes that incorporation is an important part of working through unresolved current life problems in dreams.[37] Koulack reviews several experiments giving conflicting indications on this question. In some cases, incorporating an anxiety- or stress-producing stimulus results in improved mood upon awakening; in other cases, incorporation seems instead to augment distress.[38] Koulack believes that mastery of a problem is best achieved by dreaming about it at the right times, but at other times avoiding it, until better prepared. "[T]here is an oscillation or interplay between mastery and avoidance" dreams.[39]

It is fair to presume that dream incubation is typically undertaken when a person is in a good frame of mind for dealing with an issue.*

---

* In a different set of studies, the stimuli are administered during rather than before sleep. Most of these in-sleep stimulus experiments explore REM sleep, for the indications about incorporation during NREM are mostly negative (A. M. Arkin & J. S. Antrobus 1991, p. 278). Most experiments involve sensory stimuli (see T. A. Nielsen 1993, pp. 100–1 for a good brief summary). Sensations of touch—from water sprays, feathers, cold drafts, etc. applied to a sleeping subject—are incorporated more readily into dreams than sounds, lights, etc. (D. Koulack 1986, p. 209). (Recall that sensations of wetness may be incorporated into dreams by bedwetters [ch. 9, p. 309n].) By one estimate (K. Trotter, K. Dallas & P. Verdone 1987), a water stimulus is incorporated at a rate of 42%, a light at 23%, a smell at 22%, and, surprisingly, a sound at only 9%. The investigators perhaps overcautiously conclude that "dreaming is not readily influenced by external stimuli of any kind" (p. 12). Tore Nielsen (op. cit.) induced "kinesthetic and orientational transformations" of dream content using blood pressure cuffs on both legs. His subjects produced a high percentage of direct incorporations of the cuffs. An impressive number of dreams correctly specified which limb was affected.

In other experiments, verbal information is played to sleepers. R. J. Berger found in 1963 that names of significance to the sleeper are no more likely to be incorporated into dreams than insignificant names (Arkin & Antrobus, op. cit., p. 272, citing Berger, "Experimental modification of dream content by meaningful verbal stimuli," *British Journal of Psychiatry* 109, pp. 722–40, 1963). However, M. Ennis & P. Fonagy (1989) report that proper names (played on tapes to sleep lab subjects) are incorporated with special ease, though not always in their proper form: the name Robert might become a robber or a rabbit. R. E. Rainville (1988, p. 33) states that a recording of one's own voice is more readily incorporated, and with more emotional salience, than someone else's voice. (Interestingly, people recognize their own voice 89% of the time while asleep, but only 36% awake.)

Laboratory effects. One influence on dreams which concerns all sleep lab researchers is that of the lab setting itself. "A Heisenberglike effect is at work here," remarks Louis Breger; "one cannot observe dreams without to some degree influencing them by the very process of observation."[40] The most conspicuous effect is incorporation of the experimental situation itself as an element in the dream: explicit references have been found in about 20 to 33 percent of lab dreams, and symbolized references inferred in an additional 15 to 33 percent.[41] Having a marked interest in the experimental situation further increases the rate of incorporation of the lab setting.[42] But having "a significant degree of life stress . . . [overrides] the situational stress" of sleeping in a lab and results in fewer incorporations.[43]

Incorporation of the setting is especially marked on a subject's first night. To circumvent this and other 'first-night effects', that night is often set aside for adaptation, and the second night is used to establish baselines, if necessary. Nonetheless, references to the lab setting tend to reappear when experimentation begins, particularly if stressful.[44]

Bill Domhoff & Joe Kamiya have found that women's and men's dreams reflect somewhat different reactions to sleep in the lab:

To examine a different variety of verbal stimulus, T. Hoelscher et al. first asked their subjects to identify their personal goals. Then during sleep, they "presented audio recordings of words or phrases descriptive of the goals to which the individual was highly committed. During REM sleep, but not during NREM sleep, these words or phrases were more likely to prompt dream images with goal related content than were words or phrases describing goals to which another individual was highly committed" (H. T. Hunt 1986, p. 232, citing T. Hoelscher, E. Klinger & S. G. Barta, "Incorporation of concern- and nonconcern-related verbal stimuli into dream content," *Journal of Abnormal Psychology* 90, pp. 88–91, 1981).

Another sort of experiment showing that people do respond to verbal information received during sleep involves overt responses not necessarily reflected in concomitant dreaming. Highly hypnotizable people are able both to receive and respond to verbal suggestions made during REM sleep, e.g., "Whenever I say the word 'pillow' your pillow will feel uncomfortable and you will want to move it with your hand." Subjects recall nothing upon awakening (F. J. Evans, L. A. Gustafson, D. N. O'Connell, M. T. Orne & R. E. Shor, "Verbally induced behavioral responses during sleep," *Journal of Nervous and Mental Disease* 150, pp. 171–87, 1970, quoted by D. Koulack 1986, p. 213).

Using a conditioning procedure, John Antrobus got sleeping subjects to incorporate a visual image by playing a tone previously associated with the image by reinforcement (R. E. Haskell 1986b, pp. 357–8, citing J. S. Antrobus, "Dreaming for cognition," in A. M. Arkin, J. S. Antrobus & S. J. Ellman, editors, *The Mind in Sleep*, Hillsdale, New Jersey: Lawrence Erlbaum, 1978). However, the stimulus image undergoes transformation, which Robert Haskell compares to the transformation of presleep thoughts in sleep onset dreams by Silberer's 'auto-symbolic' process (p. 358) (ch. 1, p. 27). For example, a tone was associated with the image of "a man cutting the bark off a tree with a cane knife." When the associated tone was played to the sleeping subject, she dreamt of "*cutting a pie with a kitchen knife*" (p. 357). For Haskell, this demonstration shows that while specific imagery is very difficult to control, structures of meaning underlying variable imagery are in fact more controllable than is usually recognized (p. 372).

Although female subjects had a few prosaic dreams about the experimental situation, . . . [generally it] was perceived as threatening and embarrassing. . . . S6 had a dream in which *she was in an experiment in which she had not fulfilled her obligation of giving information or learning something*. . . . S10 related the experiment to her work as a newspaper reporter when she dreamed that *her newspaper had photographed her while she was dreaming*. Her most traumatic dream in the laboratory concerned *an experimental psychologist who was sinking ships in Lake Michigan*. At home [later] S10 had two violent dreams about the experiment. In the first *she was in an experiment in which all subjects died. She had only gone through the first phase, removal of the outer skin, and had been sent home to become blind and deaf*. In the second dream *a guillotine sliced off the top of her head in an experiment*. . . .

While some male subjects perceived the situation as threatening, it seemed to be more of an annoyance and a test or exhibition for men. . . . S5 dreamed *he had electrodes on and could not do an intellectual task*. S9 dreamed that *the experimenter was disappointed because he had failed to dream*. S27 had one dream in which *all the subjects had the names of race horses, and someone was rooting for one to come in ahead of the other* (more than one subject was sometimes studied on an experimental night). In another dream S27 *put himself to sleep twice a day on the front lawn for everyone to see*.[45]

Richard Fox et al. report on a male subject whose lab dreams happened to conform to the same pattern ("test or exhibition"), but only as long as the experimenter was also a male:

> In contrast, the themes of dreams reported to the female experimenter made repeated reference to experiences in which the subject was or potentially could be hurt. These included *being in a combat situation, having a bloody nose,* and *being laughed at by women*.

This shows that the experimenter's gender can modify a dreamer's ostensible style. On alternating nights for a week, Fox's two subjects came into contact with experimenters of their own or the opposite gender:

> The dreams of the female subject, the nurse, . . . focused around dependency issues. Many of her dreams were set in the hospital ward situation where she appeared to view the male experimenter, a doctor, as one of the ward physicians whose major function was fulfilling her patients' needs. With the female experimenter, however, there were frequent dreams of waiting for doctors to meet patients' needs and in later dreams this was associated with anger at the doctor for not being available.
>
> This difference in the dependency expression between the two sets of dreams can be demonstrated by the symbol of intravenous fluids and apparatus which appeared in five of her dreams. In three dreams with the male experimenter *the intravenous fluid was running smoothly*. In contrast, in one dream reported to the

female experimenter *the intravenous tubing was not connected to the bottle* and in another dream *the bottle was running dry.*[46*]

Fox's observations establish no general pattern of dreaming, but rather show how circumstances in the dreamer's situation can alter dream content in idiosyncratic ways.

A content analysis comparing men's lab dreams and home dreams does reveal patterns of difference, some of which can be attributed to the lab situation in evident ways.[47] The lab dreams of Domhoff & Kamiya's subjects had more characters (2.63 per dream) than their home dreams (1.95). Likewise, they dreamt more of certain elements, such as buildings and printed matter, and more of the activities of sleeping and recreation. Lab dreams also have much less sex, aggression, and personal misfortune, and somewhat less good fortune as well.[48] There seems to be a general flattening of dreams in the lab. Note that nightmares seldom occur there, and are even much reduced for chronic sufferers such as those with posttraumatic nightmares.[49] Wet dreams are also rare in the lab.[50] Domhoff & Kamiya do assert that lab dreams are more bizarre; but Hunt disagrees, and so does Foulkes, who reasons that lab dreams are less bizarre simply because they comprise a more representative sample.[51**]

Cultural effects. Another place to look for the "natural tendency" to incubate, to dream of what occupies our minds, is in the area of cultural influences (chapter 5). Culture partially determines the dreams people actually

---

[*] Edith Sheppard (1969, pp. 228–9) noticed that when the experimenter in contact with a dream lab subject is of the opposite gender, "genitality" scores go up.

[**] Foulkes (1985, p. 4) argues that lab collection is indispensable for describing dreams and discovering their functions. Most home dreams are forgotten, and those recalled are reported in ways distorted by time lapse (as well as by desire to please, embarrassment, etc.). The lab provides a truly representative sample, not just specially memorable dreams. From comparison of REM awakenings with recall of the same dreams in the morning, it appears that bizarre dream elements are twice as well remembered in the morning as non-bizarre ones (C. Cipolli, R. Bolzani, C. Cornoldi, R. De Beni & I. Fagioli 1993, pp. 163 and 168). In agreement with Foulkes in most respects, Cartwright (1977, p. 17) comments further that one can obtain a whole night's series, not just "a chapter out of context." Disadvantages of lab collection include causing biases of content of the kind mentioned in the text. Further, Cartwright acknowledges that lab collection can create artificial tensions which impact on subsequent dreaming; and that awakenings can truncate dreams as well as prematurely terminate series (p. 30). Joel Covitz (1990, pp. 72–3), a Jungian, argues that lab-collected dreams are atypical, because the unconscious "is most certainly aware of who will be viewing or reviewing the dream" and produces dreams not "intended by the mind for interpretation." One can add that longitudinal studies of individual dreamers are impractical for the lab. Furthermore, spontaneous amnesia for dreams is a natural dimension of the overall dream experience, with a dynamic of its own which cannot be duplicated with lab awakenings. If one wants to investigate how people ordinarily have and 'use' their dreams, dreams from home are more to the point. But of course there is no need to exclude any source of information about dreams.

dream, as well as those selected unconsciously for recall and consciously for sharing. Further, conscious and unconscious editing and embellishing of the report often reflect cultural expectations. Some cultural influences are part of the general background of people's lives, which we do not normally connect with our dream lives, but which results in cultural dream styles. There are also explicit influences, which result in so-called culture pattern dreaming in traditional societies.

General cultural effects are revealed by cross-cultural comparisons. Certain differences, for example, are found in the dreams of U.S. women and Gusii women of Kenya.[52] Not much thought is needed to connect the U.S. profile to influences of our cultural milieu:

U.S. Women	Gusii Women
assertive	self-restrained
more aggressive; more verbally so	less aggressive; more physically so
many more failure themes	many fewer failure themes
many sex dreams	few sex dreams
predominantly apprehensive	predominantly sad

General cultural effects also show up in comparisons of sub-groups within a given society. Thus while U.S. whites and U.S. blacks both dream of the other as violent, whites in Robert Haskell's sample are also violent toward blacks, but blacks seldom dream of being violent toward whites. And whites dream of blacks as animalistic sex objects, whereas blacks dream of defending their mates against white sexual attack, according to Haskell.[53]

As for class differences, adolescent working class boys' dreams are more hostile than friendly, middle class boys' dreams not so.[54] Upper middle class dreams have fewer characters, and less death anxiety; in lower middle class dreams (even more than lower class dreams) there is more misfortune.[55]

Jayne Gackenbach, known for her research in lucid dreaming, has testified to the impact of cultural milieu upon herself personally, during the time she spent with the Cree of Alberta: "Initially Ravenwoman's object based interpretations made me uncomfortable as they tend to be at once specific yet vague. But then my dreams began to evidence more and more animals, Natives, and most recently elders. Clearly my work with Natives was bleeding into my deep unconscious so it made increasing sense for me to use cultural interpretations."[56] Along the same lines, John McCall writes: "When in the course of ethnographic research one becomes immersed in another culture, . . . [i]t is enthralling and profoundly disturbing to find oneself dreaming in a new and unfamiliar way, and to be compelled to reflect on those dreams on their own terms."[57]

'Culture pattern dream' usually refers to an important dream (or vision), with determinate characteristics, which is deliberately sought, or incubated. But dreams with such traits also occur unsought, and culture patterning affects ordinary as well as important dreams.[58] "Believing that a certain dream image has a specific meaning sometimes leads people to dream within that framework, accepting the cultural dream language as their own," says Garfield.[59] For instance, the dreaming mind sometimes detects the hidden onset of an illness (chapter 8). If one believes, through acculturation, that certain dreams predict certain illnesses, such dreams become more probable. So in cultures with stable traditions of dream symbology, codified interpretations may be justified, though for reasons other than those locally believed.[60]*

Sought culture pattern dreams are those for which incorporation from the pool of traditional motifs is fully intended. They include initiation dreams, power dreams, curative dreams, and so on. Sometimes the formula is quite general, sometimes remarkably exact.** "A would-be conjurer" of a certain Native American tribe "must have *four* dreams with specific characters, in a specific setting, in a specific order."[61] A certain amount of the prescribed material may get added during the telling,[62] or the criteria for deciding when a given motif has appeared may seem to us lax.[63]*** But, says Robert Dentan, even in those cultures where elders pressure the young "to cast their dreams or visions into acceptable form," they rarely lie about it; that is, they substantially do actually have the dreams expected of them.[64]

But even when dreams are "manipulat[ed] as social assets," that does not obviate their genuine embeddedness in the dreamer's "experience of self and reality."[65]

Doctrinal compliance. Dentan calls attention to a similarity between cultural influences in traditional societies and clinical influences in ours, where

---

* "Dream code books therefore are useless for interpreting dreams unless the dreamer is aware of the dream code" (M.-T. B. Dombeck 1991, p. 130).

** The same range of prescriptions, general to exact, is found in various religious movements in which conversion dreams qualify new members (R. T. Curley 1992, p. 139).

*** Similar considerations apparently prevailed when one of Vincent Crapanzano's (1975, p. 151) Moroccan Arab informants related that he and his wife had had the "same" dream on a momentous topic. It turned out that the dreams were the same only insofar as both dealt with the theme of departure, on a night when a momentous departure was anticipated for the following morning. On another occasion (p. 149), his hosts said that his visit had been foretold to them in dreams. Inquiry revealed that the dreams had no evident connection with the visit; rather, the host was in all likelihood simply expressing conventional hospitality. (See B. Secunda 1993, for an arrival purportedly foretold in dreams by Huichol Indians of Mexico.)

"clients undergoing a particular psychotherapy tend to report dreams significant to that therapy."[66] This phenomenon is called 'doctrinal compliance' (a term coined by Ian Ehrenwald[67]): clients of Jungians tend to have archetypal dreams, clients in Feeling Therapy have dreams about feelings, etc., in order "to please and impress" their respective therapists.[68] Clients may also 'comply' with the idiosyncracies of an individual therapist, whose taste for literature, say, may elicit client dreams "in rather literary language and in poetic form."[69] So comment Edward Tauber & Maurice Green, adding that compliance should not be viewed always as neurotic, as "the unconscious need of the patient to submit to the authority of the analyst" while evading real self-disclosure, something which it can accomplish. Compliance can also constitute a legitimate, if unconscious, attempt to communicate "in a language or dream symbology which might make it easier for the analyst to understand him."[70] This amounts to a sort of unconscious incubation. In this light, doctrinal compliance only expresses a healthy tendency to harmonize dream life with social life, a tendency whose stultification in Euro-American culture is so regretted by Montague Ullman and others (chapter 5).

One place where doctrinal compliance becomes problematical is where compliant dreams are offered as evidence for the dream theories to which they comply. If the speculation of Erik Erikson is true, the whole of modern dream theory is founded on such a dream, or a remarkable variant of it. The principle "dream specimen" of Freud's *The Interpretation of Dreams*, the first dream he related there and the one chiefly relied upon to illustrate the theory, is Freud's own dream of "Irma's injection." Erikson argued in 1954 that Freud, at the moment when his ideas were coalescing, dreamt this particular dream in order to be able to analyze it, and with the analysis, work out and substantiate his ideas. This amounts to an unconscious incubation, by Freud, of a dream in compliance with his own nascent theory. The ironic implication here that the whole dream—not the dream-thought but the dream as a coherent whole—served purposes of Freud's ego beyond the kind which the theory itself understood.[71]*

---

* At another level, Erikson proposed that for Freud to 'know' the dream—"Irma's injection" and dreams in general—meant symbolically for him to 'know' mother. Erikson (1954, pp. 45-6) cited Freud's famous caveat: "Every dream has at least one point at which it is unfathomable; a *central point*, as it were, connecting it with the unknown." Erikson pointed out that "central point" in Freud's German is "Nabel," i.e., 'navel' (cf. the slightly different translation of this sentence in my introduction, p. 4, from S. Freud 1953 [1900], p. 524). "This statement, in such intimate proximity to allusions concerning the resistance of Victorian ladies (including the dreamer's wife, now pregnant) to being undressed and examined, suggests an element of transference to the Dream Problem as such: the Dream, then, is just another haughty woman, wrapped in too many mystifying covers and 'putting on airs' like a Victorian lady. Freud's letter to Fliess spoke of an 'unveiling' of the

Asclepian Incubation

Undoubtedly, humans have long been incubating dreams. Richard Jones thinks that the wall-painted caves of Europe may have served as incubation chambers, being dark, hard of access, confining, and rich with symbolism.[72] But archaic incubation need not necessarily have been any more formalized than our own sometimes is. In New Guinea, a Tangu "faced with a problem retires for the night with the hope that a dream will shed light on the matter and present him with a directive. . . ."[73] There is no knowing how long we have been practicing such incubation-by-intention. Beyond that, common traditional means of inducing dreams include isolation, prayer, sacrifice, drugs, fasting, sexual abstinence, and self-inflicted pain.[74] Most of these features are contained in the tradition surrounding Asclepius, which is the tradition of incubation closest to Euro-American culture.

Asclepian incubation blended indigenous Greek practices with adoptions from Egypt, which itself had assimilated Mesopotamian influences.[75] Egyptian "dream-inspiring temples" date back at least to 3000 B.C.[76]

Here are some Egyptian incubation instructions: "To obtain a vision from (the god) Besa. Make a drawing of Besa on your left hand and enveloping your hand in a strip of black cloth that has been consecrated to Isis . . . lie down to sleep without speaking a word, even in answer to a question. . . ."[77]

The first known dream book, which rated dream motifs as either "good" or "bad," is in the Chester Beatty papyrus from about 2000 B.C.[78] This key was presumably intended to be used by privileged individuals,[79] or by dream priests, called "Scribes of the Double House of Life," "Masters of the Secret Things,"[80] and "The Learned Men of the Magic Library."[81]

Incubation was practiced in temples where one went specially in order to dream, assisted by a potion. Dreams were interpreted by the priests, who also administered medical treatments which, according to their interpretations, the gods had prescribed.

There were numerous Egyptian gods of dreams. One was Serapis. Another was Imhotep, the precedent if not the pattern for Asclepius. "Imhotep . . . lived about 2980-50 B.C., was a noted architect . . . , an important medical man, and one of the astrologers of the priests of Ra. After his death he was gradually elevated to the status of a deity. . . ."[82]

---

mystery of the dream, which was accomplished when he subjected the Irma Dream to an exhaustive analysis. In the last analysis, then, the dream itself may be a mother image; she is the one, as the Bible would say, to be 'known'. It is at this level, of "[s]pecial transferences to one's dream life," that Erikson explicitly compared Freud's behavior surrounding the Irma dream with culture pattern dreaming, as well as with doctrinal compliance.

Like Imhotep, Asclepius is thought to have started out as a human physician, around 1100 B.C.[83] He became "a chthonic oracular demon . . . or hero," and later still an Apollonian deity.[84*] In some versions of his myth, he was killed by Zeus for daring to bring the dead to life, then made a deity by Zeus to console his father Apollo, a god of healing. "[W]ithin the world of late pagan antiquity, Asclepius achieved the highest divine rank . . . and became the strongest rival of Christ next to Mithras."[85]

In fact, the cult of Asclepius was partially assimilated by early Christianity. "In th[e] struggle for supremacy over the ancient deities, the followers of Christ met the pagans on their own ground and adopted their tactics. . . . The methods of the later pagan incubation are found to a great extent unchanged at the shrines of Christian saints."[86] In Greece and Asia Minor, incubation was practiced in formerly Asclepian temples, but in the names of Saints Cosmas, Damian, and others. Although dreams and incubation have always been important for Islam, there were in actuality more Christian than Muslim incubation temples in the Near East.[87**] In St. Jerome's time (400 A.D.), "dreams became reclassified almost exclusively with witchcraft" by the Church.[88] Yet Asclepian influences persisted. In medieval Europe, Asclepius survived in the legends of miraculous cures by saints and the incubations for curing practiced in certain churches, despite official disapproval.[89]

There are many warnings in the Talmud against visiting Asclepian temples and other incubation temples. This must indicate that the practice was widely adopted among the Hebrews, who were enjoined rather only to pray to have good dreams and to be spared bad ones. "[A]s time went on, however, it [temple incubation] became a partly approved practice."[90]

---

* Unless otherwise attributed, information about Asclepius is from C. A. Meier (1967 [1949]) or M. Hamilton (1906).

** A traditional Muslim incubation practice is called "Istikhārah (lit. 'asking for the best choice', 'seeking goodness')[, a] practice, based upon the Sunnah, of asking God for guidance when faced with important decisions or perplexing situations. Istikhārah consists of praying a [certain] prayer immediately before retiring to sleep along with a . . . personal prayer . . . in which one presents the problem to God and asks for guidance: a response may come in the form of a dream, a sign, or a sudden certitude" (C. Glassé 1989). Istikhārah is still practiced by traditional Muslims, though not by the educated classes (Fazlur Rahman, personal communication, 1986). Among Moroccan Muslim Arabs, "stikhara" refers to recitation of the "profession of faith, other verses of the Koran, or sacred formulae or prayers . . . [one] happens to know" to encourage dreaming on a certain topic, or simply to encourage dreaming. "'Stikhara' also refers to the very important practice of visiting a saint's tomb, or some other sacred place, in order to have a dream" (V. Crapanzano 1975, p. 148), a practice also of Moroccan Jews (Y. Bilu & H. Abramovitch 1985).

Covitz (1990, pp. 135-9) discusses traditional Jewish formulae for inviting dream answers to "dream questions," including one from 1698 four pages long. He also contributes his own Judeo-Jungian incubation procedure, consisting of bedtime relaxation exercises and a petition (pp. 139–41).

Asclepian temples remained active for a thousand years, up until the late A.D. 400s. The oldest known temple was at Tricca in Thessaly, but the cult center was Epidaurus (600 B.C.), located two and a half hours' journey from Athens. Most of the 400 odd Asclepian temples were affiliated with Epidaurus. All were remotely situated, and always at cold springs, water being an element of the cult, together with trees and snakes, all symbols of earth and life (tame tree snakes were kept in the temples.) "It was very unusual for an epiphany of Asclepius to take place outside of the healing sanctuaries."[91]

The chief purpose of Asclepian incubation was the cure of physical disorders and illnesses. But "bodily illness and psychic defect were for the ancient world an inseparable unity."[92] C. A. Meier considers cure by incubation to have been a variety of mystery initiation. "Incubation rites induced . . . an artificial *mania*, in which the soul spoke directly."[93] We tend to associate the Greek attitude to dreams with Aristotle's rational-empirical approach. However, the Greeks also belonged to the general Mediterranean tradition,[94] and "[i]ncubation became such an element in everyday life that it was among the most popular and persistent of religious rites. . . ."[95] Indeed, "[t]he Greek thinker who did not accept the curative power of Asclepian visions was the exception, not the rule."[96] Recall Socrates's dying words: "Crito, I owe a cock to Asclepius; will you remember to pay the debt?"[97]

There were, actually, many other cults of incubation in the region besides that of Asclepius. These included cults of Diana, Io, and others, as well as those of Imhotep, Serapis, and Isis borrowed directly from Egypt. The Asclepian cult somewhat merged Asclepius with these gods,* together with other, local deities connected with an older fertility religion. The most famous Asclepian centers seem originally to have been earth oracles,[98] where one slept in contact with "Sacred Mother Earth, who sends the dreams."[99] "Two of the chief faculties of the earth were the power of sending dreams," commented Mary Hamilton, "and the gift of healing. As a giver of dreams she is apostrophized in the *Hecuba* of Euripides (l. 70):—'O Lady Earth, sender of black-winged dreams.'"[100]

Asclepius was always associated with female figures, Hygieia, Panacea, and others, who were variously regarded as his wife or daughter. An important function of Asclepian incubation, as of incubation practices around the

---

* Initially, according to Mary Hamilton (1906, pp. 100–1), the Asclepian cult influenced that of Serapis at Alexandria, a Greco-Egyptian city; later, the influence passed back. Isis and Serapis were widely successful throughout the A.D. Greco-Roman world. "The temples of Isis and Serapis grew to surpass in number and fame those of any other god" (p. 103). Serapis and Asclepius were commonly linked together, on coins, with adjoining temples, with inscriptions mentioning both, or in joint appearances in visions.

world, was reversal of infertility.[101] Nevertheless, women near childbirth, as well as the dying, were prohibited from entering the sanctuary for reasons of ritual cleanliness.

"Go in good, come out better" read the inscription at one Asclepieium.[102] To enter the precinct to incubate, it was necessary first to have been invited by the god in a dream. John Sanford compares the invitational dream to an initial dream in psychotherapy (chapter 11).[103] A person too sick to travel could send a stand-in dreamer, a custom borrowed from Egypt, perhaps.[104] The supplian was required to abstain from food for one day preceding the rite, and from wine for three days. In one story, Asclepius refuses to treat an alcoholic, referring him instead to a certain mortal physician.[105] Nonetheless, prepatory rites included psychotropic ointments and drinks,[106] as well as wine. Music further added to the conducive atmosphere.* The supplian purified her/himself by bathing in cold spring water** and, according to some accounts, by performing an animal sacrifice at a statue of Asclepius shortly before sleep-time.[107]

Our word 'clinic' derives from the Greek for 'couch', upon which a person lay to incubate in the inner sanctuary, the dreamery, termed the 'abaton' (or 'adytum': "place not to be entered unbidden").[108] There—always at night —s/he might receive a regular dream, a waking vision, or a hypnagogic experience.[109] If no appropriate dream came, the incubation was deemed a failure. In earlier centuries, the incubant came and went in a day. But in later centuries the ill person remained, sometimes for months or even years, until the auguries were favorable for further incubation.

The "curative factor" was the dreaming experience itself.[110] The "patient woke cured."[111] Originally, the priests were neither dream interpreters nor physicians; rather "[t]hey guided one to experience one's own personal encounter."[112] There was, however, a trend over time away from immediate

---

* The combination of wine with music suggests to C. A. Meier (1967 [1949], pp. 86–8) an integration of Dionysian and Apollonian energies in Asclepian ritual. Both were gods of healing.

** Tore Nielsen (1989, p. 6 passim) discusses the fact that incubation rites around the world typically involve physical procedures with spiritual effects. Of his four categories of procedures, three pertain to Asclepian practices. (1) "[S]leep in sacred precincts." Nielsen compares the effect of sleeping in the special environment to the "first-night effect" of sleeping in a dream lab. (2) "[C]utaneous stimulation." Asclepian prepatory rites included cold baths and ointments. (3) "[P]ain induction." Although it is nothing compared to the chopping off of fingers by certain Plains Indians in quest of visions, Nielsen includes fasting in this category. The fourth category, not mentioned by Meier or my other sources as part of Asclepian practices, is "use of bodily icons." The Egyptian ritual, mentioned above, of drawing the god Besa on the hand falls in this category, as does the custom once practiced by young women in the U.S. of sleeping with a piece of wedding cake under the pillow to induce dreams of the future spouse (P. Garfield 1988a, p. 99).

miraculous cures, toward the finding of diagnoses and prescriptions of hygienic measures and medicines in dreams where healing was not achieved by the dream per se. Occasion arose for expert priestly interpretations and treatments,[113] perhaps even for surgery,[114] and even for dreaming on the part of priests on behalf of suppliants.* These modifications show, in addition to predictable routinization, the influence of the Egyptian cults.

Those who obtained a cure had to record their dreams. There were two sorts of inscriptions: official ones, on stone slabs or pillars (stelae) conspicuously placed to impress suppliants, which memorialized traditions concerning cures achieved long before at the temple, as well as contemporary cases; and testimonials from individuals inscribed on tablets. Many also left votive offerings in the form of models, mostly in clay, of the cured body part. "Almost every outer part and inner organ of the human anatomy is represented, from head and hair to feet and toes."[115] The patient was also obliged to pay a fee, determined by ability to pay. Beyond that, s/he had to make a thanks offering, perhaps the sacrifice of a cock or a small gift, or, if so advised by Asclepius in a dream, a literary production such as a paean to the god or the donation of a building to the temple. The offering was due within one year, on pain of relapse.

As for the dreams, Asclepius might appear in any of his guises: as bearded man, young man, boy, snake, or dog. Often he came accompanied by his female companions and his sons. In the commonest type of curative dream, he "*touched* the affected part of the incubant's body and then vanished."[116] One inscription reads:

> Alecetes of Alicos, blind, dreamed *Asclepius opened his eyes with his fingers.* The next day he could see.[117]

In the case of barren women, the healing touch often took the form of sexual intercourse and impregnation by the god, especially in the guise of snake. Homosexual intercourse with the god as boy is also recorded:

> A man with a stone in his penis. He had a dream. He dreamt *he was having intercourse with a beautiful boy, and in ejaculating he ejected the stone, picked it up,* and emerged holding it in his hand.[118]

---

* Besides in Egypt, this practice, says Scott Cunningham (1992, p. 38) had earlier existed in Babylon, where the priests who dreamt for supplicants were specialists, different from the priests who interpreted the dreams. Z. A. Piotrowski (1986, p. 12), without mentioning his source, describes a sort of Asclepian dream drama: "In the morning, the priest not only listened to the dream reports but made the patients actually act out all the roles they had performed in their night dreams, as actors on a stage; the priest would assume the role of other characters from the same dreams."

And here is an interesting variant of the god's touch:

> Diaitos of Kirrha. He was paralyzed in the knees. In his sleep here he had a dream. He dreamt *the god bade his attendants lift him up, carry him out of the adytum and set him down in front of the temple; when they had done so, the god yoked horses to a chariot, drove around him in a circle three times, and trampled him with his horses; and immediately he regained control of his knees.* When day came he emerged healthy.[119]*

Apparently not everyone who came to an Asclepian temple believed firmly in the efficacy of that approach to illness, as can be inferred from inscriptions recording cures received by surprised skeptics:

> Ambrosia, from Athens, blind in one eye. She came as a suppliant to the god. As she walked about the sanctuary she laughed at some of the cures as being incredible and impossible, for example that the lame and the blind should become sound just by seeing a vision in their sleep. But in her sleep here she saw a vision. She dreamt *the god appeared to her and said he would make her sound, and as his fee she would have to dedicate in the sanctuary a silver pig as a memorial of her ignorance; so saying, he cut open her diseased eyeball and poured in some drug.* When day came she emerged healthy.[120]

Inscriptions also show that people came with nonmedical problems: broken objects were restored, lost relatives located, etc. Other variants include: miraculous cures (sight restored to a man without eyeballs; a five year pregnancy brought to a happy issue); curative dreams dreamt at places other than a temple; and relapses as punishment for evaded payments. There were even cures without benefit of dreams: "A dog cured a boy from Aigina. He had a growth on his neck. He came to the god and in broad daylight one of the sacred dogs healed him with its tongue and made him well."[121]

As mentioned above, in later centuries the Asclepian cure was sometimes effected, not by the dream per se but by a prescription set out in the dream:

> A man named Julian hemorrhaged from the lungs. In a dream *he was told to go to the altar, mix pine nuts with honey, and eat them for three days.* He was cured.[122]

---

* Meier made a Jungian amplification of this dream (1967 [1949], p. 28): "Asclepius . . . learned the art of healing from Chiron the centaur. Chiron was incurably wounded by the poisoned arrows of Hercules. Thus, here is another healer who is himself in need of healing. . . . Welcker [A mid-nineteenth century German author] makes an interesting observation on the centaur nature of Chiron: '. . . the practical side of medicine is to be understood by the irrational part of Chiron (the horse) and the scientific side by the human part.' . . . We may then say that what *works* in medicine is irrational. The horse, like the serpent and the dog, is a chthonic animal. Thus it can heal or ward off evil."

Other prescriptive dreams are commented upon interestingly by Meier:

> Some of the detailed reports of cures which have come down to us prefigure the dialectical procedure of modern psychotherapy. These accounts often have a humorous flavor. . . . *When Asclepius commanded a certain Plutarchus to eat swine's flesh, the patient objected: "Lord, what would you have prescribed for a Jew?" Asclepius obligingly acquiesced in the witty objection of the Neo-Platonist and altered the treatment. . . .* An authoritative method is used instead of a dialectical one in those cases where it was necessary to heal by means of paradoxes. This was always the case when a taboo had to be broken that a cure might be effected. . . . [I]t recalls the principle . . . that the poison, the forbidden thing, is at the same time the remedy. Examples of this are when a Syrian had to eat pork, a Jewess had to anoint her child with swine's fat, and a Greek woman, who was a devotee of Adonis, had to eat the flesh of a wild boar. . . . ("And it is in fact the paradox which is the highest thing in the god's cure" [Aristides]). Thus, for example, in the depth of winter *Aristides is required amidst ice and snow to go down into the city and bathe in the river.* "Still full of warmth from the sight of the god" he did so. For all the rest of the day he was filled with a sense of inexpressible well-being, so entirely was he "with the god."[123]

It may be interesting to bridge to the upcoming section on contemporary incubation with a contemporary 'Asclepian' dream. This dream, as Sanford amplifies, contains an archetypal image paralleling the snake in the cult of Asclepius. The dream was not deliberately incubated, but was certainly induced by waking preoccupations, and probably by presleep prayer:

> A strange event occurred in my ministry some years ago that illustrates the enduring symbol of the serpent as a healing power. A young woman in my congregation called me one day in great anguish. Her five-year-old son had been stricken with spinal meningitis and was acutely ill. . . . She was requesting the prayers of the congregation, and of course prayers were said for her and her son. Early the next morning she called me again, terrified because of the following dream that had come to her during the night:
>
> *My husband and I were outside, looking into the [hospital] room where my son was asleep. I saw to my horror a great snake on the floor, crawling toward the boy, and cried out to my husband to go in the room and stop him. But the snake reached the boy first, and bit him on the forehead between the eyes. My husband emerged with the boy, bleeding slightly, and I was terrified.* I awoke, certain he would now die.
>
> In fact, her son did not die but began to recover that very day; eventually he made a total recovery. . . . To this woman, with her Christian prejudices against the snake, the dream was threatening, but had the dream come to an ancient Greek it would have been greeted with joy, for the snake would have been recognized as Asklepius himself who had come to heal the child.[124]

Contemporary Incubation

Letting 'incubation' be understood to include all presleep preparations for dreaming, then incubation is a regular feature of contemporary dreamwork, whether in the form of specific procedures with definite purposes, or, simply, of a general orientation to dreaming.

Holding what can be considered a general incubatory attitude are some, even, who pointedly discourage 'control' as being a misguided imposition of ego consciousness on the spontaneous dream process. Here can be included those who think that the helpfulness of dreams is enhanced by anticipating help from them,[125] as well as Jungians who find that openness to dreams facilitates the compensatory function.[126] Others advise that dream life is favorably influenced by waking psychospiritual development. That is the gist of the Islamic story related by Fritz Meier:

> When, after forty years of nocturnal vigils, the mystic ash-Shāh al-Kirmānī (ca. 900) finally fell asleep and saw God in a dream *he asked God why He appeared in a dream after he had sought him so long awake. God answered, "It is only thanks to your vigil that this fulfillment is granted you in your dream."* On the degree of purity of the dreamer's soul depended, so it was thought, the very quality of the dream.[127]

Very much the same idea is voiced, but in a secular mode, by Ullman in answer to the question, "Can we program or control our dreams?" "No, not *consciously.* If we look upon a dream as a kind of natural resource flowing within us, . . . a river shaped by our life experience, then its flow will not be changed simply by having someone on the shore urge a new direction on it. But if the person on the shore does the work necessary to make a change in direction possible, the flow will alter as desired. . . . [T]here has to be more than conscious intent to influence the flow. There has to be a genuine emotional investment."[128] And Garfield, a well-known advocate of deliberate control of dreams by incubation as well as in lucidity, also urges us to consider the general effect our waking lives have on dreams: "The brighter and more creative our waking minds become, the wider and wilder our nighttime jaunts."[129]

As for deliberate incubation procedures,* mention should first be made of Henry Reed's adaptation of Asclepian (plus Native American) techniques, discussed in chapter 5 (p. 190) in connection with the social sanctioning of

---

* Scrima (1984, p. 215) warns people who have trouble getting to sleep or remaining asleep that deliberate incubation activities may have the unwelcome effect of aggravating their sleeplessness, so should be avoided by them.

dreamwork. Reed, who gives credit to Gayle Delaney (see below) for "the initial inspiration that dream incubation was a human possibility,"[130] devised a four-stage process with Asclepian features.

(1) An invitational dream.

(2) Preparative meditation regarding purpose, with the choosing of personal symbols (equivalents to the god Asclepius and his temple).

(3) Incubation proper: 4–6 hours spent with the guide in discussion and then guidance into sleep.

(4) Discussion of the dream once dreamt.

(Reed has devised another incubation procedure as part of a four-week program for using dreams to find solutions to life problems. The incubation portion calls for composing a petition, copying it as a letter to be placed under the pillow at night "as an aid to concentration," and an "incubation reverie" involving relaxation exercises and rehearsal of the petition.[131])

Another adaptation of Asclepian and Native American traditions is that of Graywolf Fred Swinney and Jeannie Eagle, who manage a "contemporary Aesculapia," a "wilderness retreat and dream sanctuary."[132] Asclepian elements include the pilgrimage to get there, the "sense of sanctuary," location by a spring, "confession" (Asclepian equivalent?), and a "ceremonial offering" as sacrifice. It is probably safe to assume that Graywolf and Eagle, as well as Reed, also conform to ancient customs by charging fees. Neither of these adaptations especially orients incubation to medical problems.

The best-known tradition of incubation within the dream movement,—or pseudo-tradition,—is that of the Senoi, briefly mentioned (ch. 5, p. 173) also in connection with social aspects of dreamwork. The supposed incubatory technique of the Senoi consists precisely of the daily socialization of dream life. However, as remarked earlier, Kilton Stewart's version of Senoi culture has been largely debunked. Dentan claims to have been first to "blow the whistle" in 1978.[133]* "A barely recognizable version of Senoi reality has affected the lives of thousands of Americans," he writes, "who should know that what they are asked to do is *not* validated by a cure-all praxis among Malaysian hill peoples."[134] William Domhoff portrays Senoi dream culture as in every respect within the mainstream of preliterate societies throughout

---

* G. William Domhoff (1985, p. 74) states, however: "Doubts were first raised in 1978 when two documentary filmmakers came back from Senoi country with the news that they could find no morning dream clinics." He cites "An illusion destroyed," *Human Nature*, p. 12, June, 1978, and continues: "However, it was not until word of my findings and those of Dentan, Faraday, and Wren-Lewis began to get around, primarily through the *Dream Network Bulletin*, that the practitioners of the new dreamwork began to downplay the Senoi. Only in 1984, for example, did the Jungian-Senoi Institute change its name to the Jungian Dreamwork Institute."

the world. Particularly, "no researcher encountered the morning dream clinics described by Stewart," and "adults deny that they ever instruct children about dreaming. . . . There is no deliberate attempt to teach children principles of dream control." At village councils, "discussions involve serious disputes, not dreams." It appears the Senoi do not even have any special belief that dreams can be controlled.[135]

As for Stewart, Domhoff depicts a well-meaning charlatan whose ideas about dream control happened to flatter our culture's faith in the malleability of human nature.[136] Stewart's version of the Senoi dovetailed with humanistic psychology in the 1960s; it suited the ambience of consciousness expansion in the U.S. then.

In the literature surrounding the Senoi, some versions emphasize waking preparations for dreams to come, or incubation;[137] others emphasize the control of dreams while dreaming, that is, "the lucidity postulated in Stewart's account";[138] while still others invoke the name of the Senoi when teaching re-entry into dreams already dreamt with the purpose of modifying future dreams.[139]* Though less so today, the Senoi have served as a touchstone validating virtually any type of dream modification going. Incubation, lucidity, and re-entry all belong in the Senoi dream culture of Stewart's portrayal, but my sense is that he emphasized a gradual socialization toward good dreaming, beginning at an early age. "The Senoi parent . . . tells the child how to change his behavior and attitude in future dreams." "[T]heir dreams consistently evolve from childhood to adolescence. Gradually, the child does do in his dreams what he is directed to do."[140]

Along with other advice on good conduct asleep and awake, a Senoi novice supposedly received the following instructions: "A. Always *confront and conquer danger* in dreams. B. Always *move toward pleasurable experience* in dreams. C. Always *make your dream have a positive outcome and extract a creative product* from it."[141] These guidelines will come up again in chapter 16 (p. 503). Suffice it to say here that while Stewart may have embroidered the Senoi, he endowed them with valid insights, ones that continue to inform the dream movement. What Krippner said about Carlos Castaneda and Don Juan applies also to Stewart and the Senoi: the account is full of errors regarding the culture, but remains useful as a metaphor.[142]

---

* In attempting to teach people to dream more pleasantly, Marie Doyle (1984) created a cocktail of techniques, including hypnotic suggestion, practice interrupting unpleasant thoughts, and waking re-entry into dreams to give them more pleasant endings, which she designated as the "Senoi strategy." Doyle reported some success. And on 6-month follow-up, the dreams of her subjects were self-reported as continuing to be more pleasant than they had been prior to training.

The remainder of this chapter describes various contemporary uses and techniques of incubation. This can only be a sampling, since ways of using incubation are virtually as diverse as dreaming itself. A book primarily for women by Koch-Sheras et al. discusses and demonstrates the following uses, among others: "life review . . . guidance and answers to practical problems . . . repeating a pleasurable dream . . . changing a dream from a destructive to a constructive resolution . . . exploring a puzzling dream symbol . . . creative work of all kinds . . . lucid or psychic dream experiments. . . ."[143] Like Koch-Sheras, David Feinstein & Krippner take the feasibility and utility of incubation almost for granted when presenting their program for evolving a "personal mythology." Among numerous other incubations, they ask their reader to incubate to discover areas of conflict and to resolve them,[144] to define one's "Quest" and to learn how to implement it,[145] to achieve integration,[146] and so on. In another book,[147] Krippner recommends incubation for purposes ranging from dreaming about next day's schedule to enhancement of creativity. Creativity is also high on Koch-Sheras's list, and is a use of incubation frequently advanced, for example by Fariba Bogzaran[148] and by Delaney. Delaney comments that although many artists and inventors report spontaneous inspiration from dreams, few actually seek that help. Exceptions are Robert Louis Stevenson and Cannon the physiologist.[149] Another important item on Koch-Sheras's list is lucidity. Although not usually identified as incubation, whatever is done before sleep to induce lucid dreams is actually a variety of incubation. Lucidity induction will be discussed in chapter 14 (p. 453 ff.), which concerns lucid dreams.

A perennial topic in writings on dreams for a general readership is how to improve dream recall. The more effective measures are probably those taken upon waking, but there are also effective measures to be taken before sleep, and these qualify as incubation—although they, like pre-sleep steps to induce lucidity, are not ordinarily identified as incubation. Some pre- and post-sleep measures to enhance recall are compiled in a footnote.*

---

* *Pre-sleep aids to recall.*

Relaxation. • Give yourself some "unwinding time" before sleep (J. Baylis 1991).

Sleep position. • If you find that you recall dreams best when sleeping in a certain position, try to sleep that way (C. S. Moss 1970, p. 123).

Alteration of sleep pattern. Such measures are especially recommended for people who never or rarely are aware that they have dreamt (G. Halliday 1990a, p. 5). • "[G]o to bed early enough to wake naturally . . ." (Baylis, op. cit.) or in some other way change your usual time of waking (R. Corriere & J. Hart 1977, p. 89). • Set the alarm for 90 minutes (Baylis, op. cit.), or 2 hours (P. O'Connor 1986, p. 229), or 4½ hours (Corriere & Hart, op. cit.) after sleep, so as to be awakened during REM. • Alternatively, have your partner wake you when s/he detects your eyelids fluttering (P. R. Koch-Sheras, E. A. Hollier & B. Jones 1983, p. 51). • Drink extra fluids before bed;

One of the best published demonstrations of dream problem-solving happens to illustrate incubation for that purpose. Morton Schatzman, a psychiatrist from the U.S. living in London, invited readers of the British periodical *New Scientist* to dream on two problems. Six people wrote in with dreamt solutions to one "brain twister," eleven with solutions to the other, which was as follows: "Using six line segments of equal length, can you construct four equilateral triangles, such that the sides of the triangles are the same length as the line segments?" A variety of dream images conveyed to dreamers—either upon awakening or while still dreaming—that the solution was to construct a three-dimensional figure, a tetrahedron. One dream showed: "*Six stereographic drawings . . . of animals.* 'As I wrote the dream down, I realized that the three-dimensional view was the clue.'" In another dream, an ingenious but erroneous attempt is rejected by a disembodied voice stating the correct solution explicitly: "*I am constructing two equilateral triangles by laying six matches on a flat mirror, so that by looking sideways I can see four triangles. At this point a voice says 'That's cheating'. After a pause a voice says 'Try three-dimensional'. At that point the solution became immediately obvious. I woke up.*"[150]

---

the urge to urinate may well interrupt REM (E. T. Gendlin 1986, p. 27). H. Reed (1991, p. 11) states that "[w]e wake up for nature's call at the end of a dream cycle," but W. C. Dement (1974 [1972], p. 36) says there is *no* relation between awakening to urinate and the rhythm of sleep stages. • Sleeping clothed on top of the blankets or anything else that changes your pattern or causes you to sleep more lightly may have a good effect (Gendlin, op. cit.). Try sleeping twice or three times a day and for shorter periods (G. Delaney 1979, p. 213).

Stimulation of imagination. • Reading a novel or watching a film before bed "provides the psyche with some images" to work on (O'Connor, op. cit.).

Auto-suggestion or intention. In Jeremy Taylor's view (1983, p. 23), all effective pre-sleep rituals have in common "a clearing away of ambivalences about the negative images that may come in dreams" and "a clear and wholehearted affirmation of the desire to remember and learn from the dreams." • Talking or reading about dreams before sleep "enhances mental set" for recall (K. L. West 1978, p. 19). • Have a clearly formulated reason for remembering your dreams, whether enjoyment, self-knowledge, or whatever (L. Reneau, no date). • Pray for dreams, if so inclined (A. Faraday 1976 [1974], p. 41). • Set up two chairs and engage your dreams in a dialogue in the Gestalt manner (chapter 6): "Dreams, why don't you come to me?" (ibid., p. 28). • Give yourself the suggestion, "When I awake I will remember my dreams vividly and completely" (Baylis, op. cit.). • "Visualize your recording equipment as a friend who is eager to hear from you, and picture yourself writing or narrating your dream in the morning" (Koch-Sheras et al., op. cit., p. 49). • "Imagine yourself remembering your dreams and enjoying a fuller life as a result" (Reneau, op. cit.). • In bed, "create a mental image of rest, peace, and beauty." This image, together with an appropriate suggestive phrase, can be used as a trigger for recall upon waking (ibid.). • Suggest to yourself that any regularly occurring morning sound—the alarm, the baby crying—is a cue to recall a dream (Koch-Sheras et al., op. cit.). • Drink half a glass of water, then leave the other half on your night table with the auto-suggestion to remember a dream when you drink the other half in the morning (L. Weiss 1986, p. 61). • Whatever other virtues it may have, a "dream pillow" made with mug-

Schatzman borrowed his experiment's "brain teaser" paradigm for incubation from William Dement. One of Dement's dreamers repeatedly failed to take hints. The puzzle to be solved was "HIJKLMNO." The dreamer had several dreams, each of which had water in it, but guessed at the solution "alphabet" rather than the correct "H2O."[151]

Deirdre Barrett had students incubate for solutions of problems of their own choice, of relevance to themselves. In one week, half the students had a dream relating to the target problem. Of these, 70% seemed to offer solutions, most often so when the problems targeted were personal rather than objective or academic.[152] One dream from Barrett's research, "Too much dieting and exercise," was quoted earlier (ch. 8, p. 274). Below is another, which Barrett introduces to caution against credulous acceptance of the reliability of solutions presented by dreams, especially when the dreamer is in a conflicted state of mind:

> There are potential dangers in automatically taking a dream as the "right answer" in making decisions. . . . [T]his experiment occurred at a religious college and several of the responses indicated a firm conviction that dreams came from God and that therefore, a dreamed solution should definitely be followed. That

---

wort, "the 'dream herb'" (ibid., p. 73) or another preparation (K. L. West 1977, p. 10) (ch. 1, p. 16n) is bound to reinforce the intention to recall. • So must wearing to bed a charm or clothing of a color which has dream associations for you (Koch-Sheras et al., op. cit., p. 72). So must the following procedure: "Tape a paper clip onto your forehead as an antennae [*sic*]. This physical sensation will trigger dream recall for some" (Baylis, op. cit.).

General conduct of life. Here are mentioned suggestions which do not pertain strictly to the period just before sleep. • Intense study of any subject, not just dreams, improves recall by stimulating the mind (Delaney, op. cit.). • Cultivate fantasy, have daydreams, make up stories while listening to music (J. Baylis 1976, p. 82). • Seek "socially and emotionally supportive contexts" for recalling dreams, e.g., join a dream group (J. Taylor 1992a, p. 72). • Respect your dreams by not telling them to people who will not consider them important (Koch-Sheras et al., op. cit.). • Meditation is widely found to improve recall (H. Reed 1973, p. 46, inter alia) (above, introduction, p. 1). • Having satisfactory interpretations of dreams stimulates recall of later ones (E. Cayce, cited by H. H. Bro 1968, pp. 122–3), by "heighten[ing] the significance of all dreams in the . . . [dreamer's] life. . ." (M. A. Mattoon, 1984 [1978], p. 148).

Post-sleep aids to recall. • People with some recall should try to awaken naturally if possible, without an alarm. Natural awakenings usually occur from REM sleep, and do not jerk the dreamer out of the dream state (P. Garfield 1976 [1974], p. 173). Alternatively, set a timer to switch on a bedside light, for a gentle waking (R. Corriere & J. Hart, op. cit., p. 89). • Upon waking, turn inward, do nothing to "dispel the afterglow" such as getting out of bed (M. Ullman & N. Zimmerman 1979, p. 93). "Let your mind wander," avoid dwelling on reality problems—except for possible dream "triggers" (R. Langs 1988, p. 95). Try free-associating (P. R. Koch-Sheras et al. op. cit., p. 50). Or imagine familiar, emotionally significant faces and places, since these may well have featured in a dream (J. Taylor 1983, p. 25; 1992a, p. 84). • Lie still: motor activity impedes recall by switching one into a more extroverted state (J. S. Singer 1975, p. 100). If that fails, adopt postures in which you usually sleep. "It would seem as if the dream were stored in a code which is most in-dreams on dichotomous problems could occur arbitrarily on either side of the ambivalence was illustrated best by the following example:

"Problem: My boyfriend plans to join the army full-time after graduation (he's in the reserves right now). He has asked me to marry him and wants me to go with him wherever he is assigned. I don't know if I want to be an army wife. I am very scared and confused about what to do. Dreams: . . . . The second night I incubated it, I dreamed *we were at the country club where I work having our wedding reception. Everyone was laughing and dancing, just having a good time. He had a tux on and I had a wedding gown on and I was very much in love with him.* I thought that was a solution. Several nights later after I had stopped incubating the problem, I dreamed *we were about to get married and I was begging the people that were with me not to make me do it. I kept saying 'Please don't make me do it! I don't want to marry him! PLEASE!' I remember feeling very frightened and very alone. I felt like if I married him my life would end.*"[153]

Here is a good place to recall Jung's warning, not "to suppose that the dream is a kind of psychopomp which, because of its superior knowledge, infallibly guides life in the right direction." And James Hall's: "[T]he ego must always take a stance toward the contents of the objective psyche . . . not simply evoke them, like the sorcerer's apprentice"[154] (ch. 3, p. 116).

One specialized technique of incubation is posthypnotic suggestion. This possibility was first demonstrated by Schroetter (1911). For example:

The following hypnotic suggestion for the next night's dreams is made: In the first half of the dream everything will be abnormally small; in the second half, abnormally large. The subject . . . brings . . . [this dream]:

---

telligible when we are in the original posture of the dream" (H. Reed 1988 [1985], p. 35). • Pay attention to your affect: it may be a lingering remnant of the dream and a trail back to its imagery (W. Bonime 1969, p. 85). Or "focus" on whatever vague "felt sense" you find in your body (E. T. Gendlin, op. cit., p. 3). • Imagine you are looking for the dream in a rearview mirror (R. E. Rainville 1988, p. 52). • Spend at least ten minutes trying to stay with the dream, to fix it in mind (A. M. Biele 1986, p. 160). If a dream is slipping away, grab hold of a "striking element" (R. Langs, op. cit.). • The last part of a dream is often remembered first; if you awaken with a fragment, therefore, try thinking backward (G. Delaney, op. cit., p. 211). This procedure, when enhanced by the "meditative practice" of reviewing one's entire day backward at bedtime, is claimed to enable morning recall of an entire night's dreams (J. Taylor 1983, p. 24). • Dreams with which we awaken during the night are better recalled in the morning, the longer we attend to them and the more we render them into verbal form (R. D. Cartwright 1977, p. 33). Some people prefer voice-activated tape recorders, but it is not difficult to learn to write in the dark with the eyes closed (P. Garfield, op. cit., p. 178). (I recommend using a pencil rather than a pen, to avoid the ink-stained bedding which can result when you drift asleep pen in hand.) Telling the dream to your bed partner also works (C. Sagan 1978 [1977], p. 80). • All recording of dreams in the morning assists in their later recall. Also, telling the dream to someone during the day often causes unrecalled details to spring to mind (R. Bosnak 1988 [1986], p. 15).

We are at Wimberger's, a restaurant in Vienna. Dr. Schroetter puts me in hypnosis; I know nothing of myself; as I wake up from the hypnosis, a priest says to me: "The soul belongs to Heaven and yours must be saved"; I do not reply. Dr. Schroetter says: "But this is my wife." Thereupon, the priest says: "The camel will more easily go through the eye of a needle than this will be your wife." I say: "Oh, I can easily crawl through the eye of a needle," whereupon, I take out a large needle and I creep through the hole. In doing so, I shrink to the size of a finger. Thereupon Dr. Schroetter says to me: "This you HAD to be able to do, you glacier flea." Then we all leave. We are very small and walk arm in arm needing a magnifying glass in order to see ourselves. Then I ask Dr. Schroetter for a cigarette. He takes out a huge one; the matchbox also is as huge as a house.[155]

One review of the topic, by Arthur Arkin & John Antrobus, indicates that posthypnotic suggestion does not necessarily achieve better results than presleep suggestion without hypnosis.[156] However, Charles Tart in his review concludes that it is "the most powerful technique for content control via presleep suggestion. . . ."[157] J. Stoyva was the first to study the technique in the sleep lab, where it works to best effect.[158] Stoyva targeted single elements "such as climbing a tree, or beating a drum. . . ."[159] Seven of 16 subjects had dreams "clearly influenced" by the suggestion 71–100% of REM awakenings. All but two subjects had at least some success. Some subjects hit the target every awakening. In a study of his own, Tart suggested to hypnotized subjects that they dream of an entire narrative. All dreamed of at least one of the 23 scorable element of the narrative; the best score was 13 of 23.[160] And in another study by Tart, in which the subincision film mentioned earlier (p. 397) was used, most subjects under posthypnotic suggestion "dreamed directly about" the film.[161] Recall that incorporation of the film without posthypnotic suggestion usually took the form either of a transformation of content or of an effect on the mood of the dream.

Posthypnotic suggestion has been used successfully to incubate dreams for purposes more practical than the incorporation of a target. Robert Davé demonstrated its benefit for problem-solving with 24 subjects "at an impasse in solving a creative problem." Subjects who were told under hypnosis that they would have "night-time dreams offering solutions" received more benefit from this procedure than did other subjects from being "offered cognitive suggestions" for solving the problem while awake.[162] And John Scott says that about 75% of patients in psychotherapy respond to the first or second hypnotic suggestion to have a night dream "relating to the problem which underlies the presenting symptom."[163] This is incubation of an initial dream.

The efficacy of presleep suggestion given to awake (not hypnotized) subjects has also been investigated experimentally. T. X. Barber et al. found the two methods equally effective, but observed that with hypnosis "authoritative" suggestion is most effective ('You will dream about . . .'), while without hypnosis, "permissive" suggestion is most effective. (These differences appear in dreams retrieved from NREM as well as REM sleep.)[164] C. Hiew studied the self-recorded home dreams of students who on three successive nights were given one of several topics to dream about: biking, fishing, a car accident, a world war. Ten of 19 dreams incorporated the suggestions. Interestingly, these subjects had more success dreaming about the pleasant than the unpleasant topics.[165] Other studies by Hiew point to "the importance of subjects' attitudes toward the task. . . ."[166] These subjective factors should be born in mind when considering the negative results obtained by Foulkes.

Foulkes & Mary Griffin conducted two studies to test Garfield's claim in *Creative Dreaming* that dream content can be programmed by "waking autosuggestion." They attempted to get dreamers to dream on selected topics. In neither the first study, where all topics were chosen by the dreamers themselves,[167] nor in the second, where experimenters as well as dreamers generated suggestions,[168] was there success above chance. "[W]hatever manner of 'dream control' may have been achieved in the few cases where targets could be identified correctly generally was indirect or symbolically mediated." They compare this to a day residue effect. "[T]arget suggestions did *not* directly organize the scenarios of sleeping consciousness." This result has to be evaluated in the light of Foulkes's low regard for dream semantics (ch. 1, p. 32 passim). Why should 'symbolic mediation' detract from the success of an incubation? And without thorough interpretation of symbolism, who is to say what organized the substance, if not the "scenarios" of the dreams?

Moreover, in *Creative Dreaming* Garfield cites research to the effect that it takes a child 2–5 weeks "to successfully self-induce a desired dream."[169] Because adults are not as suggestible as children, she concludes that it takes adults longer. By these standards, Foulkes's experiments are not a fair test. Also, even if dreaming of a desired target is infrequent, there can be a large positive effect on vividness and intensity when it does occur.[170]

More weighty than experimental results either way is the wealth of clinical and anecdotal testimony for the efficacy of incubation. Certainly therapy where dreams are used becomes, in effect, an incubatory setting, as the occurrence of doctrinal compliance (see above) implies. Therapy is often described as a 'container'; that container is an 'incubator' for dreams where the client is always under the suggestion, implicit or explicit, to bring in a dream which will contribute to treatment.

One example of implicit incubation is the use of dreams in Masters and Johnson sex therapy in cases when work on unconscious psychodynamics is indicated. Alexander Levay & Josef Weissberg say that dreams while in sex therapy reflect conflicts generated by the therapeutic directive to have pleasure. Such dreams tend to be vivid, undisguised, and closely connected to waking events. Dreams of manifestly sexual content yield important indications of "preferred methods of arousal as well as areas of inhibition":[171]

A young professional couple presented because of the wife's unresponsiveness and anorgasmia. She was quite averse to touching the husband's genitalia. Upon forcing herself conscientiously to complete the sensate focus exercise, including genital stimulation, she had two dreams.

Dream 1: *She was playing with her father's penis and he had an erection. She was aroused, fascinated, and curious, not at all frightened.*

Dream 2: *She and her brother were playing with each other sexually. Their mother came in and was furious.*

Here the exercise stimulated dreams of incestuous activity in the patient's childhood, indicating strong positive unconscious sexual desires for the penis (albeit the father's), combined with maternal disapproval and threatened retaliation. Clarifying the fact that her husband's penis, in contrast to her father's, was in reality hers to enjoy produced a dramatic break in her resistance to this phase of treatment. . . .

. . . [T]he [first] dream indicated a desire to play with a penis in contrast to the woman's waking aversion to such activity. In dealing with the dream, this element was emphasized, with only passing mention of the woman's erotic attachment to her father.[172]

A simple example of a therapist's explicit suggestion serving to incubate a dream is the following from Lillie Weiss:

Joan, a woman who was working in therapy on her eating problems, was asked to have a dream about the role that food played in her life. She recounted the following dream:

All the people in my house—my husband and my daughters—are in the living room doing something. I am in a corner of the house, off to the side, and my project is to put these rectangular food shapes, one on top of the other, so that they fit exactly.

Joan's dream succinctly encapsulated the essence of her dilemma. Her pattern was to be off to the side, engaging in some meaningless food activity, while the rest of her family were in the mainstream of life.[173]

Most dream incubation happens outside of therapy, and is initiated by no one's suggestion but the dreamer's own. Self-suggestion may consist of just a thought, or may take the form of a ritual or procedure; but in all cases, the essence of the incubation is the *intention* to dream about a given matter. "Through dream incubation," asserts Koch-Sheras, "you can program your dreaming mind to give you any kind of dream you want."[174] "It's so easy," says Delaney. "Most people can do it like that (snaps fingers) on most topics."[175] Perhaps it is not quite that easy, except if the criteria for success are stretched, but it certainly is not arcane, nor even unusual.

A simple and usually spontaneous form of incubation often takes place by merely paying close attention to previous dreams.[176] Recall the dreams from Ella Sharpe (ch. 2, p. 55) which illustrated reversal ("Woman's front clothed," and "Woman's back naked"). The dreamer awoke with a dream and "thought, 'What can there be in a dream like this to make me wake?' She fell asleep and again woke suddenly. This time she had further dreamt" a dream which led to an explanation of the first.[177]

Sometimes people have dreams which feel unfinished. These may be interrupted dreams, says Koch-Sheras, or dreams whose endings one blocked from memory or awoke to forestall, for example a falling dream: "You may have unconsciously awakened yourself just before the most revealing moment, afraid of discovering something 'at the bottom' of yourself that you might not be ready to examine. . . . Before going to sleep the following night tell yourself, 'I will complete this dream, and will remember it in vivid detail.' Then review the unfinished dream in your mind as you fall asleep, and repeat the process on consecutive nights if the dream still seems unfinished. A clear resolution to the unfinished dream may appear in a different form, rather than resuming where the first one left off."[178]

Joan Windsor provides several examples of what she calls "progressive" or "serial" dreaming, among them this classic, where a dream resumes in exactly its previous form:

> The dream series in question unfolded when Grace was a mere child of ten, but the lesson for the psyche imparted by the serialization remains etched in her mind to this day. . . .
>
>   Dream I—The Tunnel. *I (Grace) am standing at the entrance to a long tunnel. The way is well-lighted and I begin to cautiously make my way down the corridor toward a closed door at the end of the passageway. An air of mystery pervades.*
>
> Here the dream ended. . . . Grace had become an avid reader of Carolyn Keene's Nancy Drew mystery books. Thus, her natural curiosity and love of detective stories led her to wonder throughout the day what might lie behind that closed door. Tantalized by the impending mystery she retired slightly earlier the following evening. **The dream continued**.
>
>   Dream II—The Key. *I find myself again in the same tunnel, but on this occasion I have arrived before the locked wooden door. A thought crosses my mind that if I possessed the key, I would be privy to what lies beyond. I reach in my pocket and retrieve a key! I place it in the lock.*

Again the dream terminates! . . . All day she waited impatiently for the arrival of evening and the eventual solution to **The Mystery Behind the Locked Door**. . . . Dream III—The Treasure. *Again I stand before the locked door. I turn the key and hear the latch click. Slowly, the door creaks open. Behind it I catch glimpses of shining treasure.*

The alarm sounded. 7:00 am. "Impossible!" cried Grace. "I was almost there!" That day she mustered all of her mental resources and determined to secure the treasure by the end of the next dream. . . . **With the coming of dawn, the treasure behind the door still eluded her**. With the passage of time the dream never reappeared and as little girls will reason, she thought the treasure was forever lost. As Grace and I have become friends . . . , it is my unwavering belief that Grace did procure the treasure she so diligently sought.[179]

Currently the best-known procedure for incubating dreams by intention, or self-suggestion, is probably Delaney's "phrase focusing." Her precedents include: Edgar Cayce the psychic, who pioneered contemporary incubation inasmuch as he urged people to formulate the guidance they needed before sleep;[180] Ann Faraday, who did not use the term 'incubation' but first popularized the idea of "Asking Your Dreams for Help," the title of a chapter;[181] and certainly Garfield, whose 1974 chapter on incubation aimed to update the Asclepian tradition. Garfield's recommendations include the use of a key phrase.[182] You are to choose a peaceful and undistracting setting. "[C]learly formulate your intended dream." "Next, put your intention into a concise positive phrase" upon which to concentrate, such as: "Tonight I fly in my dream." "Your body should be in a deeply relaxed state" while reiterating the phrase and/or visualizing the intended dream. Importantly, "[b]elief is what makes dream induction possible." Dreams come from a power higher than the ego. We can address a god, if we are so inclined; but "[t]he faith that I am urging is really a faith in yourself"—"your subconscious mind or your dream state. . . ."[183]*

Garfield speaks of 'posing questions' to and 'obtaining answers' from the dream state through incubation, but her emphasis seems to fall more on gen-

---

* Further (P. Garfield 1976 [1974], pp. 29 and 32), "[y]ou can do several things with the dreams you now have that will help you to be more successful in inducing future dreams." These things include holding conversations with dream characters a la Gestalt, paying special attention to "unusual and positive images," and sharing your dreams with others. Finally, "make observations or involve yourself in activities that are relevant to your desired dream." Recently (1991, pp. 250–1), Garfield added this advice: "Look at pictures or books, or engage in activities that are relevant to your goal. Repeat your incubation request several times during the day. . . . Write your incubation request in your dream journal, along with your notes about your emotional state and activities during the day. . . . Picture your question being answered or your request being fulfilled as you fall asleep, but leave yourself open to whatever response the dream may provide."

erating specific desired dreams. Delaney also promotes both functions, but
with more emphasis on the one of problem-solving. She claims a very high
success rate for "phrase focusing," or "secular incubation." However, her
criteria for success are generous. Incubation can be successful, she advises,
even though no dream whatever is recalled. When, for example, Delaney incubated a dream to help her figure out how to begin her book, "[t]he next
morning I awoke with a total blank on my mind, or so it seemed." But then
a beginning came to her. "I recalled no specific dream, but the idea filled
my consciousness as if the entire chapter outline had already been planned
in detail." She continues: "Insights and solutions you receive in both incubated and spontaneous dreams may not be recalled in dream form."[184]* The
principle, which is consistent with Jung's point that unremembered dreams
can be understood subliminally and work an effect (ch. 3, p. 115),[185] is certainly true, but obviously has to be treated cautiously when judging the success rate of incubation. In some other of Delaney's examples, the success
of the incubation seems more an artifact of the interpretive process than anything else. That said, it remains that Delaney's book contains many interesting and persuasive incubations.

The procedure of phrase focusing is as follows.[186] Choose the right night.
Before sleep, write something about your thoughts, feelings, and actions of
the day. Discuss the focal issue as thoroughly as you can with yourself, and
write five or ten lines about it. Distill the issue to an "incubation phrase."
Now go to sleep repeating the incubation phrase silently for as long as you
can, returning to it whenever your mind wanders. In the morning, record
your dream.

First, here is a brief example which undoubtedly shows the importance
of choosing the right night. The dreamer in this case asks for a specific sort
of dream, rather than for the solution to a problem:

A middle-aged man who had begun to feel that his spiritual and emotional life
was stagnating incubated a dream, asking that it remind him of the vivid beauty
of the inner world. He said that he had forgotten "the first and most important
part of the dream" but that he remembered this much:
*I am on a hike in a new and beautiful land. I pass a tree with incredibly gor-
geous birds in it. The birds are different vivid living colors: reds, roses, oranges,
and purples. I am enchanted by their beauty and the peace and happiness which
surrounds them. I lie down under the tree to rejoice in their lovely song. Then I*

---

* Patricia Maybruck (1991, p. 26) makes the same point: "In all probability, you dreamed about
the problem, your dreams suggested the solution which best acknowledged your feelings, and your
mind integrated the decision so that you knew what action to take when you awoke—even though
you may not have recalled the dream."

wonder if, by wishing it, I could turn their song into classical music with familiar instruments interpreting their song. Yes! What a joy! I have never heard music so heavenly. I feel a contentment and participation in the beauty of the universe that fills my soul with great happiness. ("Classical Birds")[187]

Next, here are two examples of incubations by women seeking guidance in their relationships. The first woman fails to heed the implicit advice of her dream:

Nina . . . incubated a dream, asking, "Where is my relationship with Scott going?" She had lived with Scott for almost a year and loved him, but the relationship was a turbulent one full of tears and fights and good times. . . .

I was somewhere, not sure where. Scott came up to me and said, "Nina, would you like to go on a voyage with me?" "What is the name of the ship?" I asked. "It's the Titanic," said he. "Oh, my!" said I, "that ship is going to sink!" "No it's not," said Scott. "Oh, yes it is, I know it. Don't you realize that?" I said. He persisted, "Well, at least come to the bon voyage party with me." I agreed. We arrived on the ship, and I found the whole scene just appalling. Everyone was wasting their time and energy. They were drinking too much, wasting their bodies. They were gambling, wasting their money. It was very depressing. I decided to leave.

The next thing I knew, I was walking down a road. Coming up the road on a tricycle was an infant. The infant was really a skeleton pedaling the bike. It had a heart which I could see. The heart had a skull and crossbones on it. It was awful. ("The Titanic")

It was clear that Nina the dream producer was telling Nina the dreamer that her relation-"ship" was not going anywhere now, and when it did go somewhere, it would go down! Nina recognized this but couldn't accept it. Still, she knew it was true.

Soon after this dream, she . . . [left Scott, but] just delayed the decision of whether or not to marry him. She spent a year trying to forget instead of trying to understand. Then one day I telephoned [Nina by mistake]. . . . She had been living with Scott again for a couple of months. I said, "But Nina, what about your Titanic dream? How is it going?" She said that things hadn't changed; that they were still at the bon voyage party. "It's funny that you should call this afternoon," she said. "Do you remember the second part of that dream? . . . I've just . . . made an appointment to have an abortion on Tuesday. I am really upset because I very much want to have a child. But I know that Scott could never be a good father for my child, and I don't want to have one on my own. Oh, Gayle, I guess it took this to make me face up to the fact that I could never marry Scott."[188]

In this final example from Delaney, the dreamer heeds her dream. Notice that the question being incubated is carried explicitly into the dream, so that to a considerable extent the dream is self-interpreting. Only the concluding passages of the dream require interpretive work, though their meanings are quite transparent:

> Kay, who had begun to fall in love was troubled by what she thought might be unfinished business with an old flame. She wanted to be free of the "what if" syndrome and her lack of commitment resulting from it. She incubated a dream, asking, "Am I free of my attachments to old boyfriends, especially Bret?" She dreamed:
>
> *I am on a beach; it is "the meeting place." All my old boyfriends are coming here. I am to meet with each one, review my relationship with him, and see if I am free of a desire to reanimate it. If I am truly unencumbered by "what if" fantasies, then I will be free to commit myself to a relationship with Michael. Then every boyfriend of my life comes before me; even ones I had crushes on in grammar school! I review our relationships, one at a time, thank each man for his contribution to my life, and move on to the next, feeling free and glad for the one before. But where was Bret? I looked for him all over the beach, hoping to find him and afraid of finding him. What if I see him again and can't resist loving him? That would ruin my relationship with Michael, and yet things could never work out well for Bret and me. I meet a sixteen-year-old girl who says she was with Bret on the boat coming here, which apparently carried my other old flames. She tells me that Bret had introduced her to the joys of sex and that she was very lucky to have met him, but she had no idea where he was now. I am continuing my search when a kind old man approaches and says, "You have just received a letter that will answer your question." ("Where Is Bret?")*
>
> When Kay awoke, she was relieved and felt she had actually worked through some old resentments, hurts, and hopes she had not even realized she was still carrying around inside herself. But what about Bret? She incubated a dream three nights in a row, trying to discover what was in the letter that was supposed to explain it all. . . . No response. She found it very maddening that a dream would tease her like this. . . . [Eventually i]t dawned on Kay that the dream itself was the letter. . . . She discovered that her dream producer was pointing out that Bret had been the perfect man for her at one point in her life. He had introduced her to a new, more adult level of love between a man and a woman, but, as the sixteen-year-old implied, the voyage together was over. This is the sort of dream which seems to consolidate past experience and open the way for new development.[189]

Patricia Maybruck teaches a variant of phrase focusing as a part of couple therapy. She has one partner vocalize the focus phrase to the other as the other falls asleep.[190]

Another, and an interesting variant of phrase focusing is "The Wish-to-Be-Different Study" published by Cartwright in 1974.[191] This study of pre-sleep stimulus incorporation tests the hypothesis that "dreams are formed to reaffirm the self-concept":

With this in mind, we looked for a stimulus that subjects would define as their own rather than as one imposed on them—one that represented . . . some unresolved tension or uncompleted task which could be brought into the focus of their attention just before sleep. . . . We . . . identified for each subject one trait which he rated as most like him now but least like his ideal for himself; this word became his presleep stimulus. As he was falling asleep, he was asked to repeat that word over and over to himself, and to wish to be more like his ideal. . . . [For example,] "I wish I were not so jealous. I wish I were not so jealous." . . . The presleep stimulus trait showed up significantly more often as a quality of the dream characters than other adjectives of equal importance to him but not used as presleep stimuli. How the dreams were formed around this target word confirmed [our hypothesis]. . . . Subjects do **not** dream that they have reformed. Instead, the dreams show that they are enjoying themselves just the way they are; the present self is reaffirmed. One subject, whose instructions were to wish she were not so sarcastic, had two dreams in which she expressed herself very sarcastically to authority figures with a good deal of satisfaction[. One of those dreams]: . . .

> *I was walking home . . . and all of a sudden I saw the whole sidewalk was covered with my bedspread and all of these people were walking on my bedspread, and all of a sudden this schoolteacher came out who was my neighbor, and I said, "Look, lady, that's kinda taking liberties on my bedspread. I ought to have you fired." And she said, "Well, I've got more brains than you," or something, and I called her a bitch or something, but she had ripped my bedspread.*
> *. . . This lady—I really wasn't very diplomatic with her, like I was immediately very mean to her—and she really snapped back and then I said something like, "Well, at least my mother's not an old biddy like you."*[192]

Cartwright concludes that the problem-addressing function of dreams works better when there has been only an indirect activation of the problem, since "[f]rontal attacks on a person's areas of vulnerability appear to provoke a dream defense of the self. . . ."[193] This bears on prospects for productive incubation, by the implication that when we intentionally incubate for self-improvement, our dreams will come to the defense of our defect of character, by gratifying it, denying it, etc. However, Cartwright's study concerns artificially prompted intentions. Her subjects had not made a pilgrimage to the temple as it were—they had not bottomed on their defects and become ready for change. These results of Cartwright's really come under the heading of Delaney's first instruction, choose the right night.

An incubation described by Linda ("Ravenwolf")" Reneau comes under the heading, be careful, you may get what you ask for:

> "I asked for information about any talents that I haven't discovered yet, and dreamed: *I'm in a large house. It's familiar to me* in this dream, though I've never been to this house while awake. *To my surprise, I find a new room, one I've*

never seen before. It has a box, or some boxes in it, and I go over to one of them to open it up. It's all beat up. When I try to open it, the top turns into a sort of mirror. I see my reflection and I'm terrified! There's some ugly black bumps all over my face. With even more terror, I see that my hands are just as bad. As I wake up, I wonder if I have some kind of disease." This dreamer discovers that her disease is a lack of self-esteem. She cannot act (hands, in dreams, are often an image of the ability to act) to develop her abilities because she doesn't believe in herself as a worthy and worthwhile person. Though she knows, deep down, that she has talents and abilities she hasn't yet discovered, she has to improve her self-image before she can see them. After understanding this, her dream goal became: "In dreaming tonight, I will experience my worthiness in specific ways, and learn what I can do to improve my self-image during the day."[194]

Another variant of phrase focusing involves incubation to stimulate or influence psi in dreams. Marcia Emery reports on what she describes as a successful preliminary study of "programming" precognitive dreams to provide information about specified future events (e.g., the cover of *Newsweek* two weeks hence). She employs Delaney's phrase focusing technique.[195]

Alan Vaughan describes himself as burdened by premonitory dreams. He had a dream predicting Robert Kennedy's assassination, he says, and was so "horrified that my dream premonition had not prevented the tragedy" that he determined to cultivate only "prophetic dreams that could help me." With the admonition that "dreams cannot be *controlled*, merely *influenced*," he recommends to other premonitory dreamers a set of welcoming and cautionary attitudes, together with advice on interpretation. The actual instructions for incubation are as follows (the phrase "dream tiger" is Vaughan's conceit for the dreaming mind):

"1. Write down an important question in your life right now, or some problem that faces you.

"2. Write out or dictate on your tape recorder the following instructions for playback or reviewing just before you go to bed: 'I need advice and guidance from my dream tiger. I need a dream that will answer my questions: (read your question). I want my dream tiger to give me the answer in simple terms that I can understand. I will arise early in the morning with the dream answer fresh in my mind. I shall be able to remember it easily and write it down. Its meaning will become clear to me. I shall follow the advice of my dream tiger.'"[196]

Vaughan's instructions are obviously suitable for incubation of any sort of dream, not just psi.

Koch-Sheras et al.[197] and Windsor discuss incubation of dreams for the sake of healing a second person, a type of psi dream. Both recommend having an item belonging to the ill person to sleep with beside one or under the pillow. Windsor advises the incubant to focus on psychic causes along with somatic ones, and to request specific remedies.[198] "As with all healing dream requests, formulate and state the health problem concisely, and petition guidance and healing insights for the afflicted soul."[199] This calls to mind shamanic dreams or visions for curing the ill, as well as the temple incubations of Egypt and Babylon, where a priest sometimes dreamt for the sake of an ill suppliant.

In his book *Sacred Sleep*, Cunningham provides incubation guidelines for "modern pagans," promising that "[o]ur personal deities can visit us in our dreams."[200]

In his book on Christian dreamwork, Russ Parker describes several incubatory prayers, including one by a minister, who "laid hands on . . . [his parishioner] and asked God to come to him when he was asleep and through the dream door give us a clue or a key. . . ."[201]

Following is a procedure for incubating "high dreams," as recommended by a psychosynthesist, Diana Whitmore. She utilizes visualization in place of verbalization to express the intention to achieve a certain result. "A powerful technique to evoke 'high dreams' or transpersonal dreams is a simple visualisation. Just before sleep imagine a thread of light, like a consciousness thread that may be followed into sleep. Imagine travelling along that thread of light to the spiritual realms, and coming back again but keeping the thread, holding onto it when falling asleep. . . . Many reported waking up with an insight or intuition which was experienced as particularly beautiful and rich, often giving creative inspiration about something important in their life."[202]

To conclude, it may be mentioned that incubation is an element in "nonorthodox healing" and other practices of traditional African-American culture. Linda Camino attended the visit of a man with "jumped-up stomach" (gastroenteritis) to a southern "root doctor." Joe the doctor diagnosed "conjuration" (a cast spell), and along with fasting, herbal tea, and bible readings prescribed an incubation:

> Next Joe asked, "You have anybody close to you that has died?"
> James: "One of my brothers."
> Joe: "You got someone on the other side. He can tell you what to do, but you got to have a way of getting through to him by way of this world. You got a graveyard near where you live?"
> James: "There's one a few blocks off."
> Joe: "Now you get some graveyard dirt [goofer dust] and get it from a newly dug grave. You take that dirt home with you and put a circle of candles around it, just candles you got in the house, light them and say your brother's name.

Then go to bed and your brother will come to you in a dream and he'll tell you what to do."[203]*

James did as prescribed. *His brother* appeared in a dream and *told him he must break it off with the woman he was seeing on the side.* At their session, Joe had already settled on this woman as the probable cause of the "devil spell," which she worked by putting "poison" in her cooking. James followed his brother's advice, and his condition improved.[204]

---

* Anthropologist Loudell F. Snow (personal communication, 1993) comments: "This continued interest on the part of the dead for the affairs of their living kin is, I think, one of the strongest links of African-Americans to the African past." (See also H. J. Fisher 1979 and articles in M. C. Jędrej & R. Shaw 1992). Harry Middleton Hyatt's (1970–1978) inimitable collection of African-American folklore contains various dream incubation instructions, including: to use graveyard dirt to obtain a dream of a dead person who will give advice for playing the numbers (vol. 2, p. 1318); to dream of a dead person by urinating on a handkerchief, letting it dry in the shade, then sleeping on it under one's pillow (vol. 2, p. 1349); and to discover a murderer in a dream by sleeping in the victim's clothes at the time of burial (vol. 4, p. 3268) (Michael E. Bell, personal communication, 1993 drew these instances to my attention).

Incubation of dreams of the dead by sleeping on or by their graves is reported from cultures as diverse as the ancient Egyptians (V. MacDermot 1971, p. 46), North American Inuits (E. F. Foulks 1992, p. 200, citing M. Eliade, *Shamanism: Archaic Techniques of Ecstasy*, Princeton: Princeton University, 1964), Talmudic Hebrews (S. Lorand 1957, p. 94, citing *Sanhedrin* 65B and *Berakoth* 18B), and modern Moroccan Jews and Muslims (Y. Bilu & H. Abramovitch 1985, p. 84; V. Crapanzano 1975, p. 146). For some interesting facts about incubation in contemporary Christian and Muslim black Africa, see H. J. Fisher (op. cit.).

□ 14 □

Lucidity

In a lucid dream, "the subject is aware that he is dreaming."[1]

Agamemnon's dream at the beginning of Book 2 of *The Iliad* can be construed as being lucid. Zeus sends Dream in the guise of Nestor to Agamemnon, to deceive him about his chances of taking Troy: *"Son of wise Atreus breaker of horses, are you sleeping?"* It was the format of Homeric dreams for a ghost, god, or messenger from the gods to let the dreamer know that s/he was asleep in this fashion.[2] Agamemnon's dream concludes: *"Keep this thought in your heart then, let not forgetfulness take you, after you are released from kindly sweet slumber."*[3]

In the fourth century B.C., Aristotle "referred to 'something in consciousness which declares that what then presents itself is but a dream.'"[4]

But although identified in the West, until recently lucid dreaming (LD)* was not cultivated as a valued skill as it was in certain other traditions. An Upanishad from about 1000 B.C. speaks thus: "Having subdued by sleep all that belongs to the body, he not asleep himself, looks down upon the sleeping senses. Having taken to himself light, he goes again to his place—the golden person, the lonely swan."[5] The passage suggests not only lucidity but out-of-body experience (OBE) and the 'clear light'. Skills in these psychological matters passed from India to Tibet with other esoteric yogas between the eighth[6] and eleventh[7] centuries A.D. Tibetan dream yoga was virtually unknown to the West until introduced by W. Y. Evans-Wentz in *Tibetan Yoga and Secret Doctrines* in 1935.[8]

The modern European pioneer of LD was a Frenchman, Hervey de Saint-Denys, whose 1867 book *Dreams and How to Guide Them* was known to, but not read by Freud.[9] The first to write in English on the subject, and the

---

* The abbreviation 'LD(s)' stands for 'lucid dreaming' or for 'lucid dream(s)', as well as for 'lucid dreamer(s)' in the form 'LDer(s)'.

one to coin the term 'lucid dream', was the Dutchman Frederik van Eedan, who published his independent discoveries to a tiny audience in a journal for psychic research in 1913.[10] Other names associated with the early modern history of LD are Yves Delage, Mary Arnold-Foster, Hugh Calloway (Oliver Fox), and P. D. Ouspensky.

Greater interest arose with the general resurgence of interest in dreams and altered states of consciousness in the 1960s. Celia Green's book *Lucid Dreams*, Charles Tart's reprinting of van Eedan's article, and especially Patricia Garfield's *Creative Dreaming* brought LD to wider attention.[11]

Just now LD is a hot topic in the world of dreams—"a dream whose time has come"[12]—, with increasing research, articles in the popular press, and how-to books written by leading LD researchers[13] as well as by others for a growing market.[14] Nevertheless, recently a student of LD commented: "It cannot be said that lucid dreaming has been embraced by mainstream dream psychology (or psychology in general) with any great enthusiasm, and the concept still effectively remains on the fringe of orthodox research."[15] LD's ambivalent position is characterized by the fact that at recent conferences of the Association for the Study of Dreams there has been a mini-conference of the Lucidity Association appended at the end. In that way LD is separated from the main conference, but also recognized as the only topic generating sufficient interest among dream specialists and enthusiasts to merit its own conference.

This chapter will discuss: the defining criteria for LD; the sleep lab profile of LD; common characteristics of LD; traits of typical LDers; activities favoring LD; techniques for inducing LDs; benefits of LD; pros and cons of controlling dreams; and, in conclusion, the relation between LD and enlightenment.

Criteria of Lucidity

Celia Green's basic definition of LD—a dream in which "the subject is aware that he is dreaming"—was quoted to open this chapter. Jayne Gackenbach & Jane Bosveld qualify: "to greater or lesser degrees" the dreamer is aware.[16] Alan Worsley and many others also emphasize that lucidity is not "an all-or-nothing affair."[17] It is typical for there to be fluctuation with respect to the certainty, intensity, and perseverance of the state. And there are hybrid varieties of consciousness during sleep.[18]

Green's early methodical treatment of LD classified a number of dream events as "pre-lucid." These include having a "false awakening," i.e., you dream that you have woken up. When LDers have that dream, they often go on to question their state, discovering that they are, in fact, still dreaming. Also pre-lucid is asking, "Am I dreaming?" without becoming aware of the correct answer, or achieving partial awareness without asking "whether the *whole* of the experience" is dream.[19]

Sheila Purcell et al. describe lucidity as a high degree of "self-reflectiveness" within the dream state. They have devised a "self-reflectiveness scale" which is in effect a scale of pre-lucidity along this dimension. Their work is a refinement of Ernest Rossi's classification of dreams by degree of self-reflectiveness, with "[n]o people or personal associations in the dream" as the lowest level, and lucidity as the highest.[20] The greater the self-reflectiveness, in Rossi's view, the greater the potential for (and evidence of) psychological growth. At Purcell's lowest level, there are no people in the dream, no dream-ego, and objects are unfamiliar. The highest level is lucidity.*

Many dream theorists (e.g., David Foulkes, Allan Rechtschaffen) stress the discontinuity between ordinary dreams and LDs. This emphasis enables them to construct their theories about the former, without taking the latter seriously into account. But viewing self-reflectiveness as a graduated quality of all dreaming reveals that "dreaming is more self-reflective than is generally thought and could possibly be much more so were cultural entrainment mechanisms operating to enhance this dream process. . . ."[21]

High "self-reflectiveness" also characterizes LD in Harry Hunt's classification of dream types. In that scheme, LD is one of three varieties of "intensified dreaming": (1) nightmares intensify the kinesthetic and emotional dimensions of the dream state; (2) archetypal dreams intensify the psyche's ability to create metaphors for life; (3) LD intensifies self-reflectiveness.[22] Gackenbach, who has written a useful review article summarizing major theoretical perspectives on LD, groups herself with Purcell and Hunt as utilizing the concept of self-reflectiveness.[23]

As Gackenbach sees it, Tart, Stephen LaBerge, and Susan Blackmore all account for the lucid state in a different way, by utilizing information pro-

---

* The Self-reflectiveness scale appears in S. Purcell, J. Mullington, A. Moffitt, R. Hoffmann & R. Pigeau (1986), p. 425, and, with minor variations of diction, in A. Moffitt, R. Hoffmann, J. Mullington, S. Purcell, R. Pigeau & R. Wells (1988), p. 431 and in S. Purcell, A. Moffitt & R. Hoffmann (1993), p. 212. "1. Dreamer not in dream; objects unfamiliar; no people. 2. Dreamer not in dream; people or familiar objects present. 3. Dreamer completely involved in dream drama; no other perspective. 4. Dreamer present predominantly as observer. 5. Dreamer thinks over an idea or has definite communication with someone. 6. Dreamer undergoes a transformation of body, role, emotion, age, etc. 7. Dreamer has multiple levels of awareness: simultaneous participation and observation; dream within a dream; notices oddities while dreaming. 8. Dreamer has significant control in or control over dream story; can wake up deliberately. 9. Dreamer can consciously reflect on the fact that he or she is dreaming."

cessing models of mind. Their explanations center on activation of a 'This is a dream' schema during sleep.

Blackmore[24] emphasizes the activation of the full model of the self during LD, as does Tart. Thus something is added by them to the "minimalist"[25] definitions of LD mentioned above. Tart writes: "Simply experiencing the dream thought, 'This is a dream,' or some variant of it, is a necessary but not a sufficient condition for a lucid dream to occur." Rather, LD entails "a complex pattern change where many of the components of mental functioning we feel characterize waking consciousness come into play together. . . . [I]t feels just like your mental functioning feels right now . . . [and this] is the crucial defining element of lucid dreaming."[26*]

Other students of LD add other elements to the minimalist definition, or else adopt scales of lucidity with levels above 'mere' lucidity. Deirdre Barrett, who herself employs a minimalist definition, calls such extras "'corollaries' of lucidity."[27] Thus, for example, Wynn Schwartz & Mary Godwyn add control. The LDer, so they stipulate, "is aware that he or she is able to choose or construct alternatives in circumstances and action."[28] Andrew Brylowski's definition includes "using th[e] knowledge ['this is a dream'] to behave more adaptively."[29] Paul Tholey, a German researcher, stipulates that a dream is to be considered lucid if and only if, in addition to being aware of the dream state and controlling the dream, "the dreamer also recalls one's waking life, [and] is in full command of one's intellectual abilities. . . ."[30] Tholey has also offered a phenomenological scale of lucidity which pertains to both waking and dreaming, but which includes a level called "Full Lucidity in Sleep" at which (1) all dream characters, not just the dream-ego, are aware they are in a dream, and (2) lucidity persists during the entire period of sleep[31] (see below).

A scale offered by Tarab Tulku XI, one based on Tibetan Buddhist dream yoga training, also puts 'mere' lucidity at a lower level.[**] E. Kellogg offers yet another scale, with these levels: pre-lucid, sub-lucid, semi-lucid, lucid, fully-lucid, and super-lucid. Kellogg also emphasizes choice: it is still only sub-lucid to "realize that I dream, but continue to follow the dream 'script'

---

* LaBerge, says Gackenbach, differs from Tart and Blackmore by having a low estimate of the inherent value of dreams, which causes his latest book on LD (S. LaBerge & H. Rheingold 1990) to read "like a computer users [sic] manual. . ." (J. Gackenbach 1991a, p. 124).

** Tarab Tulku XI (1989). (1) "[H]olding the dream" entails "training to both remember dreams and go consciously into the dream state." (2) "[M]astering the dream" involves "knowing the dream is a dream while dreaming" and "using his/her dream body with volition" (p. 53). (3) "[C]hanging the dream" involves breaking illusions about reality: solidity of objects, linearity of time, fixity of objects (p. 55). (4) "[M]erge with the unity of the subtle mind/body" (p. 56).

. . . [with] no conscious choice." Super-lucidity involves self-integration and "[e]xtraordinary (even for dream reality) abilities and experiences. . . ."*

The difference between minimalist definitions of LD and these progressively more demanding definitions is, when all is said, mostly only a matter of definition. It is like defining art: should the definition broadly embrace as much as possible, or only 'true' or 'good' art? All sides appreciate good art; likewise, for the most part all these dream investigators appreciate the 'higher' potentialities of LD experience which only some incorporate in their definitions.

For example, while Tart's definition of LD states that "it feels like your mental functioning feels right now," his chief interest in lucidity, says Gackenbach, is the 'I am' or 'being' experience, often described for LD, which is closely related to waking 'peak experience'.[32] Many, including LaBerge—for whom, in Gackenbach's view, "dreams are not a priori meaningful"[33]—, acclaim the feelings of exaltation or inspiration which some LDers experience.[34] Gackenbach herself, whose own definition of lucidity is inclusive, believes that Eastern traditions are correct in thinking that minds achieve developmental stages higher than ordinary adult consciousness, and that LD represents "a bridge to higher states of consciousness."[35]

This chapter concerns the whole gamut of LD—it adopts an inclusive, or minimalist, definition. Remember, as an demonstration of the fact that LDs can be perfectly mundane, the dream quoted in chapter 10 (p. 353): "I have a recurrent dream in which *I am always surprised to find myself dreaming* when I am dreaming it, but when I wake up I never can remember what it is."[36] Many times lucidity is transient and unremarkable, or it comes in the form, 'Thank God it's only a dream!' leading to a grateful awakening.

On the other hand, LDs can be remarkable indeed. Examples could be cited from many sources;[37] here is one dreamt by a prominent researcher, LaBerge, from his chapter on "Dreaming, Death, and Transcendence":

Late one summer morning several years ago, I was lying quietly in bed, reviewing the dream I had just awakened from. A vivid image of *a road* appeared, and by focusing my attention on it, I was able to enter the scene. At this point, *I was no longer able to feel my body, from which I concluded I was, in fact, asleep. I*

---

* E. W. Kellogg, III (1989), pp. 87–8. To complete the scale: "PRE-LUCID" involves noticing bizarreness or variance from ordinary reality, without drawing the implication. "SEMI-LUCID" and "LUCID" involve lesser and greater degrees of control. "FULLY-LUCID - fully aware that I dream and the location and state of my physical body; also remember any lucid dream tasks that I had earlier decided to try (lucid dream healing, intentionally changing body form, precognition, etc.). SUPER-LUCID - aware of self as an integrated whole: self-remembering. Thinking, feeling, creating aspects of self working as a unified whole. . . ."

*found myself driving in my sportscar down the dream road, perfectly aware that I was dreaming. I was delighted by the vibrantly beautiful scenery my lucid dream was presenting. After driving a short distance farther, I was confronted with a very attractive, I might say a "dream" of a hitchhiker beside me on the road just ahead. I need hardly say that I felt strongly inclined to stop and pick her up. But I said to myself, "I've had **that** dream before. How about something new?" So I passed her by, resolving to seek "The Highest" instead. As soon as I opened myself to guidance, my car took off into the air, flying rapidly upward, until it fell behind me like the first stage of a rocket. I continued to fly higher into the clouds, where I passed a cross on a steeple, a star of David, and other religious symbols. As I rose still higher, beyond the clouds, I entered a space that seemed a vast mystical realm: a vast emptiness that was yet full of love; an unbounded space that somehow felt like home. My mood had lifted to corresponding heights, and I began to sing with ecstatic inspiration. The quality of my voice was truly amazing—it spanned the entire range from deepest bass to highest soprano—and I felt as if I were embracing the entire cosmos in the resonance of my voice. As I improvised a melody that seemed more sublime than any I had heard before, the meaning of my song revealed itself and I sang the words, "I praise Thee, O Lord!"*

Upon awakening from this remarkable lucid dream, I reflected that it had been one of the most satisfying experiences of my life. It **felt** as if it were of profound significance. However, I was unable to say in exactly what way it was profound, nor was I able to evaluate its significance. When I tried to understand the words that had somehow contained the full significance of the experience—"I praise Thee, O Lord!"—I realized that . . . I only now understood the phrase in the sense it would have in our realm. It seemed the esoteric sense that I comprehended while I dreamed was beyond my cloudy understanding while awake. About what the praise did not mean, I can say this: in that transcendent state of unity, there was no "I" and "Thee." . . . My personal "I," my dream-ego sense of individuality, was absent. . . . [I]t should be clear why I have called this lucid dream a transpersonal experience.[38]

Sleep Lab Profile of Lucid Dreaming

LD can occur at sleep onset,[39] and during NREM sleep,[40] but "rarely"[41] —about 5% of LDs occur in NREM, by one sampling.[42] Most LDs occur in ascending stage 1 REM sleep[43] and, not surprisingly therefore, during the second half of the night, and especially toward morning.[44*] The EEG pattern is "that of typical" REM sleep.[45]

---

* Garfield (1976 [1974], p. 128) says that most LDs come between 5 and 8 A.M. Keith Hearne's survey indicates that half occur between 2 and 5 A.M. (J. Gregory 1984, citing K. Hearne, "Investigating structural characteristics of lucid dreams," *Dream Network Bulletin* 1(11), 1983).

Whether there are finer EEG correlates of LD, however, has not been resolved.[46] The REM sleep state during LD has been characterized as "somewhat enhanced and intensified."[47] Evidently LDs occur during the "most intensely activated parts of REM periods."[48] Increased alpha has been detected during pre-lucidity, a state which has been "likened . . . to the access phases of waking meditation,"[49] but alpha enhancement during LD is in debate.[50] Electrical activity of the brain may show "increases in interhemispheric coherence over normal REM levels similar to those reported during key points in meditation."[51]*

Respiration rate, heart rate, and electrical skin potential, as well as the density of eye movements, all rise with the onset of LD. The average lucid episode in the sleep lab lasts for only about two minutes.[52] Body paralysis is even more complete during lucid than ordinary REM dreaming.[53]**

Signalling lucidity from sleep. Formerly it was maintained by some that since lucidity is like being awake while dreaming, LDs must actually occur during mini-awakenings. That in fact they occur during proper REM sleep was established in experiments where the sleeping subject voluntarily makes preagreed eye movements as a signal of becoming lucid. Tart was first to float the suggestion that since s/he is conscious, the LDer might be able to communicate by giving a physical signal.[54] The eye movement experiments were conducted independently and almost simultaneously by LaBerge in the U.S. and Keith Hearne in Great Britain. Priority belongs to Hearne, who in 1975 used Worsley as his subject.[55]

This was not, however, the very first time subjects had performed actions from sleep. A forerunning experiment in 1960 demonstrated the "ability of subjects to make instrumental responses during REM sleep. . . ."[56] The first actual *signals* from sleep were elicited in 1965 by Judith & John Antrobus & Charles Fisher. "By using a microswitch taped to his index finger, the subject attempts, while asleep, to signal ongoing dreaming . . . or nondreaming . . . mental events."[57] A higher rate of "dreaming" signals came during REM sleep. However, it appears that the signals may have been delivered during mini-awakenings.*** Moreover, in this and a replication study[58] it is

---

* Gackenbach (1990d) thinks women are more adept at LD because they naturally have more EEG coherence.

** But Worsley (1988, p. 338ff.) has had some success making voluntary large muscle movements (kicking) during LDs.

*** J. S. Antrobus, J. S. Antrobus & C. Fisher (1965), pp. 398–400: "[A]t the time of signalling the subject's sleep is slightly disturbed . . . for an average of 11.5 seconds. . . . [T]he subject has moved in the direction of wakefulness. . . . [However,] 68% of the D signals were followed within a few seconds by a continuation of the REM-period." Comparably, while attempting to signal from

not stated that subjects knew what they were doing as they were doing it. The results have been called "equivocal at best."[59]

Arthur Arkin et al. took a different approach. In 1966, they applied post-hypnotic suggestion to induce a subject with a history of spontaneous sleep-talking to describe his dreams as they were happening. The subject produced sleep speeches during both NREM and REM. Awakened shortly after speaking, his reports corresponded closely to his sleep speeches:

> [NREM speech:] *Now viewing a film of past experiences in gallery for small admission charge.*
>
> [Waking report:] Uh—(pause)—*there's a theatre that you pay admission charge and they run films of your life*—that's all I remember except that *I was in one of those theatres* a minute ago. . . .
>
> [REM speech:] *Claudette Colbert is trying to seduce me into a dream and I think she's **horrible** but has a friend—a **beautiful** girl from the University of California and—*
>
> [Waking report:] Mbl (pause) noot (?)—*Claudette Colbert—trying to put the make on me conversationally and she was so ugly—but she brought her daughter from U.C. and we were hitting it off and joking around Claudette and we were getting in elevators and things and we would come out and there would be Claudette—and other kinds of illusions—elusive methods—going through tunnels*—that's about all I can remember.[60]

But while these authors employ the terms "REMP" and "Non-REMP," electrophysiologically the subject was somewhere intermediate between "sleep and post-hypnotic state" when he sleep-spoke.[61]

LaBerge's and Hearne's intriguing experiments were the first where normal subjects unequivocally signalled during REM sleep, consciously knew that they were dreaming at the time, and also knew that they were signalling to an awake observer, and did so reliably. LaBerge has extended his experiments to more complex tasks. For example, he proved that during lucidity subjective elapsed time is the same as real clock time by having subjects signal the start of an interval, count to 10 or other agreed number of seconds in their dream, then signal again. On average, subjects estimate 10 seconds to last 13, the same error they make awake. LDers have also been able to hold or accelerate their actual breathing during 5 second intervals—marked by eye movements—during which they did the same in their dream. Counting tasks such as these are accompanied by activation of the left hemisphere

---

sleep concurrently with profound Transcendental Meditation, a subject wakes up momentarily (J. Gackenbach, W. Moorcroft, C. Alexander & S. LaBerge 1987). This does not happen when signalling from LD.

of the brain, just as in waking; singing—also marked by eye movements—involves the right hemisphere, also as in waking.[62]

Characteristics of Lucid Dreams

This section adds to what has already been suggested about common (and some less common) characteristics of LDs.

Sensation. Green says that the LDer often enjoys a range of sensory faculties comparable to waking and greater than ordinary dreaming.[63] Gackenbach refines this assessment.[64] Taste, smell, and pain are actually reported more from non-lucid dreams. LDs are, however, more auditory, tactile, and kinesthetic. And as for vision, she reports that "the better controlled studies clearly indicate no difference" respecting "general vision, color, brightness, and clarity of imagery." LDs *can* be as vague as ordinary dreams can be, while non-lucid "archetypal" dreams rank as more "visual" than LDs.* Yet many LDers celebrate the visual intensity of their dreams. Gackenbach believes this quality is present in early LDs, but tends to fade with habituation. Intense light experiences are, however, prominent in the LDs of those few who use LDs in the development of an advanced meditative practice.[65]

Bizarre or realistic? A Calvin Hall-style content analysis found no difference between lucid and ordinary dreams in the quality of bizarreness.[66] Differences emerge under closer analysis, however. Many pre-lucid dreams[67] and those at "state transitions"[68] are notably bizarre (incongruous, inconsistent). Bizarreness is a common 'trigger' of lucidity, since it causes a flash of realization, or leads to analysis or acute attention, which in turn ushers in lucidity. But once the lucid state becomes stabilized, LDs are if anything more realistic, more like being in the waking world than other dreams.[69]

At the same time, the "felt" quality of reality may possess the intensity of a "peak" experience.[70]

The bizarreness of pre-lucidity is ordinary bizarreness. But when the capacity for lucidity is highly developed, it may bring "psychedelic" bizarreness,[71] "with strikingly spiritual or archetypal forms of dream content . . . [which include] flying and floating, . . . geometric imagery, encounters with mythological beings, and the white light or luminosity experiences described

---

* J. Gackenbach (1990a), p. 3. In comparing several dream types—lucid, archetypal, nightmare, and ordinary—for various qualities, six qualities were found to have a statistically significant variance according to dream type. "In all cases, archetypal dreams . . . contained more of the quality than the other three forms." The qualities are (without clarification): visual, color, emotion (positive), sound, taste/smell, and transpersonal. LD ranked second for visual, emotion (+), taste/smell, and transpersonal; third for sound; fourth for color.

in classical mysticism—all with corresponding feelings of special portent and meaning."*

Control. A common trait of lucidity is "an ability to react to the dream events by making choices which to some extent effect the direction in which the dream develops. . . ."[72] However, control is not invariably available or exploited. In a sample by Hearne, a quarter of LDers had never attempted control, and a full two-thirds said that they had not "experimented" with the dream.**

It is not unusual to exercise some control over dream action without the full realization, "This is a dream" (one of Tart's criteria of lucidity), "the full lucidity 'sense'" (Hunt), or full "self-reflectiveness" (Purcell).[73] Only pre-lucidity is necessary for Senoi-type dream guidance, according to Gayle Delaney.[74] As Garfield describes it, "the dreamer knows in a vague way that he is dreaming, but the awareness is not central. He is focused on the action required."[75] In Garfield's *Creative Dreaming*, the chapter on Senoi dream control precedes the chapter on lucidity. And Rosalind Cartwright has written a book largely about changing dreams "in progress" in which the word 'lucid' does not appear in the index.***

But although lucidity and control can and do occur independently of each other, each tends to trigger the other. And "[a]t the highest levels of these capacities, each may be maximized in the presence of the other."[76] To perform such feats as arbitrary manipulation of the dream scene or redreaming past dreams at will,[77] lucidity seems indispensable. Tholey has deliberately achieved such remarkable effects as 360 degree vision.[78] Worsley can create a television set, on the screen of which he displays any device he wishes to experiment with. He retrieves the device by opening the screen.[79] Both he

---

* H. T. Hunt (1986), p. 271. It is not perfectly clear whether these effects are due to well-developed lucidity per se, or to the long-term meditative practices of Hunt's subjects, or both.

** J. Gregory (1984), p. 15, citing K. M. T. Hearne. Interestingly, a majority of Hearne's respondents also said that they had never flown in their LDs.

*** Cartwright (R. Cartwright & L. Lamberg 1992) writes about "RISC," a technique which "enables people to stop bad dreams while they are in progress and rewrite the scripts" (p. 32). RISC is an acronym for Recognize, Identify, Stop, Change. You need to *"Recognize . . . while you are dreaming that the dream is not going well. . . . Identify* what it is about the dream that makes you feel badly. . . . *Stop* any bad dream. . . . *Change* negative dream dimensions into their opposite, positive sides. At first you may need to wake up and devise a new conclusion before returning to sleep. With practice, you will be able to instruct yourself to change the action while remaining asleep" (pp. 105-6). Most of Cartwright's examples involve waking re-entry into a previous dream (see chapter 15) with a view to incubating a new and better dream. Only a few of her examples actually involve in-dream control, e.g., this case of a recurring nightmare (p. 154): *"When I realized the train was about to crash, I said to myself, 'I have to do something to keep this from happening.'"* And she does.

and George Gillespie[80] describe solidity experiments—putting a hand through glass, through one's other arm, etc.

To dream a particular dream if presleep incubation fails, LaBerge recommends that the LDer spin until the scene changes to the desired one. Imagining the dream scene to be a switchable television channel and other tricks can also be used to manipulate the action.[81*]

But by all accounts, complete and utter control is impossible, and there is great variability in the freedom to introduce or to efface characters and scenes, to guide action, and to awaken voluntarily.[82] There are two things LDers find it especially hard to do despite conscious efforts: to change the level of illumination, and to read more than a few words—a dreamer may, in fact, read more competently in ordinary dreams.[83] And, as awake, it is easier to control one's own behavior than that of others. Control improves with practice, but attempts can prove unpredictable,[84] as Jorge Luis Borges testifies:

> Asleep, I'm amused by some dream and suddenly I know that it's a dream. I usually think then: *This is a dream, a pure diversion of my will, and since I have unlimited power, I'm going to create a tiger.*
>
> Oh, incompetence! My dreams never know how to engender the wished for beast. *A tiger appears, yes, but desiccated and weak, or with impure variations of form, or of an inadmissible size, or too fleeting, or turning into a dog or a bird.*[85]

Further examples of imperfect lucid control will be introduced below, under the heading of the pros and cons of controlling one's dreams.

Cognition. Memory. It is the capacity to recall intentions formed before sleep which enables LDers to perform in the signalling experiments. LDers sometimes have access to their waking memory store, though not often without gaps, lapses, and mistakes. The more complete one's memory, the more control one can exercise.[86**] Memory is better, says Green, for generalities than for specific facts. There is "positive resistance" to accurate recall for "the most immediate and specific concrete details of the subject's life," and especially for the day or so immediately preceding the dream.[87] Typical errors of memory occur in LDs as in other dreams: getting one's age wrong,

---

* My then six-year-old friend Alice Colman said, "When I want to change my dream I blink my eyes—it's like changing channels." "Do you ever change what happens *without* changing channels?" "Yes." "How?" "By rolling over. And if you want to change it more, you roll over twice."

** A further indication of a connection between memory and control is that high dream recallers have more control in their dreams than low recallers (S. Purcell, J. Mullington, R. Hoffmann & A. Moffitt 1986, p. 18).

talking with the dead, etc. All the same, the state-specific amnesia between dream and waking is greatly mitigated. It is also mitigated in the direction from sleeping to waking. While LDs can be as fleeting upon awakening as other dreams,[88] often they are recalled as if they were waking experiences,[89] with the same "authenticity."[90] The dreamer can even scrutinize the dream environment with a view to recalling it later awake.*

Cognitive skills. With the exception of the ability to process language,[91] LDers often have "a sense of being . . . able to exercise one's normal intellectual faculties,"[92] or even of thinking thoughts "clearer than their waking thoughts."[93] Lucid reasoning is not always impeccable, however—as "when the *lucid dreamer saves a dream sandwich to eat after awakening.*"[94] Like other lucid aptitudes, reasoning improves with practice. LaBerge contends that practiced LDers, but only they, do actually function at a waking cognitive level.[95] There are, however, very practiced LDers who do not function at a waking level,[96] even though they believe they are doing so at the time of dreaming.[97] But the fact remains that Saint-Denys, LaBerge, Worsley and others like them function well enough to carry out psychological investigations and other problem-solving while lucid dreaming.[98]

Self-reflectiveness. Accurate self-reflectiveness while dreaming, or lucidity, means that the dream-ego recognizes its true state—being in a dream—and maintains that recognition. But it is precisely in the area of the relation between waking and dream that reasoning seems most to waver.[99] For one thing, lucidity tends to be intermittent. Gordon Globus[100] attributes this to the absence of corrective sensory inputs, without which the mind gravitates toward "single-mindedness"**—whereas self-reflectiveness involves "at least two levels of awareness."[101] And self-reflectiveness itself tends to be flawed. Recall the dream sandwich. And in the following account, Saint-Denys "was by no means convinced that the dream was entirely false" (note also the apparent out-of-body experience, or OBE):

---

* Saint-Denys (1982 [1867], p. 75) wrote of yet another memory enhancement: the ability to recall (and redream) other dreams of which he had had no prior waking recall.

** Allan Rechtschaffen (1978) introduced the idea of the "single-mindedness" of dreams, i.e., "the strong tendency for a single train of related thoughts and images to persist over extended periods without disruption or competition from other simultaneous thoughts and images" (p. 97). Self-reflectiveness is one such competing train. "The occurrence of a lucid dream is usually greeted with surprise, sometimes delight, which shows how well we implicitly accept the more characteristic non-reflectiveness of dreams" (p. 99).

Loss of waking self-reflectiveness and other deficits of judgment during dreaming are due, in Allan Hobson's view (1989, pp. 164–5), to (1) absence of inputs from external reality, (2) a different mix of sensory activations from that in the waking state, but chiefly to (3) deficits during sleep of a chemical neurotransmitter—which also explains amnesia for dreams, in Hobson's view.

Last night I dreamed that *my soul had left my body, and that I was travelling through vast spaces with the rapidity of thought. First I was transported into the midst of a savage tribe. I witnessed a ferocious fight, without being in any danger, for I was invisible and invulnerable. From time to time I* **looked** *towards myself, or rather towards the place where my body would have been if I had had one, and was able to reassure myself that I did not have one. The idea came to me to visit the moon, and immediately I found myself there. I saw a volcanic terrain with extinct craters and other details, obviously reproduced from books and engravings I had read or seen, but singularly amplified and made more vivid by my imagination. I was well aware that I was dreaming, but I was by no means convinced that the dream was entirely false. The remarkable clarity of everything I saw gave rise to the thought that perhaps my soul had temporarily left its terrestrial prison, an occurrence that would be no more remarkable than so many other mysteries of creation. I remembered some of the opinions of the ancient authors on the subject, and then this passage from Cicero:*

. . . If someone had risen into the heavens and had seen close up the sun, the moon and the stars, he would draw no pleasure from the experience unless he had someone to tell it to. . . .

Immediately I wished to return to earth; I found myself back in my bedroom. For a moment I had the strange sensation of looking at my sleeping body, before taking possession of it again. Soon I thought that I had got up and with pen in hand was noting down in detail everything I had seen. Finally I awoke, and a thousand details which had recently been so clear in my mind faded almost instantly from my memory.[102]

Confusions easily arise about the reality status of dream companions and one's relation to them, as Saint-Denys illustrates:

Even when I am perfectly conscious of the fact that I am dreaming, I find it extremely difficult to recognize that when some imaginary companion is sharing my illusions with me, he is only a shadow, forming part of the vision. I dream for example that *I have climbed up the tower of a church with one of my friends and we marvel at the panorama which meets our gaze.* I know very well that it is only a dream, but nevertheless I say to the friend who is with me: *"Please make sure you remember this dream, so that we can talk about it tomorrow when we are awake."*[103]

Barrett has studied whether certain aspects of "clear thinking" do or do not usually accompany knowing 'this is a dream'. LDers, she determined, are more likely to realize that dream characters are unreal than they are to possess intact waking memories, or to realize that the laws of physics need not apply (even though they are relatively likely to realize that material objects are unreal). She answers the question, "'how lucid are lucid dreams'" by answering, "'not very.'"[104]

It was mentioned above that on Tholey's scale of lucidity, "full" lucidity requires that all dream personnel, not just the dream-ego, be lucid. Tholey presents an interesting variant of this phenomenon, a dream recorded in the dissertation of J. Reis. It shows another way in which LD self-reflectiveness may be partial or imperfect:

> [M]any dream figures seem to perform with a "consciousness" of what they are doing. . . . [Usually] the dream-ego becomes lucid first. This is followed by the other dream figures attaining lucidity. On the other hand, we have many examples of reverse order. We can illustrate this by means of an example in which another dream character not only becomes lucid before the dream-ego, he also possesses a higher degree of lucidity than the dream-ego later achieves. This abbreviated form of the dream was reported by a woman . . . :
>
> > *I dreamed that I had forced myself through a grey and slimy mass. I didn't know then and I still don't know what it was. It was unpleasant, but for some reason I had to force myself through it in order to advance further. Then, in the midst of this grey slime, I came to a brightly lit place with a person standing in the center. I could see that it was Mr. Spock, the scientist of the Enterprise (the spaceship of the television series 'Startrek'). He told me, 'There is no reason to worry because you are dreaming!' I did not believe him and asked him what it was that I had just passed through. He answered that I had just passed through my own brain, or my own mind. I did not believe him, but he knew so much more than I did and he told me he would jump up and then remain in mid-air, just so that I would be able to see that we were part of a dream. Only after this actually took place was I convinced that I was in a dream. Then I said that I would never have found out by myself that I was dreaming. He replied that he knew that and that was why he was there. He also said that he knew much more than me anyway and that was the way it should be right then. He explained the meaning of my path in a very plausible manner... He also explained why it was not necessary to know all this right from the start and that he only explained it later on so that I wouldn't be afraid anymore. Anyway, he told me all kinds of things and showed me things that I did not believe right away.* I think it was great to have someone acting in a dream who knew much more than I did."[105]*

Out-of-body experience. Not always, but not uncommonly, the LDer obtains a locus of consciousness apart from and aware of her/his body lying there sleeping (cf. Saint-Denys's dream, top of p. 443). This phenomenon closely resembles out-of-body experience (OBE). People prone to OBE are also prone to LD,[106] and there are often "continuous transitions between the

---

* Barrett (1992, p. 227) gives another example of a dream character informing the dream-ego that the dream state prevails.

two states. . . ."[107]* But in LD the person is asleep dreaming and knows it, while an OBE is delusional.[108] And although the greatest number of OBEs are said to occur during sleep,[109] subjectively, "persons who have had out-of-body experiences are quite unanimous in being certain that these were *not* dreams."[110] In fact, some of the few OBEs captured in the lab do, and some do not occur during ascending stage 1 REM sleep.[111]

Nevertheless, many writers on the subject insist on an overlap if not identity of the two states. For Scott Sparrow, the only difference is whether the person believes the experience was "objective" (OBE), or "an outgrowth of one's own mental content" (LD).[112]** For LaBerge, also, OBE and LD are "necessarily distinguished" only by whether the person believes her/himself to be asleep or awake at the time.[113] Moreover he classifies OBEs as dreams occurring outside of REM sleep.[114] For Green, they are "philosophically indistinguishable."[115] For Hunt, both include "the unusual development of a detached observational attitude and its tenuous balance with participatory involvement. In addition, if the out-of-body experience ends in 'dream travel' to a setting that no longer includes the imagistic construction of one's own body percept, it is indistinguishable from lucid dreaming; and if the lucid dreamer attempts to become fully aware of his/her sleeping body, the situation may be indistinguishable from classic out-of-body accounts."[116]

While as Blackmore states, OBE and LD "can feel the same," the brain seems to have more of its waking faculties in OBE.[117] And certain other tendencies have been noted. Green finds that an OBE is more likely to occur in a field identical to waking reality, and is less likely to be hazy or symbolic. The feeling of complete disembodiment—rather than seeming to have a second body located in the dreamscape—is much more common in OBE than in LD. Green also says that OBE is thought a superior experience by those familiar with both, with respect to the degree of control over unfolding action, freedom to move at will through space, and "the intensity of . . . emo-

---

* Lynne Levitan & LaBerge (1991a, p. 2) say that people prone to OBEs are also prone to return to an earlier dream after waking and falling back to sleep. They are also prone to sleep paralysis, a not uncommon condition in which the motor inhibition of sleep persists into waking. Phenomena often reported for both OBE and sleep paralysis include "feelings of separation from the body," "vibrations," and "strange noises."

** All of the writers cited in this section discount the naive belief that OBEs 'really happen'. Blackmore (1989a, p. 7), reflecting on her own powerful OBE experiences (including the white light, tunnel, and other attributes of near-death experiences), hypothesizes: "It comes about when for some reason the brain or information processing system is unable to construct a good sensory-based model from eye-level and opts instead for a memory-[and imagination-]based view from above." Affirmations of the authenticity of OBEs have been asserted by the little-known writer on dreams C. A. Cannegieter (1985, pp. 39–40) and by the well-known Delaney (1979, p. 176).

tions of joy, liberation, and so on."[118] In the same vein, Ann Faraday compares OBE to "high" LD.[119]*

Emotion. In contrast to ordinary dreams, where apprehensions predominate, the majority of LDs are pleasant, according to LaBerge.[120] Likewise Harry Stefanakis et al. find LDs "strongly correlated" with "success, good fortune experiences and positive affect. . . ."[121] Green states that the "emotional quality" runs from "neutral" through "surprise" and "excitement" to "liberation."[122] Gackenbach also finds that LDs are more positive, but at the same time more negative.[123]** In any event, LDs are more emotional than ordinary dreams: positive and negative emotions are both sharper.[124]

The emotionality of LDs is important, because intense emotion tends to interrupt lucidity, leading either to loss of self-reflectiveness or to awakening, as in this dream recounted by D. W., in *NightLight*:

I was standing in a field in an open area when my wife pointed in the direction of the sunset. I looked at it and thought, "How odd, I've never seen colors like that before." Then it dawned on me: "I must be dreaming!" Never had I experienced such clarity and perception—the colors were so beautiful and the sense of freedom so exhilarating that I started racing through this beautiful golden wheat field yelling at the top of my voice and waving my hands in the air, "I'm dreaming! I'm dreaming!" All of a sudden I was losing it, it must have been the excitement. I tried the spinning technique [see below] but it was too late, I instantly woke up.[125]

D. W.'s account resembles one by Oliver Fox, the LD pioneer, which concludes: "The sensation was exquisite beyond words; but it lasted only a few moments, and I awoke. As I was to learn later, my mental control had been overwhelmed by my emotions. . . ."[126]

Sex. Garfield contrasts her own experience to Fox's, when she puts forward a different view. She acknowledges that the literature agrees with Fox, "that intense emotion or even a mild physical touch terminate[s] the [lucid] dream state." "I believe, however, that these people had not developed the lucid dream state until it was habitual. With practice, it is possible to experience strong emotion, even orgasm, and continue to dream."[127] Persistence of lucidity through orgasm is, perhaps, the acid test that intensity need not abort lucidity.

---

* Jill Gregory (1984), however, dissents in the opposite direction: for herself, a marked subjective difference is that in LD she feels "in her element," in OBE "out of her element."

** But there is more positive emotion in non-lucid archetypal dreams than in LDs (J. Gackenbach 1990a, p. 3). And contrary to Stefanakis et al., Gackenbach (1988b, p. 208) finds that LDs score higher in "obstacles" and lower in "success achievement outcomes" than ordinary dreams.

Going further, Garfield even conjectures that *"[o]rgasm is a natural part of lucid dreaming."*[128*] "When lucid dreams endure beyond a certain point, at least for me, orgasm is almost inevitable."[129**] As of 1979, when *Pathway to Ecstasy* appeared, two-thirds of her LDs were sexual, half of these orgasmic.[130] However, content surveys by Gackenbach suggest that Garfield's experience is not normative: sexual interactions are no more frequent in LDs than in ordinary dreams.[131] In a group of long-term meditators, Gackenbach found a reference to sex in only 1 of 150 LDs.[132***] Nevertheless, Garfield's experiences are indicative of LD potentialities, and are certainly tantalizing:

> Most often, Zal [Garfield's mate] is my lover. But he is not always so—images of other men, imaginary or real, appear. Once, I confess, *it was my father, although I had to tell myself repeatedly that his image was a part of myself that I had to integrate—the father part—to make intercourse possible.* Other dream lovers have included a kind of male angelic creature, a rare woman, or half man-half woman, and myself. Animals, plants, and objects all become more sexualized in my lucid dreams. A pink rosebud, a sparkling fountain, a pipe with its bowl warm from being smoked. . . .
>
> I have been made love to by some strange beasts in these dreams. The ultimate of the animal-intercourse series was *a strange sort of horse-goat who made love to me from behind. It might have been frightening, but I was amused to see, by peeping over my shoulder, that the tip of his gray beard was like Zal's and the edge of the Ben Franklin-style spectacles he wore were like those Zal wears.*
>
> Sometimes I am my own lover in lucid dreams. Once, *like a hermaphrodite, I found I possessed a penis myself and by bending into a circle could take the silky organ into my own mouth to climax.* More often, I am airborne while the waves of sexual energy rise higher, and at some ultimate moment the tension is broken by a body movement. *I will be climbing upward or hovering in the air, and suddenly arch backwards into orgasm. Or I lie upon my stomach as I float and merely lift my legs up behind me as I burst.* During these ecstatic episodes, I often gaze upon beautiful sights. Once, for example, *I watched a golden yellow*

---

* By having LDers in the sleep lab signal their sexual state to the experimenter, LaBerge (1985, pp. 82-7) has established that people have the same physiological correlates to sexual arousal and orgasm during LDs as they do awake. The qualification to this finding is that, while women have bona fide orgasms, men do not actually ejaculate, even though they feel as though they do.

** "Some women report achieving orgasm remarkably quickly—five to fifteen seconds after starting sexual play" (S. LaBerge 1990, p. 2).

*** LaBerge (S. LaBerge & H. Rheingold 1990, p. 76) comments that Gackenbach's results are based on experiments with "a straight-laced group of midwestern meditators. . . ." But with Gackenbach (S. LaBerge & J. Gackenbach 1986, p. 169) he had earlier quoted another LDer who describes LDs as inherently mystical (Garfield would not disagree) but "resistant to anything erotic." They cite the contrast to Garfield as showing that the mind set of the dreamer determines the form taken by the dream (thus they seem implicitly to reject a compensatory theory of dream formation).

egg that hung in the air near me; it was etched with a castle scene, an intricate, tiny world. Or I roll over and over, spinning in space. Once, *as I lay on my back in the air, I circled round and round clockwise. At the instant of orgasm, I opened and shut my fingers rapidly as my body shattered.* Often *I will bring on the orgasm by ascending to great heights and then turning, plummet back to earth or ocean. On impact with land or water, I explode into orgasm. . . .*

The pleasure that shudders through my body is not limited to the genital area. Like a pebble dropped into a pool, the ripples start from that spot and spread outward in great waves of bliss. During the most intense of these nocturnal orgasms, even my vision is involved. Whatever scene is before my sleeping eyes, its color and pattern will break into parts, flash, and spin. This kind of "visual orgasm" is indicative of the totality of the response.[133]

Maintaining techniques. Garfield's capacity for lucidity undisrupted by orgasmic intensity may not be unique, but is surely exceptional. Most LDers —Garfield herself, for that matter—can benefit from techniques which maintain and prolong lucidity on the threshold of being lost. Garfield advises the neophyte: "Keep a balance between becoming so emotional that you awaken, or so unfocused that you forget you're dreaming."[134] Techniques to accomplish this, which in addition can forestall simple awakening, exploit the LDer's ability to control her/his conduct in the dream.

One group of maintaining techniques involves *motion.* LaBerge discovered spinning to be effective.[135] Others do somersaults, whirl the arms, etc. Gackenbach believes motion works by stimulating the vestibular system.[136]

A second group of techniques involves *concentration*: stare at a body part such as the hand (Carlos Castaneda); stare at the ground (Harald von Moers-Messmer); focus on a point in the environment (Saint-Denys); concentrate on a sense other than vision (Linda Magallón).[137]* Sparrow thinks that concentration works by anchoring lucidity to something relatively constant.[138] LaBerge explains both motion and concentration techniques as working by involving the dreamer more deeply in the LD[139] and/or by "loading the perceptual system so it cannot change its focus. . . ."[140]

A third technique involves *self-persuasion* by means of verbal reminding: "'This is a dream.'"[141] "It may help to 'talk yourself down,' with a litany like: 'Yes, this is a lucid dream. This is great, but I don't want to wake up, so keep cool. Don't let the other dream characters know. . . .' If you think of your lucidity as a secret you are likely to adopt a useful amount of restraint."[142]

---

* Garfield (1989 [1979], p. 132) attributes the technique of focusing visually on a fixed point in the dream environment to Saint-Denys (1982 [1867]). See also L. Levitan (1990a).

All these techniques work against loss of lucidity by toning down the intensity of the experience. Such suppressing and/or avoiding is what Green has in mind when she underscored "emotional detachment": "Habitual lucid dreamers almost unanimously stress the importance of emotional detachment in prolonging the experience and retaining a high degree of lucidity."[143] Obviously this strategy shares little in common with ecstatic lucid indulgences such as Garfield's. But there is another sense of 'detachment' which is not inconsistent with her descriptions, a sense well-known to anyone interested in meditation. In fact, Hunt's characterization of what LD and OBE have in common—"the unusual development of a detached observational attitude and its tenuous balance with participatory involvement"[144]—also captures those practices where the meditator means to achieve concentrated 'one-pointedness' while simultaneously keeping permissive interest in the transient play of mind. LaBerge writes in the same vein as Hunt about "[t]his detached but not disinterested frame of mind . . ."[145]: "The combination of these two perspectives [participant and observer] is characteristic of lucid dreaming and allows the lucid dreamer to be 'in the dream, but not of it.'"[146] Just as the meditator experiences intensely without breaching the meditative state, so the accomplished LDer is able to maintain lucidity through very intense episodes. S/he does so, not by resistance to intensity—which nonetheless has its timely applications—but by surrender to self-reflectiveness. Garfield calls orgasmic lucidity a "mini-enlightenment."[147]

Traits of Lucid Dreamers

Spontaneous rates of lucid dreaming. The following statistics, although compiled from sources which utilize varying criteria of lucidity, give a general picture of spontaneous LD rates. Fifty percent of people report at least one LD experience in their lives.[148] Many young children often dream with degrees of lucidity and do not find this especially remarkable, as Garfield notes in her book *Your Child's Dreams*:

> Erin, 8, dreamed, *"I was in bed and I got up because I wanted a drink of water
> . . ."*; Matthew recalls that his earliest dream was of *being asleep and watching
> "green ticklemen" emerge from his bedroom wall*; a 5-year-old stated, *"Once I
> was sleeping in my room and I was scared to death—I saw some mummy cases"*;
> 8-year-old Vikram in India said, *"I am sleeping, and I see that Lord **Krishna** is
> in my room, and he has a packet full of balls for me."*[149]

By age 11–13, 10% of dreams still have this feature.[150] But thereafter, the tendency to lucid dream seems to go dormant for most people. Only 1–3%

of young adults' dreams are lucid. In the sleep lab, REM awakenings yield LDs at a rate of 1–2%[151] (but as high as 10%, when leading questions and marginal criteria for lucidity are applied[152]). 20% of "university students" and "persons with an expressed interest in dreaming" report lucid dreaming "with relative frequency."[153] 13% of dreams recorded in dream diaries have been found to be lucid.[154] Of people who do dream lucidly, 40% do so once or more per week.[155] A few do so every night.[156]

Lucid dreamer profile. Unless otherwise attributed, information in this section is from Gackenbach & Jane Bosveld's chapter, "The Right Stuff." They include an aptitude test along with the explanation of "what it takes to be a lucid dreamer."[157] But aspirants should not become discouraged if they do not match the profile, nor complacent if they do. The profile is no more than suggestive.

Good dream recall is "the single most powerful predictor of lucidity."[158] What is not clear is whether recalling many dreams actually causes lucidity, "or if some other factor leads to both. . . ."[159]*

Another important characteristic is a *good sense of balance* and "a lack of balance-related problems" (frequent ear problems or motion sickness; visual or physical handicap impeding movement). Gymnasts have five times more LDs than control subjects, but not more nightmares, another type of "intensified dream" by Hunt's description.[160] So good balance seems specifically connected to lucidity. Gackenbach conjectures that a neural connection of the vestibular system to a part of the brain stem associated with lucidity is in some way involved.** She thinks that, in psychological terms, the ves-

---

* However, the correlation of good recall to LD is not confirmed by S. Purcell, A. Moffitt & R. Hoffmann (1993, p. 227). As for other correlates in the general dream lives of LDers, S. Purcell, J. Mullington, A. Moffitt, R. Hoffmann & R. Pigeau (1986, p. 434) report that dreams of LDers as a group score slightly higher than those of non-LDers in a number of traits. LDer dreams tend to be longer, more colorful, more verbal, and more emotional. (LDers are also more likely to discuss their dreams with others, and to experience insomnia.) However, A. L. Zadra, D. C. Donderi & R. O. Pihl (1992) report that the non-lucid dreams of LDers are actually less vivid than dreams of non-LDers. Also, LDers have more nightmares (p. 92). Like Ernest Hartmann's typical nightmare-prone people (ch. 9, p. 310), LDers have "'thin' or 'permeable' boundaries" (p. 95).

** Hunt maintains in his book (1989) that nightmares are related to a *lack* of good balance. He proposes balance training both to increase LD and to reduce nightmares.

Thomas Snyder & Gackenbach (1991): "Five lines of indirect evidence support the proposed association between lucid dreaming and vestibular activation." (1) LDs, especially with onset during dreaming, "often include fictive body movements and perceptions known to involve the vestibular system during wakefulness, e.g., controlled spinning." (2) "[T]he vestibular nuclei in the brain stem become intensely activated during stage 1 sleep. . . ." (3) Vestibular systems of frequent LDers have lower thresholds of stimulation, and (4) LDers do better on balance tests than do non-LDers. (5) "[S]elf-reported vestibular dysfunction is more prevalent among" non-LDers (p. 58).

tibular system's role in spatial orientation translates to the real-seeming spatial orientation typical of LDs. It is probably relevant that LDers have *vivid auditory and kinesthetic imaginations*. Furthermore, Gackenbach sees a connection between physical balance and the "emotional" and "intellectual" balance needed to maintain lucidity without either waking up from excitement or fading back into ordinary dreaming.

LDers are *attuned to their inner lives*; non-LDers tend to be more socially oriented. And LDers are *internal risk-takers*. They may prefer to avoid external, physical risks, but are open to mind-altering experiences such as hypnosis and, of course, lucidity.[161]

Women dream lucidly more than men. But a more interesting gender trait is *"androgyny"*: men do better if they possess the 'female' trait of attending to inner processes; women do better if they possess the 'male' trait of risk-taking.

Another 'male' trait associated with lucidity in both women and men is so-called *field independence*, i.e, to depend more on information from one's body than from external senses for correct orientation in space. Field independent people have "the ability to remove self from surroundings,"[162] and tend "to rely primarily on . . . the self in psychological functioning."[163]

LDers score well on indices of *imagination*, such as mentally rotating a three-dimensional object. They are more prone than non-LDers to hypnagogic imagery, daydreams, and other spontaneous imagery, including OBEs. In the case of induced visualizations, LDers have more vivid imagery, but are no better able to control it.[164]

LDers are said to be *intelligent* and *creative*.

LDers are *able to become deeply absorbed*. Good meditators make good LDers.

LDers tend *not* to be *anxious* people.

Miscellaneous other correlations include *having a near-death experience* and *suffering from migraines*.[165]

"[W]e suspect that the phenomenal experience of consciousness during sleep is a portal to a brain system which has evolved for spatial representation and exploration. The essential behavior for this system is spatially oriented bodily movement, behavior which man experienced long before the evolution of language. . . . Through encephalization, and in particular the evolution of cortically mediated language functions, conscious access to subcortical movement patterns has been reduced. During sleep, however, . . . the prepotency of language-mediated self-awareness is attenuated or altered so that vestibular-bound imagery and movement patterns . . . assume prominence . . . and spontaneously can result in lucidity. . ." (pp. 56-7, citing T. Snyder & J. Gackenbach 1988).

Interestingly, those who have "spontaneous mystical and peak experiences" also tend to have good balance (H. T. Hunt 1986, p. 272, citing P. Swartz & L. Seginer, "Response to body rotation and tendency to mystical experience," *Perceptual and Motor Skills* 53, pp. 638-83, 1981).

Demographically, besides being a woman, being *unmarried* favors lucidity. So do being *young* and being *firstborn*.[166]

In one survey, more *blacks* than whites report having dreamed lucidly at
least once.[167]

Activities Favoring Lucidity

Certain waking activities have been found associated with the occurrence
of dream lucidity. These are not induction techniques per se, although they
may be exploited as such.

It is often mentioned that dream recall is stimulated by thinking, talking
and reading about dreams. Such occupation is said to stimulate LD also.[168]
However, Lynne Levitan, a colleague of LaBerge's, writes that *interest* in
LD "is not necessarily accompanied by a high rate of lucid dreaming. We
take this to mean that lucid dreaming is a skill that takes some training to
acquire."[169] Nevertheless, one finds many references to people having their
first LD immediately after learning that such a thing exists. (Many others
have their first without knowing of the possibility beforehand.)

All sorts of *experimentation with altered states of consciousness*, such as
psychotropic drugs, fasting, etc.—anything which brings consciousness into
greater contact with the unconscious—is said by Jill Gregory to contribute
to acquiring lucidity.[170] Long-term meditators have been found by Hunt to
have more LDs, and fewer non-LDs, than others.[171]*

Gackenbach & LaBerge say that numerous forms of *activity and arousal*
bringing "alert wakefulness" favor LD.[172] *Physical* activities do[173] (related
to vestibular stimulation?). So do "cross sex activities" as against "sex appropriate" ones.[174] Simply *being very busy* during the day increases LD. So
does *making love in the middle of the night*.[175] Love-making is of course a
physical activity, but it also entails a *period of wakefulness* during the night
before falling back to sleep, something which can be sustained to good effect by reading, meditating, etc. as well.[176] For Sparrow, an intense *feeling
of love* is often followed by LD.[177]

Certain other factors connected with increments of LD may also work via
arousal. *Life changes in progress*—pregnancy, job change, etc.—are arous-

---

* However, R. F. Price & D. B. Cohen (1988) say that the rate of LD for Hunt's meditators is
not significantly higher than that for good dream recallers. And P. A. Faber, G. S. Saayman & R.
K. Papadopoulos (1983, p. 147) report that while experienced meditators require less sleep overall
and spend less of their sleep time in REM, "[t]here [i]s also a significantly higher dream recall rate
and amount of dream content."

ing.[178] So are *unpleasant interactions*.[179] On the other hand, Faraday finds that lucidity happens to her as a reward of *integration*, the "coming together of head and heart somewhere in waking life during the course of the day."[180]

Lucid Dream Induction

For novices, there is no sure-fire technique of inducing (incubating) LDs. No technique is clearly superior to the others; what works for one person may not for another.[181] Adepts learn which techniques work best for them; and all techniques become more effective with practice.[182] But success rates differ greatly, even among LD cognoscenti who cultivate their natural aptitudes assiduously. Saint-Denys claimed that virtually all his dreams became lucid; Garfield's average rate stabilized at 4–5 LDs per month; while Gregory's reached just 1.7 per month.[183]

Robert Price & David Cohen categorize induction techniques as follows: "(1) lucid-awareness training; (2) intention and suggestion techniques; and (3) cue 'REM-minding' techniques."[184] These distinctions will be observed here, but under two other headings: whether lucidity commences (1) during sleep, after a period of non-lucid sleep and/or dreaming (the usual case), or (2) in direct transition from wakefulness to dreaming sleep while maintaining some continuity of ego consciousness (less usual). LaBerge designates these *DILDs* ("dream-initiated") and *WILDs* ("wake-initiated lucid dreams"), respectively. His chapters on induction constitute probably the best manual of the principal techniques.[185] What follows is a quite comprehensive survey, but those seeking more detailed instructions for the techniques compiled here should consult their authors, especially Gackenbach, Tholey, and LaBerge.

Dream-Initiated Lucid Dream Induction Techniques.

Intention and suggestion. These include ways of establishing a favorable climate for LD, intending to dream lucidly, and forming detailed intentions about dream content.

Establishing a favorable climate. (1) Included here are all the *activities promoting lucidity*, when pursued for the purpose during the day or before sleep: being active, studying about LD, experimenting with altered states, etc. (2) Diverse pre-sleep *mood-setting rituals* have been recommended. Fariba Bogzaran increases her LD production by entering "a shamanic state" by chanting and drumming. Linda Reneau prays. Jeremy Taylor performs personal rituals, then intones a mantra.[186] (3) LaBerge recommends that, prior to sleep and in conjunction with any other procedure, one should use a *deep relaxation* technique. He gives protocols for two.[187]

Intention. Starting with Saint-Denys, there is wide agreement that merely suggesting to oneself to have LDs is moderately effective, as long as high motivation is maintained.[188] Using this method, Garfield "obtained a classical learning curve, increasing the frequency of prolonged lucid dreams from a baseline of zero to a high of three per week."[189] LaBerge, whose lab found no effect from simple "autosuggestion" in one study,[190] recommends "goal setting" as applied in sports psychology: goals should be both long-term and short-term; should be explicit and specific (e.g., to lucid dream this week); and should be difficult, but realistic.[191] Tholey advises that autosuggestion works best when applied immediately before sleep.[192] Both he and LaBerge have found that a willful, effortful state of mind is counterproductive—it is the suggestion per se which is effective, and the "expectation" of success.[193]

For highly hypnotizable subjects, posthypnotic suggestion to have LDs is also effective,[194] more so than simply being given waking instructions.[195]

Detailed intention (incubation). Carrying detailed intentions pertaining to lucidity into sleep increases the likelihood of becoming lucid. (1) In a sleep lab, being under instructions to signal when lucid itself helps to induce lucidity.[196] (2) Subjects encouraged to find a "personalized 'dream symbol'" under hypnosis are aided in becoming lucid "by altering dream content in a form which the individual [i]s trained to recognize. . . ." These subjects are "instructed to ask for their symbol's help in becoming lucid during their dreams that night."[197] This protocol of posthypnotic suggestion yielded LDs of longer duration and with strong personal relevance.[198] (3) Of widest application is the intention to have a certain perception or to perform a certain action, which will serve as a reminder to become lucid. Thus Don Juan tells Castaneda to look at his own hands while dreaming to trigger lucidity.[199]

But perhaps more important than devising lucidity triggers is learning to recognize them when they occur spontaneously. So triggers will be discussed further under 'lucid awareness training'.

Lucid awareness training. Besides learning to recognize triggers (including, as a special case, stimuli applied from outside the dream), a number of related techniques can be practiced while awake so as to enhance awareness of one's state while dreaming: reality-testing, dream re-entry, and treating reality as if it were a dream. The practice of these techniques is especially helpful for novices.

Trigger training. As noted above, recognition of bizarreness (incongruity, inconsistency) in a dream is very often what triggers lucidity. Following are a few triggers excerpted from dreams published in *NightLight*:

> *I am on a street lined with trees. The same scene switches from daylight to night several times. This triggers my knowledge that I am dreaming.*[200]

I am in our old apartment, with my wife, Y, who is deceased. As I often do, *I become lucid because I realize that since she is dead, this must be a dream.*[201]

Walking alone on a hill of soft, green grass, I look up and notice fantastic bubbles of gigantic proportions floating in the sky. Immediately I become lucid and feel as if this is a dream come true, for just yesterday, as I gazed out of the window of an airplane, I had fantasized about cavorting in the cumulus clouds that floated majestically beside me in the brilliant blue sky.[202]

Many triggers might not necessarily be classified bizarre, but still involve a certain deviation from baseline reality. (1) One common trigger is *very intense emotion*, particularly apprehension, from which "unsophisticated subjects" usually escape by waking up with the thought "I'm only dreaming."[203] (2) "*Changes in sensation*" seem to Garfield frequently to precede lucidity.* (3) Another common trigger is "recognition that the situation possesses the quality of 'dreamlikeness'."[204] *Dreamlikeness* comprehends bizarreness, but also includes dream events such as noticing a familiar dream motif, being in a recurrent dream, or finding oneself analyzing a dream in progress.[205] The three most common spontaneous triggers—bizarreness, apprehension, and dreamlikeness—probably reflect different cognitive styles.[206]

Some LDs begin lucid or simply turn lucid. Purcell finds that LD is more likely to start from "complete absorbtion in the dream" than to be triggered by an oddity.[207] But since many LDs are triggered, it is well worth cultivating awareness of potential triggers. Trigger training amounts to: talking and reading about trigger types;** identifying one's personal symbol vocabulary

---

* Under the heading "*Changes in sensation*" Garfield (1989, pp. xxxii–iii; see also 1991, p. 254) lists the following items (punctuation, format, and italics revised): "The feeling of *wind* blowing in your face or a cool draft. A *tingling* of your skin (this often involves the image of light rain or drizzle). A *sound or vibration*, like a combined buzzing-tingling or a buzzing light. A patch, crack, or hole of *light that appears* (sometimes as a window). The sense that a dream story is beginning again (what I call *doubleness*, rather like a waking déjà vu). An intense staring or focusing of your eyes (what I call *fixedness*). *Rhythmic movements* (such as dancing, spinning, swimming, or pelvic thrusting). A *shift in consciousness* within the dream (a sense that you are going to sleep, waking up, going into a trance, feeling lightheaded, or feeling tired). *Suspension in the air* (such as flying, floating, or levitating)." Garfield mentions elsewhere (1976 [1974], p. 138) that watching the flight of others can also act as a trigger.

** LaBerge & Levitan (1989a) outline triggers under the main headings "Dream Ego," "Dream Characters," "Dream Objects," and "Dream Settings." The inventory in S. LaBerge & H. Rheingold (1990), pp. 36–8, using the headings "Inner Awareness," "Action," "Form," and "Context" is more accessible. (Punctuation, format, italics revised; further examples deleted.) •INNER AWARENESS. **Thoughts.** *I'm trying to figure out where the house and furnishings are from, and I realize this is an odd thing to be thinking about.* **Emotions.** *I am filled with extreme anxiety and remorse.* **Sensations.** *A strong wave of sexual arousal comes over me.* **Perceptions.** *Somehow I could see perfectly without my glasses.* •ACTION. **Ego action.** *I'm riding home on a unicycle.* **Character action.**

and typical dream situations;[208] and paying attention to bizarre happenings, not only in recalled dreams but daily experience also.[209]

A special class of triggers is *external stimuli* which one has been taught to expect, administered "to cue the dreamer to recognize that he or she is dreaming"[210] (Price & Cohen's "REM-minding"). Varying success has been achieved with olfactory, tactile, and visual stimuli, as well as auditory stimuli, including musical phrases and tones and recorded verbal reminders that "This is a dream."[211] Most such procedures require a laboratory. However, Hearne has devised for home use a "dream machine" which administers a mild electric shock during REM.[212] And LaBerge has produced a family of electronic sleep masks, sold under the trade names "DreamLight," "Dream-Link," and "NovaDreamer." They emit a calibrated red signal during REM which gets incorporated into the dream, and which the dreamer trains to expect as a lucidity trigger.[213]

Tholey thinks that external stimuli are good for introducing the inexperienced to the possibility of LD.[214] With reference to LaBerge's mask, however, Gackenbach considers it more useful for the experienced, to prompt LD when particularly desired. She believes that many dreamers resist acknowledging the external prompt as a trigger.[215] Moreover, she thinks the quality of externally prompted LDs may be inferior. LaBerge disputes this.[216]

Reality-testing. Tholey has developed the "reflection technique" of lucid awareness training, which is the model for this important group of induction techniques. While *awake*, one asks oneself questions such as 'Am I dreaming?' 'Is this a dream?' etc. "If a subject develops while awake a critical reflective attitude toward his momentary state of consciousness . . . , then this attitude can be transferred to the dream state."[217] Asking the question gets to be a habit, which hopefully clicks on while dreaming.*

The hairdresser refers to a blueprint to cut my hair. **Object action.** *The bologna lights up.* •FORM. **Ego form.** *I am Mozart.* **Character form.** *Contrary to reality, G's hair is cut short.* **Setting form.** *The drafting room was the wrong shape.* **Object form.** *I see a tiny purple kitten.* •CONTEXT. **Ego role.** *We're fugitives from the law.* **Character role.** *Reagan, Bush, and Nixon are flying jets.* **Character place.** *Madonna was seated on a chair in my room.* **Object place.** *My bed was in the street.* **Setting place.** *I'm on the ocean, by myself, at night.* **Setting time.** *I'm in a grade school.* **Situation.** *A commercial is being filmed at my house."*

* If you find yourself really wondering whether you are dreaming, then you almost certainly are —really wondering, therefore, is actually a good trigger (S. LaBerge & J. Gackenbach 1986, p. 162 and J. R. Malamud 1986, p. 605, both citing C. McCreery, *Psychical Phenomena and the Physical World*, London: Hamish Hamilton, 1973). Acquiring the custom of performing a certain "state test" is recommended by LaBerge (S. LaBerge & L. Levitan 1990), namely, to attempt to read any writing or numbers twice. In a lucid dream, the material will almost certainly undergo change from one reading to the next. This technique is especially useful for seeing through false awakenings.

Reality-testing works best if performed frequently during the day, and especially in situations with some likeness to dreams (bizarre, symbolic, etc.). It should be performed close to sleep-time as well.

Various reminders to test reality have been suggested: putting a rubber band on the wrist or string on the finger; setting a wrist watch alarm; writing something on the back of one's hand.

Beyond asking the basic question, it helps to become reflective about the nature of waking and dreaming and how if at all they can be told apart. One can search experience for nuances associated with the lucid state.[218] And in addition to such an "active critical attitude," "a passive receptive focus on current experience" has also been said to encourage lucidity somewhat.[219]

Dream re-entry or review. Sparrow and Judith Malamud both induced LD by teaching novices to re-enter dreams they have previously dreamt, then re-dream them in imagination as if they were lucid.[220] LaBerge recommends re-entry as a medium for practicing reality-testing.[221] Hildegard Klippstein has her subjects re-enter dreams while under light hypnotic trance, as a way of familiarizing themselves with a duality of consciousness comparable to LD (experiencing trance in itself conveys this benefit, dream re-entry aside).[222] Taylor simply imagines, while reviewing an ordinary dream, how he would have behaved differently in it had he been lucid.[223]

Reality treated as if a dream. Taylor also sharpens lucid acuity by imagining how he would have behaved differently in waking events, if they had been dreams. Reneau tells herself, "'This, too, is my created reality, just as my dreams are my creations. . . .' The goal is to get in touch with the sense of creation from within."[224] She also pretends that she is somewhere other than where she is, a practice elaborated to a fault by Keith Harary & Pamela Weintraub, who would have us script whole pretend dreams to be acted out in the real world, complete with co-actors, costumes, etc.[225]

Combined techniques. Treating reality as a dream, LaBerge reminds us, is a feature of the dream yoga of Tibetan Buddhism. He contrived a simple adaptation of this part of the yoga. It combines (a) reality-testing, and (b) looking upon waking experience as essentially dream, with (c) the sleep-time intention to understand the true state of affairs while dreaming.[226]

Another combined technique was developed by Sheila Purcell et al. Their subjects wear a wrist band which reminds them to reality-test frequently; are encouraged to intend to become lucid; and are given regular trigger training sessions.[227] About 13% of dreams of their subjects are lucid, and about half of the subjects report at least one LD.[228]

But the most comprehensive combined technique is Tholey's.[229] It is a 9-step approach which incorporates all of the items thus far discussed under the headings 'intention' and 'lucid awareness training': reality-testing (1); treating reality as a dream (2); trigger training (3–5); dream re-entry (6); establishing a favorable climate (7, plus advice to use "special relaxation techniques"); intention (8); and detailed intention, i.e., "resolve to carry out a particular action while dreaming" (9).

Return-to-sleep techniques. LDs are usually easier to achieve after several hours of sleep. Moreover, a considerable number of spontaneous LDs occur after one has awakened and returned to sleep.[230] LaBerge has developed induction techniques which exploit these favorable conditions.

Mnemonic Induction of Lucid Dreams (MILD). MILD is an intention plus re-entry technique, but practiced only during the sleep night, after awakening with a dream.[231] The dreamer (1) recalls the dream in detail, fixing it in mind; (2) concentrates on the intention, "Next time I'm dreaming, I want to remember I'm dreaming"; (3) vividly imagines her/himself back in the dream, but this time lucid; and (4) repeats the previous two steps, until sleep returns. Re-entry is not a device to cause an actual subsequent redreaming of the same dream, but a vehicle for forming a strong association between the experience of being lucid, as simulated in step 3, and the intention, reinforced in step 2, to *remember* actually to be lucid in a dream—hence the name, "mnemonic induction."

Research has failed to demonstrate the "unique effectiveness" of MILD, perhaps the best publicized technique around.[232] LaBerge would not dispute this. His lab finds reality-testing marginally more effective than MILD, especially for those not yet proficient as LDers and/or not especially good at visualizing.[233] MILD is difficult and requires intense concentration; on the other hand, reality-testing "has the problem of being easily reduced to an ineffective habit. . . ."[234]

MILD and the DreamLight mask work equally well, and enhance each other when combined.[235] It is probably safe to say that all techniques work better when combined with others. A recent version of MILD adds trigger training exercises during the day, coupled with selection of an intended trigger during the re-entry step.

LaBerge also advises that the longer one can remain awake before falling back to sleep, the better the chance of success, a circumstance which led to the following experiments.

Nap technique. "Participants got up two hours earlier than usual in the morning and took two hour naps either two or four hours after rising."[236] Both procedures worked, but the nap after two hours awake was especially successful, producing over three times as many LDs as an ordinary night of sleep. A further experiment established that it is in fact the period of wakefulness itself which is effective, not the other variables involved (earlier than usual awakening, etc.). Good results were obtained when participants got up one and a half hours earlier than usual, stayed awake one and a half hours, and returned to sleep using a modified MILD procedure.[237]

Parenthetically, some people find it easiest to become lucid during daytime naps.[238]

Wake-Initiated Lucid Dream Induction Techniques.

The goal is to pass from wakefulness to dreaming with continuity of ego consciousness, an event perhaps related to entering a trance or vision,[239] but involving descending stage 1 sleep. LaBerge outlines this group of methods: one lies abed, relaxed though "vigilant," while focusing upon a continuous mental task. "In essence, the idea is to let your body fall asleep while you keep your mind awake."[240]

Tholey has contributed most to developing these techniques, which he regards as more suitable for advanced LDers.[241] They are harder to learn, but once acquired, he says, offer almost foolproof access to lucidity. He distinguishes these techniques by "whether one concentrates while falling asleep on hypnagogic images, one's body, or one's 'thinking ego.'"[242]

Body techniques. These techniques require one to concentrate on one's body, whether impromptu (Tholey), or concentrating on any of the chakras (Warman[243]), or using a prescribed relaxation procedure (LaBerge[244]). One enters motor inhibition (sleep paralysis) and then seems to pass beyond it, in the sense that the imaginal dream body becomes mobile. With experience, says Tholey, one can pass into LD quickly, bypassing the sensation of immobility.

One-body. "[O]ne merely makes the immobile body (appear to be) moveable again. The subject attempts to imagine that he is in a different situation or in a different place from the physical body, which is sleeping in the bed. . . . Another method . . . consists in (apparently) dissolving it [the body] into an 'airy' form and then solidifying it to a moveable body."

Dual-body. This is like an OBE or astral projection, but Tholey is careful to emphasize that "no real processes" are occurring, but only dream events. "The only important thing is to imagine intensively that one has a second, moveable body with which one can float out of . . . or in some fashion detach oneself from the immobile body."[245]

Ego-point technique. "[C]oncentrate while falling asleep on the thought that the body will soon no longer be perceived. As soon as this state is reached, it is possible to float freely as an ego-point in a space which seems to be identical with the room in which one went to sleep."[246] LaBerge calls this the "no body technique."[247]

Imagery techniques. *Image technique.* This is perhaps the most accessible technique of this group. One "concentrates while falling asleep only on visual images."[248] One maintains ego consciousness even as the mind passes through its sleep onset deconstruction (ch. 1, p. 28), deliberately cultivating the hypnagogic images. "Lucid hypnogogia," as Gregory terms it,[249] is the natural mode of reaching lucidity for many LDers, as it was for Edgar Allan Poe,[250] Ouspensky,[251] and others. Gregory gives this account of how she, as an already knowledgeable dreamer and accomplished LDer, first experienced and cultivated hypnagogic lucidity:

> *I am in the hypnagogic state experiencing apparently random and brief images. In one image, I see a red and yellow bow on a large white package. I notice the hands which are tieing the bow. To my surprise, they are my hands! I ask myself "Why am I tieing a bow on a package?" There is no response from the imagery. I follow my automatic responses and let the image expand. Carefully I curl the short ends of the ribbons under and tape them to the package. I don't want any loose ends. Using more and more tape, the bow becomes more and more secure although it looks less and less attractive. I am very concerned about getting this bow on this package. "Why is this such a big deal to me?" I ask myself. "This package must be something very important to me." I ask myself what is the most important thing in my life currently and I immediately answer myself that it is my lucid dream B.A. thesis. Suddenly I understand what was meant by the importance of tieing up the loose ends! That is exactly what is on my mind nearly all of the time. I realize in the image of the well-taped bow, I am showing myself the importance of making the finishing touches of my project secure—secure, meaning able to withstand criticism. I want my conclusions to be carefully tied or fastened to my data. What a beautiful image! Then I ponder the significance of the colors. Red and gold are such vibrant exciting colors. I note that these colors contrast to the plain white box that they adorn. What makes my thesis exciting both to me and potentially to others is how I tie it together—how I **present** it! I am amused by the pun.*
>
> *Suddenly I realize the importance theoretically of the state of consciousness which I am currently experiencing! I am expanding a hypnagogic random, condensed image into a lucid dream via employing lucid dreamwork techniques upon the single image. I feel that I am lucid dreaming or about to lucid dream! Very excited I look ahead of me to see what imagery will next appear. It is a completely different scene, one which I am unable to immediately connect to the thesis and ribbon-tieing scene. Oh! "This must still be the hypnagogic state," I tell myself. I decide to continue to practice applying my lucid dreamwork techniques to this new image as well.[252]*

Combined techniques. Tholey combines the image technique with each of his other techniques for reaching lucidity directly from waking. In the resulting *image-body technique*, "the subject concentrates not only on visual images but also equally strongly on his own body. If the subject suggests to himself in a relaxed state that his own body is light and can move freely, then it can occur that his phenomenal body begins to move. It seems to glide into the dream scenery. . . ."[253] In the *image-ego-point technique*, "[i]f a visual dream scenery has become established, then it is possible [for the ego-point] to travel into this scenery."[254]

Visualization. An image technique not in Tholey's repertory is visualization of purposely chosen—not spontaneous—imagery. This approach comes from Tibetan Buddhist dream yoga. LaBerge is probably right in remarking that only some of the more straightforward instructions from the yoga will be of much use to the average inquisitive Westerner.[255] These would include the instructions, previously mentioned, to resolve to see through the unreality of both waking and dreaming experience. Possibly also of practical use is the advice to sleep on one's right side.* And for those whom it suits, LaBerge offers simplified Tibetan visualizations adapted from Evans-Wentz's translation and from Tarab Tulku XI: the *white dot technique*, the *black dot technique*,[256] and the *dream lotus and flame technique*.[257] Those interested should consult LaBerge, or his sources, or Garfield's lively rendition of Tibetan practices.[258] But bear in mind, as Gillespie reminds us, that like other

---

* A connection between nasal passage dominance and autonomic functioning is an ancient teaching of the Hindu science of breath control, confirmed in experiments by Deborah Werntz showing that breathing through one nostril favors dominance of the opposite cerebral hemisphere (E. Rossi 1985, pp. 221–2, citing D. Werntz, *Cerebral Hemispheric Activity and Autonomic Nervous Function*, Ph.D. dissertation, University of California, San Diego, California, 1981). Lying on one side causes the nasal passage on that side partially to close, and the opposite passage to expand. The Hindu belief has been that breathing through the left nostril favors dreaming, so to encourage dreaming one should sleep on the right side (O. Garrison, 1983 [1964]). Rossi assumes that the positive effect is due to consequent right hemispheric dominance, though the connection between dreaming and hemispheric dominance is by no means settled. In any event, Moroccan Muslim Arabs sleep on the right side to encourage good dreams (V. Crapanzano 1975, p. 148), while Tibetan Buddhist dream yoga gives the same advice, for achieving lucidity. Evans-Wentz quotes and comments: "'Sleep on the right side, as a lion doth. With the thumb and ring-finger of the right hand press the pulsation of the throat-arteries; stop the nostrils with the fingers [of the left hand]; and let the saliva collect in the throat.' As a result of these methods, the *yogin* enjoys as vivid consciousness in the dream-state as in the waking-state; and in passing from one state to another experiences no break in the continuity of memory. Thereby the content of the dream-state is found to be quite the same as that of the waking-state, in that it is wholly phenomenal and, therefore, illusory" (W. Y. Evans-Wentz 1958 [1935], p. 216). LaBerge's laboratory finds that subjects do have more LDs sleeping on the right side than on the left. They believe that there are circulatory effects on the CNS which account for this effect, possibly not related to nostril dominance (L. Levitan 1991b).

A caveat: in the same study, sleeping on the back also favored LD. The adept Worsley (1988, p. 325) reports that although he normally sleeps on his side, he lucid dreams more readily sleeping face down with his head supported by his fists. Taylor recommends the left side (1992a, p. 215).

esoteric texts, the dream yoga instructions were purposely left incomplete. They were meant to be fleshed out by gurus who pass along certain specifics as well as general expertise by word of mouth.[259]

Counting technique. Another method contributed by LaBerge, one with the virtue of simplicity, is the "count yourself to sleep technique." "As you are drifting off to sleep, count to yourself, '1, I'm dreaming; 2, I'm dreaming, . . . ,' and so on, maintaining a degree of vigilance. . . . After continuing the counting and reminding process for some time, you will find that at some point, you'll be saying to yourself, 'I'm dreaming . . . ,' and you'll notice that you *are* dreaming!"[260] LaBerge recommends this technique for good hypnagogic imagers who fall asleep readily.[261]

Return-to-sleep techniques. Most spontaneous wake-initiated LDs occur, not at first sleep onset, but after being asleep and awakening briefly, during the REM-rich end of a night's sleep.[262] But not necessarily. Gregory's spontaneous hypnagogic lucidity (above, p. 460), which she prolonged into a full LD, occurred at sleep onset.[263] The wake-initiated induction techniques just listed by and large suit both conditions. Thus LaBerge applies the counting technique or the body technique after awakening with a dream and then intending to "return to dreaming, remembering that I'm dreaming." He calls this the "re-entry induction technique"—"re-entry" here means into stage 1 NREM or the REM state, not into the previous dream.[264]

Benefits of Lucid Dreaming

Claims for LD run from the modest statement that it "may be associated with more adaptive functioning"[265] to the assertion that it is equivalent to or next thing to enlightenment. Enlightenment will be considered separately below. Here, roughly the same benefits as those listed for ordinary dreaming in chapter 11 will be discussed, under the headings 'medical healing', 'practice effects', 'problem-solving', 'creativity', and 'psychological benefits'.

The claims of LD advocates vis-a-vis ordinary dreaming can be summed up: anything-you-can-do-I-can-do-better.

Medical Healing. Gackenbach begins her chapter on "The Healer Within" with this anecdote about the efficacy of lucidity in a dream incubated for medical healing:

[D]uring a heated arm-wrestling match, he [David Pack] injured his arm, and despite medical treatment it was still hurting him badly enough six months later that he was unable to continue working in the construction business. As an act of desperation he suggested to himself before falling asleep that his arm be healed. "I recall *a man* in my dream state *twisting and poking around on my elbow and it hurt,"* Pack explains. *"I asked him what he was doing, and he said, 'You have received two healings.'"* It was at this point that Pack realized that he was dreaming.

Upon awakening, Pack discovered that his right arm was tingling as though it had gone to sleep. But when the tingling was gone so was the pain. His arm was, as he put it, as "good as new." He was curious, though, about why the voice had proclaimed two healings. He found out the same week when a cyst in his back, which had been bothering him on and off for ten years, finally burst, relieving his chronic pain.[266]

Gackenbach reviews the medical benefits of imagery therapies, including guided fantasy, hypnosis, and meditation. She states that all of the elements of imagery found to be instrumental for healing exist in LD, most notably control;* and claims that LD may well be the most accessible form of healing imagery: all people dream, and many find it easier to cultivate lucidity than to imagine vividly while awake, enter deep hypnosis, or devote time to advanced meditation techniques.[267]

Garfield writes: "The potential for healing in lucid dreams is enormous. Lucid dreams are much more intense than waking visualizations. . . . Yet waking visualizations alone have been found to improve health conditions. Lucid dream visualizations should be even more effective."[268] The curious thing is that Garfield, an expert at LD as well as incubation, does not make any reference to using these measures herself in her recovery from a broken wrist, though her dream life surrounding that accident forms the backbone of her book on *The Healing Power of Dreams.*

Imagery treatments are known for assisting the immune system, a claim for LD made explicit by Garfield.[269] LaBerge, in his chapter "The Healing Dream," relates how *while lucid dreaming, a woman visualized the lump in her breast as a beautiful structure, like a "geodesic" cathedral, which she proceeded to deconstruct.* The lump disappeared in a week. LaBerge is careful to point out that such reports are only anecdotal, and that the efficacy of lucid healing needs to be evaluated scientifically.[270]

Practice effects. Skills can to an extent be honed and even acquired by imaginary practice. In this connection, LD is again promoted as an especially effective imagery technique. Whatever can be accomplished through waking imagery-rehearsal can be better accomplished through LD, because the

---

* J. Gackenbach & J. Bosveld (1989), p. 111: "1. The image should be vivid and resonant for the individual. 2. Being involved in the process of imaging is more important than the image itself. 3. The image should be spontaneous and chosen by the individual so that he or she is comfortable with it. 4. The imager/dreamer should feel in control of the process. This is particularly applicable to lucid dreaming." See also J. Achterberg (1985).

experience has more felt actuality.[271] Anything can be rehearsed in LD, to improve skill, reduce anxiety, and build confidence: a business meeting, surgery, exams, theatrics, quitting smoking, etc.

Gackenbach reviews Tholey's work in LD athletic training, including skiing, riding, sailing, skateboarding, martial arts, etc.[272] Championship form can be emulated and to an extent acquired in the midst of sleep immobility. The important thing is to "let your ego and body boundaries dissolve. You are the skier, the skis, the snow, the trees, the mountain, the wind." Such absorption, which Gackenbach relates to Zen, can be achieved in LD more readily than in waking because, she believes, the lucid state inherently entails a weakening of boundaries between self and other.

Problem-solving. Jack Maguire tells this anecdote:

> A member of the Brooklyn Dream Community was undecided about which of three presents to give her boyfriend for Christmas: a lounging robe, a set of oil-painting supplies, or fishing gear. In the course of a lucid dream, *she presented all three of these items to her boyfriend and asked him to choose one.* When it came time to make her waking-life purchase, her mind was at ease. She went for what her boyfriend had gone for in the dream: the oil-painting supplies.[273]

Creativity. Again, Gackenbach and LaBerge both have chapters on creative applications of LD, and others have written on the subject. One example without pretension or inflation will suffice to illustrate the possibilities. The LDer is identified by LaBerge as M. C.:

> I do this frequently. I have a certain computer program to design. At night I will dream that *I am sitting in a parlor (an old-fashioned one that Sherlock Holmes might use). I'm sitting with Einstein, white bushy hair—in the flesh. He and I are good friends. We talk about the program, start to do some flowcharts on a blackboard. Once we think we've come up with a good one, we laugh. Einstein says, "Well, the rest is history." Einstein excuses himself to go to bed. I sit in his recliner and doodle some code in a notepad. Then the code is all done. I look at it and say to myself, "I want to remember this flowchart when I wake up." I con-centrate very hard on the blackboard and the notepad.* Then I wake up. It is usu-ally around 3:30 A.M. I get my flashlight (which is under my pillow), get my pencil and notepad (next to my bed), and start writing as fast as I can. I take this to work and usually it is 99 percent accurate.[274]

Interestingly, of the twenty-six writers whom Naomi Epel interviewed on the subject of their dreams in relation to writing, only Amy Tan spoke about having LDs. Spalding Gray mentioned interest in other people's LDs, while Gloria Naylor specifically volunteered that she does not dream lucidly.[275]

Psychological benefits. Tholey shames non-LDers with this assertion: "We consider the mere induction of dreaming lucidly as a step toward healing. The usual dream state . . . we regard as a form of consciousness disorder. . . ."[276]

However that may be, LD is said to be associated with "a high degree of self-knowledge, emotional strength, honest self-expression, the ability to reflect on your experience, and the discipline to use what you've learned" (Reneau). LD augments "mental flexibility" and "mindfulness" (LaBerge). Positive LD experiences build confidence (Tholey). The exercise of control in LD reinforces our sense of responsibility for what happens awake (Malamud). And LD facilitates the integration of past traumas (Hall & Brylowski) and provides the LDer with "continuous opportunity to unify his personality" (Garfield).[277]

Given self-reflectiveness, memory for waking life, and control, psychological work can be carried on while in the lucid state. And just as there are interpretive and non-interpretive approaches to ordinary dreams, so work in lucidity can be interpretive or not.

In-dream interpretation. Level 6 on Tholey's scale of lucidity is "lucidity about what the dream or the imagined world symbolizes. . . ."[278] Gregory, in approximately a third of her lucid dreams, practices "within-the-dream psychotherapy."[279] She seeks to understand the meaning of the dream while still dreaming it. Over half the time, she finds the meaning to her own satisfaction, as in the lucid hypnagogic dream "Bow and box" (above, p. 460). For further illustration of in-dream interpretation, here is part of a dream series from Garfield, from a time when she was curious about the prevalence of the color red in her dreams:

> *I once found myself in a lucid dream in a bedroom with two women. As one of them had red hair, I immediately seized the lucid opportunity to inquire, "What's the significance of red hair in my dreams?" She replied rather saucily, "It depends. It's not always the same. You don't control all the dream, you know." Soon I was in a car with Zal and some other men, lapping some luscious honey,* oblivious to any dream symbolism, *and floating away on ripples of rapture. . . .*
>
> . . . [Yet red] has a precise symbolic meaning that I came to understand in a particular lucid dream. There, *already conscious that I was dreaming, I was making love with Zal. We had somehow arranged our bodies so that he was lower than I and I could look into a mirror while he caressed me. Watching my image as I felt the passion flow, I could see my face change. I was surprised to see how reddish-auburn my hair was. In a flash I realized that all the redheaded people in my dreams are myself! "Red is my natural color!" I exclaimed in a burst of insight. As the fire mounted in my body, and I grew slightly dizzy, even my cheeks took on a rosy flush. Red, I understood, is my sexual color; it is the red of passion, the redness of my thoughts extending to the tip of each hair. I melted down to where Zal was. . . .*[280]

But the potential of lucid in-dream interpretation needs to kept in proportion. Some ordinary dreams, if not literally self-interpreting (because awareness of the dream state is lacking), are potentially as plain to the awakened dreamer as Gregory's and Garfield's examples. Carlotte Beradt says of the dreams she gathered in Nazi Germany (ch. 5, p. 206) that they use imagery "whose symbols need no interpretation and whose allegories need no explanation. . . . These dreams adopt forms and guises which are no more complicated than the ones used in caricature or political satire, and the masks they assume are just as transparent as those worn at carnivals."[281]

Recall Bernard Siegel's and other dreams of verbal reference to medical symptoms (ch. 8, pp. 273-4). Meredith Sabini provides other examples of self-explanatory ordinary dreams about medical symptoms. Such a dream, dreamt by Mark Pelgrin a month before his death, "gives an astonishingly frank assessment of the functions and meanings of his illness," with a cogency usually associated with lucidity:

> [This] dream had to do with *telling the friend about the cancer, and he is annoyed and says that I am dramatizing too much. Could it be, I asked, that I have "invented" the cancer as an excuse for not really facing my inner problems? The way a little child "eats worms?" I had to admit that I got a kind of secret, dramatic, and morbid excitement out of the thought of my dying in such a way. Maybe I had projected my problems, as a man often does with the feminine, onto the body. Certainly all the intestinal troubles were not necessarily linked to cancer, even according to the "cold surgeon." It could, he said, be psychosomatic.*[282]

Pelgrin did not take his dream at face value.* Not so the next two dreamers. Their dreams are more typically dreamlike, but just as transparent. The first belongs to Faraday, the second is reported by Janice Baylis:

> Some dreams are very simple to understand and require no interpretation. . . .
>
> . . . For example, many years ago while still married to my first husband, I dreamed of *creeping up on him while he slept and bashing him to death with a carpet sweeper.* . . . My husband was, in fact, insisting that I relinquish my career in order to look after the home and family, a prospect that was evidently making me feel murderous toward him, although I had not consciously faced the full extent of my hostility.[283]

> *I had sent flowers* (love) *to my boyfriend. But the flowers came back in the mail* (male), *marked "Return to Sender". I felt very sad as I looked at what I had given him. I knew he didn't want my love and I was very sad!*

---

* See also M. Sabini & V. H. Maffly (1981), where it is clear that Pelgrin's pattern of resistance to the promptings of his unconscious was maintained throughout illness and therapy, in spite of his recognition of the pattern.

The dream made her take a different look at their relationship. Now she consciously realized that it was true, he didn't need or want her love. They broke up.[284]

Both these dreams are self-evidently compensatory. Both are "turning point dreams"—a type of dream which, even in the view of a contemporary psychoanalyst, Silas Warner, is often transparent in meaning from "manifest" content alone.[285] It has to be acknowledged, however, that seemingly obvious meanings are often not understood by the dreamer, and not necessarily due to repression. Alan Siegel gives three instances of dreams of men during the late pregnancies of their partners, dreams which make obvious reference to pregnancy, e.g.:

Late in pregnancy, one man dreamed that *while he was fishing, a large bubble emerged from underwater and out of it popped a furry animal that had lived underwater for a long time.* . . . Despite the transparent symbolism . . . , none of these three men spontaneously linked their dream to pregnancy or birth. They were all surprised and delighted when I suggested the possible connection of the dreams to the birth process and to their emotional involvement with the pregnancy and their child.[286*]

Siegel's fathers were apparently naive dreamers. In contrast, people sophisticated enough to incubate (chapter 13) sometimes receive dreams which are as clear to them as any LDer's in-dream interpretation. Gayle Delaney:

A year after meeting Steve, my fiancé, I began to worry that my relationship with him was going too smoothly. Was I just fooling myself or was our love as wonderful as it seemed? I asked my dream producer, "Can a relationship this happy last?" She responded with this dream:
I saw in a beautiful, sunny, redwood forest two magnificent redwood trees dancing in the wind. They were young, graceful, and majestic. I realized that the taller tree symbolized Steve, the smaller beside it, myself. Then I was aware of our having become these trees. We were at peace with the world and would grow in the forest for centuries to come. ("Dancing Redwoods")[287]

A second reservation about the potential of in-dream interpretation is that lucidity does not bestow omniscience. In fact the quality of insight does not necessarily exceed that which would have been available to the dreamer, reflecting awake upon a similar but non-lucid scenario. Such is the case with Garfield's dream "Red is my natural color!" (above, p. 465). Or the inter-

---

* Other dreams with overt meanings missed by dreamers, evidently not due to repression, are the dreams about "conception and children" (ch. 13, p. 393), and the "brain teaser" dreams, where the dreamer missed that water = $H2O$ = H to O (ch. 13, p. 417). (See also ch. 4, p. 144.)

pretation may actually fall short in obvious ways, yet persuade the dreamer by the enthusiasm of the lucid state, which has the *Aha!* built in. Gregory's interpretation in the dream "Bow and box" (above, p. 460), it seems to me, failed to take account of a pivotal detail: the more secure the bow became, the less attractive it looked. And here, from a LDer named Lois Gordon, is an in-dream interpretation where euphoria precluded critical analysis:

> I had a vivid lucid dream some time back, which began with *me running through a maze, room after room. Each room was a scene from life, and always something was pursuing me or pushing me forward. Suddenly I stopped and said, "This is silly. I don't want to keep running through this maze. Why am I here, and how do I get out? Must I die?" A voice then said to me, "You know what to do!" and suddenly I ran to a side rail and saw the maze was not everything. It sat atop a huge expanse, and there was a valley below and more beyond that. I leapt up on the wall and said, "Yes, I know this is a dream! I can fly out of here!" whereupon I was soaring like an eagle over the maze and seeing everything with a new perspective. I tumbled and spun and was totally exhilarated, for I felt I had learned something very essential to my being.*
>
> *The voice then said, "And do you know what this dream means?" I said, "Yes, dreams are the true reality, for ordinary reality is the maze we run through, never knowing, just running all the time, but in dreams there are no walls, no obstacles, and we can see everything." I felt, somehow, that I had discovered the meaning of life!*[288]

It may well have been psychologically appropriate for Gordon to shake off her waking problems at that juncture; but the dubious conclusion makes one wonder if the dreamer was avoiding something in the maze of scenes from life.

Non-interpretive approaches to psychological work in lucidity. Recall first of all what advocates of non-interpretive work in general have to say (chapter 12). LaBerge believes that LDs (even if controlled) are just as interpretable as other dreams;[289] but he also believes resolution of psychological issues at the level of imagery is more profitable than interpretation, especially when achieved within the lucid dream state itself. "Waking analysis (or interpretation while in the dream) may help you understand the source of your anxieties but will not necessarily help you outgrow them."[290]

In lucidity, Taylor writes, we can realize that "all we behold is a mirror in which our own interior being is reflected in metaphoric form. We realize consciously in the dream that it is aspects of our own being that we are seeing and dealing with. In this sense, the act of repression is withdrawn, becomes conscious, and ceases to be repression."[291] This awareness can lead to in-dream interpretation of projections in a fashion familiar from waking dreamwork;[292] or it can lead to non-interpretive but salubrious interaction, a sort of in-dream dream drama or Gestalt workshop, though perhaps building upon interpretive insights. The dream images retain autonomy, remarks Sparrow, but the dream-ego acquires autonomy in relation to them.[293] It is the interaction which brings psychological benefit.

This important subject will be touched upon in the next section, and treated again in chapter 16.

Pros and Cons of Controlling Dreams

Pro. The benefits of LD—in-dream psychological work, creativity, problem-solving, practice, healing—all depend to varying extents upon control of the dream. The very exercise of control in dreams, says Garfield, restores a sense of control in waking life to those who feel anxious or powerless; it shows what can be accomplished from personal resources.[294] Lucidity with control, claims Rossi, is an indicator of personal growth—a position held by Rudolf Steiner, the Anthroposophist.[295]

Con. Advocates of LD occasionally caution us about potential hazards and abuses of LD and, especially, of control. Garfield advises those with a tenuous hold on reality not to become involved. Gackenbach warns that for certain people, control can produce rather than alleviate anxiety. She also notes the risk of becoming addicted.[296] These cautions ought to be born in mind. Two additional cautions, however, need to be considered more closely. These pertain to lucid control in a more general way. And they parallel those concerns, on the basis of which certain critics discourage us from all attempts at dream control.

The first caution is that control, as Gackenbach notes, can be used inappropriately as a defense to avoid the substance of our dreams, by "turning nasty things into sweet things . . . excessively"[297] (as with the dream "She escapes the maze of ordinary reality," above, p. 468). The wish to control dreams is seen by some as colored by avoidance of negative material.[298]

The second caution is related to the first, but emphasizes that control can interfere with the spontaneous healing attributes of dreams. To control outcomes may give pleasure or reassurance, but "can be destructive to the benefit of dreams" (Walter Bonime). The worst of all options is to give all bad dreams happy endings: one should "explore the dream rather than control it" (Delaney). Or: "The focus in dream control should be on learning how to control one's response to dream events, not on controlling the creation of those events" (Gackenbach). Otherwise, dreamers show an inappropriate desire for mastery, a disrespect to the unconscious (Sparrow).[299]

Many (though not all[300]) Jungians discourage control, and even disparage LD on this basis—no doubt influenced by the fact that Jung's own remarkable dream life did not feature lucidity. They can point to such statements from Jung as this: "The unconscious is an autonomous psychic entity; any efforts to drill it are only apparently successful, and moreover are harmful to consciousness. It is and remains beyond the reach of subjective arbitrary control. . . ."[301] In one place, James Hall expresses skepticism that LD control is even possible.[302] Other Jungians—Hall himself, elsewhere—concede that point,[303] but could never sympathize with the project to "free ourselves from" the unconscious through LD, as Tholey desires.[304] Jane White Lewis and others consider dreaming to be a read-out from the objective psyche, always telling us something we do not know. Why interfere? We should trust the unconscious. If there is fear, we need to go through it, not evade it by changing the dream.[305] Lewis (or White-Lewis) writes:

> At the end of an Association for the Study of Dreams (ASD) conference in Ottawa, I was sitting in the cafeteria and overheard a woman, a "lucid" dreamer, describing a troubling nightmare to a friend. In her upsetting dream, *she had been caught in a swimming pool filled with garbage.* She boasted that, thanks to lucid dreaming techniques, *she had been able to clean up the garbage and change the image of the dream.* She was pleased and proud of her success, but I, as a Jungian with a deep respect for the unconscious, was startled. Why would she want to do that—change or throw away the image of the dream and, at the same time, throw out the possibility of understanding its meaning. . . .
>
> . . . I was amazed to discover that there were people in the world who attended to their dreams and clearly valued them, but who did not trust the unconscious to speak/reveal truth in its own way. To violate a dream by altering the text or image seemed not only irresponsible but psychologically dangerous.[306]

Dreamworkers of other schools make the same and related points. Robin Shohet thinks lucidity and control conflict with "being receptive to the actual messages that can be learnt."[307] Katherine West expresses "an abhorrence" of it, because "it smacks of a subtle ego control."[308] Speaking from a Native American perspective, Edwin Richardson suggests that the move to control dreams reflects a need to control everything, typical of Euro-American culture.[309] The existentialist Eric Craig, himself not inexperienced with lucidity, nicely compares the dream to a wilderness, about the only one we have left; manipulating dreams is like building a college there: a beautiful setting, but no longer a wilderness.[310] Johanna King also believes control violates the essence of dreaming, which is its involuntariness. To the contention that LD is an excellent place for unconscious-conscious dialogue, she answers that the ego is flawed and does not know how to conduct such a dialogue.[311]

Pro. Garfield rejoins that lucid dreaming is not something done every night, nor (except rarely) every dream of a night. One's ordinary dream life goes on. Moreover, since not everything in a dream can be controlled, LDs themselves retain their interpretability in the conventional sense.[312]

The psyche appears to protect itself from over-control. Hunt & Robert Ogilvie point out that engrossment in manipulation of the dream scene often leads to loss of all but "a merely vestigial, liminal sense of lucidity," while on the other hand the full sense of lucid presence often is so prepossessing as to eliminate the desire to control things.[313]

The psyche also protects itself by balking or protesting. Responding to similar objections to control by incubation, Delaney says that excess brings either failure of the attempt or "messages" to stop or change the process.[314] Gackenbach & Bosveld relate a LD which fits this description:

> One of the authors of this book prompted herself before falling asleep to fly in her dreams and wound up *on the outside of a rocket, holding on for dear life, as it blasted off.* Not exactly the sort of flying she had in mind.[315]

Along the same lines, Linda Magallón explains that when she over-controls LD action, "my dream characters turn around and give me a bad time." In this way the process shows itself to be "wise and self-regulating."[316] Price & Cohen illustrate the fallibility of lucid control with another (hypothetical?) flying dream apparently serving such a compensatory function: "the dreamer may succeed in a wish to *become airborne only to be startled by an onlooker's angry reaction.*"[317] And Taylor addresses the issue with yet another flying dream:

> There are certain people who are reluctant to attempt to become lucid in their dreams, for fear that the intrusion of an element of waking consciousness usually absent from dreams might tend to "poison the well"—to dominate and control the dream experience so that the spontaneous unconscious will have an even harder time bringing the "natural" healing, compensatory, balancing energies into the experience of the dream. . . . To imagine that the dreaming unconscious could be totally overwhelmed and controlled by even the most practiced and disciplined lucidity seems to me to be simple hubris at worst, and at best a failure of perception and imagination. . . .
>
> . . . For a period of time I became very excited about flying in my dreams. I would attempt to incubate lucid dreaming with the focus of attention that I would fly. Eventually I had a dream in which *I was cheerfully flying and altering both my dream body and the landscape over which I flew, when I encountered a group of "older, wiser magicians" whose disparaging thoughts I telepathically overheard. "There he goes," they said to one another with a tone of resignation and disappointment, "flying again." I was taken aback in the midst of the lucid*

dream and realized that I was indeed becoming distracted from more serious and important matters by my exclusive focus upon the act of flying. This experience suggests strongly to me that the naturally self-correcting and self-criticizing quality of dreams pervades the dreams of even lucid dreamers.[318]

It is noteworthy that these three examples all involve flying. They go some way to answer a concern of Lewis, that preoccupation with flying, so common with LDers, leaves them "ungrounded."[319] However, the examples do beg the question, and the hazard of ego inflation should certainly be kept in view.

As her discussion of the dream "She cleans up the garbage" (above, p. 470) indicates, Lewis also worries that control enables LDers defensively to evade constructive pain. Granted that this can occur, the concern can be answered in various ways. One is that changing outcomes can itself be psychologically beneficial (see chapter 16). But equally important, to exercise control in a dream does not necessarily imply avoidance or even manipulation. It can, in fact, permit an anxious or fearful dreamer *not* to avoid. Restraint is also a form of control. Such control can consist precisely in staying with and living through the pain brought by the spontaneous dream.

Globus & Melissa Derfler designate as "receptive lucidity" that state in which in-dream meditation becomes possible, sometimes bringing with it visual experiences of white light or mandala patterns. These experiences lose intensity if an effort is made to manipulate them.[320] LaBerge contends that surrender of control is actually what brings a LDer to the threshold of "transcendental" experiences.[321] The restrained or receptive state of mind is not indiscriminately passive, but rather requires what, in applying Globus's concept, Garfield terms "receptive control." In this lucid state one can present requests to the psyche, such as "Take me where I need to go."[322] This combination of willingness and control entails just the openness to dream experience, the restraint from flight which Lewis asks for.

Is Lucid Dreaming 'Enlightened'?

Enlightenment—the ultimate benefit—is connected by the lucidity literature with LD. An LDer "is allowed to . . . attain enlightening experience. . ." (Henry Reed). "[L]ucid dreaming may lead an individual through various recognizable stages of the enlightenment process. . ." (Sparrow). "The Way of the Dream Mandala is a path to enlightenment" (Garfield). "To be lucid means to be clear, full of light, or enlightened" (Kenneth Kelzer).[323] The final sentence of LaBerge's *DreamLink Operation Manual* offers the hope that users' "hearts [will] be enlightened thereby. . ." (Levitan). While other au-

thors may approach it more circumspectly (see below), the linkage with enlightenment is often not far away.

LD theorists are drawn to this Eastern concept by lucidity's legitimacy
in Hindu and Buddhist traditions, especially in the dream yoga of Tibetan
Buddhism. LD is regarded there as an opportunity for in-sleep meditation,
undertaken to bring realization that phenomena are illusory: "Whatever be
seen during sleep is not something apart from mind. Similarly, all phenomena of the waking-state are but the dream-content of the Sleep of Obscuring
Ignorance."[324] Much the same perspective is found in the other traditions,
in all of which the main technique for reaching realization, or enlightenment,
is meditation.

Western theorists perceive a natural connection between meditation and
LD. Apart from the fact that one can opt to meditate *while* lucid dreaming,
some regard LD as *itself* meditative,[325] "a spontaneous form of the state of
mind *sought* within so-called 'insight' or 'mindfulness' traditions. . . ."[326] In
its detachment, its clarity about illusion, and its exhilaration, LD seems to
be inherently like meditation, and therefore inherently enlightening (if not
enlightened).

Detachment. As pointed out above in the section on maintaining lucidity,
maintaining requires a special detachment, a "tenuous balancing of a detached 'receptive' attitude with ongoing participation" which is also characteristic of meditation.[327] Delaney makes this connection: "It may be that lucidity
depends not on avoiding the experience of strong emotion but on maintaining a constant awareness or observation that you are experiencing it. This
would be similar to being both the witness and the experiencer of your emotions and thoughts, as is suggested in several forms of meditation."[328*] And
Gackenbach: "[T]o become aware [in meditation] of each passing moment
and thereby become detached from the events . . . is a state strikingly similar
to that found in lucid dreaming. . . ."[329]

Blackmore concludes her interesting remarks in an interview concerning
LD and OBE with this comment on meditation: "I'm certainly not doing it

---

[*] Hunt & Ogilvie (1988, p. 405) compare the difficulty of maintaining lucidity with the ardors
of meditation in a different respect: "Most lucid dreaming probably does end in slipping back into
ordinary dream realism or premature arousal. It is this tenuous, transitional quality, [which is] itself
so reminiscent of the subjective difficulties of meditation practice where the meditator struggles back
and forth between drowsiness and ordinary everyday obsessions. . . ."

Gackenbach (1990d, pp. 244-5) calls attention to psychological parallels between meditators and
LDers. Both "exhibit fewer stress-related personality characteristics . . . , both . . . are able to become highly focused on one activity, are able to become 'caught up' in an experience, and are aware
of their inner thoughts and internal processes." In addition, both have good dream recall and are
field-independent.

because I want to get enlightened. I do it almost as a practice because it releases one from wanting."[330] But of course such release is both a classic aim of meditation and a classic attribute of enlightenment. To attain detachment in waking life is also an aspect of what is sometimes called "lucid living"[331] in the lucidity literature. Lucid living is said to come as a consequence of developing dream lucidity.

Clarity about illusion. To be enlightened is to be "conscious of the illusion always. . . ."[332] This is Buddhism's doctrine .* Awareness of the illusion of the dream state in LD is what, in the tradition of the dream yoga, makes dream lucidity valuable practice for waking insight. LD and waking meditation are practiced in tandem: "By a careful analytical study of dreams and psychological experimentation on himself as the subject, the *yogin* at last comes actually thus to realize, and not merely believe, that the total content of the waking-state as well as of the dream-state is, in fact, illusory phenomena."[333]

Exhilaration. "[A]n electrifying sensation of rebirth" promises LaBerge. "*I have never been awake before*" reports an LDer. And another: "*It's as if I was seeing the invisible relationships connecting all things—the intimate molecular level superimposed over the vast and limitless Universe.*"[334] And "the glory, ah, the glory," muses Garfield, who believes it "quite possible that in lucid dreaming we are stimulating an area of the brain, or chain of responses, that is associated with ecstatic states of all sorts."[335] Globus considers lucid euphoria to be direct apprehension of the "natural harmony" of the "neural net" of the nervous system (ch. 1, p. 40). Hunt regards such LD experiences as spontaneous occurrences of what is sought in meditation.[336]

The spiritual exhilaration of accomplished meditation can be taken as given. What perhaps needs to be clarified is that the detachment and absolute disillusionment of the waking 'enlightened' condition are not supposed to be alienated and indifferent, but joyous and engaged. So versifies the early Tibetan master Milarepa:

> A grassy slope with flowers of many hues,
> With glades where fair trees dance
> And monkeys ply their sports,
> Where resound the many songs of birds
> And bees hover in their flight,

---

* W. D. O'Flaherty (1984), p. 12 passim. Buddhists cannot even entertain the Hindu notion that the world as we know it is the dream of god. Since Buddhists hold that there is no ultimate reality, there can be no ultimate dreamer (p. 244). "For the Buddhists do not have the theological hypothesis to fall back upon" (p. 245).

Where day-in day-out a rainbow quivers,
Where Summer and Winter a sweet rain falls,
And Spring and Autumn a thick mist clings.
It is in such a lonely place as this
That I, the yogin Mila Repa,
Am joyous in the Clear Light of realization of the Void,
Joyous exceedingly at its many ways of appearance, . . .[337]

The adept does not cling to forms, but forms delight: "far from blunting his senses, he develops a higher awareness and a deeper insight into the real nature of the world and his own mind. And this shows him that it is as foolish to run *away* from the world as to run *after* the world. . ." (Lama Govinda). Spiritual practice "leads to an epiphany of the phenomenal world as radiant with the 'Absolute'" (June Singer). 'Things' are not less than we perceive them to be, but more (Boss).[338] Compare this to epiphanous LDs, such as some quoted above, or this of Fox's, when he realized, "*I was dreaming!*":

> *With the realization of this fact, the quality of the dream changed in a manner very difficult to convey to one who has not had this experience. Instantly, the vividness of life increased a hundred-fold. Never had sea and sky and trees shown with such glamorous beauty; even the commonplace houses seemed alive and mystically beautiful. Never had I felt so absolutely well, so clear-brained, so inexpressibly free!*[339]

But to emphasize these connections is not necessarily to imply that LD *is* enlightened. "I'm not saying that lucid dreaming is the same thing as *enlightenment*," qualifies LaBerge; "I do not regard lucid dreaming as a complete path to enlightenment. . . . I see it primarily as a signpost pointing to the possibility of higher consciousness. . . ."[340] And Gackenbach "stresses the importance of placing dream lucidity in the context of a program of self development such as dream work, psychotherapy or meditation." LD should be applied first "to work through normal day to day problems before undue focus is placed on lucidity as a vehicle for seeking the spiritual highest."[341] This is consistent with the parent spiritual traditions.[342]

Within those traditions, it is important to understand, dream lucidity is not the highest level of consciousness and therefore cannot be sufficient for enlightenment. Through the Upanishadic-Vedantic tradition, from about 700 B.C., they "speak of four states of being: waking, dreaming, dreamless sleep (all natural states), and the supernatural, transcendent fourth state, the identity with Godhead."[343] The fourth state, enlightenment, is a sort of "sleepless sleep . . . realized when the veil of ignorance which causes . . . [dreamless] sleep, dream and waking, is lifted."[344] The four levels "suggest a technique of realization, a means of approaching enlightenment."[345] Dreaming gives practice reality-testing for the illusion of the world (lower samadhi); dreamless sleep is practice for the higher disillusionment of enlightenment (higher samadhi).[346]* This is the philosophy which along a certain line of development culminated with Tibetan Buddhist dream yoga.

It is not immediately obvious where LD fits into the four-level scheme. In Gillespie's experience, dreamless sleep is a "home base," from which he moves out into dream or into waking, and back again. Gillespie's implication is that everyone has dreamless sleep, but not everyone is conscious of it: "[T]he normal sleeper does not reach the state lucidly and is not aware of it." Samadhi is lucid dreamless sleep, the state before ultimate liberation. The yogin is able to achieve lucid dreamless sleep, if s/he can "disrupt a lucid dream. . . ."[347] So LD per se is evidently a wrung or more lower.

Transcendental Meditation (TM) introduces the concept of 'witnessing' which is helpful here. Above ordinary dreaming, Gackenbach distinguishes: (1) LD, in which you know you are dreaming but are completely absorbed in the dream action—though with enough detachment to maintain lucidity; (2) witnessed dreaming, in which a part of the mind is truly detached from the dream action and is tranquil, even while another part in engaged; and (3) witnessed dreamless sleep, a sort of pure expansive awareness, often described as "bliss."[348] Whereas the Upanishads differentiate dreamless sleep (the third state) from enlightenment, TM appears to regard witnessed dreamless sleep as enlightened,[349] and refers to it as "the fourth state."[350] Or perhaps I misunderstand, and something else called "pure consciousness" is the fourth state, which, when it accompanies other (including higher) states is called witnessing.[351] Be that as it may, witnessing is a "higher" state than simple lucidity.[352]** In Gackenbach's descriptions, witnessing of dreams, witnessing of dreamless sleep, and abstract experiences of light and form run together in a continuum of states above basal LD.[353]

Witnessing sounds to be a sort of all-night lucidity, something reported in the LD literature, either as an alternation between dreaming and dreamless sleep, or as persistent dreamless sleep. Delaney has given an account of what seems to be the former, one of her occasional spontaneous nights of unbroken consciousness, which she explicitly compares to the deliberate achievements of dream yoga practitioners. *She alternately hears her mind*

---

* In terms of Hindu theology, "dreamless sleep gives us a glimpse of the true *brahman* [godhead], the divine mind that does not create; dreaming sleep gives us a glimpse of the god (Vi[shn]u or Rudra) who creates us by dreaming us into existence" (W. D. O'Flaherty 1984, p. 15).

** See also E. Bruce Taub-Bynum's (1984, p. 83ff.) discussion of the "Yoga Nidra."

busily at work or chattering, experiences dreams of various lengths (and repeats some of them at will), practices French ad nauseam, practices skiing (sometimes at the same time as French), and so on—and finds herself unable to lose consciousness even when she tires and wants to.[354] And here are two other brief descriptions of the experience, showing both the affinity to and difference from ordinary lucidity. The first is reported by Gregory, as the spontaneous experience of an 11-year-old boy (if the wording is really his own, he is obviously very bright):

I am lucid all night long. I observe my dreams as they go by, staying lucid even between dreams. I feel that the awareness is located in my head and feel as though I am in a dark room where things happen. As I am falling asleep and then repeatedly through the night I hear two or three voices speaking random words. In between dreams I am aware of random background noise which congeals into visuals which are dreams. I try to wake up but can't, so I just flow with the experience.

At this point Eric stops lucid dreaming and begins active lucid dreaming. He reports: *I grab the last dream of the night, climb onto it, enter it and dream it. I'm very excited by the experience.*[355]

The second is reported by Gackenbach et al. It is the experience of a TM meditator:

Often during dreaming I am awake inside, in a very peaceful, blissful state. Dreams come and go, thoughts about the dreams come and go, but I remain in a deeply peaceful state, completely separate from the dreams and the thoughts. My body is asleep and inert, breathing goes on regularly and mechanically, and inside I am just aware than I am.[356]

Then there is dreamless sleep, persistent through all sleep stages[357] and different from mere dreamlessness because it is recallably conscious. Gackenbach supplies the example, from a "long-term meditator":

*It begins with an awareness that I am **not** dreaming, and I know I am **not** awake. I become aware of a whirlpool of vast energy and sound—rising and falling—oscillating within itself. I experience it as a natural part of myself. I feel completeness, as though I had arrived home after a long and tiring journey. I feel a deep silence, even in the midst of all this motion, and at this point I have a strange awareness that the life I live here on earth is just a dream, and that this vast field of energy is who I really am. Through all of this I don't forget who I am as a person, or the fact that I know I am not dreaming.*[358*]

** For further comments on completely dreamless but conscious sleep, see also: ibid., p. 184; M. Serrano (1968 [1966]), p. 59, reporting a conversation with Krishna Murti; R. Mehta (1978), p. 95; J. Taylor (1983), pp. 32–3; S. LaBerge (1985), pp. 123–4.

In Tibetan Buddhism, "[d]reamless sleep is described in terms of a series of eight visual experiences, consisting only of light and darkness."[359] Gillespie synopsizes Evans-Wentz on these stages of sleep consciousness above lucidity, which are realized by joining the dream yoga with the "Yoga of the Clear Light."[360] I will somewhat abridge Gillespie's account of these supposedly predictable ascending stages of dreamless sleep:

> Now that the [lucid] dream image has disappeared and the dreamer (if we may still call her that) has fallen into dreamless sleep, she begins to see a series of phenomena . . . not considered to be dreams. They are signs that one's meditation is leading one toward experience of the voidness which lies behind all worldly manifestations. They are the same signs that are seen in successful day-time meditation and at the . . . time of death.
>
> . . . The first four are thought of as successively brighter. . . . [They resemble: 1] the haziness of an apparent lake in a desert . . . [2] the billowing of smoke . . . [3] fireflies or sparks within smoke . . . [4] the sputtering light of a butter lamp, or according to others a steady lamplight. . . .
>
> The four experiences of voidness that follow are visions of solid light or darkness. . . . [They resemble: 5] a moonlit night sky . . . [6] a glaring, sunny sky. The sun itself is not present . . . [7] complete darkness. . . . [8] The last experience is of a very bright lasting light, compared to the light of dawn. This is the light of the universal void, the light from which all else comes forth. It is translated as the clear light or the radiant light. If the dreamer holds onto this light, she experiences **nirvana**, liberation. **Nirvana** is beyond dreamless sleep. These experiences of voidness are associated with feelings of bliss, the greatest bliss being in the final experience of light.[361]

Clearly, the tradition recognizes a hierarchy of experiences above LD. But Gillespie goes on to say that from our point of view it does not much matter if we regard these experiences as dreamt or as 'dreamless', and that similar phenomena, if not with the same regularity or sequence, are reported in the contemporary LD literature.[362] Gillespie reviews five experts (van Eedan, Sparrow, Garfield, Kelzer, and himself) who discuss personal LD light experiences, and five who do not, or who at any rate do not give them much prominence (Green, Faraday, LaBerge, Gackenbach, and Hunt).[363] Of himself Gillespie writes: "I have felt devotion and joy and 'awareness' of the presence of God in the full light." "The fullness of light is an intense, vibrant white light filling the visual field and seeming to surround me. It is accompanied by uncontrollable joy and devotion and a feeling of the presence of God." Kelzer relates that "the whole experience is permeated with overwhelming feelings of joy, ecstasy, loving power, and the overriding desire for one thing only: to be one with the Light!" And Garfield, who is more faithful than most others to Tibetan sources, writes: "At the fourth level of interaction, we move into a full-blown mystical, ecstatic experience within the dream. Forms disappear and all is radiance. We are part of a single life force. I glimpse the brilliance of this level fleetingly, at one with the universe. These are the dream experiences of light."[364]

Gillespie's recommendation not to feel bound by the categories of an esoteric yoga is no doubt sound. This comports with LaBerge's advice mentioned earlier, that only selected elements of the yogic procedures are suitable for adoption by his U.S. readers. It should be realized that the original context for the dream yoga comprised the whole commitment and training of a Buddhist monk. In that training, the attempt to control dreams had to be preceded by several rather extraordinary accomplishments, called *siddhi*, "marvellous powers [which] follow automatically from success in the ascetic and mystical techniques undertaken."[365] The siddhi included "tummo," or "psychic heat," whereby one can live out of doors and dry wet sheets with body heat during Himalayan winter, without feeling cold.[366*] Once proficient, the dream yogi "could make the object of his dream materialize when he woke up,"[367] and could even pass from life to death and back again without loss of consciousness.[368] The yogi could also be *observed* to levitate, fly through the air, pass through objects, and so on.[369] The siddhi obviously bespeak a cultural gulf, too wide for most of us to bridge.

Yet, to pick and choose accessible elements from a culturally integrated path of enlightenment begs the question. If my then six-year-old friend Alice Colman experienced dreamless sleep, was it because she was a spiritually advanced person?[**] Or if an adult's first, spontaneous LD is a light experience, is s/he enlightened? Sparrow, whose book is subtitled *Dawning of the Clear Light*, recounts the first LD of a young woman:

> I seemed to be responsible for a baby which was very messy and sitting on a pot. My concern was to find a bathroom and clean it up without others noticing it. As I held the baby, I distinctly felt that it should be older and better trained. I looked closely into its face which was full of wisdom and suddenly I knew I was dreaming.
>
> Excitedly, I tried to remember the advice in the article [about lucidity she had read] and the only thought I had was "Ultimate Experience." A blissful sensation

---

* Psychic heat is called "tapas" in India. "In the myth of the *Vedas*, such energy is employed by the gods themselves, especially for the purpose of creation. The creator god heats himself and produces the universe by internal incandescence" (M. Zeller 1990 [1975], p. 166, citing H. Zimmer, *Myths and Symbols in Indian Art and Civilization*, New York: Harper Torchbooks, 1962).

** "When I'm asleep," Alice told me, "I look for a dream." "So sometimes, when you know that you're asleep, you're *not* dreaming?" "Uh-huh." "Do you ever change your dreams?" "Uh-huh. But first you have to find a dream."

took over—of blending and melting with colors and light—opening up into a total "orgasm." I gently floated into waking consciousness.[370]

Sparrow's own first LD was also a fortuitous light experience:

> *It seems that I have come home from school. I become aware that I'm dreaming as I stand outside a small building which has large black double-doors on its eastern side. I approach them to enter. As soon as I open them, a brilliant white light hits me in the face. Immediately I am filled with intense feelings of love.*
>
> *I say several times, "This can't be a dream!" The interior resembles a small chapel or meeting room. It has large windows overlooking barren land like the Great Plains. I think to myself that this is somehow **real** in a three-dimensional sense. Everything is amazingly clear and the colors brilliant.*
>
> *No one is with me, yet I feel that someone needs to be there to explain the sense of purpose that seems to permeate the atmosphere.*
>
> *At one point I walk holding a crystal rod (or wand) upon which a spinning crystal circlet is poised. The light passes through it and is beautiful.*[371]

Sparrow virtually equates lucid light dreams to enlightenment, but grafts the yogic concept to Caycean Christianity. A believer, Sparrow takes Jesus as his guide (guru) in pursuit of the experience. Thus he does provide—to the extent that he discusses it—a replacement context, but one also separated by a gulf from many readers. Even Gillespie, himself a missionary by profession, finds that Sparrow "presented the experience of light in lucid dreams as more mystical than I was willing to accept." Gillespie's interest in LD is religious, but with this reservation: "As a dreamer, I cannot but uncritically accept what happens. Upon awaking, I still cannot but be the critic of both the dream and the dreamer. I am happy with this arrangement. As long as dreamer and critic can respect each other, the conflict is minimized."[372]*

Recall LaBerge's caution, that LD is not "a complete path to enlightenment"; and Gackenbach's, that LD needs to be supported by "a program of self development" (above, p. 475). The difficulty is that the lucidity advocates do not generally put it adequately into such a context. One has no right to expect it of them; the reader must rely on her/his own spiritual devices. But the consequence is that LD really is made to seem to promise more than it can provide. The perceived need to express cautions implies as much. The very introduction of the concept of enlightenment into the discussion of LD

---

* Four years later (1992, p. 171), Gillespie writes: "But I did eventually accept on faith that the experiences of the fullness of light were what they seemed to be—experiences of the God who transcends. . . . But I continue to concur . . . with Steven Katz's summation that 'we can never be *certain* that any of our experiences have their source in a transcendental reality'. . . . To believe so is a step of faith" (quoting S. T. Katz, "Editor's introduction," in S. T. Katz, editor, *Mysticism and Philosophical Analysis*, New York: Oxford University, p. 8, 1987).

has that effect. It is remarkable that nowhere in this Western literature is the concept of enlightenment itself questioned.

Although most of the advocates are serious, even sanctimonious about the spirituality of LD, there is a strong tendency for LD itself to turn—in Eastern terms—into black magic, that is, into an abused siddhi, a "marvellous power" employed as an end in itself. "[T]he yogi is in danger of yielding to the temptation of magic; of being content to enjoy the marvellous powers instead of sticking to his spiritual work and obtaining the final liberation."[373] "These considerations," quips Wendy Doniger O'Flaherty, "led Buddha to ground his monks."[374] And so it is that Gackenbach, Taylor, Craig, Blackmore and others warn that LD is not a spiritual end in itself, and that it can become a spiritual distraction, a fetish, even a narcissistic escape from self-awareness.[375]

LaBerge puts it that "the semi-lucid ego is inclined to use 'magical powers' to seek its own ends," causing "a grandiose expansion of self-esteem, the condition Jung referred to as 'inflation.'"[376] But why "semi-lucid"? The implication creeps back in, that full lucidity can be regarded as enlightened or something very close to it.

Moffitt borrows Trungpa's notion of "spiritual materialism"[377] in characterizing the attitude that LDs (and other "spiritual" dreams) are higher and better than other types of dreams. For an individual or a culture, one type may work better than another in promoting personal development; not to acknowledge this is "spiritual materialism and cultural chauvinism."[378] Along the same lines, Gackenbach remarks that LD "should not be looked upon as some sort of merit badge, or as a sign of spiritual superiority."[379] And Delaney: "I don't go for the big dream argument—or that certain dreams are more spiritually advanced than others—because we don't know."[380]

Contrast this with LaBerge's claim, that LD is "the most advanced product of millions of years of biological evolution."[381] And Sparrow compares people who dream without lucidity to infants and primitives, for whom the world is just beginning to emerge as an object distinct from the ego; for the ordinary dreamer, the inner self has yet to emerge as something clearly apprehended.[382]

It ought to give Sparrow pause, that Jung was a virtuoso of archetypal, but not of lucid dreaming. Recall that non-lucid archetypal dreams are typically more "transpersonal" than LDs.[383] Hunt affirms that archetypal dreams can be as much "peak experiences" as LDs can be, and mentions that Jung appears not to have had LDs, "or if he did he didn't find them interesting enough to report."[384] Mattoon imagines that he found LDs less real-seeming and less impactful than ordinary dreams.[385] Yet Sparrow quotes Jung out of

context in explaining psychological resistance to lucidity; while LaBerge ap-
propriates Jung's 'path' of individuation, by associating the lucid dream state
with "the culmination of the individuation process. . . ."[386] Obviously not for
Jung, at any rate.

LD, as a peak experience—which usually it is not—, is only one variety
of peak experience, a fact brought out by some LD authors, notably Hunt.[387]
Bear in mind that even seemingly supernatural light experiences, bringing
bliss and perfect acceptance, can occur in ordinary dreams, without lucidity.[388] What is more, an unreconstructed Euro-American might even maintain
that a peak experience awake—that is, awake-awake, as opposed to asleep-
awake—obtains a certain authenticity or legitimacy thereby.

Some draw a sort of equation between lucid living and lucid dreaming,
or believe them to be mutually enhancing.[389] On the one hand, waking lucidity ("the difficult-to-maintain sense 'this is a life'"[390]) is said to potentiate,[391]
or even to be "essential to lucid dreaming."* This is the basis of reality-testing LD induction techniques. On the other hand, LD is said—by Judith Malamud, among others—to foster waking lucidity. This is the basis for saying
that to dream lucidly is enlightening.** But while this idea is intuitively appealing, it is not fully borne out by psychological studies, where high levels
of "dream self-reflectiveness" are not found consistently to correlate with
high levels of "daytime self-reflectiveness."[392] Presumably LDs, even peak
LDs, are no more enlightening than many other illuminating and peak experiences.

It is also of interest that Gackenbach, a leading scholar and practitioner
of LD, has this to say about its exhilaration and clarity: "But it fades. I'm
convinced that developmentally you can't stay with it. It withdraws and with
rare exceptions, you can't maintain the exhilaration. It's generally no longer

---

* L. Reneau (no date), p. 3, italics deleted. Reneau's assertion that "lucid living is essential to
lucid dreaming" is less persuasive than Taylor's observation (1991, p. 12) that "spontaneous lucidity" often occurs following "moments of lucidity in waking life . . . [w]hen a person realizes that
his or her true circumstances are in fact substantially different from what he or she had always supposed. . . . Most often, this happens when a person withdraws a set of habitual projections in a waking-life situation." See also J. Taylor (1992a), p. 203.

** J. R. Malamud (1986). For Malamud, ordinary waking in which we naively accept objective
reality is equivalent to ordinary dreaming, while "waking lucidity," i.e., recognizing while awake
that our minds create a subjective world, is equivalent to LD. Going to the final step—achieving an
"'Awakened Life'" (really really recognizing subjectivity)—is equivalent to waking from sleep (p.
590). I am not sure how much weight this construct bears. After all, we wake effortlessly from sleep
at least once a day, while Malamud herself does "not recall ever having Awakened from my own
waking life," i.e., "Enlightenment" (p. 594). Nevertheless, she holds that LD is a natural path to
that awakening to ultimate reality.

with me and I know it's no longer with other long term lucid dreamers. The consciousness remains, but it's no longer unique and novel and fun. Sometimes it's not nice."[393] This sounds remarkably like a typical course of drug addiction: the initial euphoria; the gradual weakening of the effect; the eventual paradoxical turn to dysphoria. And in fact, as already mentioned, Gackenbach states elsewhere that LD can become destructively addictive.[394] Any variety of peak experience can be abused if it is pursued for its own sake. Of LD sought for "spiritual superiority," Gackenbach says: "Those who are truly on a spiritual path recognize that authentic personal growth is a holistic affair that encompasses all aspects of an individual's life."[395]

Returning once more to the Buddhist dream yoga, the "holistic" tradition from which the connection between lucidity and enlightenment has chiefly been absorbed, it is worth keeping in mind that while the yoga is a technic to help achieve enlightenment, enlightenment itself begins in suffering and culminates—short of Buddhahood—in compassion. Yet the crucial Buddhist concept of compassion is scarcely mentioned in the LD literature. Some, including LaBerge, Kelzer, and especially Sparrow, recount LD experiences of profound love.[396] But, firstly, in the Buddhist scheme of things love is not compassion; and, secondly, the object is to behave compassionately in waking life.

I have noticed very few references to Buddhist compassion in the LD literature, and two are from Tibetan sources. In one, *Gackenbach* quotes a Tibetan monk, that when attempting to induce LDs, one should meditate "for the sake of wanting to benefit all sentient beings."[397] These words are a formula understood to concern compassion.

Along this line, *Taylor* calls attention to the 'bodhisattva vow' (conspicuous in some schools of Buddhism) by which all devotees regularly vow to forego Nirvana in the event of achieving enlightenment. The motivation for this sacrifice is compassion for all suffering beings: the bodhisattva returns from death to be of service so long as there remain unenlightened beings. Taylor asserts, but without really justifying the assertion, that "[t]he most important meditative discipline that supports this pledge is the cultivation of what is now being called lucid dreaming in the West. . . ."[398]

Kelly *Bulkeley* raises the matter of compassion, in his discussion of LaBerge. In a note, Bulkeley glancingly makes much the same criticism which I am making here: "The root metaphor of lucid dreaming, in LaBerge's formulation of it, seems irrelevant to the important concerns of most people's daily lives. Buddhists, however, do address the issue of the relevance of their root metaphors, as they offer traditional teachings on the moral virtue of compassion. . . ."[399]

The other Tibetan source is *Lama Lodö*, who when asked, "What would you advise someone who is interested in studying their dreams?" responds: "Somebody will say, 'I want to practice that [dream yoga],' and I will say, 'Go back and start at the beginning. Develop your devotion and compassion. Purify yourself.'"[400]

The final reference to compassion is by *Garfield*. Her book *Pathway to Ecstasy*—though too 'far out' for some tastes—is at once the most readable, eloquent, and sustained attempt to give LD a spiritual context for Western readers. Garfield integrates elements of Tibetan Buddhism, Kundalini yoga, and Taoism with Western psychology in a testimonial of personal development. It is a courageous book where Garfield exposes not only her passions but also her addictions and inflations—and a book overflowing with beauty. That said, here is her mention of compassion. It comes while she is discussing an important dream, "The Strawberry Lady": "Tibetan Buddhists believe that passion can become compassion. . . . My own view is somewhat different. The Strawberry Lady symbolizes for me the height of sexual passion; she is a contrast to Amitabha, who symbolizes for Tibetan Buddhists the *conqueror* of passion. However, I see these figures as comparable. For it is *by means of* my passion that I am able to go beyond passion. I am no celibate cut off from intercourse by rules and oaths. Joyful in my relationship with my husband, I find I can 'conquer' passion with passion. Like followers of some of the Tantric and Taoist cults, I can use the very sexual energy within my body to obtain a higher kind of ecstasy. Sexual energy, I find, is intimately connected to spiritual energy."[401]

No doubt. In fact, Tibetan Buddhism incorporates the yoga of sex, the Tantra,[402] and it is curious that Garfield does not mention it. But aside from that: what became of compassion? It appears that in her understandable preoccupation with ecstasy she, like others, loses track of the ethical grounding of the tradition on which she is leaning. Those ethics are not merely marginal to enlightenment. Even where, in Buddhism and Hinduism, insight is emphasized over service, the way of insight is embedded in a cultural context where the ethics are foundational and universal. Those who lack that cultural foundation are especially at risk of treating the vehicle, in this case lucidity, as a spiritual end in itself.

None of these qualifications constitute reasons for denying the spiritual value, or just the psychological value of LD in our culture—as long as we do not fall into thinking that lucidity is any spiritual panacea; that, say, the DreamLight goggles might be an enlightenment machine. "If we learn to use it [lucid dreaming] well," as Gackenbach says, "we do not yet know how far along the path of self-enlightenment it will carry us."[403]

Certainly many people (but by no means all) find peak experience more accessible in LD than by other means. It is safer than drugs, less demanding than prolonged meditation, more dependable than spontaneous illumination. In our culture, with its penchant for borrowing (some say parasitizing) elements from other cultures, one could do worse than cultivate lucidity for the sake of enlightenment.

Only I will close the discussion with this warning from Vishnu to Narada the sage in an Indian tale, as told by O'Flaherty: "[He] warned me never to say that I had conquered illusion, since no one, not even the gods, could conquer illusion."[404]

□ 15 □

Re-entry

Chapters 13 and 14 treated two of the time frames in which dreams can be controlled: (1) before dreaming, by incubation, and (2) during dreaming, by lucid control. This chapter takes up the third time frame in which dreams can be controlled, or guided, or allowed to change: (3) after dreaming, by *re-entry*. I am using the term as the generic for all the dreamwork methods —"fantasy," "imaginary-dream state," "waking-dream state," "rehearsal,"[1] "active imagination" (see below), and so on—calling for substantial recreation in imagination of all or part of a recalled dream. The imagining may be kept inside, or verbalized, or enacted in some way. Re-entry shades toward simple vivid recall, but what usually sets it apart is deliberate readiness to cause or allow the imagery or feeling tone of the dream to evolve.

There are venerable precedents for modern incubation and lucidity techniques, notably in the cultures stretching from North Africa and Greece to South Asia and Tibet. But quite possibly re-entry has the oldest provenience, if contemporary preliterate cultures give an indication. A shaman's dream or vision is sometimes enacted by her/himself and others of the group, and may become transformed into an enduring item of ritual. And a shaman often self-induces trance to re-enter the spirit world, as revealed in a previous dream or vision, in order to accompany or retrieve the soul of a patient.

Certain dreamwork methods already discussed can be viewed as re-entry. These include 'dream drama' and other expressive techniques discussed in chapter 12, as well as Gestalt (chapter 6). However, the modern originator is (once again) Jung, with the technique of 'active imagination'.

Active Imagination

"[A]ctive imagination," wrote Jung, "is a method (devised by myself) of introspection for observing the stream of interior images. One concentrates one's attention on some impressive but unintelligible dream-image, or on a spontaneous visual impression, and observes the changes taking place in it. Meanwhile, of course, all criticism must be suspended. . . ."[2]

Jung observed that "*looking*, psychologically, brings about the activation of the object; it is as if something is emanating from one's spiritual eye that evokes or activates the object of one's vision. . . . That is the case with any fantasy image; one concentrates upon it, and then finds that one has great difficulty keeping the thing quiet, it gets restless, it shifts, something is added, or it multiplies itself. . . ."[3] "This autonomy of non-ego elements . . . [shows] the intrinsic autonomous activity of the unconscious. . . ."[4]

The raw material for active imagination can be any experience subject to introspection: a dream, a fantasy, a mood, or for that matter a waking life memory. When the starting place is a dream, change often takes the form of a continuation of the dream from the point where the original ended. But the body of the dream itself can also undergo change. Moreover, it is also possible, note Edward Whitmont & Sylvia Perera, to go "backwards from the beginning of a dream, in order to find out how the opening situation itself came into existence."[5] One way or the other, "[u]sually it will alter," observes John Sanford, "as the mere fact of contemplating it animates it."[6]

In the following passage, Robert Bosnak discusses a dream continuation. He emphasizes the "image consciousness" required to perform active imagination:

> It is advantageous to begin a process of active imagination with a dream image, because the sharpened memory of the dream reality can change naturally into active imagination. . . .
>
> . . . [I]t is important first to alter our state of awareness into an image consciousness. We can accomplish this through the very detailed recall of a dream image. . . .
>
> . . . After this reconstruction, which often begins with the vague remnants and ruins of a dream, it is possible to continue dreaming the dream. . . .
>
> . . . In contrast to passive daydreaming, during which images are merely perceived, in this disciplined imagination an active interaction with the image world takes place. . . .
>
> . . . [T]he I-figure can begin to move **through** the space of the image.
>
> . . . [I]t is rather as if you participate in two equally true realities simultaneously: the world that is actively imagined **and** the world in which you know that you are involved in active imagination. . . .
>
> Take, for example, this dream told by a nurse:
> *I'm on the night shift and have to make my rounds. The room where I find myself is brightly lit. First I go to Room 1. It's dark in the corridor. I go into the room. Here it is very dark. Vaguely I see an old woman standing with her*

back toward me near her bed. I switch on my flashlight. I see that she has a
big black-and-blue mark on her neck.

We start our work on this dream with the nurse's room. The light is bright, almost glaring. The desk she is standing next to is white formica. It reflects the neonlike light. The room is rather small. The corridor has a grayish floor covering. The dreamer cannot clearly see where the light is coming from; it is rather dark. The door of Room 1 is bare wood. The doorknob is to the right and is silver-colored. Inside it is pitch dark. There is a hospital bed and a night stand, but nothing is clearly visible. Once the flashlight is on, the dreamer sees the old woman at a distance of about eight feet. The old woman is thin. She's wearing hospital pajamas. The nurse does not know the woman. From that distance she clearly sees the black-and-blue mark on the woman's neck. At this point the dream memory ends. The dream memory has led her to an image that feels very real.

Now the active imagination begins. The transition from dream memory to active imagination is hardly noticed by the dreamer. She begins to move toward the woman. The black-and-blue mark is now extremely clear. The old woman is still standing with her back toward the nurse. The nurse is now so close that she can touch the woman's neck, which she does. Then the old woman turns around. Her face expresses endless sorrow. The old woman and the nurse gaze at each other for a long time. They both stand without speaking and feel the sadness.[7]

The state, described by Bosnak, of participating simultaneously in two realities—that of the imaginer and that of the imagined—calls to mind both lucid dreaming and waking meditation (chapter 14). Active imagination has been compared to meditation,[8] and Jung evidently valued it for some of the reasons others value meditation and lucidity. "Although Jung held dreams in high regard," says Robert Johnson, "he considered Active Imagination to be an even more effective path to the unconscious. The difference is this: When you dream, you receive signals from the unconscious, but the conscious mind does not participate. . . . In Active Imagination, by contrast, the conscious mind is awake. It participates consciously in the events."[9]

The involvement of consciousness causes the images generated by active imagination to be more readily interpretable than dream images.[10] In comparison to night dreams, said Jung, with their "superficial associations, . . . condensations, irrational expressions, confusion, etc.," the images forthcoming from active imagination "acquire a more ordered character: they become dramatically composed and reveal clear sense connections and the valency of association increases."[11]

However, active imagination demands ego strengths and a psychological balance which few beginning analysands possess. Jung usually encouraged patients to begin active imagination late in analysis, to practice it outside of sessions (to affirm their new psychological capacities and their independence from the analyst), and to continue active imagining after termination (to further their individuation).[12]

Sanford stresses the point "that the term is *active* imagination. . . . [T]he ego asserts itself in the process, and the demands of the unconscious must be measured against the reality of the ego."[13] Johnson agrees: "We must participate completely."

"There is, however, one line that should not be crossed," Johnson continues. "We must not stray from the zone of participation into the *zone of control*. . . . We have to let the imagination flow where it will . . . without trying to determine in advance what is going to happen. . . ."[14] "Above all," counselled Jung, "don't let anything from outside, that does not belong, get into it, for the fantasy-image has 'everything it needs.' In this way one is certain of not interfering by conscious caprice and of giving the unconscious a free hand."[15] However, in the context of emphasizing that ethical standards cannot be ignored when a therapist conducts an active imagination, Johnson offers examples from both his own and Jung's practice where control of outcomes was urgently encouraged. In Jung's case:

> Jung told of a young man who dreamed that *his girlfriend slid into an icy lake and was drowning beneath the water*. Jung said, in effect, that the man could not just sit and let the cold forces of fate kill the inner feminine. He advised the man to go into Active Imagination, get something to pull her out of the water, build a fire for her, get some dry clothes for her, and save her life. This is the ethical, moral, and human thing to do. It is as much the ego's duty to bring this sense of responsibility to the creatures of the inner world as it is for us to tend to the welfare of our fellow humans in the outside world. It is the health of our own, inner selves that is at stake.[16]

Lastly, a word about modalities for performing active imagination. Classically, it is an interior act of imagination. As a wrinkle, one can project the dream onto an imaginary movie or TV screen and watch "to see how the action develops further."[17] One can also write the imagining down in progress: "In this way conscious and unconscious are united, just as a waterfall connects above and below."[18] But if writing distracts too much from a meditative state, one can wait till after. Writing, thinks Sanford, is important. It "gives reality," "keeps us from cheating," and "strengthens the hand of the ego and develops our conscious position in the face of the unconscious."[19]

The imagining can be further exteriorized by being performed in some medium. The dreamer can stage the dream. This can be a pantomime, "to avoid intellectualizing or premature" interpretations.[20] In a group setting, a psychodrama can be performed. Or the dreamer can dialogue in the manner of Gestalt. In classic Gestalt, one 'becomes' dream components, whereas in active imagination, one remains oneself and lets the components speak for themselves, if they will. But Whitmont's use of the term 'active imagination' embraces Gestalt devices, as well as psychodrama, and drawing, and other media.[21] For Harry Wilmer, "Active imagination can be painting, drawing, sculpting, poetry, drama, dancing, or any other use of color and form."[22]

So there is no clear boundary nowadays between active imagination and the many modes of dreamwork which have been influenced by Jung's original techniques, to which James Hall and Andrew Brylowski adhere: "In pure active imagination the process takes place entirely in a subjective, intrapsychic manner, allowing the fullest play of the imaginal abilities of the psyche without restraints caused by resistances in the medium of expression, as can occur in painting, poetry, sandplay, and the like."[23]

Re-entry Miscellany

This section gives a sampling of various other dream re-entry techniques. These techniques differ according to the amount of control over content they employ. They also differ according to the amount of explicit interpretation they introduce, but all more or less depend for their healing/curing/integrating efficacy on resolutions achieved at an imagic, nonconceptual level.

In 1972, Ernest Rossi discussed the "psychosynthesis" which results from a "dream and imaginative experience." Such moves of imagination were evidently so unfamiliar to a professional readership two decades ago, that Rossi felt obliged to point out that the dreamer "*never* used psychedelic drugs":

[The dreamer is] a medical technician . . . who had finally made a good marriage at the age of 32 only to find she could not become pregnant. In her first therapy session it was immediately obvious that her femininity had been hurt by her background that fostered the development of masculine and competitive values. In her second therapy session she reports the following dream.

Dream: . . . *Many people try to get under a bridge to escape the war. They were being bombed but the bombs were funny. They were circular and then I saw the bomb was a huge apple with a bite out of it. Big and round apple about three feet high.*

The bomb that is actually a huge apple is obviously the most idiosyncratic aspect of the dream so it was suggested that she close her eyes and imagine she was the apple.

Psychosynthetic experience: ("How do you **feel** as an apple?") I feel fat, tasty, afraid to be bitten—Yes; there are really teeth marks in the apple—I'm jumping in and out between being the apple and not. (As usual there is a spontaneous alternation between experiencing the fantasy on the levels of sensation, emotion and imagery and observing the experience on a more cognitive level.)

Just black where it was bitten. It's dark but sunshine is around the rest of the apple.—I'm fighting to close the gap of darkness but it keeps—("Do the opposite, let the darkness come out.")

No, I feel the apple striving to get out of the black area. (Therapist obviously made an error in suggesting she let the darkness come out. Perhaps this is why she now turns to her husband for help.) I feel my husband trying to pull me out—He did it! (She laughs softly) He did it. Darkness just playing around the edge now in wiggly lines—hm—sure is a fight!—it's interesting—the bite—the bite is healing!—The area is growing over so the bite's not there any more . . . that darkness reminded me of cancer cells trying to come out over healthy cells.

She felt a bit awed by this experience because she could hardly believe . . . [it] was really taking place by itself. . . . [S]he confessed that she had kept interrupting it in a conscious way just to see if it would then really continue by itself. And continue by itself, she found, it really did. We would thus say that an autonomous process was truly activated in this light-dark conflict and she (via the image of her husband) successfully interacted with it. The amazing process of healing over of the bitten area of the apple after she succeeded in getting it pulled into the light was also an autonomous process. Was this healing imagery . . . an actual process of healing in her identity on the phenomenological level?[24]

This example of re-entry is like active imagination, with respect to imaginative immersion, but like Gestalt insofar as the person is prompted to identify with a dream element, rather than to enter the dream scene as herself. The process, as Rossi says, is autonomous, yet he initiates it and tries to guide it; and while the resolution is noncognitive, interpretive assumptions are implicit in Rossi's guidance.

Interpretation in the ordinary sense is also prominent in Eugene Gendlin's application of "focusing" to dreamwork, in which focusing amounts to re-entry. The method can be practiced solo, or with the guidance of a dreamwork partner or a therapist. The flexible set of procedures Gendlin recommends always begins with associations, and at any appropriate juncture one may identify day residues and other life themes connected with the dream's place, story line, characters, symbols, etc. Associations are also drawn from the "felt sense" of the dream. One investigates this felt sense by re-entry. "Sense the feel-quality of the dream." "[L]et a felt sense of it come in your body." "*Then ask:* What in your life feels like that? Or: . . . When did you ever feel like that? Or: What is new for you in that felt sense?" One can get further in touch with the felt sense by playing the part of a dream character or other element. One pretends to be rehearsing a play. "*Let the feel-quality of being that person come in your body.*" "Exaggerate it." "Don't make it up. Wait and see what words and moves come from the body-feel." Alternatively, one can "visualize the end, or any one important scene of the dream. Feel it again. . . . [J]ust watch it and wait for something further to happen."

Gendlin credits these re-entry steps of his method to Perls (Gestalt) and Jung (active imagination).[25] The aim of the method is both cognitive and visceral: "An interpretation is sure if, and only if, you have a breakthrough, *a physical felt shift.*"[26]*

Ann Sayre Wiseman is another dreamworker who also, among several re-entry techniques, employs a blend of active imagination (inward immersion) and Gestalt (role-taking), aimed at a visceral-interpretive outcome. In this example of group dreamwork, Wiseman gives the dreamer some guidance (control). The dreamer, age 60, has had a recurring dream for thirty years:

> "I dream that *I hear a baby crying in a room of my old house. I get up and look in every room, never finding the room or the child but still hearing its crying. It calls to me in such a deep way that I would go round and round the rooms again and never find the child, never find the room.*" I asked Cora to close her eyes, become the lost child, and ask herself to find the lost room; simply see herself in the lost room. As she closed her eyes giving herself to this suggestion, tears began to flow. She was asked not to leave the scene until she understood it. She held her face and sobbed, as we waited silently. When she opened her eyes, she said the child was herself. She found it on the other side of the mirror, where it had been crying since she was seven. It wanted to be an artist and had waited all those years for her to find **room for her**.[27]

Next, in doing psychodrama with dreams, says Helmut Barz, there can come about "an active further dreaming of the dream," "an expansion of the dream text."[28] Barz is a Jungian analyst, who also leads long-term psychodrama groups with his wife. One acts as "director," the other as "Auxiliary-Ego." The director is the overall guide, initially probing for associations and proceeding as in analysis, except that the director must "refrain from making a verbal interpretation. . . . [S/]he seeks out a symbolic scene in which

---

* Alvin Mahrer (1971), who cites Gendlin's early work, describes a method similar to Gendlin's, with a major exception. Having identified the "critical recent life event" (p. 330) the dream refers to, and having discerned the dominant motivational tenor of the dream, one carries the latter (Gendlin's "felt sense" of the dream) into an imaginary re-entry of the *life event*, rather than of the dream. "Experiencing the motivation means stepping aside, giving up your typical way of being, letting the motivation completely take you over, own you" (p. 331). The consequence is a spontaneous change of behavior in the imaginarily re-entered life situation, along the lines of one's true motivation, with wholesome effect. Elsewhere (1989) Mahrer prescribes an "experiential" technique of dreamwork involving re-entry into peak moments in the dream itself—as dream-ego, as dream figure, or as observer—as well as into related episodes of one's personal past (including before birth) and into future possible real life situations.

the current problem of the Protagonist [the dreamer] can be represented." When working with dreams, the scene usually suggests itself, so the director "can leave unfolding events up to the dream, to the Protagonist supported by the Auxiliary-Ego, and to the participation of the group.

The Auxiliary-Ego is the co-director, who "speaks . . . in the first person through the Protagonist, and each time s[/]he speaks, s[/]he lays her hands upon his or her shoulders. Insofar as the Auxiliary-Ego not only draws upon training and experience as an analyst, but also upon a great deal of empathy and intuition, the Auxiliary-Ego becomes a decisive therapeutic agent of the psychodrama. S[/]he questions the persona, supports or protects the ego, offers—with great caution—aspects of the shadow to consciousness, and takes over, as a Protagonist once expressed it, the function of guardian angel."[29] Barz's chapter concludes with this compressed example:

> A young man, a loner, withdrawn, shy and sensitive, wanted to work through a dream which he had already dreamt several times. In this dream *he took leave of his parents and undertook, alone, an expedition to the South Pole.* Each time *the dream ended with him sitting before a glacier crevice with the certain feeling that he must venture to jump into it, in order to reach something unknown but supremely important. Nevertheless, he is* always *unable to find the courage to do this,* waking up tormented instead.
>
> The dream was played out in psychodrama. Both parents were led in, the dreamer bade them farewell extremely coolly and arrived at the glacier crevice at the South Pole. Both directors and most certainly all group members are conscious of the enormous danger inherent in the situation, and the Auxiliary-Ego is—wordlessly—concerned to the utmost with lending the Protagonist warmth and support.
>
> After sitting for a long time, the Protagonist says very quietly, "It won't work. I have to go home." He goes back, stands silently before his parents, then he says suddenly, "I will try again, but not alone."
>
> He now chooses for himself two male companions for the new expedition, the one whom he liked the most in the group and another, with whom he was least sympathetic. He addresses them with their real names and asks them if they are prepared to come with him. The two agree. They play the trip to the South Pole essentially more realistically than he had done previously, taking sleds, provisions, and furs along with them, and finally they sit with him before the crevice.
>
> . . . All three tremble from the cold and wrap themselves in blankets. . . . Now the protagonist says, "Wait. I will make a fire." His pantomime is so perfect that soon all three sit before a crackling fire holding their outstretched hands to the flames. A long silence ensues.
>
> Then the protagonist gets up very quietly, grasps the other two by the hands and they stand in a circle around the fire. Finally he says quietly but firmly, "It's good now. That was it. I did it. Thank you."

Whoever has shared such a dream drama will never doubt that it can be a healing thing to share a dream with a group.[30]*

Many dreamworkers use techniques involving a more active intervention in the outcome of the re-entered dream. In the case of illness dreams, Patricia Garfield suggests we "visualize a way to make the [dream] situation better."[31] With nightmares, Garfield teaches children and adults to "redream" or "replay" them. Children can "[t]urn it [a nightmare] into a good dream" in imagination, then draw a picture of it. Adults can visualize "the changes that most appeal to you taking place" as a means of incubating subsequent dreams with a better outcome.[32] Waking "rehearsal" of recurrent nightmares brings relief, suggests Stephen LaBerge, even if the sufferer only repeats, "It's just a dream," but all the more so if the person conjures "triumphant" or "masterful endings"[33] (see chapter 16). Similarly, Rosalind Cartwright assists recurrent nightmare sufferers to incubate new endings by having them first imagine satisfactory endings while awake.[34]

Louis Savary et al. suggest two "rewriting" techniques. "1. Imaginatively reinsert yourself in the dream at a place *before the destructive patterns or painful feelings would have taken over*, and then . . . write out a new scenario . . . in order to bring about a satisfying ending. You may also spell out in the text how the revised behavior and feelings might continue to be a part of your waking personality as well as of your dream ego. 2. An alternative approach is to rewrite the dream as a life story, myth, or folk tale, including in it a healthy resolution."[35]

These authors also recommend "dream re-entry," an active imagination whose "purpose is not to manufacture a happy ending . . . but to allow an authentic response to develop."[36] However, Strephon Williams, one of the coauthors, elsewhere prefers a more "direct intervention" than do "orthodox Jungians. . . . If you just let the unconscious unfold, these people would say, healing will naturally take place. I for one would like to see direct and specific evidence that this *laissez-faire* approach works with dreams or anything else for that matter."[37]

Williams thinks that dream modification is more effective with waking re-entry than with lucidity, because more intentionality and choice are usually possible, and because one can share the actual process with others.[38]

As mentioned above, Wiseman employs several re-entry techniques. One she calls "restaging": "Dream Restaging is a way of laying out the issue visibly on a sheet of paper, using paper objects [pictures and colored papers]

---

* For other examples of dramatic enactment of dreams, see J. Morris (1987 [1985]), pp. 152-9, and, in chapter 12 (p. 381), H. R. Ellis (1988a and 1991).

to represent the images in the dream, thus showing rather than describing the issue and the relationships as well as the options that could lead to a satisfactory resolution. This permits both the dreamer and the guide to observe the action, as the dreamer plays all the roles. . . . This is a mini psychodrama. . . . As all objects have a point of view the client is able to visibly witness their own projections as well as explor[e] their own feelings and reactions to alternate solutions."[39]

Wiseman also applies the term 'restaging' to her work with posttraumatic nightmares, those recurring dreams which revive the traumatic incident. To re-enter the dream in these cases amounts to re-entering the incident. Wiseman describes work with rape victims, soldiers, and, here, with an accident victim:

> Susan is 23. *Susan had been buried alive in an avalanche under deep snow for four hours.* She suffered recurring nightmares that made her relive this terror. She . . . agreed to re-enter the terror and experience it consciously with my guidance. All I did was lead her through the four hours keeping her conscious of time passing, and the fact that help was on its way. She was asked to describe every detail of how she found her body positioned, how she was able to melt snow in her mouth, how she managed to breathe. I asked her to make it easier to breathe in that confined space. She repositioned her body to give herself more room and reduce her panic to conserve the oxygen, which helped her relax the frightened body until she could detect the sound of the shovels that would dig her out. By doing this she changed the experience.
>
> The re-staging of this terror helped her re-claim her body which panic had made her jump out of. When panic makes us jump out of our body we need to go back and re-enter it safely.[40]

This is a very carefully managed and guided re-entry. In contrast, Linda ("Ravenwolf") Reneau recounts an almost casual re-entry. It illustrates the way work with dreams becomes integrated into the waking life of a seasoned dreamworker:

> You can re-structure dream events at odd moments during the day. You don't need to go into a trance and have complete privacy and peace. Snatches of dream experience often present themselves to consciousness in the midst of daily activities, and when they do, you can turn them about in your mind and respond to them. It may only take a split second. For example, I was walking to the store yesterday when such a fragment presented itself: *I'm on the back porch, trying to sweep up some dirt, and all I have is this wire broom that just scratches the floor and moves the dirt around.* I knew that the fragment referred to "making a clean sweep" of some "negative" memories (dirt) I'd been dwelling on the day before, and it indicated that I was using the wrong tool (too much force) to get rid of them. Mentally, I turned the stiff, wire broom into a soft, straw broom,

and visualized myself easily sweeping up the dirt—and to my surprise, the image of a flower garden immediately popped into my mind! Of course, I thought; that was the proper way to use dirt. Grow some beautiful things in it, Linda! Use the knowledge you gained from those negative experiences . . .[41]

Re-entry will be treated further in the following chapter, as will lucidity and incubation.

□ 16 □

The Bo Tree Principle

A Buddhist tradition tells us that after the Buddha-to-be, Gautama, had mastered asceticism, scholarship, and all other recognized paths without attaining the enlightenment he sought, he determined to sit and meditate for once and all, until he reached his goal or died. He sat down beneath a bo tree, and meditated.

When he was finally on the verge of attainment, the devil Mara ordered a throng of demons to terrify and distract him. The demons cast their spears and shot their arrows. But as the weapons entered the mental field surrounding Gautama, they turned into flowers which fell softly on the ground. Thus Gautama attained Buddhahood while meditating under a bo tree (bo = bodhi = enlightenment).

The principle dramatized in this story permeates Buddhism, that sitting through fear is transforming. We all have our demons of fear, which hold bound and unavailable "the force that will ultimately lead us toward enlightenment. . . ." Unless we recognize our demons as "emanations of our own mind,"[1] we remain, in the Buddhist belief, trapped in the cycle of rebirth, which is to say, we do not progress psychologically. In Tibetan tradition, immediately upon death we enter a kind of nightmare, the Bardo, a realm so horrible that the unenlightened flee back to life and common suffering, through reincarnation. The dread can only be overcome by realizing that the Bardo manifests our own thought forms—that is, by experiencing something directly like Buddha's enlightenment. This aptitude is cultivated in life with the dream yoga.[2]

The English word 'nightmare' and its counterparts in other European languages are interesting in this connection. 'Mare' in 'nightmare' comes from an Old English word, 'mare,' meaning the demon which assaults people in their sleep. The Old English word comes from Early Teutonic 'mar', devil, which in turn derives from Sanskrit 'mara,' "the destroyer."[3] Therefore, our word 'nightmare' is related, at least etymologically, to Buddha's vision of demons sent by Mara during his enlightenment.[4]*

The bo tree story illustrates an often-stated principle of much contemporary dreamwork, particularly with nightmares:

"Most scary dreams bring something good which is not yet in a form the person can use. . . . Resistance? Welcome the resistance: what does it have to say?" (Eugene Gendlin). "Remember: The 'worst' dreams are really the best for you" (Harold Ellis). "We dream of violence and aggressiveness, but if we release that aggressiveness, it turns into confidence and strength of will" (James Hadfield). "Approach your fear and it will vanish. You will pass through your frozen implosive self, enter and overcome death, emerge into life and joy" (Jack Downing). "[N]othing can destroy you; nothing intends your destruction though these are the very words it utters. What is intended is your ends, not your end: finally your enlightenment and placement in the cosmos" (Richard Grossinger).[5]

The bo tree principle is obviously not the only paradigm by which dreamworkers operate, yet it underlies a surprising amount of dreamwork, for example in the last three dream readings in chapter 15: "He cannot jump into crevice" (p. 494) (Helmut Barz), "She is buried alive in avalanche" (p. 496) (Ann Sayre Wiseman), and "Wire broom does a bad job" (p. 496) (Linda "Ravenwolf" Reneau).

In these and other cases, dreamers employ various tactics for responding to a negative image, but underlying all tactics is this imperative: Do not flee or evade. If, broadly speaking, all possible responses fall into 'approach' or 'avoidance', then the ruling strategy becomes: Do not avoid, but rather approach (or, importantly, allow approach). Distinctions have only to do with alternative manners of approach. Consider two dreams in chapter 12 where the principle is clearly at work: in "She falls into monster's jaws" (p. 387) (Katherine West), the dreamer re-enters the dream to confront and attack the threat; in "Difficult bluebird" (p. 385) (Jill Gregory), the dreamer re-enters to befriend the threat.

Each of these variants generates a positive transformation of dream affect and imagery. In place of the unpleasantness or catastrophe anticipated by a dream-ego in avoidance comes a sudden turn for the better, an 'anastrophe', when the threat is no longer avoided but confronted. So the bo tree principle can be concisely diagrammed as: *approach → transform.*

---

* English 'mare', female horse, is from Old English 'myre' of that meaning (F. Galvin & E. Hartmann 1990, p. 237). French for 'nightmare': 'cauchmar'. German: 'Nachtmar'. Swedish: 'mara' or 'mardröm'. Danish: 'mareridt'. Norwegian: 'mare'. Russian: 'кошмар' (*kashmar*). Polish: 'zmora'.

While fear on the dreamer's part causes a threatening figure to become more threatening (Paul Tholey),[6] "[w]hat is more horrible is to escape to a lesser mode, where the dangers appear to be less. Instead there is a greater fragmentation and greater danger" (Grossinger).[7] Courage causes a threatening figure to diminish or shrink,[8] or to change into a benevolent or benign form, as in Gautama's vision of weapons turning into flowers. In that event, the negative quality of the dream diminishes or ceases, and the dreamer's well-being is enhanced. If there has been a series of nightmares, very likely it will cease.

LaBerge and Tholey are so persuaded of the psychological benefit of such outcomes that they urge LDers (lucid dreamers) to "look for trouble."[9]* But all of us practice the principle each time we 'approach' any negative dream image or dream, whether still dreaming or awake.

The principle is usually understood to work without need of dream interpretation. For instance, Scott Sparrow advocates confronting threats in LDs with the understanding that a threat image represents an estranged part of oneself which can be reconciled by imagic interaction. So he asks us to understand projection, but not to analyze our projections, simply to let them play out.[10] Many others, and perhaps Sparrow, would say that the principle works even without that much psychological sophistication, autonomously. On the other hand, there is nothing to prevent combining the *approach* → *transform* principle with interpretation, as Gayle Delaney points out, while moderating expectations: "I am not suggesting that you can solve the problem by magically confronting it in your dream, but that your willingness to face it in your dream will help you to face it and understand it in your waking life."[11]

The benefits of *approach* → *transform* are described in various interrelated ways. Just mentioned were the integration of disowned parts and the mobilization of psychological resources. But probably the description closest to the spirit of the bo tree story is that of a liberation of energy bound in a negative form. Ann Faraday puts it that "all evil is potential vitality in need of transformation. . . ." Working with nightmares can lead to "the release of an enormous amount of energy for constructive living."[12] Of "horrifying" images, Patricia Garfield says: "Their power to terrify has the same degree of force as their power to teach. Their energy can become your personal

---

*Ronald J. Brown and D. C. Donderi (1986, pp. 617-8) report the interesting finding that while "psychological well-being" scores are below the norm for recurrent nightmare dreamers, they are higher than the norm for *past* recurrent nightmare dreamers, whose scores even exceed those who have never had such recurrent dreams. The past recurrent nightmare dreamers even have more pleasant everyday dreams than the other groups.

vigor."[13] Children who can tame wild animals in dreams "are transforming their instinctual energy. Rather than dreams of being chased and attacked by wild creatures, indicating what they perceive to be destructive energy (in themselves or people around them), their vital forces are becoming constructive."[14] Paco Mitchell, a Jungian therapist, warns that staying with an image of this type over a series of dreams without a fundamental change of attitude "can be very upsetting indeed," causing a release of "demonic . . . energy or libido," ranging "from a mild disturbance to a full-blown psychotic episode." But "a transformation of the demonic element in the dream releases . . . an 'angelic' potential."[15]

Some authors prescribe different approach tactics (see below) depending on what the dream threat is perceived to represent, but many do not. Commonly it is problematical to say just what the image does represent. Apart from the general opacity of dreams, these images often contain tensions or polarities of meaning. Thus an image of fire in a dream discussed by Arnold Mindell[16] can be construed as the dreamer's repression of his life force, or as the life force itself, or as the constellation of both (see below). Thus John Shaffer interprets a certain threatening figure as a token of the dreamer's inhibitions, while Robert Bosnak interprets a comparable figure as betokening the dreamer's spontaneity.[17] And these readings could probably be reversed without mischief. Similarly, Garfield says that a dreamer's nightmare about her mother with vampire features detected the mother's real hostility, while the devil in a dream discussed by Adam Zwig symbolized "the dreamer's own capacity to be direct, honest, and even negative"[18]—probably Garfield's vampire also contained the dreamer's own negativity, while Zwig's devil also had a real-world pedigree.

Miscellaneous other renderings of the significance of threatening images in various contexts include: conscience (John Sanford); the Guiding Self—but possibly also spoiling elements (Edward Whitmont & Sylvia Perera); ignored potentials (Erik Craig); sexuality (Stanley Krippner & Joseph Dillard); creativity (Phyllis Koch-Sheras et al.); positive anima (the Clifts); positive animus (Krippner & Dillard); an alienated father archetype (Linda Leonard); an introjected father (Tholey); topdog—but elsewhere, underdog (Faraday); self-doubt (Strephon Williams); inappropriate survival strategy (Wiseman); a whole neurosis (Emil Gutheil).[19] The literal images of posttraumatic nightmares replay the traumatic events, but often "inter-digitated" with other psychological issues (Milton Kramer).[20]

It will have occurred to some readers that this chapter might have been entitled "The Shadow Principle," after Jung's very influential concept of a psychic structure which behaves like Mara's demons: "To the degree that we repress it, its danger increases. But the moment the patient begins to assimilate contents that were previously unconscious, its danger diminishes" (Jung). As for the shadow in dreams, a threatening image "may seem to oppose the dream-ego while its true purpose is to enlarge or transform the ego in relation to the Self" (James Hall). "One of the reasons why Shadow figures are so persistent and inexorable is that they all have gifts to give and they cannot be freed from their negative shapes and forms until the gifts are delivered" (Jeremy Taylor). "[I]t is quite obvious from dreams that when one faces a shadow which one has denied or run from it diminishes in power, and size, and ultimately becomes a positive force." Jung applied the term "'*enantiodromia*, a running contrariwise'" to "this business of everything turning into its opposite" (Harry Wilmer).[21]

A particular value of the shadow construct is to remind us that shadow contents can never entirely be integrated (except by Buddhas). "[T]he 'little devils' that go to make up the personal shadow [can be integrated], but not when it is a question of the *principle* of evil (the *archetypal* aspect of evil)" (Marie-Louise von Franz).[22] So "the shadow will always be there, always be part of our psyche" (Wilmer).[23]

The problem with the shadow concept for the present discussion is that Jung objected to intentional manipulation of dream imagery, which has increasingly come into fashion since he wrote and which figures in the dreamwork being discussed here. Also, I see no reason to freight the discussion with the baggage of 'archetypes', when many dreamworkers practice the bo tree principle without it.

This chapter might also be called "The Senoi Principle," after the (in)famous people whose affinity with Jung is signalled by the title of Williams's book, *The Jungian-Senoi Dreamwork Manual*. The Senoi's purported dreamwork philosophy came up earlier in connection with the cultural context of dreams (ch. 5, p. 173) and dream incubation and control (ch. 12, p. 390 and ch. 13, p. 413). Pertinent here is the rule attributed to them, always to "*confront and conquer* danger in a dream."[24]* "The Senoi . . . refer to these negative images as the 'evil spirits of the dream universe.' They believe that, if ignored, these hostile spirits will join forces with one another and forever hold power over the dreamer in both the dream universe and in waking life" (Koch-Sheras).[25] But "all dream characters are good if you outface them and

---

* In the sci fi movie *Dreamscape* of 1984, sleep scientist Max von Sydow invokes the Senoi rule when he convinces his favorite psychic, Dennis Quaid, to enter the nightmare of a boy to help him confront whatever psychological devil it is that troubles him. As Quaid restrains the "Snakeman," the boy decapitates it, and his nightmares are cured. Quaid later confronts his own snakeman.

bend them to your will. If you run away from them or disregard them, they will plague you forever, or until you rediscover and outface them." When attacked, one should fight to the death: if one conquers, the energy of the antagonist is released for good; if one is killed, one is immediately reborn, while the struggle "permanently exhausts the force of the adversary" (Kilton Stewart).[26]

Besides *"confront and conquer* danger" and *"give your dreams a positive outcome,"* Garfield's synopsis of the Senoi rules includes: "Always *move toward pleasurable experiences* in dreams."[27] It should be raised in this connection that Mara tempted Buddha Gautama with beautiful demons, as well as assailed him with frightening ones.* The Buddha's resistance to temptation thus puts him at odds with the Senoi rule. And in fact Garfield, in her brilliant assimilation of Tibetan Buddhism with contemporary dreamwork, separates herself from Buddhism on just this point[28] (ch. 14, p. 484). Here, the Senoi sensibility seems more congenial to our times. The problem with the Senoi is—besides their dubious authenticity—a limiting emphasis on confrontation as the response to danger. Buddhism does have a place for confrontation, as symbolized by 'the sword of Manjushri,' who is one of the five primary bodhisattvas.** However, Gautama's response to danger while he sat meditating under the bo tree was not confrontation but restraint, or self-containment. Thus I chose the caption "The Bo Tree Principle," feeling that it does more justice to the full range of productive ways of dealing with threat in dreams. I also chose it for the appeal of the story, for its sheer antiquity, and for the thread running from Mara the devil to our word 'nightmare'.

The bo tree principle, *approach → transform,* is embedded in European spiritual traditions as well. Jung quoted Hölderlin, "Where danger is, there

---

* Jeremy Taylor (1983, p. 149) tells the Hindu story about the origin of the demons whom Mara sends against Gautama: "Brahma sits absorbed in yogic trance. All that is in himself, and as he becomes increasingly aware of the infinite depths, he manifests the forms and existences of the other gods. He is the 'Father of All,' but even he does not know what he will manifest out of his unconscious depths as he meditates. So he is greatly surprised when suddenly he manifests 'Dawn,' the first goddess, and the morning light simultaneously." She is beautiful and Brahma falls in love with her. But he realizes that the incest taboo forbids it. "Brahma exerts his will and controls his desire, but the effort is so great that it causes beads of sweat to break out all over his body. These beads of sweat roll down his body and transform into all the 'demons of desire.' They march off his body shouting and chanting, 'Fear! Rage! Lust! War! Greed! Murder! Suicide!'" These are the demons Mara sends against Gautama; and, Taylor extrapolates, by resisting them he redeemed the original sin of Brahma, much as Jesus did that of Adam and Eve.

** Manjushri, the bodhisattva of wisdom, "is iconographically represented not only as bearing in his left hand a lotus blossom upon whose open petals rests a book . . . but also as wielding with his right hand a flaming sword. While the first symbolizes the establishment of Truth the second symbolizes the destruction of untruth. . ." (Sangharakshita 1980, p. 429).

is salvation also," and Jung retrieved from obscurity the symbolism of creative destruction in European alchemy.[29]

C. A. Meier discusses the Greek oracle, "He who wounds also heals," in connection with Asclepius. To the concept of the wounded healer we can add that of the wounding healer. This is "a clear form of homeopathy, the divine sickness being cast out by the divine remedy. . . . *He* was the sickness *and* the remedy."[30]* This ambivalence of harming and healing is sometimes a feature of shamanism.[31]

Sanford, in the Judeo-Christian tradition, compares the shadow to Jacob's angel. Sanford says: "God assails us in our life as our shadow, seeming to be an adversary, but desiring our fundamental change." "[I]f man will only wrestle consciously with the adversary in himself he will be blessed, for he will be wrestling with God."[32] And of projection, Taylor says: "The Christian admonition to 'Love your enemies' is then at this level a psychological necessity. . . . The 'others' whom we hate and fear are, at one level, invariably mirrors of our own repressed energies and potentials."[33]

Before discussing tactical options for responding to threats in dreams, it ought to be emphasized that, as a strategy of dreamwork, the principle *approach → transform* can effectively be cultivated because it is a natural, often observed feature of dream life. Indeed, it is a naturally occurring feature of image-life in general, as its cultural history reveals. Downing describes an LSD experience, for example: *when confronted by a "bat-like monster" he begins to panic and run away, but is urged by a loving God to approach it instead, whereupon it vanishes and is replaced by "an awesomely tender, beautiful triple image": a cathedral, a forest, and a woman.*[34] And in Bosnak's *Dreaming with an Aids Patient*, Christopher relates a recurring waking vision, here edited down from two pages:

> This is not a dream. It happens when I'm sitting in the living room close to the television. . . . *I become very frightened because I realize that the presence behind me is not human. . . . Then I remember the times that I've been afraid of dream images—and that I looked at them anyway. I realize that I have to look. So I turn around. . . .*
>
> *I look at him, and he is so dark. . . . He is enshrouded in some kind of cape made of scales, like a dragon or a giant serpent. . . .*
>
> *Then suddenly I know: this is the Spectre of Aids! . . . [N]ow I must face Aids. I keep looking at him. . . .*

---

* According to Apollodorus, Asclepius "used blood from the left side [of the dead Gorgon] for plagues for mankind, and he used that from the right for healing and to raise men up from the dead" (C. A. Meier 1967 [1949], p. 34).

Then I cried. When I stopped crying he had gone. For several days it went on like that. . . . But it was different, because I invited him. Somehow that made me less scared of him. . . . Then yesterday *he comes again.* . . . *I feel freezing cold, looking at the Angel of Darkness. Then, very rapidly, I have three memories. First I remember how Satan comes disguised as an angel of light. Then I remember a picture by William Blake of a father image who had cloven hooves and a serpentine body and who came to frighten and terrify. And finally Christ as serpent in the wilderness.*

. . . I know that to really love God, I have to love Him when His face is averted. . . . With this insight, something has changed about the spectre. I begin to see light. The light is coming from behind the scaly mantle. He is opening up his mantle, and I see eyes, thousands of eyes looking at me. I know that these are the eyes of the Shekhina, the female aspect of God dwelling in the world. The light is magnificent, and I feel seen. I feel totally seen. And I feel love.[35]

As for dreams, people may spontaneously discover the bo tree principle for themselves. Many children do.[36] As a child, the novelist Graham Greene "had a recurring nightmare of *a witch jumping on him from behind, digging her nails into him*: one time he dreamt that *he turned and fought her*, and after that he never had that nightmare again."[37]

Charles Tart, the investigator of states of consciousness, revealed his vocation at an early age by inventing the principle for himself: "I discovered this technique myself as a child of about 8, when I was troubled by nightmares. Feeling that the nightmares were *my* dreams and so should be responsive to me instead of frightening, I taught myself to go back to sleep and into the dream as quickly as possible, and either conquer the frightening image or make friends with it. After fewer than a dozen dreams where I did this, nightmares became a very rare occurrence with me, and my dreams took on a very positive, happy tone."[38]

With psychological work, even that not explicitly aimed at dream modification, the principle is observable at play in consequent changes in dreams. Such changes show up in dream series. In chapter 4 (p. 152), a series from Craig was presented: in the first dream ("Humiliated at family gathering"), *the dreamer is belittled and humiliated by relatives*; later on in therapy, he dreams that *he challenges a sibling and takes charge* ("He shows his sister out").[39] In the pages where Sanford likens the shadow to Jacob's angel, he relates his client's presenting dream: *"I saw myself in a warlike situation. Then a sinister adversary appeared. He had a gun or a knife. I fled but he pursued me and finally killed me. "* Then this dream came after much therapy and psychological hard work: *"Again I was in a warlike situation. My enemy again approached me with a knife. He wanted to kill me. I started to run, but then I stopped and, facing him, said instead, 'All right, kill me if you want to.' The enemy also stopped and paused. Then he smiled and, turning, walked away.* "[40] Finally, Will Phillips sketches a not dissimilar series which evolved without the regimen of therapy:

> For openers, your dreams will evolve, just from remembering and recording them. Just by owning your dreams, you accept them as an accurate picture of your current inner reality. This provides the foundation for change. For example, I had a series of *Nazi-capture-torture-death* dreams. Over a period of years, without doing dreamwork and without analysis or intuitive understanding, I gradually became less of a victim. In one dream *I was rescued by German villagers.* In a later dream *I killed my attacker, experiencing relief but no joy.* In the final dream of the series *a German commandant and I repeatedly wrestled to exhaustion and then formed an alliance based on mutual respect.* It wasn't until the series was over that I realized the meaning of the dreams. As a cabinet-maker my association to Germans was that they produced my finest tools. German meant not accepting anything but perfection. Through the dreams I came to terms with my own perfectionism.[41]

In some series, such as Craig's, the final dream begins as well as ends with a better tone. Krippner & Dillard talk about another such series, where *a rapist* gradually evolves over several dreams into *a lover,* who finally *reveals himself to be the dreamer herself.*[42] In other series, the ultimate dream begins as did the earlier one(s), but then makes the turn toward anastrophe mid-dream. Sanford's series is like that. Phillips's series is intermediate.

Certainly the effect of the transformation appears most dramatic when it takes place mid-dream. That is how most examples get into print (though it is a good bet most of these dreams actually occurred as the culmination of an unrecorded series). For example, from Richard Corriere et al.: "*I am being chased by a gorilla. He is very large and menacing. I run away. Finally I realize I must face him or keep running away. As I stop and face him he turns into a man who tells me—I must be more specific when talking about my feelings.*"[43]

This dream—an apparent instance of doctrinal compliance to Corriere et al.'s 'feeling therapy'—is presented by them to exemplify what that doctrine regards as a desirable "shift from symbolic to nonsymbolic dreaming within a dream." Some dreams do shift in that direction, as for example a dream discussed by the Clifts where *a wild, slobbering pig was doing mischief in the house. It eluded capture, but when it "dashed out the front door, running down the street, . . . it seemed to turn into a woman with long flying hair and white filmy dress or scarf streaming out behind her. . . .*"[44]

But many bo tree transformations make not even that much of a shift toward realism. Kathy Belicki confirms that symbolic, nonrealistic resolutions can work at depth with abuse victims, that is, even in cases where the dream threat is not—at least not entirely—a projection of intrapsychic content, but rather represents a traumatizing real-world threat.[45] And here, from Charles Rycroft, is a case of transformation from one symbol to another, where intrapsychic content *is* represented:

> A young man dreamt that *a bull charged down a village street, plunged into a pond, and turned into a swan which swam gracefully and serenely upon the water.* This dream expresses, I think, the wish to acquire poise, to achieve ego-mastery of aggressive and libidinal impulses, to change from being a country bumpkin and a bull in a china shop into someone who is in the swim and in control of himself; and, more specifically sexually, that passion can be assuaged.[46]

This dream illustrates another point, that the bo tree principle fits cases where the dream-ego is not directly being attacked by a Nazi, rapist, gorilla, etc. A further example of this, as well as of symbolic (not realistic) transformation, is a dream of Garfield's where *with the help of a guiding figure she brings up a "pusball" which turns into a metal bell and then into a flower.* Still dreaming, Garfield makes an interpretation: "*I have removed a source of infection from within me that had been deeply buried for a long time. . . .* Needless to say, this dream renewed me. . . . Awake, I felt as though I had completed, with the help of the female guide, some crucial life's work."[47]

Lastly, we can look at a dream where the desirable transformation gets aborted. The dream nicely verifies Faraday's saying, that "the 'bugs' of our psyche are our potential butterflies."[48] From Ernest Rossi:

> The transformation of the frightening and ugly to the beautiful is . . . experienced for "one flash of a second" in the following dream but is lost again:
> *Big bugs the size of ashtrays. I was invaded by them and try to kill them. I hit one hard. He is a giant mosquito like a praying mantis. And all stuff flew out when I hit it and it turned into butterflies of blue and green diamond beauty for one flash of a second and then it turned back into bug guts again.*[49]

Tactics: From Annihilation to Golden Light

The purpose of this section is not to propose hard rules for realizing the bo tree principle, nor to establish a hierarchy of preferred tactics,* but only to sample options discussed by dreamworkers. Many of these options have

---

* Speaking about shadow monsters, Jung (1984 [1938], p. 681) said: "The trouble is that no general prescription is possible. In certain cases, one has to say: now kill it, just stamp it out. In another case, quite the contrary. Therefore I give no advice at all."

already been touched upon; they will be reviewed now a little more systematically.

The topic here is not primarily the cure of nightmares, though that enters into it: a recent survey of nightmare cure techniques could be stretched to cover most if not all the tactics mentioned below.* However, the *approach* → *transform* principle applies to dreams which are far less distressing than nightmares—except if 'nightmares' be defined as inclusively as by Garfield: "All nightmares are characterized by feelings of fear that range from moderate discomfort or frustration to outright terror. There is usually a sensation of helplessness and hopelessness in the dreamer."[50] (Garfield's own dream "Pusball → bell → flower" mentioned above is such a non-nightmarish nightmare which seems to begin with only "moderate discomfort.") Furthermore, the focus here is only secondarily on the relief of distress per se, but primarily on the psychodynamic benefits of the processes bringing relief.

Conquest and/or annihilation. This is the basic face-and-conquer tactic with its variations, as illustrated by Garfield when discussing children's bad dreams:

> When your child is victimized by ghostly creatures, he or she needs to learn how to take action. Mark, for example, helps himself in this spooky dream:
> My recent dream was when *I went to this haunted and good house. It was half haunted and half good. The haunted side had all kinds of ghosts, goblins, and other scary things. The other side had all kinds of good things. One time lots of people were there so I went there and told every person to get out. Then I got an M-16 and I blew the house to bits. Then we just built the good side back.*
> Here Mark appears to be trying to deal with some aspects of himself or his environment that feel contradictory. By eliminating the "bad side" in his dream, he is more likely to be able to cope with those elements while awake.[51]

Koch-Sheras et al. urge: "Try burning, exploding, incinerating, killing, melting, eliminating, or defecating out the negative images in your dreams. . . . [Y]ou are *changing a part of you that is no longer useful,* so that you can bring it back in a more useful form." They give an example of a dream re-entry where the distressing consequences of destroying a negative image are apparently counteracted by saving what is positive in the image first:

---

* Gordon Halliday "categorizes treatment techniques into these classes: desensitization and related behavioral procedures; psychoanalytic and cathartic techniques; story-line alteration procedures; and 'face [the danger] and conquer [it]' approaches" (F. Galvin & E. Hartmann 1990, p. 240, quoting G. Halliday, "Direct psychological therapies for nightmares: a review," *Clinical Psychology Review* 7, pp. 501–23, 1987 [brackets Galvin & Hartmann's]). See also G. Halliday (1985).

If you still feel reluctant to destroy a negative or unhelpful dream figure, make sure there isn't something more it has to give or to say to you. After receiving that final gift or message, then it's time to let it go. . . .

> *I see Joe sitting with Mary at a table. Mary has on a long, midnight blue velvet dress. I try to sit with them; it is for some reason impossible. I feel excluded. I strangle Mary—I see that I am killing her. I'm glad. All the people in the room come toward me in a threatening way and seem to collapse in on me. I wake up screaming.*

In working on this dream, I discovered that Mary represented a cold, frigid part-of-me that stood between me and Joe. I decided I wanted to get rid of that part of me, but when I recreated the dream in fantasy, I didn't feel comfortable killing Mary. I felt there was a part of her I wanted to keep. A friend suggested I have Mary give me a gift. . . . I went back into the fantasy and had Mary give me the dress she was wearing. The part of her I wanted to keep was her calmness, her self-possession, her attractiveness, her thinness—and the dress embodied those qualities for me. Then I strangled Mary, in my fantasy, without a qualm.[52]

Returning to children's dreams, West calls attention to a "particularly innovative suggestion from Caroline DeClerque [which] is to mold the image of the frightening symbol in cookie dough, bake it, and then gain true mastery as it is joyfully ingested!"* This tactic of ingestion hints that, as a symbolic act, to conquer is to identify with the thing conquered. The dream-ego victor would then be atavistic cousin to the primitive hunter or warrior who acquires the power of an adversary by killing and eating, perhaps cannibalizing the adversary.

LaBerge, among others, states that people who suffer nightmares from rape, abuse, and such causes may do well by "overcoming, destroying, and transforming" the source of fear in the nightmare.[53] But he expresses a reservation: a fear thus disposed of may return with vengeful intensity; therefore other tactics are preferable. LaBerge nevertheless endorses examples of annihilation, as he exemplifies with a dream of his own where, *with lucid control, he sets fire to three muggers, then grows flowers from their ashes.* LaBerge "awoke feeling filled with vibrant energy."[54]

Faraday recommends quite different tactics, depending whether a dream threat is an underdog (shadow figure) or a topdog (secret saboteur) (ch. 6, p. 220; ch. 7, p. 246). A welcoming attitude will usually mollify and integrate an underdog (Faraday invokes *Beauty and the Beast*), but as for a topdog pursuer, "this is the last thing you should do. He too is a part of you,

---

* K. L. West (1978), p. 44, citing C. B. DeClerque, "Dream on: educating children to use dreams," *Sundance Community Dream Journal* 2(1), pp. 62–70, Winter, 1978. DeClerque also led the children she worked with, age 6–8, to create alternative endings for their dreams.

but you *cannot* agree with him, for his aim is to rule you completely, and the more you try to agree with him, the more his demands increase—in contrast to underdog, whose raging character disappears as soon as you pay attention to his needs. Topdog must be confronted, overcome. . . ."[55]

Delaney acknowledges these same alternatives of embracing or overcoming,[56] but again warns that "slain dream enemies keep popping up in future dreams in various guises. . . ." She questions whether violent conquest really assimilates the psychological substance of a dream threat. "[V]ery much more is to be gained by confronting threatening dream images with a desire to understand rather than to demolish them."[57]

Tholey notes that while the aggressive option can "have a [euphoric and] cathartic effect over a short period of time,"[58] it can also bring on feelings of fear and guilt which may persist upon awakening, as well as set the stage for a vengeful return.[59] Such untoward consequences may ensue, Tholey believes, because hostile dream figures most often symbolize parts of the self; therefore, "one should never resort to aggression" in dealing with them.[60]

As these reservations about the tactic of conquest and annihilation are being registered, we should remember James Hillman's (ch. 3, p. 118 and ch. 7, 247) critique of heroic battles to overcome enemies in the dream world, where such postures of the "heroic ego" are not, in Hillman's view, appropriate.[61] Less radically, Sparrow advises us just not to get stuck at the level of destroying the adversary,[62] which tactic stands, after all, in a relationship of polarity to fearful flight.

Self-assertion and mastery. A dreamer often faces obstacles in circumstances where a violent response would seem disproportionate. Williams instructs such a dreamer to assert herself:

> *I was walking down a road with my mother and needed to get her to an inn before nightfall. However, road workmen would not let me through even though the road was clear. I asked permission and they said 'yes' if I would not touch any of their equipment.*
> . . . This dreamer was new to dream session. We did not go into her outer life of the previous day or into her thoughts and feelings about her mother or the workmen. . . .
> **Dream Task** Re-enter the dream again in your imagination but this time do not ask permission to use the road. Tell them you need to go through, and that you are going through, and see what happens.
> . . . The dreamer did as suggested in the task. The workmen did not stop her. They let her pass and she went to the inn with her mother.
> . . . She felt good about the experience and realized that if she asserted herself it would not necessarily mean others would oppose her. It felt better as an adult to assert her equality and 'right to the road'.[63]

Sometimes a dreamer is psychologically unready to follow the instruction to confront and conquer danger. In that event, s/he can endeavor to make some other change in the dreamscape as a way to introduce a sense of mastery. Gordon Halliday demonstrates:

> [A] female patient in her 20s reported twice-nightly traumatic nightmares, primarily of *her molestation as a child*. . . . Dream lucidity techniques were discussed with her at the second therapy session. . . . She was uncomfortable with the idea of standing up to her attacker in her dream but she was able to make use of the idea of changing one detail. Thus, in the third session, she mentioned *she changed the color of a doll and of a bedspread in her abuse dream that made the dream not as bad*. She explained that this process caused her to focus on what she was doing, rather than just attending to the action of abuse. She accomplished this color change in two different dreams that week. At the seventh session, she mentioned she had had no recurrence of the traumatic molestation nightmare for about 2 week.[64]

Sometimes mastery is well served by getting the dream threat under control without annihilating it. Eileen Palace and Charlotte Johnston describe a successful employment of "dream reorganization," a modified re-entry approach combining "systematic desensitization" (gradual exposure to a frightening stimulus) and "coping self-statements" ("It's only a dream," etc.) with "story-line alteration" ("guided rehearsal of mastery endings"):

> The case involved a 10-year-old boy . . . [whose] nightmares and subsequent fear appeared directly related to two real-life traumatic events [involving auto accidents]. . . .
>
> . . . He described nightly visits to his parents' room following recurrent nightmares with the theme of *bad guys killing his friends or trying to hurt him*. . . .
>
> Working in collaboration with the therapist, the client constructed 10 anxiety-provoking scenes based on disturbing themes, images, and auditory stimuli recollected from his recurrent nightmares. . . . For example, scene #7 read as follows:
>
> You and your friend face a man dressed all in black, stealthily approaching you on the street. He wears a black ski mask covering his face with the exception of a hole at the side of the mask revealing a missing ear, and a bruised and bloody hole. With deformed hands, each missing the index finger, the man reaches into a black bag to withdraw one of an unending number of silver axes. As he hurls the weapons at the crowds of helpless victims, he proceeds with a steady gaze to walk toward you.
>
> **Treatment.** . . . [After other intervening treatment, the client was guided to re-enter the scenario with this new ending:]
>
> As he reaches into the black bag with his deformed hands, and hurls an axe into the air, you transform into Jake Rockwell who wears a cast iron exoframe armed with artillery. You coolly call Crystal on your wristcom to send

down the heavy assault system, and fire the freeze machine, automatically freezing in space the bad guy and his axes. The intruder is arrested, and placed under surveillance. The onlookers cheer—you, Jake Rockwell, have saved them all."[65]

Dialogue and conciliation. Tholey recommends always to act with courage: fight back if attacked, but do not attempt to kill. Better still, resist with a verbal counterattack. But the best option, believes Tholey, is to open a dialogue.[66] A good way to begin is with an inquiry: What do you want? What is your message? Who are you? (or Who am I?).[67] What ensues may be an argument, a conversation, or a negotiation.[68] "Ideally," concurs Jayne Gackenbach, "reconciliation should be the outcome of such dream dialogue." "If the dialogue is productive you may see the dream character change shape, become less fearsome, get smaller, disappear or merge with your 'self' in the dream."[69] Tholey observes that affinitive approaches tend to cause transformations of hostile figures "from lower-order into higher-order creatures," such as animal into human, whereas aggressive reactions tend to cause the opposite transformations.[70]

Tholey concedes, however, that constructive dialogue is not always possible, as he illustrates with a lucid dream of his own, with *an unappeasable dog-headed antagonist who identifies himself as "a top dog."* Though one should never flee, he says,[71] a tactical withdrawal from such an adversary is in order (rather than a confrontation, as per Faraday). *When the dreaming Tholey interpreted the top dog as certain professional inhibitions of his and then removed himself from the scene, the top dog "was transformed into a tiny puppy, which finally disappeared."*[72]

Here is a dream of Tholey's which illustrates dialogue and conciliation:

After my father's death in 1968, he often appeared to me in my dreams as a dangerous figure, who insulted and threatened me. When I became lucid, I would beat him in anger. He was then sometimes transformed into a more primitive creature, like a dwarf, an animal, or a mummy. Whenever I won, I was overcome by a feeling of triumph. Nevertheless, my father continued to appear as a threatening figure in subsequent dreams. Then I had the following decisive dream. *I became lucid, while being chased by a tiger, and wanted to flee. I then pulled myself together, stood my ground, and asked, "Who are you?" The tiger was taken aback but was transformed into my father and answered, "I am your father and will now tell you what you are to do!" In contrast to my earlier dreams, I did not attempt to beat him but tried to get involved in a dialogue with him. I told him that he could not order me around. I rejected his threats and insults. On the other hand, I had to admit that some of my father's criticism was justified, and I decided to change my behavior accordingly. At that moment, my father became friendly, and we shook hands. I asked him if he could help me, and he encouraged me to go my own way alone. My father then seemed to slip into my own body, and I remained alone in the dream.*[73]

Restraint. Often, simply managing to restrain precipitate responses urged by fear seems sufficient to produce a transformation. Restraint in this sense may actually go to the essence of the bo tree principle. Faraday thinks the dreamer's best option in a lucid nightmare is to confront and "see what happens";[74] and Gackenbach, "to go with the dream as it unravels, rather than try to direct the content."[75] LaBerge likewise speaks about "self-control" in contrast to controlling dream action, and of a "receptive strategy," an "intentional acceptance and assimilation."[76] (The pros and cons of control were discussed in chapter 14, p. 469ff.)

Sparrow tells a dream where his fear precipitated evasion despite lucid awareness of invulnerability ('It's only a dream'). He awoke feeling he had "avoided a necessary confrontation." Then he returned to sleep:

From a distance I see the same group of men who were in the previous dream. As they approach, I decide not to escape. They come up to me like a group of dogs, just waiting for a wrong move. But as I laugh nervously, they begin to slap me on the back, and smile in a playful manner.[77]

Hervey de Saint-Denys related a recurring non-lucid nightmare of *"hideous pursuers" who kept gaining on him* until he awakened. He cured himself during the fourth recurrence (here abridged), when *he turned lucid*:

Instead of fleeing, and by . . . an effort of will, I leaned against the wall and resolved to contemplate with the closest attention the phantoms that I had so far only glimpsed rather than seen. . . . I fixed my eyes on my principal attacker, who somewhat resembled the grinning, bristling demons which are sculpted in cathedral porticos, and as the desire to observe gained the upper hand over my emotions, I saw the following: the fantastic monster had arrived within several feet of me, whistling and cavorting in a manner which, once it had ceased to frighten me, appeared comic. . . . The attention I had concentrated on this figure had caused its companions to disappear as if by magic. The figure itself seemed to slow down in its movements, lose its clarity and take on a woolly appearance, until it changed into a kind of floating bundle of rags. . . .[78]

This dream calls to mind the transformation of incoming weapons to harmless flowers in Gautama's vision.

Being annihilated. In the Senoi dream theory (i.e., Stewart's influential version of it), after the dreamer her/himself is killed by an adversary in a dream, s/he is immediately reborn, and the fight "permanently exhausts the adversary."[79] Tart writes that an alternative to conquering or befriending a source of threat is to "be conquered by and absorbed by it, as a third way of healing the split" with the symbolized part of oneself one had "not come to grips with. . . ."[80] Likewise, Denyse Beaudet observes that "engulfment" is one of the three successful responses children spontaneously develop to deal with dream "monsters" (broadly defined), along with the responses of "combat" and "taming."[81]

Tarab Tulku XI recommends annihilation as a preferred tactic, based no doubt on the Buddhist doctrine of the unreality of the self (*anatman* or *anatta*). Dream threats represent the dreamer's "fear of having his/her self-image destroyed." The best choice is "to let the negativity destroy him/herself. In other words, unite with the negativity." "When the negativity destroys the dream subject, . . . [he/she] reaches a more authentic layer of his/her being. . . . Through this act, it seems to me, he/she has solved the underlying psychological problems."[82]

But Tholey warns that allowing oneself to be killed can lead to fear and discouragement.[83] It is a tactic to use with caution, or perhaps under guidance—the Tibetan adept, after all, trains under a guru. However, Mindell illustrates how annihilation, or at least openness to the possibility of it, can work for the good in a Western therapy, his "dreambody work" (see below) with its style of dream re-entry:

> Just this evening I was working with a man who is . . . dying of leukemia, he is so sick he can hardly talk, and he's lying in his bed, barely moving. You can't talk much to him, . . . he's too exhausted. He was supposed to have died some weeks ago, but he's still holding on, for God knows what reason. He had just the vaguest fragment of a dream in which *there's a woman being burned alive in a fire.* So, I said to him, "Don't talk to me, just feel your body. What is it that you're experiencing in your body, and do it exactly." . . . He said: "Well, warmth." And I said "Where are you feeling the warmth?" Though it was difficult for him, he pointed with one of his fingers to a place between his legs. . . . And so I said to him: "Well, just concentrate on that, and watch what happens with it." After a few minutes, suddenly he takes a deep breath—and of all things —he starts to smile, and he says: "Well, it feels like heat, something like fire burning up inside my body and trying to reach my chest." And I said "Well, what happens now?" He said: "Feels like I'm on fire and burning." And I said: "Well, go ahead and burn! What happens then?" Then, he sits up in bed—and you have to imagine, this is a very frail man—and he starts to yell: "LIFE, YOU HAVE TO GRAB IT! LIFE IS EVERYTHING! YOU HAVE TO GRAB IT!"[84]

Morton Kelsey relates another beneficial re-entry of a dream of fire. In this instance, the threat of annihilation is less absolute: it is directed not to the dreamer himself but to something belonging to him, and the good effect comes from cooperating in the annihilation:

I had frequently dreamed that *my childhood home was on fire.* In most dreams *I attempted to put out the fire.* I finally spoke to a friend about it. He suggested to me that it was important to allow the house to burn down. . . . I imagined once more the dream of the burning house, and in my imagination I allowed the house to burn to the ground. Afterward, I kicked the ashes with my foot in order to be completely sure that the house had actually burned down. Through this dream, I integrated the idea that I consciously wanted to get away from my childishness. After this I tried to change my outward childish behavior that the dream had made me aware of. I never again dreamed that that house was burning.[85]

Identification. Like Hillman, Mary Watkins seeks to lead us away from partiality to the "heroic ego": "One identifies with the dream ego to such an extent that one can only feel identity as a victim, not as the other images that victimize." When one "sides with some images against others, their victory must signal a defeat in some other corner." "But what if the threatening images are granted as much reality as the ego? If both are to be understood to be aspects of the personality with the same quality of realness?"[86]

This is of course an underlying conception of Perls's Gestalt dreamwork. "You never overcome *anything* by resisting it. You only can overcome anything by going deeper into it." "If you are pursued by an ogre in a dream, and you *become* the ogre [when you work with the dream], the nightmare disappears. You re-own the energy that is invested in the demon."[87]

Peter Fellows describes an approach called "aspect integration," a sort of intensified Gestalt work carried on within the lucid dream state. He suggests that by imaginally entering into another dream character (threatening, or not) and directly experiencing its point of view while still dreaming, one integrates that split-off aspect of oneself into one's personality.[88]

Care-giving, compassion and love. Max Zeller relates the dream of a woman about 40 who *encounters an "ancient, irascible, gnarled old witch . . . covered over the chest with huge repulsive brown scabs. She seems helpless and abandoned."* Though repulsed, the dreamer ministers to the sores. *"She protests heartily. As I continue, her skin becomes clear and clean and white. . . . Then as I wash the last scab from under her chin, she turns into a beautiful boy-child of about three years of age."* Zeller concludes, after interpreting the dream: "A shadow aspect reveals the positive and helpful side that is vitally necessary to the totality of life. When it then changes into a beautiful boy-child, it points to her creative spiritual potential."[89] The woman was encouraged by the dream to undertake analysis.

Sparrow relates a bo tree dream where compassion does the trick:

The following dream of a young woman is one of a long series of dreams in which she continually fled from an aggressive, somewhat mentally unbalanced man. This dream was the first in which she became lucid; and, as we might expect, it was one of the last in this series.

> *I'm in a dark, poor section of the city. A young man starts chasing me down an alley. I'm running for what seems to be a long time in the dream. Then I become aware than I am dreaming and that much of my dream life is spent running from male pursuers. I say to myself, "I'm tired of this never-ending chase." I stop running, turn around and walk up to the man. I touch him and say, "Is there anything I can do to help you?" He becomes very gentle and open to me and replies, "Yes. My friend and I need help." I go to the apartment they share and talk with them both about their problem, feeling compassionate love for them both.*[90]

"When you meet a monster in your lucid dream," recommends LaBerge, "sincerely greet him like a long-lost friend, and that is what he will be. . . . You don't need to talk to shadow figures to make peace with them. If you can find it in your heart to genuinely love your dream enemies, they become your friends. Embracing the rejected with loving acceptance symbolically integrates the shadow into your model of yourself. . . ."[91] He tells a dream (here abridged) where *he was beset by an ogre in the midst of a riot*:

> *As soon as I realized the struggle was a dream, I knew that as a matter of principle, the conflict was with myself. . . .*
>
> *. . . I tried to feel loving as I stood face to face with my ogre. At first I failed utterly, feeling only disgust and repulsion for the ogre. . . . But I tried to ignore the image and seek love within my own heart. Finding it, I looked my ogre in the eyes, trusting my intuition to supply the right things to say. Beautiful words of acceptance flowed out of me, and as they did, he melted into me. As for the riot, it had vanished without a trace.* The dream was over, and I awoke feeling wonderfully calm."[92]

When listing alternative tactics for bo tree situations, Garfield presents what amounts to a ranking of options: to face; to confront and conquer; to befriend; to reconcile; and on top, to love.[93] Besides being incomplete, this ordering is of course debatable. Garfield herself varies it: to confront and conquer; to reconcile; to befriend; and "[p]erhaps the highest step in the hierarchy of potential responses by the dreamer to a negative dream figure is that of merging with it."[94]* In another place, she seems to back away from the idea of a hierarchy: "The crucial point, it seems to me, is not so much *which* action is taken toward the hostile dream figure—whether we eradicate them, challenge them, stare them into submission, reconcile with them, or

---

* "In some cases—such as sexual abuse of the dreamer—merging with a hostile dream figure that represents a threat to the dreamer in waking life would be inadvisable" (P. Garfield 1988b, p. 295).

love them—but that *some* action is taken."[95] Still, love again tops this list of bo tree responses. However, this does not mean that she considers love the highest level of dream experience of all kinds—that place, she reserves for "full-blown mystical, ecstatic experience within the dream. . . . These are the dream experiences of light."[96] She briefly mentions the possibility of using light as a bo tree tactic: "One theorist suggests surrounding the threatening image with golden light."[97]

Incubation, Lucidity, Re-entry

Of the sample of bo tree dream transformations mentioned thus far, about a fifth occurred spontaneously in ordinary dreams. The remainder involved some degree of deliberate control or intention: a third took place during lucid consciousness, and a fifth during waking re-entries, but only one or two items possibly involved incubation. Though these ratios may crudely indicate something about the relative efficacy of these modalities for the purpose, it was in the context of incubation (as attributed to the Senoi) that the bo tree principle first became popularized.

With children suffering bad dreams, Garfield encourages what amounts to an incubation by advising them that in future dreams they can fight or befriend dangerous enemies. And she suggests that they call upon dream helpers when threats arise.[98] One helper she recommends is Pac-man, in reality based on a traditional Japanese spirit figure, "Baku," a name which derives from a verb meaning "to eat very fast." Japanese children say "Devour, O *Baku!*" when awakened by nightmares.[99]

Patricia Maybruck has found that pregnant women who assert and defend themselves in response to dream threats often have shorter and easier labors than do dream victims. She advises her childbirth training groups to incubate with the thought that they will not be victimized in their dreams, not even in nightmares. "Actually writing down, before going to bed, 'I will not be victimized in my dreams tonight,' helps imprint this intention."[100]

Koch-Sheras relates a dream series where a woman deliberately revisited a recurring nightmare from her adolescence: "*[A] man [is] standing over my bed with an axe. . . .*" In the course of doing dreamwork as an adult, she realized she had to deal with old sexual conflicts, and "resolved to incubate a dream where I would meet my nightmare man again." She successfully incubated a dream in which the attacker appeared as a "*fossil, who becomes a half-senile man sunning on a park bench.*" And in a sequel several months later, she dreamt *she did battle with a sword-wielding man, who in the end consented to beheading.*[101]

Carrying an incubated intention into sleep seems often to result in pre- or semi-lucidity. Krippner talks about an artist who recurrently *fled in terror from "a huge ugly monster. "* Awake, she tried to draw the elusive image, but failed. "The next time she had the dream, *Maggie was so determined to remember what the creature looked like that she actually turned to face it, but the monster disappeared. "* In a later dream, *with perseverance she succeeded in catching and touching the monster,* whereupon "*it turned into a beautiful horse-like creature" and then into a lover.*[102]

Another example of a semi-lucid determination to carry out an intention from waking is related by Faraday, who "*was being pursued one night (for the umpteenth time) by an enormous uncouth bruiser figure . . . [when] I suddenly remembered my principle and turned around, not without some trepidation, and asked him what he wanted. He immediately doffed his cap and asked me into a sleazy café for a talk. . . .*"[103]

Lucidity per se does not, it should be realized, automatically bring amelioration of a bad dream, much less bring a bo tree solution. In her survey of lucid phenomena, Celia Green gives the example of a dreamer who knew he was in a recurrent nightmare but who remained powerless either to wake himself or to modify the scenario. And she makes it clear that the majority of dreamers who become lucid in threatening dreams only use lucidity to escape by waking.[104] Halliday points out that lucidity strategies do not always help nightmares, even with the intervention of a therapist.[105]

Several of the failures Halliday mentions involve clinically depressed patients. Lynne Levitan & LaBerge confirm that even less severe depression is a factor associated with inability to improve or escape from a bad dream situation—although usually even depressed people experience *some* amelioration when nightmares turn lucid. But "[w]hen lucid in nightmares, depressed people are likely to think, 'Here I am in a nightmare again. I am scared and there is nothing I can do. I can never end these dreams. I am no good.'" The remedy suggested is a sort of in-dream cognitive therapy: "[I]t's only a dream and cannot really hurt me. If I face this fear I will gain strength and increase my ability to handle situations that cause me anxiety." Such positive thinking sets the stage for tactical options of approach.[106]

To treat recurrent nightmares, Antonio Zadra has joined lucidity induction (Tholey's combined technique) with incubation in the more usual sense and with guided imagery. He trains patients to induce lucidity at a critical moment in their recurrent dream by using a trigger, such as looking at their hands. Therapist and patient work out in advance how they want to alter the nightmare, whether by changing the scene, or by a bo tree tactic such as befriending or fighting a threat, if there is one in the nightmare (some nightmares, such as those of grief, do not contain a threat in the obvious sense). Before sleep, the patient does a relaxation exercise and visualizes the nightmare, the lucidity cue, and the plot alteration.

Zadra emphasizes that it is control over the dream's outcome which has a curative effect, not lucidity per se, which only sets up conditions for control.[107] He points to cases where "lucidity without the element of control actually worsened the nightmare."[108]

Outside of the lucidity literature, re-entry seems to be the most frequently employed modality for deliberately exercising the bo tree principle. This is presumably because it is the most reliable and accessible of the three modalities.

Individuals may react differently, however. An incest survivor with posttraumatic recurrent nightmares found it too overwhelming to confront her abuser in waking visualization, yet could do so in LD because it was "only a dream." Initially, *she controlled the LD outcome by dismissing the abuser.* Subsequently, *she could allow the interaction to follow its own course, and could even ask the figure for a gift.*[109] Thus individuals may idiosyncratically find one or another modality more congenial. Nevertheless, re-entry is probably the easiest way to change outcomes for most people, just because, as Eva Neu remarks, it does not have to be done in sleep:

> *A small boy was pursued* in his dreams *by a terrible bear.* At last, with the support of a wise therapist, he decided to look the bear in the eye and ask him what he wanted. He didn't have to do this in his sleep. He saw himself and the bear, stopped running, turned and spoke. The bear stopped dead in his tracks and said to him, "I just wanted to play."[110]

Re-entry for the purpose of approach and transformation can be done on one's own or with different degrees of guidance: anything from a friend's suggestion (Koch-Sheras's "Blue velvet dress" and Kelsey's "He tries to put out fire in childhood home") to quite detailed guidance by a therapist. As an example of detailed guidance, Shaffer guides a dreamer in a "transformational fantasy" of another dialogue with another bear:

> [Sam] had a recurring nightmare in which *grizzly bears were continually on the prowl outside his house. He wanted to be free to leave his house to go to town, but he never could because those bears were always out there. One big bear was particularly terrifying, although,* in his dreams, *he could never see it clearly.* As Sam was reliving the nightmare in fantasy, the therapist asked him to call out to the fearsome bear and ask it to have a chat. So Sam said to the bear, "Why are you bothering me this way?" "Because you're a coward," snarled the bear in reply. "Can't I ever be free to leave this house?" "No, you're too cowardly," growled the bear.

At this point, the guide suggested that Sam open the door and go out to face the bear. He was very reluctant but finally agreed. The bear growled menacingly in front of the open door. The guide suggested that Sam take a step toward the bear. The bear kept growling but did not move. Sam took another step and then another and one more. Suddenly, he was only a few feet from the bear and could see it clearly for the first time. "Why it's only a teddy bear," he gasped. Facing up to this bear helped him to overcome his passive relationship with people. He never had the dream again.[111]

As always with imaginal dreamwork, the question arises whether a non-interpretive procedure should stand alone or should be combined with other work. An example of the former is the desensitization treatment for nightmares by A. Eccles et al. They conduct "*in vivo* desensitization." For example, a woman was cured of recurring nightmares of *snake attacks* by leading her through eleven stages of approach, from being shown a real caged snake across the room to actually handling it. Her nightmares ceased without relapse following the third session. Eccles also uses "imaginal desensitization" in which the person is led through the same sort of gradual approach, but by guided visualization alone. This method has the advantage of logistical convenience, as when a woman received some relief from recurrent phobic nightmares of *crossing bridges*.[112]

But Diana Whitmore, a psychosynthesist, insists that facing the shadow or other dream transformations wrought by re-entry "must of course be followed up to ground them in the individual's 'real' life."[113] And Henry Reed uses re-entry as just one component of a larger self-development program which is in large part interpretive of the dreams on which it centers. Reed employs re-entry as a form of incubation: as part of one's "incubation reverie" just before sleep, one should "visualize the troubling image" from a previous dream "having itself transform into something positive."[114]

An interesting way of using re-entry as a form of incubation is "dream substitution," Burr Eichelman's procedure. The dream is re-entered and re-dreamt in altered form under hypnosis. "Dream substitution uses the observation that hypnotic dreams can be incorporated into nocturnal dreaming." Eichelman considers this merely as symptom relief for posttraumatic stress disorder nightmares in preparation for "more protracted and traditional kinds of therapeutic interventions."[115] One of his examples nicely echoes the story of the weapons of Mara's devils turning into flowers:

Mr. B dreamt of *being shot by a Viet Cong sniper. He would hear the shot and see the bullet coming to kill him,* awakening just before *the bullet was going to strike his head.* He had dreamt this nearly nightly for 12 years. In the alteration of the dream, it was allowed to proceed in hypnotic trance until *the bullet became visible about 50 yards away. At this point the bullet was transformed into a whipped cream pie, much in the manner of the old-time silent movies. The pie was then slowed and returned to the Viet Cong sniper. It struck the sniper in the face, so startling him that he fell from the tree. The event was so improbable that the Viet Cong and Mr. B broke into outrageous laughter and walked off together in disbelief. . . .* Mr. B rehearsed the substituted dream at home with self-hypnosis. The revised dream was dreamt at night several times, replacing the traumatic dream. After this replacement the traumatic dream disappeared. It reappeared for two periods subsequently in the next 2 years but was again removed with a rehearsal of the altered dream.[116]

Mindell's 'dreambody work'.   A dream discussed in connection with the tactic of annihilation, "A woman is being burned alive," gives an example of what Mindell calls *dreambody work*, or *process work*, or *process oriented psychology.*[117]

Dreambody work is something of a loose end here, which makes it not a bad place to end a digressive book on what is the always elusive topic of dreams. Mindell trained as a Jungian, yet Zwig's recent chapter summarizing this approach does not mention Jung.[118] Mindell's work usually concerns medical symptoms, so might have been discussed in my chapter 8—yet it did not seem to fit there either, perhaps for the same reasons that Garfield does not mention Mindell in her two recent books, one on dreams and the body, the other on dreams and healing.[119] His work can involve a variant sort of dream re-entry, so could have been raised in chapter 15, but it goes better here for the reason that dreambody work follows the principle of *approach → transform*—though not so much of approach to dream threat images as to whatever subjective experience occupies the foreground while working on a symptom and—just if there happens to be one—a dream.

Mindell also makes a good place to end because he exemplifies both the bad and good of contemporary dreamwork. On the first score: there is a bit of flim-flam about Mindell. And he conspicuously overemploys the first person singular while extolling non-ego functions. Also, he interprets disease processes so positively that they begin to lose their catagogic authenticity. But on the second score: he is inventive, creative, intuitive, holistic, and affirmative. He breaks down prevailing categories and finds authentic meanings where our culture traditionally does not. And he helps people.

Mindell posits the existence of the "dreambody, an entity which is dream and body at once." "The dreambody is a term for the total, multi-channeled personality."[120] It is the gestalt of one's being, insofar as that actualizes itself to awareness in diverse channels of information. Dreambody work can be done in any prevailing channel. By 'dream', Mindell sometimes means just that, as when he writes that "dreams are processes trying to happen in consciousness," or "are also visualizations of body experiences."[121] More often, however, Mindell uses 'dream' figuratively. For example, "sickness can be a stroke of luck. It's a dream in the body, use it to wake up,"[122] or "couples dream; when two people get together, they do unconscious things together, they create a dream together, they create their signals. . . ."[123] The dream proper is just one parallel or confluent channel of information composing this figurative dream, or dreambody.

However, actual dreams are given special notice, inasmuch as they provide, when available, "a visual map or guide in the work."[124] "The patterns contained in dreams and in body symptoms inevitably mirror each other."[125]

To illustrate this parallelism: Mindell had a session with a woman complaining of "too much milk in her breasts." She was resistant and hostile to any sort of psychological work. After irritably fending off questions for a while, she eventually confided that she hated her husband. "He never touches or caresses me, and he never has time to spend with me. I hate him." She said she could not talk to him about it because "[h]e's too stupid." Mindell suggested to her that she was projecting an insensitive, uncaring aspect of herself onto her husband. This drew a belligerent response, but then: "One thing I can tell you about myself that you should know, is that I had a dream in which *I was an abandoned child.*" Discussion of the dream rapidly led her to understand her symptom: "I know why I have too much milk, it's because I'm not drinking it, I ought to be mothering myself more." She was, concludes Mindell, "in some ways a typical medical case whose symptoms were trying to motivate her to completely change her personality."[126] This example is atypical insofar as Mindell did not get the person to work directly with a body feeling, but it well illustrates how dream and symptom can convey the same message, and how the dream can serve as guide to understanding the symptom.

More typically, as with "A woman is being burned alive," Mindell tries to get the body to deliver the message. For Mindell, a symptom itself constitutes information which diagnoses the symptom's own psychological causes. Disease is the psyche seeking expression; disease is therefore an inherently "meaningful experience that is constantly pressing" the ill person "towards consciousness." "A terrifying symptom is usually your greatest dream trying to come true."[127]

This sense of the eloquence of symptoms has much in common with shamanism, mankind's oldest medicinal doctrine, where illness reflects one's spiritual condition. Speaking of the Greek development of this perspective, which animated Greek incubation practices (chapter 13), Russell Lockhart says that "[d]isease and affliction were a consequence of improper relationship to the divine. The purpose of sickness, the meaning of affliction, was to force the individual to confront his disconnection from the Gods."[128] Nowadays, some who desire to restore this dimension to modern allopathic medicine may retain an edge of credulity about extrapsychic spiritual agencies,[129] but usually the theme is transposed along intrapsychic lines. Thus Sanford, though a clergyman, calls illness "an invitation to become a whole person, and often such illnesses can be cured only when seen in that light."[130]

Sanford's language tips his Jungian commitments. Jung is also Mindell's main influence. Mindell's central proposition, that all channels of the dreambody convey information to a receiver who evidently stands apart from those channels, derives from Jung's theory of the Self (chapter 3): the Self not only frames the ego and models the ego, but purposefully communicates with the ego as well. Illness is one of the Self's (the dreambody's) channels of information, and it compensates the ego just as dreams do. As another Jungian, Meredith Sabini, comments, "when one notes the similarity between a physical symptom and a dream image, the symbolic quality of the symptom often becomes apparent."[131]

However, Sabini does not psychologize every illness, nor did Jung. Mindell comes perilously close to doing so. What is more, Sabini makes it clear that the psychological function of illness is not uniformly anagogic. Indeed, in her final remarks about a certain dream, she says that while the dreamer's fatal cancer "functioned as an attempt to bring childhood wounds to light," it simultaneously "functioned as an excuse for not facing those problems." Sabini thus respects the ambiguity of psychologically based illness, which "may be brought about through the intervention of the invisible authority of the Self," but also through "stress and repression."[132] Mindell does not emphatically establish such balance. What he does do, however, is to provide a method for working with symptoms.

"The central intervention used in process work is called amplification."[133] Amplification can be achieved indirectly, explains David Roomy, by "slight resistance" which causes the person involuntarily to strengthen the channel or switch channels. If Mindell sees someone's foot rising as s/he speaks, he might press the foot downward, eliciting a counteraction. Or amplification can be accomplished directly, by asking "Could you make that stronger?"[134] If there is pain, for example, Mindell invites the person to go with and exaggerate the pain. This is the 'approach' aspect of Mindell's version of the bo tree principle. Amplification helps information "encoded in the symptom to unfold and reveal itself."[135] The symptom's message heals the psyche; and the symptom may even heal itself, once it is no longer needed to carry the message.[136] This is the 'transform' aspect of Mindell's version of the bo tree principle.

The 'dreambody' often switches channels, from pain to a visual image or a movement, for example. Though a symptom is usually the starting point, these other channels should also be amplified. One utilizes whatever channel occupies the foreground, just as in Gestalt work. An important channel is the dream proper. In the case of "A woman is being burned alive," discussion of a dream led to a body feeling which was then worked with. In the following and concluding example, Zwig describes Mindell's amplification of a symptom, which leads to recall of a dream, which is then worked with by re-entry:

Esther . . . was a well-behaved, well-adapted, accommodating woman. She had considerable difficulty being direct and honest with people, especially if it involved negative feelings. In one session, Esther complained to Mindell of "pressing pains" extending from her neck down to her lower back which had been preventing her from sleeping. As she said this, she placed her hand on the back of her neck. Mindell noticed this and suggested that he place his hand on her neck and that she direct his hand.

Esther agreed to the idea and asked Mindell to apply pressure to her neck. He did so; however, it was not intense enough for Esther. She kept asking for more and more pressure until eventually, Mindell was pressing her neck right to the floor. At that point, Esther spontaneously recalled a recent dream in which *a devil had thrown her into a hole.* She said that Mindell's actions reminded her of the devil figure...and she was being put into a hole!

Mindell then suggested that Esther play the part of the devil. She stood up and while pressing his neck to the floor, said, "Either you take me with you when you go out or you will have to remain in a hole." With this statement, Esther had an insight into her process. The devil in the dream was her own capacity to be direct, honest, and even negative with people. In contrast with her usual adapted and accommodating behavior, she considered this "devilish." The "devil" part of her was demanding to be noticed and utilized.[137]

List of Dreams

PAGE	SOURCE	TOPIC	DREAM

Italicized page numbers indicate dreams to be found in footnotes which begin on those pages.

Chapter 1 • REM, etc.

PAGE	SOURCE	TOPIC	DREAM
15	Mack, in Hunt (1989)	Dreams of very young children	"Boom! boom!"
15	Isaacs, in Beaudet (1990)	Dreams of very young children	A rabbit was about to bite her
15	Fraiberg, in Beaudet (1990)	Dreams of very young children	"Let me down"
19	Arkin et al. (1970b)	Stage 4 sleep talk	"No, wait Sam!"
20	Schenck et al. (1989)	REM sleep behavior disorder	Breaking the neck of a deer
20	Dement & Wolpert (1958a)	Scanning hypothesis: yes	Leaflets dropped from blimp
21	Dement & Kleitman (1957a)	Scanning hypothesis: yes	Two people throwing tomatoes
21	Roffwarg et al. (1962)	Scanning hypothesis: yes	Watching TV
21	Moscowitz & Berger (1969)	Scanning hypothesis: no	Vertical row of buttons
21	Schatzman et al. (1988)	Scanning hypothesis: yes, in lucid dreams	Triangles
23	Cartwright (1977)	REM/NREM dreams compared	1. Skiing—holy smokes! 2. Thinking about skiing
23	Rechtschaffen et al. (1963)	NREM dreams: thoughtlike	Thinking about various interests
24	Foulkes (1985)	NREM dreams: isolated images	1. Pen writing on a drum 2. Shelves with jars 3. Big piece of yellow cake
25	Faraday (1972)	NREM dreams: 'dreamlike'	1. "Go here, go there" 2. Drinking milk in bed
26	Foulkes (1978)	Hypnagogic dreams: vivid isolated images	1. Number hanging in mid-air 2. Train and strawberries
26	Ullman & Krippner (1970)	Hypnagogic dreams: bizarre sequences	Dogs fighting → Storming the barricades → Hemiplegic → Cube
27	Ullman & Zimmerman (1979)	Hypnagogic dreams: presleep preoccupation	Tossing the ball to Bob
27	Silberer (1955 [1918])	Hypnagogic dreams: auto-symbolic: thought content	Planing a piece of wood
27	Silberer (1955 [1918])	Hypnagogic dreams: auto-symbolic: thought process	Sullen officer refuses information
27	LaBerge (1985)	Hypnagogic dreams: well-developed	Huge torso with golden disc

527

PAGE	SOURCE	TOPIC	DREAM
28	Vogel et al. (1966)	Sleep onset stages	1. Thinking about clippings 2. Inside a pleural cavity 3. Driving a car
30	Piaget (1962 [1945])	Hypnopompic dreams: auto-symbolic: somatic	He was himself the frog
30	Foulkes (1985)	Waking dream: realistic episodes	Back in her home town *etc.*
31	Foulkes & Fleischer (1975)	Waking dream: transient images	Inside a refrigerator
31	Foulkes & Fleischer (1975)	Waking dream: bizarre images	This animal kind of thing

Chapter 2 • Freud

53	Fromm (1951)	Representation	Transformed into a chicken
53	Stekel (1943)	Condensation	Girl wears two bathing suits
53	Gillman (1987)	Condensation: pun	Undercover agents
53	Namrow (1980)	Condensation: pun	Going to Budapest
53	Cartwright (1977)	Condensation: pun	Her "assets were frozen"
54	Maguire (1989)	"Kiddie hangover" dreams	1. Round John Vershun 2. In the mist of his enemies
54	Altman (1969)	Displacement	He gives the ball a hard kick
55	Sharpe (1978 [1937])	Reversal	1. Woman's front clothed → 2. Woman's back naked
56	Shohet (1985)	Reversal: pun	Two youths drive at her
65	Freud (1953 [1900])	Dream-thought and wish	She abandons wish to give supper-party
66	Freud (1953 [1900])	Reductionism	Little one run over
71	Freud, in Wolff (1972 [1952])	Freud's spirituality	1. He turns aside into beer cellar 2. He pretends to be blind

Chapter 3 • Jung

81	Whitmont & Perera (1989)	Mythic images in modern guise	Zeus the electrician
83	Whitmont (1978)	Amplification	He doesn't deserve the 'fasz'
86	Clift & Clift (1984)	Persona	Gold dress from years ago
87	Bennet, in Rycroft (1981)	Shadow	Intruder bursts in
88	von Franz (1980b)	Shadow	1. He drives over a child 2. Raging wild animals in cage
90	Allenby (1985 [1955])	Animus	1. Neighbor landowner returns 2. She dances with the Chinese emperor
98	Hauri, in Breger et al. (1971)	Compensation: of physical exercise	Hammock on a tropical isle
99	Gutheil (1967 [1951])	Compensation: and repression	Covered with a black cloth

PAGE	SOURCE	TOPIC	DREAM
100	Hall (1983)	Compensation: obvious	"Don't smoke dope"
101	Dement (1974 [1972])	Compensation: obvious	Ominous chest X-ray
101	Taylor (1991)	Compensation: obvious	Puff the Magic Dragon
101	Stone, in Epel (1993)	Compensation: obvious	Smoking again
101	Denzin (1988)	Compensation: obvious	The mantle caught on fire
101	Anonymous (personal communication)	Wish-fulfilling variant on addiction theme	Just enjoy it
101	Signell (1990)	Compensation: obvious	"Absolutely No"
101	Covitz (1990)	Compensation: obvious	"Mary, if not him, who?"
101	Jung (1965 [1961])	Compensation: small adjustment	He has to look up to see her
102	A. Siegel (1990)	Compensation: large adjustment	The fallen idol
102	Diamond (1983)	Compensation: access to feelings	There was blood all over
103	Volkan & Bhatti (1973)	Compensation: access to feelings	He saw the death of a brother
103	Jung (CW 16)	Compensation: context important	His father is driving drunk
104	Marjasch (1966)	Compensation: interpreted by amplification	The family-chorus calls "Come back!"
106	Aumüller, in Sanford (1977)	Compensation: not infallible	1. White uniform black brother 2. Black camp garb white sister 3. White prisoners black Hitler
110	Jung (CW 16)	Jung's foresight (cp. Freud's hindsight)	He mounts upward on empty air
113	Whitmont & Perera (1989)	Classical dramatic structure of dreams	Floating like Ophelia
116	Jung, in Grant (1986)	Protecting the dreamer	He channels water back into the ground
117	Jung (1965 [1961])	Protecting the dreamer	Chamber with monumental phallus
119	Zeller (1975)	Transformative symbolic experience	1. "The creative spirit" 2. Mother's gift: a compass
127	Zeller (1975)	Jung's religiosity	A temple of vast dimensions
127	Jung (1965 [1961])	Clairvoyance	Figure like his wife rises in white gown
128	Jung (1965 [1961])	Jung's experiences of the dead	Parade of peasant boys
129	Serrano (1968 [1966])	Jung's deathbed dream	A sign of Wholeness and Oneness

Chapter 4 · Existentialism

134	Gold (1979)	Adler: dream reflects life-style	"Take anything you want"
137	Adler (1958 [1931])	Adler: self-deception	He was a murderer
139	Dreikurs, in Shulman (1969)	Adlerian: dream prompts change of life-style	He was in jail
145	Boss (1977)	Against symbolic interpretations	His pet turtle's shell torn away
145	Boss (1977)	Analogy, not symbolism	Rubbish heap near his church
146	Boss (1977)	Boss's dreamwork style	She declines a Latin noun
150	May & Yalom (1989)	Existential anxiety	Photo slide of her son juggling

PAGE	SOURCE	TOPIC	DREAM
152	Craig (1987)	Dream functions of discovery and rehearsal	1. Humiliated at family gathering 2. He falls from a turret toward a moat 3. He shows his sister out

Chapter 5 • Culturalism

PAGE	SOURCE	TOPIC	DREAM
161	Gillman (1987)	Reversal of dream feeling	The Mona Lisa was missing
162	Rossi (1985 [1972])	Subtleties of dream feelings	Irate husband walks out
163	Bonime (with Bonime) (1982 [1962])	Symbolized feelings	1. Feces on her leg 2. Steam valve on his penis 3. Her heavy leaden feet
163	Bonime (with Bonime) (1982 [1962])	Symbolized and experiential feelings	Popping cap annoys him
164	Bonime (with Bonime) (1982 [1962])	Bonime's dreamwork style	Three people wearing condoms
175	Inter-Tribal Council of Nevada (1976)	Big dreams	God gives him the Ghost Dance
177	Eliade (1966)	Culture pattern dreams: shamanic initiation	Dismemberment and reassembly
178	Merrill (1992 [1987])	Culture pattern dreams: shamanic initiation	God offers light-colored pieces of paper
178	Lincoln (1970 [1935])	Culture pattern dreams: dream quest	1. He refuses beautiful bird's gift 2. He accepts white loon's gift
179	Borges (1976)	Recent big dreams: Mossadegh	The dream of oil
180	von Grunebaum (1966)	Turn of century big dream: Shah of Persia	Sack of gold and silver
180	Friedman (1990)	Recent big dreams: Saddam	Mohammed: missiles pointed the wrong direction
181	Mbiti (1976)	Recent big dreams: Amin	1. He would be Uganda's ruler 2. God: Expel the Asians
181	Cooper et al., in Signell (1990)	Recent big dreams: Aquino	Ninoy's coffin was empty
181	Taylor (1992a)	Recent big dreams: Gandhi	Festival of all religions
181	Rich, in Koch-Sheras et al. (1983)	Recent big dreams: Rich	The lyrics of a blues song
182	Priess (1993)	Recent big dreams: Priess	Animals in spilled oil
182	Aldighieri & Tripician (1991)	Recent big dreams: Sapiel	"The whole country's on fire"
182	Shafton (forthcoming)	Recent big dreams: Stamps	Four-day feast
184	Ullman & Zimmerman (1979)	Ullman groups; dreams about relating to groups	1. "I am alone" [#1] 2. "I am alone" [#2] 3. Circles and squares
188	Zimmermann (1967)	Group dreams	Horrible octopus fights a man
190	Reed (1988 [1985])	Incubation with Native American and Asclepian borrowings	1. Pitiful creatures adrift at sea 2. He cuts a path for himself

PAGE	SOURCE	TOPIC	DREAM
191	Reed (1987 [1977])	Caution: transpersonal inflations	Each his own shield
195	Savary et al. (1984)	Dreams with societal dimensions understood religiously	She is offered a gift puppy
199	Koch-Sheras et al. (1983)	Feminist issues	The carpenter
200	Ullman & Zimmerman (1979)	Racial issues	He wants to be the center of action
201	Wikse (1988)	Racial issues	"Jack Wis"
205	Bilu (1989)	Dreams of Palestinian and Jewish children	1. Terrorists sneak into kibbutz 2. Israeli army attacks at night 3. The governess of Palestine 4. Dream with no end
206	Beradt (1968 [1966])	Dreams under Hitler: cooptation, complicity	"The Abolition of Walls"
207	Beradt, in Shohet (1983)	Dreams under Hitler: cooptation, complicity	1. She talks Russian in sleep 2. Barbed wire in hospital ward 3. Hitler the clown: not so bad 4. Her bus goes to 'Heil Hitler'
207	Beradt (1968 [1966])	Dreams of Jews under Hitler	The Last country that tolerates Jews refuses him too
207	Gill (1985)	A typical dream for exiles	The exile's dream
207	Beradt (1968 [1966])	Dreams of Jews under Hitler	"I Make Room for Trash"
208	Scholl, in Beradt (1968 [1966])	Dreams of political resistance	The other side of the abyss
208	Watkins (1992)	Dreams of political resistance	Her own small newspaper
209	Harrington (1991)	Dreams of political resistance	Initiation: ideals of Star Trek

Chapter 6 · Gestalt

216	Perls (1969)	Feeding back the experience	Train tracks
218	Downing & Marmorstein (1973)	Attention to the body	A threatening building
218	Perls (1969)	Physical enactment	A steel band around her chest
219	Perls (1969)	Playing both parts	Going home to see parents
223	Stekel (1943 [1929])	Objective and subjective interpretation	He destroys the lock
228	Perls (1969)	Perls's dreamwork style	With father during air raid

Chapter 7 · Catagogic/Anagogic

241	Boss (1959 [1938])	Catagogic dreams	1. A cow is to be slaughtered 2. She murders mother, is raped 3. Obscenities with her father
241	Gutheil (1967 [1951])	Anxious anagogic dreams	He delays delivering flowers
242	French, in Fliess (1953)	Anxious anagogic dreams	Washing himself in his own shit

PAGE	SOURCE	TOPIC	DREAM
246	Garfield (1984)	Dark wish-fulfillment dreams	Separated from her sister
250	Kalsched (1992)	Catagogic or anagogic?	He comes down with an axe on her neck

Chapter 8 • Dream and Symptom

PAGE	SOURCE	TOPIC	DREAM
253	Stekel (1943 [1913])	Whole neurosis personified	Attempt on King Alfonso's life
254	Stekel (1943 [1913])	Whole neurosis personified	Lillie goes on living
254	Rosenbaum, in Gutheil (1967 [1951])	Dreams which paraphrase the neurosis	He is eating a dead body
255	Feinstein (1990)	Old personal myths personified	"You're coming with us"
255	Weiss (1986)	Defining a pattern	She serves others
256	Pomer & Shain (1980)	Dream/symptom parallels	The cat comes back to life
257	Gutheil (1967 [1951])	Symptom portrayed: fugue	Falling into unconsciousness
257	Catalano (1990)	Dream indicators of concurrent childhood sexual abuse	1. He and Mom get lost from each other 2. He drowns unheeded
257	Taylor (1992a)	Dream indicators of a history of childhood sexual abuse	Blistering white paint
257	Frederickson, in Friedman (1992)	Dream indicators of a history of childhood sexual abuse	Standing in front of a particular building
257	Cartwright & Lamberg (1992)	Dream indicators of a history of childhood sexual abuse	Stained glass windows
258	Stekel (1943 [1935])	Symptom portrayed: impotence	He can't open the door
260	Levitan (1967)	Blank dream (variant)	A huge butter cookie
260	Levitan (1981b)	Blank dream (variant)	A huge navel orange
261	Roheim (1969 [1952])	Body symbolism: basic dream	Getting down the mountain
261	Roheim (1969 [1952])	Body symbolism: masturbation	She tries to hold onto the car
261	Lewin (1958)	Body sensation → spatial image	Axe falls in House of Lords
262	Silberer (1955 [1918])	Body sensation → spatial image	Lifting table on high
262	Piaget (1962 [1945])	Body sensation → spatial image	Wet moss between two rocks
262	Cartwright (1977)	Body sensation → symbolic equivalent	Her "assets were frozen"
264	Breger et al., in Haskell (1985c)	Symptom imaged: 1. circulatory 2. bowel	1. A half dried river bed 2. Plugged pipes
264	Haskell (1985c)	Symptom imaged: hypoglycemia with diarrhea	Dog defecation like maple sugar
264	Whitmont & Perera (1989)	symptom imaged: stroke	Her roof pierced by windblown branches
264	Hunt (1989)	Symptom imaged: fever	Oscillating rattlesnake
265	Epstein (1964)	Symptom imaged: epilepsy	Fall between stars and moons
265	Maybruck (1991)	Symptom imaged: 1. ulcer 2. torn sutures	1. Peasants stomp grapes in his stomach 2. Dress seams had come apart
266	Windsor (1987)	Symptom imaged: dead fetus	Baby doing dead-man's float
266	Van de Castle, in Garfield (1991)	Symptom imaged: dead fetus	1. The baby is too cold 2. Infant in refrigerator

PAGE	SOURCE	TOPIC	DREAM
266	Garfield (1991)	Symptom imaged: 1. sore throat 2. hemorrhoids 3. broken ribs 4. hysterectomy	1. Pink stairwell 2. Impaled in the anus 3. Broken bannister 4. Jagged fender comes out her vagina
267	Jung, in Davie, in Lockhart (1977)	Archetypal medical diagnosis	Extinct animals in a drained pond
268	Jung (CW 16)	Archetypal medical diagnosis	1. Suicide of her mother 2. Suicide of a horse
268	von Franz (1986 [1984])	Archetypal medical diagnosis	Dead horse in a lead cellar
269	Ziegler, in Sabini (1981a)	Heart patient aporetic dreams; buildings as body analogs	She sinks into the mire
271	Savitz, in Haskell (1985c)	Heart disease: squeezing motif	He is squeezed between yacht and pier
271	Rainville (1988)	Heart disease: squeezing motif	Choking the hamster
273	B. Siegel (1984)	Verbal reference: medical symptoms	1. 'Cancer' written on her head 2. No cancer 3. "That's what's wrong with you"
274	Windsor (1987)	Verbal reference: medical symptoms	1. "You hurt your back picking up the brown suitcase" 2. "Your blood does not circulate well"
274	Garfield (1991)	Verbal reference: medical symptoms	1. "That's my broken arm!" 2. "You're pregnant" 3. No more migraines
274	Barrett (1993)	Verbal reference: medical symptoms	Too much dieting and exercise
275	Sabini (1981b)	Verbal reference: psychosomatic symptoms	Passing through a transition
276	Gutheil (1967 [1951])	1. Psychosomatic symptom and 2. underlying conflict symbolized	1. Mute paralysis 2. Her envied sister drowns
277	Schneider (1973)	Unadorned impulses of psychosomatics: sadomasochism	He blows his brains out
278	Levitan (1981a)	Unadorned impulses of psychosomatics: incest	His daughter wants to have sex
278	Levitan (1981a)	Inability of psychosomatics to feel emotions	Her brother bursts into tears
280	Rossi & Cheek (1988)	Physical harm from dreams	I am dying of cancer
281	Snow (unpublished)	Dreams psychodynamically mediate body symptoms	A big nice fish
283	Levitan (1984)	Premigraine dreams: terror with uncompleted threat	A Nazi shoots at her
283	Warnes & Finkelstein (1971)	Premigraine dreams with completed threat	She is shot in the head
284	Gutheil (1967 [1951])	Migraine dreams: disgust	Eating a live animal

PAGE	SOURCE	TOPIC	DREAM
284	Gutheil (1967 [1951])	Migraine dreams: disgust	She has diarrhea over her groceries
284	Levitan (1984)	Premigraine dreams: outsized creatures	Huge animal blocks the door
285	Alexander, in Warnes & Finkelstein (1971)	Peptic ulcer dreams: intaking tendencies	Not enough food
285	Warnes & Finkelstein (1971)	Peptic ulcer dreams: symptom symbolized	His house is burning
285	Warnes & Finkelstein (1971)	Ulcer dreams: images of physical trauma	1. His leg is amputated 2. He is attacked by cats 3. He tears his own teeth out 4. His stomach ruptures
285	Warnes & Finkelstein (1971)	Asthma dreams: oedipal conflict	Her mother brings water
286	Warnes & Finkelstein (1971)	Asthma dreams: symptom symbolized	A machine to suffocate people under water
286	Warnes & Finkelstein (1971)	Premigraine dreams: accidental aggression	She shoots her husband by accident
286	Gutheil (1967 [1951])	Premigraine dreams: accidental aggression	He accidentally splits his sister's head
287	Kirsch, in Sabini (1981a)	Multiple sclerosis: psychological preconditions symbolized	She stamps on a tarantula
287	Ziegler (1962)	Cardiac infarct: anagogic	Evil incarnated in a giant
289	Sabini & Maffly (1981)	The cancer pattern	He never reaches his destination

Chapter 9 • Dream Styles

299	Garfield (1988)	Menstrual dreams	A huge red purse
299	Stukane (1985 [1983])	Dreams announcing pregnancy	Two moons
300	Maybruck (1990)	Pregnancy: typical motifs	Swimming in the ocean
301	Stukane (1985 [1983])	Expectant fathers' dreams	He dances on moonlit rooftop
304	Rainville (1988)	Allo-/autocentric senses in sighted/early-blind dreams	1. Up a tree 2. Raspy tongue
305	Blank (1958)	Nonvisual dreams of early-blind	Mrs. Jones in an elevator
306	Rainville (1988) and Kirtley, in Rainville	Grand spatial imagery in dreams of late-blind	1. Bubble on the moon 2. Drifting aimlessly in space 3. The end of the earth
306	Furness, in Blank (1958)	Dreams of seeing of late-blind	He knows he is really blind
307	Shulman (1979)	Dreams of blind-deaf	Hard, heavy, and thick
310	Hartmann (1984)	Nightmares from stranger face	1. Face changes into a monster 2. Face became larger 3. Not friend but a monster 4. Not husband but an android
313	Hartmann (1984)	Posttraumatic nightmares: fading into ordinary dreams	He manages to ignore old attackers

PAGE	SOURCE	TOPIC	DREAM
313	Wilmer (1986a)	Posttraumatic nightmares: unreal elements	Heads with big holes in them
314	Ziegler (1962)	Viewpoint shift	Evil incarnated in a giant
314	Craig (1987)	Viewpoint shift	He falls from a turret toward a moat
314	Saint-Denys (1982 [1867])	Dual perspective dreams	He launches into the abyss → he observes a fallen corpse
315	Author	Dual perspective dreams	1. He is afraid of falling → 2. He watches someone fall
315	Raintree (1988)	Multiple self-representation	On the team
316	Salley (1988)	Multiple personality	1. Voices shout "Yes!"/"No!" 2. "Leave Frank alone!" 3. Crowd argues on corner 4. Chased in the woods as boy 5. A boy happy in the woods 6. Ferris wheel of faces 7. Don't party at a church
319	Lavie & Kaminer (1991)	"Dreams that poison sleep"	Selection at Auschwitz
320	Bonime (with Bonime) (1980)	Moderate depression: dependency themes	Someone else puts out the fire
321	Cartwright & Lamberg (1991)	Moderate depression: self-blame	It was my fault
323	Kramer et al. (1965)	Deep depression: escape dreams	Happy with father on a train
324	Miller (1969)	1-4. Deep depression: pleasant or bland dreams / 5-6. Improving depression: distressing dreams	1. Beautiful girls in Venice 2. Happy travelling in a car 3. New apartment 4. His wife's shortcomings 5. Made to stay on shore 6. He attends his own funeral
327	Dement (1955)	Chronic schizophrenia: bland dreams	1. A trunk and curtain rods 2. A hat 3. A shelf 4. A ripped coat 5. A suitcase
327	Biddle, in Cartwright (1972)	Chronic schizophrenia: bland dreams	1. A wash rag 2. A dilapidated house 3. An empty field
328	Cartwright (1977)	Acute schizophrenia: bland dreams	1. Good times at work 2. At home, afraid 3. Will doctor sign a pass?
328	Frosch (1976)	Schizophrenia: dreams mistaken for reality	1. Mother has intercourse with her 2. He chokes his brother-in-law
329	Kafka (1980)	Schizophrenia: reality mistaken for dream	[No dream]
329	Boss (1959 [1938])	Schizophrenia: realistic dream terrifying	A nurse straightens her pillow

PAGE	SOURCE	TOPIC	DREAM
329	Boss (1959 [1938])	Schizophrenia: progressive deterioration toward undisguised dreams	1. A cow is to be slaughtered 2. She murders mother, is raped 3. A million dollars 4. He strangles her husband
332	Carrington (1972)	Schizophrenia: overwhelming environmental threats	1. Volleyball pulverizes girl 2. Eaten alive by alligator 3. Head pressed into quicksand
332	Carrington (1972)	Schizophrenia: human physical deficit states; mutilation imagery	1. A penis torn off 2. Her veins and flesh exposed 3. Body parts in camels' heads 4. Body parts down the toilet 5. Body parts on racks 6. Decapitated, picked clean
333	Carrington (1972)	Schizophrenia: morbid dreams	1. Man sweeps up girl's bones 2. Flesh decaying in layers 3. She lies in parents' coffin 4. Ten-foot piece of decaying feces

Chapter 10 • Dream Residues

PAGE	SOURCE	TOPIC	DREAM
337	Féré, in Leveton (1961)	Dream leading to psychosomatic symptom	Men try to stab her
337	Bartemeier (1950)	Dream → psychosomatic symptom	"You had better tell me"
338	Levitan (1976/77b)	Dream → compulsive neurosis	Visualizes himself as skeleton
339	Levitan (1974)	Dream → phobia	At each obstacle an orgasm
340	Bartemeier (1950)	Dream → depression	Her girlfriend was murdered
340	Frosch (1976)	Dream → schizophrenia	Rotten tree of life
341	Seidenberg (1958)	Dream → psychotic breakdown	He feels himself dying
341	Levitan (1976/77a)	Dream → depersonalization	Into a thousand pieces
342	Levitan (1968)	Dream → depersonalization	Steel case falls over him
342	Leveton (1961)	Recurrent dream → schizophrenia	The devil takes his body over
343	Shulman (1969)	Latency between dream and onset of psychotic relapse	He walks through door in side of cliff
344	Boss (1959 [1938])	Latency between dream and onset of psychosis	1. The ship sinks, he drowns 2. Eclipse of the sun 3. A little black cat drowns 4. Last bubble rises from skull
345	Mack (1969)	Psychosis portrayed literally	His illness had returned
346	Boss, in Lehmann (1969)	Dreams foreshadowing psychosis	1. World turns into stone 2. World turns into skeletons 3. World engulfed by emptiness
346	Jung (1965 [1961])	Latent psychosis revealed	1. Idiot child smeared with feces 2. Pursued by dangerous maniac
347	Friedman (1992)	Latent psychosis revealed	1. She twists pets' necks 2. White of eye turns to jelly

PAGE	SOURCE	TOPIC	DREAM
348	Raphling (1970)	1. Presuicidal: destruction motif 2-3. Presuicidal: death motif	1. Trapped by insane killer 2. Drowning watched helplessly 3. Aunt comes back from death
348	Hendin, in Friedman (1992)	Presuicidal: death symbolized, idealized	A couple stands over a manger
349	Gutheil (1967 [1951])	Presuicidal: various motifs	There is nothing ahead
350	Litman (1980)	Presuicidal: literal preparation	She drives over cliff and dies
350	Lebe (1980)	Anagogic: literal preparation	He understood the math
352	Freud (1953 [1900])	Recall as dream continuation	Some gaps in the dream
353	Kanzer (1955)	Recall as dream continuation	Something about his girl friend
353	Wolff (1972 [1952])	Recall as dream continuation	Surprised to be dreaming
353	Stekel (1943)	Association as continuation	Savage lions and tigers
354	Frosch, in Mack (1969)	Acting out dreams	She becomes a prostitute
354	Sterba (1946)	Acting out dreams	He takes off his spectacles
355	Whitmont & Perera (1989)	Acting out dreams	The door is wide open
356	Roth (1958)	Acting out dreams	Golf ball hits the door frame
357	Mack (1989 [1970])	Acting out dreams	He left his slides at home
357	Volkan & Bhatti (1973)	Acting out dreams	Kirk Douglas falls in a mud puddle
358	Kelman (1975)	Acting out dreams	A little creature who levitates
359	Lebe (1980)	Acting out dreams	Crosswalks are for protection
360	Williams (1986 [1980])	Actualizing dreams	1. Her suitcases are overpacked 2. She packs correctly
360	Johnson (1986)	Ritualizing dreams	Junk food
361	Morris (1987 [1985])	Ritualizing dreams	She can ride a bicycle

Chapter 11 • Initial and Termination Dreams

PAGE	SOURCE	TOPIC	DREAM
364	Ullman (1986b)	Dreams for another: psi	Mass in mother's womb
364	Snow (1993)	Dreams for another: U.S. black folk beliefs	She is fishing in a front yard puddle
365	Garfield (1988a)	1. Permission dreams 2. Emotional healing dreams	1. Permission for new love 2. Poison ivy sore drains clean
365	Krippner & Dillard (1988)	Breakthrough dreaming	She blasts through the ceiling
365	Garfield (1988a)	Breakthrough dreaming	Through crystal shell
366	Morrison (1989)	Addiction recovery dreams	Moving to a higher floor
368	Saul et al., in Rangell, in Kelman (1975)	Initial dreams	She takes a trip with a free ticket
368	Weiss (1986)	Initial dreams	Getting the troubleshooter
369	Jung, in Mattoon (1984 [1978])	Initial dreams	1. Can't cross the frontier [#1] 2. Can't cross the frontier [#2] 3. She crosses the Swiss frontier
370	Stekel (1943)	Initial dreams	Dark cave
371	Bosnak (1989)	Initial dreams	He visits Aunt Lib

PAGE	SOURCE	TOPIC	DREAM
372	Whitman (1980)	Reparative fantasy dreams	Cauterized lesion amazes him
372	Whitman (1980)	Pseudocurative fantasy dreams	Two farmhouses
372	Whitman (1980)	Curative fantasy dreams	She dances with her therapist
373	Kirsch (1979)	1. An early dream contrasts with: 2. a termination dream	1. Problems meeting therapist 2. She shows him her kitchen
373	Cavenar & Spaulding (1978)	Termination dreams	1. Blue washes away forever 2. Cracked window is repaired
374	Mankowitz (1984)	Termination dreams	Club of her old friends

Chapter 12 • The Non-interpretation of Dreams

377	Beck (1977)	Dream-telling without interpretation in family therapy	1. Toilet too tall [Son] 2. Toilet too tall [Mother]
381	Delaney (1991)	Dream interviewing	Huge sports arena
381	Ellis (1988a)	Dream drama	He's in the back seat, bored
383	Koch-Sheras et al. (1983)	Dream drawing	Ma Bell
385	Jung (1984 [1938])	Dream music	Socrates, make more music
385	Gregory (1988a)	Dreamwork with children	Difficult bluebird
386	Wiseman (1987)	Dreamwork with children	Her house is on fire
387	West (1978)	Dreamwork with children	She falls into monster's jaws
391	Solovey & Milechnin, in Haskell, in Garfield (1991)	Medical healing in dreams	She beat the animal with her bad arm
392	Fellows (1988)	Lucid dream control: benefits	To simply walk ahead

Chapter 13 • Incubation

393	Koulack (1986)	Dreams about daytime preoccupations	1. Bull semen for insemination 2. Looking for tricycles
397	Goodenough et al., in Koulack (1986)	Incorporation	Parachutists jump from airplane
398	Antrobus, in Haskell (1986b)	Incorporation by conditioning	Cutting pie with a kitchen knife
400	Domhoff & Kamiya (1964b)	1-5. ♀ reactions to sleep lab 6-9. ♂ reactions to sleep lab	1. Unfulfilled obligation 2. Photographed dreaming 3. Psychologist is sinking ships 4. All subjects die 5. Guillotine tops her head 6. Intellectual failure 7. He disappoints experimenter 8. Subjects horse-race 9. Sleeping on the front lawn
400	Fox et al. (1968)	1-3. ♂ dreamer, ♀ experimenter 4. ♀ dreamer, ♂ experimenter	1. In a combat situation 2. He has a bloody nose 3. He is laughed at by women 4. Intravenous runs smoothly

PAGE	SOURCE	TOPIC	DREAM
400	Fox et al. (1968) *(continued)*	5-6. ♀ dreamer, ♀ experimenter	5. Intravenous not connected 6. Intravenous running dry
409	Krippner & Dillard (1988)	Asclepian incubation: the god's touch	Asclepius opened his eyes with his fingers
409	Lewis (1976)	Asclepian: sexual contact	He ejaculates the stone
410	Lewis (1976)	Asclepian: the god's touch	The god's horses trample his paralyzed knee
410	Lewis (1976)	Asclepian: cured skeptics	She must dedicate a silver pig
410	Krippner & Dillard (1988)	Asclepian: dream prescriptions	Pine nuts with honey
411	C. A. Meier (1967 [1949])	Asclepian: dream prescriptions	1. "Lord, what for a Jew?" 2. A winter bath in the river
411	Sanford (1977)	Contemporary Asclepian	The snake bites her ill son
412	F. Meier (1966)	Islamic spiritual preparation	He finally sees God in a dream
416	Schatzman (1983)	Incubated solutions to brain teaser	1. Stereographic drawings 2. "Try three-dimensional"
417	Barrett (1993)	Incubation to solve a conflict: conflicting answers	1. Country club wedding 2. "I don't want to marry him!"
418	Schroetter, in Silberer (1955 [1918])	Incubation by posthypnotic suggestion	Abnormally small, abnormally large
421	Levay & Weissberg (1979)	Sex therapy as implicit dream incubation	1. She plays with father's penis 2. Sex play with brother
421	Weiss (1986)	Explicit incubation in therapy	Off to the side with the food
422	Windsor (1987)	Incubation of serial dreams	1. The tunnel → 2. The key → 3. The treasure
424	Delaney (1979)	Phrase focusing: the right night	Classical birds
425	Delaney (1979)	Dream advice unheeded	The Titanic
426	Delaney (1979)	Dream advice heeded	Where is Bret?
427	Cartwright (1977)	Incubating on character defects	She is not very diplomatic
427	Reneau (no date)	Unexpected answer incubated	Black bumps all over her face
430	Camino (personal communication)	Incubation in African-American non-orthodox healing	Brother: break it off with the woman

Chapter 14 • Lucidity

431	Lattimore (1951)	Ancient LDs	"Are you sleeping?"
435	Wolff (1972 [1952])	Mundane LDs	Surprised to be dreaming
435	LaBerge (1985)	Transpersonal LDs	"I praise Thee, O Lord!"
438	Arkin et al. (1966)	Sleep speech dream reports	1. A film of past experiences 2. Colbert puts on the make
440	Cartwright & Lamberg (1992)	Control without full lucidity	"I have to do something"
441	Borges (1976)	Lucid control imperfect	A desiccated tiger
442	Price & Cohen (1988)	LD cognitive skills	Saving a dream sandwich
443	Saint-Denys (1982 [1867])	LD self-reflectivity; out-of-body experience	Visit to the moon

PAGE	SOURCE	TOPIC	DREAM
443	Saint-Denys (1982 [1867])	LD self-reflectivity	"Make sure you remember this dream"
444	Reis, in Tholey (1989)	LD self-reflectivity	Mr. Spock: "You're dreaming"
446	D. W. (1989)	Emotion defeats lucidity	He loses it from the excitement
447	Garfield (1989 [1979])	Orgasmic LDs	1. It is her father 2. Horse-goat in Zal's glasses 3. Hermaphroditic autoeroticism 4. Arching backward 5. Floating 6. Watching a golden egg 7. Circling 8. Plummeting
449	Garfield (1984)	Children's LDs	1. He gets up for drink of water 2. Watching green ticklemen 3. Looking at mummy cases 4. Looking at Lord Krishna
454	T. P. (1989)	Lucidity triggers	Daylight switches to night
455	K. S. (1989)	Lucidity triggers	His dead wife is there alive
455	P. K. (1991)	Lucidity triggers	Giant bubbles
455	LaBerge & Rheingold (1990)	Lucidity triggers	[Miscellaneous]
460	Gregory (1984)	Lucid hypnagogic dreams	Bow and box
462	Gackenbach & Bosveld (1989)	LD for medical healing	"You have received two healings"
463	LaBerge & Rheingold (1990)	LD for medical healing	Geodesic breast lump
464	Maguire (1989)	LD for problem-solving	Which of three presents?
464	LaBerge & Rheingold (1990)	Creative applications of LD	Programming with Einstein
465	Garfield (1989 [1979])	Lucid in-dream interpretation	1. "Significance of red hair?" 2. "Red is my natural color!"
466	Pelgrin, in Sabini (1981a)	Self-explanatory nonlucid dreams	It could be psychosomatic
466	Faraday (1976 [1974])	Self-explanatory nonlucid dreams	She bashes him to death
466	Baylis (1976)	Self-explanatory nonlucid dreams	Flowers: "Return to Sender"
467	A. Siegel (1992)	Self-explanatory nonlucid dreams	Furry animal in a water bubble
467	Delaney (1979)	Self-explanatory nonlucid dreams	Dancing redwoods
468	Gordon (1991)	Lucid in-dream interpretation	The maze of ordinary reality
470	White-Lewis (1992)	Lucid control: dangerous	She cleans up the garbage
471	Gackenbach & Bosveld (1990)	Psyche safe from over-control	Scary blast-off
471	Price & Cohen (1988)	Psyche safe from over-control	An onlooker's angry reaction
471	Taylor (1983)	Psyche safe from over-control	"There he goes, flying again"
474	LaBerge (1985)	LD exhilaration	Never been awake before
474	LaBerge & Rheingold (1990)	LD exhilaration	The invisible relationships
475	Fox, in LaBerge (1988a)	LD exhilaration	So inexpressibly free

PAGE	SOURCE	TOPIC	DREAM
476	Delaney (1979)	Witnessing; dreamless sleep	Practicing French *etc.*
477	Gregory (1988c)	Witnessing; dreamless sleep	Lucid all night long
477	Gackenbach et al., in Alexander et al. (1986)	Witnessing; dreamless sleep	Awake inside in a blissful state
477	Gackenbach & Bosveld (1989)	Witnessing; dreamless sleep	Not dreaming, not awake
478	Gillespie (1985)	Clear Light dreamless sleep	The Clear Light
479	Sparrow (1982 [1976])	First LD a dream of light	Blending, melting colors, light
480	Sparrow (1982 [1976])	First LD a dream of light	Brilliant white light

Chapter 15 • Re-entry

PAGE	SOURCE	TOPIC	DREAM
488	Bosnak (1988 [1986])	Active imagination	Black-and-blue on her neck
490	Jung, in Johnson (1986)	Active imagination	His girlfriend is drowning
491	Rossi (1985 [1972])	Active imagination and Gestalt	Bomb is huge bitten apple
493	Wiseman (1987)	Active imagination and Gestalt	She never finds the crying child
494	Barz (1990)	Psychodrama	He cannot jump into crevice
496	Wiseman (1991)	Restaging	She is buried alive in avalanche
496	Reneau (no date)	Re-structuring	Wire broom does a bad job

Chapter 16 • The Bo Tree Principle

PAGE	SOURCE	TOPIC	DREAM
505	Downing & Marmorstein (1973)	Bo tree experience under LSD	Bat-monster → awesome triple image
505	Bosnak (1989)	Bo tree waking vision series	1. The Spectre of Aids → 2. Shekhina
506	Greene, in Grant (1986 [1984])	Spontaneous discovery of the bo tree principle in childhood	1. Witch jumps on him → 2. He turns to face the witch
506	Craig (1987)	Bo tree series in therapy	1. Humiliated at family gathering → 2. He shows his sister out
506	Sanford (1984 [1966])	Bo tree series in therapy	1. Enemy kills him → 2. Enemy smiles, walks away
507	Phillips (1989)	Bo tree series from keeping dream diary	1. Nazi-capture-torture-death → 2. Rescued by Germans → 3. Kills attacker: no joy → 4. Alliance with commandant
507	Krippner & Dillard (1988)	Bo tree series: gradual transformation of dream tone	1. Rapist → 2. Lover → 3. Herself
507	Corriere et al. (1980)	Transformation mid-dream	Gorilla → helpful man
507	Clift & Clift (1984)	Transformation mid-dream	Wild pig → beautiful woman
508	Rycroft (1981 [1979])	Transformation mid-dream	Charging bull → Graceful swan
508	Garfield (1989 [1979])	Transformation mid-dream	Pusball → bell → flower

PAGE	SOURCE	TOPIC	DREAM
508	Rossi (1985 [1972])	Transformation mid-dream: abortive	Bug → butterflies → bug
509	Garfield (1984)	Tactic: annihilation	He blows house to bits, rebuilds good half
510	Koch-Sheras et al. (1983)	Tactic: annihilation	Blue velvet dress
510	LaBerge (1985)	Tactic: annihilation	Muggers → flowers
511	Williams (1986 [1980])	Tactic: self-assertion	She needs permission to use the road
512	Halliday (1988)	Tactic: mastery	1. Molested as a child → 2. She changes some colors
512	Palace & Johnston (1989)	Tactic: mastery	Bad guys kill his friend and hurt him
513	Tholey (1988)	Tactic: tactical withdrawal	Top dog → tiny puppy
513	Tholey (1988)	Tactic: dialogue and conciliation	Pursuing tiger → friendly father
514	Sparrow (1982 [1962])	Tactic: restraint	Hostile men → become playful
514	Saint-Denys (1982 [1867])	Tactic: restraint	Hideous pursuers → bundle of rags
515	Mindell (1990)	Tactic: being annihilated	A woman is being burned alive
516	Kelsey (1978)	Tactic: being annihilated	He tries to put out fire in childhood home
516	Zeller (1990 [1975])	Tactic: care-giving	Gnarled witch → beautiful boy
516	Sparrow (1982 [1976])	Tactic: compassion	Pursuer → friend
517	LaBerge (1985)	Tactic: love	Ogre → dreamer himself
518	Koch-Sheras et al. (1983)	Incubation	1. Man with axe over bed → 2. Fossil → half-senile man → 3. He consents to be beheaded
519	Krippner & Dillard (1988)	Incubation and semi-lucidity	1. She flees from monster → 2. The monster disappears → 3. Monster → horse → lover
519	Faraday (1976 [1974])	Incubation and semi-lucidity	Bruiser → becomes civil
520	Anonymous (personal communication)	Lucidity	1. She dismisses the abuser → 2. She asks for a gift
520	Neu (1988)	Re-entry	He is pursued by a terrible bear
520	Shaffer (1986)	Re-entry: guided	Grizzlies prowl outside
521	Eccles et al. (1988)	Re-entry: desensitization	1. Snakes attack 2. Crossing bridges
521	Eichelman (1985)	Re-entry under hypnosis, as incubation	1. He sees the bullet coming → 2. Bullet → whipped cream pie
523	Mindell (1985)	Dreambody work	She is an abandoned child
525	Mindell, in Zwig (1990b)	Dreambody work	The devil has thrown her into a hole

Notes

Introduction

1. A. Moffitt (1990). **2.** W. Stekel (1943), p. 329. **3.** H. T. Hunt (1989), p. 3. **4.** M.-T.B. Dombeck (1991). **5.** S. Freud, *Fragment of an Analysis of a Case of Hysteria*, 1905, quoted by H. Fiss (1979), p. 64. **6.** S. Freud (1953 [1900]), p. 525. **7.** C. G. Jung, *Modern Man in Search of a Soul*, New York: Harcourt, Brace and World, p. 11, 1933, quoted by M. Ullman & N. Zimmerman (1979), p. 53. **8.** B. Kilborne (1992 [1987]), p. 173. **9.** H. T. Hunt (1989), p. 174. **10.** Ibid., pp. 96 and 101. **11.** J. Taylor (1983), p. 52. **12.** H. T. Hunt (1989), p. 4. **13.** G. G. Globus (1991), p. 32. **14.** C. A. Meier (1969), p. 101. **15.** M. Ullman (1987 [1978]), p. iv. **16.** M. Ullman (1982 [1962]), p. xvi. **17.** L. van den Daele (1992), p. 100. **18.** M. Boss (1977), pp. 4-7, citing articles by M. D. Zane and M. H. Eckhardt in J. H. Masserman, editor, *Dream Dynamics (Scientific Proceedings of the American Academy of Psychoanalysis, Science and Analysis*, vol. 19), New York: Grune & Stratton, 1971. **19.** P. Berry (1974), pp. 59-60. **20.** G. Levitte & G. Caseril, "Les rêves et leurs interprétations dans les textes post-biblique" (quoting *Berakhot* 55B), *Evidences* II, p. 20, 1960, quoted by R. Caillois (1966), p. 26. See also S. Lorand (1957), p. 96. **21.** 1. S. Krippner (1990b), p. 90. **2.** H. Warnes & A. Finkelstein (1971), p. 318. **3.** H. Warnes & A. Finkelstein (1971), p. 317-8. **4.** Respectively: J. A. Hadfield (1954), p. 169; C. Sagan (1978 [1977]), pp. 87-8. **5.** S. Freud (1953 [1900]), p. 271. **6.** H. Kohut, cited by J. E. Gedo (1980), p. 196. **7.** W. Stekel, cited by E. A. Gutheil (1967 [1951]), p. 219. **8.** Respectively: H. L. Levitan (1967), pp. 316-7; L. J. Saul & B. A. Fleming (1959), p. 502; S. Krippner (1990b), p. 90; J. A. Hadfield (1954), p. 169. **9.** A. Adler, cited by E. A. Gutheil (1967 [1951]), p. 219. **10.** S. Freud (1953 [1900]), p. 394. **11.** Respectively: M. Ullman & N. Zimmerman (1979), p. 108; W. Karle, R. Corriere, J. Hart & L. Woldenberg (1980), p. 71. **12.** L. Gold (1979), p. 336. **13.** P. Garfield (1984), p. 66. **14.** S. Krippner (1990b), p. 90. **15.** E. T. Gendlin (1986), p. 88. **16.** G. Delaney (1991), p. 369. **17.** A. Faraday (1976 [1974]), p. 71. **18.** G. Delaney (1991), p. 369. **19.** Respectively: S. Freud (1953 [1900]), p. 394; A. B. Siegel (1990), p. 47; H. Silberer (1955 [1918]), p. 382. **20.** A. Faraday (1976 [1974]), p. 72. **21.** G. Delaney (1979), p. 175. **22.** C. E. Green (1969), p. 55. **23.** P. Garfield (1984), p. 66. **24.** Respectively: J. Campbell (1980), p. 68; S. Krippner (1990b), p. 90. **22.** M. Sabini, personal communication, 1993, reacting to this passage. **23.** R. D. Cartwright (1977), p. 89. **24.** E. A. Gutheil (1967 [1951]), p. 178. **25.** H. T. Hunt (1989), p. 75. **26.** W. Wolff (1972 [1952]), p. 1. **27.** E. T. Gendlin (1986), p. 2.

Chapter 1 • REM, etc.

1. H. Fiss (1979), p. 21. **2.** W. C. Dement (1974 [1972]), p. 25. **3.** E. Aserinsky & N. Kleitman (1953). **4.** For example, A. Garma (1987 [1978]), p. 16. **5.** C. Binz, *Über den Traum*, Bonn, 1878, quoted by S. Freud (1953 [1900]), p. 77. **6.** T. Melnechuk (1983), p. 32, citing F. Crick & G. Mitchison (1983). **7.** S. Freud (1953 [1900]), p. 63. **8.** For example, J. A. Sanford (1984 [1966]). **9.** P. Garfield (1989 [1979]), p. 128. **10.** A. Faraday (1972), p. 22. **11.** E. Hartmann (1984), p. 18. **12.** W. C. Dement (1974 [1972]), p. 25. **13.** W. C. Dement (1966), p. 83. **14.** M. Jouvet & F. Michel, "Nouvelles recherches sur les structures responsables de la 'phase paradoxale' du sommeil," *Journal de Physiologie* (Paris) 52, pp. 130-1, 1960, cited by W. C. Dement (1966). **15.** J. A. Hobson (1988), pp. 146 and 150. **16.** Ansevics, cited by H. Doweiko (1982), p. 32. **17.** W. C. Dement (1974 [1972]), p. 26. H. Fiss (1979), p. 27. **18.** P. Hauri, *The Sleep Disorders*,

Kalamazoo: Upjohn, 1982 and other sources cited by W. Moorcroft & J. Clothier (1986), p. 33. **19.** Respectively: E. Hartmann (1984), p. 17; R. Greenberg, C. A. Pearlman & D. Gampel (1972), p. 29; E. Hartmann (1967), p. 92; M. Stern, D. H. Fram, R. Wyatt, L. Grinspoon & B. Tursky (1969), pp. 471-3. **20.** W. Dement & N. Kleitman (1957a), p. 342. **21.** R. D. Cartwright (1978), p. 12. **22.** Respectively: D. G. Schwartz, L. N. Weinstein & A. M. Arkin (1978), p. 150, citing F. Snyder, "The phenomenology of dreaming," in H. Madow & L. H. Snow, editors, *The Psychodynamic Implications of the Physiological Studies on Dreams*, Springfield, Illinois: Charles C. Thomas, 1970; W. C. Dement (1966), p. 99, citing W. Dement & E. A. Wolpert (1958). **23.** T. Allison & H. Van Twyver (1974 [1970]), p. 348. **24.** N. Kleitman, *Sleep and Wakefulness*, Chicago: University of Chicago, 1963, cited by D. F. Kripke (1972). **25.** R. D. Cartwright (1977), p. 125. **26.** S. LaBerge (1985), p. 49. **27.** A. Rechtschaffen & P. Verdone (1964), p. 955. **28.** C. Dreyfus-Brisac, "The EEG of the premature infant and the full term newborn," in P. Kelloway & I. Peterson, editors, *Neurological and Electroencephalographic Correlative Studies of Infancy*, Philadelphia: Grune & Stratton, 1964. A. Parmalee, "Maturation of EEG activity during sleep in premature infants," *Electroencephalography and Clinical Neurophysiology* 24, p. 319. Both cited by R. D. Cartwright (1977), p. 10. **29.** H. Fiss (1979), p. 26. **30.** 26th week: I. Lewin & J. L. Singer (1991), citing R. L. Williams, I. Karacan & C. J. Hursch, *Electroencephalography (EEG) of Human Sleep: Clinical Applications*, New York: Wiley, 1974. 32nd week: T. Verny with J. Kelly, *The Secret Life of the Unborn Child*, New York: Delta, pp. 41-2, 1981, cited by P. Garfield (1988a), p. 206. **31.** J. A. Hobson (1988), p. 292, citing A. H. Parmalee, Jr., W. H. Wenner, Y. Akiyama, M. Schultz & E. Stern, "Sleep states in premature infants," *Developmental Medicine and Child Neurology* 9, pp. 70-7, 1967. **32.** A. Moffitt, M. Kramer & R. Hoffmann (1993b), p. 7. **33.** Respectively: D. Foulkes (1985), p. 121; W. C. Kohler, R. D. Coddington & H. W. Agnew, Jr. (1968). **34.** P. Garfield (1988a), p. 311. **35.** R. L. Williams, I. Karacan & C. J. Hursch, *Electroencephalography (EEG) of Human Sleep: Clinical Applications*, New York: Wiley, 1974. R. Spiegel, *Sleep and Sleeplessness in Advanced Age*, Jamaica, New York: Spectrum, 1981. Both cited by P. Garfield (1988a), p. 18. **36.** A. Rechtschaffen & P. Verdone (1964), p. 952. **37.** E. Hartmann (1966). **38.** R. Greenberg, C. A. Pearlman & D. Gampel (1972), p. 29. **39.** P. Wood, *Dreaming and Social Isolation*, Ph.D. dissertation, University of North Carolina, 1962, cited by P. Garfield (1976), p. 69. **40.** J. Taylor (1992a), pp. 86-7. **41.** G. Delaney (1991), p. 19. **42.** S. Shulman (1979), p. 190. **43.** S. Davies & A. Stewart (1987), p. 109. **44.** P. Hauri, *The Sleep Disorders*, Kalamazoo: Upjohn, 1982, cited by W. Moorcroft & J. Clothier (1986), p. 39. **45.** S. C. Gresham, W. B. Webb & R. L. Williams (1963), p. 1227. **46.** M. Kramer (1991c), p. 178. **47.** J. Taylor (1992a), p. 87. **48.** A. J. Ziegler (1976), p. 62. **49.** J. Kales, C. Allen, T. A. Preston, T.-L. Tan & A. Kales (1970). **50.** J. Taylor (1992a), p. 87. J. Eisen, J. MacFarlane & C. M. Shapiro (1993). **51.** D. Koulack (1991), pp. 102-3. **52.** J. Eisen, J. MacFarlane & C. M. Shapiro (1993). D. Riemann, C. Lauer, B. Dippel & M. Berger (1989), p. 4. **53.** H. Greenhouse (1974b), p. 391. **54.** J. Taylor (1992a), p. 87. J. Eisen, J. MacFarlane & C. M. Shapiro (1993). **55.** C. Idzikowski & C. M. Shapiro (1993). **56.** S. C. Gresham, W. B. Webb & R. L. Williams (1963), p. 1227. **57.** S. Kendall (1994), citing Quentin Regestein, director of the Sleep Disorder Service at Brigham and Women's Hospital, Cambridge, Massachusetts; Q. Regestein (personal communication, 1994). **58.** N. MacKenzie (1965), p. 263. **59.** B. Zilbergeld, *Male Sexuality*, New York: Bantam, 1968, cited by P. Maybruck (1991), p. 168. **60.** C. Fisher, J. Gross & J. Zuch (1965), p. 33 passim. I. Karacan, D. R. Goodenough, A. Shapiro & S. Starker (1966), p. 184 passim. **61.** R. E. Rainville (1988), p. 9. **62.** M. D. Wasserman, M. R. Pressman, C. P. Pollak, A. J. Spielman, L. DeRosairo & E. D. Weitzman (1982). **63.** P. Garfield (1988a), p. 105ff. **64.** C. Fisher, H. D. Cohen, R. C. Schiavi, D. Davis, B. Furman, K. Ward, A. Edwards & J. Cunningham, "Patterns of female sexual arousal during sleep and waking: vaginal thermo-conductance studies," *Archives of Sexual Behavior* 12(2), pp. 97-122, 1983, cited by P. Garfield (1988a), pp. 107-8. C. Fisher, "dreaming and sexuality," in R. M. Loewenstein, editor, *Psychoanalysis—A General Psychology*, New York: International Universities, 1966, cited by D. Koulack (1991), p. 53. **65.** E. Sheppard (1969), pp. 249-50. **66.** C. Fisher, J. Gross & J. Zuch, "Cycle of penile erection synchronous with dreaming (REM) sleep," *Archives of General Psychiatry* 12, pp. 29-45, 1965, cited by E. Hartmann (1967), p. 130. **67.** I. Karacan, D. R. Goodenough, A. Shapiro & S. Starker (1966), p. 187. **68.** E. Kahn & C. Fisher (1968). **69.** A. Rechtschaffen (1978). **70.** C. Fisher, J. Gross & J. Byrne (1965), "Dissociation of penile erections from REMP and rebound effect," paper presented to the Association for the Psychophysiological Study of Sleep, Gainesville, Florida, 1965, cited by R. D. Cartwright (1977), p. 60. **71.** P. Garfield (1989 [1979]), p. 139. **72.** J. A. Hobson (1988), p. 207. **73.** W. Dement & N. Kleitman (1957b), p. 682. **74.** W. Dement & E. A. Wolpert (1958). **75.** W. Dement & N. Kleitman (1957b), p. 682. **76.** R. Gardner, W. I. Grossman, H. P. Roffwarg & H. Weiner (1975), pp. 155-6. **77.** S. LaBerge (1988b), p. 148. **78.** M. Gerne & I. Strauch, "Psychophysiological indicators of affect patterns and conversational patterns during sleep," in W. P. Koella, E. Ruther & H. Schulz, editors, *Sleep '84*, Stuttgart: Gustav Fischer, pp. 367-9, 1985, cited by T. A. Nielsen (1988). **79.** F. Heynick (1991), p. 88. **80.** A. M. Arkin, M. F. Toth, J. Baker & J. M. Hastey (1970a). See also A. M. Arkin, *Sleeptalking: Psychology and Psychophysiology*, Hillside, New Jersey: Lawrence Erlbaum. 1981. **81.** A. M. Arkin, M. F. Toth, J. Baker & J. M. Hastey (1970b), pp. 382 and 392. **82.** A. Jacobson & A. Kales, "Somnambulism: all-night EEG and related studies," in S. S. Kety, E. V. Evarts & H. L. Williams, editors, *Sleep and Altered States of Consciousness*, Baltimore: Williams & Wilkins, 1967, cited by E. R. Hilgard (1977), p. 95. **83.** R. Cartwright & L. Lamberg (1992), p. 242. **84.** C. H. Schenck, D. M. Milner, T. D. Hurwitz, S. R. Bundlie & M. W. Mahowald (1989), p. 1171. **85.** Ibid., pp. 1168-9. **86.** Ibid., p. 1171. **87.** R. Cartwright & L. Lamberg (1992), p. 242. **88.** J. E. Mack (1989 [1970]), p. 194. **89.** G. T. Ladd (1892). **90.** W. Dement & E. A. Wolpert (1958), p. 548. **91.** W. Dement & N. Kleitman (1957a), p. 344. **92.** H. P. Roffwarg, W. C. Dement, J. N. Muzio & C. Fisher (1962), pp. 245-6. **93.** J. A. Hobson (1989), pp. 156-7. The quote comes from (1988), p. 166. **94.** D. Koulack (1991), p. 52. **95.** J. H. Herman, M. Erman, R. Boys, L. Peiser, M. E. Taylor & H. P. Roffwarg (1984), p. 61. **96.** L. D. Jacobs, M. Feldman & M. B. Bender (1970). **97.** E. Moscowitz & R. J. Berger (1969), p. 614. **98.** S. LaBerge (1988b), p. 148. **99.** M. Schatzman, A. Worsley & P. Fenwick (1988), pp. 156-7. **100.** M. Jouvet, "Telencephalic and rhombencephalic sleep in cat," in G. Wolstenholme & M. O'Connor, editors, *Ciba Foundation Symposium on Nature of Sleep*, London: J. & A. Churchill, 1961, pp. 188-200, cited by C. Fisher, J. Gross & J. Zuch (1965), p. 43. **101.** D. Foulkes (1985), p. 57. **102.** J. A. Hobson (1988), p. 143. **103.** H. Fiss (1979), p. 45. D. Foulkes (1985), p. 63. **104.** W. Dement (1955), p. 265. **105.** M. Koukkou-Lehmann (1990). **106.** J. A. Hobson (1989), p. 154. **107.** R. D. Cartwright (1977), p. 9. **108.** R. T. Pivik & D. Foulkes (1968). **109.** A. Faraday (1972), pp. 41-2. Punctuation added. **110.** A. Rechtschaffen, P. Verdone & J. Wheaton (1963), p. 411. **111.** J. Antrobus, "REM and NREM sleep responses: comparison of word frequencies by cognitive classes," *Psychophysiology* 20, pp. 562-8, 1983, cited by H. T. Hunt 1989, p. 163. **112.** H. T. Hunt (1989), p. 163, citing D. Foulkes & M. Schmidt, "Temporal sequence and unit composition in dream reports from different stages of sleep," *Sleep* 6, pp. 265-80, 1983 and H. S. Porte & J. A. Hobson, "Bizarreness in REM and NREM sleep reports," *Sleep Research* 15, p. 81, 1986. **113.** D. Foulkes (1985). **114.** W. B. Zimmerman (1970), p. 545. **115.** R. D. Cartwright (1977), pp. 110-1. **116.** W. C. Dement (1974 [1972]), p. 92. **117.** R. Cartwright & L. Lamberg (1992), p. 57. **118.** S. Purcell, J. Mullington, A. Moffitt, R. Hoffmann & R. Pigeau (1986), p. 434. **119.** Non-lucidity: G. Delaney (1979), pp. 94-5 and 99; M. A. Mattoon (1984), pp. 85-6. Semi-lucidity: E. Rossi (1985), pp. 156-7. Lucidity: P. Garfield (1989 [1979]), pp. 132-3; J. Gregory (1984), pp. 364-5. **120.** J. A. Hobson (1988), p. 143. **121.** D. Foulkes (1985), pp. 58-9. **122.** H. Fiss, G. S. Klein & E. Bokert (1966), p. 545. **123.** D. Foulkes (1985), p. 62. **124.** Ibid., p. 59. **125.** L. J. Monroe, A. Rechtschaffen, D. Foulkes & J. Jensen (1965). **126.** K. M. T. Hearne, *Lucid Dreams: An Electrophysiological and Physiological Study*, Ph.D. dissertation, University of Liverpool, 1982, pp. 151 and 212, cited by M. Schatzman (1982), p. 6. **127.** G. Delaney (1979), pp. 168-70. S. LaBerge (1985), pp. 123-4. J. Gregory

(1988c), p. 8. **128.** H. Shevrin (1986), p. 392, citing H. Shevrin & C. Fisher, "Changes in the effects of a waking subliminal stimulus as a function of dreaming and non-dreaming sleep," *Journal of Abnormal Psychology* 72, pp. 362-8, 1967. **129.** W. Dement & N. Kleitman (1957a), p. 34. **130.** W. Dement (1966), pp. 96-7, quoting D. Foulkes, "Dream reports from different stages of sleep," *Journal of Abnormal and Social Psychology* 65, pp. 14-25, 1962. **131.** G. W. Domhoff (1 985), p. 102, citing C. S. Hall, unpublished data. **132.** R. T. Pivik (1991), p. 217. **133.** A. Faraday (1972), pp. 42-3. **134.** G. W. Domhoff (1985), p. 102. **135.** D. Foulkes (1985), p. 60. **136.** R. L. Tracy & L. N. Tracy (1974), p. 647. **137.** D. Foulkes (1978), p. 91. **138.** M. Ullman & S. Krippner (1970), p. 40. **139.** M. Ullman & N. Zimmerman (1979), p. 66. **140.** H. Silberer (1955 [1918]), pp. 365. This material was first published in "Bericht . . . " etc., 1909, quoted by S. Freud (1953 [1900]), p. 344. **141.** Ibid., p. 368. **142.** Ibid., p. 370. **143.** C. S. Moss (1970), p. 19. **144.** L. N. Weinstein, D. G. Schwartz & A. M. Arkin (1991), pp. 207-8, citing P. Cicogna, C. Cavallero & M. Bosinelli, "Different access to memory traces in the production of mental experience," *International Journal of Psychophysiology* 4, pp. 209-16, 1986. **145.** P. Cicogna, C. Cavallero & M. Bosinelli (1991), p. 421. **146.** H. T. Hunt (1989), p. 181, citing C. Green & C. McCreery, *Apparitions*, London: Hamish Hamilton, 1975. **147.** H. T. Hunt, R. Ogilvie, K. Belicki, D. Belicki & E. Atalick (1982), p. 581. This and subsequent quotes are reproduced with permission of the author and publisher. See credit page. **148.** S. LaBerge (1985), p. 48. **149.** G. Vogel, D. Foulkes & H. Trosman (1966). Also see E. Gibson, F. Perry, D. Redington & J. Kamiya (1982). **150.** Ibid., p. 242. **151.** D. Foulkes, P. S. Spear & J. D. Symonds (1966). **152.** D. Foulkes (1985), pp. 70-1. **153.** J. Piaget (1962 [1945]), p. 200. **154.** D. Foulkes & G. Vogel (1965). D. Foulkes & S. Fleischer (1975). D. Foulkes (1985), pp. 71-7. **155.** D. Foulkes (1985), p. 72. **156.** D. Foulkes & S. Fleischer (1975), p. 72. **157.** Ibid. **158.** S. Freud (1953 [1900]), p. 576. **159.** H. Shevrin (1986). **160.** C. G. Jung, *Seminar on Children's Dreams, 1938-9*, unpublished, quoted by C. Rycroft (1981 [1979]), p. 32. **161.** L. J. West, "A clinical and theoretical overview of hallucinatory phenomena," in R. K. Siegel & L. J. West, editors, *Hallucinations: Behavior, Experience, and Theory*, New York: Wiley, 1975, quoted by R. F. Price & D. B. Cohen (1988), p. 108. **162.** D. Meltzer (1984), p. 38. **163.** R. Rados & R. D. Cartwright (1982), p. 433, citing E. Klinger, *Structure and Function of Fantasy*, New York: Wiley, 1970. **164.** J. Tolaas (1986), p. 368. **165.** D. Foulkes & S. Fleischer (1975), p. 74. **166.** D. Foulkes (1985), p. 1. **167.** Ibid., p. 76. **168.** Respectively, e.g.: B. Tedlock (1991) and (1992a [1987]); R. L. Jones (1980). **169.** D. Foulkes (1985), p. 123. **170.** D. Foulkes (1978). **171.** Ibid., p. 47. **172.** D. Foulkes (1985), p. 200. **173.** Respectively: P. O'Connor (1986), p. 88; E. C. Whitmont & S. B. Perera (1989), p. 7. **174.** D. Foulkes (1993). **175.** D. Foulkes (1985), p. 205. **176.** Ibid., p. 209. **177.** J. S. Antrobus (1977) and (1986). **178.** J. A. Hobson (1988), p. 180ff. **179.** H. Fiss (1986), p. 167. S. Purcell, A. Moffitt & R. Hoffmann (1993), pp. 200 and 244. See also M. Ullman (1959), p. 144. **180.** H. Zepelin (1992). **181.** R. W. McCarley & E. Hoffman (1981). **182.** J. A. Hobson & R. W. McCarley (1977), p. 1339. **183.** Ibid., p. 1347. **184.** R. W. McCarley & J. A. Hobson (1979), p. 125. **185.** J. A. Hobson & R. W. McCarley (1977), p. 1347. **186.** R. W. McCarley & J. A. Hobson (1979), p. 114. **187.** H. T. Hunt (1991a), pp. 236-7. **188.** J. A. Hobson & R. W. McCarley (1977), p. 1347. **189.** J. A. Hobson (1989), p. 166. **190.** J. A. Hobson (1990), pp. 223 and 221. **191.** J. A. Hobson (1988), pp. 16, 81, 228 and 281. **192.** A. Moffitt, M. Kramer & R. Hoffmann (1993b), pp. 4 and 3. See also R. E. Haskell (1986a), p. 151. **193.** J. A. Hobson (1988), quoted by K. Bulkley (1991b), p. 227. **194.** J. A. Hobson, interviewed by D. Goleman, "Do dreams really contain important secret meaning?" *New York Times*, July 10, 1984, quoted by S. LaBerge (1985), p. 188. **195.** J. A. Hobson (1988), p. 12. **196.** K. Bulkley (1991b), p. 228, quoting J. A. Hobson (1988), pp. 11 and 258. **197.** J. A. Hobson (1991), p. xix. **198.** D. Foulkes (1991), p. 246. **199.** D. Foulkes (1990), pp. 40-1. **200.** J. A. Hobson (1989), p. 151. **201.** J. A. Hobson (1988), p. 135. **202.** R. Cartwright & L. Lamberg (1992), pp. 10-1. **203.** H. T. Hunt (1991a), p. 237. **204.** H. T. Hunt (1989), p. 8. **205.** Ibid., pp. 188-9. **206.** Ibid., pp. 208 and 211. **207.** C. R. Evans (completed by P. Evans), *Land-*

of the Night, New York: Viking, 1984, pp. 141 and 155, quoted by G. Globus (1987), pp. 100-1. **208.** B. O. States (1988), pp. 12 and 32. **209.** F. Crick & G. Mitchison (1983). **210.** S. Freud (1953 [1900]), p. 79, citing W. Robert, *Der Traum als Naturnotwendigkeit Erklärt*, Hamburg, 1886. **211.** T. Melnechuk (1983), p. 22. **212.** H. Fiss (1979), p. 40, citing C. R. Evans & E. A. Newman, "Dreaming: an analogy from computers," *New Scientist* 419, pp. 577-9, 1964. **213.** F. Crick & G. Mitchison (1986), p. 235. F. Crick (1988). **214.** A. Moffitt, M. Kramer & R. Hoffmann (1993b), pp. 4 and 7. **215.** M. Blagrove (1990), pp. 1-2, citing J. Hopfield, D. Feinstein & R. Palmer, "'Unlearning' has a stabilizing effect in collective memories," *Nature* 304, pp. 158-9, 1983. **216.** A. Faraday (1972), p. 82. **217.** G. G. Globus (1993), p. 127. **218.** Ibid., p. 120. **219.** Ibid., pp. 128 and 127. **220.** H. Fiss (1979), pp. 36-7. C. Smith (1993), pp. 341-2. **221.** M. Jouvet, "The function of dreaming: a neurophysiologist's point of view," in M. Gazzinaga & C. Blakemore, editors, *Handbook of Psychobiology*, New York: Academic Press, 1975, cited by E. Rossi (1985), p. 205. **222.** K. Lorenz (1965). **223.** R. D. Cartwright (1977), p. 86 passim. **224.** B. Lerner (1967). **225.** M. J. McGrath & D. B. Cohen (1978), p. 51, reviewing various studies. **226.** L. Scrima (1984), p. 211, citing R. Heine. **227.** J. DeKoninck, G. Lorrain, G. Christ, G. Proulx & D. Couloumbe, "Intensive language learning and increases in rapid eye movement sleep," *International Journal of Psychophysiology* 8, pp. 43-7, 1989, cited by G. Delaney (1991), p. 5. **228.** R. Greenberg (1987a), p. 48, citing J. DeKoninck, G. Proulx, W. King & L. Poitras, "Intensive language learning and REM sleep," *Sleep Research* 7, p. 146, 1977. **229.** R. Greenberg (1987b), p. 134. **230.** L. Scrima (1984), pp. 212-3. **231.** M. J. McGrath & D. B. Cohen (1978), pp. 49-50, reviewing various studies. **232.** L. Breger, I. Hunter & R. W. Lane (1971). **233.** H. Fiss (1986), p. 167, citing J. Zimmerman, J. Stoyva & D. Metcalf, "Distorted visual feedback and augmented REM sleep," *Psychophysiology* 7, p. 298, 1970. **234.** I. Lewin & J. L. Singer (1991), citing various studies. **235.** F. M. C. Watson & J. P. Henry (1977). **236.** W. Dement (1960), p. 1707. **237.** F. Snyder (1963), p. 384. A. Kales, F. S. Hoedemaker, A. Jacobson & E. L. Lichtenstein (1964). **238.** W. C. Dement (1974 [1972]), p. 91. **239.** W. Moorcroft (1986), p. 18, citing F. R. Freemon, *Sleep Research: A Critical Review*, Springfield, Illinois: Charles C. Thomas, 1972. **240.** W. Moorcroft (1986), p. 19, citing R. D. Cartwright (1978). **241.** D. Koulack (1991), p. 148, citing H. Sampson, "Psychological effects of deprivation of dreaming sleep," *Journal of Nervous and Mental Disease* 143, pp. 305-17, 1966. **242.** R. D. Cartwright (1977), p. 50. **243.** H. W. Agnew, Jr., W. B. Webb & R. L. Williams (1967). **244.** N. Kleitman, *Sleep and Wakefulness*, Chicago: University of Chicago, 1963, cited by W. Moorcroft (1986), p. 18. **245.** W. Domhoff (1985), pp. 102-3. **246.** H. Fiss (1986), pp. 169-70, citing H. Fiss, S. Ellman & G. Klein, "Waking fantasies following interrupted and completed REM periods," *Archives of General Psychiatry* 21, pp. 230-9, 1969. **247.** T. Pivik & D. Foulkes (1966). **248.** H. Fiss (1979), p. 55. **249.** C. Fisher, "Experimental and clinical approaches to the mind/body problem through recent research in sleep and dreaming," paper presented to the Michigan Psychiatric Association, Aruba, 1974, cited by H. Fiss (1979), p. 34. **250.** S. LaBerge (1985), p. 192. **251.** C. Sagan (1978), p. 138. **252.** W. C. Dement (1974 [1972]), p. 3. **253.** I. Lewin & H. Glaubman (1975), p. 350. **254.** C. Grieser, R. Greenberg & R. A. Harrison (1972), p. 280. **255.** R. Greenberg, R. Pillard & C. Pearlman (1972). **256.** R. Greenberg & C. A. Pearlman (1975), p. 441. **257.** D. R. Cann & D. C. Donderi (1986), p. 1028, citing various sources. **258.** R. Cartwright (1986), p. 415, citing L. Breger, "Dream function: an information processing model," in L. Breger, editor, *Clinical-Cognitive Psychology*, Englewood Cliffs, New Jersey: Prentice-Hall, 1969. **259.** L. Breger, I. Hunter & R. W. Lane (1971), p. 7. **260.** R. Cartwright (1986), p. 415. **261.** L. Breger, I. Hunter & R. W. Lane (1971), pp. 10 and 15. **262.** Ibid., p. 22. **263.** Ibid.,pp. 190-1. **264.** S. R. Palombo (1978), p. 10. **265.** S. R. Palombo (1987a), p. 60. **266.** S. R. Palombo (1978), p. 5.

Chapter 2 • Freud

1. S. Freud, letter of June 12, 1900, *Aus den Anfängen der Psychoanalyse*, London, 1950, quoted by J. Strachey, editor, in S. Freud (1953 [1900]), p. 121 n. The plaque is translated with slight differences in M. Bonaparte, A. Freud & E. Kris, editors, *The Origins of Psycho-Analysis: Letters to Wilhelm Fliess, Drafts and Notes: 1887-1902 by Sigmund Freud*, New York: Basic, 1954, p. 322. **2.** S. Freud (1953 [1900]), p. 579. **3.** E. Fromm (1951), p. 71. **4.** D. Foulkes (1978), p. 63. **5.** W. Stekel (1943), p. 221. **6.** R. D. Gillman (1987), p. 30. **7.** A. Namrow (1980), p. 156. **8.** R. D. Cartwright (1977), p. 10. **9.** S. Freud (1953 [1900]), p. 284. **10.** W. Bonime (with F. Bonime) (1982 [1962]), pp. 39-40. See also A. Faraday (1976 [1974]), p. 104. **11.** L. L. Altman (1969), p. 13. **12.** S. Freud (1953 [1900]), p. 327. **13.** Ibid., pp. 136-41, 245-6 and 400, respectively. **14.** G. Roheim (1969 [1952]), p. 7. **15.** S. S. Feldman, "Interpretation of a typical and stereotyped dream met with only during psychoanalysis," *Psychiatric Quarterly* 14, 1945, cited by R. Fliess (1953), p. 27. **16.** E. A. Gutheil (1967), p. 49. **17.** S. Freud (1980 [1901]), p. 65. **18.** E. F. Sharpe (1978 [1937]), pp. 47-8 and 51. **19.** Ibid., p. 38. **20.** R. Shohet (1985), p. 111. **21.** J. D. Clift & W. B. Clift (1984). L. Hudson (1985). **22.** E. F. Sharpe (1978 [1937]). **23.** E. Fromm (1951). **24.** E. S. Tauber & M. R. Green (1959). **25.** A. Adler (1958 [1931]), p. 102. **26.** S. Freud (1980 [1901]), pp. 60-3. **27.** S. Freud (1953 [1900]), p. 97. **28.** S. Freud, *Introductory Lectures on Psycho-analysis*, 1916-7, Standard Edition, vol. 22, London: Hogarth, pp. 181-2, quoted by J. Spanjaard (1969), p. 221. **29.** D. Deslauriers (1988). **30.** S. Breznitz (1971). **31.** M. H. Stein (1989), pp. 70-7. **32.** S. Freud (1953 [1900]), p. 449. **33.** Ibid., p. 206. **34.** J. Spanjaard (1969), p. 225. **35.** S. Freud (1953 [1900]), p. 174. **36.** S. Freud, *Fragment of an Analysis of a Case of Hysteria*, Standard Edition, vol. 7, London: Hogarth, 1953 [1905], p. 68, quoted by H. Fiss (1979), p. 64. **37.** S. Freud (1953 [1900]), p. 266. **38.** Ibid., p. 594. **39.** S. Freud (1980 [1901]), p. 114. **40.** Ibid., p. 29. **41.** S. Freud, "Two encyclopaedia articles," Standard Edition, vol. 28, London: Hogarth, 1953 [1923], p. 241, quoted by J. Spanjaard (1969), p. 226. **42.** S. Freud (1980 [1901]), p. 114. **43.** S. Freud (1953 [1900]), p. 175. **44.** Ibid., p. 589. **45.** L. L. Altman (1969), p. 8. **46.** L. Breger, I. Hunter & R. W. Lane (1971), p. 15. **47.** S. Freud (1953 [1900]), p. 594. **48.** Ibid., p. 106ff. **49.** J. Spanjaard (1969), p. 224. **50.** W. McGuire (1974), p. 392. **51.** Ibid., p. 395. **52.** S. Freud (1953 [1900]), p. 146ff, for example. **53.** R. M. Jones (1979a), p. 280. **54.** S. Freud, "Two encyclopedia articles," 1923, quoted by J. Spanjaard (1969), p. 226. **55.** S. Freud (1966b [1920]), p. 32. **56.** L. Breger, I. Hunter & R. W. Lane (1971), p. 10. **57.** S. Freud (1966c [1923]). **58.** M. N. McLeod (1992), pp. 41-4. **59.** R. M. Friedman (1992), p. 13. **60.** S. Freud (1950 [1923]), p. 138. **61.** S. Freud (1953 [1900]), p. 552. **62.** Ibid., pp. 269-71. **63.** Ibid., pp. 146-8. **64.** R. Fliess (1953), p. 46. **65.** S. Freud, "Fragment of an analysis of a case of hysteria," Standard Edition. vol. 7, London: Hogarth, 1953 [1905], quoted by H. Fiss (1979), p. 64. **66.** S. Freud (1965 [1900]), pp. 362-4. **67.** E. Sharpe (1978 [1937]), p. 21. **68.** Ibid., p. 91. **69.** M.-T. B. Dombeck (1991), p. 16. **70.** G. Roheim (1969 [1952]), p. 29. **71.** C. G. Jung [1944], CW 12, para. 79. **72.** E. H. Erikson, *Young Man Luther: A Study in Psychoanalysis and History*, New York: Norton, 1962, quoted by A. Stevens (1983), p. 33. **73.** G. Roheim (1969 [1952]), pp. 200-1. **74.** R. Grossinger (1971a), p. 23. **75.** Ibid., p. 26. **76.** L. Hudson (1985), p. 56, quoting S. Freud (1966b [1920]). **77.** H. C. Curtis & D. M. Sachs (1976), p. 344, paraphrasing A. Garma's contribution to a panel discussion. **78.** A. Garma (1987 [1978]), p. 28. **79.** C. Rycroft (1981 [1979]), p. 4. **80.** E. H. Erikson (1954), p. 35. **81.** D. Meltzer (1984), p. 37. **82.** K. Horney (1970 [1950]), p. 14. **83.** J. Hillman (1979), p. 8. **84.** Heracleitos of Ephesos, quoted by B. D. Lewin (1958), p. 11. **85.** S. Freud, quoted by L. Hudson (1985), p. 26. **86.** E. Fromm (1951), p. 56. **87.** K. Horney (1970 [1950]), pp. 378 and 15. **88.** K. Stern, quoted by A. Stevens (1983 [1982]), p. 33. **89.** W. Wolff (1972 [1952]), pp. 131-55. **90.** Ibid., p. 146. **91.** S. Freud (1953 [1900]), p. 470. **92.** W. Wolff (1972 [1952]), p. 155, quoting and commenting upon H. Meng, "Notes and comments," *American Journal of Psychotherapy* 4, pp. 510-1, 1950. **93.** S. Freud (1953 [1900]), p. 399. **94.** Ibid., pp.

409 and 408. **95.** L. Hudson (1985), p. 24. **96.** H. Kelman (1944), p. 96. **97.** E. R. Neu (1988), p. 60. **98.** R. Grossinger (1971a), p. 26.

Chapter 3 • Jung

1. C. G. Jung, "The aims of psychotherapy" [1931], CW 16, para. 86. **2.** M. Ullman & N. Zimmerman (1979), p. 56. **3.** E. C. Whitmont & S. B. Perera (1989), p. 6. **4.** M. A. Mattoon (1984 [1978]), p. 5. **5.** J. A. Hall (1983). **6.** C. G. Jung (1974). **7.** M.-T. B. Dombeck (1991). **8.** A. Koestler (1967), p. 100. **9.** E. C. Whitmont (1987 [1978]), p. 61. **10.** C. G. Jung [1921], CW 6, para's 789-91. **11.** C. G. Jung [1951], CW 9-II, para. 2. **12.** J. Jacobi (1959 [1957]), p. 34. **13.** C. G. Jung (1965 [1961]), p. 161. **14.** C. G. Jung, "The significance of the father in the destiny of the individual" [1909/1949], CW 4, reprinted as C. G. Jung (1985 [1949]), where the quoted passage appears on p. 240. **15.** A. Samuels, B. Shorter & F. Plaut (1985), p. 251. **16.** M. A. Mattoon (1984 [1978]), p. 21ff. See also J. Jacobi (1959 [1957]), pp. 39-46. **17.** A. Stevens (1983 [1982]). **18.** C. G. Jung, "Foreword to Harding: 'Woman's Mysteries'" [1949], CW 18, para. 1228. **19.** J. A. Hall (1983), p. 11. **20.** C. G. Jung [1921], CW 6, para. 747. **21.** C. G. Jung, "Wotan" [1936], CW 10, para. 389. **22.** J. Singer (1977), p. 260. M. Stein (1990), p. 19. **23.** J. Jacobi (1959 [1957]), p. 39 passim. **24.** C. G. Jung [1944], CW 12, para. 113. **25.** J. A. Hall (1983), pp. 78 and 38. **26.** E. C. Whitmont & S. B. Perera (1989), p. 97. **27.** R. A. Johnson (1986), p. 60. **28.** J. A. Hall (1983), p. 76. **29.** K. Asper (1992a [1988]), p. 24. **30.** H. Stefanakis, A. Zadra & D. Donderi (1990), p. 2. **31.** R. J. Brown & D. C. Donderi (1986), p. 620. See also D. R. Cann & D. C. Donderi (1986). **32.** C. G. Jung, "Analytical psychology and education: three lectures" [1926/1946], CW 17, para. 208. **33.** P. O'Connor (1986), p. 208. **34.** J. A. Hall (1983), p. 34. **35.** K. Asper (1992b), p. 86. **36.** E. C. Whitmont & S. B. Perera (1989), pp. 53 and 109. **37.** R. Cahen (1966), p. 127. **38.** E. C. Whitmont (1987 [1978]), pp. 59-60. **39.** C. G. Jung, "The practical use of dream-analysis" [1934], CW 16, para. 320. **40.** T. A. Greene (1979), p. 311. **41.** C. G. Jung [1921], CW 6, para. 803. **42.** M. A. Mattoon (1984 [1978]), p. 17. **43.** J. D. Clift & W. B. Clift (1984), p. 54. **44.** Ibid., pp. 55-7. **45.** C. G. Jung, as told by M.-L. von Franz, *The Shadow and Evil in Fairytales*, Zurich: Spring, 1974, quoted by A. Stevens (1983 [1982]), p. 215. **46.** J. W. Lewis (1991), p. 2. **47.** P. O'Connor (1986), p. 135. **48.** C. Rycroft (1981 [1979]), pp. 34-5, citing E. A. Bennet, *What Jung Really Said*, London: Macdonald, 1966. **49.** C. G. Jung, *Aion* [1951], CW9-II, excerpted in V. S. de Laszlo (1958), where the quoted phrase appears on p. 7. **50.** C. G. Jung, *On the Psychology of the Unconscious* [1917/1943], CW 7, para. 103, note 5. **51.** M.-L. von Franz (1980b), p. 59. **52.** C. G. Jung (1984 [1938]), p. 53. **53.** C. G. Jung, "Marriage as a psychological relationship" [1925], CW 17, para. 338. **54.** J. A. Hall (1983), p. 120. **55.** C. G. Jung, *Aion* [1951], CW9-II, excerpted in V. S. de Laszlo (1958), where the quoted phrase appears on p. 15. **56.** A. Samuels, B. Shorter & F. Plaut (1985), p. 250. **57.** A. Allenby (1985 [1955]), pp. 139-40 and 144-5. **58.** C. G. Jung [1921], CW 6, para. 803. **59.** C. G. Jung (1984 [1938]), p. 52. **60.** J. A. Hall (1983), p. 68. **61.** C. G. Jung [1955-6], CW 14, para. 129. **62.** J. A. Hall (1983), p. 10. **63.** E. C. Whitmont (1987 [1978]), p. 60. **64.** C. G. Jung [1921], CW 6, para. 706. **65.** J. A. Hall (1983), p. 105. **66.** C. G. Jung, *Aion* [1951], CW9-II, excerpted in V. S. de Laszlo (1958), where the quoted phrase appears on p. 3. **67.** Ibid., p. 5. **68.** A. Stevens (1983 [1982]), p. 141. **69.** H. A. Wilmer (1987), pp. 81-2. K. A. Signell (1990), p. 50 passim. **70.** P. Teilhard de Chardin (1959 [1955]). **71.** A. Stevens (1983 [1982]), pp. 70-1. **72.** C. G. Jung (1965 [1961]), pp. 255, 279 and 326, respectively. **73.** Ibid., p. 3. **74.** Ibid., p. 326. **75.** J. A. Sanford (1984 [1966]), p. 84. **76.** E. C. Whitmont (1987 [1978]), p. 53. **77.** A. Stevens (1983 [1982]), p. 141. **78.** C. G. Jung, "The practical use of dream-analysis" [1934], CW 16, para. 330. **79.** C. G. Jung, "General aspects of dream psychology" [1916/1948], CW 8, para. 444. **80.** C. S. Hall (1966a [1953]), p. 12. **81.** Ibid., p. 11. **82.** C. S. Hall & V. J. Nordby (1972), p. 104. **83.** Ibid., p. 184. **84.** Ibid., p. 105. **85.** Ibid., p. 104. **86.** C. S. Hall & R. L. Van de Castle, (1966). **87.** G. W.

Domhoff (1985), p. 104. P. Garfield (1984), p. 34. **88.** P. Garfield (1984), p. 34. **89.** S. Roll, R. Hinton & M. Glazer, "Dreams and death: Mexican Americans vs. Anglo-Americans," *International Journal of Psychology* 8, pp. 111-5, 1974, cited by L. Weiss (1986), p. 23. **90.** A. T. Beck & C. H. Ward (1961), p. 466. **91.** J. B. Miller (1969), p. 563. **92.** P. Ben-Horin, *The Relationship Between Some Personality Variables in Wakefulness, Fantasy, and Dreams*, Ph.D. dissertation, University of Chicago, 1967, cited by C. Winget & M. Kramer (1979), pp. 193-4. **93.** P. R. Robbins (1988), p. 69, citing P. R. Robbins & R. H. Tanck, "Sexual gratification and sexual symbolism in dreams: some support for Freud's theory," *Bulletin of the Menninger Clinic* 44, pp. 49-58, 1980. **94.** S. B. Sarason (1959 [1944]). C. Winget & M. Kramer (1979), p. 26. **95.** S. J. Meer (1955), p. 74. **96.** D. Foulkes, J. D. Larson, E. M. Swanson & M. Rardin, "Two studies of childhood dreaming," *American Journal of Orthopsychiatry* 39, pp. 627-43, 1969, cited by C. Winget & M. Kramer (1979), p. 250. **97.** H. L. Pope, *Prohibitions, Self-conceptions, and Dreams*, Ph.D. dissertation, Western Reserve University, 1952, cited by C. Winget & M. Kramer (1979), p. 234. **98.** M. Kramer & T. Roth (1979), p. 372, citing S. Grand, N. Freedman & S. Jortner, "Variations in REM dreaming and the effectiveness of behavior in group therapy," *American Journal of Psychotherapy* 23:667-680, 1969. **99.** S. Starker (1974). **100.** Respectively, e.g.: J. M. Nanda (1974); W. Y. Evans-Wentz (1958 [1935]). **101.** L. Reneau (no date), p. 4. **102.** M. C. Jędrej & R. Shaw (1992b), pp. 1-5. **103.** D. Price-Williams (1992 [1987]), p. 259. Reprinted with permission. See credit page. **104.** M. C. Jędrej & R. Shaw (1992b), pp. 1-5. **105.** J. Frazer, *The Golden Bough*, pp. 172-3, 1890, cited by J. S. Lincoln (1970 [1935]), p. 52. **106.** C. G. Seligman, Huxley Lecture, 1932, cited by J. S. Lincoln (1970 [1935]), p. 52. **107.** J. Frazer, *The Golden Bough*, cited by C. W. O'Nell (1976), p. 22. **108.** R. Caillois (1966), pp. 29-30. **109.** G. Roheim (1969 [1952]), p. 193. **110.** M. Boss (1965). **111.** M. Boss (1977). **112.** M. Boss & B. Kenny (1987 [1978]), p. 159. **113.** Ibid., p. 150. **114.** A. Adler (1958 [1931]). **115.** L. Gold (1979), p. 321. **116.** W. Bonime (1969). W. Bonime (1982 [1962]) and (1978). **117.** M. Ullman (1982 [1962]), p. xi. **118.** S. Freud (1953 [1900]), p. 128. **119.** P. Wood, *Dreaming and Social Isolation*, Ph.D. dissertation, University of North Carolina, 1962. P. Hauri, *Effects of Evening Activity on Subsequent Sleep and Dreams*, Ph.D. dissertation, University of Chicago, 1967. Both cited by L. Breger, I. Hunter, & R. W. Lane (1971), pp. 26-7. **120.** P. Hauri, *Effects of Evening Activity on Subsequent Sleep and Dreams*, Ph.D. dissertation, University of Chicago, 1967, cited by L. Breger, I. Hunter & R. W. Lane (1971), p. 27. **121.** S. J. Wolin & N. K. Mello (1973), pp. 282-3. **122.** A. F. Paolino (1964), pp. 224-5. **123.** J. E. Leman, Jr., *Aggression in Mexican-American and Anglo-American Delinquents and Non-delinquents as Revealed in Dreams and Thematic Apperception Test Responses*, Ph.D. dissertation, University of Arizona, 1966, cited by C. Winget & M. Kramer (1979), p. 316. **124.** P. R. Robbins & R. Tanck "Community violence and aggression in dreams. An observation," *Perceptual and Motor Skills* 29, pp. 41-2, 1969, cited by C. Winget & M. Kramer (1979), p. 288. **125.** E. M. Swanson & D. Foulkes (1968), p. 361. **126.** E. A. Gutheil (1967 [1951]), pp. 204-5. **127.** M. A. Mattoon (1984 [1978]), p. xii. **128.** R. D. Cartwright (1977), p. 44. See also p. 58. **129.** L. Hudson (1985), p. 162. **130.** M. A. M. Holmes, *REM Sleep Patterning and Dream Recall in Convergers and Divergers*, Ph.D. dissertation, Edinburgh University, 1976, cited by L. Hudson (1985), p. 136ff. **131.** D. Foulkes, "Personality and dreams," in E. Hartmann, editor, *Sleep and Dreaming*, Little Brown, pp. 147-53, 1970, cited by D. Foulkes (1978), p. 94. **132.** R. D. Cartwright (1977), p. 31. **133.** E. C. Whitmont (1987 [1978]), pp. 61 and 53. **134.** C. G. Jung, "The Tavistock lectures" [1935], CW 18, para. 248. **135.** M. A. Mattoon (1984 [1978]), p. 131, quoting C. G. Jung, "Psychological commentary on 'The Tibetan Book of the Great Liberation'" [1939/1954], CW 11, para. 779. **136.** C. G. Jung, "General aspects of dream psychology" [1916/-1948], CW 8, para. 488. **137.** J. A. Hall (1983), pp. 84-6. **138.** C. G. Jung (1965 [1961]), p. 133. **139.** A. B. Siegel (1990), p. 103. **140.** R. C. Diamond (1983), pp. 79-80. **141.** V. D. Volkan & T. H. Bhatti (1973), p. 273. **142.** C. G. Jung, "General aspects of dream psychology" [1916/-1948], CW 8, para. 489. **143.** C. G. Jung, "The practical use of dream-analysis" [1934], CW 16, para's 335-7. **144.** J. A. Hall (1983), p. 24. **145.** S. Marjasch (1966), pp. 153-5. **146.** D. Koulack (1993), p. 323. **147.** D. G. Schwartz, L. N. Weinstein & A. M. Arkin (1978), pp. 226-7. **148.** M. Barad, K. Z. Altshuler & A. I. Goldfarb (1961). **149.** C. G. Jung, "General aspects of dream psychology" [1916/1948], CW 8, para. 488. **150.** Ibid., para. 546. **151.** E. C. Whitmont & S. B. Perera (1989), p. 56, quoting C. G. Jung [1944], CW 12, para. 48. **152.** S. K. Williams (1986 [1980]), p. 263. **153.** C. G. Jung [1944], CW 12, para. 48. **154.** C. G. Jung, "General aspects of dream psychology" [1916/1948], CW 8, para. 500. **155.** M. A. Mattoon (1984 [1978]), pp. 49 and 142-5. **156.** Ibid., pp. 49 and 139-42. **157.** E. C. Whitmont & S. B. Perera (1989), p. 56. **158.** J. A. Hall (1983), p. 60. **159.** M. Woodman (1985), p. 163. **160.** E. T. Gendlin (1986). **161.** R. A. Johnson (1986), p. 97. **162.** C. G. Jung, "General aspects of dream psychology" [1916/-1948], CW 8, para. 492. **163.** R. A. Johnson (1986), p. 73. **164.** C. G. Jung (1984 [1938]), p. 530. **165.** C. G. Jung, "On the nature of dreams" [1945/1948], CW 8, para. 547. **166.** R. Cahen (1966), p. 133. **167.** J. A. Sanford (1977), pp. 13-4, quoting A. Aumüller, "Jungian psychology in wartime Germany," *Spring*, pp. 12-31, 1950. **168.** E. C. Whitmont & S. B. Perera (1989), p. 9. **169.** R. Bosnak (1988 [1986]), p. 28. **170.** J. Hillman (1979), p. 141. **171.** C. G. Jung, "The significance of constitution and heredity in psychology" [1929], CW 8, para. 230. **172.** R. A. Johnson (1986), p. 94. **173.** E. T. Gendlin (1977). **174.** E. T. Gendlin (1986), p. 80. **175.** Ibid., p. 39. **176.** Ibid. **177.** G. Globus (1987), p. 151. **178.** C. G. Jung, "The relations between the ego and the unconscious" [1928], CW 7, para. 218. **179.** C. G. Jung, *Aion* [1951], CW 9-II, excerpted in V. S. de Laszlo (1958), where the quoted phrase appears on p. 19. **180.** A. Mankowitz (1984), p. 29. **181.** R. A. Johnson (1986), p. 4. **182.** E. C. Whitmont (1987 [1978]), p. 61. **183.** R. Cahen (1966), p. 123. **184.** C. G. Jung, *L'homme à la découverte de son âme*, Geneva: Mont-Blanc, p. 201, 1962, quoted by R. Cahen (1966), p. 122. **185.** M.-L. von Franz (1980a [1978]), pp. 167 and 168. **186.** C. G. Jung, "Dogma and natural symbols, "*Psychology and Religion*, New Haven: Yale, p. 45, 1938, quoted by E. Fromm (1951), p. 96. Also in CW 11. **187.** C. G. Jung, "General aspects of dream psychology" [1916/1948], CW 8, para. 488. **188.** W. H. Thorpe (1966 [1956]). A. Shafton (1976). **189.** C. G. Jung, "General aspects of dream psychology" [1916/1948], CW 8, para. 456. **190.** G. Sommerhoff, *Analytical Biology*, Oxford, 1950, quoted by W. H. Thorpe (1966 [1956]), p. 6. **191.** S. E. Pulver (1978), p. 682n, quoting M. Choisy, *Sigmund Freud: A New Appraisal*, New York: Philosophical Library, 1963. **192.** C. G. Jung, "The practical use of dream-analysis" [1934], CW 16, para's 323-4. **193.** C. G. Jung, "General aspects of dream psychology" [1916/1948], CW 8, para. 462. **194.** T. A. Greene (1979), p. 315. **195.** J. A. Hall (1983), p. 60. **196.** C. G. Jung, "General aspects of dream psychology" [1916/1948], CW 8, para. 497. **197.** Ibid., para. 496 and "Analytical psychology and education: three lectures" [1926/1946], CW 17, para. 196. **198.** M. A. Mattoon (1984 [1978]), p. 126. **199.** C. G. Jung (1965 [1961]), p. 162. **200.** M. A. Mattoon (1984 [1978]), p. 100, quoting C. G. Jung, CW 13, para. 469. **201.** M. A. Mattoon (1984 [1978]), p. 171. **202.** C. G. Jung (1965 [1961]), p. 163. **203.** C. G. Jung [1951], CW 9-II, para. 315n. **204.** W. Stekel (1943 [1913 and later]). W. Wolff (1972 [1952]). E. Fromm (1951). **205.** S. Freud (1953 [1900]), p. 54. **206.** C. G. Jung (1965 [1961]), pp. 161-2. **207.** C. W. Jung, *Analytical Psychology*, London: Balliére, Tindall & Cox, 1916, quoted by J. A. Hadfield (1954), p. 135. See also C. G. Jung, "General aspects of dream psychology" [1916/1948], CW 8, para. 505. **208.** C. G. Jung, "The practical use of dream-analysis" [1934], CW 16, para. 319. **209.** C. G. Jung, "The meaning of psychology for modern man" [1933/1934], CW 10, para. 304. **210.** For example, E. Sheppard & L. J. Saul (1958); D. Foulkes & A. Rechtschaffen (1964); P. Carrington (1972); C. S. Hall & V. J. Nordby (1972); W. Karle, R. Corriere, J. Hart & L. Woldenberg (1980). **211.** C. S. Moss (1970), p. 20. **212.** L. Breger, I. Hunter & R. W. Lane (1971), pp. 179-80. **213.** E. Rossi (1985); J. Hillman (1979); S. Purcell, J. Mullington, A. Moffitt, R. Hoffmann & R. Pigeau (1986); P. E. Craig (1987); H. T. Hunt (1989); P. Garfield (1991). **214.** E. C. Whitmont (1987 [1978]), p. 53. **215.** J. A. Hadfield (1954), pp. 135-6; H. T. Hunt, R. Ogilvie, K. Belicki, Dennis Belicki & E. Atalick (1982), p. 566; K. Asper (1992a [1988]), pp. 9 and

20. **216.** T. A. Greene (1979), p. 307. See also C. A. Meier (1990 [1972]), p. 89. **217.** E. C. Whitmont & S. B. Perera (1989), p. 74. **218.** Ibid., p. 129. **219.** H. T. Hunt, R. Ogilvie, K. Belicki, D. Belicki & E. Atalick (1982), p. 608. **220.** C. G. Jung, "The Tavistock lectures" [1935], CW 18, para. 52. **221.** R. D. Cartwright (1977), pp. 46-7. **222.** C. G. Jung, *Aion* [1951], CW9-II, excerpted in V. S. de Laszlo (1958), where the quoted phrases appear on pp. 19-20. **223.** C. G. Jung, "General aspects of dream psychology" [1916/1948], CW 8, para's 466-8. **224.** C. G. Jung, "Symbols and the interpretation of dreams" [1961], CW 18, para. 596. **225.** E. C. Whitmont (1987 [1978]), p. 67. J. A. Hall (1983), p. 65. **226.** K. A. Signell (1990). **227.** M. A. Mattoon (1984 [1978]), p. 65, quoting C. G. Jung, CW 17, para. 208. **228.** C. G. Jung, quoted by M. A. Mattoon (1984 [1978]), p. 1. **229.** C. G. Jung, "Concerning rebirth" [1940/1950], CW 9-I, para. 211. **230.** C. G. Jung, "On the nature of dreams" [1945/1948], CW 8, para. 560. **231.** C. G. Jung (1984 [1938]), p. 225. **232.** J. D. Clift & W. B. Clift (1984), p. 13. **233.** C. G. Jung, "General aspects of dream psychology" [1916/1948], CW 8, para. 494. **234.** C. G. Jung, "On the nature of dreams" [1945/1948], CW 8, para. 568. **235.** J. A. Hall (1983), pp. 14 and 103. **236.** C. G. Jung, "De la nature des reves," *Revue Ciba*, p. 1612, 1945, quoted by L. M. Savary, P. H. Berne & S. K. Williams (1984), p. 133. **237.** J. A. Hall (1983), p. 34. **238.** Ibid., p. 78. **239.** J. Grant (1986 [1984]), p. 45, citing C. G. Jung. **240.** C. G. Jung (1965 [1961]), pp. 11-5. **241.** Ibid., p. 41. **242.** C. A. Meier (1969), p. 105. **243.** C. G. Jung (1965 [1961]), p. 141. **244.** K. A. Signell (1990), p. 62. **245.** M. A. Mattoon (1984 [1978]), p. 68. **246.** C. G. Jung (1965 [1961]), p. 187. **247.** C. G. Jung, *Aion* [1951], CW9-II, excerpted in V. S. de Laszlo (1958), where the quoted sentence appears on p. 24. **248.** J. Hillman (1979), p. 112. **249.** Ibid., pp. 114-5. **250.** Ibid., p. 132. **251.** R. Bosnak (1988 [1986]), p. 120. **252.** C. G. Jung, "On the nature of dreams" [1945/1948], CW 8, para. 568. **253.** J. A. Hall (1983), p. 29. **254.** M. Zeller (1975), pp. 75-6. **255.** C. G. Jung, "On the nature of dreams" [1945/1948], CW 8, para. 557. **256.** M. Sabini & V. H. Maffly (1981), p. 145. **257.** A. Stevens (1983 [1982]), p. 141. **258.** M. Zeller (1990 [1975], p. 90). **259.** J. Hillman (1979), p. 23. **260.** B. Malinowski, *Sex and Repression in Savage Societies*, London: Routledge & Kegan Paul, 1927. **261.** J. S. Lincoln (1970 [1935]), p. 22 passim. **262.** M. Ullman (1969a), pp. 96-7. **263.** M. Eliade (1960 [1957]), p. 19. **264.** C. G. Jung, "On the nature of dreams" [1945/1948], CW 8, para. 568. **265.** C. G. Jung, *Aion* [1951], CW9-II, excerpted in V. S. de Laszlo (1958), where the quoted phrase appears on p. 23. **266.** C. G. Jung (1965 [1961]), p. 325. **267.** R. A. Johnson (1986), p. 11. **268.** C. G. Jung, "Archetypes of the collective unconscious" [1934/1954], CW 9-I, para. 198. **269.** C. G. Jung (1965 [1961]), p. 297. **270.** Ibid., p. 354. **271.** D. S. Wehr (1985), p. 28. **272.** Bill Wilson, letter of Jan. 23, 1961 to Jung, quoted in Anonymous (1984), p. 382. **273.** C. G. Jung, letter of Jan. 30, 1961 to Bill Wilson, quoted in Anonymous (1984), pp. 383-4. Also in C. G. Jung, *Letters*, vol. 2, Princeton: Princeton University, 1975. **274.** A. Govinda (1984 [1966]), pp. 163-4. **275.** C. G. Jung (1965 [1961]), p. 35. **276.** M. Zeller (1975), pp. 74-5; also (1990 [1975], pp. 1-7. **277.** C. G. Jung (1965 [1961]), p. 303. **278.** C. G. Jung, *Letters*, vol. 1, Princeton: Princeton University, pp. 257-8, 1973, quoted by M.-L. von Franz (1986 [1984]), pp. 113-4. **279.** C. G. Jung (1965 [1961]), pp. 229-31. **280.** C. G. Jung, *Letters*, vol. 1, Princeton: Princeton University, pp. 257-8, 1973, quoted by M.-L. von Franz (1986 [1984]), pp. 113-4. **281.** C. G. Jung (1965 [1961]), p. 295. **282.** M.-L. von Franz (1986 [1984]), p. 156. **283.** C. G. Jung, *Letters*, vol. 2, Princeton: Princeton University, p. 561, 1975, quoted by M.-L. von Franz (1986 [1984]), pp. 149-50. **284.** M. Serrano (1968 [1966]), p. 104.

Chapter 4 • Existentialism

1. S. Freud (1966a [1914]), p. 60. **2.** J. L. Fosshage & C. A. Loew, editors (1987a [1978]). Republished with an additional chapter: J. L. Fosshage (1987a). **3.** M. A. Mattoon (1984 [1978]), p. 5. **4.** A. Adler, *Social Interest: A Challenge to Mankind*, London: Faber & Faber, p. 255, 1938, quoted by L. Gold (1979), p. 332. **5.** A. Adler (1958 [1931]), p. 52. **6.** G. Kaufman (1985 [1980]),

p. 8. **7.** A. Adler (1958 [1931]), p. 53. **8.** A. Adler (1958 [1931]), p. 50. **9.** Ibid., p. 98. **10.** L. Gold (1979), pp. 320-1. **11.** M. Ullman (1982 [1962]), p. x. **12.** H. H. Mosak (1989), p. 81. **13.** M. Ullman (1982 [1962]), p. x. **14.** L. Gold (1979), p. 319. **15.** A. Adler (1958 [1931]), pp. 95-6. **16.** L. Gold (1979), p. 321. **17.** A. Adler (1958 [1931]), p. 99. **18.** H. H. Mosak (1989), p. 87. **19.** A. Adler (1958 [1931]), pp. 98-9. B. Shulman (1969), pp. 120-1. **20.** A. Adler (1958 [1931]), p. 99 and *Social Interest: A challenge to Mankind*, London: Faber & Faber, 1938, quoted by B. Shulman (1969), p. 118. **21.** L. Gold (1979), p. 335. **22.** A. Adler (1958 [1931]), p. 53. **23.** Ibid., p. 94. **24.** Ibid., p. 101. **25.** Ibid. **26.** Ibid., pp. 105-7. **27.** B. Shulman (1969), p. 132. **28.** A. Adler (1958 [1931]), p. 101. **29.** A. Adler, "On the interpretation of dreams," *International Journal of Individual Psychology* 1, pp. 3-16, 1936, quoted by B. Shulman (1969), p. 126. **30.** Ibid. Brackets Shulman's. **31.** A. Adler (1958 [1931]), pp. 103-4. **32.** L. Gold (1979), pp. 324-5. **33.** B. Shulman (1969), p. 132. **34.** Ibid., pp. 131-2. **35.** A. Adler, *Problems of Neurosis*, New York: Harper Torchbooks, 1967, quoted by B. Shulman (1969), p. 127. **36.** B. Shulman (1969), p. 121. **37.** Phyllis Bottome, *Alfred Adler: A Biography*, New York: Putnam, p. 199, 1939, quoted by H. H. Mosak (1989), p. 72. **38.** H. E. Lehmann (1969), p. 143. **39.** P. E. Craig (1990a). **40.** M. Boss (1977), p. 3. **41.** M. Boss & B. Kenny (1987 [1978]), p. 151. **42.** P. E. Craig (1987), p. 39. **43.** M. Boss & B. Kenny (1987 [1978]), p. 150. **44.** H. E. Lehmann (1969), p. 144. **45.** M. Boss (1977), p. 183. **46.** H. E. Lehmann (1969), p. 144. **47.** P. E. Craig (1987), p. 41. **48.** M. Boss (1977), p. 190. **49.** P. E. Craig (1992). **50.** P. E. Craig (1990b), p. 73. **51.** M. Boss, *The Analysis of Dreams*, London: Rider, p. 210, 1958, quoted by W. Karle, R. Corriere, J. Hart & L. Woldenberg (1980), p. 26. **52.** Ibid. **53.** H. E. Lehmann (1969), p. 147. **54.** R. Corriere, W. Karle, L. Woldenberg & J. Hart (1980), p. 88. **55.** M. Boss, *The Analysis of Dreams*, London: Rider, pp. 210-1, 1958, quoted by R. Corriere, W. Karle, L. Woldenberg & J. Hart (1980), p. 84. **56.** D. Foulkes (1985). **57.** H. T. Hunt. R. Ogilvie, K. Belicki, D. Belicki & E. Atalick (1982), p. 568. **58.** Ibid., p. 627. **59.** A. Rechtschaffen (1978). **60.** G. Globus (1987), p. 80ff, citing A. Rechtschaffen (1978). **61.** Ibid., p. 91ff. **62.** Ibid., p. 99. **63.** M. Boss (1965), p. 112. **64.** Ibid., p. 189. **65.** J. H. Van Der Berg, *The Phenomenological Approach to Psychiatry*, Springfield, Illinois: Charles C. Thomas, p. 83, 1955, quoted by M. Ullman (1982 [1962]), p. x. **66.** P. E. Craig (1987), p. 35. **67.** M. Boss, *The Analysis of Dreams*, London: Rider, p. 9, 1958, quoted by R. Corriere, W. Karle, L. Woldenberg & J. Hart (1980), pp. 83-4. **68.** M. Boss (1977), pp. 31-2. **69.** P. E. Craig (1987), p. 40. **70.** M. Boss (1977), pp. 180-1. **71.** H. E. Lehmann (1969), p. 143. **72.** H. T. Hunt (1989), p. 36. **73.** M. Boss (1977), p. 183. **74.** Ibid., p. 10. **75.** W. M. Mendel (1980), p. 396. **76.** M. Boss & B. Kenny (1987 [1978]), p. 149. **77.** M. Boss (1977), pp. 74-5. **78.** H. T. Hunt, R. Ogilvie, K. Belicki, D. Belicki & E. Atalick (1982) and (1989). **79.** G. Globus (1987), pp. 150-1. **80.** M. Boss (1977), p. 76. **81.** Ibid., p. 212. **82.** Ibid., pp. 202-3. **83.** P. E. Craig (1990a). **84.** M. Boss (1977), pp. 59-63. **85.** C. Downing (1977), p. 100. **86.** Ibid., p. 197ff. M. Boss & B. Kenny (1987 [1978]), p. 153ff. **87.** R. May & I. Yalom (1989), p. 377, quoting J. P. Sartre, *Being and Nothingness*, New York: Philosophical Library, 1956, p. 631. **88.** Ibid., p. 364. **89.** M. Boss & B. Kenny (1987 [1978]), p. 159. **90.** Ibid., p. 175. **91.** H. H. Mosak (1989), p. 92. **92.** M. Boss (1977), p. 24. **93.** R. May & I. Yalom (1989), pp. 364-5. **94.** Ibid., p. 376, citing I. Yalom, *Existential Psychotherapy*, New York: Basic Books, 1981. **95.** Ibid., pp. 389 and 365, respectively. **96.** Ibid., pp. 391-3, citing I. Yalom, *Existential Psychotherapy*, New York: Basic Books, 1981. **97.** Ibid., pp. 382 and 369, respectively. **98.** M. Boss (1977), p. 172. **99.** P. E. Craig (1990b), p. 71. **100.** P. E. Craig (1987), pp. 49-52. **101.** R. May & I. Yalom (1989), p. 363. **102.** M. Boss (1977), p. 171. **103.** R. May & I. Yalom (1989), p. 363. **104.** Ibid., p. 374. **105.** Ibid., p. 364. **106.** H. E. Lehmann (1969), p. 153. **107.** Ibid., quoting J. Needleman, *Being-in-the-World*, New York: Basic Books, 1963, who is commenting on L. Binswanger. **108.** R. May & I. Yalom (1989), p. 375. **109.** L. Caligor & R. May (1968). **110.** R. May & I. Yalom (1989), pp. 370-1. **111.** R. Corriere, W. Karle, L. Woldenberg & J. Hart (1980), p. 8. **112.** Ibid., p. 54. **113.** Ibid., p. 20. **114.** Ibid., p. 147. **115.** Ibid., p. 61. **116.** W. Karle, R. Corriere, J. Hart & L. Woldenberg (1980),

p. 7. **117.** R. Corriere, W. Karle, L. Woldenberg & J. Hart (1980), p. 8. **118.** H. T. Hunt (1989), p. 231. **119.** R. May (1968), pp. 2-8, 82, 128 passim. **120.** R. May & I. Yalom (1989), p. 399.

Chapter 5 • Culturalism

1. W. Bonime (1969), p. 79. **2.** M. Ullman (1982 [1962]), p. x. **3.** B. Shulman (1969), p. 128. **4.** W. Bonime (with F. Bonime) (1982 [1962]), p. xxi. **5.** W. Bonime (1969), p. 79. **6.** W. Bonime (with F. Bonime) (1982 [1962]), p. xxi. **7.** M. Ullman (1982 [1962]), p. xi. **8.** W. Bonime (with F. Bonime) (1987 [1978]), p. 81. **9.** W. Bonime (with F. Bonime) (1982 [1962]), p. 53. **10.** W. Bonime (1969), p. 82. **11.** W. Bonime (with F. Bonime) (1987 [1978]), pp. 81-2. **12.** W. Bonime (with F. Bonime) (1982 [1962]), p. 9. **13.** Ibid., p. 49. **14.** Ibid., p. 9. **15.** Ibid., p. 50. **16.** M. Ullman (1982 [1962]), p. xv. **17.** W. Bonime (with F. Bonime) (1982 [1962]), p. 50. **18.** D. Foulkes (1978), p. 73, citing S. Freud (1965 [1900]). **19.** C. S. Moss (1970), p. 112. **20.** S. Freud (1953 [1900]), pp. 471. L. L. Altman (1969), pp. 24-5. E. A. Gutheil (1967 [1951]), p. 41. **21.** M. A. Mattoon (1984 [1978]), p. 107. **22.** W. Bonime (with F. Bonime) (1982 [1962]), p. 53. **23.** R. W. McCarley & J. A. Hobson (1979), p. 121. **24.** E. Rossi (1985), p. 177. **25.** W. Bonime (with F. Bonime) (1980), p. 145. **26.** W. Bonime (with F. Bonime) (1982 [1962]), pp. 50-1. **27.** Ibid., pp. 50-2. **28.** Ibid., p. 130. **29.** Ibid., pp. 153-5. **30.** H. H. Mosak (1989), pp. 65-6. **31.** Ibid., p. 81. **32.** A. Adler (1958 [1931]), p. 8. **33.** H. H. Mosak (1989), pp. 67-8. **34.** E. Fromm (1955), pp. 168-9. **35.** H. H. Mosak (1989), p. 93. **36.** Ibid., p. 80. **37.** W. Bonime (with F. Bonime) (1982 [1962]), pp. 64-6. **38.** Ibid., pp. 66-7. **39.** Ibid., p. 86. **40.** E. Fromm (1951), p. 29. **41.** E. Fromm (1955), p. viii. **42.** Ibid., p. 25. **43.** W. Bonime (with F. Bonime) (1982 [1962]), pp. 178-9. **44.** E. Fromm (1951), pp. 196, 204-5. **45.** M. Ullman (1982 [1962]), pp. viii-ix. **46.** E. Fromm (1951), pp. 33-4. **47.** E. Fromm (1955), p. 11. **48.** Ibid., p. 17. **49.** Ibid., p. 361. **50.** M. Ullman (1969a), p. 97. **51.** M. Ullman (1973), pp. 287-8 and (1988c), p. 291. **52.** M. Ullman (1988c), p. 280. **53.** M. Ullman (1988b), p. 5. **54.** M. Ullman & N. Zimmerman (1979), p. 82. **55.** M. Ullman & S. Krippner (1970), p. 30. See also M. Ullman (1988b), p. 3. **56.** M. Ullman & S. Krippner (1970), p. 108. **57.** M. Ullman (1988c), p. 280. **58.** M. Ullman & N. Zimmerman (1979), p. 30. **59.** M. Ullman (1987b), p. 147. **60.** M. Ullman & N. Zimmerman (1979), p. 58. **61.** M. Ullman (1988c), p. 280. **62.** M. Ullman (1988b), p. 4. **63.** M. Ullman (1969b), pp. 697-8. **64.** M. Ullman (1962), p. 25. **65.** W. Bonime (1969), p. 82. **66.** M. Ullman (1969b), p. 700. **67.** M. Ullman (1988c), p. 290. **68.** M. Ullman & S. Krippner (1970). M. Ullman, S. Krippner & A. Vaughan (1989). See also: J. Tolaas & M. Ullman (1979); M. Ullman (1981), (1984) and (1986b); J. Tolaas (1986). **69.** M. Ullman & S. Krippner (1970), p. 111. **70.** M. Ullman & N. Zimmerman (1979), p. 63. **71.** M. Ullman, personal communication, 1993. **72.** M. Ullman (1962), p. 22. **73.** M. Ullman & S. Krippner (1970), p. 30. **74.** M. Ullman (1969b), p. 699. **75.** M. Ullman & N. Zimmerman (1979), p. 83. **76.** M. Ullman (1987a [1978]), p. ii. **77.** M. Ullman (1982 [1962]), pp. viii-x. **78.** R. Bastide (1966), p. 200. **79.** K. R. Stewart, "Dream theory in Malaya," *Complex* 6, pp. 21-33, 1951, cited by G. W. Domhoff (1985). **80.** P. Garfield (1976 [1974]). S. K. Williams (1986 [1980]). **81.** G. W. Domhoff (1985). **82.** B. Tedlock (1981) and (1992d [1987]). **83.** B. Secunda (1993), p. 19. **84.** M. M. Mpier (1992), pp. 100 and 108. **85.** L. N. Degarrod (1990). **86.** B. Tedlock (1992b), p. ix. This and subsequent quotes reproduced with permission. See credit page. **87.** B. Tedlock (1992c [1987]), p. 24. **88.** B. Tedlock (1992b), p. x and (1992c [1987]), p. 21. **89.** B. Tedlock (1991), p. 161. **90.** G. Herdt (1992 [1987]), p. 76. This and subsequent quotes reproduced with permission. See credit page. **91.** Ibid., pp. 55 and 63. **92.** J. P. Kiernan (1985), p. 304. **93.** M.-T. B. Dombeck (1991), p. 19 passim. **94.** O. Garrison (1983 [1964]), p. 181. **95.** See articles in G. E. Von Grunebaum & R. Caillois (1966). **96.** J. S. Lincoln (1970 [1935]), p. 47. **97.** Inter-Tribal Council of Nevada (1976), p. 55, quoting J. Mooney, "The Ghost-Dance religion and the Souix outbreak of 1890," Accompanying Paper, *Fourteenth Annual Report (Part 2) of the Bureau of Ethnology to the Smithsonian Institute, 1892-3 by J. W. Powell, Di-*

rector, Washington, D.C.: Government Printing Office, 1896. **98.** W. Doniger & K. Bulkley (1993), p. 71. **99.** V. Lanternari (1963 [1960]). **100.** Ibid., p. 123ff. **101.** Ibid., pp. 70 and 87. **102.** R. K. Dentan (1986), p. 325. **103.** J. G. Neihardt (1979 [1932]), p. 270. **104.** M. Eliade (1966), p. 332. **105.** For example: B. Kilborne (1981); S. Charsley (1992); M. C. Jędrej & R. Shaw (1992b). **106.** B. Tedlock (1992c [1987]), p. 21. **107.** W. Kracke (1992 [1987]), p. 41. **108.** E. B. Basso (1992 [1987]), p. 99. **109.** W. Merrill (1992 [1987]), pp. 204-5. This and subsequent quotes reproduced with permission. See credit page. **110.** M.-T. B. Dombeck (1991), p. 16. **111.** J. S. Lincoln (1970 [1935]), pp. 275-6. **112.** H. Reed (1988 [1985]), p. 74. **113.** M. Ullman (1988a), pp. viii-ix. **114.** N. MacKenzie (1965), p. 215. **115.** M. Mossadegh, session of the Iranian Parliament, May 13, 1951, quoted by J. L. Borges (1976), p. 139. My translation. **116.** See chapters in G. E. von Grunebaum & R. Caillois (1966). **117.** G. E. von Grunebaum (1966), pp. 19-20, quoting Great Britain, Public Record Office 070, F.O. 60/660; A. Hardinge to the Marquess of Lansdowne, Tehran, Feb. 27, 1902, No. 32, Secret. **118.** T. J. Friedman (1990). **119.** J. S. Mbiti (1976), p. 41. **120.** N. Cooper (with M. Liu, W. Lin & R. Vokey), "The remarkable rise of a widow in yellow," *Newsweek* 107(10), p. 34, March 10, 1986, quoted by K. A. Signell (1990), pp. 9-10. **121.** J. Taylor (1992a), pp. 118-20. **122.** A. Rich, *On Lies, Secrets and Silence—Selected Prose 1966-78*, New York: Norton, p. 35, 1979, quoted by P. R. Koch-Sheras, E. A. Hollier & B. Jones (1983), p. 14. **123.** T. Priess (1993), p. 12. **124.** M. Aldighieri & J. Tripician (1991), pp. 9-10. **125.** A. Shafton (forthcoming). **126.** J. Taylor (1983), pp. 100-6. **127.** C. Upton (1988a) and (1988b). **128.** D. J. Hillman (1988), p. 124. **129.** J. Maguire (1989), p. 22. **130.** D. J. Hillman (1990), p. 14. **131.** A. Faraday (1972) and (1976 [1974]). **132.** P. Garfield (1976 [1974]). G. Delaney (1979). **133.** G. Delaney (1990c), p. 25. **134.** D. J. Hillman (1988), p. 121. **135.** J. Taylor (1992a), pp. 64-5 and 229-34. **136.** L. L. Magallón & B. Shor (1990), p. 254 and p. 253. **137.** M. Ullman (1986a), pp. 538 and 551. **138.** Respectively: J. Dodd (1988); H. Fagin (1988); J. Walsh (1988); S. Knapp (1988). **139.** A. Hazarika (1992). **140.** J. Maguire (1989), pp. 23-4. **141.** M. Ullman & N. Zimmerman (1979), pp. 268-70. **142.** R. Shohet (1985). See also R. Shohet (1981). **143.** S. Andrews (1983). H. Scaife (1983). **144.** M. Ullman & N. Zimmerman (1979), pp. 245-6. **145.** M. Ullman (1990), p. 20. **146.** V. J. Gold (1973). J. M. Natterson (1980b). **147.** E. Klein-Lipshutz (1953). See also N. Locke, "The use of dreams in group psychoanalysis," *American Journal of Psychotherapy* 11, pp. 98-110, 1957, cited by V. J. Gold (1973), p. 396. **148.** L. Breger, I. Hunter & R. W. Lane (1971). V. J. Gold (1973), pp. 401-4. **149.** T. M. French & E. Fromm (1964), p. 59. **150.** R. M. Whitman (1973). **151.** V. J. Gold (1973), p. 395. **152.** Ibid., p. 396, citing S. Foulkes, *Therapeutic Group Analysis*, New York: International Universities Press, 1964. **153.** S. R. Kaplan (1973), p. 421. **154.** R. M. Whitman (1973). J. M. Natterson (1980b). **155.** M.-T. B. Dombeck (1988), p. 97. **156.** C. G. Jung (1984 [1938]), p. 35. **157.** D. Zimmermann (1967), pp. 526 and 531-3. **158.** For example: I. Markowitz, G. Taylor & E. Bokert (1968); H. W. Beck (1977); D. Cirincione, J. Hart, W. Karle & A. Switzer (1980); E. B. Taub-Bynum (1984). **159.** P. Maybruck (1991), p. 138 passim. **160.** For example: P. Garfield (1988a); R. Parker (1988), pp. 69-74; G. Delaney (1991). **161.** R. Corriere, W. Karle, L. Woldenberg & J. Hart (1980), p. 8. **162.** Ibid., p. 90. **163.** Ibid., p. 88. **164.** For example: J. Hart, "Dreams in the classroom," *Experiment and Innovation: New Directions in Education at the University of California* 4, pp. 51-66, 1971, cited by P. Garfield (1976 [1974]), p. 232; R. Shohet (1985), p. 98ff; J. Gregory (1988a) and (1988b); C. Pacosz (1990); J. Taylor (1992b); J. White-Lewis (1993); K. Bulkeley (1994), Ch. 20. **165.** R. M. Jones (1979b), (1987) and (1988). **166.** J. Maguire (1989). **167.** A. Singer (1988). R. W. Krajenke (1987). A. B. Siegel (1990), p. 257. Graywolf (1992). Temagami Vision Quest, c/o Donna Giovaniello, 100 Churn Road, Matteson, Illinois 60443. J. Zimmerman (1991). Cogburn, described in J. Puzen & M. Fulmer (1990). **168.** J. Maguire (1989), p. 22. **169.** H. Reed (1976) and (1988 [1885]), p. 71ff. **170.** H. Reed (1988 [1985]), pp. 89-90. **171.** M. Ullman, S. Krippner & A. Vaughan (1989), pp. 106-18. **172.** C. Hall & R. L. Van de Castle (1965) and (1966). **173.** H. Reed (1987 [1977]) and (1988 [1985]). **174.** H. Bro (1968). **175.** T. Yellowtail (with O. F. Fitzgerald) (1991). **176.** H. Reed (1987 [1977]), p. 335. **177.** H. Reed (1988 [1985]), p. 102. **178.** H. Reed (1987 [1977]), p. 342. **179.** Ibid., pp. 343-4. **180.** H. Reed, quoted by R. W. Krajenke (1987), p. 347. **181.** H. Reed (1987 [1977]), p. 342. **182.** M. King, quoted by W. Churchill (1990). **183.** R. Means, quoted by W. Churchill (1990). **184.** A. Smith (1992). **185.** W. LaDuke (1990), p. 32. **186.** Traditional Circle of Elders (1986). **187.** A. Smith (1992). **188.** V. Lanternari (1963 [1960]), p. 82. **189.** Terri Strauss, Native American Educational Services College, Chicago, personal communication, 1990. **190.** W. Churchill (1990). **191.** W. LaDuke (1990), pp. 33-4. **192.** A. Smith (1992). **193.** For example: J. A. Sanford (1984 [1966]); M. Kelsey (1978); J. Taylor (1983); J. D. Clift & W. B. Clift (1984); L. M. Savary, P. H. Berne & S. K. Williams (1984). **194.** R. Parker (1988), pp. 78-9. **195.** J. Taylor (1983), p. 17. **196.** L. M. Savary, P. H. Berne & S. K. Williams (1984), p. 179. **197.** Ibid., pp. 176-7. **198.** J. Covitz (1990). **199.** A. Jaffé (1965 [1961]), p. xi. **200.** J. Hillman (1979), p. 23. **201.** M. Ullman & N. Zimmerman (1979), p. 56. **202.** J. Hooper & D. Teresi (1990), p. 80. **203.** M. Ullman & N. Zimmerman (1979), p. 56. **204.** R. Bastide (1966). **205.** M. Ullman (1973), p. 284. **206.** M. Ullman (1969a), p. 98. M. Ullman & N. Zimmerman (1979), pp. 194-5. **207.** M. Ullman (1973), p. 284. **208.** M. Ullman (1969a), p. 97. **209.** M. Ullman (1973), p. 285. **210.** M. Ullman & N. Zimmerman (1979), p. 200. M. Ullman (1988c), p. 290. **211.** M. Ullman (1973), p. 285. **212.** M. Ullman (1992), p. 3. **213.** D. J. Hillman (1990), p. 17. See also (1988). **214.** M. Ullman (1992), p. 3. **215.** For example, J. M. Natterson & B. Gordon (1977). **216.** M. Ullman (1973), p. 287 and (1988c), p. 291. **217.** M. Ullman & N. Zimmerman (1979), p. 184. **218.** Ibid., p. 200. **219.** M. Ullman (1988c), p. 281. **220.** M. Ullman & N. Zimmerman (1979), p. 195. **221.** Ibid., p. 184. **222.** M. Ullman (1988c), pp. 290-1. **223.** M. Ullman (1969a), p. 97. **224.** M. Ullman (1973), p. 290. **225.** M. Ullman (1988c), p. 282. **226.** M. Ullman & N. Zimmerman (1979), p. 184. **227.** K. A. Signell (1990), p. 83 passim. **228.** P. R. Koch-Sheras, E. A. Hollier & B. Jones (1983), p. 219. **229.** Ibid., "Preface" (no page number) and p. 11. **230.** Ibid., p. 3. **231.** For example: C. S. Rupprecht (1985); J. Taylor (1992a), p. 242 passim. **232.** P. R. Koch-Sheras, E. A. Hollier & B. Jones (1983), pp. 157-74. **233.** Ibid., pp. 157-8. **234.** M. Ullman & N. Zimmerman (1979), pp. 192-4. **235.** J. R. Wikse (1988), p. 196. **236.** Ibid., pp. 209-10. **237.** For example: C. Winget, M. Kramer & R. M. Whitman (1972); T. Gregor (1983); R. E. Haskell (1985a). **238.** For example: P. Maybruck (1991), pp. 45-8; J. Taylor (1992a), p. 100ff. **239.** C. Payne, personal communication, 1990. **240.** L. Flowers, personal communication, 1990. **241.** William M. Banks, personal communication, 1990. **242.** Gerald G. Jackson, personal communication, 1990. William D. Pierce, personal communication, 1990. **243.** J. L. White (1984), p. 19. **244.** G. G. Jackson (1980a), p. 296. **245.** W. M. Banks (1980). **246.** For example: W. W. Nobles (1974), (1978), (1980a) and (1980b); J. A. Baldwin (1981). **247.** For example: C. A. Diop (1974 [1955 & 1967]) and (1990 [1959]); M. Karenga (1990). **248.** W. W. Nobles (1980a), p. 29. **249.** G. G. Jackson (1980b), p. 317. **250.** W. W. Nobles (1980a). **251.** I. L. Toldson (1973). **252.** W. M. Banks (1980). **253.** W. W. Nobles (1980a), p. 23. **254.** J. L. White (1984), p. 150. **255.** R. E. Haskell (1985a). **256.** M. Watkins (1992), p. 118. **257.** K. A. Signell (1990), p. 2. **258.** M. Watkins (1992), p. 112. **259.** J. King (1993). **260.** K. Bulkley (1993). **261.** K. Bulkeley, personal communication, 1994. **262.** W. R. Stimson (1982). **263.** Y. Bilu (1989), p. 365. **264.** Ibid., p. 374. **265.** Ibid., p. 379. **266.** Ibid., pp. 378, 381 and 382. **267.** Ibid., p. 382. **268.** Ibid., p. 386. **269.** C. Beradt (1968 [1966]), p. 9. **270.** Ibid., p. 18. **271.** Ibid., p. 21. **272.** R. Shohet (1983), pp. 98-101, citing C. Beradt (1968 [1966]). **273.** C. Beradt (1968 [1966]), pp. 139-40. **274.** Ibid., pp. 134-5. **275.** Ibid., pp. 107-8, quoting I. Scholl, *Die Weisse Rose*. **276.** M. Watkins (1992), p. 117. **277.** J. W. Lewis (1991), p. 6. **278.** Ibid., pp. 9-10. **279.** J. L. Harrington (1991). **280.** M. Ullman & N. Zimmerman (1979), p. 195. **281.** M. Ullman (1992), p. 3. **282.** M. Ullman (1973), p. 292. **283.** M. Ullman (1988c), p. 293. **284.** M. Ullman (1973), p. 287. **285.** T. Burrow, *The Social Basis of Consciousness*, New York: Harcourt Brace, 1927. A. Angyal, *Foundations for a Science of Personality*, New York: The Commonwealth Fund, 1941. Both cited by M. Ullman (1973), pp. 286-7. **286.** H. H. Mosak (1989), p. 80. **287.** Ibid., pp. 65-6.

Chapter 6 • Gestalt

1. G. M. Yontef & J. S. Simkin (1989), p. 330, citing F. S. Perls, R. F. Hefferline & P. Goodman, *Gestalt Therapy*, New York: Julian Press, 1951. **2.** Ibid., p. 329. **3.** R. E. Fantz (1987 [1978]), p. 197. **4.** G. M. Yontef & J. S. Simkin (1989), p. 350, citing F. S. Perls, "Group vs. Individual Therapy," *ETC* 24, pp. 306-12, 1967. **5.** A. Faraday (1972), p. 145. **6.** F. S. Perls (1992 [1969]), p. 94. **7.** G. M. Yontef & J. S. Simkin (1989), pp. 330-1 and 350. **8.** F. S. Perls (1992 [1969]), p. 21. **9.** G. M. Yontef & J. S. Simkin (1989), pp. 355-6. **10.** D. Whitmore (1981), p. 113. **11.** G. M. Yontef & J. S. Simkin (1989), p. 323. **12.** F. S. Perls (1992 [1969]), p. 36. **13.** Ibid., p. 30. **14.** A. Faraday (1972), p. 146. **15.** G. M. Yontef & J. S. Simkin (1989), p. 340. **16.** F. S. Perls (1992 [1969]), p. 26. **17.** G. M. Yontef & J. S. Simkin (1989), p. 334. **18.** F. S. Perls, quoted by A. Faraday (1972), pp. 190-1. **19.** G. M. Yontef & J. S. Simkin (1989), pp. 324-5. **20.** F. S. Perls (1992 [1969]), p. 63. **21.** Ibid., p. 179. **22.** A. Faraday (1972), p. 146. **23.** Ibid. **24.** G. M. Yontef & J. S. Simkin (1989), p. 336. **25.** R. E. Fantz (1987 [1978]), p. 195. **26.** S. Knapp (1979), p. 343. **27.** M. Boss (1977), p. 54. **28.** F. S. Perls (1992 [1969]), p. 35. **29.** G. M. Yontef & J. S. Simkin (1989), p. 331. **30.** L. Perls, "Some aspects of Gestalt therapy," paper presented to the Orthopsychiatric Association, p. 3, 1973, quoted by G. M. Yontef & J. S. Simkin (1989), p. 333. **31.** A. Faraday (1972), p. 146. **32.** F. S. Perls (1992 [1969]), p. 31. **33.** Ibid., p. 114. **34.** J. L. Fosshage & C. A. Loew (1987b [1978]), p. 264. **35.** F. S. Perls (1992 [1969]), p. 60. **36.** Ibid., p. 37. **37.** Ibid., p. 23. **38.** R. Corriere, W. Karle, L. Woldenberg & J. Hart (1980). A. Mindell (1985). E. T. Gendlin (1986). **39.** R. E. Fantz (1987 [1978]), p. 196. **40.** F. S. Perls (1992 [1969]), p. 241. **41.** Ibid., p. 122. **42.** J. Downing & R. Marmorstein (1973), pp. 45-6. Wide ellipsis authors'. **43.** F. S. Perls (1992 [1969]), p. 215. **44.** G. M. Yontef & J. S. Simkin (1989), p. 336. **45.** R. E. Fantz (1987 [1978]), p. 192. **46.** F. S. Perls (1992 [1969]), p. 87. **47.** Ibid., p. 143. **48.** Ibid., pp. 291-3. **49.** A. Faraday (1976 [1974]), p. 170 **50.** Ibid., p. 175-6. **51.** F. S. Perls (1992 [1969]), p. 38. **52.** R. E. Fantz (1987 [1978]), p. 196. **53.** R. E. Fantz (1987 [1978]), p. 196. **54.** J. L. Fosshage & C. A. Loew (1987b [1978]), p. 278n. **55.** A. Faraday (1972), p. 153. **56.** R. E. Fantz (1987 [1978]), p. 193. **57.** F. S. Perls (1992 [1969]), p. 146. **58.** J. L. Fosshage & C. A. Loew (1987b [1978]), p. 260. **59.** F. S. Perls (1992 [1969]), p. 171. **60.** C. G. Jung, "General aspects of dream psychology" [1916/1948], CW 8, para. 509. **61.** H. E. Lehmann (1969), p. 141. **62.** R. W. Emerson, in R. L. Woods & H. B. Greenhouse (1974), pp. 175-6. **63.** E. A. Gutheil (1967 [1951]), pp. 185-6, quoting S. Freud. **64.** For example: W. Stekel (1943 [1913 and later]), p. 152 passim; E. A. Gutheil (1967 [1951]), p. 185ff; E. H. Erikson (1954), p. 31; K. Horney (1970 [1950]); S. E. Pulver (1978), p. 681. **65.** W. Stekel (1943 [1914]), p. 61. **66.** W. Stekel (1943), p. 536. **67.** W. Stekel (1943 [1929]), p. 152. **68.** C. G. Jung, "General aspects of dream psychology" [1916/1948], CW 8, para. 510. **69.** C. G. Jung, CW 10, quoted by T. A. Greene (1979), p. 304. **70.** M. A. Mattoon (1984 [1978]), pp. 115 and 200. **71.** C. G. Jung, "General aspects of dream psychology" [1916/1948], CW 8, para. 519. **72.** R. A. Johnson (1986), p. 69. **73.** C. G. Jung, "General aspects of dream psychology" [1916/1948], CW 8, para. 517. **74.** R. H. Hopcke (1990), p. 60. **75.** C. G. Jung, "General aspects of dream psychology" [1916/-1948], CW 8, para. 498. **76.** C. G. Jung [1944], CW 12, para. 346. **77.** T. A. Greene (1979), p. 313. **78.** E. C. Whitmont (1987 [1978]), p. 56. **79.** M.-L. von Franz (1980a [1978]), p. 7ff. **80.** J. S. Singer (1975), p. 209. **81.** A. Stevens (1983 [1982]), p. 292. **82.** C. A. Meier (1959), p. 22. **83.** W. Bonime (with F. Bonime) (1982 [1962]), p. 268. **84.** M. Boss & B. Kenny (1987 [1978]), p. 169. **85.** F. S. Perls (1992 [1969]), p. 57. **86.** Ibid., p. 314. **87.** C. G. Jung, "General aspects of dream psychology" [1916/1948], CW 8, para's 507 and 517. **88.** C. G. Jung (1965 [1961]). **89.** M.-L. von Franz (1980a [1978]), p. 13. **90.** R. Lind (1985). **91.** M.-L. von Franz (1980a [1978]), p. 13. **92.** F. S. Perls (1992 [1969]), p. 39. **93.** Ibid., p. 60. **94.** Ibid., p. 265. **95.** M.-L. von Franz (1980a [1978]), pp. 158-9. **96.** W. Y. Evans-Wentz (1969 [1928]). **97.** R. Bosnak (1988 [1986]), p. 66. **98.** F. S. Perls (1992 [1969]), p. 87. **99.** R. E. Fantz (1987 [1978]), p. 193. **100.**

F. S. Perls (1992 [1969]), p. 87. **101.** R. E. Fantz (1987 [1978]), p. 193. **102.** J. Downing & R. Marmorstein (1973), p. 7. **103.** F. S. Perls (1992 [1969]), p. 87. **104.** J. A. Hall (1983), p. 14. **105.** F. S. Perls (1992 [1969]), pp. 250-5. **106.** E. R. Neu (1988), p. 37ff. **107.** A. Faraday (1976 [1974]), pp. 157-8. **108.** F. S. Perls (1992 [1969]), p. 76. **109.** Ibid., p. 89-90.

Chapter 7 • Catagogic/Anagogic

1. S. Freud (1953 [1900]), p. 88. **2.** Ibid., pp. 90. **3.** C. S. Rupprecht (1990), p. 119. **4.** S. Freud (1953 [1900]), p. 92. **5.** Ibid., pp. 579, 567, 267 and 54, respectively. **6.** J. E. Mack (1989 [1970]), p. 159, quoting S. Freud, *An Outline of Psychoanalysis*, Standard Edition, vol. XXIII, p. 195, 1964 [1938]. **7.** S. Freud (1953 [1900]), p. 270 fn. **8.** J. A. Hadfield (1954), p. 32, citing S. Freud, *Introductory Lectures*, p. 440, 1932 edition. **9.** C. Rycroft (1981 [1979]), p. 4. **10.** T. A. Greene (1979), p. 302. **11.** C. G. Jung, "The state of psychotherapy today" [1934], CW 10, para. 361, quoted by J. A. Sanford (1977), p. 105. **12.** R. A. Johnson (1986), p. 10. **13.** E. Hartmann (1967), p. 82, citing C. G. Jung, *The Psychology of Dementia Praecox*, New York: Journal of Nervous and Mental Disease Publishing Co., 1944 (CW 3). **14.** R. Cahen (1966), p. 133. **15.** M. Ullman (1987a [1978]), p. v. **16.** W. D. O'Flaherty (1984), pp. 19-20 passim. **17.** J. S. Lincoln (1970 [1935]), pp. 66, 209-13 and 268. **18.** D. Eggan (1974 [1952]), p. 242. **19.** C. W. O'Nell (1976), p. 26. **20.** *Genesis* 41, discussed by J. Covitz (1990) and many others. **21.** N. MacKenzie (1965). **22.** W. Wolff (1972 [1952]), pp. 10-1. **23.** James Hastings, editor, *Encyclopedia of Religion and Ethics*, vol. V, New York: Scribners, 1914, quoted by W. Wolff (1972 [1952]). p. 9. **24.** Plato, *Republic* and *Phaedo*, Jowett translations, quoted by W. Wolff (1972 [1952]), p. 16. **25.** M. Ullman & N. Zimmerman (1979), p. 40. **26.** E. Fromm (1951), p. 126, citing Cicero, *On Divination*, in R. L. Woods (1947). **27.** Ibid., p. 125. See Artemidorus Daldianus, *The Interpretation of Dreams*, R. J. White, translator, Park Ridge, New Jersey: Noyes Press, 1975. **28.** S. Parman (1991), pp. 35-6. **29.** *Jeremiah* 29. **30.** J. Covitz (1990), p. 2. **31.** M. Kelsey (1978). **32.** E. Fromm (1951), p. 130, citing Synesius of Cyrene, *On Dreams*, in R. L. Woods (1947). **33.** M. Ullman & N. Zimmerman (1979), p. 43, citing M. T. Kelsey, *Dreams: The Dark Speech of the Spirit*, New York: Doubleday, 1968. **34.** M. Kelsey (1978), p. 76. **35.** E. Fromm (1951), pp. 134-5. M. Kelsey (1978), pp. 76-7. M. Ullman & N. Zimmerman (1979), p. 44. **36.** J. S. Lincoln (1970 [1935]), pp. 8-9, citing Philip Goodwin, "The mystery of dreams historically considered," 1865. **37.** G. E. von Grunebaum (1966) p. 5ff. **38.** S. Freud (1965 [paragraph added in 1919]), p. 562, citing H. Silberer, *Probleme der Mystik und ihrer Symbolik*, Part II, section 5, Vienna and Liepsig, 1914. **39.** W. Stekel (1943), p. 538. **40.** S. Freud (1965 [paragraph added in 1919]), p. 562. **41.** E. A. Gutheil (1967 [1951]), p. 31 passim. W. Wolff (1972 [1952]), p. 50 passim. **42.** W. Stekel (1943), p. 538. **43.** W. Stekel (1943 [1914]), p. 62. **44.** W. Stekel (1943), p. x. **45.** Ibid., p. 507. **46.** W. Stekel (1943 [1914]), p. 76. **47.** W. Wolff (1972 [1952]), p. 53. **48.** Ibid., p. 52. **49.** Ibid., p. 68. **50.** M. Boss (1959 [1938]), pp. 160-2. **51.** E. A. Gutheil (1967 [1951]), pp. 167-8. **52.** M. M. R. Khan (1976). **53.** R. Fliess (1953), pp. 46-9, quoting T. M. French, "Reality testing in dreams," *Psychoanalytic Quarterly* 6:62-77, 1937. **54.** L. S. Kubie (1975 [1958]), p. 3. **55.** Ibid., p. 20. **56.** E. S. Tauber & M. R. Green (1959), p. 171. **57.** J. L. Fosshage (1987b), pp. 29 and 33. **58.** E. Fromm (1951), p. 47. **59.** K. Horney (1970 [1950]), p. 188. **60.** Ibid., pp. 349-50. **61.** T. French & E. Fromm (1964), pp. 66-7. **62.** H. Segal, "The function of dreams," in *The Works of Hanna Segal*, New York: Aronson, p. 90, 1981, quoted by L. Grinberg (1987), p. 156. **63.** D. Meltzer (1984), p. 91. **64.** Ibid., p. 88. **65.** Ibid., pp. 94-5. **66.** S. Gabel (1985), p. 86, citing C. Grieser, R. Greenberg & R. A. Harrison, "The adaptive function of sleep: the differential effects of sleep and dream on recall," *Journal of Abnormal Psychology* 80, pp. 280-6, 1972. **67.** L. Breger, I. Hunter & R. W. Lane (1971), pp. 51 and 59. **68.** S. Gabel (1985), pp. 86-7, citing I. Lewin & H. Glaubman, "The effect of REM deprivation: Is it detrimental, beneficial, or neutral?" *Psychophysiology* 12, p. 349, 1975. **69.** M. Kramer (1991a), pp. 280 and 284. **70.** J. Piaget (1962 [1945]), p. 209. **71.** H. T.

Hunt (1989), p. 194. **72.** M. Ullman (1962), p. 22. S. R. Palombo (1987b), p. 135. D. Kuiken & S. Sikora (1993), p. 426. J. L. Fosshage (1987a), p. 303 and (1987b), p. 29. K. Kelzer (1992). J. McManus, C. D. Laughlin & J. Shearer (1993), p. 29. R. Cartwright & L. Lamberg (1992), p. 95. D. Feinstein (1990), pp. 28-32. K. Belicki & M. A. Cuddy (1991), p. 111. **73.** D. Whitmore (1981), p. 108. See also R. Assagioli (1971 [1965]). **74.** P. Garfield (1976 [1974]). **75.** P. Garfield (1984), pp. 158-9. **76.** Ibid., p. 161. **77.** A. Faraday (1972). **78.** A. Faraday (1976 [1974]), p. 68. **79.** Ibid., p. 253. **80.** Ibid., p. 228. **81.** A. Mankowitz (1984), p. 29. **82.** R. A. Johnson (1986), p. 4. **83.** E. T. Gendlin (1986), p. 40. **84.** J. Taylor (1983), p. 75. See also (1992a), pp. 77 and 183. **85.** J. Hillman (1979), p. 2. **86.** Ibid., p. 41. **87.** Ibid., p. 48. **88.** Ibid., p. 43. **89.** W. A. Shelburne (1984), p. 44. **90.** J. Hillman (1979), p. 164, citing C. G. Jung, "A psychological view of conscience" [1958], CW 10, para. 835. **91.** G. Delaney (1979), p. 6. **92.** Ibid., p. 12. **93.** Ibid., pp. 9-10. **94.** Ibid., p. 176. **95.** R. Langs (1988), p. 9. **96.** D. E. Kalsched (1992), pp. 91-3, citing J. Grotstein, *Splitting and Projective Identification*, New York: Jason Aronson, 1981.

Chapter 8 • Dream and Symptom

1. W. Stekel (1943 [1913]), pp. 11-3. **2.** Ibid., pp. 15-6. **3.** Ibid., p. 19. **4.** E. A. Gutheil (1967 [1951]), pp. 294-5. **5.** Ibid., p. 159, citing E. Rosenbaum, "Zur 'aktiven' Traumdeutung," *Fortschr. d. Sexualw. u. Psa.*, 1931. **6.** D. Feinstein (1990), p. 27. **7.** L. Weiss (1986), p. 80. **8.** H. Reed (1991), pp. 68-70. **9.** S. L. Pomer & R. A. Shain (1980), pp. 186-7. **10.** E. A. Gutheil (1967 [1951]), p. 371. **11.** Ibid., pp. 417-9. **12.** W. Stekel (1943 [1935]), p. 25. **13.** Ibid., p. 40. **14.** S. Freud (1953 [1900]), passim, citing K. A. Scherner, *Das Leben des Traumes*, Berlin, 1861, and J. Volkelt, *Die Traum-Phantasie*, Stuttgart, 1875. **15.** Ibid., p. 225. **16.** Ibid., pp. 85-6 and 225. **17.** Ibid., p. 346. **18.** Ibid., p. 85. **19.** Ibid., p. 83. **20.** G. Roheim (1969 [1952]), p. 36. **21.** Ibid., p. 18. **22.** Ibid., p. 27. **23.** Ibid., p. 50. **24.** P. Garfield (1988a). **25.** B. D. Lewin (1958), pp. 20-1. **26.** H. Silberer (1955 [1918]), pp. 366-7. **27.** J. Piaget (1962 [1945]), pp. 199-200. **28.** R. D. Cartwright (1977), p. 10. **29.** F. Crick & G. Mitchison (1986), p. 240. **30.** C. S. Rupprecht (1990), p. 121, quoting Thomas Nashe, *Terrors of the Night, Or, A Discourse of Apparitions*, 1594. **31.** J. Taylor (1992a), p. 12. **32.** H. T. Hunt (1986), p. 264. **33.** H. Silberer (1955 [1918]), p. 379. **34.** V. Kasatkin (1984), p. 104. **35.** P. Garfield (1991), p. 360, note 3, quoting E. Rossi & D. Cheek, *Mind-Body Therapy*, New York: Norton, p. 377, 1988. **36.** Ibid., p. 62. **37.** Ibid., p. 60ff. **38.** H. Fiss (1993), p. 395ff and p. 387. **39.** R. E. Haskell (1985c), p. 114, quoting L. Breger, I. Hunter & R. W. Lane (1971). **40.** R. E. Haskell (1985c), p. 115. **41.** E. Whitmont & S. B. Perera (1989), p. 138. **42.** H. T. Hunt (1989), p. 80. **43.** A. W. Epstein (1964), pp. 26 and 28. **44.** P. Maybruck (1991), pp. 29 and 71. **45.** Ibid., p. 146. **46.** J. Windsor (1987), p. 112. **47.** P. Garfield (1991), p. 123, citing R. Van de Castle, "Pregnancy dreams," paper presented to the Association for the Study of Dreams, Ottawa, 1986. **48.** Ibid., p. 82. **49.** E. Stukane (1985 [1983]), pp. 16 and 72. **50.** Ibid., p. 52. **51.** P. Garfield (1991), pp. 82, 116-7 and 153, respectively. **52.** Ibid., pp. 75-6 and 124ff. Italics omitted. **53.** Ibid., p. 80. **54.** R. A. Lockhart (1977), pp. 9-10, quoting T. M. Davie, "Comments upon a case of periventricular epilepsy," *British Medical Journal*, 1935, pp. 296-7; and quoting C. G. Jung, *Analytical Psychology: Its Theory and Practice*, New York: Pantheon, pp. 73-4, 1968. **55.** M. Sabini (1981a), p. 85. **56.** C. G. Jung, "The practical use of dream-analysis" [1934], CW 16, para's 343-50. **57.** M.-L. von Franz (1986 [1984]), p. 19. **58.** M. Sabini (1981a), p. 94, citing A. Ziegler, "Heart-failure and aporetic dreams," *Psychosomatische Medizin* 9, pp. 66-71, 1980. **59.** C. G. Jung, "Psychological interpretations of children's dreams," unpublished notes on lectures given at Eidgenössische Technische Hochschule, Zurich, pp. 81-2, 1938-9, quoted by M. Sabini (1981a), p. 95. **60.** C. G. Jung, "The practical use of dream analysis" [1934], CW 16, para. 349. **61.** E. Whitmont & S. B. Perera (1989), p. 135. **62.** P. Garfield (1991), p. 301. **63.** R. E. Haskell (1985c), p. 111, citing H. A. Savitz, "The dream as a diagnostic aid in physical diagnosis," *Connecticut Medicine* 33, pp. 309-10, 1969. **64.** R. E. Rainville (1988), p. 191.

65. R. C. Smith (1984), (1985) and (1990). **66.** R. C. Smith (1987). **67.** R. C. Smith (1986), pp. 397, 406 and 407. **68.** R. C. Smith (1984), p. 174, citing A. Kardiner, "The bio-analysis of the epileptic reaction," *Psychoanalytic Quarterly* 1, pp. 375-483, 1932. **69.** R. C. Smith (1990), p. 228. **70.** Ibid., p. 229. **71.** D. Koulack (1991), p. 107. **72.** R. C. Smith (1984), p. 174, citing H. L. Levitan (1976/77a). **73.** S. Resnik (1987), p. 33. **74.** M. Sabini (1981a), p. 88 passim. See also M. Sabini (1981b). **75.** B. Siegel (1984), pp. 1-2. **76.** J. Windsor (1987), p. 109. **77.** P. Garfield (1991), pp. 91 and 165, respectively. **78.** Ibid., p. 200. **79.** D. Barrett (1993), p. 119. **80.** M. Sabini (1981b), p. 31. **81.** H. Warnes & A. Finkelstein (1971), p. 322. **82.** S. Resnik (1987), p. 85, citing W. Bion. **83.** E. A. Gutheil (1967 [1951]), pp. 386-7. **84.** H. Warnes (1982), p. 155. **85.** Ibid., p. 156. **86.** H. Warnes & A. Finkelstein (1971), p. 322. **87.** H. Warnes (1982), p. 156. **88.** H. L. Levitan (1981a), p. 2. **89.** D. E. Schneider (1973), p. 364. Ellipsis Schneider's. **90.** H. L. Levitan (1981a), p. 5. Ellipses Levitan's. **91.** Ibid., pp. 3-4. Ellipses Levitan's. **92.** A. B. Siegel (1990), pp. 235-7. **93.** H. L. Levitan (1981a), p. 6. **94.** E. Hartmann (1967), p. 104ff. **95.** R. E. Rainville (1988), p. 202. **96.** R. E. Haskell (1985c), p. 120. **97.** R. Haskell (1985b), pp. 50-1. **98.** E. L. Rossi & D. B. Cheek (1988), pp. 389-99. **99.** Ibid., pp. 389-91. **100.** D. B. Cheek (1969). **101.** D. Koulack (1991), p. 108. **102.** R. E. Rainville (1988), p. 191. **103.** E. Hartmann (1967), p. 118, citing R. H. Armstrong, D. Burnap, A. Jacobson, A. Kaies, S. Ward, & J. Golden, "Dreams and gastric secretions in duodenal ulcer patients," *The New Physician* 14, pp. 241-3, 1965. **104.** H. Warnes & A. Finkelstein (1971), p. 317, citing M. Andrisani, "Nocturnal angina pectoris," *Journal of the American Medical Association* 203, p. 152, April 7, 1969. See also J. B. Nowlin, W. G. Troyer, W. S. Collins, G. Silverman, C. Nichols, H. McIntosh, E. Estes & M. Bogdonoff, "The association of angina pectoris with dreaming," *Annals of Internal Medicine* 63, p. 1040, 1965. **105.** A. Potamianou (1990), pp. 285 and 290. **106.** L. F. Snow, unpublished, part of the original manuscript of (1993). **107.** H. L. Levitan (1984), p. 161, citing D. S. Dexter & E. D. Weitzman, "The relationship of migraine to sleep stages," *Neurology* 20, p. 513, 1970; and citing L. K. G. Hsu et al., "Nocturnal plasma levels of catecholamines, tryptophane, glucose and fatty acids and the sleeping encephalographs of subjects experiencing early morning migraine," in Raymond Greene, editor, *Current Concepts of Migraine Research*, New York: Raven Press, 1978. **108.** H. L. Levitan (1984), p. 162. **109.** Ibid., pp. 162-3. **110.** H. Warnes & A. Finkelstein (1971), p. 319. **111.** E. A. Gutheil (1967 [1951]), p. 310ff. **112.** Ibid., p. 310. **113.** Ibid., p. 315. **114.** Ibid., p. 310. **115.** Ibid., p. 314. **116.** H. L. Levitan (1984), p. 162. **117.** Ibid., p. 165, citing C. W. Lippman, "Recurrent dreams in migraine," *Journal of Nervous and Mental Diseases* 120, p. 273, 1954. **118.** P. Garfield (1991), pp. 314-5. **119.** H. Warnes & A. Finkelstein (1971), p. 318, quoting F. Alexander & G. W. Wilson, "Quantitative dream studies: A methodological attempt at a quantitative evaluation of psychoanalytic material," *Psychoanalytic Quarterly* 4, pp. 371-407, 1935. **120.** Ibid., p. 319. **121.** Ibid., pp. 319-20. **122.** C. M. Shapiro, J. R. Catterall, I. Montgomery, G. M. Raab & N. J. Douglas (1986). **123.** M. Katz & C. M. Shapiro (1993), p. 994, citing C. M. Shapiro & N. J. Douglas, "Psychophysiology of asthma patients at night," in C. von Euler & M. Katz-Solamon, editors, *Respiratory Psychophysiology*, Basingstoke: Macmillan, 1988. **124.** B. Bressler & N. Mizrachi (1978a), p. 179 and (1978b), p. 1, citing T. M. French, *Psychoanalytic Interpretations: The Selected Papers of Thomas M. French*, Chicago: Quadrangle, 1970. **125.** F. Alexander, quoted by A. Gutheil E. (1967 [1951]) p. 342. **126.** H. Warnes & A. Finkelstein (1971), p. 318, citing T. M. French & F. Alexander, "Psychogenic factors in bronchial asthma" (Parts I & II), *Psychosomatic Medicine Monographs, II*, no. 1 & 2, 1941. **127.** W. Stekel (1943 [1935]), p. 26ff. E. A. Gutheil (1967 [1951]), p. 341ff. **128.** H. Warnes & A. Finkelstein (1971), p. 319. **129.** Ibid., p. 320. **130.** J. M. Wood, R. R. Bootzin, S. F. Quan & Mary E. Klink (1993), pp. 232-5. **131.** Ibid., p. 234, citing E. Hartmann (1984), pp. 253-4. **132.** H. L. Levitan (1984), p. 166, citing H. L. Levitan, "Dreams which precede asthma attacks," in Kimball & Krakowski, editors, *Psychosomatic Medicine: Theoretical, Clinical and Transcultural Aspects*, New York: Plenum, 1983. **133.** H. Warnes & A. Finkelstein (1971), p. 320. **134.** E. A. Gutheil (1967 [1951]), p. 316. **135.** C. Winget & M. Kramer (1979),

p. 58, citing L. J. Saul, E. Sheppard, D. Selby, W. Lhamon, D. Sachs & R. Master, "The quantification of hostility in dreams with reference to essential hypertension," *Science* 119, pp. 382-3, 1954 (also reprinted in M. F. DeMartino 1959). See also: L. Saul, "Utilization of early recurrent dreams in formulating psychoanalytic cases," *Psychoanalytic Quarterly* 9, pp. 453-69, 1940; L. J. Saul & E. Sheppard, "An attempt to quantify emotional forces using manifest dreams," *Journal of the American Psychoanalytic Association* 4, pp. 486-502, 1956; and E. Sheppard & L. J. Saul (1958). **136.** H. Warnes & A. Finkelstein (1971), p. 318, citing L. J. Saul, "Utilization of early current dreams in formulating psychoanalytic cases," *Psychoanalytic Quarterly* 9, p. 453, 1940. **137.** M. Sabini (1981a), p. 92, quoting J. Kirsch, "The role of instinct in psychosomatic medicine," *American Journal of Psychotherapy* 3, p. 257, 1949. **138.** A. Ziegler (1962), pp. 142-7. **139.** M. Sabini & V. H. Maffly (1981), p. 124. **140.** Ibid., pp. 126-7. **141.** Ibid., p. 149.

Chapter 9 • Dream Styles

1. H. L. Levitan (1976/77b), p. 126. **2.** P. Garfield (1984), p. 270. **3.** G. W. Domhoff (1985), pp. 108-10, citing C. S. Hall & B. Domhoff, "The dreams of Freud and Jung," *Psychology Today*, pp. 42-5 and 64-5, June, 1968. **4.** H. T. Hunt, R. Ogilvie, K. Belicki, D. Belicki & E. Atalick (1982), p. 608. H. Hunt (1992). **5.** C. Winget, M. Kramer & R. M. Whitman (1972), p. 204. **6.** The following is from D. Foulkes (1978), (1979) and (1985). See also *Children's Dreams: Longitudinal Studies*, New York: Wiley, 1982. **7.** C. Winget & M. Kramer (1979), p. 24, citing C. S. Hall & B. Domhoff, "Aggression in dreams," *International Journal of Social Psychiatry* 9, pp. 259-67, 1963. **8.** D. Foulkes (1978), p. 136. **9.** C. S. Hall & V. J. Nordby (1972), pp. 86-7. **10.** D. Foulkes (1979), pp. 147-8. **11.** M. Kramer (1970), p. 151. **12.** C. S. Hall (1966a [1953]), p. 17. **13.** T. A. Nielsen, D. Deslauriers & G. W. Baylor (1991), p. 291. **14.** C. S. Hall & R. L. Van de Castle (1966), p. 189. **15.** C. S. Hall (1966a [1953]). **16.** C. S. Hall & B. Domhoff (1974 [1968]). **17.** C. S. Hall (1966a [1953]). **18.** C. S. Hall (1966a [1953]). M. Kramer (1970). C. Winget, M. Kramer & R. M. Whitman (1972). C. Winget & M. Kramer (1979). H. Zepelin (1980-1) and (1981). **19.** M. Barad, K. Z. Altshuler & A. I. Goldfarb (1961), p. 420. **20.** E. Kahn, C. Fisher & L. Lieberman (1969). J. B. Howe & K. A. Blick (1983). P. Garfield (1988a), pp. 334 and 383. **21.** K. Z. Altshuler, M. Barad & A. I. Goldfarb (1963), pp. 34-5. **22.** M. Katz & C. M. Shapiro (1993), p. 994, citing R. J. Nathan, C. Rose-Itkoff & G. Lord, "Dreams, first memories and brain atrophy in the elderly," *Hillside Journal of Clinical Psychiatry* 3, pp. 139-48, 1981. **23.** D. Foulkes (1985), p. 133. **24.** R. E. Rainville (1988), pp. 82-3. **25.** U. Niederer (1990). **26.** R. Armitage (1992), p. 140. **27.** J. Taylor (1983), p. 28. **28.** P. Garfield (1991), p. 189. **29.** E. Hartmann, R. Elkin & M. Garg (1991), p. 312. **30.** P. R. Koch-Sheras & A. Hollier (1985), p. 8. **31.** C. Winget & R. A. Farrell (1974 [1971]), p. 25. **32.** P. R. Koch-Sheras, E. A. Hollier & B. Jones (1983), p. 21. **33.** P. Garfield (1984), p. 288. R. Levin & J. Rosenblatt (1990). **34.** A. Moffitt (1990). M. Cuddy, *Predicting Sexual Abuse from Dissociation, Somatization and Nightmares*, Ph.D. dissertation, York University, Downsview, Ontario, 1990, cited by A. Moffitt, M. Kramer & R. Hoffmann (1993b), p. 4. **35.** E. Hartmann (1984), p. 33. **36.** K. J. Schultz & D. Koulack (1980), p. 436. **37.** P. Garfield (1988a), p. 280, citing J. Thomson & I. Oswald, "Effect of estrogen on the sleep, mood and anxiety of menopausal women," *British Medical Journal* 2, pp. 317-9, 1977, and J. Thomson, J. Maddock, M. Aylward & I. Oswald, "Relationship between nocturnal plasma oestrogen concentration and free plasma tryptophan in post-menopausal women," *Journal of Endocrinology* 72, pp. 395-6, 1977. **38.** P. Garfield (1984), p. 14. **39.** J. Gackenbach (1990b). **40.** E. Hartmann (1967), p. 111. **41.** E. M. Swanson & D. Foulkes (1968), p. 361. **42.** C. Winget & M. Kramer (1979), p. 38, citing R. L. Van de Castle, personal communication, 1972. **43.** D. Koulack (1991), p. 105, citing K. J. Schultz & D. Koulack (1980). **44.** J. Gackenbach (1990b). **45.** C. Winget & M. Kramer (1979), p. 41, citing R. L. Van de Castle, personal communication, 1972. **46.** W. Bucci, M. L. Creelman & S. K. Severino (1991), p. 273. **47.** J. Gackenbach & J. Bosveld (1989), p.

108, citing R. L. Van de Castle. **48.** P. R. Koch-Sheras, E. A. Hollier & B. Jones (1983), p. 22, citing R. L. Van de Castle, *The Psychology of Dreaming*, Morristown, New Jersey: General Learning, 1971. **49.** C. Winget & M. Kramer (1979), p. 189, citing R. L. Van de Castle, personal communication, 1972. **50.** E. M. Swanson & D. Foulkes (1968), p. 361. **51.** L. Dudley & M. Swank (1990), p. 3. **52.** P. R. Koch-Sheras, E. A. Hollier & B. Jones (1983), p. 22, citing R. L. Van de Castle, *The Psychology of Dreaming*, Morristown, New Jersey: General Learning, 1971. **53.** J. Gackenbach (1990b). **54.** P. Garfield (1988a), pp. 48-96. **55.** Ibid., pp. 48-9. **56.** Ibid., pp. 161-209. **57.** E. Stukane (1985 [1983]), p. 31. **58.** P. Maybruck (1990), pp. 143-4. **59.** Ibid., pp. 148-9. **60.** E. Stukane (1985 [1983]), pp. 15-6. **61.** P. Maybruck (1990), p. 146. **62.** E. Stukane (1985 [1983]). P. Garfield (1988a), pp. 161-209 and 366. S. Krippner & J. Dillard (1988), p. 60, citing S. Krippner, N. Posner, W. Pomerance & S. Fischer, "An investigation of dream content during pregnancy," *Journal of the American Society of Psychosomatic Dentistry and Medicine* 21, pp. 111-123, 1974. E. Cortopassi, R. Dalle Luch, N. Cascella & C. Maggini (1989). R. Cartwright & L. Lamberg (1992), p. 157, citing R. L. Van de Castle, personal communication. See also P. Maybruck, *Pregnancy and Dreams*, Los Angeles: Jeremy P. Tarcher, 1989. **63.** P. Maybruck (1990), p. 146. **64.** A. Siegel (1990), pp. 8 and 59-94, and (1992). See also L. Zayas, "Thematic features in the manifest dreams of expectant fathers," *Clinical Social Work Journal* 16, pp. 282-96, 1988, cited by R. Cartwright & L. Lamberg (1992), p. 157. **65.** A. Siegel (1990), p. 86, citing J. Clinton, "Expectant fathers at risk for couvade," *Nursing Research* 35, pp. 290-5, 1986. **66.** E. Stukane (1985 [1983]), p. 35. **67.** Ibid., pp. 59-60. **68.** C. Winget, M. Kramer & R. M. Whitman (1972), p. 203. **69.** R. E. Rainville (1988), pp. 127-9. **70.** P. Maybruck (1991), p. xv. **71.** R. E. Rainville (1988), p. 101. **72.** P. Maybruck (1991), p. 169. **73.** S. LaBerge (1985), p. 82. **74.** C. S. Hall, G. W. Domhoff, K. A. Blick & K. E. Weesner (1982). **75.** L. Dudley & M. Swank (1990). **76.** V. K. Tonay (1990-1)). **77.** P. R. Koch-Sheras, "A re-examination of the difference between men's and women's dreams," paper presented to the Association for the Study of Dreams, Charlottesville, Virginia, 1985, cited by L. Weiss (1986), pp. 22-3. **78.** M. Lortie-Lussier, C. Schwab & J. De Koninck (1985). **79.** B. Meier & I. Strauch (1990). **80.** P. Cramer, "Fantasies of college men: then and now," *Psychoanalytic Review* 73, pp. 163-74, 1986, cited by K. Rubenstein (1990), p. 139. **81.** M. Kramer, L. Kinney & M. Scharf, "Sex differences in dreams," *Psychiatric Journal of the University of Ottawa* 8, pp. 1-4, 1983, cited by K. Rubenstein (1990), p. 139. **82.** N. Rinfret, M. Lortie-Lussier & J. De Koninck (1991), pp. 180-1. **83.** S. Krippner & K. Rubenstein (1990), p. 4. **84.** N. Rinfret, M. Lortie-Lussier & J. De Koninck (1991), pp. 188. **85.** P. Garfield (1988a), p. 11, citing L. A. Kilner (1987). **86.** P. R. Koch-Sheras, E. A. Hollier & B. Jones (1983), pp. 24-5. **87.** H. R. Blank (1958), p. 159. **88.** R. E. Rainville (1992). **89.** R. E. Rainville (1988), pp. 206-7 and 216. **90.** J. Gross, J. Byrne & C. Fisher (1965). See also W. Offencrantz & E. Wolpert, "The detection of dreaming in a congenitally blind subject," *Journal of Nervous and Mental Disease* 136, pp. 88-90, 1963. **91.** D. G. Schwartz, L. N. Weinstein & A. M. Arkin (1978), p. 185. **92.** N. H. Kerr, D. Foulkes & M. Schmidt (1982), p. 286. **93.** R. W. McCarley & J. A. Hobson (1979), p. 121. R. W. McCarley & E. Hoffman (1981), p. 908. **94.** D. G. Schwartz, L. N. Weinstein & A. M. Arkin (1978), p. 185. **95.** H. R. Blank (1958), p. 159. **96.** R. E. Rainville (1988), pp. 24-6 and 207. **97.** Ibid., pp. 207-8. **98.** N. H. Kerr, D. Foulkes & M. Schmidt (1982), p. 293. **99.** H. R. Blank (1958), pp. 162-3. **100.** Ibid., p. 159. **101.** N. H. Kerr, D. Foulkes & M. Schmidt (1982), p. 293. **102.** Ibid., p. 286. P. R. Robbins (1988), pp. 48-9, citing D. Kirtley & K. Cannistraci, "Dreams of the visually handicapped: toward a normative approach," *American Foundation for the Blind Research Bulletin* 27, pp. 111-133, 1974. **103.** R. E. Rainville (1988), pp. 210-11. **104.** D. D. Kirtley, *The Psychology of Blindness*, Chicago: Nelson-Hall, 1975, quoted by R. E. Rainville (1988), p. 208. **105.** R. E. Rainville (1988), p. 209, quoting D. D. Kirtley, *The Psychology of Blindness*, Chicago: Nelson-Hall, 1975. **106.** R. E. Rainville (1988), p. 211ff. **107.** R. Furness, "Dreams without sight," *The Beacon* 5(58), p. 16, 1921, quoted by H. R. Blank (1958), p. 168. **108.** R. E. Rainville (1992). **109.** R. E. Rainville (1988), pp. 213-4. **110.** J. H. Mendelson, L. Siger & P. Solomon (1974 [1960]), p. 365. **111.** J. Grant (1986 [1984]), pp. 17-21. **112.** S. Shulman (1979), p. 81. **113.** M. J. Thorpy (1990). **114.** E. Hartmann (1984). F. Galvin & E. Hartmann 1990, p. 235, citing R. Broughton, "Sleep disorders: disorders of arousal?" *Science* 159, pp. 1070-8, 1968, and C. Fisher, J. V. Byrne, A. Edwards & E. Kahn, "A psychophysiological study of night-mares," *Journal of the American Psychoanalytical Association* 18, pp. 747-82, 1970. **115.** E. Hart-mann (1984), p. 21. **116.** M. Ullman & N. Zimmerman (1979), p. 25. **117.** R. A. Bonato, A. R. Moffitt, R. F. Hoffmann, M. A. Cuddy & F. L. Wimmer (1991), p. 59. **118.** E. Hartmann (1984), p. 195. G. Halliday (1985), p. 4. **119.** F. Galvin & E. Hartmann (1990), p. 237. **120.** J. M. Wood & R. R. Bootzin (1990). **121.** E. Hartmann (1984), pp. 31-2. **122.** Ibid., p. 157. **123.** Ibid., p. 36. **124.** K. K. Dunn & D. Barrett (1988), p. 92. **125.** E. Hartmann (1984), p. 23 passim. **126.** A. Moffitt (1990). **127.** K. K. Dunn & D. L. Barrett (1987), p. 5. **128.** E. Hartmann, R. Elkin & M. Garg (1991). **129.** J. M. Wood & R. R. Bootzin (1990). **130.** D. A. Belicki (1987). J. M. Wood & R. R. Bootzin (1990). K. Belicki (1992a). **131.** J. E. Mack (1969), pp. 207-8. **132.** E. Hartmann (1984), p. 23. **133.** R. Levin & J. Rosenblatt (1990). R. Levin, J. Galin & B. Zywiak (1991), p. 70. **134.** J. S. Singer (1975), p. 194. **135.** K. Belicki & M. A. Cuddy (1991), p. 108. See also K. Belicki (1992a). **136.** E. Hartmann (1984), p. 188. **137.** R. Cartwright & L. Lamberg (1992), p. 186. **138.** M. R. Lansky & C. R. Bley (1990). **139.** H. A. Wilmer (1982). **140.** M. R. Lansky & C. R. Bley (1993). **141.** R. Cartwright & L. Lamberg (1992), p. 213. **142.** J. Haw-kins (1991), p. 46, citing J. L. Herman. **143.** E. Hartmann (1984), p. 210. **144.** Ibid., p. 192. El-lipsis Hartmann's. **145.** R. E. Rainville (1988), pp. 198-9. **146.** H. A. Wilmer (1986a), pp. 126 and 132. **147.** H. A. Wilmer (1982). S. S. Brockway (1987). **148.** D. Shapiro, D. Notowitz & G. W. Domhoff (1990). **149.** E. Hartmann (1984), p. 245. **150.** J. Hawkins (1991), p. 49, citing J. L. Herman. See also J. L. Herman, *Trauma and Recovery: The Aftermath of Violence*, New York: Basic, 1992. **151.** M. Prince, *The Dissociation of Personality*, New York: Meridian, p. 342, 1957 [1906], quoted by Z. A. Piotrowski (1986), p. 56. **152.** S. S. Marmer (1980), p. 173. **153.** A. L. Carlisle (1988), p. 10. **154.** M. Goldberger (1989), p. 402. **155.** S. Freud (1953 [1900]), p. 316. **156.** A. Ziegler (1962), pp. 142-4. **157.** H. de Saint-Denys (1982 [1867]), pp. 61-2. **158.** R. E. Rainville (1988), pp. 81-2. **159.** A. L. Carlisle (1988), p. 10. **160.** R. D. Salley (1988), p. 112. **161.** Ibid., p. 112, citing G. B. Greaves, "Multiple personality: 165 years after Mary Reynolds," *Journal of Nervous and Mental Disease* 168, pp. 577-96, 1980. **162.** Ibid., p. 112, citing R. Allison, "A new treatment approach for multiple personalities," *American Journal of Clinical Hypnosis* 17, pp. 15-32, 1974. **163.** R. D. Salley (1988), pp. 112-5. **164.** H. L. Levitan (1976/77b), p. 126. **165.** J. Frosch (1976), p. 46, citing E. Hartmann (1967). **166.** M. Kramer & T. Roth (1979), p. 381. **167.** E. Sheppard (1963), pp. 267-8. **168.** R. M. Benca, W. H. Obermeyer, R. A. Thisted & J. C. Gillin (1992), p. 661. **169.** Respectively: A. T. Beck & C. H. Ward (1961); W. Bonime (with F. Bonime) (1980); D. Barrett & M. Loeffler (1990). **170.** R. D. Cartwright, S. Lloyd, S. Knight & I. Trenholme (1984), pp. 255-8. **171.** R. D. Cartwright (1991), citing respectively: D. Cohen & C. Cox, "Neuroticism in the sleep laboratory: implications for representational and adaptive properties of dreaming," *Journal of Abnormal Psychology* 84, pp. 91-108, 1975; L. Breger, I. Hunter & R. W. Lane (1971); C. Winget & F. T. Kapp, "The relationship of the manifest content of dreams to duration of childbirth in primiparae," *Psychosomatic Medicine* 34, pp. 313-9, 1972. **172.** R. E. Rainville (1988), p. 159. **173.** E. Hartmann (1991), p. 24. **174.** R. D. Cartwright, S. Lloyd, S. Knight & I. Trenholme (1984), pp. 252-3. **175.** R. Cartwright (1986), p. 420. **176.** D. Barrett & M. Loeffler (1990), p. 4. **177.** W. Bonime (with F. Bonime) (1980), pp. 132-3. **178.** Ibid., pp. 131-6. **179.** J. A. Hall (1983), p. 45; R. D. Cartwright, S. Lloyd, S. Knight & I. Trenholme (1984), pp. 252-3. **180.** A. T. Beck & C. H. Ward (1961), p. 462. **181.** Ibid., p. 464. **182.** R. Cartwright & L. Lamberg (1992), p. 124. **183.** Ibid., p. 70. **184.** A. T. Beck & C. H. Ward (1961), p. 466. **185.** Ibid., p. 466. **186.** R. D. Cartwright (1992), pp. 80 and 84. **187.** R. J. Langs (1966), p. 638. E. Friess, B. Dippel, D. Riemann & M. Berger (1989), p. 10. **188.** M. Kramer & T. Roth (1973), p. 326. **189.** M. Kramer, R. M. Whitman, B. Baldridge & L. Lansky (1965),

p. 412. **190.** R. M. Benca, W. H. Obermeyer, R. A. Thisted & J. C. Gillin (1992), pp. 660-1. **191.** E. Hartmann (1967), p. 92. R. D. Cartwright, S. Lloyd, S. Knight & I. Trenholme (1984), p. 252. M. Koukkou-Lehmann (1990). R. M. Benca, W. H. Obermeyer, R. A. Thisted & J. C. Gillin (1992). R. Cartwright & L. Lamberg (1992), p. 138. **192.** R. Cartwright & L. Lamberg (1992), p. 138, citing D. Kupfer, "REM latency: a psychobiologic marker for primary depressive disease," *Biological Psychiatry* 11, pp. 159-74, 1976. **193.** R. Cartwright & L. Lamberg (1992), p. 138. **194.** M. Kramer (1991c), pp. 175-6. **195.** R. Cartwright & L. Lamberg (1992), pp. 139-40. **196.** G. W. Vogel, A. Thurmond & P. Gibbons, "REM sleep reduction effect in depressive syndromes," *Archives of General Psychiatry* 32, pp. 765-77, 1975, cited by D. Riemann, C. Lauer, B. Dippel & M. Berger (1989), p. 4. **197.** G. W. Vogel (1983). J. C. Gillin (1983). S. Krippner & J. Dillard (1988), pp. 91-2, citing G. W. Vogel, "REM sleep reduction effects on depression syndromes," *Archives of General Psychiatry* 33, pp. 96-7, 1975 and "Evidence for REM sleep deprivation as the mechanism of action of anti-depressant drugs," *Progress in Neuropsychopharmacology and Biological Psychiatry* 7, pp. 343-9, 1983. **198.** R. J. Langs (1966), p. 638. **199.** M. Kramer, R. M. Whitman, B. Baldridge & L. Lansky (1965), p. 414. **200.** E. Friess, B. Dippel, D. Riemann & M. Berger (1989), 10. **201.** M. Kramer & T. Roth (1973), p. 326. **202.** R. J. Langs (1966). M. Kramer, B. J. Baldridge, R. M. Whitman, P. H. Ornstein & P. C. Smith (1969), p. 129. **203.** F. Galvin & E. Hartmann (1990), p. 238. **204.** M. Kramer, R. M. Whitman, B. Baldridge & L. Lansky (1965), p. 413. **205.** R. J. Langs (1966), p. 638. **206.** M. Kramer, B. J. Baldridge, R. M. Whitman, P. H. Ornstein & P. C. Smith (1969), p. 129. **207.** M. Kramer & T. Roth (1979), p. 378. **208.** M. Kramer & T. Roth (1973), p. 327. **209.** M. Kramer, R. M. Whitman, B. Baldridge & L. Lansky (1965), p. 414. **210.** Ibid., p. 413, footnote 3. **211.** J. B. Miller (1969), pp. 561-3. **212.** R. D. Cartwright (1977), pp. 106-7. **213.** J. E. Mack (1969), pp. 217-8. M. Kramer & T. Roth (1973). **214.** S. Resnik (1987), p. 135. **215.** M. Kramer (1970), p. 154. **216.** M. Kramer, R. Hlasny, G. Jacobs & T. Roth (1976), pp. 779-80. **217.** P. Carrington (1972), p. 349. **218.** T. Okuma, Y. Sunami, E. Fukuma, S. Takeo & M. Motoike (1970). **219.** M. Kramer & T. Roth (1979), p. 378. **220.** M. Kramer, B. J. Baldridge, R. M. Whitman, P. H. Ornstein & P. C. Smith (1969), p. 129. **221.** T. Okuma, Y. Sunami, E. Fukuma, S. Takeo & M. Motoike (1970). **222.** S. C. Chang, "Dream recall and themes of hospitalized schizophrenics," *Archives of General Psychiatry* 10, pp. 119-22, 1964, cited by C. Winget & M. Kramer (1979), p. 314. **223.** C. Winget & M. Kramer (1979), p. 74, citing R. L. Van de Castle, personal communication, 1972. **224.** R. D. Cartwright (1972) and (1977), p. 105ff. **225.** M. Kramer (1991c), p. 179. **226.** R. M. Benca, W. H. Obermeyer, R. A. Thisted & J. C. Gillin (1992), p. 652. **227.** M. Stern, D. H. Fram, R. Wyatt, L. Grinspoon & B. Tursky (1969). R. D. Cartwright (1977), p. 107. **228.** V. Zarcone, G. Gulevitch, T. Pivak & W. Dement, "Partial REM phase deprivation and schizophrenia," *Archives of General Psychiatry* 18, pp. 194-202, 1968, cited by R. D. Cartwright (1972). R. D. Cartwright (1977), p. 111. **229.** R. D. Cartwright (1972), p. 276. **230.** R. D. Cartwright (1977), p. 117. **231.** W. Dement (1955). **232.** Ibid., p. 266. **233.** L. Sussmann, 1936, quoted by G. A. Richardson & R. A. Moore (1963), p. 283. **234.** W. E. Biddle, "Images," *Archives of General Psychiatry* 9, pp. 464-70, 1963, quoted by R. D. Cartwright (1972), p. 275. R. D. Cartwright (1977), pp. 112-3. **236.** J. S. Kafka (1980), p. 104. **237.** J. E. Mack (1969), pp. 208 and 218-9, and (1989 [1970]), pp. 169-71 passim. **238.** J. Frosch (1976), p. 50. **239.** J. S. Kafka (1980), p. 105. **240.** J. E. Mack (1989 [1970]), pp. 169-71. **241.** M. Boss (1959 [1938]), p. 168. **242.** Ibid., p. 164. **243.** Ibid., p. 162. **244.** D. Noble, "A study of dreams in schizophrenia and allied states," *American Journal of Psychiatry* 107, pp. 612-6, 1950-1, cited by G. A. Richardson & R. A. Moore (1963), p. 283. **245.** G. A. Richardson & R. A. Moore (1963). **246.** R. J. Langs (1966), p. 639. M. Kramer, B. J. Baldridge, R. M. Whitman, P. H. Ornstein & P. C. Smith (1969), p. 129. **247.** P. Carrington (1972), p. 343. M. Kramer & T. Roth (1979), p. 375. **248.** R. D. Cartwright (1972), p. 276ff. **249.** M. Kramer, R. Whitman, B. Baldridge & P. Ornstein, "Dream content in male schizophrenics," *Diseases of the Nervous System* 31, pp. 51-8, 1970, cited by R. D. Cartwright (1977), p. 109. **250.** C. S. Hall (1966b), p. 135.

251. T. Okuma, Y. Sunami, E. Fukuma, S. Takeo & M. Motoike (1970), p. 153. **252.** C. S. Hall (1966b), p. 136. **253.** T. Okuma, Y. Sunami, E. Fukuma, S. Takeo & M. Motoike (1970), p. 153. **254.** D. G. Schwartz, L. N. Weinstein & A. M. Arkin (1978), p. 171. **255.** R. D. Cartwright (1977), p. 109. D. G. Schwartz, L. N. Weinstein & A. M. Arkin (1978), p. 168. **256.** R. D. Cartwright (1977), pp. 107-10. **257.** P. Carrington (1972), pp. 346-7. **258.** Ibid., p. 348. **259.** Ibid., pp. 347-9. **260.** Ibid., p. 347. **261.** M. Boss (1977), p. 124. **262.** J. Frosch, cited without source by J. E. Mack (1969), p. 208. **263.** P. Carrington (1972), p. 348. **264.** S. Krippner (1990c), pp. 192-3, citing various sources. **265.** P. Carrington (1972), p. 349. **266.** W. Dement (1955), p. 266. **267.** R. D. Cartwright (1977), pp. 112-3. **268.** M. Boss (1959 [1938]), p. 162. **269.** J. Frosch (1976), p. 50. **270.** T. Okuma, Y. Sunami, E. Fukuma, S. Takeo & M. Motoike (1970), p. 153. **271.** R. J. Langs (1966), p. 639. M. Kramer, B. J. Baldridge, R. M. Whitman, P. H. Ornstein & P. C. Smith (1969), p. 129. **272.** R. D. Cartwright (1977), pp. 107-10. **273.** P. Carrington (1972), pp. 346-7. **274.** Ibid., p. 343. M. Kramer & T. Roth (1979), p. 375. **275.** G. A. Richardson & R. A. Moore (1963). **276.** R. D. Cartwright (1977), pp. 107-10. **277.** J. S. Kafka (1980), p. 104. **278.** For example, M. Boss (1959 [1938]), pp. 167-8. **279.** M. Kramer (1970), p. 154. **280.** M. Kramer, B. J. Baldridge, R. M. Whitman, P. H. Ornstein & P. C. Smith (1969), pp. 128-9.

Chapter 10 • Dream Residues

1. W. Bonime (with F. Bonime) (1982 [1962]), pp. 42-4. F. S. Perls (1992 [1969]). S. K. Williams (1986 [1980]), p. 167. J. Taylor (1983), p. 122. A. Mindell (1985). E. T. Gendlin (1986), p. 79. **2.** For example, D. Feinstein & S. Krippner (1988). **3.** M. Watkins (1984 [1976]), p. 129. **4.** S. Freud (1953 [1900]), p. 165. **5.** M. Watkins (1984 [1976]), p. 130. **6.** A. F. Leveton (1961). **7.** L. S. Kubie (1975 [1958]), p. 3. **8.** C. Féré, "Note sur un cas de paralysie hystérique consécutive à un rêve," *Soc. biolog.* 41, Nov. 20, 1886, cited by S. Freud (1953 [1900]), p. 89. C. Féré, "A contribution to the pathology of dreams," *Brain* 9, p. 488, 1887, cited by A. F. Leveton (1961), p. 508. **9.** L. H. Bartemeier (1950), pp. 9-10. **10.** H. L. Levitan (1976/77b), p. 127. **11.** H. L. Levitan (1974), p. 315. **12.** Ibid., pp. 316, 321. **13.** S. Freud (1953 [1900]), pp. 89. **14.** L. H. Bartemeier (1950), p. 10. **15.** J. Frosch (1976), p. 53. **16.** H. Seidenberg (1958), p. 225. **17.** H. L. Levitan (1976/77a), pp. 4-5. **18.** H. L. Levitan (1968), p. 57. Ellipsis Levitan's. **19.** A. F. Leveton (1961), p. 507. **20.** B. Shulman (1969), p. 126. **21.** M. Boss (1959 [1938]), pp. 169-70. **22.** J. E. Mack (1969), p. 208. **23.** H. E. Lehmann (1969), p. 151, citing M. Boss, *Der Traum und Seine Auslegung*, Switzerland: Verlag Hans Huber, p. 189, 1953. **24.** C. G. Jung (1965 [1961]), pp. 135-6. **25.** E. Whitmont & S. B. Perera (1989), pp. 129-30. **26.** R. M. Friedman (1992), p. 21. **27.** D. L. Raphling (1970), p. 407. **28.** R. M. Friedman (1992), p. 26, quoting H. Hendin, "The psychodynamics of suicide," *Journal of Nervous and Mental Disease* 136, pp. 236-44, 1963. **29.** R. E. Litman (1980), p. 294. **30.** Ibid., p. 283. **31.** R. M. Friedman (1992), p. 25. **32.** R. E. Litman (1980), p. 283. **33.** E. A. Gutheil (1967 [1951]), pp. 445-7. Ellipses in dream report Gutheil's. **34.** R. E. Litman (1980), p. 287. **35.** D. Lebe (1980), p. 212. **36.** E. Hartmann (1967), p. 97, citing T. Detre, J. Davis & P. Spaulding, "Sleep disturbance in mental patients," report to the Association for the Psychophysiological Study of Sleep, Washington, D. C., March, 1965. **37.** K. E. Belicki (1986). **38.** S. Freud (1953 [1900]), p. 590. **39.** R. A. Schonbar (1959) and (1961). R. D. Cartwright (1972), pp. 37-8. A. Faraday (1972), p. 54. H. Fiss (1979), pp. 45-7. L. Hudson (1985), p. 140. **40.** D. Koulack (1991), p. 143. **41.** S. Freud (1953 [1900]), p. 520. **42.** O. Garrison (1983 [1964]), p. 171. **43.** Respectively: H. Fiss (1979), p. 46, citing R. M. Jones, *The New Psychology of Dreaming*, New York: Grune & Stratton, pp. 134-66, 1970; C. A. Meier (1969), p. 105; J. Taylor (1983), p. 31; M. Koukkou & D. Lehmann (1993), pp. 80-1. **44.** D. B. Cohen (1970) p. 434, citing D. R. Goodenough, H. B. Lewis, A. Shapiro, L. Jaret & F. Sleser, "Dream reporting following abrupt and gradual awakenings from different types of sleep," *Journal of Personality and Social Psychology* 2, pp. 170-9, 1965. **45.** D. B. Cohen (1974), p. 50. **46.** J. H. Mendelson, L.

Siger & P. Solomon (1974 [1960]), p. 367. **47.** R. E. Rainville (1988), p. 43. P. R. Robbins (1988), pp. 54-5, citing: B. Barber, *Factors Underlying Individual Differences in Rate of Dream Reporting*, Ph.D. dissertation, Yeshiva University, New York, 1969. S. S. Anish, *The Relationship of Dream Recall to Defensive Mode*, Ph.D. dissertation, University of Pittsburgh, 1969. T. L. Cory, D. W. Ormiston, E. Simmel & M. Dainoff, "Predicting the frequency of dream recall," *Journal of Abnormal Psychology* 84, pp. 261-6, 1975. R. Martinetti, "Cognitive antecedents of dream recall," *Perceptual and Motor Skills* 60, pp. 395-401, 1985. **48.** K. E. Belicki (1986), p. 189. **49.** D. B. Cohen (1970), p. 435. J. Trindler & M. Kramer (1971), p. 298. P. Hauri & R. L. Van de Castle (1973), p. 299. D. G. Schwartz, L. N. Weinstein & A. M. Arkin (1978), p. 147, citing various sources. G. W. Domhoff (1985), p. 98. D. Koulack (1991), p. 136, citing B. Barber, *Factors Underlying Individual Differences in Rate of Dream Reporting*, Ph.D. dissertation, Yeshiva University, New York, 1969. **50.** A. Rechtschaffen & P. Verdone (1964). M. A. Mattoon (1984 [1978]), p. 148, citing J. S. Antrobus, W. Dement & C. Fisher "Patterns of dreaming and dream recall: an EEG study," *Journal of Abnormal and Social Psychology* 69, pp. 341-4, 1964, and citing D. R. Goodenough, A. Shapiro, M. Holden & L. Steinschriber "A comparison of 'dreamers' and 'nondreamers': eye movements, electroencephalograms, and the recall of dreams," *Journal of Abnormal and Social Psychology* 59, pp. 295-302, 1959. **51.** R. D. Cartwright (1977), p. 34. **52.** K. E. Belicki (1986), p. 189 and 193. **53.** Z. Z. Cernovsky (1984). **54.** Ibid., p. 190. **55.** D. B. Cohen (1974), pp. 52-3. **56.** R. E. Rainville (1988), pp. 43-5. **57.** A. Moffitt & R. Hoffmann (1986), p. 159. **58.** D. B. Cohen (1974), p. 54. **59.** L. DeGennaro & C. Violani (1990), p. 7, citing C. Violani, L. DeGennaro & L. Solano, "Hemispheric differentiation and dream recall: subjective estimates of sleep and dreams in different handedness groups," *International Journal of Neurosciences* 39, pp. 9-14, 1988. **60.** D. B. Cohen (1970), p. 437. J. Trindler & M. Kramer (1971), citing B. Domhoff & A. Gerson, "Replication and critique of three studies on personality correlates of dream recall," *Journal of Consulting Psychology* 31, p. 431, 1967. G. W. Domhoff (1985), p. 98. **61.** B. D. Lewin (1946), p. 420. **62.** D. Barrett (1988). **63.** Ibid., p. 1, citing D. R. Goodenough "Dream recall: history and current status of the field," in A. M. Arkin, J. S. Antrobus & S. T. Ellman, editors, *The Mind in Sleep: Psychology and Psychophysiology*, Hillsdale, New Jersey: Lawrence Erlbaum, 1978. **64.** S. Freud (1953 [1900]), p. 332-3. **65.** M. Kanzer (1955), p. 262. **66.** W. Wolff (1972 [1952]), p. 90. **67.** L. Breger (1980), p. 10. **68.** R. A. Johnson (1986), p. 52. **69.** S. Lowy, quoted by W. Stekel (1943), p. 566. **70.** W. Stekel (1943), pp. 242-3. **71.** L. Grinberg (1987), p. 170. **72.** B. D. Lewin (1946), cited by N. Roth (1958), p. 548. **73.** J. Frosch, cited by J. E. Mack (1969), pp. 208-9. **74.** R. Sterba (1946), pp. 175-6. **75.** E. Whitmont & S. B. Perera (1989), p. 123. **76.** N. Roth (1958), pp. 547 and 549. **77.** Ibid., pp. 550-2. **78.** J. E. Mack (1989 [1970]), p. 52. **79.** V. D. Volkan & T. H. Bhatti (1973), pp. 269 and 273-4. **80.** H. Kelman (1975), p. 209. **81.** Ibid., pp. 211-2. **82.** D. Lebe (1980), pp. 210-1. **83.** Ibid., p. 220. **84.** S. K. Williams (1986 [1980]), p. 121ff. **85.** Ibid., p. 134. **86.** R. A. Johnson (1986), p. 97. **87.** Ibid., pp. 196-7. **88.** Ibid., p. 98. **89.** J. Morris (1987 [1985]), pp. 148-9.

Chapter 11 • Initial and Termination Dreams

1. G. Delaney (1991), pp. 384-6. **2.** L. Flowers (1988), cited by G. Delaney (1991), p. 384. **3.** J. Windsor (1987), p. 162. **4.** Ibid., p. 109. **5.** H. H. Bro (1968). **6.** P. Garfield (1988a), p. 128. **7.** Ibid., pp. 149-50. **8.** S. Krippner & J. Dillard (1988), p. 113. R. Corriere & J. Hart (1977). G. Delaney (1991). **9.** S. Krippner & J. Dillard (1988), p. 113. **10.** P. Garfield (1988a), pp. 155-6. **11.** G. Delaney (1990b [1986]), p. 5. **12.** Respectively: K. Paley & T. A. Nielsen, editors (1989); H. R. Ossana, editor (1991b). **13.** R. Morrison (1989), p. 1. See also R. Morrison, "Dream mapping in chemical dependency recovery," *Alcoholism Treatment Quarterly* 7(3), pp. 113-20, 1990. **14.** Ibid., pp. 1-2. **15.** L. S. Leonard, *Witness to the Fire: Creativity and the Veil of Addiction*, Boston: Shambhala, 1989, quoted by N. Piaget (no date). **16.** K. Bulkley (1991), p. 10. **17.** H. Roberta

Ossana (1991a), p. 4. **18.** G. Delaney (1990c), p. 27. **19.** S. Krippner & L. Stoller, "Sleeptalking and creativity: a case study," *Journal of the American Society of Psychosomatic Dentistry and Medicine* 20, pp. 107-14, 1973, cited by S. Krippner & J. Dillard (1988), pp. 3-4. **20.** I. L. Child (1985), p. 1224. **21.** M. Ullman & S. Krippner (1970). M. Ullman, S. Krippner & A. Vaughan (1989). **22.** H. A. Abramson & L. W. Krinsky (1975), p. 221. **23.** J. A. Sanford (1977), p. 55. **24.** L. J. Saul, T. R. Snyder & E. Sheppard, "On reading manifest dreams and other unconscious material," in panel report by L. Rangell, "The dream in the practice of psychoanalysis," *Journal of the American Psychoanalytic Association* 4, pp. 122-37, 1956, cited by H. Kelman (1975), p. 216. **25.** L. Weiss (1986), pp. 40-1. **26.** C. G. Jung, "The practical use of dream-analysis," CW 16, para's 307-12. And "The Tavistock lectures, lecture 5," CW 18, para's 346-8. Quoted in edited composite by M. A. Mattoon (1984 [1978]), pp. 140-1. **27.** M. A. Mattoon (1984 [1978]), p. 141. **28.** H. Dieckmann (1985), p. 219. **29.** W. Stekel (1943), p. 250. **30.** J. L. Henderson (1980), p. 370. **31.** L. L. Altman (1969), p. 51. **32.** R. Bosnak (1989), pp. 3, 8, 28 and 89. **33.** R. Bosnak (1988 [1986]), p. 52. **34.** R. M. Whitman (1980), p. 53. **35.** Ibid., p. 47. **36.** Ibid., p. 49. **37.** Ibid., p. 46. **38.** T. B. Kirsch (1979), pp. 150-1. **39.** J. O. Cavenar & J. G. Spaulding (1978), pp. 60-2. **40.** A. Mankowitz (1984), pp. 99-102.

Chapter 12 • The Non-interpretation of Dreams

1. H. A. Wilmer (1986b), p. 54. **2.** H. W. Beck (1977), p. 56. **3.** H. C. Curtis & D. M. Sachs (1976), p. 344. **4.** M.-T. B. Dombeck (1991), pp. 105-6. **5.** R. A. Russo (1987b), p. 1. **6.** M. A. Mattoon (1984 [1978]), p. 134. **7.** J. A. Hadfield (1954), pp. 96-7. **8.** J. D. Clift & W. B. Clift (1984), p. 13. **9.** M. Zeller (1975). **10.** R. Shohet (1985), p. 30. **11.** C. G. Jung, quoted by R. A. Johnson (1986), p. 56. **12.** Expressions quoted variously from: C. G. Jung, "The practical use of dream-analysis" [1934], CW 16, para. 337; E. Cayce, quoted by H. H. Bro (1968), p. 146; C. A. Meier (1990 [1972]), p. 120; A. Faraday (1976 [1974]), p. xiv; M. Ullman & N. Zimmerman (1979), p. 29; J. Taylor (1983), p. 37 and (1992a), p. 12; D. Deslauriers (1986), p. 19; E. T. Gendlin (1986), p. 1; J. Maguire (1989), p. 30; E. Whitmont & S. B. Perera (1989), p. 14; D. Koulack (1991), p. 4; P. Maybruck (1991), p. 41; R. Cartwright & L. Lamberg (1992), p. 72. **13.** A. R. Mahrer (1989), p. 289. See also (1971) and (1990). **14.** G. Delaney (1991), p. 9. **15.** Ibid., p. 10. **16.** Ibid., p. 37. **17.** P. E. Craig (1990a) and (1992). **18.** G. Delaney (1991), p. 181. **19.** G. Delaney (1979), pp. 15-6. Ellipsis Delaney's. **20.** H. R. Ellis (1991), pp. 3-4. **21.** H. R. Ellis (1988), p. 16. **22.** H. R. Ellis (1991), pp. 2-3. **23.** F. Bogzaran (1990), p. 8. **24.** D. Deslauriers (1989), p. 2. **25.** F. Bogzaran (1990), p. 9. **26.** D. Deslauriers (1989), p. 3. **27.** P. R. Koch-Sheras, E. A. Hollier & B. Jones (1983), pp. 68-9. **28.** J. Morris (1987 [1985]), pp. 67-8 and 169-70. **29.** R. A. Johnson (1986), pp. 196-7. **30.** Ibid., p. 90. **31.** Ibid., p. 99. **32.** S. K. Williams (1986 [1980]), p. 28. **33.** Ibid., p. 192. **34.** L. M. Savary, P. H. Berne & S. K. Williams (1984), p. 18. **35.** S. K. Williams (1986 [1980]), p. 123. **36.** J. Baylis (1976), p. 62. **37.** C. G. Jung (1984 [1938]), p. 11. **38.** D. Beaudet (1990), p. 124. **39.** J. Gregory (1988a), p. 13. **40.** A. S. Wiseman (1987), pp. 79 and 88-9. Reprinted in A. S. Wiseman, *Nightmare Help*, Berkeley: Ten Speed, 1989. **41.** K. L. West (1978), p. 6. **42.** Ibid., pp. 45-7. **43.** C. D. Warner (1992). **44.** K. Belicki & M. A. Cuddy (1991), p. 109. **45.** J. Hillman, "Further enquiry into images," *Spring*, p. 87, 1977, quoted by W. A. Shelburne (1984), p. 46. **46.** M. Watkins (1984 [1976]), pp. 36-7. **47.** Ibid., p. 53. **48.** Ibid., pp. 54-9. **49.** Ibid., p. 59. **50.** Ibid., pp. 59-63. **51.** M. Eliade (1960 [1957]), p. 117. **52.** M. Watkins (1984 [1976]), p. 63ff. **53.** R. Assagioli (1971 [1965]). **54.** E. Rossi (1985). **55.** J. S. Singer (1975), p. 215ff. **56.** J. Achterberg (1985). **57.** P. R. Koch-Sheras, E. A. Hollier & B. Jones (1983), pp. 71-2. **58.** P. R. Koch-Sheras, E. A. Hollier & B. Jones (1983), p. 105. **59.** C. T. Tart (1979) and (1988). **60.** P. Garfield (1989), p. xxv. **61.** S. K. Williams (1986 [1980]), p. 181. **62.** R. Cartwright & L. Lamberg (1992), p. 35. **63.** Z. A. Piotrowski (1986), p. 47. **64.** J. Gackenbach & J. Bosveld (1989), p. 91. **65.** H. Stefanakis, A. Zadra & D. Donderi (1990), p. 2. **66.** P. Garfield (1976 [1974]), p. 94. **67.** Ibid., p. 172. **68.** J. I. Gackenbach (1985-86), p. 42. **69.** S. La-Berge (1985), p. 161. **70.** Ibid., p. 163. **71.** P. Fellows (1988), p. 303. **72.** Ibid., p. 302.

Chapter 13 • Incubation

1. F. X. Newman, *Somnium: Medieval Theories of Dreaming and the Form of Vision Poetry*, Ann Arbor: University Microfilms International, p. 19, 1983, quoted by C. S. Rupprecht (1990), p. 121. **2.** J. King (1990). **3.** D. Koulack (1986), pp. 214-5. **4.** S. Krippner & J. Dillard (1988), pp. 176-7. **5.** P. R. Koch-Sheras, E. A. Hollier & B. Jones (1983), p. 100. **6.** P. Garfield (1988a), p. 99. **7.** S. Cunningham (1992), p. 163, citing I. Opie & M. Tatem, editors, *A Dictionary of Superstitions*, Oxford: Oxford University, p. 343, 1989. **8.** J. Maguire (1989), p. 144. **9.** S. Freud (1953 [1900]), p. 166. **10.** Ibid., p. 174. **11.** R. Corriere, W. Karle, L. Woldenberg & J. Hart (1980). **12.** S. Freud (1953 [1900]), pp. 18-9. **13.** R. D. Gillman (1980), p. 29. **14.** D. Foulkes (1979), p. 154. **15.** C. Fisher (1974 [1960]). **16.** C. Winget & M. Kramer (1979), p. 287, citing E. Hartmann, "The day residue: time distribution of waking events," paper presented to the Association for the Psychophysiological Study of Sleep, Denver, Colorado, 1968. **17.** Ibid. **18.** For example, discussing their own research and various sources: R. Rados & R. D. Cartwright (1982); A. M. Arkin & J. S. Antrobus (1991), p. 294; M. Kramer (1993), p. 151. **19.** L. Scrima (1984), p. 212. **20.** V. Natale & D. Battaglia (1990-1). P. Cicogna, C. Cavallero & M. Bosinelli (1991). **21.** J. A. Davison & B. D. Kelsey, "Incorporation of recent events in dreams," *Perceptual & Motor Skills* 65, p. 114, 1987, cited by T. A. Nielsen & R. A. Powell (1989), p. 561. **22.** M. Jouvet, "Mémoire et 'cerveau dédoublé' au cours du rêve a propos de 2525 souvenirs de rêve," *L'année du Practicien* 29, pp. 27-32. 1979, cited by T. A. Nielsen & R. A. Powell (1992), p. 71. **23.** T. A. Nielsen & R. A. Powell (1989) and (1992). **24.** R. D. Cartwright (1977), p. 81. **25.** D. Foulkes & A. Rechtschaffen (1964). **26.** D. R. Goodenough, H. A. Witkin, D. Koulack & H. Cohen, "The effects of stress films on dream affect and on respiration and eye-movement activity during rapid-eye-movement sleep," *Psychophysiology* 12, pp. 313-20, 1975, quoted and cited by D. Koulack (1986), pp. 215-6. **27.** D. Koulack (1991), pp. 71-2. **28.** T. A. Nielsen & R. A. Powell (1992), p. 74. **29.** D. Koulack (1991), pp. 74-5. **30.** D. B. Cohen & C. Cox, "Neuroticism in the sleep laboratory: implications for representational and adaptive properties of dreaming," *Journal of Abnormal Psychology* 84, pp. 91-108, 1975, cited by T. A. Nielsen & R. A. Powell (1989), p. 564. **31.** R. Rados & R. D. Cartwright (1982), p. 433, citing W. Webb & R. D. Cartwright, "Sleep and dreams," *Annual Review of Psychology* 29, pp. 223-52, 1978. **32.** D. Koulack (1986), pp. 217-8. **33.** L. Breger, I. Hunter & R. W. Lane (1971), p. 82. **34.** K. A. Carpenter (1988). **35.** R. D. Cartwright (1977), p. 81. **36.** K. A. Carpenter (1988). **37.** R. D. Cartwright (1991). **38.** D. Koulack (1991), p. 166, citing D. B. Cohen & C. Cox, "Neuroticism in the sleep laboratory: implications for representational and adaptive properties of dreaming," *Journal of Abnormal Psychology* 84, pp. 91-108, 1975, and p. 167, citing D. Koulack, F. Prevost & J. De Koninck, "Sleep, dreaming, and adaptation to a stressful intellectual activity," *Sleep* 8, pp. 244-53, 1985, respectively. **39.** Ibid., p. 183. **40.** L. Breger, I. Hunter & R. W. Lane (1971), p. 34. Among others, C. S. Moss (1970, pp. 286-7) has made the same analogy. **41.** B. Domhoff & J. Kamiya (1964b), p. 526. R. P. Fox, M. Kramer, B. J. Baldridge, R. M. Whitman & P. H. Ornstein (1968), pp. 698 and 700 (with further references). **42.** M. Kramer (1970). **43.** R. Cartwright (1986), p. 418. **44.** D. Koulack (1991), p. 62. **45.** B. Domhoff & J. Kamiya (1964b), pp. 526-7. **46.** R. P. Fox, M. Kramer, B. J. Baldridge, R. M. Whitman & P. H. Ornstein (1968), p. 700. **47.** B. Domhoff & J. Kamiya (1964a). **48.** Ibid. Institute of Dream Research, *Studies of Dreams Reported in the Laboratory and at Home*, Felton, California: Big Trees, cited by C. Winget & M. Kramer (1979), p. 41. A. Ziegler J. (1976), p. 58. **49.** R. Greenberg, C. A. Pearlman, & D. Gampel (1972). E. Hartmann (1984) p. 37. **50.** P. Garfield (1976 [1974]), p. 12. **51.** H. T. Hunt, R. Ogilvie, K. Belicki, D. Belicki & E. Atalick (1982), p. 606. D. Foulkes (1985), p. 4. **52.** L. A. Kilner (1987) and (1988). **53.** R. E. Haskell (1985a). **54.** D. Foulkes (1979), p. 159.

55. C. Winget, M. Kramer & R. M. Whitman (1972), p. 204. **56.** J. Gackenbach (1993), p. 18. **57.** J. C. McCall (1993), p. 57. **58.** D. Eggan (1966), p. 261. **59.** P. Garfield (1988a), p. 118. **60.** W. Morgan (1932), p. 394. **61.** P. Garfield (1976 [1974]), p. 66. **62.** G. Devereux (1970), p. vii. C. W. O'Nell (1976), p. 60. **63.** S. Charsley (1992), p. 155. **64.** R. K. Dentan (1986), p. 327. **65.** M. C. Jędrej & R. Shaw (1992b), p. 14. **66.** R. K. Dentan (1986), p. 325. **67.** I. Ehrenwald, *New Dimensions of Deep Analysis*, London: Allen & Unwin, 1954 [1952], quoted by C. A. Meier (1990 [1972]), p. 121. **68.** E. H. Erikson (1954), p. 46. **69.** E. S. Tauber & M. R. Green (1959), p. 156, citing Wittels. **70.** Ibid., p. 162. **71.** E. H. Erikson (1954), p. 8 passim. **72.** R. Jones (1979b), pp. 132-3. **73.** R. K. Dentan (1986), p. 329, citing K. O. L. Burridge, "Social implications of some Tangu myths," in J. Middleton, editor, *Myth and Cosmos: Readings in Mythology and Symbolism*, Garden City, New York: The Natural History Press, 1967. **74.** Ibid., p. 331. **75.** N. MacKenzie (1965), p. 30. **76.** W. Wolff (1972 [1952]), p. 10. **77.** W. B. Webb (1979), p. 4. **78.** N. Lewis (1976), pp. 7-15. **79.** S. Cunningham (1992). p. 28. **80.** N. MacKenzie (1965), p. 30. **81.** W. Wolff (1972 [1952]), p. 10. **82.** N. MacKenzie (1965), p. 30. **83.** Ibid., p. 43. **84.** C. A. Meier (1967 [1949]), p. 23. **85.** C. A. Meier (1967 [1949]), p. 118. **86.** M. Hamilton (1906), pp. 109 and 114. **87.** J. Lecerf (1966), p. 378. **88.** M. Ullman & N. Zimmerman (1979), p. 43. **89.** C. W. O'Nell (1976), p. 35. **90.** S. Lorand (1957), pp. 93-4. **91.** S. M. Oberhelman (1983), p. 38, note 16. **92.** C. A. Meier (1967 [1949]), p. xv. **93.** Ibid., p. xiv. **94.** A. Brelich (1966). C. A. Meier (1966). **95.** N. MacKenzie (1965), p. 43. **96.** S. M. Oberhelman (1983), p. 39. **97.** M. A. Jowett (1937 [1892]), para. 118. **98.** N. MacKenzie (1965), p. 43. **99.** C. A. Meier (1967 [1949]), p. 93. **100.** M. Hamilton (1906), pp. 2-3. **101.** MacKenzie, N. (1965), p. 43. **102.** C. A. Meier (1967 [1949]), p. 54. **103.** J. A. Sanford (1977), p. 55. **104.** S. Krippner & J. Dillard (1988), p. 13, citing R. L. Van de Castle, *The Psychology of Dreaming*, Morristown, New Jersey: General Learning press, pp. 3-4, 1971. **105.** C. A. Meier (1967 [1949]). p. 57. **106.** N. MacKenzie (1965), p. 44. S. Resnik (1987), p. 31. **107.** N. MacKenzie (1965), p. 44. **108.** Ibid., p. 56. **109.** Ibid., p. 59. J. Achterberg (1985), p. 55. **110.** H. Reed (1988 [1985]), p. 12. **111.** C. A. Meier (1966), p. 315. **112.** P. Welch (1991), p. 52. **113.** H. Reed (1976), p. 53. **114.** J. Achterberg (1985), p. 56. **115.** N. Lewis (1976), p. 36. **116.** C. A. Meier (1967 [1949]), p. 59. **117.** E. Sechrist, *Dreams: Your Magic Mirror*, New York: Cowles, pp. 73-4, 1968, quoted by S. Krippner & J. Dillard (1988), p. 174. **118.** N. Lewis (1976), p. 39. **119.** Ibid., p. 42. **120.** Ibid., p. 37. **121.** Ibid., p. 40. **122.** E. Sechrist, *Dreams: Your Magic Mirror*, New York: Cowles, pp. 73-4, 1968, quoted by S. Krippner & J. Dillard (1988), p. 174. **123.** C. A. Meier (1967 [1949]), pp. 69-70. **124.** J. A. Sanford (1977), p. 52. **125.** R. Corriere & J. Hart (1977). **126.** P. O'Connor (1986). **127.** F. Meier (1966), p. 422. **128.** M. Ullman & N. Zimmerman (1979), pp. 23-4. **129.** P. Garfield (1984), p. 33. **130.** H. Reed (1976), p. 54. **131.** H. Reed (1991), p. 5 passim. **132.** P. Welch (1991), pp. 20 and 59. See also Graywolf (1992). **133.** R. Dentan (1987), p. 14. **134.** R. Dentan (1988), p. 38. **135.** G. W. Domhoff (1985), pp. 28-30. **136.** Ibid., p. 67. **137.** P. Garfield (1976 [1974]). **138.** R. K. Dentan (1988), p. 59. **139.** M. C. Doyle (1984). **140.** K. Stewart (1954), pp. 396 and 401. **141.** P. Garfield (1976 [1974]), p. 112. **142.** S. Krippner (1990d). **143.** P. R. Koch-Sheras, E. A. Hollier & B. Jones (1983), pp. 215 and 100-1. **144.** D. Feinstein & S. Krippner (1988), pp. 64-5 and 150. **145.** Ibid., pp. 59-60 and 177. **146.** Ibid., p. 133. **147.** S. Krippner & J. Dillard (1988). **148.** F. Bogzaran (1990). **149.** G. Delaney (1991), p. 24. **150.** M. Schatzman (1983). See also by Schatzman: "Solve your problems in your dreams," *New Scientist*, 9 June, pp. 692-3, 1983; "Dreams and problem solving," *International Medicine* 4, pp. 6-9, 1984; "The meaning of dreams," *New Scientist*, 25 December, pp. 36-9, 1986. **151.** D. Barrett (1993), pp. 116-7, citing W. C. Dement (1974 [1972]). **152.** D. Barrett (1993). **153.** Ibid., p. 121. **154.** C. G. Jung, "General aspects of dream psychology" [1916/1948], CW 8, para. 494). J. A. Hall (1983), p. 14. **155.** H. Silberer (1955 [1918]), p. 372, quoting (without reference) K. Schroetter, "Experimentelle Traüme," *Zentralblatt für Psychoanalyse* 2, pp. 638-48, 1911. **156.** A. M. Arkin & J. S. Antrobus (1991), pp. 300-3. **157.** C. T. Tart (1988), p. 99. **158.** P. C. Walker & R. F. Q. Johnson

(1974). **159.** C. T. Tart (1988), p. 86, citing J. Stoyva, "Posthypnotically suggested dreams and the sleep cycle," *Archives of General Psychiatry* 12, pp. 287-94, 1965. **160.** Ibid., pp. 86-7, citing C. Tart, "A comparison of suggested dreams occurring in hypnosis and sleep," *International Journal of Clinical and Experimental Hypnosis* 12, pp. 263-89, 1964. **161.** Ibid., p. 93. **162.** S. Krippner & J. Dillard (1988), p. 31, citing R. Davé, "Effects of hypnotically induced dreams on creative problem solving," *Journal of Abnormal Psychology* 88, pp. 293-302, 1979. **163.** J. A. Scott, Sr. (1982), p. 89. **164.** P. C. Walker & R. F. Q. Johnson (1974), p. 365, citing T. X. Barber, P. C. Walker & K. W. Hahn, Jr., "Effects of hypnotic induction and suggestions on nocturnal dreaming and thinking," *Journal of Abnormal Psychology* 82, pp. 414-27, 1973. **165.** C. Hiew, "The influence of presleep suggestions on dream content," paper presented to the Brunswick Psychological Association, Bathurst, NB, Canada, 1976, cited by C. T. Tart (1988), p. 82. **166.** C. T. Tart (1988), p. 83. **167.** D. Foulkes & M. L. Griffin (1976), p. 129. **168.** M. L. Griffin & D. Foulkes (1977). **169.** P. Garfield (1976 [1974]), p. 33, citing I. S. Wile, "Auto-suggested dreams as a factor in therapy," *American Journal of Orthopsychiatry* 4, pp. 449-63, 1934. **170.** C. T. Tart (1979), p. 241. **171.** A. Levay & J. Weissberg (1979), p. 335. **172.** Ibid., pp. 337-9. **173.** L. Weiss (1986), pp. 79-80. **174.** P. R. Koch-Sheras, E. A. Hollier & B. Jones (1983), p. 99. **175.** G. Delaney (1990c), p. 27. **176.** P. Garfield (1976 [1974]), p. 32. **177.** E. F. Sharpe (1978 [1937]), p. 48. **178.** P. R. Koch-Sheras, E. A. Hollier & B. Jones (1983), pp. 93-4. **179.** J. Windsor (1987), pp. 141-3. **180.** H. H. Bro (1968). **181.** A. Faraday (1976 [1974]), p. 142. **182.** P. Garfield (1976 [1974]), pp. 18-36. Italics deleted from quotations. **183.** Ibid. **184.** G. Delaney (1979), p. 26. **185.** C. G. Jung, "The Tavistock lectures" [1935], CW 18, para. 52. **186.** G. Delaney (1979), p. 21ff, (1990d) and (1991), p. 26. **187.** G. Delaney (1979), pp. 138-9. **188.** Ibid., pp. 18-9. **189.** Ibid., pp. 94-5. **190.** P. Maybruck (1991), p. 186. **191.** R. D. Cartwright (1974). **192.** R. D. Cartwright (1977), pp. 86-7. Ellipses in dream report Cartwright's. **193.** Ibid., p. 89. **194.** L. Reneau (no date), p. 58. **195.** M. R. Emery (1989) and (1991). **196.** A. Vaughan (1991). **197.** P. R. Koch-Sheras, E. A. Hollier & B. Jones (1983), p. 147. **198.** J. Windsor (1987), p. 121. **199.** Ibid., p. 118. **200.** S. Cunningham (1992), pp. 86 and 11. **201.** R. Parker (1988), p. 24 passim and p. 36. **202.** D. Whitmore (1981), p. 111. **203.** L. A. Camino (1986), p. 233. **204.** Ibid., p. 231 and personal communication, 1994.

Chapter 14 • Lucidity

1. C. E. Green (1968), p. 15. **2.** B. Kilborne (1981), p. 167, citing E. R. Dodds, *The Greeks and the Irrational*, Berkeley: University of California, 1951. **3.** R. Lattimore (1951). **4.** P. Garfield (1989), p. xxvii, quoting Aristotle, *On Dreams*. **5.** *Brihadaranyaka Upanishad*, quoted by O. Garrison (1983 [1964]), p. 170. **6.** S. LaBerge (1988a), p. 13. **7.** G. Gillespie (1988a), pp. 27-8. **8.** W. Y. Evans-Wentz (1958 [1935]). **9.** H. de Saint-Denys (1982 [1867]). **10.** F. Van Eedan, "A study of dreams," *Proceedings of the Society for Psychical Research* 26, pp. 431-61, 1913, cited by C. T. Tart (1988). **11.** C. E. Green (1968). F. Van Eedan, "A study of dreams," in C. Tart, editor, *Altered States of Consciousness: A Book of Readings*, New York: Wiley, 1969, cited by C. T. Tart (1988). P. Garfield (1976 [1974]). **12.** J. Gackenbach & S. LaBerge (1984). **13.** S. LaBerge (1985). J. Gackenbach & J. Bosveld (1989). S. LaBerge & H. Rheingold (1990). **14.** K. Harary & P. Weintraub (1989). **15.** R. Rooksby (1989), p. 75. **16.** J. Gackenbach & J. Bosveld (1989), p. 9. **17.** A. Worsley (1988), p. 326. **18.** J. Gregory (1984), p. 86 passim. **19.** C. E. Green (1968), pp. 23-7. **20.** E. Rossi (1985), pp. 131-41. **21.** S. Purcell, A. Moffitt & R. Hoffmann (1993), pp. 205ff. and 213, citing D. Foulkes (1985), pp. 44-5 and A. Rechtschaffen (1978). **22.** H. T. Hunt (1989). **23.** J. Gackenbach (1991a), p. 118. **24.** S. Blackmore (1989a) and (1989b). **25.** A. Moffitt, R. Hoffmann, J. Mullington, S. Purcell, R. Pigeau & R. Wells (1988), p. 430. **26.** C. T. Tart (1979), p. 255 and (1988), p. 94. **27.** D. Barrett (1992), p. 222. **28.** W. Schwartz & M. Godwyn (1988), p. 425. **29.** A. Brylowski (1990), p. 79. **30.** P. Tholey (1988), p. 269. **31.** P. Tholey (1989), p. 12.

32. J. Gackenbach (1991a), p. 123. **33.** Ibid., p. 124. **34.** S. LaBerge (1985), pp. 242-6. **35.** J. Gackenbach (1991a), p. 118. **36.** W. Wolff (1972 [1952]), p. 90. **37.** For example: G. S. Sparrow (1982 [1976]); P. Garfield (1989 [1979]); K. Kelzer, *The Sun and the Shadow*, ARE Press, 1986, quoted by K. Kelzer (1987). **38.** S. LaBerge (1985), pp. 244-6. **39.** P. Tholey (1983). **40.** J. Dane, "Non-REM lucid dreaming," *Lucidity Letter* 5(1), pp. 133-45, 1986, cited by H. T. Hunt (1989), p. 232. **41.** J. Gackenbach (1991a), p. 123. **42.** S. LaBerge, L. Levitan & W. C. Dement (1986), p. 252. **43.** J. Gackenbach & S. LaBerge (1984), p. 4. **44.** C. E. Green (1968), p. 128. **45.** M. Schatzman (1982), p. 6, citing K. M. T. Hearne, personal communication and *Lucid Dreams: an Electrophysiological and Physiological Study*, Ph.D. dissertation, University of Liverpool, pp. 151 and 212, 1978. **46.** H. T. Hunt (1990b). **47.** J. Gackenbach (1991a), p. 119, citing S. LaBerge (1988b). **48.** L. Levitan (1990c), p. 9, citing S. LaBerge, L. Levitan & W. C. Dement, "Lucid dreaming: physiological correlates of consciousness during REM sleep," *Journal of Mind & Behavior* 7, pp. 251-8, 1986. **49.** J. Gackenbach (1991a), p. 120, citing H. T. Hunt & R. D. Ogilvie (1988) and other papers by these authors and collaborators. **50.** S. LaBerge (1988b), p. 146. R. D. Ogilvie, H. T. Hunt, P. D. Tyson, M. L. Lucescu & D. B. Jeakins (1982), pp. 799-800. **51.** J. Gackenbach (1991a), p. 120. **52.** S. LaBerge, L. Levitan & W. C. Dement (1986), p. 255. **53.** J. Gackenbach & J. Bosveld (1989), p. 148, citing A. Brylowski, "H-reflex in lucid dreams," *Lucidity Letter* 5(1), pp. 116-8, 1986. **54.** C. Tart, "Towards the experimental control of dreaming: a review of the literature," *Psychological Bulletin* 64, pp. 81-91, 1965, cited by K. M. T. Hearne (1987), p. 76. **55.** A. Worsley (1988), p. 323. **56.** R. F. Price & D. B. Cohen (1988), p. 126, citing I. Oswald, A. Taylor & M. Treisman, "Discriminative responses to stimulation during human sleep," *Brain* 83, pp. 440-53, 1960. **57.** J. S. Antrobus, J. S. Antrobus & C. Fisher (1965), p. 395. **58.** J. Salamy (1970). **59.** D. Koulack (1991), p. 49. **60.** A. M. Arkin, J. M. Hastey & M. F. Reiser (1966), p. 305. **61.** Ibid., p. 309. **62.** S. LaBerge (1985), pp. 76-82. **63.** C. E. Green (1968). **64.** J. Gackenbach (1988b), pp. 183-4. **65.** J. Gackenbach & J. Bosveld (1989), p. 45. **66.** J. Gackenbach (1988b), p. 193. **67.** H. T. Hunt (1986), p. 270. **68.** J. Gackenbach (1988a), p. 3. **69.** P. Garfield (1976 [1974]), pp. 128-9. H. T. Hunt (1986), p. 270. **70.** H. T. Hunt & R. D. Ogilvie (1988), p. 391. **71.** Ibid. **72.** C. E. Green (1968), p. 6. **73.** C. T. Tart (1988), p. 95. H. T. Hunt & R. D. Ogilvie (1988), p. 397. A. Moffitt, R. Hoffmann, J. Mullington, S. Purcell, R. Pigeau & R. Wells (1988), p. 431. **74.** G. Delaney (1979), p. 160. **75.** P. Garfield (1976 [1974]), p. 120. **76.** S. Purcell, A. Moffitt & R. Hoffmann (1993), pp. 198 and 240. **77.** H. de Saint-Denys (1982 [1867]), p. 75. **78.** P. Tholey (1989), p. 14. **79.** A. Worsley (1988), p. 328. **80.** G. Gillespie (1988b). **81.** S. LaBerge & H. Rheingold (1990), p. 134. **82.** M. Schatzman (1982), p. 9. **83.** S. LaBerge (1985), p. 102. **84.** J. Gackenbach & J. Bosveld (1989), p. 19. **85.** J. L. Borges (1976), p. 121. My translation. **86.** J. Gackenbach & J. Bosveld (1989), p. 55. **87.** C. E. Green (1968), pp. 84, 90 and 159. **88.** H. de Saint-Denys (1982 [1867]), pp. 20 and 24. **89.** P. Garfield (1976 [1974]), p. 176. S. LaBerge (1985), p. 3. **90.** C. E. Green (1968), p. 79. **91.** J. Gackenbach (1988b), p. 185. **92.** C. E. Green (1968), p. 6. **93.** J. Gackenbach (1988b), p. 185. **94.** R. F. Price & D. B. Cohen (1988), p. 108. **95.** S. LaBerge (1985), p. 98. **96.** J. Gregory (1984), p. 4, citing G. Gillespie, "Memory and reason in lucid dreams: a personal observation," *Lucidity Letter* 2(4), pp. 8-9, 1983. **97.** Ibid., pp. 4-5. **98.** H. de Saint-Denys (1982 [1867]). S. LaBerge (1985). A. Worsley (1988). **99.** C. E. Green (1968), p. 91. **100.** G. Globus (1987). **101.** S. Purcell, J. Mullington, A. Moffitt, R. Hoffmann & R. Pigeau (1986), p. 424. **102.** H. de Saint-Denys (1982 [1867]), pp. 161-2. **103.** Ibid., p. 150. **104.** D. Barrett (1992), pp. 221 and 226. **105.** P. Tholey (1989), p. 16, quoting J. Reis, *Affektive Verlaufsphänomene des Klartraums*, Ph.D. dissertation, University of Frankfurt am Main, 1989. **106.** C. E. Green (1968), p. 20. **107.** H. T. Hunt (1989), p. 121. **108.** S. Blackmore (1989a), p. 7. **109.** R. D. Salley (1982), p. 161, citing D. Sheils, "A cross-cultural study of beliefs in out-of-body experiences, waking and sleeping," *Journal of the Society for Psychical Research* 49, pp. 697-741, 1978. **110.** S. LaBerge (1985), p. 211. **111.** R. D. Salley (1982), p. 162, citing several sources. **112.** G. S. Sparrow (1982 [1976]), p. 66. **113.** S. LaBerge (1985),

p. 211. **114.** L. Levitan & S. LaBerge (1991b), p. 3. **115.** C. E. Green (1968), p. 20. **116.** H. T. Hunt (1989), p. 121. **117.** S. Blackmore (1989a), pp. 7-8. **118.** C. E. Green (1968), p. 20. **119.** A. Faraday (1976 [1974]), p. 339. **120.** S. LaBerge (1985), p. 175. **121.** H. Stefanakis, A. Zadra & D. Donderi (1990), p. 3. **122.** C. E. Green (1968), p. 98. **123.** J. Gackenbach (1988b), p. 186, citing J. I. Gackenbach & B. Schillig, "Lucid dreams: the content of conscious awareness of dreaming during the dream," *Journal of Mental Imagery* 7(2), pp. 1-14, 1983. **124.** J. Gackenbach & J. Bosveld (1989), p. 43. **125.** D. W. (1989). **126.** O. Fox, *Astral Projection*, New York: University Books, p. 33, 1962, quoted by C. E. Green (1968), p. 99. **127.** P. Garfield (1989 [1979]), p. 134. **128.** Ibid., p. 44. **129.** P. Garfield (1989 [1979]), p. 134. **130.** P. Garfield (1989 [1979]), pp. 134-5. **131.** J. Gackenbach (1988b), p. 200. **132.** J. Gackenbach & J. Bosveld (1989), p. 57. **133.** P. Garfield (1989 [1979]), pp. 135-7. **134.** Ibid., p. xxxiv. **135.** S. LaBerge (1985), pp. 119-23. S. LaBerge & H. Rheingold (1990), pp. 117-21. **136.** J. Gackenbach & J. Bosveld (1989), p. 48. **137.** S. LaBerge & H. Rheingold (1990, pp. 115-6) cite: C. Castaneda, *Journey to Ixtlan*, New York: Simon & Schuster, 1972. H. von Moers-Messmer, "Träume mit der gleichzeitigen Erkenntnis des Traumzustandes," *Archiv für Psychologie* 102, pp. 291-318, 1938. L. Magallon, "Awake in the dark: imageless lucid dreaming," *Lucidity Letter* 6, pp. 86-90, 1987. **138.** G. S. Sparrow (1982 [1976]). **139.** L. Levitan (1990b), p. 4. **140.** S. LaBerge & H. Rheingold (1990), p. 116. **141.** Ibid., p. 121. **142.** L. Levitan (1990b), p. 4. **143.** C. E. Green (1968), p. 99. **144.** H. T. Hunt (1989), p. 121. **145.** S. LaBerge (1985), p. 11. **146.** Ibid., p. 97. **147.** P. Garfield (1989 [1979]), p. 44. **148.** J. Gackenbach & S. LaBerge (1984), p. 4. **149.** P. Garfield (1984), p. 85. Ellipsis Garfield's. **150.** Ibid., citing D. Foulkes, *Children's Dreams: Longitudinal Studies*, New York: John Wiley & Sons, p. 189, 1982. **151.** S. Purcell, J. Mullington, R. Pigeau, R. Hoffman[n] & A. Moffitt (1984). S. Purcell, J. Mullington, A. Moffitt, R. Hoffmann & R. Pigeau (1986). A. Moffitt, R. Hoffmann, J. Mullington, S. Purcell, R. Pigeau & R. Wells (1988). **152.** A. Rechtschaffen (1978), p. 98, citing W. B. Zimmerman, "Sleep mentation and auditory awakening thresholds," *Psychophysiology* 6, pp. 540-9, 1970. **153.** T. Snyder & J. Gackenbach (1988), p. 221. **154.** Ibid., p. 230. **155.** J. Gregory (1984), p. 15, citing K. Hearne, "Investigating structural characteristics of lucid dreams," *Dream Network Bulletin* 1(11), 1983. **156.** K. M. T. Hearne (1987), p. 75. **157.** J. Gackenbach & J. Bosveld (1989), pp. 155-76. **158.** J. Gackenbach (1988a), p. 3. **159.** L. Levitan (1989), p. 9. **160.** H. T. Hunt (1990a), citing J. Gackenbach. **161.** J. Gackenbach (1988a), p. 3. T. Snyder & J. Gackenbach (1988), p. 250. **162.** J. Gackenbach (1988a), p. 3. **163.** H. A. Witkin & D. R. Goodenough, *Cognitive Styles: Essence and Origins*, New York: International Universities Press, p. 1131, 1981, quoted by T. Snyder & J. Gackenbach (1988), p. 248. **164.** T. Snyder & J. Gackenbach (1988), p. 238ff. **165.** S. LaBerge & J. Gackenbach (1986), pp. 174 and 176, respectively, citing H. J. Irwin, "Migraine, out-of-body experiences, and lucid dreams," *Lucidity Letter* 2(2), pp. 2-3, 1983, and R. L. Kohr, "A survey of psi experiences among members of a special population," *Journal of the American Society for Psychical Research* 74, pp. 295-411, 1980. **166.** T. Snyder & J. Gackenbach (1988), p. 238ff. **167.** Ibid., citing J. Palmer, "A community mail survey of psychic experiences," *Research in Parapsychology* 3, pp. 130-3, 1974. **168.** M. Schatzman (1982). S. Purcell, J. Mullington, A. Moffitt, R. Hoffmann & R. Pigeau (1986). **169.** L. Levitan (1989), p. 9. **170.** J. Gregory (1984), p. 47ff. **171.** H. T. Hunt (1986), p. 270. **172.** J. Gackenbach & S. LaBerge (1984), p. 7. **173.** R. F. Price & D. B. Cohen (1988), p. 109. **174.** J. Gackenbach (1990b), p. 6. **175.** P. Garfield (1989 [1979]), pp. 122-3. **176.** R. F. Price & D. B. Cohen (1988), p. 109. **177.** G. S. Sparrow (1982 [1976]), p. 6. **178.** J. Gregory (1984), p. 58. **179.** J. Gackenbach (1985-6), p. 46. **180.** A. Faraday (1976 [1974]), p. 57. **181.** R. F. Price & D. B. Cohen (1988), p. 131. J. Gackenbach & J. Bosveld (1989), p. 21. **182.** L. Levitan (1989), p. 12. **183.** H. de Saint-Denys (1982 [1867]), p. 25. P. Garfield (1989 [1979]), p. 120. J. Gregory (1984), p. 69. **184.** R. F. Price & D. B. Cohen (1988), p. 112. **185.** S. LaBerge & H. Rheingold (1990). **186.** J. Gackenbach & J. Bosveld (1989), p. 23, citing F. Bogzaran. L. Reneau (no date), p. 150. J. Taylor (1983), p. 203. **187.** S. LaBerge & H. Rheingold (1990), pp. 44-7. **188.** J. Gackenbach (1985-6), p. 44. **189.** P.

Garfield, "Psychological concomitants of the lucid dream state," *Sleep Research* 4, p. 184, 1975, quoted by S. LaBerge & H. Rheingold (1990), p. 67. **190.** L. Levitan (1989), p. 10. **191.** S. LaBerge & H. Rheingold (1990), pp. 39-41. **192.** P. Tholey (1983), p. 81. **193.** S. LaBerge & H. Rheingold (1990), pp. 67-8. S. LaBerge (1992). **194.** J. Gackenbach (1985-6), p. 45. **195.** J. R. Dane & R. Van De Castle (1984). **196.** Ibid. **197.** Ibid. **198.** R. F. Price & D. B. Cohen (1988), p. 121, citing J. Dane, *An Empirical Evaluation of Two Techniques for Lucid Dream Induction*, Ph.D. dissertation, Georgia State University, Atlanta, 1984. **199.** C. Castaneda, *Journey to Ixtlan: The Lessons of Don Juan*, New York: Simon & Schuster, 1972, cited by P. Tholey (1983). **200.** T. P. (1989). **201.** K. S. (1989). **202.** P. K. (1991). **203.** C. E. Green (1968), p. 45. **204.** Ibid., p. 34. **205.** Respectively: S. LaBerge (1985), p. 113; C. E. Green (1968), p. 45; P. Garfield (1989), p. xxxiv. **206.** S. LaBerge & J. Gackenbach (1986), pp. 162-3. **207.** M. Darling, R. Hoffmann, A. Moffitt & S. Purcell (1993), pp. 16 and 18. **208.** J. Gackenbach & J. Bosveld (1989), p. 27, citing J. Gregory. J. R. Malamud (1988), p. 311. **209.** J. R. Malamud (1988), p. 314. **210.** J. Gackenbach (1985-6), p. 48. **211.** S. LaBerge (1987). R. F. Price & D. B. Cohen (1988), p. 125ff. **212.** K. M. T. Hearne (1983). **213.** S. LaBerge & H. Rheingold (1990), p. 73ff. **214.** P. Tholey (1983). **215.** J. Gackenbach & J. Bosveld (1989), pp. 36-7. **216.** Ibid., p. 57. S. LaBerge & H. Rheingold (1990), p. 76. **217.** P. Tholey (1983), p. 80. This and subsequent quotes reproduced with permission of author and publisher. See credit page. **218.** S. LaBerge (1985), p. 113. P. Tholey (1983), pp. 11-2. **219.** R. F. Price & D. B. Cohen (1988), p. 113. **220.** J. R. Malamud, "Training for lucid awareness in dreams, fantasy, and waking life," *Lucidity Letter* 1(4), pp. 7-12, 1982. G. S. Sparrow, *An exploration into the inducibility of increased reflectiveness and 'lucidity' in nocturnal dream reports*, Ph.D. dissertation, College of William and Mary, Williamsburg, Virginia, 1983. Both cited by R. F. Price & D. B. Cohen (1988), pp. 115-6. **221.** S. LaBerge & L. Levitan (1990), p. 7. **222.** H. Klippstein, "Hypnotherapy: a natural method of learning lucid dreaming," *Lucidity Letter* 7(2), pp. 79-88, 1988, cited by J. Gackenbach & J. Bosveld (1989), pp. 34-5. **223.** J. Taylor (1983), p. 202. **224.** L. Reneau (no date), p. 118. **225.** K. Harary & P. Weintraub (1989), pp. 16-8. **226.** S. LaBerge & H. Rheingold (1990), p. 55. **227.** S. Purcell, J. Mullington, A. Moffitt, R. Hoffmann & R. Pigeau (1986). **228.** S. Purcell, A. Moffitt & R. Hoffmann (1993), pp. 230 and 241. **229.** P. Tholey (1983), pp. 81-2. **230.** S. LaBerge & L. Levitan (1991), p. 3. **231.** S. LaBerge (1985), pp. 140-3. S. LaBerge & H. Rheingold (1990), pp. 61-6. **232.** J. Gackenbach (1985-6), p. 45. See also R. F. Price & D. B. Cohen (1988), p. 119ff. **233.** L. Levitan (1989). **234.** S. LaBerge & L. Levitan (1990), p. 5. **235.** S. LaBerge & H. Rheingold (1990), p. 74. **236.** L. Levitan (1990c), pp. 9-10. **237.** L. Levitan (1991a). **238.** J. Campbell (1980), p. 27. **239.** C. E. Green (1968), p. 37. M. Watkins (1984 [1976]), passim. **240.** S. LaBerge (1985), p. 137. **241.** P. Tholey (1989), p. 19. **242.** R. F. Price & D. B. Cohen (1988), p. 130, citing P. Tholey (1983). **243.** B. S. L. Warman (1947). **244.** S. LaBerge & H. Rheingold (1990), pp. 45-7, citing S. Rama, *Exercise Without Movement*, Honesdale, Pennsylvania: Himalayan Institute, 1984. **245.** P. Tholey (1983), p. 84. **246.** Ibid., p. 85. **247.** S. LaBerge & H. Rheingold (1990), pp. 97-8. **248.** P. Tholey (1983), p. 83. **249.** J. Gregory (1984), p. 86. **250.** J. Grant (1986 [1984]), pp. 84-6. **251.** C. E. Green (1968), p. 37, citing P. D. Ouspensky, *A New Model of the Universe*, London: Routledge & Kegan Paul, 1960 [1931]. **252.** J. Gregory (1984), p. 398. **253.** P. Tholey (1983), p. 84. **254.** Ibid., p. 85. **255.** S. LaBerge (1985), p. 130. **256.** S. LaBerge & H. Rheingold (1990), pp. 84-7, citing W. Y. Evans-Wentz (1958 [1935]). **257.** S. LaBerge & H. Rheingold (1990), pp. 87-8, citing Tarab Tulku XI, *Openness Mind*, Berkeley: Dharma Publishing, 1978. **258.** P. Garfield (1976 [1974]), chapter 7. **259.** G. Gillespie (1988a), p. 29. **260.** S. LaBerge & H. Rheingold (1990), p. 90. **261.** S. LaBerge (1985), p. 135. **262.** S. LaBerge & H. Rheingold (1990), p. 80. L. Levitan (1990c), p. 9. **263.** J. Gregory, personal communication, 1992. **264.** S. LaBerge & L. Levitan (1991). **265.** H. Stefanakis, A. Zadra & D. Donderi (1990), p. 3. **266.** J. Gackenbach & J. Bosveld (1989), pp. 100-1. **267.** Ibid., p. 107. **268.** P. Garfield (1991), p. 256. **269.** P. Garfield (1988b), p. 291. **270.** S. LaBerge & H. Rheingold (1990), p. 226. **271.** Ibid., p. 153ff. **272.** J. Gackenbach & J. Bosveld

(1989), p. 70ff. **273.** J. Maguire (1989), pp. 202-3. **274.** S. LaBerge & H. Rheingold (1990), p. 178. **275.** N. Epel (1993). **276.** P. Tholey (1988), p. 273. **277.** Respectively: L. Reneau (no date), p. 2; S. LaBerge & H. Rheingold (1990), p. 220; P. Tholey (1988), p. 273; J. R. Malamud (1988), p. 310; J. A. Hall & A. Brylowski (1990), pp. 36-7; P. Garfield (1976 [1974]), p. 14. **278.** P. Tholey (1989), p. 12. **279.** J. Gregory (1984), p. 99. **280.** P. Garfield (1989 [1979]), pp. 132-3. Ellipses terminating dream texts Garfield's. **281.** C. Beradt (1968 [1966]), p. 16. **282.** M. Sabini (1981a), p. 101, quoting M. Pelgrin, *And a Time to Die*, Wheaton, Illinois: Theosophical Publishing House, p. 113, 1962. **283.** A. Faraday (1976 [1974]), pp. 51-2. **284.** J. Baylis (1976), p. 11. **285.** S. L. Warner (1987), p. 105. **286.** A. B. Siegel (1992), p. 12. **287.** G. Delaney (1979), p. 99. **288.** L. M. Gordon (1991), p. 15. **289.** S. LaBerge & H. Rheingold (1990), p. 27. **290.** Ibid., p. 185. **291.** J. Taylor (1983), p. 196. **292.** J. Gregory (1984), pp. 364-5. **293.** G. S. Sparrow (1982 [1976]), pp. 16-7. **294.** P. Garfield (1990). **295.** E. Rossi (1985), p. 20. R. Steiner (1971), p. 48. **296.** J. Gackenbach (1990c). **297.** J. Gackenbach (1989), p. 65. **298.** J. King (1990). **299.** W. Bonime (1990). J. Gackenbach & J. Bosveld (1989), p. 87, quoting G. Delaney. J. Gackenbach & J. Bosveld (1989), p. 94. G. S. Sparrow (1982 [1976]), p. 8. **300.** J. D. Clift & W. B. Clift (1984), p. 126. **301.** C. G. Jung [1944], CW 12, para. 51. See also (1984 [1938]), p. 4. **302.** J. A. Hall (1983), p. 91. **303.** M. A. Mattoon (1984 [1978]), p. 33. J. A. Hall & A. Brylowski (1990), pp. 40-2. **304.** P. Tholey (1989), p. 13. **305.** J. W. Lewis (1990). E. T. Gendlin (1990). J. Gollnick (1987), p. 32. **306.** J. White-Lewis (1992), pp. 98-9. **307.** R. Shohet (1985), p. 45. **308.** K. L. West (1977), p. 61. **309.** E. S.-L. Richardson (1991), p. 12. **310.** P. E. Craig (1990). **311.** J. King (1990). **312.** P. Garfield (1990). **313.** H. T. Hunt & R. D. Ogilvie (1988), p. 397. **314.** S. Krippner & J. Dillard (1988), p. 170, citing G. Delaney (1979). **315.** J. Gackenbach & J. Bosveld (1989), p. 19. **316.** L. Magallon, interviewed in J. Gregory (1987), p. 16. **317.** R. F. Price & D. B. Cohen (1988), p. 108. **318.** J. Taylor (1983), pp. 201-2. See also (1992a), pp. 218-20. **319.** J. W. Lewis (1990). **320.** G. G. Globus & M. Derfler (1990). See also H. T. Hunt (1989), p. 120. **321.** S. LaBerge (1985), p. 243ff. **322.** P. Garfield (1990). **323.** H. Reed (1988 [1985]), p. 25. G. S. Sparrow (1982 [1976]), p. 4. P. Garfield (1989 [1979]), p. 17. K. Kelzer (1987), p. 271. **324.** W. Y. Evans-Wentz (1958 [1935]), p. 146. **325.** G. S. Sparrow (1982 [1976]), p. 52. J. Gackenbach (1989), p. 63. **326.** H. T. Hunt (1986), p. 269. See also H. T. Hunt (1991b). **327.** H. T. Hunt & R. D. Ogilvie (1988), p. 391. **328.** G. Delaney (1979), p. 168. **329.** J. Gackenbach & J. Bosveld (1989), p. 125. **330.** S. Blackmore (1989a), p. 10. **331.** For example, S. LaBerge (1985), p. 248. **332.** J. Gackenbach & J. Bosveld (1989), p. 125. **333.** W. Y. Evans-Wentz (1958 [1935]), p. 165. **334.** Respectively: S. LaBerge (1985), p. 8; Ibid., p. 9; P. K., quoted by S. LaBerge & H. Rheingold (1990), p. 229. **335.** P. Garfield (1989 [1979]), pp. 128 and 44-5. **336.** G. G. Globus & M. Derfler (1990). H. T. Hunt (1986), p. 269. **337.** Milarepa, translated by E. Conze (1964 [1954]), p. 258. **338.** Lama A. Govinda (1984 [1966]), pp. 100-1. J. Singer (1977 [1976]), p. 180. M. Boss (1965), pp. 134-5. **339.** O. Fox, *Astral Projection*, New York: University Books, 1962, quoted by S. LaBerge (1988a), p. 20. **340.** S. LaBerge & H. Rheingold (1990), p. 243. **341.** J. Gackenbach (1991a), p. 124 and (1989), p. 63, respectively. See also J. Gackenbach & J. Bosveld (1989), p. 98. **342.** Tarab Tulku XI (1989), p. 48. **343.** W. D. O'Flaherty (1984), p. 15. **344.** J. M. Nanda (1974), pp. 48 and 17. **345.** W. D. O'Flaherty (1984), p. 17. **346.** J. M. Nanda (1974). **347.** G. Gillespie (1991), pp. 226, 227 and 230. **348.** J. Gackenbach & J. Bosveld (1989), p. 187. **349.** C. N. Alexander (1990). **350.** C. N. Alexander, R. W. Cranson, R. W. Boyer & D. W. Orme-Johnson (1986), p. 302. **351.** G. Gillespie (1992), pp. 172-3, citing J. Gackenbach & J. Bosveld (1989), p. 136 and C. Alexander, R. Boyer & D. W. Orme-Johnson, "Distinguishing between transcendental consciousness and lucidity," *Lucidity Letter* 4(2), pp. 68-85, 1985. **352.** C. N. Alexander, R. W. Cranson, R. W. Boyer & D. W. Orme-Johnson (1986), p. 296ff. **353.** J. Gackenbach (1991b). **354.** G. Delaney (1979), pp. 168-70. **355.** J. Gregory (1988c), p. 8, quoting Eric Snyder. **356.** J. Gackenbach, R. Cranson & C. N. Alexander, "Lucid dreaming, witnessing dreaming, and the Transcendental Meditation technique: A developmental relationship," paper presented to the Association for the Study of Dreams, Ontario, Canada, 1986, quoted by C. N. Alexander, R. W. Cranson, R. W. Boyer & D. W. Orme-Johnson (1986), p. 295. **357.** C. N. Alexander (1990). **358.** J. Gackenbach & J. Bosveld (1989), p. 49. **359.** G. Gillespie (1992), p. 168. **360.** W. Y. Evans-Wentz (1958 [1935]), p. 223ff. **361.** G. Gillespie (1985), pp. 6-7. **362.** G. Gillespie (1988b), p. 349. **363.** G. Gillespie (1992), p. 169. **364.** G. Gillespie (1988b), p. 349 and (1992), p. 170. K. Kelzer (1987), p. 260, first published in K. Kelzer, *The Sun and the Shadow*, Virginia Beach, Virginia: ARE Press, 1986. P. Garfield (1989 [1979]), p. 54. **365.** M. Eliade (1960 [1957]), pp. 89-91. **366.** W. Y. Evans-Wentz (1958 [1935]). **367.** W. D. O'Flaherty (1984), p. 26. **368.** W. Y. Evans-Wentz (1958 [1935]). **369.** M. Eliade (1960 [1957]), pp. 89-91. Lama A. Govinda (1984 [1966]). **370.** P. L., quoted by G. S. Sparrow (1982 [1976]), pp. 26-7. **371.** G. S. Sparrow (1982 [1976]), p. 5. **372.** G. Gillespie (1988b), p. 350. See also G. Gillespie (1988c). **373.** M. Eliade (1960 [1957]), p. 91. **374.** W. D. O'Flaherty (1984), p. 182. **375.** J. Gackenbach & J. Bosveld (1989), pp. 28-9. J. Gregory (1984), p. 53, citing J. Taylor. P. E. Craig, quoted by J. Gackenbach (1989), pp. 65-6. S. Blackmore (1989a), p. 8. **376.** S. LaBerge (1985), p. 239. **377.** C. Trungpa (1973). **378.** A. Moffitt (1990). **379.** J. Gackenbach & J. Bosveld (1989), pp. 28-9. **380.** G. Delaney (1990c), p. 26. **381.** S. LaBerge (1985), p. 200. **382.** G. S. Sparrow (1982 [1976]), pp. 18 and 25. **383.** J. Gackenbach (1990a), p. 3. **384.** H. T. Hunt (1989), p. 119 and (1990a). **385.** M. A. Mattoon (1984 [1978]), p. 106. **386.** S. LaBerge (1985), p. 16, citing J. Fabricius, "The symbol of the self in the alchemical 'proiectio'," *Journal of Analytical Psychology* 18, pp. 47-58, 1973. **387.** H. T. Hunt (1989). **388.** For example, K. Asper (1992a [1988]), p. 114. **389.** E. Rossi (1985). **390.** H. T. Hunt, R. Ogilvie, K. Belicki, D. Belicki & E. Atalick (1982), p. 592. **391.** H. P. Wilberg (1981), p. 120. **392.** J. Mullington, M. Cuddy, A. Moffitt, R. Hoffman[n] & L. Pickavance (1988), p. 4. **393.** P. Kugler, J. Gackenbach & H. Hunt (1987), p. 9. **394.** J. Gackenbach & J. Bosveld (1989), p. 95. **395.** Ibid., p. 29. **396.** S. LaBerge & H. Rheingold (1990), p. 239. K. Kelzer (1987 [1986]), p. 260. G. S. Sparrow (1982 [1976]), passim. **397.** J. Gackenbach & J. Bosveld (1989), p. 23. **398.** J. Taylor (1992a), pp. 212-3 and 240 passim. **399.** K. Bulkeley (1994), chapter 17, note 5. **400.** Lama Lodö (1990), p. 12. **401.** P. Garfield (1989 [1979]), p. 138. **402.** O. Garrison (1983 [1964]). **403.** J. Gackenbach & J. Bosveld (1989), p. 99. **404.** W. D. O'Flaherty (1984), p. 81.

Chapter 15 • Re-entry

1. Respectively: P. R. Koch-Sheras, E. A. Hollier & B. Jones (1983), p. 93; Tarab Tulku XI (1989), p. 56; L. M. Savary, P. H. Berne & S. K. Williams (1984), p. 167; I. Marks (1978). **2.** C. G. Jung, "The psychological aspects of the Kore" [1941], CW9-I, para's 319-20, quoted by H. A. Wilmer (1987), p. 125. **3.** C. G. Jung, quoted by M. Watkins (1984 [1976]), p. 43. **4.** J. A. Hall & A. Brylowski (1990), p. 37. **5.** E. C. Whitmont & S. B. Perera (1989), p. 47. **6.** J. A. Sanford (1977), p. 142. **7.** R. Bosnak (1988 [1986]), pp. 39 and 43-4. **8.** A. Mankowitz (1984), p. 71. **9.** R. A. Johnson (1986), p. 139. **10.** S. Peterson, *A Catalogue of Ways People Grow*, New York: Ballantine, p. 162, 1971, cited by M. Watkins (1984 [1976]), p. 48. **11.** C. G. Jung, "The transcendent function" [1957], CW 8, para. 152. **12.** M. Watkins (1984 [1976]), pp. 46-50. **13.** J. A. Sanford (1977), p. 148. **14.** R. A. Johnson (1986), p. 182. **15.** C. G. Jung [1955-6], CW 14, para. 749, quoted by J. A. Sanford (1977), p. 142. **16.** R. A. Johnson (1986), p. 190, citing C. G. Jung. **17.** E. C. Whitmont & S. B. Perera (1989), p. 47. **18.** J. A. Sanford (1977), p. 142. **19.** Ibid., p. 144. **20.** E. C. Whitmont & S. B. Perera (1989), p. 48. **21.** Ibid., p. 9. **22.** H. A. Wilmer (1987), p. 125. **23.** J. A. Hall & A. Brylowski (1990), p. 39. **24.** E. Rossi (1985), pp. 200-2. Ellipses in transcript of conversation and dream text Rossi's. **25.** E. T. Gendlin (1986), pp. 10-3. **26.** Ibid., p. 1. **27.** A. S. Wiseman (1987), p. 76. **28.** H. Barz (1990), pp. 169 and 174. **29.** Ibid., pp. 166-7. **30.** Ibid., pp. 178-9. **31.** P. Garfield (1991), p. 145. **32.** P. Garfield (1984), p. 286 and (1991), p. 249. **33.** S. LaBerge & H. Rheingold (1990), p. 203, citing J. H. Geer & I. Silverman, "Treatment of a recurrent nightmare by behaviour modification procedures," *Journal of Abnormal Psychol-*

ogy 72, pp. 188-90, 1967, I. Marks, "Rehearsal relief of a nightmare," *British Journal of Psychiatry* 135, pp. 461-5, 1978, and citing N. Bishay, "Therapeutic manipulation of nightmares and the management of neuroses," *British Journal of Psychiatry* 147, pp. 67-70, 1985. **34.** S. Shulman (1979), pp. 206-7, citing R. D. Cartwright. **35.** L. M. Savary, P. H. Berne & S. K. Williams (1984), p. 124. **36.** Ibid., p. 167. **37.** S. K. Williams (1986 [1980]), p. 170. **38.** Ibid., pp. 191-2. **39.** A. S. Wiseman (1987), p. 15. **40.** A. S. Wiseman (1991), p. 17. See also A. S. Wiseman, *Nightmare Help: A Guide for Parents and Teachers*, Berkeley: Ten Speed Press, 1989. **41.** L. Reneau (no date), p. 79. Ellipsis Reneau's.

Chapter 16 • The Bo Tree Principle

1. Lama A. Govinda (1984 [1966]), p. 175. **2.** J. Taylor (1983), p. 198 and (1992a), p. 209. **3.** J. E. Mack (1989 [1970]), p. 3, citing J. Shipley, *Dictionary of Word Origins*, New York: Philosophical Library, 1945. **4.** S. Shulman (1979), p. 12. R. Broughton, "The incubus attack," in E. Hartmann, editor, *Sleep and Dreaming*, Boston: Little, Brown, 1970, cited by P. R. Robbins (1988), p. 80. **5.** E. T. Gendlin (1986), pp. 39 and 77. H. R. Ellis (1989), p. 3. J. A. Hadfield (1954), p. 93. J. Downing & R. Marmorstein (1973), p. 39. R. Grossinger (1971b), pp. 151-2. **6.** P. Tholey (1983), p. 87. **7.** R. Grossinger (1971b), pp. 151-2. **8.** P. Tholey (1983), p. 87. **9.** S. LaBerge & H. Rheingold (1990), p. 214. P. Tholey (1988). **10.** G. S. Sparrow (1982 [1976]). **11.** G. Delaney (1991), p. 365. **12.** A. Faraday (1976 [1974]), pp. 304 and 233. **13.** P. Garfield (1989), p. xxxv. **14.** P. Garfield (1984), p. 266. **15.** P. Mitchell (1990), p. 28. **16.** A. Mindell (1990), p. 34. **17.** J. T. Shaffer (1986), p. 347. R. Bosnak (1988 [1986]), p. 41. **18.** P. Garfield (1988a), p. 68. A. Zwig (1990b), p. 84. **19.** J. A. Sanford (1984 [1966]), p. 28. E. C. Whitmont & S. B. Perera (1989), p. 125. P. E. Craig (1990b), p. 73. S. Krippner & J. Dillard (1988), pp. 122-3. P. R. Koch-Sheras, E. A. Hollier & B. Jones (1983), p. 32. J. D. Clift & W. B. Clift (1984), pp. 68-9. S. Krippner & J. Dillard (1988), pp. 142-3. L. S. Leonard (1985 [1982]), pp. 96-7. P. Tholey (1988), p. 265. A. Faraday (1976 [1974]), pp. 264-5. S. K. Williams (1986 [1980]), pp. 179-80. A. S. Wiseman (1989), p. 1. E. A. Gutheil (1967 [1951]), p. 131. **20.** M. Kramer (1991a), pp. 283-4. **21.** C. G. Jung, "The practical use of dream-analysis" [1934], CW 16, para. 329. J. A. Hall (1983), p. 49. J. Taylor (1983), p. 68. H. A. Wilmer (1987), pp. 101 and 112, quoting C. G. Jung, *On the Psychology of the Unconscious* [1917/1926/1943], CW 7, para. 111. **22.** M.-L. von Franz (1980a [1978]), p. 119, citing C. G. Jung [1951], CW9-II, para. 209ff. **23.** H. A. Wilmer (1987), p. 103. **24.** P. Garfield (1989 [1979]), p. xxii. **25.** P. R. Koch-Sheras, E. A. Hollier & B. Jones (1983), p. 95. **26.** K. Stewart (1954), pp. 392 and 399. **27.** P. Garfield (1989), p. xxii. **28.** P. Garfield (1979), p. 138. **29.** Respectively: C. G. Jung (1965 [1961]), p. 245; C. G. Jung, CW 12 and CW 13. **30.** C. A. Meier (1967 [1949]), p. 5. **31.** W. Z. Park (1975 [1938]), pp. 84-5 and 87. **32.** J. A. Sanford (1984 [1966]), pp. 28 and 167. **33.** J. Taylor (1983), p. 56. **34.** J. Downing & R. Marmorstein (1973), pp. 38-9. **35.** R. Bosnak (1989), pp. 90-1. **36.** D. Beaudet (1990). **37.** J. Grant (1986 [1984]), p. 183, citing G. Greene, *A Sort of Life*, London: Bodley Head, 1971. **38.** C. T. Tart (1988), p. 98. **39.** P. E. Craig (1987), pp. 49-52. **40.** J. A. Sanford (1984 [1966]), pp. 22 and 26. **41.** W. Phillips (1989), p. 5. **42.** S. Krippner & J. Dillard (1988), pp. 142-3. **43.** R. Corriere, W. Karle, L. Woldenberg & J. Hart (1980), p. 63. **44.** J. D. Clift & W. B. Clift (1984), pp. 68-9. **45.** K. Belicki, personal communication, 1992. **46.** C. Rycroft (1981 [1979]), p. 88. **47.** P. Garfield (1979), pp. 196-7. **48.** A. Faraday (1976 [1974]), p. 304. **49.** E. Rossi (1985), p. 17. **50.** P. Garfield (1991), p. 167. **51.** P. Garfield (1984), p. 150. **52.** P. R. Koch-Sheras, E. A. Hollier & B. Jones (1983), p. 97. **53.** S. LaBerge & H. Rheingold (1990), p. 196. **54.** S. LaBerge (1985), p. 161. **55.** A. Faraday (1976 [1974]), p. 235. **56.** G. Delaney (1991), p. 205. **57.** G. Delaney (1979), p. 161. **58.** P. Tholey (1988), p. 280. **59.** Ibid., pp. 269-70. **60.** J. Gackenbach & J. Bosveld (1989), p. 90, citing P. Tholey. **61.** J. Hillman (1979), p. 113. **62.** S. Sparrow, cited by J. Gackenbach & J. Bosveld (1989), p. 86. **63.** S. K. Williams (1986 [1980]), p. 179. **64.**

G. Halliday (1988), p. 306. **65.** E. M. Palace & C. Johnston (1989), pp. 220-4. **66.** P. Tholey (1983), p. 88 and (1988), pp. 271 and 274. **67.** Respectively: R. Bosnak (1988 [1986]), p. 41; B. Tedlock (1981), p. 326; P. Tholey (1988), p. 274. **68.** J. R. Malamud (1988), p. 313. **69.** J. Gackenbach (1989), p. 66. **70.** P. Tholey (1988), p. 272. **71.** Ibid., p. 274. **72.** Ibid., p. 266. **73.** Ibid., p. 265. **74.** A. Faraday (1976 [1974]), p. 263. **75.** J. Gackenbach & J. Bosveld (1989), p. 56. **76.** S. LaBerge (1985), pp. 106 and 161. **77.** G. S. Sparrow (1982 [1976]), p. 24. **78.** H. de Saint-Denys (1982 [1867]), pp. 58-9. **79.** K. Stewart (1954), p. 399. **80.** C. T. Tart (1988), p. 98. **81.** D. Beaudet (1990), p. 28 passim. **82.** Tarab Tulku XI (1989), p. 54. **83.** P. Tholey (1988), pp. 269-70. **84.** A. Mindell (1990), p. 34. See also (1989). **85.** M. Kelsey (1978), pp. 48-9. **86.** M. Watkins (1984 [1976]), p. 147. **87.** F. S. Perls (1992 [1969]), pp. 241 and 190. **88.** P. Fellows (1988), pp. 302-3. **89.** M. Zeller (1990 [1975]), pp. 187 and 200. **90.** G. S. Sparrow (1982 [1976]), p. 31. **91.** S. LaBerge & H. Rheingold (1990), pp. 210-1. **92.** S. LaBerge (1985), pp. 11-2. **93.** P. Garfield (1991), pp. 167-8. **94.** P. Garfield (1988b), pp. 294-5. **95.** P. Garfield (1989 [1979]), pp. xxv-xxvi. **96.** Ibid., p. 54. **97.** P. Garfield (1988a), p. 205, citing P. Étévenon, personal communication. **98.** P. Garfield (1984), p. 283. **99.** Ibid., pp. 366-7. **100.** P. Garfield (1988a), p. 203-4, citing P. Maybruck, personal communication. See also Maybruck, *Pregnancy & Dreams*, Los Angeles: Jeremy P. Tarcher, 1989. **101.** P. R. Koch-Sheras, E. A. Hollier & B. Jones (1983), pp. 102-3. **102.** S. Krippner & J. Dillard (1988), p. 122. **103.** A. Faraday (1976 [1974]), p. 260. **104.** C. E. Green (1968), pp. 45-6. **105.** G. Halliday (1988), p. 306. **106.** L. Levitan & S. LaBerge (1990), p. 10 passim. **107.** A. L. Zadra (1990). **108.** A. L. Zadra & R. O. Pihl (no date), p. 14, citing G. Halliday (1988) and A. L. Zadra (1990). **109.** Anonymous, personal communication. **110.** E. R. Neu (1988), p. 43. **111.** J. T. Shaffer (1986), p. 347. **112.** A. Eccles, A. Wilde & W. L. Marshall (1988), pp. 285-6, citing I. Silverman & J. H. Geer, "The elimination of a recurrent nightmare by desensitization of a related phobia," *Behaviour Research and Therapy* 6, pp. 109-11, 1968. **113.** D. Whitmore (1981), p. 112. **114.** H. Reed (1991), p. 109. **115.** B. Eichelman (1985), pp. 113-4. **116.** Ibid., p. 113. **117.** A. Zwig (1990a). **118.** A. Zwig (1990b). **119.** P. Garfield (1988a) and (1991). **120.** A. Mindell (1985), pp. 8 and 39. **121.** A. Mindell (1989), pp. 23 and 104. **122.** A. Mindell (1985) , p. 70. **123.** A. Mindell (1990), p. 34. **124.** A. Zwig (1990b), p. 85. **125.** Ibid., p. 84. **126.** A. Mindell (1985), pp. 18-20. **127.** Ibid., pp. 10 and 27. **128.** R. A. Lockhart (1977), p. 7. **129.** H. P. Wilberg (1981), p. 122. **130.** J. A. Sanford (1977), p. 33. **131.** M. Sabini (1981a), p. 87. **132.** Ibid., p. 101. **133.** A. Zwig (1990b), p. 85. **134.** D. Roomy (1990), p. 14. See also A. Mindell (1989), p. 26. **135.** A. Zwig (1990b), p. 85. **136.** A. Mindell (1985), p. 15. **137.** A. Zwig (1990b), p. 84, quoting A. Mindell, *River's Way: The Process Science of the Dreambody*, London: Routledge and Kegan Paul, pp. 34-6, 1985.

References

Ablon, Steven Luria & John E. Mack (1980). Children's dreams reconsidered. *Psychoanalytic Study of the Child* 5:179-217.

Abramson, Harold A. & Leonard W. Krinsky (1975). The first dream as the chief complaint of the unconscious, and its utilization by the primary physician. *Journal of Asthma Research* 12:221-36.

Achterberg, Jeanne (1985). *Imagery in Healing: Shamanism and Modern Medicine*. Boston: Shambhala.

Ackerknecht, Lucy K. (1985). Creative dream work in high and low synergy cultures. *Individual Psychology* 41:340-8.

Adams, Michael Vannoy (1990). Dreams as complexes: Jung's dream of the brown horse and heavy log. *Quadrant* 24(1):45-63.

Adler, Alfred (1958 [1931]). *What Life Should Mean to You*. New York: Capricorn.

Agnew, H. W., Jr., W. B. Webb & R. L. Williams (1967). Comparison of stage four and 1-REM sleep deprivation. *Perceptual and Motor Skills* 24:851-8.

Aldighieri, Merrill & Joe Tripician (1991). *METAPHORIA* (video). New York: Co-directions.

Alexander, Charles N. (1990). Panel discussion. See Alexander et al.

Alexander, Charles N., Robert W. Cranson, Robert W. Boyer & David W. Orme-Johnson (1986). Transcendental consciousness: a fourth state of consciousness beyond sleep, dreaming, and waking. In Gackenbach.

Alexander, Charles N., Fariba Bogzaran, Melissa Derfler, Jayne Gackenbach & Harry T. Hunt (1990). Is lucid dreaming related to higher states of consciousness? Panel discussion at the conference of the Lucidity Association, Chicago.

Allenby, Amy (1985 [1955]). The father archetype in feminine psychology. In Samuels (1985a).

Allison, Truett & Henry Van Twyver (1974 [1970]). The sleep and dreams of animals (II). *Natural History* 79:56-65. Excerpted in Woods & Greenhouse.

Allison, Truett & Domenic V. Cicchetti (1976). Sleep in mammals: ecological and constitutional correlates. *Science* 194:732-4.

Altman, Leon L. (1969). *The Dream in Psychoanalysis*. New York: International Universities.

Altshuler, Kenneth Z., Martin Barad & Alvin I. Goldfarb (1963). A survey of dreams in the aged, Part II: Noninstitutionalized subjects. *Archives of General Psychiatry* 8:33-7.

Andrews, Shelagh (1983). Teenage girls' dream group. *Self and Society* 11:84-8.

Anonymous (1984). *"Pass It On"—Bill Wilson and the A.A. Message*. New York: Alcoholics Anonymous World Services.

Antrobus, John S. (1977). The dream as metaphor: an information-processing and learning model. *Journal of Mental Imagery* 2:327-38.

Antrobus, John S. (1986). Dreaming: cortical activation and perceptual thresholds. *Journal of Mind and Behavior* 7:193-211.

Antrobus, John (1987). Cortical hemisphere assymetry and sleep mentation. *Psychological Review* 94:359-68.

Antrobus, John (1993). Dreaming: could we do without it? In Moffitt et al. (1993a).

Antrobus, Judith S., John S. Antrobus & Charles Fisher (1965). Discrimination of dreaming and nondreaming sleep. *Archives of General Psychiatry* 12: 395-401.

Arkin, Arthur M. & John S. Antrobus (1991). The effects of external stimuli applied prior to and during sleep on sleep experience. In Ellman & Antrobus.

Arkin, Arthur M., John M. Hastey & Morton F. Reiser (1966). Post-hypnotically stimulated sleep-talking. *Journal of Nervous and Mental Disease* 142:293-309.

Arkin, A. M., M. F. Toth, J. Baker & J. M. Hastey (1970a). The frequency of sleep talking in the laboratory among chronic sleep talkers and good dream recallers. *Journal of Nervous and Mental Disease* 151:369-74.

Arkin, A. M., M. F. Toth, J. Baker & J. M. Hastey (1970b). The degree of concordance between the content of sleep talking and mentation recalled in wakefulness. *Journal of Nervous and Mental Disease* 151:375-93.

Armitage, Roseanne (1992). Gender differences and the effect of stress on dream recall: a 30-day diary report. *Dreaming* 2:137-41.

Aserinsky, E. & N. Kleitman (1953). Regularly occurring periods of eye motility, and concomitant phenomena during sleep. *Science* 118:273-4.

Ashanti, Faheem C. (1990). *Rootwork & Voodoo in Mental Health*. Durham, North Carolina: Tone.

Asper, Kathrin (1992a [1988]). *The Inner Child in Dreams*. Boston: Shambhala.

Asper, Kathrin (1992b). Beyond Freud and Jung: seven analysts discuss the impact of new ideas about dreamwork. A response by Kathrin Asper. *Quadrant* 25(2):86-9.

Assagioli, Roberto (1971 [1965]). *Psychosynthesis*. New York: Viking Compass.

Baldwin, Joseph A. (1981). Notes on an Africentric theory of black personality. *Western Journal of Black Studies* 5:172-9.

Banks, William M. (1980). The social context and empirical foundations of research on black clients. In Jones.

Barad, Martin, Kenneth Z. Altshuler & Alvin I. Goldfarb (1961). A survey of dreams in aged persons. *Archives of General Psychiatry* 4:419-23.

Barnouw, Victor (1975 [1966]). *Dream of the Blue Heron*. New York: Dell Yearling.

Barrett, Deirdre (1987). Dreams of death. *Association for the Study of Dreams Newsletter* 4(3):1-2.

Barrett, Deirdre (1988). The ostrich policy: the repression hypothesis revisited. *Association for the Study of Dreams Newsletter* 5(5):1-3.

Barrett, Deirdre (1992). Just how lucid are lucid dreams? *Dreaming* 2:221-8.

Barrett, Deirdre (1993). The "committee of sleep": a study of dream incubation for problem solving. *Dreaming* 3:115-22.

Barrett, Deirdre & Michael Loeffler (1990). The effect of depression on dream content. *Association for the Study of Dreams Newsletter* 7(2):4,16.

Bartemeier, Leo H. (1950). Illness following dreams. *International Journal of Psycho-Analysis* 31:8-11.

Barz, Helmut (1990). Dreams and psychodrama. In Schwartz-Salant & Stein.

Basso, Ellen B. (1992 [1987]). A progressive theory of dreaming. In Tedlock (1992a [1987]).

Bastide, Roger (1966). The sociology of the dream. In Grunebaum & Caillois.

Baylis, Janice (1976). *Dream Dynamics and Decoding: An Interpretation Manual.* Huntington Beach, California: Sun, Man, Moon.

Baylis, Janice (1991). Aids to dream recall. *Dream Network Journal* 10(2 & 3): 49.

Beaudet, Denyse (1990). *Encountering the Monster: Pathways in Children's Dreams.* New York: Continuum.

Beck, Aaron T. & Clyde H. Ward (1961). Dreams of depressed patients. *Archives of General Psychiatry* 5:462-7.

Beck, Henry W. (1977). Dream analysis in family therapy. *Clinical Social Work Journal* 5:53-7.

Belicki, Denis A. (1987). Relationship of nightmares to psychopathology, stress, and reactivity to stress. *Association for the Study of Dreams Newsletter* 4(1): 10.

Belicki, Kathryn E. (1986). Recalling dreams: an examination of daily variation and individual differences. In Gackenbach.

Belicki, Kathryn (1992a). The relationship of nightmare frequency to nightmare suffering with implications for treatment and research. *Dreaming* 2:143-8.

Belicki, Kathryn (1992b). Survivors of sexual abuse and their dreams. Address to the Association for the Study of Dreams, Santa Cruz.

Belicki, Kathryn & Marion A. Cuddy (1991). Nightmares: facts, fictions and future directions. In Gackenbach & Sheikh.

Benca, Ruth M., William H. Obermeyer, Ronald A. Thisted & J. Christian Gillin (1992). Sleep and psychiatric disorders: a meta-analysis. *Archives of General Psychiatry* 49:651-68.

Beradt, Carlotte (1968 [1966]). *The Third Reich of Dreams.* Chicago: Quadrangle.

Berry, Patricia (1974). An approach to the dream. *Spring:* 58-79.

Biele, Albert M. (1986). Principles and problems in the clinical use of PDS for manifest dreams. In Piotrowski, pp. 158-76.

Bilu, Yoram (1989). The Other as a nightmare: the Israeli-Arab encounter as reflected in children's dreams in Israel and the West Bank. *Political Psychology* 10:365-89.

Bilu, Yoram & Henry Abramovitch (1985). In search of the Saddiq: visitational dreams among Moroccan Jews in Israel. *Psychiatry* 48:83-92.

Blackmore, Susan (1989a). Dreaming, out-of-body experience, and reality: an interview with Susan Blackmore. [Interview by Tore Nielsen.] *Association for the Study of Dreams Newsletter* 6(6):7–10.

Blackmore, Susan (1989b). Mental models in sleep: why do we feel more conscious in lucid dreams? *Lucidity Letter* 8(2):31–46.

Blagrove, Mark (1990). A critical review of neural net theories of REM sleep. *Association for the Study of Dreams Newsletter* 7(1):1–2.

Blagrove, Mark (1992). Dreams as the reflection of our waking concerns and abilities: a critique of the problem-solving paradigm in dream research. *Dreaming* 2:205–20.

Blank, H. Robert (1958). Dreams of the blind. *Psychoanalytic Quarterly* 27: 158–74.

Blum, Harold (1976). The changing use of dreams in psychoanalytic practice: dreams and free association. *International Journal of Psycho-Analysis* 57:315–24.

Bogart, Gregory Charles (1993). Seven dreams in a case of childhood sexual abuse and adult homophobia. *Dreaming* 3:201–10.

Bogzaran, Fariba (1990). Expressive dream art. *Association for the Study of Dreams Newsletter* 7(2):8–9.

Bonato, Richard A., Alan R. Moffitt, Robert F. Hoffmann, Marion A. Cuddy & Frank L. Wimmer (1991). Bizarreness in dreams and nightmares. *Dreaming* 1:53–61.

Bonime, Walter (1969). A culturalist view. In Kramer.

Bonime, Walter (with Florence Bonime) (1980). The dream in the depressive personality. In Natterson (1980a).

Bonime, Walter (with Florence Bonime) (1982 [1962]). *The Clinical Use of Dreams*. New York: Da Capo.

Bonime, Walter (with Florence Bonime) (1987 [1978]). Culturalist approach. In Fosshage & Loew (1987a [1978]).

Bonime, Walter (1990). Panel discussion. See Gackenbach et al.

Borges, Jorge Luis (1976). *Libro de Sueños*. Buenos Aires: Torres Agüero Editor.

Bosinelli, Marino (1991). Chapter 3 update: recent research trends in sleep onset mentation. In Ellman & Antrobus.

Bosnak, Robert (1988 [1986]). *A Little Course in Dreams*. Boston: Shambhala.

Bosnak, Robert (1989). *Dreaming with an Aids Patient*. Boston: Shambhala.

Boss, Medard (1959 [1938]). The psychopathology of dreams in schizophrenia and organic psychosis. In DeMartino.

Boss, Medard (1965). *A Psychiatrist Discovers India*. London: Oswald Wolff.

Boss, Medard (1977). *"I dreamt last night . . ."* New York: Gardner.

Boss, Medard & Brian Kenny (1987 [1978]). Phenomenological or Daseinsanalytic approach. In Fosshage & Loew (1987a [1978]).

Breger, Louis (1980). The manifest dream and its latent meaning. In Natterson (1980a).

Breger, Louis, Ian Hunter & Ron W. Lane (1971). *The Effect of Stress on Dreams.* New York: International Universities.

Brelich, Angelo (1966). The place of dreams in the religious world concept of the Greeks. In Grunebaum & Caillois.

Brenneis, Brooks (1970). Male and female ego modalities in manifest dream content. *Journal of Abnormal Psychology* 76:434–42.

Bressler, Bernard & Nan Mizrachi (1978a). The first dream as a psychodiagnostic tool: its use by the primary physician with his psychosomatic patients. *Journal of Asthma Research* 15:179–89.

Bressler, Bernard & Nan Mizrachi (1978b). The first dream as a psychodiagnostic tool: II. Parameters. *Journal of Asthma Research* 16:1–14.

Breznitz, Shlomo (1971). A critical note on secondary revision. *International Journal of Psycho-Analysis* 52:407–12.

Briggs, John (1988). This*Other-ness and dreams. In Ullman & Limmer.

Brink, T. L. & F. Matlock (1982). Nightmares and birth order: an empirical study. *Individual Psychology* 38:47–9.

Bro, Harmon H. (1968). *Edgar Cayce on Dreams.* New York: Warner.

Brockway, Stephen S. (1987). Group treatment of combat nightmares in post-traumatic stress disorder. *Journal of Contemporary Psychotherapy* 17:270–84.

Brown, Ronald J. & D. C. Donderi (1986). Dream content and self-reported well-being among recurrent dreamers, past-recurrent dreamers, and nonrecurrent dreamers. *Journal of Personality and Social Psychology* 50:612–23.

Brylowski, Andrew (1990). Nightmares in crisis: clinical applications of lucid dream techniques. *Psychiatric Journal of the University of Ottawa* 15:79–83.

Bucci, Wilma, Monica L. Creelman & Sally K. Severino (1991). The effects of menstrual cycle hormones on dreams. *Dreaming* 1:263–76.

Bulkeley, Kelly (1994). *The Wilderness of Dreams.* Albany: State University of New York.

Bulkeley, Kelly (forthcoming). Dreaming is play. *Psychoanalytic Psychology.*

Bulkley, Kelly (1990). The meaning of dreaming. Panel discussion at the conference of the Association for the Study of Dreams, Chicago.

Bulkley, Kelly (1991a). Dreaming to heal the earth. *Dream Network Journal* 10 (2 & 3):8–10,55.

Bulkley, Kelly (1991b). Interdisciplinary dreaming: Hobson's successes and failures. *Dreaming* 1:225–34.

Bulkley, Kelly (1993). Preface to a new feature column by Kelly Bulkley: "Dreaming Life, Waking Life." *Dream Network Journal* 12(1):23.

Burton, Dee (1984). *I Dream of Woody.* New York: William Morrow.

Cahen, Roland (1966). The psychology of the dream: its instructive and therapeutic uses. In Grunebaum & Caillois.

Caillois, Roger (1966). Logical and philosophical problems of the dream. In Grunebaum & Caillois.

Caligor, Leopold & Rollo May (1968). *Dreams and Symbols: Man's Unconscious Language.* New York: Basic.

Calverley, P. M. A. & Colin M. Shapiro (1993). Medical problems during sleep. *British Medical Journal* 306:1403–5.

Camino, Linda Anne (1986). *Ethnomedical Illnesses and Non-orthodox Healing Practices in a Black Neighborhood in the American South: How They Work and What They Mean.* Unpublished Ph.D. dissertation, University of Virginia.

Campbell, Jean (1980). *Dreams Beyond Dreaming.* Virginia Beach, Virginia: Donning.

Cann, Douglas R. & D. C. Donderi (1986). Jungian personality typology and the recall of everyday and archetypal dreams. *Journal of Personality and Social Psychology* 50:1021–30.

Cannegieter, C. A. (1985). *Around the Dreamworld.* New York: Vantage.

Carlisle, Al L. (1988). Dreams of multiple personality disorder. *Association for the Study of Dreams Newsletter* 5(3):2,10.

Carpenter, Kimberly A. (1988). The effects of positive and negative pre-sleep stimuli on dream experiences. *Journal of Psychology* 122:33–7.

Carrington, Patricia (1972). Dreams and schizophrenia. *Archives of General Psychiatry* 26:343–50.

Cartwright, Rosalind Dymond (1972). Sleep fantasy in normal and schizophrenic persons. *Journal of Abnormal Psychology* 80:275–9.

Cartwright, Rosalind Dymond (1974). The influence of a conscious wish on dreams: a methodological study of dream meaning and function. *Journal of Abnormal Psychology* 83:387–93.

Cartwright, Rosalind D. (1977). *Night Life: Explorations in Dreaming.* Englewood Cliffs, New Jersey: Prentice-Hall.

Cartwright, Rosalind D. (1978). *A Primer on Sleep and Dreaming.* Reading, Massachusetts: Addison-Wesley.

Cartwright, Rosalind (1986). Affect and dream work from an information processing point of view. *Journal of Mind and Behavior* 7:411–27.

Cartwright, Rosalind D. (1991). Dreams that work: the relation of dream incorporation to adaptation to stressful events. *Dreaming* 1:3–9.

Cartwright, Rosalind D. (1992). "Masochism" in dreaming and its relation to depression. *Dreaming* 2:79–84.

Cartwright, Rosalind & Lynne Lamberg (1992). *Crisis Dreaming: Using Your Dreams to Solve Your Problems.* New York: HarperCollins.

Cartwright, Rosalind D., Stephen Lloyd, Sara Knight & Irene Trenholme (1984). Broken dreams: a study of the effects of divorce and depression on dream content. *Psychiatry* 47:251–9.

Cartwright, Rosalind D., Lynda Weiner Tipton & Jane Wicklund (1980). Focusing on dreams: a preparation program for psychotherapy. *Archives of General Psychiatry* 37:275–7.

Catalano, Stephen (1990). *Children's Dreams in Clinical Practice.* New York: Plenum.

Cavenar, Jesse O. & Jean G. Spaulding (1978). Termination signal dreams in psychoanalytic psychotherapy. *Bulletin of the Menninger Clinic* 42:58–62.

Cernovsky, Zack Zdenek (1984). Dream recall and attitude toward dreams. *Perceptual and Motor Skills* 58:911-4.

Charsley, Simon (1992). Dreams in African churches. In Jędrej & Shaw (1992a).

Cheek, David B. (1969). Significance of dreams in initiating premature labor. *American Journal of Clinical Hypnosis* 12:5-15.

Child, Irvin L. (1985). Psychology and anomalous observations: the question of ESP in dreams. *American Psychologist* 40:1219-30.

Choi, Sei Y. (1973). Dreams as a prognostic factor in alcoholism. *American Journal of Psychiatry* 130:699-702.

Churchill, Ward (1990). Spiritual hucksterism. *Z Magazine* 3(12):94-8.

Cicogna, Piercarla, Corrado Cavallero & Marino Bosinelli (1991). Cognitive aspects of mental activity during sleep. *American Journal of Psychology* 104: 413-25.

Cipolli, Carlo, Roberto Bolzani, Cezare Cornoldi, Rossana De Beni & Igino Fagioli (1993). Bizarreness effect in dream recall. *Sleep* 16:163-70.

Cirincione, Dominic, John Hart, Werner Karle & Alan Switzer (1980). The functional approach to using dreams in marital and family therapy. *Journal of Marital and Family Therapy* 6:147-51.

Clift, Jean D. & Wallace B. Clift (1984). *Symbols of Transformation in Dreams*. New York: Crossroads.

Cohen, David B. (1970). Current research on the frequency of dream recall. *Psychological Bulletin* 73:433-40.

Cohen, David B. (1974). To sleep, perchance to recall a dream. *Psychology Today* 7(12):50-4.

Conze, Edward (1964 [1954]). *Buddhist Texts Through the Ages*. New York: Harper & Row.

Cooper, Arnold M. (1983). The place of self psychology in the history of depth psychology. In Goldberg.

Corriere, Richard & Joseph Hart (1977). *The Dream Makers: Discovering Your Breakthrough Dreams*. New York: Funk & Wagnalls.

Corriere, Richard, Werner Karle, Lee Woldenberg & Joseph Hart (1980). *Dreaming and Waking: The Functional Approach to Dreams*. Culver City, California: Peace Press.

Corsini, Raymond J. & Danny Wedding, editors (1989). *Current Psychotherapies*, 4th edition. Itasca, Illinois: F. E. Peacock.

Cortopassi, E., R. Dalle Luch, N. Cascella & C. Maggini (1989). Some features of dreams in the last trimester of pregnancy. *Association for the Study of Dreams Newsletter* 6(4):1-3.

Covitz, Joel (1990). *Visions of the Night: A Study of Jewish Dream Interpretation*. Boston: Shambhala.

Craig, P. Erik (1987). The realness of dreams. In Russo (1987a).

Craig, P. Erik (1990a). Dreaming your possibilities. Workshop at the Association for the Study of Dreams Conference, Chicago.

Craig, P. Erik (1990b). An existential approach to dreamwork. In Krippner (1990a).

Craig, P. Erik (1992). The existential stuff of dreams. Address to the Association for the Study of Dreams, Santa Cruz.

Crapanzano, Vincent (1975). Saints, Jnun, and dreams: an essay in Moroccan ethnopsychology. *Psychiatry* 38:145–59.

Crick, Francis (1988). Neural networks and REM sleep. *Bioscience Reports* 8: 531–5.

Crick, Francis & Graeme Mitchison (1983). The function of dream sleep. *Nature* 304:111–4.

Crick, Francis & Graeme Mitchison (1986). REM sleep and neural nets. *Journal of Mind and Behavior* 7:229–49.

Cuddy, Marion A. & Kathryn Belicki (1992). Nightmare frequency and related sleep disturbance as indicators of a history of sexual abuse. *Dreaming* 2: 15–22.

Cunningham, Scott (1992). *Sacred Sleep: Dreams & the Divine*. Freedom, California: Crossing.

Curley, Richard T. (1992). Private dreams and public knowledge in a Camerounian Independent Church. In Jędrej & Shaw (1992a).

Curtis, Homer C. & David M. Sachs (1976). Dialogue on "the changing use of dreams in psychoanalytic practice." *International Journal of Psycho-Analysis* 57:343–54.

Dane, Joseph R. & Robert Van de Castle (1984). A comparison of waking instruction and posthypnotic suggestion for lucid dream induction. *Association for the Study of Dreams Newsletter* 1(4):4–8.

Darling, Mary, Robert Hoffmann, Alan Moffitt & Sheila Purcell (1993). The pattern of self-reflectiveness in dream reports. *Dreaming* 3:9–19.

Davies, Stephen & Alan Stewart (1987). *Nutritional Medicine*. London: Pan.

Degarrod, Lydia Nakashima (1990). Coping with stress: dream interpretation in the Mapuche family. *Psychiatric Journal of the University of Ottawa* 15:111–6.

DeGennaro, Luigi & Cristiano Violani (1990). White dreams: the relationship between the failure in dream recall and degree of hemispheric lateralization. *Association for the Study of Dreams Newsletter* 7(5):7.

Delaney, Gayle M. V. (1979). *Living Your Dreams*. San Francisco: Harper & Row.

Delaney, Gayle (1990a). Dreams and the recollection of incest. *Association for the Study of Dreams Newsletter* 7(1):5–6.

Delaney, Gayle (1990b [1986]). Dreams and healing. *Association for the Study of Dreams Newsletter* 7(4):4–5.

Delaney, Gayle (1990c). An interview with Gayle Delaney. [Interview by H. Roberta Ossana.] *Dream Network Journal* 9(3):13, 24–7.

Delaney, Gayle (1990d). Personal and professional problem solving in dreams. In Krippner (1990a).

Delaney, Gayle (1991). *Breakthrough Dreaming*. New York: Bantam.

DeMartino, Manfred F., editor (1959). *Dreams and Personality Dynamics.* Springfield, Illinois: Charles C Thomas.

Dement, William (1955). Dream recall and eye movements during sleep in schizophrenics and normals. *Journal of Nervous and Mental Disease* 122:263–9.

Dement, William (1960). The effect of dream deprivation. *Science* 131:1705–7.

Dement, William C. (1966). The psychophysiology of dreaming. In Grunebaum & Caillois.

Dement, William C. (1974 [1972]). *Some Must Watch While Some Must Sleep.* San Francisco: W. H. Freeman.

Dement, W. & N. Kleitman (1957a). The relation of eye movements during sleep to dream activity: an objective method for the study of dreaming. *Journal of Experimental Psychology* 53:339–46.

Dement, W. & N. Kleitman (1957b). Cyclic variations in EEG during sleep and their relation to eye movements, body motility, and dreaming. *Electroencephalography and Clinical Neurophysiology* 9:673–90.

Dement, William & Edward A. Wolpert (1958). The relation of eye movements, body motility, and external stimuli to dream content. *Journal of Experimental Psychology* 55:543–53.

Dentan, Robert K. (1986). Ethnographic considerations of the cross cultural study of dreams. In Gackenbach.

Dentan, Robert (1987). You can never find a cop when you need one: a response to Faraday. *Association for the Study of Dreams Newsletter* 4(2):14–6.

Dentan, Robert K. (1988). Lucidity, sex, and horror in Senoi dreamwork. In Gackenbach & LaBerge.

Denzin, Norman K. (1988). Alcoholic dreams. *Alcoholism Treatment Quarterly* 5:133–9.

Desjarlais, Robert R. (1991). Dreams, divination, and Yolmo ways of knowing. *Dreaming* 1:211–24.

Deslauriers, Daniel (1986). A "waker's" perspective on dream interpretation. *Association for the Study of Dreams Newsletter* 3(4):1–2,19–20.

Deslauriers, Daniel (1988). Scripts and script deviations in men's REM dream reports. *Association for the Study of Dreams Newsletter* 5(6):1–3,13.

Deslauriers, Daniel (1989). A creative journey into dreams with Fariba Bogzaran: where beauty meets power. *Bulletin of the Montreal Centre for the Study of Dreams* 3(3–4):1–3.

Devereux, George (1970). Preface. In Lincoln.

Diamond, Randa Carmen (1983). Persephone today: use of dreams, imagery, and myth in the treatment of raped women. *Clinical Social Work Journal* 11:78–86.

Dieckmann, Hans (1985). Some aspects of the development of authority. In Samuels (1985a).

Diop, Cheikh Anta (1974 [1955 & 1967]). *The African Origin of Civilization, Myth or Reality.* Chicago: Lawrence Hill.

Diop, Cheikh Anta (1990 [1959]). *The Cultural Unity of Black Africa.* Chicago: Third World.

Dodd, Jenny (1988). A mothers' dream group. In Ullman & Limmer.

Dombeck, Mary-Therese Behar (1988). Group mythology and group development in dream sharing groups. *Psychiatric Journal of the University of Ottawa* 13:97–106.

Dombeck, Mary-T. B. (1991). *Dreams and Professional Personhood: The Contexts of Dream Telling and Dream Interpretation among American Psychotherapists*. Albany: State University of New York.

Domhoff, G. William (1985). *The Mystique of Dreams: A Search for Utopia through Senoi Dream Theory*. Berkeley: University of California.

Domhoff, Bill & Joe Kamiya (1964a). Problems in dream content study with objective indicators, I: A comparison of home and laboratory dream reports. *Archives of General Psychiatry* 11:519–24.

Domhoff, Bill & Joe Kamiya (1964b). Problems in dream content study with objective indicators, II: Appearance of experimental situation in laboratory dream narratives. *Archives of General Psychiatry* 11:525–8.

Doniger, Wendy & Kelly Bulkley (1993). Why study dreams? A religious studies perspective. *Dreaming* 3:69–73.

Doweiko, Harold (1982). Neurobiology and dream theory: a rapprochement model. *Journal of Individual Psychology* 38:55–61.

Downing, Christine (1977). Poetically dwells man on this earth. In Scott (1977a).

Downing, Jack & Robert Marmorstein (1973). *Dreams and Nightmares*. New York: Perennial Library.

Doyle, Marie C. (1984). Enhancing dream pleasure with Senoi strategy. *Journal of Clinical Psychology* 40:467–74.

Druss, Richard G. & Donald S. Kornfeld (1967). The survivors of cardiac arrest: a psychiatric study. *Journal of the American Medical Association* 201: 291–6.

Dudley, Linda & Michelle Swank (1990). A comparison of the dreams of college women in 1950 and 1990. *Association for the Study of Dreams Newsletter* 7(5):3,16.

Dunn, Karen Kincaid & Deirdre L. Barrett (1987). Personality characteristics of nightmare subjects and descriptions of nightmares. *Association for the Study of Dreams Newsletter* 4(4):4–6.

Dunn, Karen Kincaid & Deirdre Barrett (1988). Characteristics of nightmare subjects and their nightmares. *Psychiatric Journal of the University of Ottawa* 13: 91–3.

D. W. (1989). The color of a dream. *NightLight* 1(1):14.

Eccles, A., A. Wilde & W. L. Marshall (1988). *In vivo* desensitization in the treatment of recurrent nightmares. *Journal of Behavior Therapy and Experimental Psychiatry* 19:285–8.

Eggan, Dorothy (1966). Hopi dreams in cultural perspective. In Grunebaum & Caillois.

Eggan, Dorothy (1974 [1952]). The culture shapes the dream. In Woods & Greenhouse.

Eichelman, Burr (1985). Hypnotic change in combat dreams of two veterans with posttraumatic stress disorder. *American Journal of Psychiatry* 142:112–4.

Eisen, Joel, James MacFarlane & Colin M. Shapiro (1993). Psychotropic drugs and sleep. *British Medical Journal* 306:1331–4.

Eisenstein, Samuel (1980). The dream in psychoanalysis. In Natterson.

Eisler, Riane (1990). Foreword. In Signell.

Eliade, Mircea (1960 [1957]). *Myths, Dreams, and Mysteries*. New York: Harper Torchbooks.

Eliade, Mircea (1966). Initiation dreams and visions among Siberian shamans. In Grunebaum & Caillois.

Ellis, Harold R. (1988). Dream drama: an effective use of dreams (part 2). *Dream Network Bulletin* 7(5):16–7,19–20.

Ellis, Harold R. (1989). Easy tips on your dreams. *Dream Switchboard* 1(2):3.

Ellis, Harold R. (1991). A presentation by the Center for Dream Drama. *Dream Switchboard* 2(4):1–6.

Ellman, Steven J. & John S. Antrobus, editors (1991). *The Mind in Sleep: Psychology and Psychophysiology*, 2nd edition. New York: John Wiley & Sons.

Ellman, Steven J. & Lissa N. Weinstein (1991). REM sleep and dream formation: a theoretical integration. In Ellman & Antrobus.

Emerson, Ralph Waldo (1974 [1884]). The witchcraft of sleep. Originally: Demonology, in *Lectures and Biographical Sketches*. Boston: Houghton, Mifflin, 1884. Excerpted in Woods & Greenhouse.

Emery, Marcia Rose (1989). Programming the precognitive dream. *Dream Network Bulletin* 8(3):9–12.

Emery, Marcia (1991). Programming the precognitive dream. *Association for the Study of Dreams Newsletter* 8(2):7–8,12–5.

Ennis, Maeve & Peter Fonagy (1989). Influence of monaural and dichotic stimuli on dreams. *Association for the Study of Dreams Newsletter* 6(3):4.

Epel, Naomi (1993). *Writers Dreaming*. New York: Carol Southern.

Ephron, Harmon S. & Patricia Carrington (1966). Rapid eye movement sleep and cortical homeostasis. *Psychological Review* 73:500–26.

Epstein, Arthur W. (1964). Recurrent dreams: their relationship to temporal lobe seizures. *Archives of General Psychiatry* 10:25–30.

Erikson, Erik Homburger (1954). The dream specimen of psychoanalysis. *Journal of the American Psychoanalytic Association* 2:5–56.

Evans-Wentz, W. Y. (1958 [1935]). *Tibetan Yoga and Secret Doctrines*. London: Oxford University.

Evans-Wentz, W. Y. (1969 [1928]). *Tibet's Great Yogi Milarepa*. London: Oxford University.

Faber, P. A., G. S. Saayman & R. K. Papadopoulos (1983). Induced waking fantasy: its effects upon the archetypal content of nocturnal dreams. *Journal of Analytical Psychology* 28:141–64.

Fagin, Helene (1988). Creativity and dreams. In Ullman & Limmer.

Fantz, Rainette Eden (1987 [1978]). Gestalt approach. In Fosshage & Loew (1987a [1978]).

Faraday, Ann (1972). *Dream Power.* London: Hodder and Stoughton.

Faraday, Ann (1976 [1974]). *The Dream Game.* New York: Perennial Library.

Feinstein, David (1990). The dream as a window on your evolving mythology. In Krippner (1990a).

Feinstein, David & Stanley Krippner (1988). *Personal Mythology: The Psychology of Your Evolving Self.* Los Angeles: Jeremy P. Tarcher.

Fellows, Peter (1988). Working within the lucid dream. In Gackenbach & LaBerge.

Fisher, Charles (1974 [1960]). Subliminal and supraliminal stimulation before the dream. In Woods & Greenhouse.

Fisher, Charles, Joseph Gross & Joseph Zuch (1965). Cycle of penile erection synchronous with dreaming (REM) sleep. *Archives of General Psychiatry* 12: 29–45.

Fisher, Humphrey J. (1979). Dreams and conversion in black Africa. In Levtzion.

Fiss, Harry (1979). Current dream research: a psychobiological perspective. In Wolman.

Fiss, Harry (1986). An empirical foundation for a self psychology of dreaming. *Journal of Mind and Behavior* 7:161–91.

Fiss, Harry (1993). The "royal road" to the unconscious revisited: a signal detection model of dream function. In Moffitt et al. (1993a).

Fiss, Harry, George S. Klein & Edwin Bokert (1966). Waking fantasies following interruption of two types of sleep. *Archives of General Psychiatry* 14:543–51.

Fitch, Thomas & Roseanne Armitage (1989). Variations in cognitive style among high and low frequency dream recallers. *Personality and Individual Differences* 10:869–75.

Fliess, Robert (1953). *The Revival of Interest in the Dream.* New York: International Universities.

Flowers, Loma K. (1988). The morning after: a pragmatist's approach to dreams. *Psychiatric Journal of the University of Ottawa* 13:65–71.

Fosshage, James L. (1983). The psychological function of dreams: a revised psychoanalytic perspective. *Psychoanalysis and Contemporary Thought* 6:641–69.

Fosshage, James L. (1987a). A revised psychoanalytic approach. In Fosshage & Loew (1987a [1978]).

Fosshage, James L. (1987b). New vistas in dream interpretation. In Glucksman & Warner.

Fosshage, James L. & Clemens A. Loew, editors (1987a [1978]). *Dream Interpretation: A Comparative Study, Revised Edition.* New York: PMA.

Fosshage, James L. & Clemens A. Loew (1987b [1978]). Comparison and synthesis. In Fosshage & Loew (1987a [1978]).

Foulkes, David (1978). *A Grammar of Dreams.* New York: Basic.

Foulkes, David (1979). Children's dreams. In Wolman.

Foulkes, David (1985). *Dreaming: A Cognitive-Psychological Analysis*. Hillsdale, New Jersey: Lawrence Erlbaum.

Foulkes, David (1990). Dreaming and consciousness. *European Journal of Cognitive Psychology* 2:39–55.

Foulkes, David (1991). Why study dreaming: one researcher's perspective. *Dreaming* 1:245–8.

Foulkes, David (1993). Data constraints on theorizing about dream function. In Moffitt et al. (1993a).

Foulkes, David & Stephan Fleisher (1975). Mental activity in relaxed wakefulness. *Journal of Abnormal Psychology* 84:66–75.

Foulkes, David & Mary Lloyd Griffin (1976). An experimental study of "creative dreaming." *Sleep Research* 5:129.

Foulkes, David & Allan Rechtschaffen (1964). Pre-sleep determinants of dream content: effects of two films. *Perceptual and Motor Skills* 19:983–1005.

Foulkes, David, Paul S. Spear & John D. Symonds (1966). Individual differences in mental activity at sleep onset. *Journal of Abnormal Psychology* 71:280–6.

Foulkes, David & Gerald Vogel (1965). Mental activity at sleep onset. *Journal of Abnormal Psychology* 70:231–43.

Fox, Richard P., Milton Kramer, Bill J. Baldridge, Roy M. Whitman & Paul H. Ornstein (1968). The experimenter variable in dream research. *Diseases of the Nervous System* 29:698–701.

Franz, Marie-Louise von (1980a [1978]). *Projection and Recollection in Jungian Psychology: Reflections of the Soul*. La Salle, Illinois: Open Court.

Franz, Marie-Louise von (1980b). *The Psychological Meaning of Redemption Motifs in Fairytales*. Toronto: Inner City.

Franz, Marie-Louise von (1986 [1984]). *On Dreams and Death*. Boston: Shambhala.

French, Thomas M. & Erika Fromm (1964). *Dream Interpretation: A New Approach*. New York: Basic.

Freud, Sigmund (1950 [1923]). Remarks upon the theory and practice of dream-interpretation. *Collected Papers*, vol. 5, pp. 136–49. London: Hogarth.

Freud, Sigmund (1953 [1900]). *The Interpretation of Dreams*. Standard Edition, vol's 4 and 5. London: Hogarth.

Freud, Sigmund (1966a [1914]). *On The History of the Psycho-Analytic Movement*. New York: W. W. Norton. Standard Edition, vol. 14. London: Hogarth.

Freud, Sigmund (1966b [1920]). *Beyond the Pleasure Principle*. Standard Edition, vol. 18. London: Hogarth.

Freud, Sigmund (1966c [1923]). *The Ego and the Id*. Standard Edition, vol. 19. London: Hogarth.

Freud, Sigmund (1980 [1901]). *On Dreams*. New York: W. W. Norton. Standard Edition, vol. 5. London: Hogarth.

Friedman, Joseph (1981). Dream groups. *Self and Society* 9:126–30.

Friedman, Robert M. (1992). The use of dreams in the evaluation of severely disturbed patients. *American Journal of Psychoanalysis* 52:13–30.

Friedman, Thomas J. (1990). A dreamlike landscape, a dreamlike reality. *New York Times*, 28 October: E3.

Friess, Elisabeth, Bertram Dippel, Dieter Riemann & Mathias Berger (1989). Interrelations of dream recall and content with depressive symptomatology. *Association for the Study of Dreams Newsletter* 6(2):10.

Fromm, Erich (1951). *The Forgotten Language: An Introduction to the Understanding of Dreams, Fairy Tales and Myths.* New York: Rinehart.

Fromm, Erich (1955). *The Sane Society.* New York: Rinehart.

Frosch, John (1976). Psychoanalytic contributions to the relationship between dreams and psychosis—a critical survey. *International Journal of Psychoanalytic Psychotherapy* 5:39–63.

Gabel, S. (1985). Sleep research and clinically reported dreams. *Journal of Analytical Psychology* 30:185–205.

Gackenbach, Jayne I. (1985–6). A survey of considerations for inducing conscious awareness of dreaming while dreaming. *Imagination, Cognition and Personality* 5:41–55.

Gackenbach, Jayne, editor (1986). *Sleep and Dreams: A Sourcebook.* New York: Garland.

Gackenbach, Jayne (1988a). Lucidity reports. *Dream Network Bulletin* 7(4):3.

Gackenbach, Jayne (1988b). Psychological content of lucid versus nonlucid dreams. In Gackenbach & LaBerge.

Gackenbach, Jayne (1989). Clinical applications for consciousness in sleep. *Lucidity Letter* 8(2):62–8.

Gackenbach, Jayne (1990a). The content of intensified dreams. *Association for the Study of Dreams Newsletter* 7(3):3,16.

Gackenbach, Jayne (1990b). Content and context of intensified dreams. Paper presented to the Association for the Study of Dreams, Chicago.

Gackenbach, Jayne (1990c). Panel discussion. See Gackenbach et al.

Gackenbach, Jayne I. (1990d). Women and meditators as gifted lucid dreamers. In Krippner (1990a).

Gackenbach, Jayne (1991a). Frameworks for understanding lucid dreams: a review. *Dreaming* 1:109–28.

Gackenbach, Jayne (1991b). A developmental model of consciousness in sleep: from sleep consciousness to pure consciousness. In Gackenbach & Sheikh.

Gackenbach, Jayne (1993). Reflections on dreamwork with Central Alberta Cree. *Association for the Study of Dreams Newsletter* 10(4):18–20.

Gackenbach, Jayne, Walter Bonime, Patricia Garfield, Johanna King, Eugene Gendlin & Jane White Lewis (1990). Should you control your dreams? Panel discussion at the conference of the Association for the Study of Dreams, Chicago.

Gackenbach, Jayne & Jane Bosveld (1989). *Control Your Dreams.* New York: Harper & Row.

Gackenbach, Jayne & Stephen LaBerge (1984). The lucid dream: a dream whose time has come. *Association for the Study of Dreams Newsletter* 1(1):1,4–5, 7–8,11.

Gackenbach, Jayne & Stephen LaBerge, editors (1988). *Conscious Mind, Sleeping Brain: Perspectives on Lucid Dreaming.* New York: Plenum.

Gackenbach, Jayne, William Moorcroft, Charles Alexander & Stephen LaBerge (1987). "Consciousness" during sleep in a TM Practitioner: heart rate, respiration, and eye movement. *Association for the Study of Dreams Newsletter* 4(5):6–9,12.

Gackenbach, Jayne & Anees A. Sheikh, editors (1991). *Dream Images: A Call to Mental Arms.* Amityville, New York: Baywood.

Galeano, Eduardo (1990 [1984]). *Memoria del fuego II: las caras y las máscaras.* Mexico City: Siglo Veintiuno.

Galvin, Franklin & Ernest Hartmann (1990). Nightmares: terrors of the night. In Krippner (1990a).

Gardner, Russell, William I. Grossman, Howard P. Roffwarg & Herbert Weiner (1975). The relationship of small limb movements during REM sleep to dreamed limb action. *Psychosomatic Medicine* 37:147–59.

Garfield, Patricia (1976 [1974]). *Creative Dreaming.* New York: Ballantine.

Garfield, Patricia (1984). *Your Child's Dreams.* New York: Ballantine.

Garfield, Patricia (1988a). *Women's Bodies, Women's Dreams.* New York: Ballantine.

Garfield, Patricia (1988b). Clinical applications of lucid dreaming: introductory comments. In Gackenbach & LaBerge.

Garfield, Patricia (1989 [1979]). *Pathway to Ecstasy: The Way of the Dream Mandala.* New York: Prentice Hall.

Garfield, Patricia (1990). Panel discussion. See Gackenbach et al.

Garfield, Patricia (1991). *The Healing Power of Dreams.* New York: Simon & Schuster.

Garma, Angel (1987 [1978]). Freudian approach. In Fosshage & Loew (1987a [1978]).

Garrison, Omar V. (1983 [1964]). *Tantra: The Yoga of Sex.* New York: Julian.

Gedo, John E. (1980). The dream in regressed states. In Natterson (1980a).

Gendlin, Eugene T. (1977). Phenomenological concept vs. phenomenological method: a critique of Medard Boss on dreams. In Scott (1977a).

Gendlin, Eugene T. (1986). *Let Your Body Interpret Your Dreams.* Wilmette, Illinois: Chiron.

Gendlin, Eugene T. (1990). Panel discussion. See Gackenbach et al.

Gibson, Elizabeth, Franklin Perry, Dana Redington & Joe Kamiya (1982). Discrimination of sleep onset stages: behavioral responses and verbal reports. *Perceptual and Motor Skills* 55:1023–37.

Gill, John (1985). Czechpoints. *Time Out.* August 22.

Gillespie, George (1985). From lucid dream to dreamless sleep. *Association for the Study of Dreams Newsletter* 2(4):6–8,10.

Gillespie, George (1988a). Lucid dreaming in Tibetan Buddhism. In Gackenbach & LaBerge.

Gillespie, George (1988b). Without a guru: an account of my lucid dreaming. In Gackenbach & LaBerge.

Gillespie, George (1988c). When does lucid dreaming become transpersonal experience. *Psychiatric Journal of the University of Ottawa* 13:107–10.

Gillespie, George (1991). Early Hindu speculation about dreams: implications for dream yoga. In Gackenbach & Sheikh.

Gillespie, George (1992). Light in lucid dreams: a review. *Dreaming* 2:167–79.

Gillin, J. Christian (1983). The sleep therapies of depression. *Progress in Neuro-Psychopharmacology & Biological Psychiatry* 7:351–64.

Gillman, Robert D. (1980). Dreams in which the analyst appears as himself. In Natterson (1980a).

Gillman, Robert D. (1987). Dreams as resistance. In Rothstein.

Glassé, Cyril (1989). *The Concise Encyclopedia of Islam.* London: Stacey International.

Globus, Gordon (1987). *Dream Life, Wake Life: The Human Condition through Dreams.* Albany: State University of New York.

Globus, Gordon G. (1991). Dream content: random or meaningful? *Dreaming* 1:27–40.

Globus, Gordon G. (1993). Connectionism and sleep. In Moffitt et al. (1993a).

Globus, Gordon G. & Melissa Derfler (1990). The lucid brain. Paper presented to the Lucidity Association, Chicago.

Glucksman, Myron L. (1987). Introduction. In Glucksman & Warner.

Glucksman, Myron L. & Silas L. Warner, editors (1987). *Dreams in New Perspective: The Royal Road Revisited.* New York: Human Sciences.

Gold, Leo (1979). Adler's theory of dreams: an holistic approach to interpretation. In Wolman.

Gold, Vivian J. (1973). Dreams in group therapy: a review of the literature. *International Journal of Group Psychotherapy* 23:394–407.

Goldberg, Arnold, editor (1983). *The Future of Psychoanalysis: Essays in Honor of Heinz Kohut.* New York: International Universities.

Goldberger, Marianne (1989). On the analysis of defenses in dreams. *Psychoanalytic Quarterly* 58:396–418.

Gollnick, James (1987). *Dreams in the Psychology of Religion.* Lewiston, New York: Edwin Mellen.

Gordon, Lois M. (1991). I sleep, perchance to lucid dream. *NightLight* 3(3):14–5.

Govinda, Lama Anagarika (1984 [1966]). *The Way of the White Clouds: A Buddhist Pilgrim in Tibet.* London: Rider.

Grant, John (1986 [1984]). *Dreamers: A Geography of Dreamland.* London: Grafton.

Graywolf (1992). Beyond the vision quest: bringing it back or did I really ask for this? *Dream Network Journal* 11(2):17–9.

Green, Celia E. (1968). *Lucid Dreams*. Oxford: Institute of Psychophysical Research.

Green, Celia (1990). Lucid dreams in relation to OBEs and other metachoric phenomena. *Association for the Study of Dreams Newsletter* 7(5):5–6.

Greenberg, Ramon (1987a). The dream problem and problems in dreams. In Glucksman & Warner.

Greenberg, Ramon (1987b). Dreams: new frontiers. Panel discussion, in Glucksman & Warner.

Greenberg, Ramon & Chester Pearlman (1967). Delirium tremens and dreaming. *American Journal of Psychiatry* 124:133–42.

Greenberg, Ramon & Chester Pearlman (1975). A psychoanalytic-dream continuum: the source and function of dreams. *International Review of Psycho-Analysis* 2:441–8.

Greenberg, Ramon, Chester A. Pearlman & Dorothy Gampel (1972). War neurosis and the adaptive function of REM sleep. *British Journal of Medical Psychology* 45:27–33.

Greenberg, Ramon, Chester Pearlman, Wynn R. Schwartz & Hildreth Youkilis Grossman (1983). Memory, emotion, and REM sleep. *Journal of Abnormal Psychology* 92:378–81.

Greenberg, Ramon, Richard Pillard & Chester Pearlman (1972). The effect of dream (REM) deprivation on adaptation to stress. *Psychosomatic Medicine* 34:257–62.

Greene, Thayer A. (1979). C. G. Jung's theory of dreams. In Wolman.

Greenhouse, H. (1974). The effects of drugs on dreams. In Woods & Greenhouse.

Gregor, Thomas (1983). Dark dreams about white men. *Natural History* 92(1): 8–14.

Gregory, Jill (1984). *Becoming a Lucid Dreamer: An Analysis of My Development in the Art and Science of Lucid Dreaming.* B.A. thesis, Dominican College.

Gregory, Jill (1987). Interview with DNB publisher Linda Magallon. *Dream Network Bulletin* 5(6):16–7.

Gregory, Jill (1988a). Bringing dreams to kids! *Dream Network Bulletin* 7(2): 12–3.

Gregory, Jill (1988b). Bringing dreams to kids! *Dream Network Bulletin* 7(3):4–7.

Gregory, Jill (1988c). The cutting edge of lucidity. *Dream Network Bulletin* 7(6): 8–9,17,20.

Gresham, Samuel C., Wilse B. Webb & Robert L. Williams (1963). Alcohol and caffeine: effect on inferred visual dreaming. *Science* 140:1226–7.

Grieser, Caroline, Ramon Greenberg & Robert A. Harrison (1972). The adaptive function of sleep: the differential effects of sleep and dreaming on recall. *Journal of Abnormal Psychology* 80:280–6.

Griffin, M. L. & D. Foulkes (1977). Deliberate presleep control of dream content: an experimental study. *Perceptual and Motor Skills* 45:660–2.

Grinberg, León (1987). Dreams and acting out. *Psychoanalytic Quarterly* 56: 155–76.

Gross, Joseph, Joseph Byrne & Charles Fisher (1965). Eye movements during emergent stage 1 EEG in subjects with lifelong blindness. *Journal of Nervous and Mental Disease* 141:365–70.

Grossinger, Richard (1971a). A history of dream. *Io* 8:14–48.

Grossinger, Richard (1971b). The dreaming. *Io* 8:141–66.

Grunebaum, G. E. von (1966). Introduction: the cultural function of the dream as illustrated by classical Islam. In Grunebaum & Caillois.

Grunebaum, G. E. von & Roger Caillois, editors (1966). *The Dream and Human Societies*. Berkeley: University of California.

Gutheil, Emil A. (1967 [1951]). *The Handbook of Dream Analysis*. New York: Washington Square.

Guthrie, Robert V. (1976). *Even the Rat Was White: A Historical View of Psychology*. New York: Harper & Row.

Hadfield, J. A. (1954). *Dreams and Nightmares*. Baltimore: Penguin.

Hajek, Peter & Michael Belcher (1991). Dream of absent-minded transgression: an empirical study of a cognitive withdrawal symptom. *Journal of Abnormal Psychology* 100:487–91.

Halifax, Joan (1982). *Shaman: The Wounded Healer*. New York: Crossroad.

Hall, Calvin S. (1966a [1953]). *The Meaning of Dreams*. New York: McGraw-Hill.

Hall, Calvin S. (1966b). A comparison of the dreams of four groups of hospitalized mental patients with each other and with a normal population. *Journal of Nervous and Mental Disease* 143:135–9.

Hall, Calvin S. & Bill Domhoff (1974 [1968]). The dreams of Freud and Jung. In Woods & Greenhouse.

Hall, Calvin S., G. William Domhoff, Kenneth A. Blick & Kathryn E. Weesner (1982). The dreams of college men and women in 1950 and 1980: a comparison of dream contents and sex differences. *Sleep* 5:188–94.

Hall, Calvin S. & Vernon J. Nordby (1972). *The Individual and His Dreams*. Bergenfield, New Jersey: Signet.

Hall, Calvin & Robert L. Van de Castle (1965). An empirical investigation of the castration complex in dreams. *Journal of Personality* 33:20–9.

Hall, Calvin & Robert L. Van de Castle (1966). *The Content Analysis of Dreams*. New York: Appleton-Century-Crofts.

Hall, James A. (1983). *Jungian Dream Interpretation: A Handbook of Theory and Practice*. Toronto: Inner City.

Hall, James A. & Andrew Brylowski (1990). Lucid dreaming and active imagination: implications for Jungian therapy. *Quadrant* 24(1):35–43.

Halliday, Gordon (1985). Direct psychological therapies for nightmares: a review. *Association for the Study of Dreams Newsletter* 2(2):4–6.

Halliday, Gordon (1988). Lucid dreaming: using nightmares and sleep-wake confusion. In Gackenbach & LaBerge.

Halliday, Gordon (1990). Dream recall for therapy or self-improvement. *Association for the Study of Dreams Newsletter* 7(1):4–5.

Hallowell, A. Irving (1975 [1960]). Ojibwa ontology, behavior, and world view. In Dennis Tedlock & Barbara Tedlock, editors (1975). *Teachings from the American Earth: Indian Religion and Philosophy.* New York: Liveright.

Hamilton, Mary (1906). *Incubation, or, The Cure of Disease in Pagan Temples and Christian Churches.* London: Simpkin, Marshall, Hamilton, Kent.

Harary, Keith & Pamela Weintraub (1989). *Lucid Dreams in 30 Days.* New York: St. Martin's.

Harrington, James Lawrence (1991). Dreams of war: the unconscious call to initiation. *Men's Council Journal* No. 8 (February):6–7.

Hart, David L. (1977). Dreams of escape from bewitchment. *Spring*: 42–5.

Hartmann, E. (1966). Dreaming sleep (the D-state) and the menstrual cycle. *Journal of Nervous and Mental Disease* 143:406–16.

Hartmann, Ernest (1967). *The Biology of Dreaming.* Springfield, Illinois: Charles C. Thomas.

Hartmann, Ernest (1984). *The Nightmare: The Psychology and Biology of Terrifying Dreams.* New York: Basic.

Hartmann, Ernest (1991). Dreams that work or dreams that poison? What does dreaming do? An editorial essay. *Dreaming* 1:23–5.

Hartmann, Ernest, Rachel Elkin & Mithlesh Garg (1991). Personality and dreaming: the dreams of people with very thick or very thin boundaries. *Dreaming* 1:311–24.

Haskell, Robert E. (1985a). Racial content and issues in dream research. *Association for the Study of Dreams Newsletter* 2(1):7–9.

Haskell, Robert (1985b). Dreaming, cognition, and physical illness: Part I. *Journal of Medical Humanities and Bioethics* 6:46–56.

Haskell, Robert E. (1985c). Dreaming, cognition, and physical illness: Part II. *Journal of Medical Humanities and Bioethics* 6:109–22.

Haskell, Robert E. (1986a). Cognitive psychology and dream research: historical, conceptual, and epistemological considerations. *Journal of Mind and Behavior* 7:131–59.

Haskell, Robert E. (1986b). Logical structure and the cognitive psychology of dreaming. *Journal of Mind and Behavior* 7:345–78.

Hauri, Peter & Robert L. Van de Castle (1973). Psychophysiological parallels in dreams. *Psychosomatic Medicine* 35:297–308.

Hawkins, Janet (1991). Rowers on the River Styx. *Harvard Magazine* 93(4): 43–52.

Hazarika, Anjali (1992). Harnessing managerial potential through dreams. *Association for the Study of Dreams Newsletter* 9(2 & 3):15.

Hearne, Keith M. T. (1983). Lucid dream induction. *Journal of Mental Imagery* 7(1):19–24.

Hearne, Keith M. T. (1987). A new perspective on dream imagery. *Journal of Mental Imagery* 11(2):75–82.

Henderson, Joseph L. (1980). The dream in Jungian analysis. In Natterson (1980a).

Hendricks, Marion & Rosalind D. Cartwright (1978). Experiencing level in dreams: an individual difference variable. *Psychotherapy: Theory, Research and Practice* 15:292–8.

Herdt, Gilbert (1992 [1987]). Selfhood and discourse in Sambia dream sharing. In Tedlock (1992a [1987]).

Herman, John H., Milton Erman, Randy Boys, Liora Peiser, Mary Ellen Taylor & Howard P. Roffwarg (1984). Evidence for a directional correspondence between eye movements and dream imagery in REM sleep. *Sleep* 7:52–63.

Heynick, Frank (1986). The dream-scriptor and the Freudian ego: "pragmatic competence" and superordinate and subordinate cognitive systems in sleep. *Journal of Mind and Behavior* 7:299–331.

Heynick, Frank (1991). Linguistic and literary creativity in dreams: a psycho-analytic and an experimental approach. In Gackenbach & Sheikh.

Hicks, Robert A., Cheryl Chancellor & Tim Clark (1987). The valence of dreams reported by type A-B college students. *Perceptual and Motor Skills* 65:748–50.

Hilgard, Ernest R. (1977). *Divided Consciousness: Multiple Controls in Human Thought and Action.* New York: John Wiley & Sons.

Hillman, Deborah Jay (1988). Dream work and field work: linking cultural anthropology and the current dream work movement. In Ullman & Limmer.

Hillman, Deborah Jay (1990). The emergence of the grassroots dreamwork move-ment. In Krippner (1990a).

Hillman, James (1979). *The Dream and the Underworld.* New York: Harper & Row.

Hobson, J. Allan (1988). *The Dreaming Brain.* New York: Basic.

Hobson, J. Allan (1989). *Sleep.* New York: Scientific American.

Hobson, J. Allan (1990). Dreams and the brain. In Krippner (1990a).

Hobson, J. Allan (1991). Foreword. In Delaney.

Hobson, J. Allan & Robert W. McCarley (1977). The brain as a dream state generator: an activation-synthesis hypothesis of the dream process. *American Journal of Psychiatry* 134:1335–48.

Holy, Ladislav (1992). Berti dream interpretation. In Jędrej & Shaw (1992a).

Hooper, Judith & Dick Teresi (1990). *Would the Buddha Wear a Walkman?* New York: Fireside.

Hopcke, Robert H. (1990). *Men's Dreams, Men's Healing.* Boston: Shambhala.

Horney, Karen (1970 [1950]). *Neurosis and Human Growth: The Struggle To-ward Self-Realization.* New York: W. W. Norton.

Howe, Joan B. & Kenneth A. Blick (1983). Emotional content of dreams recalled by elderly women. *Perceptual and Motor Skills* 56:31–4.

Hudson, Liam (1985). *Night Life: The Interpretation of Dreams.* London: Weid-enfeld & Nicolson.

Humbert, Elie G. (1990). Dream experience. In Schwartz-Salant & Stein.

Hunt, Harry T. (1985). Do animals dream? The significance of an evolutionary perspective to dreaming and its human symbolic potential—a reply to Foulkes. *Association for the Study of Dreams Newsletter* 2(1):5–6.

Hunt, Harry (1986). Toward a cognitive psychology of dreams. In Gackenbach.

Hunt, Harry T. (1989). *The Multiplicity of Dreams: Memory, Imagination, and Consciousness*. New Haven: Yale University.

Hunt, Harry T. (1990a). Commenting on Gackenbach (1990b).

Hunt, Harry T. (1990b). Panel discussion. See Alexander et al.

Hunt, Harry T. (1991a). Dreams as literature/science of dreams: an essay. *Dreaming* 1:235–42.

Hunt, Harry T. (1991b). Lucid dreaming as a meditative state: some evidence from long-term meditators in relation to the cognitive-psychological bases of transpersonal phenomena. In Gackenbach & Sheikh.

Hunt, H. (1992). Dreams of Freud and Jung: reciprocal relationships between social relations and archetypal/transpersonal imagination. *Psychiatry* 55:28–47.

Hunt, Harry (1993). A conversation with Harry Hunt, Ph.D. [Interview by Tracey Kahan.] *Association for the Study of Dreams Newsletter* 10(1):6–9.

Hunt, Harry T. & Robert D. Ogilvie (1988). Lucid dreams in their natural series: phenomenological and psychophysiological findings in relation to meditative states. In Gackenbach & LaBerge.

Hunt, Harry T., Robert Ogilvie, Kathy Belicki, Dennis Belicki & Ernest Atalick (1982). Forms of dreaming. *Perceptual and Motor Skills* 54:559–633.

Hyatt, Harry Middleton (1970–1978). *Hoodoo, Conjuration, Witchcraft, Rootwork*. 5 volumes. Hannibal, Missouri: Western.

Idzikowski, Chris & Colin M. Shapiro (1993). Non-psychotropic drugs and sleep. *British Medical Journal* 306:1118–21.

Inter-Tribal Council of Nevada (1976). *Numa: A Northern Paiute History*. Reno: Inter-Tribal Council of Nevada.

Jackson, Gerald G. (1980a). The emergence of a black perspective in counseling. In Jones.

Jackson, Gerald G. (1980b). The African genesis of the black perspective in helping. In Jones.

Jacobi, Jolande (1959 [1957]). *Complex/Archetype/Symbol in the Psychology of C. G. Jung*. Princeton: Princeton University.

Jacobs, L. D., M. Feldman & M. B. Bender (1970). The pattern of human eye movements during sleep. *Transactions of the American Neurological Association* 95:114–9.

Jaffé, Aniela (1965 [1961]). Introduction. In Jung (1965 [1961]).

Jędrej, M. C. (1992). Ingessana dreaming. In Jędrej & Shaw (1992a).

Jędrej, M. C. & Rosalind Shaw, editors (1992a). *Dreaming, Religion and Society in Africa*. Leiden: E. J. Brill.

Jędrej, M. C. & Rosalind Shaw (1992b). Introduction: dreaming, religion and society in Africa. In Jędrej & Shaw (1992a).

Johnson, Robert A. (1986). *Inner Work: Using Dreams and Active Imagination for Personal Growth*. San Francisco: Harper & Row.

Jones, Reginald L., editor (1980). *Black Psychology*, 2nd edition. New York: Harper & Row.

Jones, Richard M. (1979a). Freudian and post-Freudian theories of dreams. In Wolman.

Jones, Richard (1979b). *The Dream Poet*. Boston: G. K. Hall.

Jones, Richard M. (1987). Dreams and creativity. In Russo (1987a).

Jones, Richard M. (1988). Dream reflection and creative writing. In Ullman & Limmer.

Jones, Russell (1979). Ten conversion myths from Indonesia. In Levtzion.

Jowett, M. A., translator (1937 [1892]). *Phaedo*. In *The Dialogues of Plato*. New York: Random House.

Jung, C. G. (1953–1976). *The Collected Works of C. G. Jung*. Bollingen Series XX, 18 volumes. Princeton: Princeton University. Cited in the text as CW.

CW 3. *The Psychogenesis of Mental Disease* (1960).

CW 4. *Freud and Psychoanalysis* (1961).

CW 6. *Psychological Types* (1971).

CW 7. *Two Essays on Analytical Psychology* (1953; 2nd edition, 1966).

CW 8. *The Structure and Dynamics of the Psyche* (1960; 2nd edition, 1969).

CW 9-I. *The Archetypes and the Collective Unconscious* (1959; 2nd edition, 1968).

CW 9-II. *Aion* (1959; 2nd edition, 1968).

CW 10. *Civilization in Transition* (1964; 2nd edition 1970).

CW 11. *Psychology and Religion: West and East* (1958; 2nd edition, 1969).

CW 12. *Psychology and Alchemy* (1953; 2nd edition, 1968).

CW 13. *Alchemical Studies* (1968).

CW 14. *Mysterium Coniunctionis* (1963; 2nd edition, 1970).

CW 16. *The Practice of Psychotherapy* (1954; 2nd edition, 1966).

CW 17. *The Development of Personality* (1954).

CW 18. *The Symbolic Life: Miscellaneous Writings* (1976).

Jung, C. G. (1965 [1961]). *Memories, Dreams, Reflections*. Recorded and edited by Aniela Jaffé. New York: Vintage.

Jung, C. G. (1974). *Dreams*. Princeton: Princeton University.

Jung, C. G. (1984 [1938]). *Dream Analysis: Notes of the Seminar Given in 1928–30*, 2nd edition. Princeton: Princeton University.

Jung, C. G. (1985 [1949]). The significance of the father in the destiny of the individual. In Samuels (1985a).

Kafka, John S. (1980). The dream in schizophrenia. In Natterson (1980a).

Kahn, Edwin & Charles Fisher (1968). Dream recall and erections in the healthy aged. *Psychophysiology* 4:393–4.

Kahn, Edwin, Charles Fisher & Lois Lieberman (1969). Dream recall in the normal aged. *Journal of the American Geriatrics Society* 17:1121–6.

Kales, A., F. S. Hoedemaker, A. Jacobson & E. L. Lichtenstein (1964). Dream deprivation: an experimental reappraisal. *Nature* 204:1337–8.

Kales, Anthony, Joyce D. Kales, Allan Jacobson, Frederick J. Humphrey II & Constantin R. Soldatos (1977). Effects of imipramine on enuretic frequency and sleep stages. *Pediatrics* 60:431–6.

Kales, J., C. Allen, T. A. Preston, T.-L. Tan & A. Kales (1970). Changes in REM sleep and dreaming with cigarette smoking and following withdrawal. *Psychophysiology* 7:347–8.

Kalsched, Donald E. (1992). Beyond Freud and Jung: seven analysts discuss the impact of new ideas about dreamwork. A response by Donald E. Kalsched. *Quadrant* 25(2):91–4.

Kanzer, Mark (1955). The communicative function of the dream. *International Journal of Psycho-Analysis* 36:260–6.

Kaplan, Seymour R. (1973). The "group dream." *International Journal of Group Psychotherapy* 23:421–31.

Karacan, I., D. R. Goodenough, A. Shapiro & Steven Starker (1966). Erection cycle during sleep in relation to dream anxiety. *Archives of General Psychiatry* 15:183–9.

Karenga, Maulana, editor (1990). *Reconstructing Kemetic Culture.* Los Angeles: University of Sankore.

Karle, Werner, Richard Corriere, Joseph Hart & Lee Woldenberg (1980). The functional analysis of dreams: a new theory of dreaming. *Journal of Clinical Psychology* 36:5–78.

Kasatkin, Vasily (1984). Diagnosis by dreams. *International Journal of Paraphysics* 18:104–6.

Katz, Mark & Colin M. Shapiro (1993). Dreams and medical illness. *British Medical Journal* 306:993–5.

Kaufman, Gershen (1985 [1980]). *Shame: The Power of Caring.* Rochester, Vermont: Schenkman.

Kellogg, E. W., III (1989). Mapping territories: a phenomenology of lucid dream reality. *Lucidity Letter* 8(2):81–97.

Kelman, Harvey (1944). A new approach to dream interpretation. *American Journal of Psychoanalysis* 4:89–107.

Kelman, Harvey (1975). The "day precipitate" of dreams: the Morris hypothesis. *International Journal of Psycho-Analysis* 56:209–18.

Kelsey, Morton (1978). *Dreams: A Way to Listen to God.* New York: Paulist.

Kelzer, Kenneth (1987). The sun and the shadow. In Russo (1987a).

Kelzer, Kenneth (1992). Dreams and the transformation of the personal shadow. Workshop presented at the conference of the Association for the Study of Dreams, Santa Cruz.

Kendall, Sandy (1994). Caffeine paradox. *Harvard Magazine* 96(1):13–4.

Kerr, Nancy H., David Foulkes & Marcella Schmidt (1982). The structure of laboratory dream reports in blind and sighted subjects. *Journal of Nervous and Mental Disease* 170:286–94.

Khan, M. Masud R. (1976). The changing use of dreams in psychoanalytic practice: in search of the dreaming experience. *International Journal of Psycho-Analysis* 57:325–30.

Kiernan, J. P. (1985). The social stuff of revelation: pattern and purpose in Zionist dreams and visions. *Africa* 55:304–18.

Kilborne, Benjamin (1981). Pattern, structure, and style in anthropological studies of dreams. *Ethos* 9:165–85.

Kilborne, Benjamin (1992 [1987]). On classifying dreams. In Tedlock (1992a [1987]).

Kilner, Linda A. (1987). Cross-cultural comparison of manifest dream content: United States and Gusii Females. *Association for the Study of Dreams Newsletter* 4(3):10.

Kilner, Linda A. (1988). Manifest content in dreams of Gussi and U.S. females: social and sexual interactions, achievement and fortune. *Psychiatric Journal of the University of Ottawa* 13:79–84. [NOTE: 'Gussi' is a misprint of 'Gusii'.]

King, Johanna (1990). Panel discussion. See Gackenbach et al.

King, Johanna (1993). Let's stand up, regain our balance, and look around before we fall (or melt) into the pool. *Association for the Study of Dreams Newsletter* 10(1):13–5,17.

Kirsch, Thomas B. (1979). Reflections on introversion and/or schizoid personality. *Journal of Analytical Psychology* 24:145–52.

Kitzinger, Sheila (1980 [1978]). *Women as Mothers*. New York: Vintage.

Klein-Lipshutz, Eva (1953). Comparison of dreams in individual and group psychotherapy. *International Journal of Group Psychotherapy* 3:143–9.

Knapp, Susan (1979). Dreaming: Horney, Kelman, and Shainberg. In Wolman.

Knapp, Susan (1988). Teaching the use of the dream in clinical practice. In Ullman & Limmer.

Koch-Sheras, Phyllis R. & Ann Hollier (1985). A re-examination of the difference between men's and women's dreams. *Association for the Study of Dreams Newsletter* 2(2):8.

Koch-Sheras, Phyllis R., E. Ann Hollier & Brook Jones (1983). *Dream On: A Dream Interpretation and Exploration Guide for Women*. Englewood Cliffs, New Jersey: Prentice-Hall.

Koestler, Arthur (1967). *The Ghost in the Machine*. New York: Macmillan.

Kohler, William C., R. Dean Coddington & H. W. Agnew, Jr. (1968). Sleep patterns in 2-year-old children. *Journal of Pediatrics* 72:228–33.

Kohut, Heinz & Ernest S. Wolf (1978). The disorders of the self and their treatment: an outline. *International Journal of Psycho-Analysis* 59:413–25.

Koukkou-Lehmann, Martha (1990). A psychophysiological model of dreaming with implications for the therapeutic effect of dreamwork. Address to the Association for the Study of Dreams, Chicago.

Koukkou, Martha & Dietrich Lehmann (1993). A model of dreaming and its functional significance: the state-shift hypothesis. In Moffitt et al. (1993a).

Koulack, David (1986). Effects of presleep and during sleep stimuli on the content of dreams. In Gackenbach.

Koulack, David (1991). *To Catch a Dream: Explorations of Dreaming*. Albany: State University of New York.

Koulack, David (1993). Dreams and adaptation to contemporary stress. In Moffitt et al. (1993a).

Kracke, Waud (1992 [1987]). Myths in dreams, thought in images. In Tedlock (1992a [1987]).

Krajenke, Robert Wm. (1987). The Mt. Rushmore full moon medicine wheel quest. In Russo (1987a).

Kramer, Milton, editor (1969). *Dream Psychology and the New Biology of Dreaming.* Springfield, Illinois: Charles C Thomas.

Kramer, Milton (1970). Manifest dream content in normal and psychopathologic states. *Archives of General Psychiatry* 22:149–59.

Kramer, Milton (1990). The relationship of pre-sleep mood to post-sleep mood. Paper presented to the Association for the Study of Dreams, Chicago.

Kramer, Milton (1991a). The nightmare: a failure in dream function. *Dreaming* 1:277–85.

Kramer, Milton (1991b). A selective mood regulatory function of sleep. In Gackenbach & Sheikh.

Kramer, Milton (1991c). The psychobiology of mental illness: changes in the physiological and psychological aspects of sleep. In Gackenbach & Sheikh.

Kramer, Milton (1993). The selective mood regulatory function of dreaming: an update and revision. In Moffitt et al. (1993a).

Kramer, Milton, Bill J. Baldridge, Roy M. Whitman, Paul H. Ornstein & Philip C. Smith (1969). An exploration of the manifest dream in schizophrenic and depressed patients. *Diseases of the Nervous System* 30:126–30.

Kramer, Milton, Robert Hlasny, Gerald Jacobs & Thomas Roth (1976). Do dreams have meaning? An empirical inquiry. *American Journal of Psychiatry* 133:778–81.

Kramer, Milton & Thomas Roth (1973). A comparison of dream content in laboratory dream reports of schizophrenic and depressive patient groups. *Comprehensive Psychiatry* 14:325–9.

Kramer, Milton & Thomas Roth (1979). Dreams in psychopathology. In Wolman.

Kramer, Milton, Roy M. Whitman, Bill Baldridge & Leonard Lansky (1965). Depression: dreams and defenses. *American Journal of Psychiatry* 122:411–7.

Kripke, Daniel F. (1972). An ultradian biologic rhythm associated with perceptual deprivation and REM sleep. *Psychosomatic Medicine* 34:221–34.

Krippner, Stanley, editor (1990a). *Dreamtime & Dreamwork: Decoding the Language of the Night.* Los Angeles: Jeremy P. Tarcher.

Krippner, Stanley (1990b). Dreams in creativity and education. In Krippner (1990a).

Krippner, Stanley (1990c). Tribal shamans and their travels into dreamtime. In Krippner (1990a).

Krippner, Stanley (1990d). Shamanism and higher consciousness. Paper presented to the Lucidity Association, Chicago.

Krippner, Stanley (1993). A conversation with Stanley Krippner, Ph.D. [Interview by Alan B. Siegel.] *Association for the Study of Dreams Newsletter* 10(3):1,17,24,27.

Krippner, Stanley & Joseph Dillard (1988). *Dreamworking: How to Use Your Dreams for Creative Problem-Solving.* Buffalo, New York: Bearly Limited.

Krippner, Stanley & Kenneth Rubenstein (1990). Gender differences in dream content. *Association for the Study of Dreams Newsletter* 7(3):4.

K. S. (1989). Beyond this world. *NightLight* 1(4):12-3.

Kubie, Lawrence S. (1975 [1958]). *Neurotic Distortion of the Creative Process.* New York: Noonday.

Kugler, Paul K. (1992). The "subject" of dreams. *Quadrant* 25(2):63-83.

Kugler, Paul, Jayne Gackenbach & Harry Hunt (1987). Jungian, Paul Kugler, on assumptions of reality. *Association for the Study of Dreams Newsletter* 4(6): 8-12,16.

Kuiken, Don & Shelley Sikora (1990). A classificatory study of impactful dreams. Paper presented to the Association for the Study of Dreams, Chicago.

Kuiken, Don & Shelley Sikora (1993). The impact of dreams on waking thoughts and feelings. In Moffitt et al. (1993a).

LaBerge, Stephen (1985). *Lucid Dreaming.* Los Angeles: Jeremy P. Tarcher.

LaBerge, Stephen (1987). Induction of lucid dreaming by luminous stimulation. *Association for the Study of Dreams Newsletter* 4(2):7.

LaBerge, Stephen (1988a). Lucid dreaming in Western literature. In Gackenbach & LaBerge.

LaBerge, Stephen (1988b). The psychophysiology of lucid dreaming. In Gackenbach & LaBerge.

LaBerge, Stephen (1990). Lucid dreaming: a healthy pleasure. *NightLight* 2(1): 1-3.

LaBerge, Stephen (1992). Experiments with the DreamLight lucid dreaming induction device. Paper presented to the Association for the Study of Dreams, Santa Cruz.

LaBerge, Stephen & Jayne Gackenbach (1986). Lucid dreaming. In Wolman & Ullman.

LaBerge, Stephen & Lynne Levitan, editors (1989a). Discovering dreamsigns: what makes a dream seem like a dream. *NightLight* 1(2):5-10.

LaBerge, Stephen & Lynne Levitan, editors (1989b). Can "false awakenings" be avoided? *NightLight* 1(4):4,15.

LaBerge, Stephen & Lynne Levitan, editors (1990). Fifteen minutes to lucid dreaming: morning vs. evening focus. *NightLight* 2(2):5-8.

LaBerge, Stephen & Lynne Levitan, editors (1991). Dream re-entry as a way to lucid dreaming. *NightLight* 3(2):5-8.

LaBerge, Stephen, Lynne Levitan & William C. Dement (1986). Lucid dreaming: physiological correlates of consciousness during REM sleep. *Journal of Mind and Behavior* 7:251-8.

LaBerge, Stephen & Howard Rheingold (1990). *Exploring the World of Lucid Dreaming.* New York: Ballantine.

Ladd, George T. (1892). Contribution to the psychology of visual imagery in dreams. *Mind* 1:299-304.

LaDuke, Winona (1990). Environmentalism, racism, and the New Age Movement: the expropriation of indigenous cultures. *Left Green Notes* #4 (September/October):15-8, 32-4. Reprinted from *Left Field: A Journal of Ideas and Polemics* #4 (Summer), 1990.

Langs, Robert J. (1966). Manifest dreams from three clinical groups. *Archives of General Psychiatry* 14:634-43.

Langs, Robert J. (1971). Day residues, recall residues, and dreams: reality and the psyche. *Journal of the American Psychoanalytic Association* 19:499-523.

Langs, Robert (1988). *Decoding Your Dreams*. New York: Henry Holt.

Lansky, Melvin R. & Carol R. Bley (1990). Exploration of nightmares in hospital treatment of borderline patients. *Bulletin of the Menninger Clinic* 54:466-77.

Lansky, Melvin R. & Carol R. Bley (1993). Delayed onset of post-traumatic nightmares: case report and implications. *Dreaming* 3:21-31.

Lanternari, Vittorio (1963 [1960]). *The Religions of the Oppressed: A Study of Modern Messianic Cults*. New York: Alfred A. Knopf.

Lanternari, Vittorio (1975). Dreams as charismatic significants: their bearing on the rise of new religious movements. In Thomas R. Williams, editor. *Psychological Anthropology*. The Hague: Mouton.

de Laszlo, Violet S., editor (1958). *Psyche & Symbol: A Selection from the Writings of C. G. Jung*. Garden City, New York: Doubleday Anchor.

Lattimore, Richard, translator (1951). *The Iliad of Homer*. Chicago: University of Chicago.

Lauter, Estella & Carol Schreier Rupprecht, editors (1985a). *Feminist Archetypal Theory: Interdisciplinary Re-Visions of Jungian Thought*. Knoxville: University of Tennessee.

Lauter, Estella & Carol Schreier Rupprecht (1985b). Introduction. In Lauter & Rupprecht (1985a).

Lauter, Estella & Carol Schreier Rupprecht (1985c). Feminist archetypal theory: a proposal. In Lauter & Rupprecht (1985a).

Lavie, Peretz & Hanna Kaminer (1991). Dreams that poison sleep: dreaming in holocaust survivors. *Dreaming* 1:11-21.

Lebe, Doryann (1980). The dream in acting out disturbances. In Natterson (1980a).

Lecerf, Jean (1966). The dream in popular culture: Arabic and Islamic. In Grunebaum & Caillois.

Lehmann, Heinz E. (1969). An existential view. In Kramer.

Leonard, Linda Schierse (1985 [1982]). *The Wounded Woman*. Boston: Shambhala.

Lerner, Barbara (1967). Dream function revisited. *Journal of Abnormal Psychology* 72:85-100.

Levay, Alexander N. & Josef Weissberg (1979). The role of dreams in sex therapy. *Journal of Sex & Marital Therapy* 5:334-9.

Leveton, Alan F. (1961). The night residue. *International Journal of Psycho-Analysis* 42:506-16.

Levin, Ross, John Galin & Bill Zywiak (1991). Nightmares, boundaries, and creativity. *Dreaming* 1:63–74.

Levin, Ross & Jodi Rosenblatt (1990). Nightmares and creativity. Paper presented to the Association for the Study of Dreams, Chicago.

Levitan, Harold L. (1967). Depersonalization and the dream. *Psychoanalytic Quarterly* 36:157–71.

Levitan, Harold L. (1968). The turn to mania. *Psychoanalytic Quarterly* 37:56–62.

Levitan, Harold L. (1974). The dreams of a phobic patient. *International Review of Psycho-Analysis* 1:313–23.

Levitan, Harold L. (1976/77a). The significance of certain catastrophic dreams. *Psychotherapy and Psychosomatics* 27:1–7.

Levitan, Harold L. (1976/77b). Dynamic and structural features of a case of compulsive neurosis as revealed in dreams. *Psychotherapy and Psychosomatics* 27: 125–132.

Levitan, Harold L. (1981a). Failure of the defensive functions of the ego in dreams of psychosomatic patients. *Psychotherapy and Psychosomatics* 36:1–7.

Levitan, Harold L. (1981b). Implications of certain dreams reported by patients in a bulemic phase of anorexia nervosa. *Canadian Journal of Psychiatry* 26: 228–31.

Levitan, Harold L. (1984). Dreams which culminate in migraine headaches. *Psychotherapy and Psychosomatics* 41:161–6.

Levitan, Lynne (1989). A comparison of three methods of lucid dream induction. *NightLight* 1(3):3, 9–12.

Levitan, Lynne (1990a). Prolonging lucid dreams. *NightLight* 2(1):9–11.

Levitan, Lynne (1990b). Questions & Answers. *NightLight* 2(1):4, 15.

Levitan, Lynne (1990c). The best time for lucid dreaming. *NightLight* 2(3):9–11.

Levitan, Lynne (1991a). Get up early, take a nap, be lucid! *NightLight* 3(1): 1–4, 9.

Levitan, Lynne (1991b). "Sleep on the right side, as a lion doth..." Tibetan dream lore still true after 10 centuries. *NightLight* 3(3):4, 9–11.

Levitan, Lynne (1993). *DreamLink Operation Manual.* Stanford: Lucidity Institute.

Levitan, Lynne & Stephen LaBerge (1990). Beyond nightmares: lucid resourcefulness vs helpless depression. *NightLight* 2(4):1–3, 9–11.

Levitan, Lynne & Stephen LaBerge (1991a). In the mind and out-of-body: OBEs and lucid dreams. *NightLight* 3(2):1–4, 9.

Levitan, Lynne & Stephen LaBerge (1991b). Mind in body or body in mind? OBEs and lucid dreams, part II. *NightLight* 3(3):1–3.

Levtzion, Nehemia, editor (1979). *Conversion to Islam.* New York: Holmes & Meier.

Lewin, Bertram D. (1946). Sleep, the mouth, and the dream screen. *Psychoanalytic Quarterly* 15:419–34.

Lewin, Bertram D. (1958). *Dreams and the Uses of Regression.* New York: International Universities.

Lewin, Isaac & Hanania Glaubman (1975). The effect of REM deprivation: is it detrimental, beneficial, or neutral? *Psychophysiology* 12:349–53.

Lewin, Isaac & Jerome L. Singer (1991). Psychological effects of REM ("dream") deprivation upon waking mentation. In Ellman & Antrobus.

Lewis, Jane White (1990). Panel discussion. See Gackenbach et al.

Lewis, Jane White (1991). Images of war: the impact of the Gulf conflict on an analytic practice. Paper presented to the Association for the Study of Dreams, Charlottesville.

Lewis, Naphtali (1976). *The Interpretation of Dreams and Portents*. Toronto: Samuel Stevens, Hakkert.

Lincoln, Jackson Stewart (1970 [1935]). *The Dream in Primitive Cultures*. New York: Johnson Reprint.

Lind, Richard (1985). The relativization of the ego. *Association for the Study of Dreams Newsletter* 2(3):5–6, 8–9.

Litman, Robert E. (1980). The dream in the suicidal situation. In Natterson (1980a).

Lockhart, Russell A. (1977). Cancer in myth and dream: an exploration into the archetypal relation between dreams and disease. *Spring*: 1–26.

Lodö, Lama (1990). We can wake up as Buddha. *Night Vision*, April/May.

Loepfe, Ariane (1989). Perceptions in REM dreams. *Association for the Study of Dreams Newsletter* 6(3):5.

Lorand, Sandor (1957). Dream interpretation in the Talmud (Babylonian and Graeco-Roman period). *International Journal of Psycho-Analysis* 38:92–7.

Lorenz, Konrad (1965). *Evolution and Modification of Behavior*. Chicago: University of Chicago.

Lortie-Lussier, Monique, Christine Schwab & Joseph De Koninck (1985). Working mothers versus homemakers: do dreams reflect the changing roles of women? *Sex Roles* 12:1009–21.

MacDermot, Violet (1971). *The Cult of the Seer in the Ancient Middle East*. Berkeley: University of California.

Mack, John E. (1969). Dreams and psychosis. *Journal of the American Psychoanalytic Association* 17:206–21.

Mack, John E. (1989 [1970]). *Nightmares and Human Conflict*. New York: Columbia University.

MacKenzie, Norman (1965). *Dreams and Dreaming*. New York: Vanguard.

Magallón, Linda (1989). Dream trek: expanding the components for a dream. *Dream Network Bulletin* 8(4–6):7.

Magallón, Linda Lane & Barbara Shor (1990). Shared dreaming: joining together in dreamtime. In Krippner (1990a).

Maguire, Jack (1989). *Night and Day*. New York: Simon & Schuster.

Mahrer, Alvin R. (1971). Personal life change through systematic use of dreams. *Psychotherapy: Theory, Research and Practice* 8:328–32.

Mahrer, Alvin R. (1989). *Dreamwork in Psychotherapy and Self-Change*. New York: W. W. Norton.

Mahrer, Alvin R. (1990). The role of dreams in psychotherapy. In Krippner (1990a).

Malamud, Judith R. (1986). Becoming lucid in dreams and waking life. In Wolman & Ullman.

Malamud, Judith R. (1988). Learning to become fully lucid: a program for inner growth. In Gackenbach & LaBerge.

Malcolm, Norman (1967 [1959]). *Dreaming*. London: Routledge & Kegan Paul.

Mankowitz, Ann (1984). *Change of Life: Dreams and the Menopause*. Toronto: Inner City.

Marjasch, Sonja (1966). On the dream psychology of C. G. Jung. In Grunebaum & Caillois.

Markowitz, I., Gwen Taylor & E. Bokert (1968). Dream discussion as a means of reopening blocked familial communication. *Psychotherapy and Psychosomatics* 16:348-56.

Marks, Isaac (1978). Rehearsal relief of a nightmare. *British Journal of Psychiatry* 133:461-5.

Marmer, Stephen S. (1980). The dream in dissociative states. In Natterson (1980a).

Martin, Stephen A. (1992). Smaller than small, bigger than big: the role of the "little dream" in individuation. *Quadrant* 25(2):31-41.

Mattoon, Mary Ann (1984 [1978]). *Understanding Dreams*. Dallas: Spring.

May, Rollo (1968). Part I: Dreams and symbols. In Leopold Calligor & Rollo May. *Dreams and Symbols: Man's Unconscious Language*. New York: Basic.

May, Rollo & Irvin Yalom (1989). Existential psychotherapy. In Corsini & Wedding.

Maybruck, Patricia (1990). Pregnancy and dreams. In Krippner (1990a).

Maybruck, Patricia (1991). *Romantic Dreams: How to Enhance Your Romantic Relationship by Understanding and Sharing Your Dreams*. New York: Pocket Books.

Mbiti, John S. (1976). God, dreams and African militancy. In J. S. Pobee, editor. *Religion in a Pluralistic Society*. Leiden: E. J. Brill.

McCall, John C. (1993). Making peace with Agwu. *Anthropology and Humanism* 18(2):56-66.

McCann, Stewart J. H. & Leonard L. Stewin (1987). Frightening dreams and birth order. *Individual Psychology* 43:56-8.

McCann, Stewart J. H., Leonard L. Stewin & Robert H. Short (1990). Frightening dream frequency and birth order. *Individual Psychology* 46:304-10.

McCarley, Robert W. & J. Allan Hobson (1979). The form of dreams and the biology of sleep. In Wolman.

McCarley, Robert W. & Edward Hoffman (1981). REM sleep dreams and the activation-synthesis hypothesis. *American Journal of Psychiatry* 138:904-12.

McCurdy, Harold Grier (1946). The history of dream theory. *Psychological Review* 53:225-33.

McGrath, Michael J. & David B. Cohen (1978). REM sleep facilitation of adaptive waking behavior: a review of the literature. *Psychological Bulletin* 85:24–57.

McGuire, William, editor (1974). *The Freud/Jung Letters: The Correspondence between Sigmund Freud and C. G. Jung.* Princeton: Princeton University.

McLeester, Dick (1991). 15 simple guidelines. *Dream Network Journal* 10(4):17.

McLeod, Malcolm N. (1992). The evolution of Freud's theory about dreaming. *Psychoanalytic Quarterly* 61:37–64.

McManus, John, Charles D. Laughlin & Jon Shearer (1993). The function of dreaming in the cycles of cognition: a biogenetic structural account. In Moffitt et al. (1993a).

Meer, Samuel J. (1955). Authoritarian attitudes and dreams. *Journal of Abnormal and Social Psychology* 51:74–8.

Mehta, Rohit (1978). *The Science of Meditation.* Oxford: Motilal.

Meier, Barbara & Inge Strauch (1990). The phenomenology of dreams: dream settings, dream characters, and self-participation. *Association for the Study of Dreams Newsletter* 7(3):5–6.

Meier, C. A. (1959). Projection, transference, and the subject-object relation in psychology. *Journal of Analytical Psychology* 4:21–34.

Meier, Carl Alfred (1966). The dream in ancient Greece and its use in temple cures (incubation). In Grunebaum & Caillois.

Meier, C. A. (1967 [1949]). *Ancient Incubation and Modern Psychotherapy.* Evanston: Northwestern University.

Meier, Carl A. (1969). A Jungian view. In Kramer.

Meier, C. A. (1990 [1972]). *The Meaning and Significance of Dreams.* Boston: Sigo.

Meier, Fritz (1966). Some aspects of inspiration by demons in Islam. In Grunebaum & Caillois.

Melnechuk, Theodore (1983). The dream machine. *Psychology Today* 17(11): 22–34.

Meltzer, Donald (1984). *Dream-Life: A Re-examination of the Psycho-analytical Theory and Technique.* Reading, U.K.: Clunie.

Mendel, Werner M. (1980). The dream in analysis of existence. In Natterson (1980a).

Mendelson, Jack H., Leonard Siger & Philip Solomon (1974 [1960]). The dream in technicolor of the congenitally deaf. In Woods & Greenhouse.

Merrill, William (1992 [1987]). The Rarámuri stereotype of dreams. In Tedlock (1992a [1987]).

Meyer, Thomas (1971). Dream essays. *Io* 8:177–82.

Mikkelsen, Edwin J. & Judith L. Rapoport (1980). Enuresis: psychopathology, sleep stage, and drug response. *Urologic Clinics of North America* 7:361–77.

Mikkelsen, Edwin J., Judith L. Rapoport, Linda Nee, Cynthia Gruenau, Wallace Mendelson & J. Christian Gillin (1980). Childhood enuresis. I. Sleep patterns and psychopathology. *Archives of General Psychiatry* 37:1139–44.

Miller, Jean B. (1969). Dreams during varying stages of depression. *Archives of General Psychiatry* 20:560-5.

Mindell, Arnold (1985). *Working with the Dreaming Body*. London: Routledge & Kegan Paul.

Mindell, Arnold (1989). *Coma: Key to Awakening*. Boston: Shambhala.

Mindell, Arnold (1990). An interview with Arnold Mindell. [Interview by H. Roberta Ossana.] *Dream Network Journal* 9(4):15,33-5.

Mitchell, Paco (1990). Demons and angels. *Dream Network Journal* 9(3):14,28.

Moffitt, Alan (1990). Dreaming: the outstanding issues. Presidential address to the Association for the Study of Dreams, Chicago.

Moffitt, Alan & Robert Hoffmann (1986). On the single-mindedness and isolation of dream psychophysiology. In Gackenbach.

Moffitt, Alan, Robert Hoffmann & Susan Galloway (1990). Dream recall: imagination, illusion and tough-mindedness. *Psychiatric Journal of the University of Ottawa* 15:66-72.

Moffitt, Alan, Robert Hoffmann, Janet Mullington, Sheila Purcell, Ross Pigeau & Roger Wells (1988). Dream psychology: operating in the dark. In Gackenbach & LaBerge.

Moffitt, Alan, Milton Kramer & Robert Hoffmann, editors (1993a). *The Functions of Dreaming*. Albany: State University of New York.

Moffitt, Alan, Milton Kramer & Robert Hoffmann (1993b). Introduction. In Moffitt et al. (1993a).

de Monchaux, Cecily (1978). Dreaming and the organizing function of the ego. *International Journal of Psycho-Analysis* 59:443-53.

Monroe, L. J., A. Rechtschaffen, D. Foulkes & J. Jensen (1965). The discriminability of REM and NREM reports. *Journal of Personality and Social Psychology* 2:456-60.

Moorcroft, William (1986). An overview of sleep. In Gackenbach.

Moorcroft, William & Jennifer Clothier (1986). An overview of the body and the brain in sleep. In Gackenbach.

Moore, Robert A. (1962). The manifest dream in alcoholism. *Quarterly Journal of Studies on Alcoholism* 23:583-9.

Morgan, William (1932). Navaho dreams. *American Anthropologist* 34:391-405.

Morris, Jill (1987 [1985]). *The Dream Workbook: Discover the Knowledge and Power Hidden in Your Dreams*. New York: Ballantine.

Morrison, Adrian R. (1983). A window on the sleeping brain. *Scientific American* 248(4):94-102.

Morrison, Reed (1989). Dreams mapping recovery from chemical dependency. *Association for the Study of Dreams Newsletter* 6(5):1-3.

Mosak, Harold H. (1989). Adlerian psychotherapy. In Corsini & Wedding.

Moscowitz, E. & R. J. Berger (1969). Rapid eye movements and dream imagery: are they related? *Nature* 224:613-4.

Moss, C. Scott (1970). *Dreams, Images, and Fantasy: A Semantic Differential Casebook*. Urbana: University of Illinois.

Mpier, Mubuy Mubuy (1992). Dreams among the Yansi. In Jędrej & Shaw (1992a).

Mullington, J., M. Cuddy, A. Moffitt, R. Hoffman[n] & L. Pickavance (1988). Continuity of self-reflectiveness across states. *Association for the Study of Dreams Newsletter* 5(5):4–5.

Myers, Isabel Briggs (with Peter B. Myers) (1985 [1980]). *Gifts Differing*. Palo Alto: Consulting Psychologists.

Myers, Wayne A. (1977). The significance of the colors black and white in the dreams of black and white patients. *Journal of the American Psychoanalytic Association* 25:163–81.

Namrow, Arnold (1980). The dream in obsessive states. In Natterson (1980a).

Nanda, Jyotir Maya (1974). *Waking, Dream and Deep Sleep*. Miami: International Yoga Society.

Natale, Vincenzo & Daniela Battaglia (1990–91). Temporal dating of autobiographical memories associated to REM and NREM dreams. *Imagination, Cognition and Personality* 10:279–84.

Natterson, Joseph M., editor (1980a). *The Dream in Clinical Practice*. New York: Jason Aronson.

Natterson, Joseph M. (1980b). The dream in group psychotherapy. In Natterson (1980a).

Natterson, Joseph M. & Bernard Gordon (1977). *The Sexual Dream*. New York: Crown.

Neihardt, John G. (1979 [1932]). *Black Elk Speaks*. Lincoln: University of Nebraska.

Neu, Eva Renée (1988). *Dreams and Dream Groups: Messages from the Interior*. Freedom, California: Crossing.

Niederer, Ursula (1990). Children's home dreams: content and relation to anxiety. *Association for the Study of Dreams Newsletter* 7(1):3.

Nielsen, Tore A. (1988). The dream research of Inge Strauch. *Association for the Study of Dreams Newsletter* 5(6):7–8.

Nielsen, Tore A. (1989). Ancient methods of dream incubation: bodily methods of inducing spiritual presence. *Bulletin of the Centre for the Study of Dreams* 3(3–4):6–10,15.

Nielsen, Tore A. (1993). Changes in kinesthetic content of dreams following somatosensory stimulation of leg muscles during REM sleep. *Dreaming* 3:99–113.

Nielsen, Tore A., Daniel Deslauriers & George W. Baylor (1991). Emotions in dream and waking event reports. *Dreaming* 1:287–300.

Nielsen, Tore A. & Russell A. Powell (1989). The 'dream-lag' effect: a 6-day temporal delay in dream content incorporation. *Psychiatric Journal of the University of Ottawa* 14:561–5.

Nielsen, Tore A. & Russell A. Powell (1992). The day-residue and dream-lag effects: a literature review and limited replication of two temporal effects in dream formation. *Dreaming* 2:67–77.

Nino-Murcia, German & Sharon A. Keenan (1987). Enuresis and sleep. In Christian Guilleminault, editor. *Sleep and Its Disorders in Children*. New York: Raven.

Nobles, Wade W. (1974). Africanity: its role in black families. *Black Scholar* 5(9):10-7.

Nobles, Wade W. (1978). Toward an empirical and theoretical framework for defining black families. *Journal of Marriage and the Family* 40:679-88.

Nobles, Wade W. (1980a). African philosophy: foundations for black psychology. In Jones.

Nobles, Wade W. (1980b). Extended self: rethinking the so-called Negro self-concept. In Jones.

Oberhelman, Steven M. (1983). Galen, *On Diagnosis from Dreams*. *Journal of the History of Medicine and Allied Sciences* 38:36-47.

O'Connor, Peter (1986). *Dreams and the Search for Meaning*. New York: Paulist.

O'Flaherty, Wendy Doniger (1984). *Dreams, Illusions and Other Realities*. Chicago: University of Chicago.

Ogilvie, Robert D., Harry T. Hunt, Paul D. Tyson, Melodie L. Lucescu & Daniel B. Jeakins (1982). Lucid dreaming and alpha activity: a preliminary report. *Perceptual and Motor Skills* 55:795-808.

Okuma, Teruo, Yuzuru Sunami, Etsuo Fukuma, Seiki Takeo & Mitsuo Motoike (1970). Dream content study in chronic schizophrenics and normals by REMP-awakening technique. *Folia Psychiatrica et Neurologica Japonica* 24:151-62.

O'Nell, Carl W. (1976). *Dreams, Culture, and the Individual*. Novato, California: Chandler & Sharp.

Ornstein, Paul H. (1987). On self-state dreams in the psychoanalytic treatment process. In Rothstein.

Ossana, H. Roberta (1991a). Planetary dream USA: editorial. *Dream Network Journal* 10(2 & 3):4-5.

Ossana, H. Roberta, editor (1991b). *Dream Network Journal* 10(4).

Ossana, H. Roberta, editor (1993). *The Art of Dream Sharing & Developing Dream Groups*. Moab, Utah: Design Publishing/Dream Network Journal.

Ostow, Mortimer (1992). The interpretation of apocalyptic dreams. *Dreaming* 2:1-14.

Pacosz, Christina (1990). Dreamsharing with children in the classroom. *Dream Network Journal* 9(2):13.

Padel, John H. (1987 [1978]). Object relational approach. In Fosshage & Loew (1987a [1978]).

Palace, Eileen M. & Charlotte Johnston (1989). Treatment of recurrent nightmares by the dream reorganization approach. *Journal of Behavior Therapy and Experimental Psychiatry* 20:219-26.

Paley, Karen & Tore A. Nielsen, editors (1989). *Association for the Study of Dreams Newsletter* 6(5).

Palombo, Stanley R. (1978). *Dreaming and Memory: A New Information-Processing Model*. New York: Basic.

Palombo, Stanley R. (1987a). Can a computer dream? In Glucksman & Warner.

Palombo, Stanley R. (1987b). Dreams: new frontiers. Panel discussion, in Glucksman & Warner.

Palombo, Stanley R. (1992). The eros of dreaming. *International Journal of Psycho-Analysis* 73:637–46.

Paolino, Albert F. (1964). Dreams: sex differences in aggressive content. *Journal of Projective Techniques and Personality Assessment* 28:219–26.

Park, Willard Z. (1975 [1938]). *Shamanism in Western North America: A Study in Cultural Relationships*. New York: Cooper Square.

Parker, Russ (1988). *Healing Dreams: Their Power and Purpose in Your Spiritual Life*. London: SPCK.

Parman, Susan (1991). *Dream and Culture*. New York: Praeger.

Perls, Frederick S. (1992 [1969]). *Gestalt Therapy Verbatim*. Highland, New York: Gestalt Journal.

Phillips, Will (1989). Bringing the dream into the world: an interview with Will Phillips by Jill Gregory. *Dream Network Bulletin* 8(2):4–5,19.

Piaget, Jean (1962 [1945]). *Play, Dreams, and Imitation in Childhood*. New York: W. W. Norton.

Piaget, Nicki (no date). Dreams and addictions: the wisdom of the dream in recovery. Unpublished manuscript.

Pierce, Chester M. (1963). Dream studies in enuresis research. *Canadian Psychiatric Association Journal* 8:415–9.

Pierce, Chester M., Roy M. Whitman, James W. Maas & Michael L. Gay (1961). Enuresis and dreaming. *Archives of General Psychiatry* 4:166–70.

Piotrowski, Zygmunt A. (1986). *Dream: A Key to Self-Knowledge*. Hillsdale, New Jersey: Lawrence Erlbaum.

Pivik, R. T. (1991). Tonic and phasic events in relation to sleep mentation. In Ellman & Antrobus.

Pivik, Terry & David Foulkes (1966). "Dream deprivation": effects on dream content. *Science* 153:1282–4.

Pivik, R. T. & D. Foulkes (1968). NREM mentation: relation to personality, orientation time, and time of night. *Journal of Consulting and Clinical Psychology* 32:144–51.

P. K. (1991). Dream zebra. *NightLight* 3(3):13.

Pomer, Sydney L. & Robert A. Shain (1980). The dream in phobic states. In Natterson (1980a).

Potamianou, Anna (1990). Somatization and dream work. *Psychoanalytic Study of the Child* 45:273–92.

Price, Robert F. & David B. Cohen (1988). Lucid dream induction: an empirical evaluation. In Gackenbach & LaBerge.

Price-Williams, Douglass (1992 [1987]). The waking dream in ethnographic perspective. In Tedlock (1992a [1987]).

Priess, Tima (1993). We come silent; we speak in dreams. *Dream Network Journal* 12(1):12–3.

Pulver, Sydney E. (1978). Book reviews. *Journal of the American Psychoanalytic Association* 26:673–83.

Purcell, Sheila, Alan Moffitt & Robert Hoffmann (1993). Waking, dreaming, and self-regulation. In Moffitt et al. (1993a).

Purcell, Sheila, Janet Mullington, Ross Pigeau, Robert Hoffman[n] & Alan Moffitt (1984). Dream psychology: operating in the dark. *Association for the Study of Dreams Newsletter* 1(4):1–4.

Purcell, Sheila, Janet Mullington, Robert Hoffman[n] & Alan Moffitt (1986). The range and manipulation of dream control. *Association for the Study of Dreams Newsletter* 3(4):9,18.

Purcell, Sheila, Janet Mullington, Alan Moffitt, Robert Hoffmann & Ross Pigeau (1986). Dream self-reflectiveness as a learned cognitive skill. *Sleep* 9:423–37.

Puzen, Julien & Maria Fulmer (1990). Dreams and drums. *Dream Network Journal* 9(3):18–9.

Rados, Robert & Rosalind D. Cartwright (1982). Where do dreams come from? A comparison of presleep and REM sleep thematic content. *Journal of Abnormal Psychology* 91:433–6.

Rainville, Raymond E. (1988). *Dreams Across the Lifespan.* Boston: American.

Rainville, Raymond E. (1992). The role of dreams in the rehabilitation of the blind. Paper presented to the Association for the Study of Dreams, Santa Cruz.

Raphling, David L. (1970). Dreams and suicide attempts. *Journal of Nervous and Mental Disease* 151:404–10.

Rapoport, Judith L., Edwin J. Mikkelsen, Anthony Zavadil, Linda Nee, Cynthia Gruenau, Wallace Mendelson & J. Christian Gillin (1980). Childhood enuresis. II. Psychopathology, tricyclic concentration in plasma, and antienuretic effect. *Archives of General Psychiatry* 37:1146–52.

Rechtschaffen, Allan (1978). The single-mindedness and isolation of dreams. *Sleep* 1:97–109.

Rechtschaffen, Allan, Marcia A. Gilliland, Bernard M. Bergman & Jacqueline B. Winter (1983). Physiological correlates of prolonged sleep deprivation in rats. *Science* 221:182–4.

Rechtschaffen, A. & P. Verdone (1964). Amount of dreaming: effect of incentive, adaptation to laboratory, and individual differences. *Perceptual and Motor Skills* 19:947–58.

Rechtschaffen, Allan, Paul Verdone & Joy Wheaton (1963). Reports of mental activity during sleep. *Canadian Psychiatric Association Journal* 8:409–14.

Reed, Henry (1973). Learning to remember dreams. *Journal of Humanistic Psychology* 13:33–48.

Reed, Henry (1976). Dream incubation: a reconstruction of a ritual in contemporary form. *Journal of Humanistic Psychology* 16:53–70.

Reed, Henry (1987 [1977]). The Sundance experiment. In Russo (1987a).

Reed, Henry (1988 [1985]). *Getting Help from Your Dreams*. New York: Ballantine.

Reed, Henry (1991). *Dream Solutions: Using Your Dreams to Change Your Life*. San Rafael, California: New World.

Reid, Clyde H. (1983). *Dreams: Discovering Your Inner Teacher*. Minneapolis: Winston.

Reneau, Linda ("Ravenwolf") (no date). *The Waking Dreamer's Manual*. Unpublished manuscript.

Resnik, Salomon (1987). *The Theatre of the Dream*. New York: Tavistock.

Richardson, Edwin Strong-Legs (1991). Dreams: a part of the spiritual reality of Native Americans. Address to the Association for the Study of Dreams, Charlottesville, Virginia.

Richardson, George A. & Robert A. Moore (1963). On the manifest dream in schizophrenia. *Journal of the American Psychoanalytic Association* 11: 281-302.

Riemann, Dieter, Christoph Lauer, Bertram Dippel & Mathias Berger (1989). Dream investigations in depressed patients. *Association for the Study of Dreams Newsletter* 6(4):4.

Rinfret, Natalie, Monique Lortie-Lussier & Joseph De Koninck (1991). The dreams of professional mothers and female students: an exploration of social roles and age impact. *Dreaming* 1:179-91.

Rivers, W. H. R. (1923). *Conflict and Dream*. London: Kegan Paul, Trubner, Trench.

Robbins, Paul R. (1988). *The Psychology of Dreaming*. Jefferson, North Carolina: McFarland.

Roffwarg, H. P., W. C. Dement, J. N. Muzio & C. Fisher (1962). Dream imagery: relationship to rapid eye movements of sleep. *Archives of General Psychiatry* 7:235-58.

Roheim, Geza (1969 [1952]). *The Gates of the Dream*. New York: International Universities.

Rooksby, Robert (1989). Problems in the historical research of lucid dreaming. *Lucidity Letter* 8(2):75-80.

Roomy, David (1990). *Inner Work in the Wounded and Creative: The Dream in the Body*. London: Arkana.

Rossi, Ernest (1985). *Dreams and the Growth of Personality*, 2nd edition. New York: Brunner/Mazel.

Rossi, Ernest Lawrence & David B. Cheek (1988). *Mind-Body Therapy: Ideodynamic Healing in Hypnosis*. New York: W. W. Norton.

Rotenberg, V. S. (1993). REM sleep and dreams as mechanisms of the recovery of search activity. In Moffitt et al. (1993a).

Roth, Nathan (1958). Manifest dream content and acting out. *Psychoanalytic Quarterly* 27:547-54.

Rothstein, Arnold, editor (1987). *The Interpretation of Dreams in Clinical Work*. Madison, Connecticut: International Universities.

Rubenstein, Kenneth (1990). How men and women dream differently. In Krippner (1990a).

Rupprecht, Carol Schreier (1985). The common language of women's dreams: colloquy of mind and body. In Lauter & Rupprecht (1985a).

Rupprecht, Carol Schreier (1990). Our unacknowledged ancestors: dream theorists of antiquity, the Middle Ages, and the Renaissance. *Psychiatric Journal of the University of Ottawa* 15:117-22.

Russo, Richard A., editor (1987a). *Dreams Are Wiser Than Men.* Berkeley: North Atlantic.

Russo, Richard A. (1987b). Introduction. In Russo (1987a).

Rychlak, Joseph F. & Jerome M. Brams (1963). Personality dimensions in recalled dream content. *Journal of Projective Techniques and Personality Assessment* 27:226-34.

Rycroft, Charles (1981 [1979]). *The Innocence of Dreams.* Oxford: Oxford University.

Sabini, Meredith (1981a). Imagery in dreams of illness. *Quadrant* 14(2):85-104.

Sabini, Meredith (1981b). Dreams as an aid in determining diagnosis, prognosis, and attitude toward treatment. *Psychotherapy and Psychosomatics* 36:24-36.

Sabini, Meredith (1988). The therapist's inferior function. *Journal of Analytical Psychology* 33:373-94.

Sabini, Meredith & Valerie Hone Maffly (1981). An inner view of illness: the dreams of two cancer patients. *Journal of Analytical Psychology* 26:123-50.

Sagan, Carl (1978 [1977]). *The Dragons of Eden.* New York: Ballantine.

Saint-Denys, Hervey de (1982 [1867]). *Dreams and How to Guide Them.* Morton Schatzman, editor. Nicholas Fry, translator. London: Duckworth.

Salamy, J. (1970). Instrumental responding to internal cues associated with REM sleep. *Psychonomic Science* 18:342-3.

Salley, Roy D. (1982). REM sleep phenomena during out-of-body experiences. *Journal of the American Society for Psychical Research* 76:157-65.

Salley, Roy D. (1985). Dream work in a case of multiple personality. *Association for the Study of Dreams Newsletter* 2(4):1-4.

Salley, Roy D. (1988). Subpersonalities with dreaming functions in a patient with multiple personalities. *Journal of Nervous and Mental Disease* 176:112-5.

Salley, Roy D. (1991). Dream work with dissociated patients and a self curative programming function of dreams. In Gackenbach & Sheikh.

Samuels, Andrew, editor (1985a). *The Father: Contemporary Jungian Perspectives.* London: Free Association.

Samuels, Andrew (1985b). The image of the parents in bed. In Samuels (1985a).

Samuels, Andrew (1992a). National Psychology, National Socialism, and analytical psychology: reflections on Jung and anti-semitism Part I. *Journal of Analytical Psychology* 37:3-28.

Samuels, Andrew (1992b). National Psychology, National Socialism, and analytical psychology: reflections on Jung and anti-semitism Part II. *Journal of Analytical Psychology* 37:127-48.

Samuels, Andrew, Bani Shorter & Fred Plaut (1985). Glossary. In Samuels (1985a).

Sanford, John A. (1977). *Healing and Wholeness*. New York: Paulist.

Sanford, John A. (1984 [1966]). *Dreams: God's Forgotten Language*. New York: Crossroad.

Sand, Shara & Ross Levin (1992). Music and its relationship to dreams and the self. *Psychoanalysis and Contemporary Thought* 15:161–97.

Sangharakshita (1980). *A Survey of Buddhism*. Boulder: Shambhala.

Sarason, Seymour B. (1959 [1944]). Dreams and thematic apperception test stories. In DeMartino.

Saul, Leon J. (1940). Utilization of early current dreams in formulating psycho-analytic cases. *Psychoanalytic Quarterly* 9:453–69.

Saul, Leon J. & Burton A. Fleming (1959). A clinical note on the ego meaning of certain dreams of flying. *Psychoanalytic Quarterly* 28:501–4.

Savary, Louis M., Patricia H. Berne & Strephon Kaplan Williams (1984). *Dreams and Spiritual Growth: A Christian Approach to Dreamwork*. New York: Paulist.

Scaife, Hilary (1983). Dream work with children. *Self and Society* 11:73–7.

Schatzman, Morton (1982). Introduction. In Saint-Denys.

Schatzman, Morton (1983). Sleeping on problems really can solve them. *New Scientist*, 11 August:416–7.

Schatzman, Morton, Alan Worsley & Peter Fenwick (1988). Correspondence during lucid dreams between dreamed and actual events. In Gackenbach & LaBerge.

Schenck, Carlos H., Donna M. Milner, Thomas D. Hurwitz, Scott R. Bundlie & Mark W. Mahowald (1989). A polysomnographic and clinical report on sleep-related injury in 100 adult patients. *American Journal of Psychiatry* 146: 1166–73.

Schneider, Daniel E. (1955). The image of the heart and the synergic principle in psychoanalysis (psychosynergy). *Psychoanalytic Review* 42:343–60.

Schneider, Daniel E. (1973). Conversion of massive anxiety into heart attack. *American Journal of Psychotherapy* 27:360–78.

Schonbar, Rosalea A. (1959). Some manifest characteristics of recallers and non-recallers of dreams. *Journal of Consulting Psychology* 23:414–8.

Schonbar, Rosalea Ann (1961). Temporal and emotional factors in the selective recall of dreams. *Journal of Consulting Psychology* 25:67–73.

Schultz, Katherine J. & David Koulack (1980). Dream affect and the menstrual cycle. *Journal of Nervous and Mental Disease* 168:436–8.

Schwartz, David G., Lissa N. Weinstein & Arthur M. Arkin (1978). Qualitative aspects of sleep mentation. In Arthur M. Arkin, John S. Antrobus & Steven J. Ellman, editors. *The Mind in Sleep: Psychology and Psychophysiology*. Hillsdale, New Jersey: Lawrence Erlbaum.

Schwartz, Wynn & Mary Godwyn (1988). Action and representation in ordinary and lucid dreams. In Gackenbach & LaBerge.

Schwartz-Salant, Nathan & Murray Stein, editors (1990). *Dreams in Analysis.*
    Wilmette, Illinois: Chiron.
Scott, Charles E., editor (1977a). *On Dreaming: An Encounter with Medard Boss.*
    Chico, California: Scholars.
Scott, Charles E. (1977b). Medard Boss. In Scott (1977a).
Scott, Edward M. (1968). Dreams of alcoholics. *Perceptual and Motor Skills* 26:
    1315-8.
Scott, John A., Sr. (1982). The principles of rapid dream analysis. *Medical Hyp-
    noanalysis* 3:85-95.
Scrima, Lawrence (1984). Dream sleep and memory: new findings with diverse
    implications. *Integrative Psychiatry* 2:211-6.
Secunda, Brant (1993). Put your dreams into the fire: an interview with Brant
    Secunda. [Interview by H. Roberta Ossana.] *Dream Network Journal* 12(4):
    18-20.
Seidenberg, Henry (1958). Predicting the onset of psychosis by a nightmare of
    death. *Psychiatry* 21:225-6.
Serrano, Miguel (1968 [1966]). *Jung and Hesse: A Record of Two Friendships.*
    New York: Schocken.
Shaffer, John T. (1986). Transformational fantasy. In A. A. Sheikh, editor.
    Anthology of Imagery Techniques. Milwaukee: American Imagery Institute.
Shafton, Anthony (1976). *Conditions of Awareness: Subjective Factors in the
    Social Adaptations of Man and Other Primates.* Portland, Oregon/Chicago:
    Riverstone.
Shafton, Anthony (1991). Why so few blacks in the dream movement? *Associ-
    ation for the Study of Dreams Newsletter* 8(4):1, 12-4.
Shafton, Anthony (forthcoming). Black dreamers in the U.S. In Kelly Bulkeley,
    editor. *Among All These Dreamers: Essays on Dreaming and Modern Society.*
    Albany: State University of New York.
Shands, Harley C. (1966). Dreams as drama. In Jules H. Masserman, editor.
    Adolescence, Dreams and Training. New York: Grune & Stratton.
Shapiro, C. M., J. R. Catterall, I. Montgomery, G. M. Raab & N. J. Douglas
    (1986). Do asthmatics suffer bronchoconstriction during rapid eye movement
    sleep? *British Medical Journal* 292:1161-4.
Shapiro, David, David Notowitz & G. William Domhoff (1990). Night wars:
    Vietnam veterans and their nightmares. Video presentation and discussion at
    the conference of the Association for the Study of Dreams, Chicago.
Sharpe, Ella Freeman (1978 [1937]). *Dream Analysis: A Practical Handbook for
    Psycho-analysts.* New York: Brunner/Mazel.
Shaw, Rosalind (1992). Dreaming as accomplishment: power, the individual and
    Temne divination. In Jędrej & Shaw (1992a).
Shelburne, W. A. (1984). A critique of James Hillman's approach to the dream.
    Journal of Analytical Psychology 29:35-56.
Sheppard, Edith (1963). Systematic dream studies: clinical judgment and objec-
    tive measurements of ego strength. *Comprehensive Psychiatry* 4:263-70.

Sheppard, Edith (1969). Dream-content analysis. In Kramer.

Sheppard, Edith & Leon J. Saul (1958). An approach to the systematic study of ego function. *Psychoanalytic Quarterly* 27:237–45.

Shevrin, Howard (1986). Subliminal perception and dreaming. *Journal of Mind and Behavior* 7:379–95.

Shohet, Robin (1981). The peer dream group. *Self and Society* 9:116–9,136–8.

Shohet, Robin (1983). The Third Reich of Dreams. *Self and Society* 11:98–101.

Shohet, Robin (1985). *Dream Sharing: How to Enhance Your Understanding of Dreams by Group Sharing and Discussion.* Wellingborough, U.K.: Turnstone.

Shulman, Bernard (1969). An Adlerian view. In Kramer.

Shulman, Sandra (1979). *Nightmare.* Newton Abbot, U.K.: David & Charles.

Shuttleworth-Jordan, Ann B. & Graham S. Saayman (1989). Differential effects of alternative strategies on psychotherapeutic process in group dream work. *Psychotherapy* 26:514–9.

Siegel, Alan B. (1990). *Dreams That Can Change Your Life: Navigating Life's Passages through Turning Point Dreams.* Los Angeles: Jeremy P. Tarcher.

Siegel, Alan B. (1992). Pregnant dreams: the secret life of the pregnant father. *Dream Network Journal* 11(2):11–3,30.

Siegel, Bernard (1984). Applications of dreams and drawings. *Association for the Study of Dreams Newsletter* 1(2):1–2.

Signell, Karen A. (1990). *Wisdom of the Heart: Working with Women's Dreams.* New York: Bantam.

Silberer, Herbert (1955 [1918]). The dream: introduction to the psychology of dreams. *Psychoanalytic Review* 42:361–87.

Singer, Alexa (1988). Dancing your dream awake. *Dream Network Bulletin* 7(3):17–8.

Singer, Jerome S. (1975). *The Inner World of Daydreaming.* New York: Harper & Row.

Singer, June (1977 [1976]). *Androgyny: Toward a New Theory of Sexuality.* Garden City, New Jersey: Anchor.

Slap, Joseph W. & Eugene E. Trunnell (1987). Reflections on the self state dream. *Psychoanalytic Quarterly* 56:251–62.

Smith, Andy (1992). For all those who were Indians in a former life. In *Conference on Genocide*, sourcebook for the conference of Women of All Red Nations, Chicago.

Smith, Carlyle (1993). REM sleep and learning: some recent findings. In Moffitt et al. (1993a).

Smith, Robert C. (1984). A possible biologic role of dreaming. *Psychotherapy and Psychosomatics* 41:167–76.

Smith, Robert C. (1985). A possible biologic role of dreaming. *Association for the Study of Dreams Newsletter* 2(2):2–3.

Smith, Robert C. (1986). Evaluating dream function: emphasizing the study of patients with organic disease. *Journal of Mind and Behavior* 7:397–410.

Smith, Robert C. (1987). Do dreams reflect a biological state? *Journal of Nervous and Mental Disease* 175:201–7.

Smith, Robert C. (1990). Traumatic dreams as an early warning of health problems. In Krippner (1990a).

Snow, Loudell F. (1993). *Walkin' Over Medicine*. Boulder, Colorado: Westview.

Snyder, Frederick (1963). The new biology of dreaming. *Archives of General Psychiatry* 8:381–91.

Snyder, Thomas & Jayne Gackenbach (1988). Individual differences associated with lucid dreaming. In Gackenbach & LaBerge.

Snyder, Thomas J. & Jayne Gackenbach (1991). Vestibular involvement in the neurocognition of lucid dreaming. In Gackenbach & Sheikh.

Sokolov, E. N. (1963). Higher nervous functions: the orienting reflex. *Annual Review of Physiology* 25:545–80.

Somers, Virend K., Mark E. Dyken, Allyn L. Mark & François M. Abboud (1993). Sympathetic-nerve activity during sleep in normal subjects. *New England Journal of Medicine* 328:303–7.

Spanjaard, Jacob (1969). The manifest dream content and its significance for the interpretation of dreams. *International Journal of Psycho-Analysis* 50:221–35.

Sparrow, G. Scott (1982 [1976]). *Lucid Dreaming: Dawning of the Clear Light*. Virginia Beach, Virginia: A.R.E.

Spero, Moshe Halevi (1984). A psychotherapist's reflections on a countertransference dream. *American Journal of Psychoanalysis* 44:191–6.

Starker, Steven (1974). Daydreaming styles and nocturnal dreaming. *Journal of Abnormal Psychology* 83:52–5.

States, Bert O. (1988). *The Rhetoric of Dreams*. Ithaca, New York: Cornell University.

Stefanakis, Harry, Antonio Zadra & Don Donderi (1990). A correlational analysis of dream content variables with measures of self-reported well-being. *Association for the Study of Dreams Newsletter* 7(4):1–3,16.

Stein, Martin H. (1989). How dreams are told: secondary revision—the critic, the editor, and the plagiarist. *Journal of the American Psychoanalytic Association* 37:65–88.

Stein, Martin H. (1991). Dreams, conscience, and memory. *Psychoanalytic Quarterly* 60:185–206.

Stein, Murray (1990). On dreams and history in analysis. In Schwartz-Salant & Stein.

Steiner, Rudolf (1971). *Methods in Spiritual Research*. Fair Oaks, California: Rudolf Steiner.

Stekel, Wilhelm (1943 [1913 and later]). *The Interpretation of Dreams: New Developments and Technique*. New York: Liveright.

Sterba, Richard (1946). Dreams and acting out. *Psychoanalytic Quarterly* 15:175–9.

Stern, M., D. H. Fram, R. Wyatt, L. Grinspoon & B. Tursky (1969). All-night sleep studies of acute schizophrenics. *Archives of General Psychiatry* 20:470–7.

Stevens, Anthony (1983 [1982]). *Archetypes: A Natural History of the Self.* New York: Quill.

Stevens, Caroline T. (1990). Some comments on knowing: discussion of "A pedestrian approach to dreams" by Thomas B. Kirsch. In Schwartz-Salant & Stein.

Stewart, Kilton (1954). Mental hygiene and world peace. *Mental Hygiene* 38: 387–403.

Stimson, William R. (1982). Dreams as a subversive activity. *Dream Network Bulletin* 1(1):1,6.

Stockholder, Kay (1987). *Dream Works: Lovers and Families in Shakespeare's Plays.* Toronto: University of Toronto.

Stukane, Eileen (1985 [1983]). *The Dream Worlds of Pregnancy.* New York: Quill.

Suinn, Richard M. (1967). Anxiety and color dreaming. *Mental Hygiene* 51:27–9.

Swanson, Ethel M. & David Foulkes (1968). Dream content and the menstrual cycle. *Journal of Nervous and Mental Disease* 145:358–63.

Sylvia, Wesley H., Philip M. Clark & Lawrence J. Monroe (1978). Dream reports of subjects high and low in creative ability. *Journal of General Psychology* 99:205–11.

Tart, Charles T. (1979). From spontaneous event to lucidity: a review of attempts to consciously control nocturnal dreaming. In Wolman.

Tart, Charles T. (1988). From spontaneous event to lucidity: a review of attempts to consciously control nocturnal dreaming. In Gackenbach & LaBerge. Revision of Tart (1979).

Taub-Bynum, E. Bruce (1984). *The Family Unconscious.* Wheaton, Illinois: Quest.

Tauber, Edward S. & Maurice R. Green (1959). *Prelogical Experience: An Inquiry into Dreams & Other Creative Processes.* New York: Basic.

Taylor, Jeremy (1983). *Dream Work: Techniques for Discovering the Creative Power in Dreams.* New York: Paulist.

Taylor, Jeremy (1991). Puff the Magic Dragon. Kicking the smoking habit: one lucid dreamer's experience. *Dream Network Journal* 10(4):11–2.

Taylor, Jeremy (1992a). *Where People Fly and Water Runs Uphill: Using Dreams to Tap the Wisdom of the Unconscious.* New York: Warner.

Taylor, Jeremy (1992b). The nagging question of "dream education." *Dream Network Journal* 11(2):20–1.

Tedlock, Barbara (1981). Quiché Maya dream interpretation. *Ethos* 9:313–30.

Tedlock, Barbara (1991). The new anthropology of dreaming. *Dreaming* 1: 161–78.

Tedlock, Barbara, editor (1992a [1987]). *Dreaming: Anthropological and Psychological Interpretations.* Santa Fe, New Mexico: School of American Research.

Tedlock, Barbara (1992b). Preface to the 1992 edition. In Tedlock (1992a [1987]).

Tedlock, Barbara (1992c [1987]). Dreaming and dream research. In Tedlock (1992a [1987]).

Tedlock, Barbara (1992d [1987]). Zuni and Quiché dream sharing and interpreting. In Tedlock (1992a [1987]).

Teilhard de Chardin, Pierre (1959 [1955]). *The Phenomenon of Man.* New York: Harper Torchbooks.

Tholey, Paul (1983). Techniques for inducing and manipulating lucid dreams. *Perceptual and Motor Skills* 57:79–90.

Tholey, Paul (1988). A model for lucidity training as a means of self-healing and psychological growth. In Gackenbach & LaBerge.

Tholey, Paul (1989). Overview of the development of lucid dream research in Germany. *Lucidity Letter* 8(2):6–30. Also in *Lucidity Letter* 10(1 & 2), 1991.

Thorpe, W. H. (1966 [1956]). *Learning and Instinct in Animals.* Cambridge: Harvard University.

Thorpy, Michael J., editor (1990). *The International Classification of Sleep Disorders.* Rochester, Minnesota: American Sleep Disorders Association.

Tolaas, Jon (1978). Rem sleep and the concept of vigilance. *Biological Psychiatry* 13:135–48.

Tolaas, Jon (1986). Vigilance theory and psi. Part I: ethological and phylogenetic aspects. *Journal of the American Society for Psychical Research* 80:357–73.

Tolaas, Jon & Montague Ullman (1979). Extrasensory communication and dreams. In Wolman.

Toldson, Ivory L. (1973). The human potential movement and black unity: counseling blacks in groups. *Journal of Non-White Concerns* 1:69–76.

Tolpin, Paul (1983). Self psychology and the interpretation of dreams. In Goldberg.

Tonay, Veronica K. (1990–91). California women and their dreams: a historical and subcultural comparison of dream content. *Imagination, Cognition and Personality* 10:85–99.

T. P. (1989). The secret of lucid dreaming. *NightLight* 1(3):13.

Tracy, Russel L. & Linda N. Tracy (1974). Reports of mental activity from sleep stages 2 and 4. *Perceptual and Motor Skills* 38:547–8.

Traditional Circle of Elders (1986). Tenth meeting of the Traditional Elders Circle, Loneman School, White Clay District, Pine Ridge, Dakota Nation, South Dakota, June 21, 1986, Communique No. 9.

Trinder, John & Milton Kramer (1971). Dream recall. *American Journal of Psychiatry* 128:296–301.

Trotter, Kimberly, Kay Dallas & Paul Verdone (1987). Olfactory and other stimuli and their effects on REM dreams. *Association for the Study of Dreams Newsletter* 4(2):6–7,12.

Trungpa, Chögyam (1973). *Cutting Through Spiritual Materialism.* Boston: Shambhala.

Tulku, Tarab, XI (1989). A Buddhist perspective on lucid dreaming. *Lucidity Letter* 8(2):47–57.

Ullman, Montague (1955). The dream process. *Psychotherapy* 1:30–60.

Ullman, Montague (1959). The adaptive significance of the dream. *Journal of Nervous and Mental Disease* 129:144–9.

Ullman, Montague (1962). Dreaming, life style, and physiology: a comment on Adler's view of the dream. *Journal of Individual Psychology* 18:18–25.

Ullman, Montague (1969a). Discussion of Bonime. In Kramer.

Ullman, Montague (1969b). Dreaming as metaphor in motion. *Archives of General Psychiatry* 21:696–703.

Ullman, Montague (1973). Societal factors in dreaming. *Contemporary Psychoanalysis* 9:282–93.

Ullman, Montague (1981). Psi communication through dream sharing. *Parapsychology Review* 12(2):1–8.

Ullman, Montague (1982 [1962]). Foreword. In Bonime (with Bonime).

Ullman, Montague (1984). Dream, metaphor, and psi. In Rhea A. White & Richard S. Broughton, editors. *Research in Parapsychology 1983*. Metuchen, New Jersey: Scarecrow.

Ullman, Montague (1986a). Access to dreams. In Wolman & Ullman.

Ullman, Montague (1986b). Vigilance theory and psi. Part II: physiological, psychological, and parapsychological aspects. *Journal of the American Society for Psychical Research* 80:375–91.

Ullman, Montague (1987a [1978]). Foreword. In Fosshage & Loew (1987a [1978]).

Ullman, Montague (1987b). Dreams: new frontiers. Panel discussion, in Glucksman & Warner.

Ullman, Montague (1988a). Introduction. In Ullman & Limmer.

Ullman, Montague (1988b). The experiential dream group. In Ullman & Limmer.

Ullman, Montague (1988c). Dreams and society. In Ullman & Limmer.

Ullman, Montague (1990). Three perspectives on dream groups, first view: an objective comparison of dream groups & therapy. *Dream Network Journal* 9(1):19–20.

Ullman, Montague (1992). Personal and social honesty and cultural differences. *Association for the Study of Dreams Newsletter* 9(2 & 3):3–4.

Ullman, Montague & Stanley Krippner (1970). *Dream Studies and Telepathy: An Experimental Approach*. New York: Parapsychology Foundation.

Ullman, Montague, Stanley Krippner & Alan Vaughan (1989). *Dream Telepathy*, 2nd edition. Jefferson, North Carolina: McFarland.

Ullman, Montague & Claire Limmer, editors (1988). *The Variety of Dream Experience: Expanding Our Ways of Working with Dreams*. New York: Continuum.

Ullman, Montague & Nan Zimmerman (1979). *Working with Dreams*. New York: Delacorte Press/Eleanor Friede.

Upton, Charles (1988a). U.S.-Soviet dream bridge. *Dream Network Bulletin* 7(3):5.

Upton, Charles (1988b). Dream bridge complete. *Dream Network Bulletin* 7(6):5.

Van de Castle, Robert L. (1990). Animal figures in dreams: age, sex and cultural differences. *Association for the Study of Dreams Newsletter* 7(2):1–2.

van den Daele, Leland (1992). Direct interpretation of dreams: some basic principles and technical rules. *American Journal of Psychoanalysis* 52:99–118.

Vaughan, Alan (1991). Training your dream tigers. In *The Power of Positive Prophecy*. London: HarperCollins.

Vaughan, Charles J. (1964). Behavioral evidence for dreaming in rhesus monkeys. *Physiologist* 7:275.

Vogel, Gerald W. (1983). Evidence for REM sleep deprivation as the mechanism of action of antidepressant drugs. *Progress in Neuro-Psychopharmacology & Biological Psychiatry* 7:343–9.

Vogel, Gerald, David Foulkes & Harry Trosman (1966). Ego functions and dreaming during sleep onset. *Archives of General Psychiatry* 14:238–48.

Volkan, Vamik D. & Tajammul H. Bhatti (1973). Dreams of transsexuals awaiting surgery. *Comprehensive Psychiatry* 14:269–79.

Walker, Priscilla Campbell & R. F. Q. Johnson (1974). The influence of presleep suggestions on dream content: evidence and methodological problems. *Psychological Bulletin* 81:362–70.

Wallerstein, Robert S. (1983). Self psychology and "classical" psychoanalytic psychology: the nature of their relationship. In Goldberg.

Walsh, John (1988). Myths, dreams, and divine revelation: from Abram to Abraham. In Ullman & Limmer.

Warman, Babu Shivbarat Lal (1947). Yoga dream doctrine. In Woods.

Warner, Carol D. (1992). The use of dreamwork in uncovering repressed memories in therapy. Paper presented to the Association for the Study of Dreams, Santa Cruz.

Warner, Silas L. (1987). Manifest dream analysis in contemporary practice. In Glucksman & Warner.

Warnes, H. (1982). The dream specimen in psychosomatic medicine in the light of clinical observations. *Psychotherapy and Psychosomatics* 38:154–64.

Warnes, H. & A. Finkelstein (1971). Dreams that precede a psychosomatic illness. *Canadian Psychiatric Association Journal* 16:317–25.

Wasserman, Marvin D., Mark R. Pressman, Charles P. Pollak, Arthur J. Spielman, Laurette DeRosairo & Elliott D. Weitzman (1982). Nocturnal penile tumescence: is it really a REM phenomenon? *Sleep Research* 11:44.

Watkins, Mary (1984 [1976]). *Waking Dreams*. Dallas: Spring.

Watkins, Mary (1992). Perestroika of the self: dreaming in the U.S.S.R. *Dreaming* 2:111–22.

Watson, Flora M. C. & James P. Henry (1977). Loss of socialized patterns of behavior in mouse colonies following daily sleep disturbance during maturation. *Physiology & Behavior* 18:119–23.

Watts, Rosemary (1992a). Dream categories: Part one. *Dream Network Journal* 11(1):25–6.

Watts, Rosemary (1992b). Dream categories: Part two. *Dream Network Journal* 11(2):28-9.

Webb, Wilse B. (1979). A historical perspective of dreams. In Wolman.

Webb, Wilse B. (1992). A dream is a poem: a metaphorical analysis. *Dreaming* 2:191-201.

Wehr, Demaris S. (1985). Religious and social dimensions of Jung's concept of the archetype: a feminist perspective. In Lauter & Rupprecht (1985a).

Weinstein, Lissa N., David G. Schwartz & Arthur M. Arkin (1991). Qualitative aspects of sleep mentation. In Ellman & Antrobus.

Weinstein, Lissa N., David G. Schwartz & Steven J. Ellman (1991). Sleep mentation as affected by REM deprivation: a new look. In Ellman & Antrobus.

Weiss, Lillie (1986). *Dream Analysis in Psychotherapy*. New York: Pergamon.

Welch, Patrick (1991). Aesculapia and Hygiea from ancient dream healing temples to contemporary dream retreat: an interview with Graywolf Fred Swinney. *Dream Network Journal* 10(2 & 3)):20-1, 52-4, 59.

Welman, Mark & Phillip A. Faber (1992). The dream in terminal illness: a Jungian formulation. *Journal of Analytical Psychology* 37:61-81.

Wessling, Noreen (1993). The adventure of starting your own dream group. *Dream Network Journal* 12(2):30-2.

West, Katherine Lee (1977). *Neptune's Plummet*. Lake Oswego, Oregon: Amata Graphics.

West, Katherine L. (1978). *Crystallizing Children's Dreams*. Lake Oswego, Oregon: Amata Graphics.

White, Joseph L. (1984). *The Psychology of Blacks*. Englewood Cliffs, New Jersey: Prentice-Hall.

White-Lewis, Jane (1992). Beyond Freud and Jung: seven analysts discuss the impact of new ideas about dreamwork. A response by Jane White-Lewis. *Quadrant* 25(2):98-100.

White-Lewis, Jane (1993). Teaching a dream course in the inner city. *Association for the Study of Dreams Newsletter* 10(4):8-10.

Whitman, Roy M. (1973). Dreams about the group: an approach to the problem of group psychology. *International Journal of Group Psychotherapy* 23: 408-20.

Whitman, Roy M. (1980). The dream as a curative fantasy. In Natterson (1980a).

Whitmont, Edward C. (1987 [1978]). Jungian approach. In Fosshage & Loew (1987a [1978]).

Whitmont, Edward C. & Sylvia Brinton Perera (1989). *Dreams, a Portal to the Source*. London: Routledge.

Whitmore, Diana (1981). A psychosynthetic view of dreams: levels of the unconscious. *Self and Society* 9:108-16.

Wikse, John R. (1988). Night rule: dreams as social intelligence. In Ullman & Limmer.

Wilberg, Henry P. (1981). The dream-art science of waking life: a new Kabbalah. *Self and Society* 9:120-5.

Williams, Strephon Kaplan (1986 [1980]). *The Jungian-Senoi Dreamwork Manual: A Step-by-Step Introduction to Working with Dreams*. Berkeley: Journey. Revised as Strephon Kaplan-Williams, *Dreamworking: A Comprehensive Guide to Working with Dreams*, San Francisco: Journey, 1991.

Williamson, L. S. [Montague Ullman] (1955). An approach to the interpretation of dreams. *Science & Society* 19:23-42.

Wilmer, Harry A. (1982). Vietnam and madness: dreams of schizophrenic veterans. *Journal of the American Academy of Psychoanalysis* 10:47-65.

Wilmer, Harry A. (1986a). Combat nightmares: toward a therapy of violence. *Spring*: 120-39.

Wilmer, Harry A. (1986b). The healing nightmare: a study of the war dreams of Vietnam combat veterans. *Quadrant* 19(1):47-61.

Wilmer, Harry A. (1987). *Practical Jung: Nuts and Bolts of Jungian Psychotherapy*. Wilmette, Illinois: Chiron.

Windsor, Joan (1987). *Dreams and Healing: Expanding the Inner Eye*. New York: Dodd, Mead.

Winget, Carolyn & Ronald A. Farrell (1974 [1971]). Homosexual dreams. In Woods & Greenhouse.

Winget, Carolyn & Milton Kramer (1979). *Dimensions of Dreams*. Gainesville: University Presses of Florida.

Winget, Carolyn, Milton Kramer & Roy M. Whitman (1972). Dreams and demography. *Canadian Psychiatric Association Journal* 17 (supplement):203-8.

Wiseman, Ann Sayre (1987). *Dreams as Metaphor: The Power of the Image*. Cambridge, Massachusetts: Ansayre.

Wiseman, Ann Sayre (1989). Earthquake nightmare help. *Association for the Study of Dreams Newsletter* 6(6):1-3.

Wiseman, Ann Sayre (1991). Nightmare help. *Dream Network Journal* 10(1): 17-8.

Wolff, Werner (1972 [1952]). *The Dream—Mirror of Conscience*. Westport, Connecticut: Greenwood.

Wolin, Steven J. & N. K. Mello (1973). The effect of alcohol on dreams and hallucinations in alcohol addicts. *Annals of the New York Academy of Sciences* 215:266-302.

Wolman, Benjamin B., editor (1979). *Handbook of Dreams: Research, Theories and Applications*. New York: Van Nostrand Reinhold.

Wolman, Benjamin B. & Montague Ullman, editors (1986). *Handbooks of States of Consciousness*. New York: Van Nostrand Reinhold.

Wood, James M., Richard R. Bootzin, Stuart F. Quan & Mary E. Klink (1993). Prevalence of nightmares among patients with asthma and chronic obstructive airways disease. *Dreaming* 3:231-41.

Wood, James M. & Richard R. Bootzin (1990). The prevalence of nightmares and their independence from anxiety. *Journal of Abnormal Psychology* 99:64-8.

Woodman, Marion (1985). *The Pregnant Virgin: A Process of Psychological Transformation*. Toronto: Inner City.

Woods, Ralph L., editor (1947). *The World of Dreams: An Anthology*. New York: Random House.

Woods, Ralph L. & Herbert B. Greenhouse, editors (1974). *The New World of Dreams*. New York: Macmillan.

Worsley, Alan (1988). Personal experiences in lucid dreaming. In Gackenbach & LaBerge.

Yellowtail, Thomas (with Michael Oren Fitzgerald) (1991). *Yellowtail: Crow Medicine Man and Sun Dance Chief*. Norman: University of Oklahoma.

Yontef, Gary M. & James S. Simkin (1989). Gestalt therapy. In Corsini & Wedding.

Young-Eisendrath, Polly (1987). The absence of black Americans as Jungian analysts. *Quadrant* 20(2):41–53.

Zadra, Antonio L. (1990). Lucid dreaming, dream control, and the treatment of nightmares. Paper presented to the Association for the Study of Dreams, Chicago.

Zadra, Antonio L., D. C. Donderi & Robert O. Pihl (1992). Efficacy of lucid dream induction for lucid and non-lucid dreamers. *Dreaming* 2:85–97.

Zadra, Antonio L. & Robert O. Pihl (no date). Lucid dreaming as a treatment for recurrent nightmares. Unpublished manuscript.

Zeller, Max (1975). The task of the analyst. *Psychological Perspectives* 6(1):74–8.

Zeller, Max (1990 [1975]). *The Dream—The Vision of the Night*. Boston: Sigo.

Zepelin, Harold (1980–1). Age differences in dreams. I: Men's dreams and thematic apperceptive fantasy. *International Journal of Aging and Human Development* 12:171–86.

Zepelin, Harold (1981). Age differences in dreams. II: Distortion and other variables. *International Journal of Aging and Human Development* 13:37–41.

Zepelin, Harold (1992). Sleep EEG and dreaming: current status of methodologies, theories, and finding. Paper presented to the Association for the Study of Dreams, Santa Cruz.

Ziegler, A. (1962). A cardiac infarction and a dream as synchronous events. *Journal of Analytical Psychology* 7:141–8.

Ziegler, Alfred J. (1976). Rousseauian optimism, natural distress, and dream research. *Spring*: 54–65.

Zimmerman, Jack (1991). The council process in dream and personal myth work: an interview with Jack Zimmerman. [Interview by H. Roberta Ossana.] *Dream Network Journal* 10(2 & 3):31–4, 50.

Zimmerman, William B. (1970). Sleep mentation and auditory awakening thresholds. *Psychophysiology* 6:540–9.

Zimmermann, David (1967). Some characteristics of dreams in group-analytic psychotherapy. *International Journal of Group Psychotherapy* 17:524–35.

Zwiebel, R. (1985). The dynamics of the countertransference dream. *International Review of Psycho-Analysis* 12:87–99.

Zwig, Adam (1990a). Dreambody work, symptoms, and illness. Workshop presented at the conference of the Association for the Study of Dreams, Chicago.

Zwig, Adam (1990b). A body-oriented approach to dreamwork. In Krippner (1990a).

Index of Authors and Names

- Endnotes are indicated by numerals following 'n' or 'nn', except where 'passim' is used. Footnotes are indicated by asterisks following 'n' or 'nn'.
- Footnotes are listed separately from endnotes for the same pages; where 'passim' is used, it pertains to endnotes only (e.g., 435-7 passim, 437nn*,***).
- A footnote which extends over more than one page is listed only by the page number on which the asterisk itself appears. Therefore, an item in such a footnote sometimes actually appears in the footnote text on a page following the one listed.
- Names in bold type also appear as main entries in the General Index.

Abboud, F. M., 279n*
Ablon, S. L., 15n**
Abramovitch, H., 430n*
Abramson, H. A., 368n22
Achterberg, J., 389n56, 409n114, 463n*
Ackerknecht, L. K., 132n*
Adams, M. V., 62n*, 89n**
Adler, A., 6n21, 57n25, 97n114, 133-9 passim, 166n32
Agnew, H. W., Jr., 15n33, 44n243
Akiyama, Y., 15n31
Aldighieri, M., 182n124
Alexander, C. N., 437n***, 476nn349-52, 477nn356-7
Alexander, F., 285nn119,125-6
Allen, C., 17n49
Allen, Woody, 198n*
Allenby, A., 91n57
Allison, R., 316n162
Allison, T., 13n*, 14n23, 40n*
Almoli, S., 239n*
Altman, L. L., 54n11, 61n45, 161n20, 352n*, 370n31
Altshuler, K. Z., 105n148, 295n19, 296n21
Ames, L. B., 395n*
Amin, Idi, 181
Andrews, S., 186n143
Andrisani, M., 281n104
Anish, S. S., 351n47
Antrobus, John S., 4n*, 23n111, 31n*, 34n177, 351n50, 396n18, 398n*, 419n156, 437n57, 437n***
Antrobus, Judith S., 437n57, 437n***
Apollodorus, 505n*
Aquino, Cory, 181
Aristotle, 239, 259, 262, 263n*, 407, 431
Arkin, A. M., 14n22, 19nn80-1, 105n147, 294n***, 304nn91,94, 331nn254-5, 351n49, 396n18, 398n*, 419n156, 438nn60-1
Armitage, R., 296n26, 310n*
Armstrong, R. H., 280n103
Arnold-Foster, M., 431

Artemidorus, 55n*, 239
Aserinsky, E., 11n3
Ashanti, F. C., 202n*
Asper, K., 82nn29,35, 112n215
Assagioli, R., 389n53
Atalick, E., 27n147, 84n*, 112n215, 114n219, 142nn57-8, 145n78, 291n4, 401n51, 482n390
Aumüller, A., 107n167
Aylward, M., 298n37

Baker, J., 19nn80-1
Baldridge, B. J., 322-3 passim, 326n220, 330n246, 331n249, 333nn271,280, 399n41, 401n46
Baldwin, J. A., 203n246
Banks, W. M., 202nn241,245, 202n*, 203n252
Barad, M., 105n148, 295n19, 296n21
Barber, B., 351n47,49
Barber, T. X., 420n164
Barnouw, V., 179n*
Barrett, D., 35n*, 270n*, 275n79, 310nn124,127, 319n169, 320n176, 352nn62-3, 417-8nn151-3, 434n27, 443n104, 444n*
Barta, S. G., 398n*
Bartemeier, L. H., 338n9, 340n14
Barz, H., 183n**, 381n**, 493-5 passim
Basso, E. B., 178n108
Bastide, R., 172n78, 197n204
Battaglia, D., 396n20
Baylis, J., 84n*, 384n36, 415n*, 467n284
Baylor, G. W., 295n13
Beaudet, D., 15n**, 385n38, 395n*, 506n36, 515n81
Beck, A. T., 95n90, 319n169, 321 passim
Beck, H. W., 188n158, 378n2
Belcher, M., 307n*
Belicki, D. A., 27n147, 84n*, 112n215, 114n219, 142nn57-8, 145n78, 291n4, 311n130, 401n51, 482n390

General Index

- A footnote which extends over more than one page is listed only by the page number on which the asterisk itself appears. Therefore, an item in such a footnote sometimes actually appears in the footnote text on a page following the one listed.
- When an item appears both on a certain page and in a footnote beginning on that same page, the footnote is not indicated separately with an asterisk.
- The indication of consecutive pages by a dash does not invariably mean that treatment of the item being referenced is continuous across those pages; the item may appear separately on the pages indicated.
- Names appearing in parentheses are in some cases those of first authors whose collaborators are not shown.

dream movement (*cont'd*)
reservations about intrapsychic analysis, 204
sanctioning of dreams restored by, 182-3, 192
social awareness too low in, 197-8, 202-4
dream quest, 32, 178-9, 189-90
dream recall
aids to, 415n*
to be avoided (Crick), 38-9
and compensation (Jung), 114-5
as dream continuation, 352-4
as dream re-entry, 153, 487-8
functionally unnecessary
Adler, cp. to today's Adlerians, 137-9
Kramer, 136n*
Lowy, 42n*
hypnosis used for (Rossi), 280
interpretable as dream element, 352
recall style, 352
and lucid dreaming
MILD (LaBerge), 458-9
rate, 450, 452n*
nonrecall, amnesia
before dire medical outcomes, 272
before suicide attempts, 350
interpretable as dream element, 352-3
neurotransmitter deficit (Hobson), 442n**
and state-specific memory, 351, 442
rates of, 350
and recall residues (Langs), 336n*
and trauma, walling off of, 319n*
various related factors
age, 16n*
brain wave profile, 351
deafness, 307, 351
deep depression, 322
dream bizarreness, 401
dream control, 441n**
dream salience and intensity, 351
ego defense profile, 352n*
gender, 296-7
Jungian typology, 291n**, 351
lucidity, 442, 473n*
manner of waking up, 351
meditation, 1, 415n*, 473n*
motivation to recall, 351
personality, cognitive profile, 310, 350-2
pregnancy, 299
REM/NREM profile, 351
repression, 16n*, 350-2
resistance, 16n*
schizophrenia, 322
stress, 296, 351
and vigilance hypothesis (Ullman), 170n*
dream re-entry, 487-97
and bo tree principle, 500, 509-12, 514-6, 518-22, 525
and control
active intervention, 490, 495-7
cp. to lucid dreaming (Williams), 495
participatory, 490

dream re-entry (*cont'd*)
defined, 487
as dream incubation technique, 495, 521-2
dream recall amounting to, 153, 487-8
by falling back asleep, 506, 514
interpretive/non-interpretive, 491-7
as lucid dream induction technique, 457-8
and nightmares, 495-6, 509-12, 514, 520-2
and Senoi, 414
in serial dreams (Windsor), 422-3
and shamanism, 487
as tool in daily life, 496-7
in various techniques and approaches
active imagination (Jung). *See* active imagination
actualizing (Williams), 384
dreambody work (Mindell), 515, 522, 525
experiential (Mahrer), 493n*
focusing (Gendlin), 492-3
Gestalt, 228
humanistic approaches (Shohet), 379
miscellaneous, 494-5
psychodrama, 490-1, 493-6
psychosynthesis (Rossi), 491-2
restaging (Wiseman), 495-6
rewriting (Savary), 495
RISC (Cartwright), 440n***
See also drama: as dreamwork technique
dream reorganization (Palace), 512-3
dream residue (Watkins), 335, 353, 357
dream screen (Lewin), 260n*
dream series, of a night
with all-night lucidity, 476-7
illustrating:
confirming an interpretation (Freud), 67
dual perspective dreams, 315
group dreamwork (Ullman), 184-6
re-entry by return to sleep (Sparrow), 514
reversal (Sharpe), 55
single preoccupation, (Koulack), 393
linked by feelings (Cartwright), 162n**
mistaken for episodes of one dream (Cartwright), 14n*
recent → distant → recent memories, 396
re-entry by return to sleep, 506, 514
repetitive-traumatic/progressive-sequential (Kramer), 244
See also dream episodes
dream series, over time
illustrating:
actualization (Williams), 360
animus (Allenby), 90-1
bo tree principle, 501, 505-7, 512-4, 516-21
catagogic trend, 240-1
compensation not infallible, 106-7
incubated dream solutions not infallible, (Barrett), 417-8
discovery and rehearsal (Craig), 152-4